PRAISE FOR

Contemporary Colleges and Universities

"In his preface to this extraordinary collection of essays, Joseph L. DeVitis writes that 'This book is both a celebration of colleges and universities and a challenge to readers to take a hard look at where they are going....' It includes a remarkable range of topics on the contemporary college and university. The volume's illustrious contributors and editor are to be commended for the wisdom and sensitivity reflected in their insightful, hopeful, splendidly written essays."

—*Robert H. Deluty, Associate Dean of the Graduate School,*
University of Maryland, Baltimore County

"Written by some of the academy's most respected thinkers and leaders, this welcome book affords an authoritative overview of crucial themes in today's postsecondary landscape. The essays examine a wide range of current issues and strategies and offer critical commentary on higher education's 'new normal.' The volume also provides reflective historical context and useful policy recommendations that make it must reading for all those who care about, study, work in, and lead our colleges and universities."

—*Sandra Jordan, Chancellor, University of South Carolina, Aiken*

Contemporary Colleges and Universities

Adolescent
Cultures,
School &
Society

Joseph L. DeVitis & Linda Irwin-DeVitis
GENERAL EDITORS

Vol. 64

The Adolescent Cultures, School & Society series
is part of the Peter Lang Education list.
Every volume is peer reviewed and meets
the highest quality standards for content and production.

PETER LANG
New York • Washington, D.C./Baltimore • Bern
Frankfurt • Berlin • Brussels • Vienna • Oxford

Contemporary Colleges and Universities

A Reader

edited by Joseph L. DeVitis

PETER LANG
New York • Washington, D.C./Baltimore • Bern
Frankfurt • Berlin • Brussels • Vienna • Oxford

Library of Congress Cataloging-in-Publication Data

Contemporary colleges & universities: a reader / edited by Joseph L. DeVitis.
p. cm. — (Adolescent cultures, school and society; vol. 64)
Includes bibliographical references and index.
1. Universities and colleges—United States. I. DeVitis, Joseph L.
II. Boeckenstedt, Jon. Outside the gates, looking in.
III. Title: Contemporary colleges and universities.
LA227.4.C67   378.73—dc23   2012042557
ISBN 978-1-4331-1602-5 (hardcover)
ISBN 978-1-4331-1601-8 (paperback)
ISBN 978-1-4539-0919-5 (e-book)
ISSN 1091-1464

Bibliographic information published by **Die Deutsche Nationalbibliothek**.
Die Deutsche Nationalbibliothek lists this publication in the "Deutsche
Nationalbibliografie"; detailed bibliographic data is available
on the Internet at http://dnb.d-nb.de/.

The paper in this book meets the guidelines for permanence and durability
of the Committee on Production Guidelines for Book Longevity
of the Council of Library Resources.

© 2013 Peter Lang Publishing, Inc., New York
29 Broadway, 18th floor, New York, NY 10006
www.peterlang.com

Printed in the United States of America

In memory of

Kingsley Blake Price,

my undergraduate mentor at
The Johns Hopkins University —
and for decades thereafter

Contents

Part Two — Faculty: Changing Roles in Today's World

Part Three: Curriculum: Transmission and Transformation

Part Four — Administration: Negotiating the Labyrinth

Part Five — Social Forces: Mirror Images and Transfigurations

Preface

JOSEPH L. DeVITIS

Twenty years from now you will be more disappointed by the things you didn't do than by the ones you did. So throw off the bowlines, sail away from the safe harbor. Catch the trade winds in your sails. Explore. Dream. Discover.
 —Mark Twain

My love affair with colleges and universities began in 1960, when I started a three-year stint as a student guidance office worker at then all-male Baltimore City College, founded in 1839, one of the oldest public high schools in America. The "Castle on the Hill," as the Collegians call it, stands about eight blocks from the stately Homewood campus of The Johns Hopkins University. I took two city buses to arrive at City College, and the second bus passed The Hopkins grounds. (Hopkins prefers to emphasize the "The" in its formal name.) Each morning and afternoon I would shake my head and murmur to myself, "Who could go to that place?" It was a statement about class and culture by a second-generation Italian American boy who grew up in a small family grocery in a low-income, racially mixed neighborhood in Fells Point, the oldest part of Charm City. Yet at least one fortuitous circumstance lent me more than a bit of "cultural capital" (a term I learned much later): By devouring college catalogs and meeting admissions representatives from Boston University to Thiel College, I acquired a firm grasp of what college was about, where colleges were, and how to get into most of them. Despite middling SAT scores, my excellent grades and extracurricular record won me a partial scholarship to Syracuse University and an almost full scholarship to JHU. It helped immensely that City College was a main "feeder" school to the nearby Hopkins campus. Indeed, its assistant director of admissions told me not to worry about my disappointing SAT (especially by JHU standards). He was impressed that I had read most everything written by the likes of Steinbeck and Saroyan. At about the same time, an admissions staff person at the University of Maryland, College Park, was placing my application file in the ashbin since I had missed its ACT cutoff score. (A similar thing happened to Joe Namath the year before—much to the delight of Bear Bryant and The University of Alabama.) I learned to take standardized tests far less seriously at a rather young age. Their predictability for my academic results was way off base; all my grades were A and B in freshman year, and I graduated with honors at one of the country's most rigorous academic institutions. (Many years later a whole host of rather prestigious colleges and universities would make admissions tests optional.)[1]

Once in college, following Twain's advice, I began to explore, dream, and discover. I was on my way, so it seemed, to fulfilling the American Dream, mid-1960s style, by way of Emersonian self-reliance. An earnest young man, I studied hard (one had to at JHU); and, as a commuter, I led a Spartan social life. Before long, I realized that cultural constraints provided heavy baggage in the parade of life. I started to slough off my previous absolutist vantage points; and a potent liberal education permitted me to view multiple perspectives, subtle ambiguities and nuances, and massive shades of gray. (In my case, William Perry's developmental model turned out to be largely accurate.)[2] Civil rights and Vietnam were becoming part and parcel of my collegiate dialogue, and my earlier abstract thought on matters of equity and social justice took on more pronounced and purposeful activism. Those attitudes and actions grew even more marked during my graduate school experience at the University of Illinois at Urbana-Champaign.

In the cornfields of central Illinois (the library at the University, one of the nation's best, sits right next to an experimental cornfield) in the early 1970s, our days were filled with a heady stream of campus protests, marches, and demonstrations. Dodging billy clubs and dashing into Altgeld Hall for refuge became nearly ritualistic. (I was still earnest in coursework and dissertation writing, finishing in three years—Secretariat-like speed by Illini standards in social foundations of education). It might sound strange today, but we did think we could change the world. We honestly believed that sea changes in intellectual patterns were altering how the world looked at political and social events. And I remained in love with academe—even as I struggled to find a first job in a terribly tight labor market. Finally, in the summer of my final year at Illinois, I landed that initial appointment. I quickly learned that higher education was not nearly as rational or fair as I had imagined in my more naïve days as an undergraduate and graduate student. Yet, after all these years and considering most other institutions in the United States, I still view the academy as the most liberating one around—one in which I can still explore, dream, and discover within limits. In my nearly 40–year career, I have had the pleasure of teaching at five academic institutions—three research universities, a regional state university, and a public liberal arts college. Compared to many of today's college students, I consider myself quite fortunate. Like most of my peers, I graduated from undergraduate and graduate studies with no worries about debt. As social mobility declines and a deep recession remains, scholarship aid is becoming harder to find, especially at state schools.[3] Loans are more typically the order of the day. Meanwhile, astounding tuition hikes continue to make the public shake their heads in despair. The days of free tuition at the University of California and the City Colleges of New York are long gone—two relics of the 1960s.

As I edit this volume, my long sojourn in higher education has also given me pause for care and concern: This book is both a celebration of colleges and universities and a challenge to readers to take a hard look at where they are going in today's fast-paced world. It affords us all an opportunity to step back, reflect, and then re-engage in the work of guiding youth, fostering wisdom (and not simply transmitting knowledge), and making our world a better place. I hope that voyage will reveal why my fondness for the academy continues despite real evidence that it has grown bigger warts and bunions since 1960. We learn, as John Dewey said, by reconstructing our knowledge.[4] It is a way back to the past, to ground us in the present, and to move us forward in the future. Improving colleges and universities is worth that journey and is the major reason for this book's inception. I hope readers accept my effort to combine some personal history with the theory and practice of academic life in this preface.

———————

In the current climate, students all too often are the losers. Today, undergraduates are aggressively recruited. In the glossy brochures, they're assured that teaching is important, that a spirit of community pervades the campus. . . . But (that is not) the reality.
—Ernest L. Boyer

———————

In 1985, Ernie Boyer informed me that most of the colleges and universities he visited while writing *College* reminded him of walking through a typical shopping mall:[5] They tended to look alike and offered students less diversity in content than their bare forms would indicate. Of course, we both viewed that circumstance as lamentable, especially given how arduously many students struggle for acceptance into the college of their choice. More positively, we surmised that there might well be dozens upon dozens of schools that could fit most of them quite comfortably. Part One of the text affords a rich panoply of perspectives on some of the major conflicts and contestations faced by today's college and university students—both inside and outside the classroom. The topics considered include an appraisal of college admissions; a comparison of four-year and community college students; how religion and spirituality affect academic careers; issues related to sexual orientation and harassment; a concerted challenge to improve Greek life; the role of athletics in campus life; and a comprehensive survey of how student affairs and services differ across the globe. Most of the essays in Part One reflect, roughly speaking, elements of an Oxfordian model of higher education. By this, I mean an emphasis on undergraduate education, a consideration of the whole student, an acknowledgment of the need for moral and civic education, the importance of broadly based educational experiences, and the significance of relationship-building among students, faculty, and staff members. There is more constituent diversity in academe today than in 1960, but we still have a long way to go in relating to each other in authentic and just ways. According to DeVitis and Rich: "In viewing the concept of equality, [we] find it to be equivocal, serving the interests of the powerful while placating the powerless. Thus, education can be equitable. . . only if just principles first govern society."[6] In higher education today, it is vitally important that any such unfair circumstances be emblazoned by equity and social justice if academe is to be considered a moral institution.

At the same time, academicians must be cognizant of recent critiques of American higher education that paint a rather dismal portrait of how little learning may actually be taking place on our campuses.[7] If those reports ring true in any legitimate sense, academe will have to defend itself against strident calls for change from policymakers and politicians of all stripes. They will be asking these kinds of questions: Are our colleges and universities justifying their exalted reputations? Do students, parents, and employers regard them as primarily credentialing institutions? Are students reading and writing far less than previous generations? In particular, are they doing less lengthy, sustained reading and writing? Has academic rigor been on the wane for some time now? If the answers to those questions prove to be affirmative, we are facing tough times in establishing any semblance of a viable civic society and a stable future for our children and grandchildren.

A university's essential character is that of being a center of free inquiry and criticism—a thing not to be sacrificed for anything else.
    —Richard Hofstadter

Ideally, professors should stand firmly for the right of faculty and students to teach and learn free from arbitrary and whimsical external and internal pressures and constraints. That is to say, they should passionately guard one another's academic freedom to explore, dream, and discover. Professors should also serve critical roles in the public arena, though the influence of "public intellectuals" seems to be waning given the pervasive dominance of specialized narratives and research. That dire message was brought home by the independent scholar Russell Jacoby in 2000: "Academics. . . create insular societies. . . . The professors share an idiom and a discipline. . . [that] constitute their own universe."[8] Part Two illustrates how academic faculty, if adequately protected (no mean task, by the way), can use their freedom to enhance learning for their students, the community, and the world. It also shows how strict adherence to a Germanic model of higher education that stresses narrow specialization can further attenuate Jacoby's vision of writing, speaking, and sharing with both college students and a larger public. The dynamics of teaching and learning can be severely shortchanged in such a framework. In a word, there are disincentives in the Germanic university that vitiate against good teaching. Truth be told, my alma mater was the first American university to adopt the Germanic model of graduate studies, research, and specialization in 1876 (the undergraduate school came along later to help finance the graduate and medical schools). Luckily, I had some exceptional professors and teaching assistants who introduced me to the life of the mind. Granted, it also helped that I was largely an independent learner. According to Ken Bain, who cares passionately about college teaching:

> For the last half century, much of the money for higher education has come through grants for research. The most successful and prestigious universities have built their reputations with those dollars. . . . So the secret is out: everyone really does care about teaching, or at least says they do, or knows they should—even within the research university. Now it's time we did something about that little secret.[9]

Yet today's glossy college videos and view books will not divulge the fact that only a small portion of university faculty have any explicit preparation in pedagogy. Some recruitment materials point to Nobel laureates, but fail to acknowledge that few undergraduates will ever meet them. What they might come to learn is that most professors are taught to be researchers and encouraged to be grant seekers. Particularly at research universities, they tend to be individual entrepreneurs who guard their scholarly time and priorities because of institutional mandates that privilege publications and grants above all else—no matter how worthy or unworthy some of those projects might be and regardless of how important teaching and service need to be. In David Thornton Moore's words, it might be heartening to see a core of faculty create "a form of discourse in which teachers and students conduct an unfettered investigation of social institutions, power relations and value commitment."[10] That kind of movement would steer the university more toward collaboration and community instead of institutionalized rugged individualism.

The college is meaningless without a curriculum, but it is more so when it has one that is meaningless.
—Mark Van Doren

Curriculum issues have perennially been at the forefront of conflict in the halls of academe. Some of those clashes highlight disciplinary and doctrinal disputes, particularly of a departmental and territorial nature; others spotlight how competing political and societal values and pressures can heavily influence what is taught, if not always what is learned. At the turn of the 20th century, Herbert Spencer posed perhaps the essential curricular question: "What knowledge is of most worth?"[11] Part Three attempts to respond to that thorny query in the following manner: It includes essays on liberal education's traditional and contemporary byways, comprehensive perspectives on multiple routes to forming academic curricula, creative ways of looking at general education, the gaps and opportunities in service learning, and the often hidden nature of curriculum in colleges and universities.

One of the more curious aspects of college curricula seems to be the lack of distinctiveness in so many of them. To corroborate Boyer's point about the shopping mall mentality of most American colleges and universities, one might randomly peruse several dozen college catalogs. The similarities in general education, distribution requirements, and even upper-division course offerings are startling. Only a minority of colleges carve out programs that are truly different and innovative, in theory if not always in practice—and some genuinely do appear to hit the target on both.[12]

It is especially imperative that we recognize that curricula, at any level of education, can deeply influence the meanings students attach to their intellectual, social, and emotional lives. As Apple and Franklin put it: "[Curricula] preserve and distribute what is perceived to be 'legitimate knowledge'—the knowledge that 'we all must have.'"[13] Indeed, that conferring of power places enormous responsibility on college faculty to do what is good, right, and just in selecting and constructing curricula. In the end, they must attempt to make curricular experiences eventuate in student growth. That is, following Dewey, learning must be educative, not miseducative or noneducative.[14]

On a good day, I view the job [of university president] as directing an orchestra. On the dark days, it is more like that of a clutch—engaging the engine to effect forward motion, while taking great friction.
—A. Bartlett Giamatti

Academic administrators typically face daily multi-faceted, often complex tasks that might drive many mortals to give up the ghost. According to Stanley Fish, a veteran university administrator and contentious public intellectual:

> In the course of making a decision, an administrator must perform a complex act of taking into account any number of goals (short and long range), constituents, interests, opportunities, costs, dangers; and at every point. . . keep constantly in mind the forces and resources that must be marshaled.[15]

Administrators must do so in a semi-domesticated environment in which they often feel as if they are herding cats. Faculty can routinely be seen to ignore them, and their relations with administrators can be frosty or adversarial. College leaders also face student and parent demands for more compliant and convenient customer service, external audiences who seek more active involvement, and athletic boosters who desire wins above all else. Hacker and Dreifus paint a portrait of university leadership in even gloomier shades than does Fish:

> The hard fact is that on the modern campus, no one really wants to be led. Every current and former college president we've met has related how every proposal he or she made was greeted by a chorus of no's or simply stone-faced resistance. Add in faculty, trustees, alumni, legislators, and nowadays students, each with their own demands. Indeed, when presidents call for something new, they usually find they have no real allies.[16]

Though the contributing administrators in Part Four realize the above concerns, they are also attuned to the need for trust among all constituencies, strategic planning, building campus relationships, nurturing town and gown interaction, and ameliorating political squabbles. Many of them step gingerly, as if on a high wire, to balance all manners of competing interests in the hope of creating a better college or university.

> Think about the big picture, the political economy of education, and the meaning of social democracy. Sharpen your pencils and back up your hard drives. . . . Universities need to move away from the old business model based on minimizing costs and maximizing revenues toward a renewed commitment to the common good.
> —Nancy Folbre

On one hand, universities tend to reproduce, usually in a lagging fashion, what the larger society is expecting of them. On the other hand, one would also anticipate that they should be aiming for more ideal contributions to the commonwealth than instantiating the status quo. That conundrum has posed persistent dilemmas about the purposes of higher education throughout the ages. In ancient Greece, the offerings of liberal education were segregated gifts to those who held wealth, status, and power. In medieval times, the interests of the Church provided the dominant rationale for the very existence of universities. In colonial America, preparation for the ministry was what sent affluent male youths to places such as Harvard and Yale. In the 19th century, many U.S. college presidents taught a senior seminar in moral philosophy. If they did so now, would public relations be a more likely theme for their instruction? Who defines the justifications for academe today? Many of the authors in Part Five lay out arguments that describe and interpret the hegemony of economic, corporate, and technocratic influences in contemporary colleges and universities. How will Twain's yearning to explore, dream, and discover fare in that kind of environment? Those who read this volume with any care will indeed be left with sobering thoughts about the present and future of higher education, an institution that still warrants our vigilance, nurture, and sustenance.

Notes

1. As of spring 2012, these are some of the prominent colleges and universities that have made admissions tests optional: Bard, Bates, Bennington, Bowdoin, Connecticut College, DePaul, Dickinson, Drew, Franklin and Marshall, Gustavus Adolphus, Hamilton, Hobart and William Smith, Holy Cross, Juniata, Knox, Lawrence, Lewis and Clark (Or.), Loyola (Md.), Middlebury, Moravian, Mount Holyoke, Muhlenberg, Pitzer, Providence, Susquehanna, Union College (N. Y.), Ursinus, and Wheaton (Ill.).
2. William G. Perry, Jr. *Forms of Intellectual and Ethical Development in the College Years: A Scheme* (New York: Holt, Rinehart, and Winston, 1970).
3. See Nancy Folbre, *Saving State U: Why We Must Fix Public Higher Education* (New York: The New Press, 2010) and Christopher Newfield, *Unmaking the Public University: The Forty-Year Assault on the Middle Class* (Cambridge, MA: Harvard University Press, 2008).
4. John Dewey, *Experience and Education* (New York: Macmillan, 1938).
5. Ernest L. Boyer, *College: The Undergraduate Experience in America* (New York: Harper and Row, 1987).
6. Joseph L. DeVitis and John Martin Rich, *The Success Ethic, Education, and the American Dream* (Albany, NY: State University of New York Press, 1996), pp. 5–6. See also Maxine Greene, "On the American Dream: Equality, Ambiguity, and the Persistence of Rage" *Curriculum Inquiry* 13 (Summer, 1983), 179–93.
7. See, for example, Richard Arum and Josipa Roksa, *Academically Adrift: Limited Learning on College Campuses* (Chicago: University of Chicago Press, 2011); and Derek Bok, *Our Underachieving Colleges: A Candid Look at How Much Students Learn and Why They Should Be Learning More* (Princeton, NJ: Princeton University Press, 2006).
8. Russell Jacoby, *The Last Intellectuals* (New York: Basic Books, 2000), p. 7.
9. Ken Bain, *What the Best Teachers Do* (Cambridge, MA: Harvard University Press, 2004), p. 178.
10. David Thornton Moore, "Experiential Education as Critical Discourse." In *Combining Service and Learning: A Resource Book for Community and Public Service*, vol. 1, Jane Kendall and associates, eds. (Raleigh, NC: National Society for Internships and Experiential Education, 1990), p. 281. See also Benjamin R. Barber, *An Aristocracy of Everyone: The Politics of Education and the Future of America* (New York: Ballantine Books, 1992); and Joseph L. DeVitis, Robert W. Johns, and Douglas J. Simpson, eds., *To Serve and Learn: The Spirit of Community in Liberal Education* (New York: Peter Lang Publishing, 1998).
11. Herbert Spencer, *Education: Intellectual, Moral, and Physical* (New York: Appleton and Co., 1909), p. 11.
12. See my *The College Curriculum: A Reader* (New York: Peter Lang Publishing, in press). In that book, I devote full chapters to some of the more distinctive colleges and universities in America: Alverno, Bennington, College of the Atlantic, Colorado College, Empire State College, Fairhaven College (Western Washington University), Goddard, Green Mountain, Hampshire, James Madison University's Integrated Science & Technology Program, John Jay College's Interdisciplinary Studies Program, Miami University (OH)'s Western Interdisciplinary Studies Program, Michigan State's James Madison College residential program, New Century College of George Mason University, Olin College of Engineering, peace studies at such institutions as Earlham College, Prescott College, required service-learning experiences (focusing on Salem College), Roanoke College's problem-based general education, St. John's College (Md. & N. M.), service academies (West Point is dealt with in the text), University of Cincinnati's COOP program, University of Redlands' Johnston Center, University of Richmond's Jepson School of Leadership Studies, Wagner College's practical liberal arts program, and the ethics-across-the-curriculum offerings at Union College (N.Y.).
13. Michael W. Apple (with Barry Franklin), "Curricular History and Social Control," in Apple, *Ideology and Curriculum*, 3rd ed. (London: Routledge, 2004), p. 74.
14. Dewey, p. 67.
15. Stanley Fish, *Save the World on Your Own Time* (New York: Oxford University Press, 2008), p. 64.
16. Andrew Hacker and Claudia Dreifus, *Higher Education? How Colleges Are Wasting Our Money and Failing Our Kids—And What We Can Do About It* (New York: Times Books/Henry Holt, 2010), p. 43.

Acknowledgments

I want to thank Christopher Myers, managing director, and the production team of Peter Lang Publishing, especially Bernadette Shade and Phyllis Korper, for their typically excellent work in helping me assemble yet another project to completion. Jennifer Giblin, a talented graduate assistant in the Higher Education Program at Old Dominion University, deserves particular praise for her diligent and exceptional copy editing. Finally, I greatly appreciate the contribution of each of the chapter authors. In their own special ways, they confirm why I have enjoyed my adventures in higher education for such a long time.

PART ONE

Students: In and Out of the Classroom

CHAPTER ONE

Outside the Gates, Looking In

JON BOECKENSTEDT

If you wish to understand the modern American university, you might best start by looking at its front door, which at most universities is the admissions office. The front door metaphor is in many ways an apt one, as the admissions office is often located in a spot on campus that is easily located and accessible to people who are not familiar with the university; and it is intended to offer easy access to what lies beyond. As with most homes, the front door grants access to the living room, a place designed to be warm and welcoming to visitors, a showcase of sorts. Finally, the admissions office is found frequently on the edge of campus, sitting somewhere on the border between academia and the world beyond: This too may be a fitting metaphor.

But truly, if you wish to understand the admissions office, you might first start with a refresher on mythology, specifically the Roman god Janus. It is both the historic role of Janus and his dualistic nature that makes him a fitting model for admissions, and helps define the admissions profession in the early part of the 21st century.

Janus is, of course, the two-faced god for whom the month of January is named. January and the start of the new calendar year represent for many a time of looking back while looking forward; and Janus, with his two faces enabling him to see in both directions simultaneously, seems especially well qualified to do just that. The parallel is clear, of course, to high school students who are looking back at what they've already accomplished, and looking forward to what they hope to experience in college.

In addition to his bi-directional vision, Janus is the god who presides—at least symbolically—over important beginnings in a person's life: Representing the transition between primitive life and civilization, between the countryside and the city, and between peace and war, while watching over the maturing of young people. And finally, he is the god of doors and gates, standing at the passage from one reality to another. If the admissions profession were to have a patron saint or god, surely Janus would be it.

This is because it is almost certainly the notion of the gatekeeper that most concretely defines the role of the admissions office in the minds of many people outside—and sometimes inside—of academia. Like Disney World employees who enforce the height requirement on rides, or the thick-necked tenders of the velvet ropes at the latest trendy Los Angeles hot spot, admissions officers do, to some real extent, simply keep out those who should not be in and grant passage to those who qualify. Of course, it is clear even to the uninitiated that the definition of "qualify" varies widely from one institution to another, just as the criteria at night clubs do; but if the standards are different, it is widely believed, the job is essentially the same.

For those who are not familiar with the day-to-day work involved in enrolling a new class each fall, the implication is clear: While the real work of the university, whether it be teaching eager minds or creating new knowledge via research, goes on *inside* the massive stone buildings covered with ivy, admissions officers merely sit on the periphery, performing the important— albeit not especially skilled—task of sorting out those who are deemed capable from those who are not—or so conventional wisdom suggests. A closer inspection might reveal otherwise.

How Admissions Work Is Done

"Guarding the gates" as reflected in the admissions processes at the almost 1,500 public and private four-year, degree-granting institutions in the United States (National Center for Education Statistics, n. d.) is hardly the sole function of the admissions office in the modern university, even if it is commonly the one most associated with it. Nor is admitting a class of new students a monolithic process or system, as a monograph published by the College Board (Perfetto, 1999) points out—diving deeply as it attempts to develop a sophisticated and nuanced taxonomy of the wide range of admissions models in place across academia. And yet, that document begins the process of the classification of admission models with a simple bifurcation:

> The most basic distinction in the admission decision-making process is the one between eligibility and selection. Pure eligibility-based admissions models are ones in which there are objective and public criteria that anyone can use to determine if a student will be admitted to the institution. All students deemed "eligible" by these criteria will be admitted; all students who fail to meet the eligibility criteria will be denied. There is no ambiguity in an eligibility-based model, and there is little in the way of a selection process per se. (Perfetto, 1999, pp. 3–4)

The spectrum between pure eligibility models at one end, and selection models at the other, affords a wide range of approaches to college admission, all of which take into account some combination of academic accomplishment, intellectual potential, and other characteristics that may be strongly or loosely tied to the institution's curricular offerings or mission. For instance, a music conservatory may have some type of academic qualification as a preliminary selection criterion and may set those standards of accomplishment high or not, based on the extent to which the non-music classes in the university curriculum might demand it. But, in the end, students are ultimately selected to enroll in a music conservatory because they have both demonstrated musical talent and have achieved some heightened level of accomplishment as a musician. National Merit or Intel Scholars may impress admissions committees at Grinnell, UCLA, or Miami; but if you cannot play the violin, Juilliard does not care. Similarly, programs that seek to develop and train practicing artists or actors may weigh innate artistic talent and accomplishment almost to the exclusion of academic ability. While being able to integrate functions or balance chemical equations probably would not have been hindrances to Picasso or Brando, neither were they especially requisite for the specialized work they did.

In a very real way, admissions models are a reflection of the philosophy embedded in the university mission, and in application the most simple and straightforward admissions models we might find working in land-grant or other public institutions are easy to explain and comprehend. There the daily or yearly routine may in fact have some resemblance to that Disney World employee tending the rides: A simple, almost perfunctory review of qualifications with no judgment beyond the quantitative measures such as high school grade point average, curriculum appropriateness, and test scores is necessary; anyone in line who measures up gets to ride, provided there are no major character flaws or criminal convictions that might make you a danger to the academic community. In models like this, the university is required to educate whoever shows up after passing admissions muster; and if necessary, the university grows in direct proportion to demand. The reputation of the university is often based on a long history of accomplishment, substantial masses of successful and enthusiastic alumni, and widespread name recognition, rather than on the quality of the students it admits or the percentage it denies.

This should not be surprising, as it is frequently in large part reflective of founding missions and state legislatures, who, with assistance from Congress, founded and funded state institutions and land-grant institutions, the latter, for instance, ". . . to teach agriculture, military tactics, and the mechanic [sic] arts as well as classical studies so that members of the working classes could obtain a liberal, practical education" (National Association of State Universities and Land-Grant Colleges, 1995, p. x). Even today, with market pressures and in the face of decreased public funding, land-grant institutions "will remain fundamentally oriented to serving our respective publics and improving the human condition. That's what [their] DNA is" (Penn State, 2011).

And that DNA plays out in tangible ways, not the least of which are the published admissions policies. Take Texas A&M University, for instance, which admits any Texas high school graduate with a designated curriculum who graduates in the top 10% of his or her class and applies on time ("Ways to be Admitted"). Similarly, the University of Arkansas admissions website lists what seem to be fairly modest requirements for "automatic admission": A grade point average of 3.0 on a 4.0 scale, 16 required academic units in high school, and a composite score of 20 on the ACT or math+verbal scores of 920 on the SAT ("New Freshmen: Admissions"). In much the same way, the University of Montana requires that applicants meet a series of requirements in each of three areas in order to be admitted ("Apply Now"). The message is clear: Do what we ask you to do, meet the clear-cut academic requirements, and we are here to serve you. The admissions process is not bathed in mystique, not run inside a black box containing curious or arbitrary algorithms.

Inside the academy, many believe it is dangerous to attempt to measure the quality of a university by input measures such as admissions standards or selectivity rates (*U.S. News and World Report* notwithstanding); and these well-known and well-respected public institutions are perhaps the best evidence to support that belief. But there is a large group of moderately selective, mostly private institutions operating in a fiercely competitive market, employing a different model in admissions that strives to first fill the class (the majority of these places are, after all, overwhelmingly reliant on tuition to balance the budget) and simultaneously to leverage greater reputational equity, driven in large part by admission rates and input measures. And whether any university administrator likes it or not, absent any meaningful way to measure the quality of an institution (and academia's lack of willingness to even admit that there might be a way to do it), the public often has little else to go on.

There is, admittedly, a bit of Groucho Marx's "I wouldn't want to belong to any club that would have me as a member" mystique among high school students and their parents that colleges in the moderately selective group have seized upon; they have responded by trying to gain a share of heart and minds by attempting to inch into the next category of selectivity. Often this involves counterintuitive approaches to selecting the class. Golden (2001), for instance, outlines the strategy at Franklin and Marshall College in Pennsylvania, a respected liberal arts college attempting to move up in the pecking order. Director of Admissions Gregory Goldsmith puts a substantial number of very well-qualified students who had applied on the admission wait list, given the general lack of interest they had shown in the college:

The prospective students submitted Scholastic Aptitude Test scores and grades well above the average for applicants to the college. In past years, Mr. Goldsmith says, the college invariably admitted similarly qualified students who, like these, hadn't bothered to interview with the school. And usually, only half a dozen or so of them would enroll. "They think they're Ivy material," Mr. Goldsmith says.

So he relegated the overachievers to the waiting list. By doing so, he wove a statistical illusion, making the liberal-arts college appear more desirable and selective without actually raising the quality of its incoming freshman class.

Franklin and Marshall is hardly alone in using methods like this to create the illusion of selectivity or prestige. In the past decade, colleges have joined The Common Application, begun using "Fast Apps" (where a student can click on a link in an email to "apply" for admission, sometimes not even knowing she's done so), using special programs that defer wealthy low-ability students to spring term admits (where their profiles are generally not reported in public calculations), or reporting "Super Scores" on standardized tests (combining subsections from multiple test administrations to raise the scores reported to the public). While little changes in reality, a great deal can change in perception. The rub here, of course, is that if all colleges act this way, the net gain is negligible, while the costs are very real.

Those institutions positioned in the great and large middle of the bell curve attempt to offer some degree of cachet and exclusivity but still operate in a generally logical and predictable way in the admissions process. Even within this large group, there are, not surprisingly, many different missions and thus many different approaches and outcomes in the admissions process. Different colleges attempt to, or are forced to, maximize different outcomes; and it is important to distinguish here between two often conflated terms: Selective Admissions, on the one hand, and Competitive Admissions on the other.

Selectivity is a function of the admissions rate, that is, the percentage of applicants who are offered admission. An institution that receives 10,000 applications and admits 7,000 has an admission rate of 70%, for example, a rate well below open admissions institutions that admit close to 100%, and far above Harvard, whose 2010 admit rate was about 7% (IPEDS). Nationally, in fact, for the 2010 admissions cycle, fewer than 50 colleges admitted less than 25% of their applicants (and because the IPEDS data set that is the source of this data is not adjudicated, a handful of the institutions reporting these figures seem suspect). About 669 four-year private and public universities fell in the large group of four-year, degree-granting private and public universities that might be labeled moderately selective, with admission rates between 50% and 75%.

On the other hand, *competitiveness* is a measure of the quality of the incoming class, i.e., not the percent admitted, but median (or 25th to 75th percentiles) on the student characteristics, including rank in class, grade point average, and standardized test scores. For example, the same IPEDS data from 2010 shows the University of Dallas admitting well over 90% of its applicants, but with an average ACT score of enrolling students of 27, meaning the average student scored at about the 87th percentile of all test takers nationally. Both numbers are due in large part to the serious and rigorous "great books" curriculum that likely scares away large numbers of weak students and typical teenagers from applying. Similarly, Calvin College, a well-known institution in Michigan with a strong Christian focus that likely limits its mass appeal, admits 92% of those who apply, but shows median SAT scores (math + verbal) of 1185, putting its average student in the same company as those of its Catholic freshman profile twin in Dallas.

If it is clear, then, that not every competitive institution is selective, it is also true that not every selective institution is competitive. St. Peter's, for instance, a Jesuit school in New Jersey, has an admit rate of 44%, which many institutions might find enviable, but lists median SAT scores (math + verbal) of under 1,000. Similarly, Graceland University, an institution affiliated with the Community of Christ (a branch of Latter Days Saints) in rural southern Iowa, admits just 39% of its applicants, yet reports median ACT composite scores of 21, just at the national average.

Of course, while admissions standards do to a large extent control who gets in, they really have little to do with what happens inside the classroom. Inputs don't necessarily determine outputs. But, again, absent any standardized measure of what happens during a student's four years in college, the objective measures about the incoming class are frequently all the public has left to use for institutional yardsticks. Frank and Cook (1995) suggest that our "Winner Take All Society" causes the media and public to focus on and obsess over the top of any distribution, and that the obsession fuels itself. Given human nature and competition, is it any wonder colleges in the great middle strive to move up in the industry?

The obsession with the top of the bell curve is evident in the media fascination with the most selective institutions in the nation. Driven by extraordinary demand, the process of admission at highly selective institutions is very different than it is at other, less selective institutions. At Dartmouth and the seven other Ivy League universities (who enroll 61,000 undergraduates, or just under 1% of all college students in four-year institutions nationwide; IPEDS), where there are far more eager potential entrants than the university could comfortably handle, the model looks more like the night club bouncer, or perhaps, more appropriately, the country club membership committee, where a first cut is made to weed out those who are obviously out of the running, and a secondary or even tertiary round of evaluation happens on softer, more subjective criteria that are certainly not published and infrequently discussed (even if they seem to be understood by high school and independent counselors). But the nature of demand and the size of the pool means that, to outsiders at least, the final decisions on the large group of well-qualified students can seem like splitting hairs at best, and downright capricious at worst.

Along these lines, there is a by-now public domain observation about selective college admissions: A dean of admissions remarked publicly that if he were to accidentally send denial letters to the 1,000 students he wants to admit, and to send accidental admission letters to the 1,000 he denied who were just on the cusp, no one would notice. When I asked a group of knowledgeable professionals who had first said it, I heard from several people that it was Fred Hargadon when he was at Princeton or Stanford; Bill Fitzsimmons at Harvard; Bruce Poch at Pomona; or Christoph Guttentag at Duke. There were a handful of others mentioned at least once—from Yale, MIT, Northwestern, the University of Chicago, and Rice. It might be that, regardless of who said it first, it is now a way to at once position yourself among the handful of super-selective institutions without making it sound like you are happy about it, i.e., expressing pride in your humility. Yet another possibility is that admissions has assumed a religion-like quality in our collective mentality, replete with its own myths.

The Ivy League institutions, all strictly private except Cornell (which is an unusual amalgamation of both public and private), have no legal charter or requirement to serve anyone other than those whom they choose to serve, no state legislature mandating service, and no legal or moral obligation to serve any one in particular. In fact, the large corporate entity Harvard University (distinguished here from Harvard College) has no formal mission statement ("Frequently Asked Questions" Harvard University) that says whom they strive to educate or how they purport to do it (or even if education is a formal part of their *raison d'être*), but Yale does: "Yale seeks to attract a diverse group of exceptionally talented men and women from across the nation and around the world and to educate them for leadership in scholarship, the professions, and society" ("University Mission" Yale University Website). As we shall see, there is far more subtle nuance and texture on the road to accomplishing this task than first meets the eye. Ivy League and other highly selective university admissions can be described as anything but predictable or rational.

Henry Park might have benefitted from this perspective: Despite mission statements, conventional wisdom, and university strategic plans that measure the success of entire enterprises by the standardized measures of the entering freshman class, it is not always the academically talented who are admitted to the most elite institutions. Park was profiled by Golden (2003) in a *Wall Street Journal* article which pointed out that his stellar record in one of the nation's most prestigious and rigorous prep schools—Groton in Massachusetts—had earned him admissions denials (otherwise known as "rejections") at six elite universities, forcing him to "settle" for a place at Case Western Reserve University (he later transferred to Johns Hopkins).

It is not just that the universities that denied admission to Park are selective or that their admissions policies are rigorous. (This is widely known, even among those who are not in pursuit of a coveted admissions slot at what Sue Biemeret, a long-time high school counselor in Illinois, calls "one of the Holy Grail Schools"; Kleiner, 2000). In 2007, for instance, Princeton rejected thousands of students who never came close to settling for an A- in high school; and Harvard denied admission to 1,100 students with math scores of 800 on the SAT (Dillon, 2007). It is the case that many of Henry Park's classmates earned spots in those most selective institutions despite records demonstrably weaker than his. How can this be?

Christoph Guttentag, of Duke University, explains that paradox by describing admissions decisions as an "equitable distribution of unhappiness. . . Ultimately. . . schools make their admissions decisions to further their own goals. 'It's about us. It's not about you, '[and] we don't do a good enough job of being honest with parents and students. [The admissions process] is not merit-based, it's interest-based, our interest. It's how we define what we want to do" ("Rethinking Admissions," 2011).

Of course, we never meet Henry Park of the article in person. Perhaps he was profoundly shy, socially awkward, rude, offensive, grating, or even downright obnoxious. Or perhaps his parents were, leaving admissions officers an easy option to give out a sacred spot to someone with more pleasing personal characteristics and better breeding—and similar stellar academic credentials. This is, of course, the luxury of selectivity: The ability of an institution that generally seeks the very best students can deny even the most accomplished and most qualified students because there are too many "qualified" applicants in the pool to go around. Of course, there are also spillover benefits to the university in doing so: They are able to fill the class with students who bring something other than raw intellectual horsepower, knowing that a class full of straight-A students might be dull; and they perpetuate the mystique of the process, and this seems, interestingly enough, to generate even more interest. After all, if the system is hard to explain, it just might favor illogical decisions, and any student's chances for admission might increase.

Gladwell (2005) sums up selective admissions and the demand for them quite well:

> Social scientists distinguish between what are known as treatment effects and selection effects. The Marine Corps, for instance, is largely a treatment-effect institution. It doesn't have an enormous admissions office grading applicants along four separate dimensions of toughness and intelligence. It's confident that the experience of undergoing Marine Corps basic training will turn you into a formidable soldier. A modeling [sic] agency, by contrast, is a selection-effect institution. You don't become beautiful by signing up with an agency. You get signed up by an agency because you're beautiful.

At the heart of the American obsession with the Ivy League is the belief that schools like Harvard provide the social and intellectual equivalent of Marine Corps basic training—that being taught by all those brilliant professors and meeting all those other motivated students and getting a degree with that powerful name on it will confer advantages that no local state university can provide. . . . The extraordinary emphasis the Ivy League places on admissions policies, though, makes it seem more like a modeling agency than like the Marine Corps.

On a personal level, I find that this question parallels a conversation I once had with my brother: One of us wondered aloud whether Mom was the way she was because Dad was the way he was, or whether Dad was the way he was because Mom was the way she was. The answer, of course, is that it is impossible to separate cause and effect when they are so co-mingled. And thus it is with selective institutions: Are their students successful because admissions does a great job of selecting those who demonstrate that they are destined for success, or because something happens while enrolled that makes them successful? No one can say for sure, despite studies that have come down on both sides of the argument. But if parents obsess over their children's future and choose to err on the side of caution absent empirical evidence, can they be blamed?

Institutions with strong reputations will always attract students, or so it seems; and the fascination with the "best" institutions is hardly a recent phenomenon. Indeed, a 1957 ranking of the Best Colleges published in the *Chicago Daily Tribune* lists Oberlin, Swarthmore, Reed, Pomona, Grinnell, and Carleton among the best coed institutions, while Haverford, Williams, Kenyon, Wesleyan and Hamilton are listed as the best men's colleges. (On the latter list, Dartmouth was excluded, the rankings say, because it had "too much of a spread between its best and poorest students"). Williams slipped into 10th place despite several scholars who said it was "definitely not" among the top 10 men's colleges. Bryn Mawr, Vassar, Wellesley, Pembroke, and Radcliffe were among the top 10 in women's colleges. These listings, of course, largely mirror almost any "top" list one can find today.

For many applicants, "the something" that makes a single student stand out in a sea of almost identical academic perfection has to do with intangible qualities: leadership, charisma, or the attainment of the title of "best" in something such as music or acting or speech or writing or entrepreneurship or debate. Whereas colleges with large numbers of applications used to look for well-rounded *students*, they now seek a well-rounded *class*, filled with students who collectively bring a wide variety of talents at which they excel individually.

But too often, as the Golden (2003) article suggests, that something is often tangential at best to academic characteristics. As the story of the Groton class unfolds, we discover some of the well-known secrets of selective college admissions: that students with "hooks" as high school counselors call them, have much better chances for admission at the universities they pursue. Legacy admission, for example (where one or both parents is an alumnus of the university), appears to give students a leg up for no other reason than accident of birth.

Similarly, parents who are identified by the advancement or alumni office as large donors (or even potentially large donors) also impart a distinct advantage to applicants. In some ways, this makes sense: Colleges and universities have reasonable interests in keeping alumni and donors happy. What seems impossible to believe is that parents of the students in Park's class at Groton who probably benefited from these policies seem, at least publicly, to be oblivious to the fact. Yet Glouberman (2011) writes candidly in his discussion of his time at Harvard in a piece that is ostensibly about the university's lack of cachet in Canada:

> When I applied, I thought it would be great because I would get to meet lots of smart people. Those were the kinds of people I liked to be friends with, and I thought there would be more of them there. That was the main reason I thought it would be a fun place to be. I don't think I was super ambitious or professional minded or even a very good student.

The thing I figured out soon after I applied was that, on *Gilligan's Island*, it wasn't the Professor who went to Harvard, it was Mr. Howell, the rich man. That was something of a revelation.

And Moll (1994), writing almost 20 years ago, portends this trend in reporting a conversation with a college counselor at a high-profile East Coast prep school for girls:

> "It's downright embarrassing to have the kids who can pay, ranking in the middle of the class, admitted to fairly selective colleges who without a wink pass by better students and sometimes more interesting girls who need considerable financial aid" she notes. "We have grown accustomed to this inconsistency when used to the advantage of students of color, and we can understand that; but to explain away inconsistencies quietly based on who can pay and who cannot is a tough task." (p. 16)

Yet still another variable, namely athletic ability, comes into play at the most selective institutions in the nation. In an article in the *New York Times* by Fiske (2001), Philip Smith, the recently retired dean of admissions at Williams, said: "Athletic recruiting is the biggest form of affirmative action in American higher education, even at schools such as ours." The trend is even more pronounced at Big Division I schools with football: The same admissions office at Notre Dame that boasts median SAT scores of 1,400 for the general student body admits football players with scores almost 400 points lower ("College Athletes' SAT and IQ Scores,"

2011), a trend mirrored to a lesser extent at every university that the *Atlanta Journal-Constitution* reported on after making freedom of information requests (Knobler, 2008).

If this seems confusing, perhaps it is meant to be. Sundry and secretive admissions approaches—even at moderately selective institutions—seem designed, on purpose, to fly in the face of conventional wisdom and common sense. When colleges and universities reserve the right to shape classes and include not just those who are academically excellent but those who can contribute something to the character, personality, or ethos of campus life, they are, they claim, doing so in order to improve the experience for all students, and at some level, this makes perfect sense. If educators believe—and most seem to—that learning happens best when new ideas are discussed, long-held beliefs are challenged, and students encounter and work with others who are not all just like them, it is difficult to argue with them. But the U.S. Supreme Court came dangerously close to eliminating the right of colleges to do just that in the 2003 cases of *Gratz v. Bollinger* and *Grutter v. Bollinger*, often referred to in admissions as "The Michigan decisions."

Without re-hashing those decisions more than has already been done, the Court ruled against the University of Michigan undergraduate admissions office and its policy of awarding points to candidates from underrepresented minority groups. Review of undergraduate applicants prior to the lawsuit was done on a strict, almost robotic, point system, with no nuance or subjectivity, except of course in the creation of the scale in the first place.

At the same time, though, the Court ruled the Law School at Michigan was operating within acceptable guidelines by considering race and ethnicity as one element of many in a holistic, more subjective, and individual review of every applicant. The Court had weighed in on the validity of a mostly subjective admissions process, narrowly clearing it after having rejected the quota system in the 1978 case *Regents of the University of California v. Bakke*, where the Harvard system on individual review was specifically mentioned as acceptable.

However, many were troubled by the premise of the lawsuit in the first place, i.e., that "qualification for admission" was strictly and rigidly argued by the narrowest of criteria, namely GPA and standardized test scores. To those who know college admission well, it was almost as if the plaintiffs were asking the court to order Michigan to institute a pure eligibility standard for admission to the nation's universities who received Title IV funding, which includes not only public institutions but the overwhelming majority of private colleges and universities as well. The plaintiffs in Michigan came very close to succeeding, losing 4–5 in the law school case after winning the undergraduate case.

Thus, the admissions profession, poised as it is between a student's high school graduation and college matriculation, and driven largely by an unknown and indefinable (some might say purposely clandestine) formula, is at the forefront of many controversies. But even if there were a way to encapsulate and articulate how admissions is done, one would still not have defined what admissions is.

A Monolithic Term, but Not a Monolithic Function

It should be clear by now that it is unfair, or even inappropriate, to speak of the admissions office and assume it is the same everywhere. There are thousands of institutions, thousands of mission statements, and probably almost as many strategic plans that contain some component of moving the college or university forward with respect to the quality of the students enrolling. In some sense, of course, this has always been the case. But even if the roles of the various and sundry offices function differently, it is equally interesting to note how they seem to be in conflict with the very things they purport to serve. This is part evolution, part response to changing markets and changing market expectations.

Consider the often-seen television ad for Subaru. It shows a man, talking to his daughter, who is seated in the driver's seat of a car. He is leaning in the open passenger-side window, giving her instructions about safe driving, but something is wrong: He sees her as a four-year-old who can barely reach the steering wheel; then we see her as a 16–year-old getting ready to drive the car for the first time. Any parent watching understands the metaphor. Even though time has changed the toddler into a young woman, the father still sees her as the child he remembers from a decade or more ago. He is unable to grasp how she has grown up before his eyes, even though he obviously knows the truth. Yet we are perfectly comfortable with the duality: She is both young woman and little girl, both ready for the world and likely unaware of what awaits her.

So it is with college admissions. Over the past few decades, the role of the admissions office within the academy has changed dramatically, yet many still view and understand the function through an outdated lens of innocence, perhaps even remembering when admissions was simply a part of the registrar's office, or, more likely, when admissions was mostly the previously mentioned "gatekeeper" function, evaluating whatever applications came in to ensure that the students were, in fact, capable of doing the work required of college students. That view of reality is seriously warped. Kirp (2003) sums it up nicely:

> A Rip Van Winkle admissions officer who fell asleep in the 1970s and awoke today wouldn't recognize his own profession. Even as students have changed—they are more willing to consider going to school away from home and apply to more schools—the easygoing world of registrars who counted things and counselors who played matchmaker has vanished. While "the general admission objectives and some of the admission folkways persist" writes Donald Stewart, the former president of The College Board, "much that is done now on the admissions landscape would be foreign territory to many of them." (pp. 16–17)

In some sense, the very phrase "admissions office" is a misnomer, for two reasons: The admissions offices at Iowa State, Occidental, and Williams carry the same title, and ostensibly carry out the same tasks—admitting and enrolling new students—even if they work in different ways. But all conduct many activities that go beyond admissions or selection work. Not only does the work that happens inside the admissions office affect what happens at the university; some suggest that there are agents of social and economic change working inside the office, and not always for the most positive purpose.

It is natural to ask how important the admissions office function is to the university. To many who know the profession, the very existence of this question misses much of the nuance and complexity embedded in the day-to-day tasks of enrolling a new class. But even if there are some elements of truth in the perception of admissions offices as gatekeepers (and those who know them would have to admit there are), no less authority than A. Michael Spence (1973), the 2001 winner of *The Sveriges Riksbank Prize in Economic Sciences in Memory of Alfred Nobel* (often called the *Nobel Prize in Economics*), suggests that selective college admissions as an efficient sorter of human capital has implications in the country's labor market: In a game in which employers are forced to hire in a context of asymmetrical information, the process of student self-sorting, and the subsequent secondary sorting of the admissions office, can signal much to an employer.

Similarly, Karabel (2005) suggests that the policies of the admissions offices at Harvard, Yale, and Princeton in the late 1900s and early part of the 20th century had as much, or even more, to do with shaping the 20th century as what actually went on inside the classrooms at those quintessential brand names in American higher education. This might seem like a formidable burden to hoist onto the shoulders of mere gatekeepers, but it exists as perhaps an excellent introduction to the widely divergent perspectives on college admissions offices today.

Thus, we again return to Janus, whose duality is appealing: Admissions work is filled with paradox, the embracing of seeming contradictions, and the creative tension between pragmatism and ideal that we find in the university admissions office in the early part of the 21st century. For to understand what goes on in a university admissions office and its peculiar place in the academy, one must, to quote F. Scott Fitzgerald, "hold two opposed ideas in the mind at the same time, and still retain the ability to function" ("Talk: F. Scott Fitzgerald" Wikiquote). In a certain sense, the way in which talented and experienced admissions professionals are capable of balancing ostensibly contradictory truths is admirable; at the same time, limiting the number of "opposed truths" to two does not do the comparison justice. Sometimes, the paradoxes consist of multiple and interwoven layers of complexity that seem to make sense only to those who manage them regularly.

Peter Senge (1990) suggests that this duality—he refers to it as creative tension—can serve as a personal propellant. For Senge, it is often a personal tension between what is and what can be. For professionals in the field of admissions, it may well be a tension between what educators perceive their work to be about, and what it actually is about.

On the Edge of Access and Economic Perpetuation

David Brooks (2005), in an op-ed piece in *The New York Times*, opens with this provocative statement: "Let's say you work at a university or college. You are a cog in one of the great inequality producing machines this country has known. What are you doing to change that?"

Ask this question of most admissions officers, and you will likely find—after shocked disbelief—that the answer is "a great deal." Based solely on my personal experience, which includes almost 30 years in the profession, the very thought that admissions officers and admissions processes might be contributing to the perpetuation of what Tom Mortenson (2005) calls "Higher Education's Gated Communities" might qualify as heresy. Most admissions officers see themselves as doing just the opposite: Encouraging education, advocating for underrepresented students, and facilitating the transition to higher education in order to change lives.

Again, it is extraordinarily difficult to separate cause and effect; but the end product is clear: The most selective and sought-after institutions in the nation are also the wealthiest, with per-capita resources that put them far beyond the fiscal realities of most universities in the nation. And yet, for their resources, these wealthy institutions do the worst job of educating poor students in America. Princeton, for example, in 2010 had net assets per full-time-equivalent (FTE) enrollment of almost $1. 9 million, yet only about 10% of its undergraduates received Pell Grants (the federal program for the most needy students, as defined by the results of the Free Application for Federal Student Aid, or FAFSA).

It is not for lack of trying, if one looks at what the richest institutions say publicly: The well-resourced institutions in the nation still hold onto the concept of "need blind" admissions, i.e., a student's ability to pay does not affect his or her chances for admission. In fact, most of the extraordinarily selective universities also guarantee to meet 100% of demonstrated financial need for those who are admitted. Harvard even goes farther, pledging that students who come from families with less than $180,000 in family income will pay no more than 10% to enroll there.

On the surface, this is quite a noble proposition—and frequently one of the things outsiders who think of students as customers cannot understand. Jesse Ventura, the former governor of Minnesota, was fairly incredulous when he was told that universities often admitted better students who could not pay over weaker ones who could. The governor, not known for subtlety, responded, "Baloney," and even seemed to doubt it when assured by experts.

Yet there are two catches in the discussion of need-blind admissions that are important to understand: First, as indicted above, the inverse of need-blind admissions often comes into play when evaluating and admitting students with extraordinary wealth; and the slots that those students take do, in a zero-sum game, take away slots that might go to low-income students. One need only look at John F. Kennedy's underwhelming application to Harvard (O'Connor, 2011) and the correspondence his father Joe had with people there to see how this effect played out in the past, even if no one believes it could happen in the same way today.

But this is a minor issue compared to the larger one: Need-blind admissions naively ignore only the income part of being poor, not the residual effects of it. Any institution that weighs standardized test scores (and thus the financial wherewithal to pay for test-prep services or to take the test several times), access to AP classes from the College Board, or even a record of out-of-class accomplishments that favor students who do not have to work, can hardly be called need-blind. Against those odds, low-income students seem to have little chance to collect the prize promised to them. It is akin to owning a restaurant and saying, "Dogs welcome, as long as they only have two legs like the rest of our customers." It may, in fact, happen that occasionally a dog has only two legs (or gets there by unthinkable means), but it is certainly not a natural state of affairs. The welcome is a hollow one.

Despite admissions officers' collective pronouncement that a student's four years in high school matter more than four hours spent on Saturday morning in a standardized test like the SAT or ACT, the importance of those test scores is still evident, if not in public pronouncements about admissions processes, then certainly in public pronouncements about the quality of the freshman class, or strategic plans that seek to increase them. The appeal of the tests is easy to understand: Who would not love to be able to sum up an extraordinarily complex variable like academic ability or intellectual capacity in a single number, especially when having to make decisions that are somewhat arbitrary and where the future of a student is at stake? The Provost of Oklahoma State University Robert Sternberg (2011) lists this and nine other reasons tests are popular, including sunk costs and superstition, for the perpetuation of the tests' popularity.

There is no shortage of test critics, of course, even though the statistical analysis talent necessary to determine whether or not they really measure anything of value is found within a relatively small group of statisticians and social scientists. Even the testing agencies themselves admit that there is a clear and pronounced correlation between income and achievement on standardized tests, yet they argue—sometimes convincingly—that these factors are mostly explained by different patterns of course selection or access to greater educational opportunity bestowed by parental wealth. What the agencies are less proud of are documents that show the tests were originally developed and used precisely to exclude or limit certain groups of students from enrolling, including Jews at Columbia, and later at Yale, populations of students who needed financial aid. In these uses of the test, there is a sort of tacit endorsement of the many studies showing little or no predictive validity of the scores as they relate to academic success in college (Soares, 2011). *Rationale for tests is reasonable*

So the current standardized testing requirement of the wealthy, selective institutions is ironically exclusionary and, in some sense, perfectly rational. Even absent any statistical analysis, it is clear that a student who scores well on such a test is likely to have some real and measureable level of intelligence, academic accomplishment, or perhaps aptitude. With thousands of 3.9 and 4.0 students vying for a small and fixed number of spaces in the freshman class, and hundreds more with one or more "hooks" a standardized test with a very low false positive helps make admissions decisions easier, and even more rational. The logical contrapositive is not true, of course, and most educators say they know lots of students with low test scores who are equally talented intellectually and on par academically with their high-scoring peers.

Serving Two Masters

Admissions ≠ Academy
- Revenue generating & marketing business unit

Is the dean of admissions now outside the academy? Moll (1994) suggests the answer is an *of university* unqualified yes, and goes a step beyond, suggesting that the admissions office has been transformed into the marketing and revenue-generating business unit of the otherwise noble university. Listing a group of admissions deans and directors who have been shown the door because they would not embrace technology or because they did not adequately balance quality, diversity, revenue, or the other demands imposed on them by presidents or trustees, he quotes one president as proof:

> "Today I expect the admissions/financial aid team to invent and oversee a marketing plan that, by the end of each recruiting year, produces a student body that achieves net tuition revenue targets. . . I hate to say it" he continues, "but we're getting to be like the airlines in creative discounting. United and Continental have all those planes that have to fly. They prosper and have the means to improve their product only if those planes are full, or nearly full. So they take a reading of the diverse populations they are happy to attract, market creatively to each of them with their eyes glued to the competition, alter pricing among the populations, walk the different groups who've paid very different prices down the red carpet, and lift off. (pp. 12–13) *yes!*

It is thus difficult to understand why the industry trade paper *The Chronicle of Higher Education* lists admissions and enrollment management positions under the "Student Services" section in its weekly jobs listing, along with positions for registrar, residence life specialists, and campus programming professionals. It is clear that the admissions office is very different from other units in the university: It must have two faces, one pointing inward at what happens in the classrooms and residence halls, and one facing outward to understand what happens outside, i.e., in markets. In fact, despite the profession's insistence on using terms such as "admissions counselors" for entry-level staff members, the annual routine of the admissions officer involves the creation of marketing materials, including printed and electronic communications and presentations for large groups, that are often developed in conjunction with volumes of

inward & outward facing unit

market research—which analyze data on the population of high school graduates in coming years, looking not just at the number of students but also their location, ethnicity, geographic mobility, and socioeconomic levels; and which study the price elasticity of last year's applicants in terms of academic ability, choice set, parental attainment, and areas of academic interest to best use institutional financial aid, manipulating cost via sophisticated price discrimination; and understanding and assessing job market data to gauge whether academic programs offered are in line with student expectations and wants.

Of course, there is no outcome at the university that is measured and discussed as much as the results of the admissions efforts each year. (It is not unreasonable to point out here that a Division I football or basketball coach might get more attention, but sports are arguably less tied to the core mission of the university than student enrollment is.) Few professors need to worry about whether an annual measure of student learning (if one happens) will cause many of them to lose their jobs. A "housecleaning" of unproductive faculty is unheard of, but not so with admissions personnel. Annual press releases tout not only the number but the quality of the students enrolling, and a number too low can result in immediate ramifications at the university. Beloit College, for instance, had to lay off 40 staff members to save a million dollars when enrollment—mostly driven by a smaller-than-expected freshman class—fell short by 36 students (Schultz, 2008). Conversely, a number too large can result in classroom overcrowding, a last-minute scramble to hire staff to cover additional sections, or strain on other systems such as housing and food services.

The magic in enrolling a freshman or transfer class of the appropriate size is both an art and a science. Deciding how many to admit is determined both by looking backwards at the size of the applicant pool (in order to keep admission rates from inching up too high) and looking forward at an anticipated "yield rate" or the number of students offered admission who decide to enroll. At DePaul University, in 2011, for example, over 16,000 students applied and about 10,000 were admitted; 2,458 enrolled, for a yield rate of 24.58%. But a swing of one percentage point on that number means 100 more or 100 less, and at $30,000 in gross tuition per student, the implications are clear. Even at a university with a $550 million dollar budget, $3 million is substantial. Consider the Navy pilot who needs to land a jet on a rainy night on an aircraft carrier pitching on a rough sea. Sometimes just a safe landing is more than enough to ask for; expecting the pilot to hit "the second wire" on the deck can be seen as unreasonable in tough conditions. Yet admissions officers need to not only land the plane (by bringing in a certain number), but also go for the second wire—hitting net revenue, quality, and diversity goals at the same time. They often have to make critical, "point of no return" decisions months ahead of time on seas that are not only rough, but prone to rapid change. The only good part is that a metaphorical crash under such circumstances carries far less risk than a literal one.

But that does not mean that the interests of admissions officers lie solely on the business side of the enterprise. In fact, it is hard to imagine anyone coming into the admissions profession (with its long hours often spent away from home, relatively low pay, and often misunderstood roles in the university) with solely materialist visions in mind. The for-profit world offers greater clarity, less need to serve sometimes conflicting objectives, and greater pay. Yet there are many loyal members of NACAC (the National Association for College Admission Counseling), which hosts over 5,000 admissions and high school guidance professionals each year, who often come together for a common cause, i.e., for the students they serve. Anyone who has been around admissions people for a while knows that there is a true sense of a higher calling that buoys the spirit and propels professional accomplishment. Thresher (1966), in a superb and almost prescient book about college admissions, says it well:

> At its lowest and least imaginative level, exchange between high school counselors and admissions people constitutes a kind of brokerage operation. At this level, the job is one of negotiation: the high school counselor tries to make the best possible bargain on behalf of his "client" for admission to a strong college. . . . The admissions officer . . . is looking for the strongest students. . . who are deemed more desirable. In such an atmosphere of negotiation it is very easy to fall into a predominately bargaining habit of thought, losing sight of the fact that both parties to the transaction are in a deeper sense obligated to ask as trustees for the student's welfare. (p. 53)

Zemsky, Wegner, and Massy (2005) recall the words of Clark Kerr, the former president of the University of California, who waxed eloquent about this tension inherent in the academy: "The cherished academic view that higher education started out on the acropolis and was desecrated by descent into the agora led by ungodly commercial interests and scheming public officials and venal academic leaders is just not true. If anything, higher education started in the agora, the market, at the bottom of the hill and ascended to the acropolis at the top of the hill."

The admissions officer, it seems, manages to balance the needs of the agora and the acropolis well, and the American university system is better for it.

References

"Apply Now | Enrollment Services-Admissions at The University of Montana." *Enrollment Services-Admissions at The University of Montana | Explore, Apply, and Experience UM*. Web. 29 Oct. 2011. <http://admissions. umt. edu/apply>.

Brooks, David. "The Education Gap." *The New York Times* 25 Sept. 2005. Web. 30 Oct. 2011. <http://select. nytimes.com/2005/09/25/opinion/25brooks.html? _r=1>.

"College Athletes' SAT and IQ Scores."*Centraltendencies.com*. Web.01 Nov. 2011. <http://centraltendencies. com/2009/01/college-athletes-sat-iq-scores/>.

Dillon, Sam. "A Great Year for Ivy League Schools, but Not So Good for Applicants to Them." Advertisement. *The New York Times* 04 Apr. 2007. Web. 29 Oct. 2011. <http://www.nytimes.com/2007/04/04/ education/04colleges.html>.

Fiske, Edward B. "Gaining Admission: Athletes Win Preference." *The New York Times* 07 Jan. 2001. Web. 29 Oct. 2011. <http://www.nytimes.com/2001/01/07/education/gaining-admission-athletes-win-preference.html? pagewanted=all>.

Frank, Robert H., and Philip J. Cook. *The Winner-take-all Society: How More and More Americans Compete for Ever Fewer and Bigger Prizes, Encouraging Economic Waste, Income Inequality, and an Impoverished Cultural Life*. New York: Free, 1995. Print.

"Frequently Asked Questions." *Harvard University*. Web. 29 Oct. 2011. <http://www.harvard.edu/faqs/mission-statement>.

Gladwell, Malcolm. "Getting In." *Gladwell.com* 10 Oct. 2005. Web. 29 Oct. 2011. <http://www.gladwell. com/2005/2005_10_10_a_admissions.html>.

Glouberman, Misha. "Harvard and Class." *Paris Review*. Ed. Sheila Heti. 11 July 2011. Web. 29 Oct. 2011. <http:// www.theparisreview.org/blog/author/mglouberman/>.

Golden, Daniel. "For Groton Grads, Academics Aren't Only Keys to Ivy Schools." *The Wall Street Journal* 25 Apr. 2003. Web. 29 Oct. 2011. <http://online. wsj.com/article/SB105122532572026400.html>.

"*Gratz v. Bollinger*." *Wikipedia, the Free Encyclopedia*. Web. 30 Oct. 2011. <http://en. wikipedia.org/wiki/Gratz_v. _Bollinger>.

"*Grutter v. Bollinger*."*Wikipedia, the Free Encyclopedia*. Web. 30 Oct. 2011. <http://en. wikipedia.org/wiki/ Grutter_v. _Bollinger>.

Hacker, Andrew, and Claudia Dreifus. *Higher Education?: How Colleges Are Wasting Our Money and failing Our Kids--and What We Can Do about It*. New York: Times, 2010. Print.

"Harvard College Admissions § Financial Aid: Harvard Financial Aid Initiative." *Harvard College Admissions § Homepage*. Web. 30 Oct. 2011. <http://www.admissions. college. harvard.edu/financial_aid/hfai/index.html>.

"Janus." *Encyclopedia Mythica: Mythology, Folklore, and Religion*. Web. 30 Oct. 2011. <http://www.pantheon.org/articles/j/janus.html>.

"Janus: Roman God of Beginnings." *Penumbra*. Web. 30 Oct. 2011. <http://www.novareinna.com/festive/janus.html>.

"Janus." *Wikipedia, the Free Encyclopedia*. Web. 30 Oct. 2011. <http://en. wikipedia.org/wiki/Janus>.

Kalafa, J. "The Answer to Notre Dame's Academic Stds Debate: The NFL Studies Degree | Bleacher Report." *Bleacher Report* 5 July 2010. Web. 29 Oct. 2011. <http://bleacherreport.com/articles/415794--college-football-schools-can-offer-majors-in-nfl-studies>.

Karabel, Jerome. *The Chosen: The Hidden History of Admission and Exclusion at Harvard, Yale, and Princeton*. Boston: Houghton Mifflin, 2005. Print.

Kirp, David L. *Shakespeare, Einstein, and the Bottom Line: The Marketing of Higher Education*. Cambridge, MA: Harvard UP, 2003. Print.

Kleiner, Caroline. "Getting in Gets Harder." *U.S. News & World Report* 14 May 2000. Web. 23 Mar. 2012. <http://www.usnews.com/usnews/edu/articles/000522/archive_017095_2.htm>.

Knobler, Mike. "AJC Investigation: Many Athletes Lag Far behind on SAT Scores." *Atlanta Journal-Constitution* 28 Dec. 2008. Web. 29 Oct. 2011. <http://www.ajc.com/search/content/sports/stories/2008/12/28/acadmain_1228_3DOT.html>.

Manley, Chesly. "Bryn Mawr: A Synonym for Brainy Women." *Chicago Daily Tribune* 2 June 1957. *ProQuest Historical Newspapers*. Web. 30 Oct. 2011.

Manley, Chesly. "Haverford College: It's Small but Famous." *Chicago Daily Tribune* 2 June 1957. *ProQuest Historical Newspapers*. Web. 30 Oct. 2011.

Manley, Chesly. "Oberlin Is Leader of Co-ed Liberal Arts Colleges." *Chicago Daily Tribune,* 2 June 1957. *ProQuest Historical Newspapers*. Web. 30 Oct. 2011.

Moll, Richard W. "The Scramble to Get the New Class." *Change* 26. 2 (1994): 10–17. Print.

Mortenson, Thomas. "The Most Exclusive Gated Communities of Higher Education." *Postsecondary Education OPPORTUNITY* 10 Dec. 2005. Web. 30 Oct. 2011. <http://postsecondaryopportunity. blogspot.com/2005/12/most-exclusive-gated-communities-of.html>.

"Myths about the Roman God Janus." *Roman Colosseum*. Web. 30 Oct. 2011. <http://www.roman-colosseum. info/roman-gods/myths-about-the-roman-god-janus.htm>.

National Association of State Universities and Land-Grant Colleges. *The Land-grant Tradition*. Washington, DC: National Association of State Universities and Land-Grant Colleges, 1995. Print.

National Association of State Universities and Land-Grant Colleges. *The Land-grant Tradition*. Washington, DC: National Association of State Universities and Land-Grant Colleges, 1995. Print.

National Center for Education Statistics. "The Integrated Postsecondary Education Data System: Home Page." *National Center for Education Statistics (NCES), a Part of the U.S. Department of Education*. National Center for Education Statistics, n. d. Web. 29 Oct. 2011. <http://nces. ed. gov/ipeds/>.

"New Freshmen | Admissions | University of Arkansas." *Home | Admissions | University of Arkansas*. Web. 29 Oct. 2011. <http://admissions. uark.edu/apply/118. php>.

O'Connor, Maureen. "JFK's Unimpressive Harvard Application." *Gawker* 14 Jan. 2011. Web. 30 Oct. 2011. <http://gawker.com/5734064/jfks-unimpressive-harvard-application>.

Penn State. –"Scholars Debate Future Role of Land-grant Universities at Penn State." *Penn State Live—The University's Official News Source* 24 June 2011. Web. 30 Oct. 2011. <http://live. psu.edu/story/53946>.

Perfetto, Greg. *Toward a Taxonomy of the Admissions Decision-making Process: A Public Document Based on the First and Second College Board Conferences on Admissions Models*. New York: College Board, 1999. Print.

Regents of the University of California v. Bakke. *Wikipedia, the Free Encyclopedia*. Web. 30 Oct. 2011. <http://en. wikipedia.org/wiki/Regents_of_the_University_of_California_v. _Bakke>.

"Rethinking Admissions » Blog Archive » It's about Us, Not You." *Rethinking Admissions*. Wake Forest University, 15 April 2009. Web. 30 Oct. 2011. <http://rethinkingadmissions. blogs. wfu.edu/2009/04/15/its-about-us-not-you/>.

Schultz, Frank. "Beloit College Announces Job Cuts." *GazetteXtra* 08 Nov. 2008. Web. 30 Oct. 2011. <http://gazettextra.com/news/2008/nov/08/beloit-college-announces-job-cuts/>.

Senge, Peter M. *The Fifth Discipline: The Art and Practice of the Learning Organization*. New York: Doubleday/Currency, 1990. Print.

Soares, Joseph A. *SAT Wars: The Case for Test-optional College Admissions*. New York: Teachers College, 2012. Print.

Spence, Michael A. "Job Market Signaling." *The Quarterly Journal of Economics* 87. 3 (1973): 355–74. Print.

Sternberg, Robert. "How to Reform Testing." *Inside Higher Ed* 01 Nov. 2011. Web.01 Nov. 2011. <http://www.insidehighered.com/views/2011/11/01/essay-difficulty-promoting-reforms-admissions-testing>.

"Talk: F. Scott Fitzgerald." *Wikiquote*. Web.01 Nov. 2011. <http://en. wikiquote.org/wiki/Talk: F. _Scott_Fitzgerald>.

Thresher, B. Alden. *College Admissions and the Public Interest*. New York: College Entrance Examination Board, 1966. Print.

"University Mission | Yale."*Yale University*. Web. 29 Oct. 2011. <http://www.yale.edu/about/mission.html>.

University of Michigan News Service. 11 May 2011. Web. 30 Oct. 2011. <http://ns. umich.edu/index.html? Releases/2003/Jun03/supremecourt2>.

"Ways to Be Admitted." *Texas A&M University*. Web. 30 Oct. 2011. <http://admissions.tamu.edu/freshmen/gettingin/waysAdmitted/default. aspx>.

Zemsky, Robert, Gregory Wegner, and William Massy. "Today's Colleges Must Be Market Smart and Mission Centered." *The Chronicle of Higher Education* 15 July 2005. Web. 30 Oct. 2011. <http://chronicle.com/article/Todays-Colleges-Must-Be/35802/>.

CHAPTER TWO

Heeding the Canary

How Higher Education Can Improve Outcomes for All Students

HEATHER D. WATHINGTON

For some reason, we were unprepared for the news. The stinging condemnation of higher learning that emerged from the controversial book *Academically Adrift: Limited Learning on College Campuses* (Arum & Roksa, 2011) stunned many educators in and outside of academia. The authors of the book, professors Richard Arum and Josipa Roksa, contend that four years of undergraduate classes make little difference in students' ability to synthesize knowledge and put complex ideas in writing. Arum and Roksa call for greater student learning accountability and for new commitments to be made to undergraduate education. While calls for undergraduate reform are not new to higher education (AAC & U, 1985), *Academically Adrift* is among the first sources to present convincing empirical research as evidence of a crisis within the ivory tower.

But this news should not have come as a total surprise. The doors to college have widened over the last century to include new populations of underserved students who are often underprepared for college expectations. Underserved students—students of color, low-income, and first generation students—have a long storied history with success in higher education and their challenges are well known to us. For example, we know that low-income students are less likely to attend college than their higher-income high school counterparts (Kahlenberg, 2004a); students of color who choose to major in STEM fields often change majors from STEM fields due to low academic performance (Betts & Morrell, 1999); and first-generation students are far more likely to drop out of college than their second- and third-generation peers. Underserved students are frequently criticized for their failure to measure up to the performance of traditional students. To help improve their access and success, educators have sympathized with their challenges and have developed special services and boutique programs here and there to serve them. But the notion that the ivory tower is somehow the problem—or at least complicit in sustaining the problem—is hardly discussed. But perhaps it should be. Perhaps underrepresented students are our canaries in the mine (Guinier & Torres, 2002). As coalminers looked to canaries with their sensitive respiratory systems to alert them to poison in the air, so we too should interpret what our underrepresented students signal about the current state of higher education. If we were to look and listen, their stressed presence within colleges says a great deal about the health and well-being of our academic institutions. However, at our own peril we choose to pathologize the canaries instead of interpreting their signals of distress as vulnerabilities in our capacity to serve them.

This essay illustrates how the challenges of our underserved students point to signs of system failure in higher education and how we cannot afford to ignore the signs. Rather, we must re-envision how we educate students for the 21st century to offer all students the opportunity to be successful in higher education. Citing recent research, I examine three broad areas of college participation in turn: access to higher education, academic progress in higher education, and attainment within higher education. Within each area, I highlight how two or three documented challenges for underserved students are not just issues of equity, but challenges for the academy. I also recommend promising programs and workable solutions that might bring about the change we need.

Access to Higher Education

Developmental Education

To be fair, higher education has fairly limited control over a major barrier to college entry—referral into developmental education. Developmental courses are pre-college courses that almost never count toward a postsecondary credential or graduation. These courses are designed for students who are underprepared for the rigors of college-level work. The need to complete these basic skills courses before starting college-level coursework delays progress to a degree or credential. And the delay for many students becomes paralyzing as most colleges and universities struggle with helping students to progress. Bailey, Jeong, and Cho (2008) show that while many students are referred to developmental education, a third of those referred fail to even enroll in these courses so they never complete a credential. For those that do enroll, too few make it through the developmental sequence into college-level coursework students.

Given that students with developmental needs are less likely to earn a credential, strengthening developmental education needs to be a focus for higher education institutions. Access, achievement, and completion in postsecondary education are all undermined by the weak academic preparation of many students. If more students are to be successful, colleges and universities must urgently develop approaches that work. While colleges and universities have experimented with various forms of developmental education reform,[1] recent research suggests that comprehensive approaches to improving developmental education might be necessary. Emerging research in developmental education suggests many reforms have modest effects—far too modest to significantly impact student outcomes (Wathington et al., 2011). Students need more than single-semester or summer developmental experiences to prepare them for the rigors of college-level work. Revamping the full first-year experience for all developmental students to include a student success course, intensive advising, and tutoring would likely prove more successful than brief intensive interventions. Other promising interventions include developing developmental modules rather than courses (the model adopted by Virginia's community colleges for developmental math) to help meet students at their immediate area of need and mainstreaming the highest-level developmental students into college-level courses to advance them onto college-level work.

Experimental Participation

Aside from developmental education, some students do not stay for a full year. Because the American higher education system has open enrollment community colleges, open access proprietary and public institutions, and the available financial aid to those that need it, we are not always mindful that access to college is a challenge for many. Researcher Clifford Adelman (2007) notes that the meaning of the phrase "college access" varies and that multiple definitions of the phrase obscure the true nature of the problem. According to Adelman, the real access conundrum refers to "threshold access" paired with "participation"—that is, students can walk through the door, enroll, and stay a while. To be clear, Adelman suggests that true access and participation in higher education is when a student matriculates at a college or university and earns more than 10 credits. But retaining students long enough to earn 10 credits can be daunting for many institutions, especially open access institutions. Examined another way, just mere time enrolled in college—more than 18 months—seems to be a hurdle that disproportionately affects first-generation students. According to the National Center for Education Statistics, of the students enrolled in the 2003 Beginning Postsecondary Students Study, 60% of students who enrolled in college for less than 18 months were first-generation compared to 32% whose parents had at least two years' higher education experience. Why do so many first-generation students try higher education and then leave empty-handed with few credits and no credential?[3]

Some research suggests lack of preparation for college-level work, finances, employment needs, and family concerns prevent full access to higher education, but there are ways institutions can minimize the "experimentation" lost time, and money that early dropouts experience. One possibility is to create shorter term credentialing opportunities—more career pathways or stackable credentials for students. The state of Ohio has designed one such model for its adult learners—but the concept, tailored to meet state or local needs, could become a promising example throughout higher education. The Ohio framework for low-skilled adults includes a progression of certificates—entry-level, intermediate, and advanced—each targeted to adults at a specific point along the education continuum. As individuals raise their academic and technical skill levels by earning a certificate, they earn an increasing number of college credits in a technical field. This also prepares them to take general education courses required for a degree. Examples of the framework for the healthcare, welding, and advanced manufacturing industries have been developed in consultation with Ohio and national education and training providers (Community Research Partners, 2008). Shorter term credentialing opportunities allow for recurrent access and credit accumulation for a large population of students.

Academic Progress in Higher Education

Changing STEM majors

Once students enter higher education, we expect them to gain academic momentum toward a credential. Two indicators of academic progress are concentrating in a major or pre-professional program (as opposed to just declaring one) and passing grades to show mastery of the subject knowledge (measured cumulatively as a grade point average). Concentrating in a major is considered an important step toward a postsecondary credential because it signals the development of interest and goals that influence learning and achievement. Psychologists explain that interest may drive knowledge acquisition, which then continues to fuel interest. Cognitive educational psychology experts, Hidi and Anderson (1992) suggest that individuals who have more interest in an area probably pay more attention to information that is to be learned.

Presumably, the relationship between interest and knowledge acquisition drives program concentration and ultimately degree completion. But within higher education, we consistently observe students changing majors despite avowed interest in a subject. To be clear, changing majors does not necessarily indicate a problem on the part of the student or the institution. But the fairly regular exodus that occurs with students of color from the science, technology, engineering, and math fields to the humanities is an area of concern, particularly as expansive efforts by the National Science Foundation and the National Institutes of Health to support underrepresented minority students (African American, Latino, Native American) in the sciences are underway.

Although a relatively high proportion of Black students enter college with the intention to major in STEM fields, relatively few graduate with STEM majors (May & Chubin, 2003). Looking at degree attainment, only 24% of underrepresented minority students who begin college as a science major complete a bachelor's degree in a science major within six years of college entry, as compared to 40% of White students (as cited in Chang, Cerna, Han, & Saenz, 2008).

A recent controversial study by scholars Arcidiacono, Aucejo, and Spenner (2011) at Duke University found that among students that declare an initial major, 76. 7% of Black males initially choose natural science, engineering, or economics majors yet only 35% finish in a natural science, engineering, or economics major. For Black females, the percentages are better but nonetheless bleak: 56% start in economics, engineering, or natural science majors yet only 27. 7% finish in these majors. In contrast, the differences between initial and finishing proportions in natural science, engineering, and economics are 69% initially for White males to a final 64%—only a five point gap. For White females, 51% initially declare a STEM or an economics major compared to a much lower 34% of White females that finish in STEM or economics.

Poor preparation for concentrating in STEM disciplines is, no doubt, a major issue for some of these students. Stinebrickner and Stinebrickner (2011), in their study at Berea College, note that a large number of all students move away from math and science after realizing that their grade performance will be substantially lower than expected. These changes in beliefs about grade performance arise because students realize that their knowledge base in math/science is lower than expected rather than because students realize that they are not willing to put substantial effort into math or science majors.

But included among those who abandon science majors and underperform in science and quantitative courses are Black students with high scholastic aptitude test (SAT) scores, impressive high school grade point averages (GPAs), and success in high school honors math and science courses (Grandy, 1998). The findings in these studies suggest that students must enter college better prepared to study math or science, *but what is equally important* is that students need better academic and social support while in college.

The point here is that higher education must endeavor to close achievement gaps between students by changing practices, policies, and programs associated with academic and social support. Lamenting that students are not well prepared for college-level work should no longer stymie action to create a STEM pipeline. Higher education has to decide to meet students where they are and help to prepare them for STEM disciplines and other rigorous majors. Institutions such as the University of Maryland Baltimore County and Xavier University have been successful with educating black students in the STEM disciplines because educators engineer a pathway and coordinate mandatory supports for students. The Meyerhoff Scholars Program at the University of Maryland Baltimore County uses a "strength-based" program model for STEM-intending students that includes a summer bridge program, financial aid, mentoring, tutoring, undergraduate research, program community, summer research opportunities, etc. This program was designed to produce minority STEM PHDs and has had remarkable outcomes (Maton & Hrabowski, 2004). In a time of cost constraints, additional program supports to produce a STEM pipeline for students like the Meyerhoff Program seems untenable, but the long-term costs of too few scientists should be of even greater concern.

Disappointing Grade Point Averages

Grade point averages (GPAs) are another measure of academic progress—one that often takes a backseat to postsecondary completion. Nevertheless, GPAs illustrate more than if students finished the race; they indicate how well the race was run. In addition, GPAs are important mid-term indicators for entry into competitive major programs and transfer to other institutions. Unfortunately, as Betts & Morell (1999) have found, college grade point averages often differ between traditional and underserved groups and reflect differences in background, preparation, high school attended, etc.

The Arcidiacono (2011) study mentioned earlier also examined college GPA and found that the gap between White and Black students' grade point averages falls by half between the students' freshmen and senior year. By the senior year, White students earned a grade point average of 3. 6 compared to Black students who earned a grade point average of 3. 3. I find this 3/10 point gap between White and Black students at Duke University, a highly selective institution, to be noteworthy. It is quite likely that the gap has implications for graduate and professional study. An 'A-' average of 3. 6 might indicate that most of the White students can advance to graduate and professional schools based on their undergraduate record (if they choose to do so). However, for Black students the 'B+' average could harm their chances for admission into top-flight graduate and professional programs. In this way, achievement gaps are replicated, not just from high school to college, but from college to graduate and/or professional school. More explicit focus on the importance of GPAs along with the necessary academic support would potentially close this gap.

Attainment within Higher Education

Finally, we examine attainment in higher education with an express focus on low-income student performance. While low-income students are less likely to enroll in college, those who manage to do so are less likely to graduate than their middle-class peers. As The Century Foundation in its report *Unequal Opportunity* (Kahlenberg, 2004b) suggests, low-income students are considerably less likely to receive a bachelor's degree or higher five years after entering college than wealthy students.

But the issue for low-income students is not one only of money, but of programs that support them and prepare them for college expectations. Although President Obama has recently increased Pell Grant Program support, other forms of social, academic, and financial support for low-income students are minimal. Kahlenberg (2004b) points out that federal programs such as TRIO and GEAR-UP remain underfunded and underdeveloped.

And while elite institutions, such as Harvard, Princeton, the University of Virginia, and the University of North Carolina open up aid programs, Kahlenberg (2004b) states that "they behave less like nonprofit educational institutions and more like market players, using financial aid as a way of attracting talented students away from competitors rather than as a method of helping those who need it most." According to the *Journal of Blacks in Higher Education* (2009), over both the short and long term, most of the nation's leading universities and colleges show significant declines in percentages of low-income students. The journal asserts that examining the period from 1993 to 2006, of the 10 colleges with the largest endowments only Harvard and Princeton have increased their percentages of low-income students. The other eight universities with the largest endowments showed declines. As the number of low-income students continues to grow, this lack of commitment is unsustainable. Colleges and universities must commit to enrolling and graduating low-income students.

Some scholars have pointed out that public higher education will have to step up to assume a greater role in graduating low-income students (Bowen, Chingos, & McPherson, 2010). Since low-income students are attending college at greater rates because more individuals are desirous of postsecondary education, the public institutions become the primary sites for accommodating this growth. Bowen et al. (2010) state that transfer policies and financial aid policies need to be strengthened to actually work for minority students and low-income students. So many students are unable to complete degrees they begin because of a lack of financial aid and broken transfer policies.

But higher education institutions can also learn how to boost low-income student graduation rates from programs such as the Posse Foundation, an innovative non-profit organization that helps students and colleges succeed at improving outcomes for low-income students. Choosing from an applicant pool of 14,000, the Posse Foundation selects nearly 600 traditional-aged students throughout eight different cities every year and sends students in small groups of approximately 10 to 40 to selective institutions who participate in the program. The summer before they attend college, the Posse Foundation offers students leadership skills, communication skills, and advanced writing skills to help them succeed. These students would likely not have been admitted by traditional means because many of them have low standardized test scores. The schools relax their admission standards, and the students succeed (Rosenberg, 2012). Ninety percent of the selected Posse scholars graduate from college. Students are financially supported by institutional scholarships and receive social support from the organization and their Posse scholar peers for all four years of their undergraduate program. The success of the Posse Foundation highlights that high standardized test scores are not a necessary condition for college graduation for low-income students. Rather, supports—financial, academic, and social—are essential and sufficient ingredients. Surely, higher education institutions can begin to learn and build from this non-profit model and incorporate practices and policies that will mirror the support that Posse students receive; the Posse Foundation model has been in place for more than 20 years.

Concluding Thoughts

The challenges for educating diverse students in higher education are significant. Many low-income, first-generation, and underrepresented minority students are not as prepared or as well-resourced as the higher education community would like, but this does not mean that they do not have a place in college. Rather, their presence within the academy makes it clear that higher education must adjust some of its assumptions and operating principles to make appropriate room for these students and their needs. Quite likely, the adjustments that are needed would benefit all students and make our higher education system better and stronger.

To be clear, the adjustments that are required are major and cannot be isolated interventions of a short duration. Special programs are of great benefit to some, but not to most students. And the impact of some specialized programs is simply too short to produce the long-term effect that is needed for all students. To produce the broad-scale change that we need, institutions of higher learning must transform into innovative, agile organizations that take new research on diverse students and small reforms to bold scale. If we just heed the canary and take the need for systemic higher education reform seriously, we can save the mine.

Note

1. Based on calculations, it is quite possible that these numbers include students who completed a certificate or award within an 18–month time frame.

References

"Disappointing Progress in Enrollments of Low-income Students at America's Most Selective Colleges and Universities." 2009. *The Journal of Blacks in Higher Education*. Retrieved February 28, 2012 from http://www.jbhe.com/features/61_lowincome.html.

Adelman, Clifford. 2007. "Do We Really Have A College Access Problem?" *Change* July/August, Vol. 39, No. 4.

Arcidiacono, Peter, Esteban Aucejo, and Ken Spenner. 2011. What Happens After Enrollment? An Analysis of the Time Path of Racial Differences in GPA and Major Choice. Working Paper, Duke University.

Arum, Richard, and Josipa Roksa. 2011. *Academically Adrift: Limited Learning on College Campuses*. Chicago: University of Chicago Press.

Association of American Colleges & Universities. 1985. *Integrity in the College Curriculum: A Report to the Academic Community*. Washington DC: AAC&U Publications.

Bailey, Thomas, Dong Wook Jeong, and Sung-Woo Cho. 2008. *Referral, Enrollment, and Completion in Developmental Education*. New York: Community College Research Center, Teachers College, Columbia University.

Betts, Julian R., and Darlene Morrell. 1999. "The Determinants of Undergraduate Grade point Average: The Relative Importance of Family Background, High School Resources, and Peer Group Effects." *Journal of Human Resources* 34 (2): 268–293.

Bowen, William, Matthew Chingos, and Michael McPherson. 2010. *Crossing the Finish Line*. Princeton: Princeton University Press.

Community Research Partners, 2008. "Ohio Stackable Certificates: Models of Success." Columbus Ohio.

Chang, Mitchell, Oscar Cerna, June Han, and Victor Saenz. 2008. "The Contradictory Roles of Institutional Status in Retaining Underrepresented Minorities in Biomedical and Behavioral Science Majors." *The Review of Higher Education*, 31 (4): 433–464.

Grandy, J. 1998. Persistence in science of high-ability minority students: Results of a longitudinal study. *Journal of Higher Education* 69: 589–620.

Guinier, Lani, and Gerald Torres. 2002. *The Miner's Canary*. Cambridge, MA: Harvard University Press.

Hidi, S., & Anderson, V. 1992. Situational interest and its impact on reading and expository writing. In K. A. Renninger, S. Hidi, & A. Krapp (Eds.), The role of interest in learning and development (pp. 215–238). Hillsdale, NJ: Lawrence Erlbaum. Associates, Inc.

Kahlenberg, Richard. 2004a. *America's Untapped Resource: Low-Income Students in Higher Education.* Washington DC: Century Foundation.

Kahlenberg, Richard. 2004b. *Unequal Opportunity.* Washington DC: Century Foundation.

Maton, Kenneth I., and Freeman A. Hrabowski III, 2004. Increasing the number of African American PhDs in the Sciences and Engineering, *American Psychologist* 59 (6): 547–556.

May, G. S., and Daryl Chubin, 2003. A retrospective on under-graduate engineering success for underrepresented minority students. *Journal of Engineering Education* 92: 1–13.

Rosenberg, T. 2012. Beyond SATs, Finding Success in the Numbers. *New York Times*, February 15. http://opinionator. blogs. nytimes.com/2012/02/15/beyond-sats-finding-success-in-numbers/

Seymour E., and N. Hewitt. 2000. *Talking About Leaving: Why Undergraduates Leave the Sciences.* 2nd ed. Boulder, CO: Westview Press.

Stinebrickner, Todd, and Ralph Stinebrickner. 2011. Math or Science? Using Longitudinal Expectations Data to Examine the Process of Choosing a College Major. NBER Working Paper 16869, National Bureau of Economic Research, Cambridge, MA.

Wathington, H., E. Barnett, E. Weissman, J. Teres, J. Pretlow, and A. Nakanishi. 2011. *Getting Ready for College: An Implementation and Early Impacts Study of Eight Texas Developmental Summer Bridge Programs.* New York: National Center for Postsecondary Research.

CHAPTER THREE

Still Trying to Be All Things to All People

What It Means for Students at Community Colleges

MITCHELL R. WILLIAMS

The history of higher education in the United States has been a story of increasing access. From the Morrill Acts to the GI Bill, from the Truman Commission Report to the Higher Education Acts, higher education has moved from serving primarily wealthy white males to providing opportunities for people of every age, ethnicity, race, and professional background. Institutions of higher education reflect the variety of people observed in American society. The diversity found on American college campuses is best reflected in the community college. From the first "junior college," founded by William Rainey Harper in Joliet, Illinois in 1901, the community college has been a uniquely American institution which has helped to democratize higher education. The number of Americans attending college increased steadily through the 20th century, and the increase in the number of community colleges has contributed significantly to this growth (Cohen & Brawer, 2008).

Enrollment in community colleges has been expanding for several decades. From 1963 to 2006, community college enrollment has increased by 741%, a much greater percentage increase than has been experienced by public (197%) or private (170%) four-year institutions (Provasnik & Planty, 2008). In recent years, over half of all students in higher education started their postsecondary education at the community college, and community colleges have made significant progress in improving graduation rates. A report from the American Association of Community Colleges pointed out that the number of community college graduates has increased in the past 20 years: between 1989 and 2009, the number of credentials awarded by community colleges increased by over 125%, while enrollment in community colleges grew by 65% (Mullin, 2011). Particularly encouraging in these figures is the significant growth in the number of graduates among students from non-dominant groups: a 283% increase in the number of degrees awarded to African Americans and a more than 400% increase in credentials earned by Hispanic students.

The growth and success of the community college is reflected in growing national recognition of the institution and its place within the higher education community. This achievement reflects current and past leaders' commitment to the community college mission of open access admission and offering a comprehensive curriculum. Can future leaders, facing declining state appropriations and expanding community demands, continue to guide institutions which strive to be "all things to all people"?

All People: Community College Students

The popular television show *Community* describes the community college as "loser college for remedial teens, 20–something dropouts, middle-aged divorcees and old people keeping their minds active as they circle the drain of eternity." While this comic description is an extreme exaggeration, it seems fair to say that most Americans do not understand community colleges or recognize the benefits that community colleges provide for their friends, neighbors, and communities. The community college serves a more diverse student population than any other type of institution of higher education. Additionally, the profile of the "typical" community college student is constantly changing.

When compared to four-year institutions, the community college has greater student diversity within categories such as age, race and ethnicity, previous academic record, and professional background (Cohen & Brawer, 2008). This significant diversity among the student population is due, in part, to open access admission or trying to serve "all people." The community college, as an open access institution, allows everyone to attend. Open admission allows the community college to not only serve people of all race and ethnic backgrounds but also all professional, educational, social, and economic backgrounds. Within the new financial reality of public funding of institutions of higher education, does the community college do a disservice to some students by trying to serve all students? Is it unfair to provide limited resources to remedial courses when the best and brightest students are attending the community college in increasing numbers? Similarly, does the community college do a disservice to society if resources are shifted away from students who are not yet ready for college-level work to provide more services to students planning to pursue a bachelor's or advanced degree?

Cohen and Brawer (2008) said two words could be used to describe community college students: number and variety. For many observers of higher education over the past century, enrollment growth has been the single most significant attribute of the community college. Nevertheless, an equally significant observation would indicate that the community college serves people of all ages, including those from all academic backgrounds and a wide variety of professional experiences. Open access admission is the key feature of the community college which creates this diversity within its student population. Open access is the primary component of the mission of the community college, and it is the attribute which distinguishes it among other institutions within the higher education community. Unlike universities which admit students based on sometimes questionable criteria such as SAT scores, applicant essays, and letters of recommendation, the community college encourages all who can benefit from its programming to enroll.

Two primary characteristics distinguish community college students from students at other postsecondary institutions. Historically, community college students are older and they tend to be part-time learners. Over time, as the average age of students went up, the number of credit hours each student attempted went down (Cohen & Brawer, 2008). There are a number of reasons for this increase in the number of part-time students. First and foremost, the community college has made deliberate efforts to attract students who have jobs, families, and other responsibilities by making it easier for them to attend. This has allowed more students to combine work and study, and it has encouraged women and people of color to participate in postsecondary education. Another consequence of this diversity is that the community college has a larger, and increasing, proportion of so-called "nontraditional" students who do not conform to the traditional profile of an 18–year old who enrolls in college on a full-time basis to pursue a baccalaureate degree (Cohen & Brawer, 2008).

The variety of students found at a community college reflects the notion that the community college is the "first choice for a second chance" for many Americans (Townsend, 2009). Students are not selected for admission to the community college based upon their academic success in high school, test scores, or other indications of potential for success in postsecondary study. Many people attending the community college are looking for a second chance; they may have lost their jobs; they may have failed in their first attempt at college; they may not be able to afford the tuition at the university; they may be unable to attend on a full-time basis, they may have had inadequate preparation in high school; they may already have a bachelor's degree but are unprepared to work in a job; they may have physical disabilities which have hindered their opportunities, or they may simply be unable to do college-level work.

The student population at the community college is diverse from another perspective. The community college student population includes students traditionally found at selective liberal arts colleges, regional comprehensive state universities, research universities, and two and four-year proprietary institutions. Due to the increased recognition of the value of community colleges and relatively low tuition, the student population of the community college currently reflects the student population of all other institutions within the higher education community. This means that more students who are bound for four-year and advanced degrees are starting their higher education journey at the community college. This is because the community college is a wise choice financially and a compelling choice academically.

All Things: The Comprehensive Curriculum

As the community college faces a declining proportion of its revenue from state appropriations, is there also increasing pressure on community college leaders to serve those who would traditionally begin their higher education at a four-year institution? At a time when public funding is decreasing and tuition increasing, difficult decisions must be made about what programs and curricula a community college can afford to offer. In order to serve "all people," the community college must offer programming that meets the needs of all. Researchers and community college leaders need to also discuss the other half of the all things to all people axiom. In the context of the modern community college, what is included within the phrase "all things"?

An issue that is often raised while questioning whether a publicly supported institution should attempt to be "all things" is whether the community college today can afford to offer a comprehensive curriculum. If an institution is truly going to claim to be "open access," it must offer a program of study that serves "all people"; there must be a curriculum that serves the needs of everyone from those not ready to do college-level work to those who need skills to find a job or get a promotion, to those who seek the credential of an associate's degree or certificate, to those who want to transfer to a four-year institution.

Debate surrounding the comprehensive curriculum required at two-year colleges has been actively engaged in for over 50 years. The junior/community college has built its reputation on open access and its ability to serve all who seek higher learning. Over 50 years ago, Medsker (1960) wrote:

> No unit of American higher education is expected to serve such a diversity of purposes, to provide such a variety of educational instruments, or to distribute students among so many types of educational programs as the junior college. . . The diversity of students to be served suggests that the public two-year college of the future must be even more comprehensive than it has been in the past. (p. 4)

A comprehensive curriculum is just as important as an open access admission policy to the core mission of the community college. That means a comprehensive curriculum which traditionally includes a number of functions:

> a transfer function for students who are earning the first two years of a bachelor's degree, a vocational function for those seeking the skills to get a job (or a higher paying job), a general education function for those who wish to pursue an associate's degree but do not intend to transfer to a four-year institution, a developmental education function for those not yet ready to do college-level work, a personal enrichment function for those who wish to improve their lives through continuing education, a contract function which provides customized programming for specific industries or businesses, and a so-called "reverse transfer" function for those who have already earned a bachelor's or advanced degree but have returned to the community college seeking skills or credentials for available jobs or advancement.

A consistent but significant challenge for today's community college leaders is whether they can maintain the comprehensive curriculum in light of decreasing state and federal appropriations for higher education. This has been a challenge for community college leaders for decades (Vaughan, 1985), but leaders today, and in the future, will be challenged by critics who feel the community college cannot meet its core mission while trying to maintain the ideal of open access admissions and a comprehensive curriculum. Critics often propose the viewpoint that the community college, more than other institutions of higher education, has been particularly threatened by declining appropriations. The students who attend community colleges are significantly affected by increases in tuition which may be necessary because of the loss of per-pupil student aid.

As the nation's economy has endured a recession and slow recovery, many community colleges have had record enrollments. This enrollment growth has been fueled by several diverse groups: laid-off workers seeking jobs skills to provide for their families, recent high school graduates who recognize that completing the first two years of a bachelor's degree at a community college is a wise financial and educational decision, and people who have already earned a bachelor's or advanced degree and return to the community college seeking the skills or credentials needed for available jobs. At the same time these institutions have been faced with declining state appropriations which have made it difficult to maintain a commitment to open access admission and the comprehensive curriculum which is required to support open access. Some community colleges have been forced to implement enrollment caps, and other colleges have eliminated some programs.

Does the attempt to be all things to all people hurt some community college students? Is it time for community college leaders to make the difficult decisions that may restrict access for some people/potential students but may mean more opportunities for success for greater numbers of other students? Are open access admission and the comprehensive curriculum ideals whose time has passed?

Criticism of the Community College

Criticism of the community college comes from a variety of sources and covers a number of academic and non-academic issues. Critics clearly question whether the community college can really serve its core constituency and mission if it continues to try to be "all things to all people" (Dougherty, 1994; Beach, 2011; Gollattscheck, 1983). Many detractors charge that the community college is actually not providing better access to higher education or social mobility. Beach (2011) wrote that community colleges have been praised as an efficient way to handle Americans looking for access to higher education and an economical path for social mobility. Nevertheless, Beach claimed: "However, it is unclear if this institution actually helps students, let alone how it might help. Scholars have never been able to completely agree on the mission of the community college, and therefore, have never been able to adequately determine what it is the community college is supposed to do" (pp. xix–xx).

Indeed, many new left critics see the community college as an unwitting contributor to America's lingering class-based and race-based societal failures. According to Beach (2011), "Community college students are offered what appears to be a chance to succeed, but when they fail to obtain success, it appears to be their own fault because of a lack of academic skills or effort" (p. 124). Beach goes on to describe the community college as a structurally limited opportunity in need of institutional reform which would include unified missions, clear goals of educational success, properly trained faculty, sufficient numbers of support staff, and adequate financial resources.

The counter-argument, however, is that if the sole, or even primary, purpose of the community colleges was to move students through to a baccalaureate degree, then the community college "is a failure by design" (Cohen & Brawer, 2008). The community college accepts those who are poorly prepared academically, those who must work full-time and study part-time, and those for whom all too often "life happens" and their academic dreams and goals are delayed. All of these characteristics are associated with a higher probability of academic failure. Community colleges should not be criticized for giving the students a better chance to succeed.

Community colleges are often criticized for low graduation rates and for their failure to close the educational achievement gap between white Americans and students from non-dominant groups. Community colleges are known for serving the types of students who are most at-risk of attrition: those who are in need of remedial education, adult learners, first-generation college students, and those from groups that are historically underserved in higher education. Minority students are more likely to enroll at the community college when they first enter the higher education system. There is a growing recognition, however, that investment in the community college is a good deal for students and our nation. Economists and sociologists point out that many of the fastest-growing jobs in today's knowledge-based economy require a two-year degree rather than a four-year degree. Additionally, there is a growing acknowledgment among political and educational leaders that successful workers in today's global economy will be lifelong learners; people will change jobs and careers several times, and successful citizens need the quick and easy access to job skills and employment upgrades provided by the community college.

During a time of economic hardship, in July 2009, President Barack Obama proposed the American Graduation Initiative with a goal of adding 5 million new college graduates by the year 2020. The program called for training millions of Americans and creating new opportunities for thousands of Americans who have never completed college degrees. Coming at a time when the United States had fallen from first to tenth place in the world in the proportion of the population with a college degree, this was a historic effort to increase the number of college graduates in America. The American Graduation Initiative (AGI) set a goal of returning the United States to the top of the world ranking in terms of the number of college graduates by the year 2020.

The Obama initiative came just over 60 years after the Truman Commission report of 1947 first recognized the potential of community colleges in promoting the nation's economic development. The Truman Commission called for a nationwide network of community colleges with little or no tuition, offering a comprehensive curriculum, and serving the specific educational and workforce training needs of specific communities in which they were located. A portion of the report said that higher education in the United States could no longer be focused on producing intellectual elite from among the nation's wealthy citizens; it called for a continued democratization of higher education in which every American was "enabled and encouraged" to pursue higher education.

It is significant that President Obama identified community colleges, which enroll 44% of all American undergraduates, as the cornerstone of this national effort, calling on them to significantly increase their graduation rates. Many in higher education questioned whether community colleges would be able to meet the challenge of the AGI because the students who are attracted to the community college are academically underprepared to do college-level work. These underprepared students are often low income, members of racial/ethnic groups that are non-dominant in society, and at risk of other academic-related barriers. Underprepared students are defined as those who require remediation. Almost 50% of all first-time community college students require some remediation, and students who place into developmental courses are less likely to persist to graduation or goal completion. To serve this large percentage of students, almost one in three community college courses are offered at the developmental level (Cohen & Brawer, 2008). Too many community college students require too many remedial courses, according to this argument. These students become discouraged with the required time and expense of taking courses which do not move them toward graduation; they become disheartened and all too often drop out of college.

Likewise, many institutions in economically depressed communities, especially poor urban centers and isolated rural areas, have difficulty affording the expenses related to serving students who lack academic abilities. Reductions in state appropriations for higher education have made it even more difficult for these community colleges to serve the increasing number of students who need remedial courses. Lower per student state funding has led to higher tuition. The higher cost to attend the college has meant that more community college students must work while taking classes. More than two-thirds of community college students work at least 20 hours per week, and a growing number of full-time community college students also have full-time jobs. There is strong evidence that as students increase the number of hours they are employed, their study time suffers; having a job while a student increases the time it takes to finish a degree and, therefore, increases the probability of a student dropping out of college. Therefore, declining state support for community colleges—and the resulting increases in tuition and in the number of hours students work per week—is indirectly working against the goals of the AGI.

Conclusion

Future community college leaders will continue to discuss, argue over, and struggle with the goal of being all things to all people—that is, to provide educational services to people from all walks of life and with all educational and professional backgrounds. There is little reason to believe there will be a significant change in the trend of reduced state appropriations for community colleges (or other public institutions of higher education). How will an institution known for providing access to higher education for the historically underserved—members of non-dominant groups and those from the lowest socio-economic quartile—be able to maintain open access admission and the comprehensive curriculum it requires? Will the community college of the future be able to serve all students, or will the attempt to serve all mean that fewer will be served effectively?

One possible response to this challenge may lie in inter-institutional collaboration among diverse colleges and universities from multiple sectors of the higher education community. Given the tradition of institutional autonomy and competition among colleges and universities, cooperation among institutions from any one sector of the higher education community (e.g., public, private, proprietary, or four-year, and two-year institutions) is difficult; attempting cooperation relationships among institutions from different sectors may be especially problematic. Institutions from different sectors of higher education vary substantially in mission, organizational structure, and degree of commitment to the basic functions of postsecondary education (Williams & Pettitt, 2003). When institutions from different sectors of higher education do cooperate, however, they create a powerful presence that can serve students at all types of institutions. When institutional leaders work to understand the diverse missions of the various types of postsecondary institutions, unique collaborations can be created which can allow the community college to maintain both open access and a comprehensive curriculum. Innovative partnerships can produce answers to challenges which individual institutions cannot generate on their own.

Finding solutions to the challenges facing higher education today requires leaders who are truly innovative thinkers with the ability to find creative collaborative answers to the complex challenges facing community colleges in the future. These collaborations could include partnerships which in the past may have been improbable: community colleges partnering with research one universities, proprietary institutions, or private liberal arts colleges.

Community colleges and universities are places where diverse groups naturally interact, and the potential for innovative approaches to outreach and engagement is greatest when a variety of institutions of higher education collaborate. Diverse missions allow dissimilar institutions to bring unique strengths to cooperative efforts to address community demands and regional needs. There is no reason why diverse institutions of higher education should not continue to engage in productive competition, but there are also many reasons why they should, at appropriate times, form inter-institutional partnerships to benefit students.

At a time when people are increasingly questioning the value of a four-year college degree, the community college offers an attractive and prudent alternative. It offers affordable tuition and programs that lead to jobs that are available and well paying. Students move quickly into the workforce and with much lower debt. It serves communities and meets the need for a trained workforce to compete in the information-based global economy.

Future students of the community college (and future leaders of these important institutions) may find comfort and support in the words of former Harvard University President Derek Bok:

> The college that takes students with modest entering abilities and improves their abilities substantially contributes more than the school that takes very bright students and helps them develop only modestly. We really need to take the focus off entering scores and put it more on how much value is added. (Brush, 2006)

References

Beach, J. M. (2011). *Gateway to opportunity? A history of the community college in the United States*. Sterling, VA: Stylus.

Brush, S. (2006). Fixing undergrad education. *U.S. News & World Report*, 140 (8), 28. Retrieved from http://www.usnews.com/usnews/news/articles/060306/6qa.htm

Cohen, A. M., & Brawer, F. B. (2008). *The American community college*. San Francisco: Jossey-Bass.

Dougherty, K. J. (1994). *The contradictory college: The conflicting origins, impacts, and futures of the community college*. Albany: State University of New York Press.

Gollattscheck, J. F. (1983). All things to all people? The third mission of the community college. *Community Services Catalyst*, 13 (1), 4–10.

Medsker, L. L. (1960). *The junior college: Progress and prospect*. New York: McGraw-Hill.

Mullin, C. M. (2011). The road ahead: A look at trends in the educational attainment of community college students (AACC Policy Brief2011–04PBL, October 2011). Washington, DC: American Association of Community Colleges.

Provasnik, S., & Planty, M. (2008). *Community colleges: Special supplement to the condition of education 2008* (NCES 2008–033). Washington, DC: National Center for Education Statistics, Institute of Education Sciences, U.S. Department of Education.

Townsend, B. K. (2009). The two-year college as a first choice, second chance institution for baccalaureate degree holders. *Community College Journal of Research and Practice, 33,* 749–764.

Vaughan, G. B. (1985). Maintaining open access and comprehensiveness. In D. E. Puyear & G. B. Vaughan (eds.), *Maintaining institutional integrity*. San Francisco: Jossey-Bass.

Williams, M. R., & Pettitt, J. M. (2003). Partnerships among institutions from different sectors of higher education: Expanding views of collaboration for outreach and community service. *Journal of Higher Education Outreach and Engagement, 8* (2), 25–40.

CHAPTER FOUR

Higher Education Student Affairs and Services Around the World

ROGER B. LUDEMAN & DENNIS E. GREGORY

In the context of unprecedented demand, increasing diversification and the vital role it plays in the economic and socio-cultural development of nations, higher education needs to address a number of challenges. These challenges include financing, equality of access, widening participation, the improvement of support and developmental services, effective use of technology including distance learning, use of new and more flexible learning formats, ensuring student attainment of new skills and increased employability, as well as the need for international cooperation.

For higher education to play its role in promoting ideals and values associated with a world culture of peace, it needs to become an agent of change, to respond to social needs and to promote the principles of solidarity and equity. One of the important ways to meet the challenges is to become more student-centered in all aspects of its activities, to encourage the development of a citizenry fully able to take its place on the community, national, regional, and international stages.

Therefore, the development of higher education must recognize the importance of making allowance for national identities. At the same time, there are universal values that transcend individual cultures and their political and economic contexts. It is these values that comprise the necessary underpinnings for a solid global education framework that advocates for peace, justice, democratic practices, human rights, and sustainable economic development for all. Student affairs and services efforts have always been at the center of recognizing cultural differences and, simultaneously, promoting universal values.

The World Declaration on Higher Education (UNESCO, 1998b) makes a strong case for the development and implementation of a highly effective student affairs and services program in higher education around the world. Each country, as a unique sector of society, must bring its own traditions, culture, social infrastructure, and priorities into the development of this invaluable array of services and programs; nevertheless, it is imperative that higher education include such services and programs to promote quality of student life, meet student needs, and enhance student learning and success.

Higher education student affairs and services are designed to provide access to higher education, enhance student retention and graduation rates, develop global citizenship skills, and provide society with new human capital and potential that can help everyone as we move forward toward a true family of nations. These services and programs vary depending on the country in which they are found. The delivery systems employed and the array of offerings available to students develop in accordance with the historical, cultural, economic, and social contexts that present themselves in the regions or countries in which they are employed.

Until the early to mid part of the 19th century, in the United States and elsewhere, the teaching faculty and a few clerical assistants handled the few non-instructional functions for students, e.g., accommodations, food service, student discipline and advising, and some activities. The earlier models of higher education did not focus on the whole student and access to an education was limited to those who could afford it. For centuries, higher education was almost exclusively the province of men. With the development of the classical European higher education system during the Middle Ages, students were those primarily training to become priests or those of noble birth who were supported by various princes. While other models were prevalent elsewhere in the world, they were virtually all based upon an academic model, and seldom included support for persons in areas not necessarily directly related to academics (Rudolph, 1990).

In the United States, teaching staff and tertiary education institutions focused on a classical education centered on the teaching of Latin and Greek. The education of young wealthy White men, the small size of the colleges around the country, the limited number of American scholars, and the diverse population alignments within the country mitigated against change or growth early in the 19th century. The Yale Report of 1828 applauded this model in the face of changing approaches, which were beginning to evolve. However, as the 19th century proceeded, different kinds of institutions began to develop. "Flagship" universities began to be established. Thomas Jefferson, for example, founded the University of Virginia, with a diverse curriculum unique to the period. The research university model was imported from Germany along with professional faculty whose focus was research, and a division between the "college" and "university" began to develop. In addition, coeducational institutions and those focusing on educating women and enrolling free Blacks arrived on the scene. With the arrival of the land grant universities in the 1860s and their spread to institutions focusing on the education of African Americans in the 1890s, a new breed of coeducational institutions began to develop (Rudolph, 1990).

Soon, the types and number of students coming to higher education began to swell (many of them women who were being admitted to higher education for the first time in several centuries). Academics, who were previously handling support functions, even though they knew next to nothing about administering such initiatives and counseling students, began calling for more assistance in carrying out these non-instructional duties. In the United States, Deans of Women, Deans of Men, and Deans of Students began to be appointed because of the increases in numbers and types of students who were enrolling in higher education. Also during the late 19th century, the teacher/scholar and research models were being adopted all over the world, moving away from a main purpose of teaching and service. Governments and communities were turning to higher education systems to generate research and development for the military, industry, health, and other social programs (Rudolph, 1990).

Therefore, in the U.S. a new profession was born: higher education student affairs and services or what was called then student personnel services. These staff members were now in charge of not only housing and feeding students, but also their physical and mental health care. These services soon became a necessity on many college campuses. Recreation, cultural activities, sports, testing, orientation, career assistance, job placement, financial assistance, and disability services all became new units in many countries. They were initiated to help meet emerging student types and their corresponding student needs.

In the U.S. professional associations began to develop around various service focuses, and umbrella organizations also began to grow. In 1937, The American Council of Education (ACE) called together a group of individuals who were charged with developing a statement that described this new profession and its goals. This statement, *The Student Personnel Point of View (SPPOV)* (ACE, 1937), became the founding ideals upon which the profession is still based. In fact, as we approach the 75th anniversary of *SPPOV*, ACPA (one of two American umbrella professional associations) has called upon professional practitioners and faculty to write about the statement, its legacy, and its future (Kate Boyle, personal communication, October 31, 2011).

Following World War II, campuses everywhere continued to become more diverse because returning war veterans were accessing higher education through the use of government benefits designed for that purpose. In 1949 a second *Student Personnel Point of View* was written, amplifying the original statement and adding a focus on national identity and the need for student personnel to also have an outward worldview (ACE, 1949).

During the last quarter of the 20th century, the variety of students coming to higher education continued to expand all around the world. Joining the traditional, well-to-do men were women students, students of color, older non-traditional students, single parents, students with disabilities, and others. As a result, new professionals were hired to work with these new groups to meet their needs and help them to become successful students, and documents were developed which focused upon the changes taking place within higher education and student affairs and services on American campuses (NASPA, 1987).

During the 1990s, the focus of student affairs and services moved toward an enhancement of student learning outcomes and working hand-in-hand with the teaching faculty and others on this objective. This development has given new hope to the idea that an integrated campus effort will produce better results for students and more efficient use of resources for all campus units (AAHE, 1991; AAHE/ACPA, 1998; ACPA, 1996; Chickering & Reisser, 1993; Evans, Forney, & Guido-DiBrito, 1998; NASPA, 1998).

The 21st century brought another wave of research and student services focused on cooperation between student affairs and other units within the university (ACPA/NASPA, 2010; Keeling, 2006; Komives & Woodard, 2003; Kuh, Kinzie, Schuh, & Whitt, 2005; NASPA/ACPA, 2004; Pascarella & Terenzini, 2005; Strange & Banning, 2001).

The degree to which the wide array of student services and programs is developed in a particular country depends on the demands for and access to higher education, the cultural context, and the ability of the infrastructure to provide this level of student support. Each part of the world, and in many cases each country, must review its commitment to higher education and include in the financial infrastructure some major provision for student affairs and services functions that will ensure student needs are being met. In addition, various student activities should be developed so that they blend well with the instructional nature of the institution and, therefore, enhance the desired student learning outcomes. Higher retention and graduation rates will be the results, justifying the commitment and the resources provided up front (Ludeman, Osfield, Hidalgo, Oste, & Wang, 2009).

The decade of the 1990s brought a revolution in the development and utilization of computing, communications, and multimedia in all aspects of society, but most assuredly in higher education. Old ways of communicating, delivering services, conducting research, and teaching have been enhanced or replaced by such phenomena as e-mail, fax, listservs or chat rooms, blogs, interactive video, online courses, online registration, and other resources on the World Wide Web. Student affairs and services employs technology in its various forms to deliver its programs and services more effectively and efficiently as demanded by students and other stakeholders. Where once students were required to come to a central location to complete a transaction, this can now be done from their residence using interactive web-based services. Examples include completing applications, responding to questionnaires, doing class assignments, watching lectures, conducting research, purchasing books and materials, and finding up-to-date information on classes and activities at their university or in their communities. On the one hand, a number of transactions can now be carried out quite efficiently at a distance through employment of the tools of modern technology. On the other, the price of efficiency carries with it a different cost: keeping up with the cost of hardware, software, training, and network administration (Junco & Mastrodicasa, 2007).

Common Principles, Values, Beliefs

In order for any part of the higher education enterprise to be applied consistently and to be of good quality, it must be grounded in a set of principles and values that takes into consideration the expressed needs of those whom it serves (that is, students; Ludeman, 2002; Ludeman et al., 2009). While specific principles, values, and beliefs might vary depending on the region or country of origin, the tenets outlined here have nearly universal appeal and allow readers to understand how they might apply to the creation and ongoing assessment of student affairs functions and services in higher education anywhere. Here are those principles, values, and beliefs:

Purposes and Partnerships
Higher education and student affairs professionals, as integral partners in providing services and programs, must be student-centered and acknowledge students as partners and responsible stakeholders in their education. Along with institutional decision-makers, government officials, and UNESCO representatives, students must also be included in the process, as well as in follow-up conferences and meetings related to the proceedings of the World Conference on Higher Education (UNESCO, 1998a). Students have the right and responsibility to organize, to participate in governance, and to pursue their personal and social interests.

1. Partnerships with all constituents, both within and beyond the academy, must be established to promote not only lifelong learning, but also learning for life. Such partnerships should include students; faculty; staff; alumni; parents; employers; social

service agencies; primary and secondary school systems; government agencies; and representatives of the local, national, regional, and global communities.

2. Student affairs functions and services must be delivered in a manner that is seamless, meaningful, and integrated with the academic mission of the institution. These practices and resulting policies must be built upon sound principles and research, and carried out by partnering with others throughout the campus community.

3. Student affairs and services professionals are key players in the advancement of the talents of all nations. This requires partnerships at the national and international levels, through cooperative exchanges, conferences, seminars, and shared research.

Access and Diversity

1. Higher learning is enhanced by creative conflict, in particular as students, faculty, and student services professionals of varying backgrounds encounter in one another differences of histories, experiences, and points of view. Thus, every effort should be made to attract and retain a diverse student body and staff.

2. The mission for student affairs functions and services must be consistent with the institutional mission, its educational purposes, the locale in which it is operating, and its student characteristics. Programs must be established and resources allocated for the purposes of meeting the ultimate goal of student affairs functions and services: enhancement of student learning and development.

Learning

1. Higher education must address the personal and developmental needs of students as whole human beings. Student affairs functions and services should assume leadership in this regard, as well as in the appropriate advocacy of students in general.

2. Students encounter three major transitions related to their higher education experience: they first move *into* higher education, second *through* their collegiate and university life, and third *from* higher education into their careers and immediate workplace. Support must be available for students during these transitions, in the form of timely and accurate information, a broad range of services, and activities that engage them in the learning process within and beyond the classroom.

3. Learning is complex and multi-faceted. For society to benefit fully, the processes of learning must be lifelong in scope and varied in contexts.

4. All higher education stakeholders must promote independent, self-directed student behavior, within a community context. Worthy citizenship and service to the community, in particular, are important values to promote during the postsecondary experience.

5. The delivery of student services and programs is based on a number of critical values, including diversity, pluralism, inclusiveness, community, high expectations, a global view, citizenship and leadership, ethical living, the inherent worth of the individual, and the idea that students can and must participate actively in their own growth and development.

6. Higher education must prioritize academic and career counseling programs to assist students in preparing for their life work, employment, and subsequent careers beyond the academy.

7. Tools of information technology should serve as means, rather than ends, in the student learning process. Student affairs and services professionals should explore ways they can enhance student learning through technology and promote effective student usage, through advising, counseling, development of appropriate systems, and training.

8. Student affairs and services professionals expect students to engage with their institution and the learning process, consistent with principles of academic and personal integrity, responsible behavior in a community setting, and the exercise of appropriate freedoms developed within a national, as well as local and institutional, context. Good practices in student affairs and services build supportive and inclusive communities locally and globally.

Resource Management

1. Student affairs functions and services must subscribe to high standards of practice and behavior, including professional preparation; assessment of professional qualifications; continuing training and development; evaluation of services, programs, and staff performances; assessment of student outcomes; adherence to codes of ethics; and use of effective management practices. All are necessary in order to deliver the best in services and programs and to remain accountable to students and other constituents.

2. Student affairs and services funding sources ideally should be diversified and include significant institutional support. Funding from outside sources, such as grants, foundations, philanthropies, cooperative relationships, and alumni donations, may be necessary in order to provide the array and level of services required.

3. Resources must be allocated to those student services and programs that enhance student learning and success in relation to demonstrated need and demand.

4. Information technology (IT) is essential to efficient and effective management of student services and programs. Therefore, IT must be made available to students and student affairs and services workers in order to achieve learning and success goals for students.

Research and Assessment

Student affairs and services professionals, along with the teaching faculty, bring to the academy a particular expertise on students, their development, and the impact of their learning environments. They gain that information through systematic inquiry, including both quantitative and qualitative research methods. They are closely aligned with the academic mission and serve as invaluable links between students and the institution. They also serve as role models with high expectations of students and their capacities for learning.

Student Affairs and Services Around the World

As indicated earlier in this chapter, the practice of student affairs and services in higher education varies greatly depending on the country, culture, and traditions in which they exist. The following summary will give the reader an idea of the delivery of this vital part of higher education in a number of countries. While the descriptions that follow are not comprehensive, a task that is beyond the scope of this chapter, we have selected program descriptions from major countries on each continent in order to show the diversity of approaches to this topic. Many additional countries around the world have well-developed or growing programs in student support services. We have not included descriptions of student affairs in the U.S. since there are thousands of articles and books which provide these, and we have addressed some of the background above. A comprehensive and inclusive set of these descriptions may be found in the book *Student affairs and services in higher education: Global foundations, issues and best practices* (Ludeman et al., 2009).

ARGENTINA

Background Information on Student Affairs/Services

The history of higher education in Argentina started with the creation of the Universidad de Cordoba in 1622. The manifesto of the First National Congress of Students in 1918 in Cordoba introduced the concept of democracy and autonomy in the university. The participation of students in the governance of the university has precipitated numerous support programs. There are some 40 public and 55 private universities.

Typical Services and Programs Offered

The Scholarship Department offers information about internal and external scholarship opportunities. Scholarships may cover expenses for transportation, copy services, housing, cafeteria, and medical assistance for the students and/or their family for emergencies during the academic year, and work study with their department. There are cash awards. There is an age limit for benefits with exceptions for students with disabilities or those from indigenous populations. There is also financial aid for students who move from their province to continue their education. Private universities have benefits for students with academic potential but low resources.

The Health and Wellness Department prepares multiple activities in addition to the regular ones: medical check-ups, nursing, emergency, control of admission medical exams for both students and personnel, and physical examinations for sport aptitude, among others. The Physical and Sport Education Department offers free classes, tournaments, and training in basketball, soccer, tennis, aerobics, chess, and swimming.

There are daycare facilities for children of students, faculty, and staff. The cafeteria is open for students with scholarships and to others for a minimum fee. There are housing services in some universities. The Student Employment Office assists graduates entering the job market through internal promotion in the industry, maintaining communication with alumni about job opportunities.

Academic Services offer quality courses in the area of information systems. There are language labs. Each one of the colleges in the national universities has a library and students can borrow material with their "Library I. D. card." The Psychology and Psycho-pedagogy Department offers vocational orientation and learning skills workshops. There is also attention given to emotional problems that may serve as an obstacle to a student's academic achievement. This unit also tracks the academic progress of students receiving tutorial services. The tutor's responsibility is to guide the students when they experience learning difficulties and in their relationship with the faculty. The Social Service Division promotes and participates in the politics of prevention and assistance to the social problems of the university. It is also involved with diagnostic research about the socio-economic and family situation of the students. One of its goals is to improve the nutritional condition of those students without economic resources.

Organizational Structure of Student Affairs/Services

In the national universities, the Secretary of University Support assists the rector and coordinates activities related to the well-being of the university community and its integration to the environment. The Secretary is responsible, among other functions, for planning actions that facilitate the socio-economic development of the students in areas such as health and family assistance for the university community, as well as in the areas of sport and recreation. It works in coordination with the Secretary of Student Affairs of each college. It maintains inter-institutional relations with the municipalities that allow them to execute diverse academic activities, training, extension, and internship of students.

AUSTRALIA

Background Information on Student Affairs/Services

In Australia the term "student services" describes student support initiatives or units. Student support, student services, and student amenities are the responsibility of three agents of service delivery: the Commonwealth Government, the universities, and student organizations. All three have made significant investments and contributions to the evolution of student support, services, and amenities since the middle of the 20th century. Student services units and programs aim to enhance the student experience and to enrich campus life. Australia has a growing number of higher education student enrollments. As of 2006 more than 984,146 students were enrolled in Australian higher education programs. International students accounted for 25.5% of the total enrolments.

Typical Services and Programs Offered

The primary goals for student services are 1) to assist students in making a successful adjustment and transition to the university environment; and 2) to reduce enrollment attrition and enhance student retention. Specific service delivery areas include academic advising, academic skills enhancement and information literacy, peer mentoring, student equity, services for students with disabilities, student social engagement activities, psychological counseling and student development services, careers and employment services, student housing services, international student services, Indigenous student support centers and Indigenous cultural programs, sports and recreation activities, and student health services. Increasingly, student services and/ or student organizations are involved in forming campus-wide policies and procedures that impact on student experience. The Director of Student Services (or the Pro Vice Chancellor [PVC] Students, or the Dean of Students) is responsible for student disciplinary procedures.

Organizational Structure of Student Affairs/Services
Typically, the head of the student services area is a Director or Associate Director reporting to a Dean of Students, an Academic Registrar, PVC (Students and Registrar), or a Deputy Vice Chancellor (Academic).

BRAZIL

Background Information on Student Affairs/Services
The history of higher education in Brazil began with the creation of the Universidade Federal do Paraná in 1892. According to a 2005 census, Brazil had over 2,165 higher education institutions, which are divided according to their funding status as private, state, federal, and municipal. Over 70% of all enrolled students attend private universities (2005 Censo da Educação Superior, Instituto Nacional de Pesquisas Educacionais).

Typical Services and Programs Offered
Most universities in Brazil started specific student assistance units in the past 10 years; and many of them already offer a variety of programs such as subsidized food services where the university operates cafeterias to provide low cost meals for students. This service is mostly available at the public universities. Low cost student housing is provided on a need basis and in most cases students must prove they do not live in the same city as the school. Scholarships and financial aid are available based on need and mostly funded by the Brazilian government. In addition, the following services are also provided: academic advisement, employment and internships placement, psychological counseling, community involvement programs where students can apply knowledge from their majors into supporting the local community, assistance for visually impaired students and students with other disabilities, and retention and financial support programs for students from Afro-Brazilian and indigenous descendents.

Organizational Structure of Student Affairs/Services
Typical units will have a Pro-Reitor as the senior student affairs officer, a number of project coordinators, social workers, and support staff members. The Pro-Reitor reports directly to the Reitor (President or Chancellor of the university).

CANADA

Background Information on Student Affairs/Services
Student affairs and service programs in universities throughout Canada formally began in the mid 1940s. Prior to this, student housing professionals, the registrar, and individuals whose

titles varied—but were predominantly entitled Dean of Men or Dean of Women—coordinated services. For purposes of this report higher education is defined as those formal programs that occur in formally recognized postsecondary institutions.

The community college structure has also enjoyed the expertise of student service professionals beginning in the early 1960s. Currently Canada has in excess of 90 universities and affiliated colleges and over 100 community colleges and institutes.

Typical Services and Programs Offered

The services traditionally offered on college and university campuses in Canada include housing, counseling, registrar, recruitment, enrollment management, chaplaincy, student success, student judicial affairs, disability, career development, cooperative education, health, scholarships and awards, aboriginal services, ancillary services, and athletics. Variations in each of these services will depend on the culture and history of the institution.

Organizational Structure of Student Affairs/Services

The organizational structure varies within each university and college. Position titles include Associate Vice President (Students), Vice Provost (Students), Dean of Students, and Director of Student Services. There appears to be a movement to ensure the portfolio is within the president's senior executive team. Hence, the title of Vice President (Students) is gaining popularity. The majority of positions report to the Vice President (Academic) or Chief Academic Officer or the President and Vice Chancellor.

CHINA

Background Information on Student Affairs/Services

In 2006, China had a total of 1,867 regular universities, of which 720 were undergraduate, four-year-institutions, and 1,147 were advanced professional institutions, typically three-year colleges. Among regular universities, 450 offer graduate degrees and 317 are research institutions offering graduate studies. There are also 444 universities for non-traditional (adult) students. The total number of students in all educational institutions is more than 25 million.

The management of students and services is known in China as "student work." The term "student affairs administration" is a relatively new concept in Chinese higher education, though many Chinese universities use "student work" and "student affairs" interchangeably. Student affairs administration is shared among the offices of "student management" (involved in "moral" education), "educational auxiliaries" (akin to "academic support" provided by schools, colleges or faculties in the universities) and logistics department (equivalent to auxiliary services in the United States, such as "dormitories" campus maintenance, housekeeping, public safety, etc), with designated individuals in charge of each office.

Typical Services and Programs Offered

Services mainly include learning support, dormitory and dining, financial aid (mostly in the form of bank loans), physical education and medical health, psychological health and counseling, career development, student entrepreneurship support, and management of student organizations.

Organizational Structure of Student Affairs/Services

In a university, there usually is a university-level leadership group or "administrative unit" for student work. One of the senior university administrators such as the Vice Secretary assumes the role of director of student work. Staff who are responsible for various offices or departments within student work report directly to the Vice Secretary. Normally, student work includes the following offices, departments, or centers: Office of Student Affairs, Office of Academic Affairs, Department of Logistics or Logistic Service Center, Psychological Counseling Center, Financial Aids Center, and Career Development Center.

FRANCE
Centre National des Œuvres Universitaires et Scolaires (CNOUS)
Centre Regional des Œuvres Universitaires et Scolaires (CROUS)

Background Information on Student Affairs/Services

Under the supervision of the *Ministère de l'enseignement supérieur et de la recherche*, the Centre National des Œuvres Universitaires et Scolaires (CNOUS) manages the Centre Regional des Œuvres Universitaires et Scolaires (CROUS) network. Its objective is to provide all students equal access to higher education and an equal opportunity for success by lending support to their everyday activities.

Born of student initiative, the university social services network took its current form under the law of March 16, 1955. The social services network predated the government's activity in the domain of social aid to students. From this beginning, the network of university social services has built a strong identity based on its core values of justice, equality, and sharing.

Typical Services and Programs Offered

Typical tasks of the network are social work, grants (grants based on social or university criteria, and study grants), cultural and student initiatives, international (14,137 foreign students holding grants managed directly by the CNOUS/CROUS network), housing (for 155,000 students), and food services (55.1 million meals served in 2006). The comprehensive regional coverage allows a local response to user needs and constitutes the core of a network of university social services.

At the national level, the CNOUS regulates and oversees the network and contributes its expertise to projects. It promotes the sharing of experience, the modernization of management, and the allocation and optimization of resources. It seeks dialogues with employee representatives and students. And it is responsible for monitoring the results of policies financed by the French government on a nationwide basis. The CNOUS supervises foreign grant holders for the *Ministère des affaires étrangères,* and it mobilizes foreign investment sources to create foreign government education grants. It negotiates projects in partnership with universities for construction of student life services.

Organizational Structure of Student Affairs/Services

National level: The CNOUS is a national independent public establishment with a civil and financial orientation. The CNOUS Administrative Council is the institution's deliberative body. It defines the general policies of the network; assures the distribution of CROUS budget allocations; and accepts and distributes donations, bequests, subsidies and other aid intended for the development of centers. The Prime Minister names the Director of the CNOUS for a period of three years at the recommendation of the Minister of Higher Education.

The CNOUS Administrative Council has 27 members: (1) the President: a leading figure in the field, well qualified, and named by the minister of higher education; (2) eight civil servants representing the national government (of whom four are designated by the minister of higher education and four are designated respectively by the budget, housing, social affairs and foreign affairs ministers); (3) eight elected student representatives; (4) three representatives of CNOUS' and CROUS' personnel designated by the most representative employee unions; (5) three university presidents or directors of establishments of higher education, of which one is from a private institution; and (6) four qualified representatives, of whom two are chosen from a list proposed by the student representatives.

Local level: The local network includes 28 regional centers (CROUS: national public administrative institutions) located concurrent with regional education authorities (académies). There are 16 local centers (CLOUS) and over 40 special branches that bring services directly to students. Each CROUS takes charge of all the students who study within the region of its académie.

A civil servant named by the Minister of Higher Education who implements the resolutions of the CROUS Administrative Council heads each CROUS. This Administrative Council is chaired by the *Recteur de l'académie*, who is the head of the regional educational administration. The council includes seven representatives of the national government, seven elected student representatives, three representatives of CROUS employees, one representative of the regional government, two university presidents (or directors of *Grandes Écoles*), and four representatives chosen by the *Recteur* for their abilities. There are nearly 12,000 employees in the network (national and local level). The CNOUS/CROUS annual budget for 2006 was €1 billion, of which 66. 10% was its own funds.

GERMANY (DEUTSCHLAND)
Deutsches Studentenwerk
Studentenwerke

Background Information on Student Affairs/Services
In Germany, the local *Studentenwerke* (*STW*)—student service organizations—perform public responsibilities related to the economic, social, health care, and cultural support of all students. These organizations are completely autonomous and fully independent from the higher education institutions that they serve, unlike colleges and universities in Anglo-Saxon countries, where departments that are an integral part of the respective university or college carry out these responsibilities.

The *STW* emerged after World War One from the students' mutual aid initiatives. With the support of the industry they founded student houses, restaurants, and loan societies, and arranged for factory work to alleviate economic hardship. Today, there are 58 local *STW* in charge of 2 million students enrolled at about 370 higher education institutions. Hence, many *STW* are simultaneously responsible for several higher education institutions and, in some cases, for institutions at various locations.

The mission of the *STW* is to contribute substantially to the realization of equal opportunities. In collaboration with the higher education institutions and the university towns, the *STW* strive to improve the social framework conditions for higher education study. The *Deutsches Studetenwerk* (*DSW*) is the voluntary national umbrella organization of the 58 *STW*.

Typical Services and Programs Offered

Typical tasks of the local *STW* are student housing, student restaurants/cafeterias, financial aid (administration of the Federal Educational Assistant Act), advisory services (for psychological problems, social and legal counseling), guiding and counseling centers for students with disabilities, international student students, cultural activities, and daycare centers for children.

On the *national level*, the *DSW* supports and coordinates the work of its members. Its main tasks are to organize the exchange and flow of experience between the local *STW* and to safeguard the social-economic policy interests of all students.

Organizational Structure of Student Affairs/Services

Local level: The *STW* are mainly independent statutory bodies of the 16 federal states (*Länder*). Their organizational structure is slightly different from federal state to federal state. In general, the *STW* have three governing bodies: the Executive Director, the Board, and the Administrative Council. Traditionally, students and professors are represented on the Board as well as in the Administrative Council (AC). Representatives of public life have often been part of the AC. The Executive Director is elected by the AC and appointed after confirmation by the respective minister. In total, the local *STW* employ approximately 15,000 people (45% are part-time staff).

National level: The *DSW* has three executive bodies: the Members' Assembly, the Executive Board, and the Secretary General. The Members' Assembly is composed of representatives of the 58 *STW* and meets annually. The Board, elected by the Members' Assembly, is comprised of three professors, three executive directors of the local *STW* and three students. The Board nominates the Secretary General who assumes the executive responsibility and heads the national office with a staff of approximately 45.

HONG KONG SAR, CHINA

Background Information on Student Affairs/Services

Eight of 12 degree-awarding public higher education institutions are funded through the University Grants Committee (UGC). In 2006–07, UGC-funded institutions accounted for 5.6% of the total government expenditure, or 24. 1% of the total expenditure on education. Since 2003, the Government provided matching grants to broaden the funding sources of these UGC-funded institutions and strengthen their fund-raising capabilities. Only about 18% of students between the ages of 17 and 20, or around 15,000, were successful in entering first-year, first-degree places in these institutions. There are 51,000 undergraduate and 10,000 postgraduate students.

Transfer of Hong Kong sovereignty to the People's Republic of China (PRC) in 1997 accelerated the linkage with China and an influx of students from PRC. Non-local students accounted for 4% of all undergraduates in 2005–06 and 6% in 2006–07. The Government is preparing to further increase the admission quotas and introduce measures to facilitate local employment of graduates in order to enhance the status of Hong Kong as an education hub that brings young, new, and high quality talents into the Hong Kong population.

Typical Services and Programs Offered

Student affairs emerged as a defined area of work in universities in the early 1970s. All student affairs offices facilitate student learning and development. They also provide health services, guidance and counseling, career and employment services, financial assistance and scholarships, sports and recreations, student amenities, residential halls and food service, co-curricular activities, leadership development, support for students with disabilities, student organizations, and international students. Cross-institutional collaboration is extensive through ventures such as joint programs, inter-varsity competitions, a job-search database system, award schemes, summer internship projects and work groups on special topics. A shift from "management and service" to an emphasis on "whole-person development" of students is continuing. There is a growing focus on the education role of student affairs practitioners, as they partner with faculty members in facilitating integrated learning of students, and an increasing emphasis on using various outcome-based assessment tools for quality assurance and service improvement.

With the impending introduction of the new senior secondary school curriculum and the transformation of undergraduate studies from three to four years in 2012 (known as the "3–3–4" academic structure), local universities are working towards new directions such as re-structuring their curriculums, in view of globalization and internationalization, to be more multi-disciplinary with greater emphasis on core curriculum or general education. There is a trend for faculty to play a more active role in transforming co-curricular activities into academic requirements or credit-bearing modules, such as service-learning and transferable skills training. Student affairs offices are expected to work collaboratively with academic departments to launch these activities. All such changes have great implications on the direction of student affairs and the roles it plays within higher education institutions.

Organizational Structure of Student Affairs/Services

As universities are restructuring themselves to meet with challenges of the new "3–3–4" academic structure, some Offices of Student Affairs are transforming themselves and undergoing service integration and introducing new services, such as support for international students or strengthening internship programs. As heads of student affairs offices retire, there is a tendency to appoint senior academic staff to serve as Dean of Students to advise the educational leader of the institution on policy formulation, resource allocation, and development strategies for supporting and developing students. The "Dean" may either serve as head of various sections of the office, or delegate this administrative role to a "Director" with Assistant or Deputy Directors responsible for specific student service areas. As residential life is considered a very important part in university education, the Government has recently allocated additional resources to expand residential facilities for students. In general, academic staff is usually appointed as Hall Wardens, with university staff or post-graduate students appointed to be tutors or senior tutors to take care of hall residents.

INDIA

Background Information on Student Affairs/Services

With more than 10 million students enrolled in over 18,000 higher education institutions, India's higher education system is the third largest in the world, after China and the United States. Despite the size of the Indian higher education system, the concept of formal Student affairs offices is a recent trend in India. Student services are more prominently provided in professional schools rather than at the university-wide level.

Typical Services and Programs Offered

Advancement in student services in higher education has been largely restricted to business schools. After the liberalization of India's industrial sector in 1991, business schools became professionalized. However, student services in most of the business schools are still limited to career employment and housing services. Student affairs gained momentum in 2001 with the start of the Indian School of Business (ISB), Hyderabad, in collaboration with global business schools. Student services at ISB include fundraising and event support to student organizations, student counseling, and health services.

Organizational Structure of Student Affairs/Services

Since the concept of "student affairs" is fairly new in India, senior positions like the Dean of Students are non-existent. The Head of Career Services usually reports to the head of an academic department or institution; all other student services report to the administrative head of the institution.

ITALY

Background Information on Student Affairs/Services

In Italy, public responsibilities related to the economic, social, health care, and cultural support of all students are mostly performed by the *Regioni* or directly by some universities. The regional administrations institute local agencies or *Enti per il Diritto allo Studio*—a major agency is located in each province capital or in the regional capital city (e.g., Torino in Piedmont). These organizations are completely autonomous and fully independent from the higher education institutions they serve, unlike colleges and universities in Anglo-Saxon countries, but their administration councils are composed of some university representatives and elected students. Recently, in some regions student welfare activities have been incorporated into the respective universities (e.g., Lombardy, Milan). Some private universities or technical universities manage their facilities directly, as well as some university campuses instituted by special national laws, e.g., the *Centro Residenziale* of the University of Calabria. The mission of the *Enti per il Diritto allo Studio* is to contribute substantially to the realization of equal opportunities. A voluntary umbrella organization, called ANDISU (*Associazione Nazionale degli Organismi per il Diritto allo Studio Universitario*) coordinates the activities of all the agencies at the national level. In collaboration with the higher education institutions and the university towns, the ANDISU strives to improve the social framework conditions for higher education study, according to the 390/91 Italian national law.

Today, there are more than 50 local agencies in charge of 1. 8 million students enrolled at about 75 higher education institutions. Hence, many *Enti* are simultaneously responsible for several higher education institutions and, in some cases, for institutions at various locations.

Typical Services and Programs Offered

Typical tasks of the local *Enti* are basic student services, housing, student canteens/cafeterias, financial aid (administration of student scholarships financed at regional, national, and local level), financial aid for international student exchanges, advisory services (for psychological problems, social and legal counseling), guiding and counseling centers for students with disabilities, job and placement orientation, and cultural activities.

On the *national level*, ANDISU supports and coordinates the work of its members. Its main tasks are to organize the exchange and flow of experience between the local *STW* and to safeguard the social-economic policy interests of all students.

Organizational Structure of Student Affairs/Services

Local level: The *Enti per il Diritto allo Studio* are mainly instrumental bodies of the 21 Italian *Regioni*. Their organizational structure is slightly different from region to region. In general, the *Enti* have three governing bodies: the President, the Executive Director, and the Administrative Council. Traditionally, students and professors are represented in the Administrative Council (AC). Representatives of public life have often been part of the AC. The local government designates the Executive Director, accordingly with the Rectors of the Universities. In total, the local *Enti* employ approximately 3,500 people.

National level: The ANDISU has four executive bodies: the Members' National Assembly, the Executive Board, the President, and the Secretary General. The Members' Assembly is composed of representatives of the 50 *Enti* (President and Director of each agency) and meets twice a year. The Board, elected by the Members' Assembly, is comprised of five Presidents and five executive directors of the local *Enti*, and its President and Secretary General. The Board nominates the Secretary General who assumes the executive responsibility.

JAPAN

Background Information on Student Affairs/Services

Student affairs programs and management in higher education in Japan are modeled after the United States. In 1958, the Student Welfare Council of the Educational Ministry published a policy white paper addressing the importance of extra-curricular programs in developing students' personalities. However, many Japanese universities continue to be faculty-centered, and extra-curricular programs are thought to complement the academic curriculum. In 2000, the University Council of the Educational Ministry (which is now known as the Ministry of Education, Culture, Sports, Science and Technology) published a report that requires universities to become student-oriented and to accept the value of co-curricular programs.

Typical Services and Programs Offered

Services and programs include advising student organizations, organizing student activities, services in student counseling, careers and employment, student housing, services for international students, sports and recreation, student health, orientation, peer mentoring, financial aid, campus amenities for disabled students, cultural events, school festivals, self-development seminars, and freshmen camps. Student cooperatives that are not part of the university have traditionally undertaken student welfare and amenities such as operating the bookstore, cafeteria, housing services, insurance business as well as administering student affairs programs. However recently, the number of universities that have established their own enterprises as part of the university organizational structure to deal with these student services is increasing.

Organizational Structure of Student Affairs/Services

Typically, the heads of a student affairs operation are a Dean of Students and a faculty member who most often report to the President. It is not uncommon for the Dean of Students to also hold the position of Vice-President. Reporting to him/her are often several sections including student life, housing/accommodations, financial aid, sport/recreation, and counseling.

KUWAIT

Background Information on Student Affairs/Services

Higher education has evolved in the state of Kuwait since the early 1960s after the founding of Kuwait University, the country's comprehensive state-supported public university. Public Authority for Applied Education and Training, established in 1982, serves as the two-year public college for the country. Kuwait students attend the state-supported institutions free of charge. Within the last 10 years, the government has provided licenses for numerous private universities and colleges. Thus far, institutions are based upon the American and Australian models of higher education with more institutions to follow. The government of Kuwait provides a scholarship program, full tuition, expenses, and stipend for talented students who have been accepted to universities in the United States, the United Kingdom, and other foreign countries. Similar scholarships are available to attend Kuwait's private colleges and universities, that are monitored by the Private University Council, a department within the Ministry of Higher Education. The prospective collegiate pool is expected to grow three-fold over the next years. No two student affairs programs within the state of Kuwait are alike, and the concept of student development is new with little understanding of its benefits. From a traditional Division of Student Affairs excluding housing to a program whereby a student committee working with the Vice President of Student Affairs plans the institution's student activities, each university provides a unique perspective of programs and services for students.

Typical Services and Programs Offered

The structure and comprehensiveness of student affairs programs and services are varied within the institutions of Kuwait. Each institution offers an iteration of the following programs and services: admissions, registration services, student activities including co- and extracurricular programming, counseling services, career services including counseling and placement, disability accommodations, housing, health services, outreach and events, alumni affairs, academic advisement, retention initiatives, academic support, student media, sports, and student associations. Most institutions focus on admissions, registration, and student activities, particularly student government and athletics.

Organizational Structure of Student Affairs/Services

There is not a typical operational structure for student affairs programs and services in Kuwait. In most cases the chief student affairs officer reports to the President of the university or college. Whereas one model may be the traditional comprehensive model of programs and services with directors of student life, admissions, registration, student success, alumni affairs, and health services, reporting to the chief student affairs officer, another typical model has a chief student affairs officer with a student advisory committee that plans college activities and professional staff that provide counseling services, advisement, and language support. Another operational structure includes only the functions of admissions, registration, and the student union. The philosophy of student affairs is new to Kuwait. As more western colleges and universities are opened, it is expected there will be more traditional operational structures.

MALAYSIA

Background Information on Student Affairs/Services

Currently, there are 17 public universities and university colleges and around 670 private colleges and universities. University colleges, unlike universities, are set up by the government to offer specialized courses or training, which at the moment are predominantly on technology and/or engineering. Public and private universities are now being coordinated and monitored by the Higher Education Department, a department within the newly established Ministry of Higher Education.

The hereditary roots as far as the student affairs profession and the setting up of the Department of Student Affairs (DSA) may be traced back to the Universities and University College Act 1971 (as amended 1975). Initially, establishment of the DSA was more geared toward regulating and monitoring student activities and movement.

Typical Services and Programs Offered

Services and programs typically include advising of student organizations, student accommodation services, counseling services, career and industry relations, student health services, sports and recreation, and in recent years, entrepreneur advisory service and support.

Organizational Structure of Student Affairs/Services

All public universities are headed by a Deputy Vice Chancellor and, in the case of university colleges, by a Deputy Rector. A Dean and/or Deputy Registrar with a number of student affairs personnel assist them in overseeing or coordinating the activities of various sections including student life and development, accommodation, counseling, career, student discipline, and judicial services. Residential colleges and their activities, which are also under the purview of the Deputy Vice Chancellor/Deputy Rector, are headed by college masters who are faculty members and assisted by fellows who are from the academia and career administrators. These officers are appointed for a fixed term and compensated, amongst other privileges, with free accommodation in residential colleges.

NEW ZEALAND

Background Information on Student Affairs/Services

Established student service groups in New Zealand (NZ) universities have existed for over 20–25 years. The extension of services occurred largely when access to tertiary institutions was widened in the 1980s. There are 31 tertiary institutions (eight universities, 20 polytechnics, three wanangas—indigenous tertiary institutions) in New Zealand with a student population of about 448,000.

Typical Services and Programs Offered

Though there is institutional variance, student services mainly consist of a mix of the following service groups: student health and counseling, learning services including mentoring, disability services and equity programs, child care, student housing, career development and employment, recreation, financial aid and advice, student administration, retention and transition/orientation programs, and international services. Services are funded and supported in many ways: through universities' operational grants, a student services levy paid directly by students, commercial income and government subsidies for health care, child care, disability services, and Maori and Pacific programs.

Organizational Structure of Student Affairs/Services

Structurally many student services are grouped together. Through a Director of that group, they report to the Teaching and Learning Pro Vice Chancellor or equivalent.

PAKISTAN

Background Information on Student Affairs/Services

Pakistan is a young country that acquired independence in 1947. At the time of independence Pakistan had only one higher education institution (*World Education News and Reviews*, January/February 2005).

Currently there are 124 public and private universities in Pakistan. The Higher Education Commission (HEC) in Pakistan recognizes these universities against set criteria. The Higher Education Commission has been set up by the Government of Pakistan to enable local universities to become world-class centers of education, research, and development. With the recent trend of globalization, few overseas universities in partnership with local universities are establishing their campuses in Pakistan. Also, some international university campuses in Pakistan are not recognized by HEC, as they do not fulfill the criteria set by HEC. To address the need to enhance the quality of higher education in terms of teaching, research, enrollment of students, facilities, and services, HEC recently developed and shared the criteria on which universities are ranked in Pakistan.

International students in Pakistan are drawn from developing countries such as Bangladesh, Afghanistan, Syria and other Middle East countries, Tajikistan, Kyrgyzstan, Kenya, Uganda, Tanzania, and Zanzibar.

The Government of Pakistan does not have officially designated student affairs offices. As a result, the Government sets no prescribed students affairs programs or activities. However, with the increasing need for student affairs services and programs, it is becoming a defined area at higher education institutions in Pakistan, particularly in the private sector and to some extent in the public sector. Recently, in 2001–2 the Government of Pakistan has started to provide interest free education loans to students through local banks. All student affairs offices facilitate student learning and development.

By 2008, not all universities in Pakistan had student affairs offices as uniform units. The responsibilities of student affairs are divided among various offices of the university, e.g., academic administrative offices, educational management office, program office, student support services office, admission office, and communication centers. General administration offices handle some services that are purely administrative such as dining, housing, and transportation.

Typical Services and Programs Offered

The primary goals for student affairs services are student recruitment, admissions, academic record keeping, course scheduling, academic progression, grades, electives, examination administration, transcripts production, management support to academic committees, and student financial assistance, grants and scholarships.

In a larger perspective student affairs practitioners design orientation programs for new students, organize English language support courses, take a lead role in policy implementation, make recommendations in policy making, offer student counseling, provide support for field-work activities for courses, play an active role in internal and external examination, course and facilitator evaluation, program evaluations and quality assurance, and manage summer intern-ship activities for students, international student services, convocation, opening and gradua-tion ceremonies, student development activities, and student social engagement activities.

Organizational Structure of Student Affairs

In general, the Registrar is head of the student affairs office. Associate and Assistant Registrars support the position. The Registrar has a reporting relationship to the Provost or Rector of the university, while the Assistant Registrar has a dotted-line relationship to Deans and Directors who are academic heads of entities. Students' residential or campus life is considered a very important part in university education. Only a few private universities are engaging themselves to deliberate on this important aspect and thinking of where to place the position within the organizational structure.

QATAR

Background Information on Student Affairs/Services

The concept of student affairs and services is a relatively recent one in Qatar. There is one public university in Qatar (Qatar University) and several other higher education institutional affiliate partners from the United States and Canada. There are approximately 13,000 university stu-dents in Qatar: 9,000 at Qatar University with the other 4,000 spread among the international institutions. Qatar University is approximately 84% Qatari; the Qatar Foundation-funded Education City has about 2,000 students and 45 nationalities across its affiliate institutions, with approximately 50% of the population Qatari. With the exception of Qatar University, all other higher education institutions have been in operation less than 11 years.

The Qatar Foundation for Education, Science, and Community Development is a private, chartered, non-profit organization founded by Sheikh Hamad Bin Khalifa Al-Thani, Emir of Qatar. Guided by the principle that a nation's greatest resource is the potential of its people, Qatar Foundation aims to develop that potential through a network of centers devoted to progressive education, research, and community development. While Qatar Foundation funds and oversees a variety of programs and entities, one of its major projects is Education City, a one-of-a-kind center for higher education in Doha, Qatar. Education City is a collection of world-renowned universities including, at present, Virginia Commonwealth University, Cor-nell University, Texas A&M University, Carnegie Mellon University, Georgetown University, and Northwestern University. These six partner institutions (and more to be added in the future) contribute their best academic programs to the students of Education City in order to provide the students of Qatar, the Arabian Gulf, and other countries around the world the chance to study together in one place with the world's greatest universities. Admission stan-dards, curriculum, and the collegiate experience for students at the partner institutions are identical to those of the home campuses.

The universities that make up Education City have been working closely with their counterparts in the United States to establish important services and programs like student activities, leadership development, disability services, counseling, athletics, and a student code of conduct. In addition, universities have been working to share with students the rich history and traditions of the home campuses. Education City is unique in that the Qatar Foundation manages residence life and campus-wide events.

The qualifications/training of student affairs professionals in Qatar varies widely. Each university has placed emphasis on different criteria, so that no two universities have the same qualifications. Some staff members have degrees in student affairs or a related field, but some come from business or psychology backgrounds. Some professionals have been hired based on their degrees from the granting institutions, while for others it is their experience in the gulf region and working with Arab students. There have been some professional development opportunities offered for student affairs practitioners in Qatar, and this trend is very likely to continue.

Typically, the head of the student services area is a Director or Assistant Dean reporting to an Associate Dean or Dean of the college.

A major challenge facing universities in Qatar is the lack of identification with a university. The institutions have a large commuter population, so there is not the built-in community that residence halls often provide. Education City has the added challenge of bringing together several diverse and unique institutions, all under the Qatar Foundation umbrella.

The work of student affairs is a distributed and shared responsibility among Education City branch partners and the Qatar Foundation. The low faculty-to-student ratio provides the opportunity for much higher levels of interaction. Active pedagogical approaches are used both in and out of class and the role of student affairs staff is to be catalysts for deeper learning everywhere.

Typical Services and Programs Offered

A full array of student affairs services and programs has been available to the students of Education City for about 10 years. Staff members who focus specifically on their own students create the unique institutional culture of each Education City branch partner. For example, Carnegie Mellon University provides a "Meeting of the Minds" poster session where students' individual or group research work is displayed in a conference setting. Northwestern University provides opportunities for students to learn about media by being involved in producing a student newspaper. Other programs such as intramural sports, Education City-wide speakers and programs, and leadership development opportunities such as the Leader Shape Institute are provided cooperatively across all the branches and with the support of Qatar Foundation staff. Services such as testing, financial aid, counseling and health, and residence halls are provided by Qatar Foundation, and students from all campuses are intermingled in their living experiences.

Because Education City is so new, many of the relationships and programs are still emerging. Qatar Foundation and the Education City branches have made a commitment to constantly seek the most effective and efficient means to provide the programs and services that are so necessary to enhancing student learning and development. The other commitment that Qatar Foundation and Education City-Branch student affairs staff members make is to keep faculty involved in the lives of students. Student affairs serves as a catalyst in retaining a commitment to holistic learning among all faculty and staff. Partnerships are being developed to provide Qatari staff the opportunity to pursue advanced degrees in student affairs. Education City also serves as a site for graduate students who seek internship-abroad opportunities. An ongoing staff learning community provides the opportunity for on-the-job development as well.

Organizational Structure of Student Affairs/Services

The Qatar Foundation and the Education City branches establish agreements that serve as a guide for the academic courses and co-curricular programs students will experience. The Foundation has a staff in the Faculty and Student Services area that coordinates key student services. The Education City branches each have additional student affairs staff members who provide co-curricular opportunities focused on the branch's own students. Where appropriate and desired, Education City branches cooperate with one another and with Qatar Foundation in providing programs for all students.

RUSSIA

Background Information on Student Affairs/Services

Student life is a complex, complicated, and many-sided process which includes academic, scientific, personal, creative, and leisure aspects. In order to develop a student and prepare a professional specialist, much attention is paid to students' extracurricular life in Russian universities. Student affairs services are distributed among and administered by various administrative and academic units of higher education institutions (commonly known as extra-educational students' activities departments). As an integrated part of the university process they create student learning through programs and services that promote leadership, development, and tolerance, and that communicate the values and standards of the university community.

The concept of student affairs/services as a formal institutionalized single unit is fairly new in Russia. It is very difficult to make any generalizations about higher education institutions in Russia; for this reason additional research is necessary. This report is based on description of current practices in the leading universities of Russia (for further information about leading Russian universities refer to http://new. hse. ru/sites/international_mobil/partners_en. aspx).

Typical Services and Programs Offered

Russian higher education institutions have prevalent, well-developed systems of extracurricular activities for/with students, which are run by special divisions for extracurricular activities. Vice Presidents and Associate Vice Presidents at the university level, and Deans in colleges, usually lead these institutions The main goal of these divisions is any work for/with students that leads to students' personal and professional advancement. These divisions are aimed at (1) commitment to extraordinary learning by students, staff, and community members—both within and outside the universities; (2) support for enterprising students and engagement with the world; (3) current and future trends affecting students and campus life to meet students' needs; (4) support of students' self-governance and initiatives; (5) ensuring social protection of students; (6) financial aid information assistance; (7) pre-admission and post-admission orientation; and (8) alumni affairs.

Academic departments are responsible for academic admission, advising, registration, and records. Students' academic life is governed through general rules and regulations and academic and examinations rules. A system of advisers (curators) is very well developed. Students' extracurricular life is commonly performed through Student Representative Councils, a variety of clubs, and different units (choirs, chorales, consorts, skiffle groups, and companies). Athletics is given much attention.

Student support networks include career development and counseling, student health clinics and medical treatment, health insurance, and scholarships and financial assistance. Student services also include accommodation, facilities, dining halls, advisory services, university preparatory services, study abroad programs, and programs for international students. They are offered through various administrative units and centers for student development at higher education institutions.

Advocacy of students' rights is primarily a goal of the students' union/students' governance. Every state university (and many private institutions) has its own Student Council. In addition to advocacy, its activities include disseminating information about available financial aid; overseeing fair student housing administration; and assisting in student job search, and organizing recreational activities.

Organizational Structure of Student Affairs/Services

Organizational structure varies in different higher education institutions, mirroring their sizes, needs, and requirements. Typically, the Vice President for Extracurricular Activities coordinates various departments that manage academic and extracurricular activities, enhancement of students' self-governance and protection of student rights, and social guarantees. This organizational structure (whatever name it has) is aimed at contributing to the general mission of the universities by providing an opportunity for students to develop their lives to become enlightened citizens and contributors to their country. Planning and administering services that contribute to the learning environment and augment the functions of teaching, research, creative scholarship, and public service accomplish this goal.

Senior positions like the Dean of Students typically do not exist. Their functions and responsibilities are distributed among the Deans of Faculties (College). The dean, who is responsible for students' academic and extracurricular activities, heads each faculty. Their main role is to directly support the faculty (college), department programs, and students. There may be some assistant deans responsible for different fields of student services.

Russian universities tend to administer their international cooperation and work with international students through a separate unit. For example, there may be an Office for Development of International Relations (IR Development Office) at the State University–High School of Economics. Typically, the office for international affairs provides assistance to international students in the following areas: admission, Russian language instruction, housing, pre-departure orientation, and staying in legal status. There may also be special offices, centers and groups. They report to the Vice President for International Affairs. The office staff may include an International Students Affairs Coordinator, Student and Faculty Advisors, and Educational and Post-Graduate International Programs Advisors.

SOUTH AFRICA

Background Information on Student Affairs/Services

African education has been influenced by colonization by the English, French, Portuguese, Belgians, Germans, and Dutch. Models of higher education adapted from these countries have impacted heavily on African universities and student affairs practice. No other continent has had so many and such diverse influences as Africa.

The concepts of student affairs and alumni affairs received only cursory attention, at least in South Africa, from 1959 (with the establishment of "non-white universities") until 1976. Student affairs generally would be catering for the following during this earlier period: residences, sports and recreation, and student government. After the Soweto uprisings (1976) and the years leading up to 1976, there were dramatic changes. In 1976, for example, counseling and judicial services were added to student affairs, as well as health services. They were followed by campus protection services and services for students with disabilities.

Typical Services and Programs Offered

Residences and Catering Services: In the main, ensuring that students live in an environment that allows them to study effectively, and have their basic needs, food and housing, adequately met.

Sports and Recreation: The adage "a healthy mind in a healthy body" applies in this instance. The following sports were played at traditionally (historically) white campuses: rugby, cricket, tennis, soccer, boxing, athletics, table tennis, basketball, baseball, gymnastics, and surfing. Historically, black campuses only had soccer, softball, netball, boxing, athletics, and tennis. Racial segregation also contributed to the type of resources students would have by way of recreational facilities.

Student Government: This area is covered in the Student Representative Councils. These are statutorily catered for in terms of the Higher Education Act of 1997.

Counseling Services: In addition to caring for the mental health needs of students, such efforts as life skills training and academic support for students struggling with their academic programs are some of the functions of Student Counseling. Trained and licensed psychologists work in these counseling centers, and they are registered with the South African Health Professionals Council (SAHPC).

Health Centre: The health centre is staffed by health personnel, usually nurses and doctors. Their raison d'être is to ensure the physical health of students and to offer prophylactic advice on health-related matters like the importance of exercise, healthy eating habits, and pursuing a healthy lifestyle. Their services, therefore, range from curative to preventive. Programs to inform students about all aspects of HIV and AIDS are high on the agenda. Preventive measures, anti-retroviral drugs, and healthy sexual choices are highlighted on many a campus health program. Health is pursued not only as the absence of disease, but rather as a state of being in optimal condition.

Campus Protection Services: Campus Protection Services are essentially about promoting law and order on campuses and ensuring the safety of students. Campuses sometimes report high incidences of vandalism, rape, stolen property, illegal residents in hostels, parking violations and infringements, lack of respect for curfews, and room searches. All the issues attendant upon a safe and accessible campus are within the remit of campus protection services.

Students with disabilities: Although the percentage of students with disabilities is between 0. 75% and 2. 5%, such students do need specialized attention. Disabilities generally catered for include visual impairments, hearing impairments, and physical impairments (quadriplegics). Advocacy for students with disabilities, educating the general university community on disabilities, and provisioning of resources (e.g., Braille texts, computers for the visually impaired, elevators with knobs written in Braille, and ramps to allow free movement of wheelchairs) are some of the challenges that are met by a department devoted to students with disabilities.

Student Judicial Services: Campuses are replete with students who get involved in infractions of the law and university policy. These students are then subjected to substantively and procedurally fair processes to strive at decisions that are fair and punishments commensurate to the infraction.

Organizational Structure of Student Affairs/Services

The vice-chancellor is the senior executive officer in South African institutions. Prior to the tertiary education institution merger of the early 2000s, most institutions had a deputy vice chancellor for student affairs. Post-merger most senior student affairs positions are now entitled Executive Dean of Students.

SPAIN
Consejo of Colegios Mayores Universitarios de España (CCMU)

Background Information on Student Affairs/Services

In mid-2007 the resident population of the Kingdom of Spain was 45,120,000, 1.5 million students, 74 universities and 165 *Colegios Mayores*, university residential centers that are integrated into the university and provide a service to the university community. *Colegios Mayores* provide lodgings and food for students and also offer a complete spectrum of academic, cultural, and sports activities.

Under Spanish law, the State has transferred all powers with regard to education and science to the different autonomous regional governments and to the universities. Thus, the universities are self-governing and have great autonomy, and so face, under the protection of the L. O. U. (Law of University Autonomy), the challenge of looking after students' social, cultural, and sport life. Most of the services that have been carried out by the *Colegios Mayores* are now being offered by the university authorities through the Vice Rectors (Vice Presidents) and other departments or offices. This results in a parallel provision of services, all within the same university community. In Spain each university decides how to structure its own student services. For this reason, services may vary from one institution to another; however, advice services are generally very well established and equipped in all universities.

Typical Services and Programs Offered

Student services within the Spanish universities support students in their academic life as well as in their social needs through the Vice Presidents of Students. This service consists of the following areas: grants and other economic aids; enquiries and documentation, legal advice, welfare centre, general affairs, orientation and information, counseling centers, disability services, health service (health services are provided by the national health system), student associations, and sports. *Colegios Mayores* are under this Vice President (or another) or directly under the Rector of the university. In many universities a special Commission of *Colegios Mayores* is chaired by the Rector.

Not all students who apply can be accommodated in the *Colegios Mayores* so Spanish universities also provide an off-campus housing service. This is a computerized database of private residences, apartments, houses, and flat shares offered by private owners in the area. The service is available via the Web pages of every university, but the university is not responsible for the applications. Applications have to be made directly to the private institutions.

All cultural activities on a broader scale such as theatre, cinema, art exhibitions, and concerts, are encouraged and promoted by another Vice President. As a complement to syllabuses and teaching curricula, students are also offered a wide range of support services to make life more agreeable and profitable during their stay at the university. When they arrive they can take advantage of orientation, advice and psycho pedagogic services, and ask for social assistance and grants where applicable. During their studies they have access to libraries, computer services, cultural and sporting activities, and lodgings services. Before they graduate they may ask for advice and help in finding employment at the Centre for the Promotion of Employment and Practice in Industry.

One point to be considered is that the Rectors of the Spanish universities and their governments are elected by all the university members—students and faculty.

Organizational Structure of Student Affairs/Services

As already mentioned above, all the education competences are the responsibility of the universities. The Ministry of Education and Science retains responsibility for very few of them. For this reason the student affairs office at each university, under a Vice Rector's supervision, carries out policy. At the same time there is a *Consejo of Colegios Mayores Universitarios de España* (Council of University Colegios Mayores of Spain), CCMU.

The CCMU is a legally constituted association according to the Spanish Constitution whose members are all the *Colegios Mayores* of Spain from all the Spanish universities, either founded by public or private institutions. The governing body is made up of one representative from each university and an Executive Board of five members is elected from among them. A General Delegate is elected mainly for international relationships.

TAIWAN

Background Information on Student Affairs/Services

Until 2006, Taiwan had 126 postsecondary institutions in total, including 89 universities, 56 colleges, and 17 junior colleges. Among them, there are 2,591 graduate schools with 177,000 graduate students. The total undergraduate enrollment is 1,296,000 students.

Nowadays, student affairs and "professional education" (undergraduate education) complement each other. In order to enable the students to acquire model characters and healthy lifestyles while pursuing professional knowledge, student affairs work should focus not only on cultivating students to become elite citizens who possess both the maturity and professional skills to equally seek the truth and pursue knowledge. It also means working with each student to have an international awareness and a spirit of service to increase the visibility of Taiwan internationally and to have a love for mankind sentence is too long.

Typical Services and Programs Offered

Programs and services include advising student life (e.g., lodging, diet, scholarship grant, student loan, student insurance, campus safety, etc.), advising for expatriate students, sports activities, health care services, psychological counseling (individual and group, personality tests), alumni career counseling (resume writing in Chinese/English, interview skills, job placement), advising extra-curricular activities, and academic advising.

Organizational Structure of Student Affairs/Services

Student affairs organizational structure varies among higher education institutions in Taiwan. At the National Chengchi University, the Dean of Students and the Vice Dean of Students oversee several "Sections" such as the Military Education Office, Life Guidance Section, Student Activities Section, Health Services, Student Housing Services, Arts and Cultural Activities, Counseling Center, and the Center of Career Development.

UNITED ARAB EMIRATES

Background Information on Student Affairs/Services

The United Arab Emirates is a small, oil-rich country located on the Persian Gulf to the East of Saudi Arabia. All UAE young people have access to higher education paid for by the government. Federal institutions of higher education are increasing. There are 12 campuses of the Higher Colleges of Technology, the very large United Arab Emirates University, and the three campuses of Zayed University developed for Emirati women only but recently opened to international students and male students as well. Emirates College of Advanced Education is a federal university located in Abu Dhabi. The private higher education sector continues to grow with the participation of both recognized and little-known institutions from the U.S., Canada, the United Kingdom, India, and Pakistan. Student affairs services vary by university and are only fully functioning in a handful of universities as the educational role of student affairs is not yet clearly understood. On each campus student affairs personnel may include two to 15 people depending on the configuration of the services provided. A recent event for student affairs professionals from throughout the country generated a group of 100, with estimates that there are at least 150–200 student affairs personnel employed at institutions in the United Arab Emirates.

Typical Services and Programs Offered

Typical services include registration services, academic advising, personal counseling services, student activities, recreational sports and activities, student housing services, international student services, disabled student services, career and placement services, and health services. While all these services are provided in at least one university within the country, most institutions provide a subsection of the services listed.

Organizational Structure of Student Affairs/Services

Typically the head of the student affairs staff, i.e., Dean of Students, Supervisor of Student Services, Director of Student Services, reports to the Chief Academic Officer. The person heading the student affairs area typically has staff reporting to him/her in a number of the specialty areas listed above including counseling, housing, activities, and recreation. The size and maturity of the institution usually determine the richness and breadth of the student services offered. Staff and administrators are hired for fixed terms and because most student affairs staff members are expatriates, the turnover of staff is higher than in countries where the student affairs staff is comprised primarily of citizens working in their home country.

UNITED KINGDOM

Background Information on Student Affairs/Services

Student services departments are now a well-established feature of higher education institutions in the UK. The function has a longer history in the former polytechnics ("new universities"), with the concept spreading across all institutions following the national restructuring of the HE sector in 1992. Typically there is some crossover of responsibility, with the department responsible for student administration often called the Academic Registrar's Department. Student associations are also active throughout the sector. These are independent organizations based on each campus with a funding subsidy from the HE institution to which they relate. Depending on the size of the university, this association (or 'union' or 'guild') may deliver a significant range of commercial and support services to students (such as catering services and housing advice) alongside the provision of student activities and social events, as well as opportunities for student development and leadership.

Typical Services and Programs Offered

These include: (1) welfare and support services, including provision for disabled students; (2) residential services and support; (3) financial assistance; (4) support for student complaints, appeals, and disciplinary/judicial procedures; (5) international student support; (6) services relating to student health and well-being, such as health promotion, medical consultation, counseling; (7) student induction and orientation; (8) study skills provision, including academic and social mentoring; (9) community liaison activity, such as student volunteering; (10) student activities and events; (11) outreach to schools and colleges, including involvement in recruitment and admissions work; (12) careers guidance; (13) agencies for part-time employment; (14) sports and recreation services; (15) childcare provision; and (16) chaplaincy and faith-related activities.

Organizational Structure of Student Affairs/Services

A typical student services department comprises a number of functional units (e.g., disability support, careers, student housing), with the manager of each unit reporting to a head of student services. Depending on the size and type of institution, the head of student services may report upwards to the head of a larger service department, a head of university administration, or to an academic manager (such as a Pro Vice Chancellor) responsible for teaching or for the student experience across the institution. A head of student services may or may not be part of the senior management group for the institution.

References

American Association of Higher Education. (1991). *9 principles of good practice for assessing student learning*. Retrieved November 1, 2011, from http://www.iuk.edu/%7Ekoctla/assessment/9principles. shtml

American Association of Higher Education, American College Personnel Association, & National Association of College Personnel Administrators. (1998*). Powerful partnerships: A shared responsibility for learning*. Retrieved November 1, 2011, from http://www.aahe.org/teaching/tsk_frce.htm

American College Personnel Association (ACPA). (1996). *The student learning imperative: Implications for student affairs*. Washington, DC: Author.

American College Personnel Association (ACPA) & National Association of Student Personnel Administrators (NASPA). (2010). *Professional competency areas for student affairs practitioners*. Retrieved November 1, 2011, from http://www.naspa.org/regions/regioniii/Professional%20Competency.pdf

American Council on Education. (1937). *The student personnel point of view.* Washington, DC: American Council on Education.

American Council on Education (1949). The student personnel point of view (rev. ed.). *American Council on Education Studies* (Series 6), *1* (3). Washington, DC: Author.

Chickering, A., & Reisser, L. (1993). *Education and identity* (2nd ed.). San Francisco: Jossey-Bass.

Evans, N. J., Forney, D. S., Guido-DiBrito, F. (1998). *Student development in college: Theory, research, and practice.* San Francisco: Jossey-Bass.

Junco, R., & Mastrodicasa, J. (2007). *Connecting to the net. generation: What higher education professionals need to know about today's students.* Washington, D C: NASPA. Available at http://blog. reyjunco.com/pdf/NetGenerationProof.pdf

Keeling, R. P. (Ed.). (2006). *Learning reconsidered 2: A practical guide to implementing a campus wide focus on the student experience.* Washington, DC: American College Personnel Association, Association of College and University Housing Officers–International, Association of College Unions–International, National Academic Advising Association, National Association for Campus Activities, National Association of Student Personnel Administrators, National Intramural-Recreational Sports Association. Retrieved November 1, 2011, from http://www.myacpa.org/pub/documents/learningreconsidered2.pdf

Komives, S., & Woodard, D. (Eds.). (2003). *Student services: A handbook for the profession* (4th ed.). San Francisco: Jossey-Bass

Kuh, G., Kinzie, J., Schuh, J., & Whitt, E. (2005). *Student success in college: Creating conditions that matter.* San Francisco: Jossey-Bass.

Ludeman, R. B. (Ed.). (2002). *The role of student affairs and services in higher education: A practical manual for developing, implementing, and assessing student affairs programs and services.* Paris: UNESCO.

Ludeman, R. B., Osfield, K. J., Hidalgo, E. I., Oste, D., & Wang, H. S. (Eds.). (2009) *Student affairs and services in higher education: Global foundations, issues, and best practices.* Paris: UNESCO. Available at http://unesdoc. unesco.org/images/0018/001832/183221e.pdf

National Association of Student Personnel Administrators (NASPA). (1987). *A perspective on student affairs: A statement issued on the 50th anniversary of the Student Personnel Point of View.* Washington, DC: Author.

National Association of Student Personnel Administrators (NASPA). (1998). *Principles of good practice for student affairs.* Retrieved November 1, 2011, from http://www.naspa.org/career/goodprac. cfm

National Association of Student Personnel Administrators (NASPA) & American College Personnel Association (ACPA). (2004). *Learning reconsidered.* Washington, DC: Authors. Retrieved November 1, 2011, fromhttp://www.naspa.org/membership/leader_ex_pdf/lr_long.pdf

Pascarella, E., & Terenzini, P. (2005). *How college affects students: Vol. 2. A third decade of research.* San Francisco: Jossey-Bass.

Rudolph, F. (1990). *The American college and university: A history.* Athens: The University of Georgia Press.

Strange, C., & Banning, J. (2001). *Educating by design: Creating campus learning environments that work.* San Francisco: Jossey-Bass.

UNESCO. (1998a). *World Conference on Higher Education: Higher Education in the Twenty-first Century; Vision and Action, Volume IV (Thematic Debate).* Paris: Author. Retrieved from http://unesdoc. unesco.org/images/0011/001166/116613m.pdf

UNESCO. (1998b). *World Declaration on Higher Education for the Twenty-first Century: Vision and Action and Framework for Priority Action for Change and Development in Higher Education.* Paris: Author.

CHAPTER FIVE

Fraternities and Sororities in the Contemporary Era

A Cause for Change

PIETRO A. SASSO

John Robson (1966), editor of Baird's *Manual of Fraternities*, authored a text, *The College Fraternity and Its Modern Role*. In it Robson concludes, "Man is a noble creature, only a little lower than the angels. A chapter made up of his tribe is the kind that has given the American college fraternity a glorious history and promises it a glorious future" (p. 112). Robson is correct in his assertion that fraternities, and even sororities, have a storied and contributing narrative in shaping higher education. The future of fraternities is one that is undeniable, as collegiate fraternal organizations are enduring and pervasive organizations that have yet to falter despite widespread criticism and public events that provide face validity to these criticisms (Sasso, 2008). This chapter will examine the role of fraternities and sororities on college campuses by providing a brief overview of fraternities and sororities which will serve as a pretext to the role of fraternities and sororities in the contemporary era. Previous research and suggestions will also be discussed to ensure that fraternities and sororities continue to offer student development opportunities.

Overview

The historical evolution of fraternities and sororities since the founding of Phi Beta Kappa has transitioned them into a form radically different than their ancestors. In the contemporary context, fraternities are social fellowship groups assembled by values, rites of passage, and rituals that remain abstruse for the rest of campus. They provide social opportunities, leadership training, and philanthropic efforts for their members (Gregory, 2003). While there may be significant elements of fraternities that remain esoteric, what has been visible to the remainder of society at large as well as other undergraduate students, are the results of alcohol-infused hazing incidents and consistent displays of alcohol use (Wechsler, Kuh, & Davenport, 1996).

Within the last 20 years, fraternities and sororities, or Greek letter organizations (GLOs), have continued to be featured in a number of high-profile incidents leading to a negative perception of these groups. News reports of incidents of alcohol-related deaths and other issues resulting from fraternity and sorority alcohol abuse provide face validity to these findings (Wall, 2006). For fraternities, these include racially charged party themes, hazing incidents, and most recently comments about women deemed offensive (Kaplin & Lee, 2006; Marcus, 2011). For sororities, hazing, public displays of intoxication, as well as destruction of public property during formal chapter events are commonplace themes (Cornwell, 2010). However, there are a number of external supports, including umbrella organizations, that work to develop fraternity and sorority chapters and individual members, against their own negative trends.

These umbrella organizations, each serving a particular population of fraternities and sororities, are numerous. They include (1) the North American Interfraternity Conference (NIC), which represents traditional fraternities; (2) the National Panhellenic Council (NPC), which represents 26 women's organizations; (3) the National Pan-Hellenic Council (NPHC), which represents nine historically African American fraternities and sororities commonly known as the "Divine Nine"; (4) the National Association for Latino Fraternal Organizations (NALFO), which encourages the advancement of Latino fraternities and sororities; (5) the National Asian Pacific Islander American Panhellenic Association (National APIA Panhellenic Association), an umbrella organization that exists to unite Asian fraternities and sororities; and (6) the National Multicultural Greek Council (NMGC), which represents 10 multicultural fraternities and sororities (Gregory, 2003).

Supporting these umbrella organizations are several incorporated leadership conferences run by professional and volunteer staff. These organizations are grouped by regions. They are (1) Association of Fraternal Leadership and Values, which serves the Midwest and West and features the National Cultural Greek Leadership Conference (NCGLC) and the National Black Greek Leadership Conference (NBGLC); (2) the Southeastern Interfraternity Conference (SEIFC) and Southeastern Panhellenic Association (SEPA), which service fraternities and sororities in the south; and (3) the Northeast Greek Leadership Association (NGLA), which serves the northeast region of the United States. Additionally supporting and coordinating the leadership conferences and campus-based professionals are two professional associations for advisors. The Association of Fraternity/Sorority Advisors (AFA) is the professional organization for campus-based fraternity/sorority advisors. The Fraternity Executives Association (FEA)coordinates the professional standards and offers professional development for staff members of national fraternities and sororities (Gregory, 2003).

These umbrella organizations traditionally meet each academic year at conferences for educational programming that run concurrently with professional development and meetings. Each organization attempts to address a number of issues that have plagued fraternities and sororities and promote a more positive fraternity and sorority experience for students.

Even with all of these umbrella organizations and leadership conferences, negative behaviors still persist. Previous research indicates that these related problems exist within the cultures of fraternities and sororities on American college campuses because of the organizations' strong association with alcohol (Pascarella, Edison, & Whitt, 1996). However, a lack of response to programs and interventions by fraternities and sororities persist regardless of their value to individual members and society (Kuh, Pascarella, & Wechsler, 1996; Wall, 2005).

Challenges to Fraternities and Sororities

Additionally, attitudes of students, administrators, faculty, and other external constituencies of a college or university in response to such data have furthered the views that sororities and fraternities are no more than speakeasies or drinking clubs (Kuh et al., 1996). This has generated the *Animal House* stereotype commonly associated with fraternities and sororities (Maisel, 1990). These perceptions, along with consistent stories of alcohol misuse, have motivated college administrators and officials to take action, but these efforts have been ineffective (Gurie, 2002). Moreover, membership in a fraternal organization has become a predictor for alcohol misuse, leading Arnold (1995) to term them "addictive organizations."

Administrators have attempted a number of measures aimed at curbing the trend of binge drinking and its associated negative effects. These efforts have included everything from mandating dry housing (Crosse, Ginexi, & Caudill, 2006) to banning common source containers such as kegs (Kilmer, Larimer, Parks, Dimeff, & Marlatt, 1999). However, these measures have been found to have little or no effect (Wall, 2006). Regardless of policy, GLOs, specifically fraternities, will continue to consume heavy volumes of alcohol (Kilmer et al., 1999). Indeed, if there are policies in place to restrict alcohol use, fraternities will increase their levels of binge drinking (Kilmer et al., 1999). Carter and Kahnweiler (2000) also found that social norming was ineffective for fraternity and sorority members. Instead individually oriented programs, with low economy of scale, such as brief motivational enhancement and cognitive-behavioral skills training, have been found to be the most effective among fraternity members (Larimer et al., 2001).

These outcomes identify the underlying trend that fraternities and sororities are resistant to change and have low response rates to interventions and programs, with those that are effective too taxing and fiscally difficult to implement. This failure is indicative of the numerous social aspects of fraternity life that can create an environment conducive to excessive alcohol use (Baer, 1994). Supporting this notion are Thombs and Briddick (2000), who found that only 25% of fraternity/sorority students reported moving into stages that involve thinking about change or action to reduce their alcohol consumption. The outcomes from these policies, programs, and interventions have not resulted in the decrease of alcohol consumption levels sought by institutions.

However, there have been small reductions with findings that the trend of binge drinking and overall volume consumption of alcohol for fraternities and sororities is decreasing (Caron, Moskey, & Hovey, 2004). Yet even with this slight decrease and despite the best efforts of fraternity/sorority organizations and their advisors, nationally and campus-based, the perception remains that alcohol use is a core component of the fraternal experience (Workman, 2001). Given these apparent problems, some administrators in higher education have called for tighter controls or even the removal of fraternal organizations from colleges (Kuh et al., 1996; Maisel, 1990; Wall, 2006).

The relevancy of fraternities and sororities on the college campus is frequently questioned. Liabilities related to recent events across the country concerning fraternities and sororities cast doubts regarding their place on the modern college campus, which threatens their existence

(Kaplin & Lee, 2006; Kuh et al., 1996). Many college administrators feel that fraternity/sorority organizations are not consistent with their individual institutional mission or that they are not related to desired learning outcomes.

This has led to the dissolution of fraternity/sorority systems at Alfred University, Amherst College, Bowdoin College, Colby College, Santa Clara University, and Williams College (Hokanson, 1992; Tolliver, 1997; and Zacker, 2001). Others have chosen to allow them to exist, but not formally recognize them, something that has occurred at Franklin and Marshall University and is currently occurring at Princeton University (Kaplin & Lee, 2006). The banning of Greek life by college administrators was made a legal option through the cases *Waugh v. Mississippi* and *Webb v. State University of New York* (Kaplin & Lee). While banning fraternities and sororities has been one method of addressing the problem, others have suggested that further in-depth studies of fraternity/sorority problems are needed to determine the most effective methods of dealing with these social organizations (Neuberger & Hanson, 1997). However, what confounds this call for research is the lack of response to interventions, as well as programming, and resistance to change demonstrated by fraternity and sorority chapters and individual members.

While these challenges are centered on a "liquid bonding" culture, change is both necessary and difficult. There are continuing operational and culture challenges that need to be addressed if fraternities and sororities are to continue to sustain themselves in the contemporary era. These challenges will now be addressed and recommendations will now be provided.

Recommendations

Recommendation One: Improve Advising Support

The support for college fraternal organizations traditionally is facilitated in the form of leadership training as well as advising. Advising is facilitated by alumni/alumnae advisors who are approved by the national organization or from an administrator who is traditionally located in a centralized "Greek Affairs" office with other related staff or within the student activities office. Within a chapter, alumni/alumnae advisors may be an individual advisor or consist of an advisory board. It is more commonplace for a sorority than a fraternity to have an alumnae advisory board; fraternities may simply have a singular advisor. NPHC and NAFLO chapters may have the local support of a graduate chapter consisting entirely of alumni/alumnae (Gregory, 2003). Formal training regarding how to advise fraternities and sororities does not exist. Therefore, it is the opinion of the author that many chapter members and student leaders are not the beneficiary of the advisors, but are the victim of their efforts. Simply put, there is a significant number of bad advisors.

On the campus side, the majority of fraternities and sororities at large universities are advised by graduate assistants who are overseen by a small, but often dedicated, staff of administrators. At smaller institutions there may be one individual responsible for advising. The age range of these individuals is traditionally under 30; many are only a few years removed from graduate school and traditionally serve in the role less than four years (Gregory, 2003). In other circumstances the advisor may be a graduate assistant, often the same age or close to the age of traditional undergraduate students.

Within the traditional national organizations or the chapter, support structures vary for advising. Sororities traditionally have an advisory board and each has a delineation of responsibility that represents a specific functional area of the chapter such as leadership or recruitment. There appears to be greater age range and more experience within sororities. These advisory boards are also supported by traveling staff members from the national headquarters who undergo extensive training. Within fraternities, support for chapters varies. Traditional fraternities have traveling staff members like sororities and traditionally have an alumni advisor. The alumni advisor appointment structure varies by organizations, but is predominantly a loosely coupled structure. Alumni advisory boards, like those found within sororities, are all too rare. In some instances it is not uncommon, in situations where the chapter has private housing, that the local incorporated housing corporation which oversees the residence assumes responsibilities for advising. NPHC and NAFLO groups are supported by a decentralized structure with volunteer-driven staff members who irregularly visit chapters. Their greatest support comes from their alumni/alumnae advisor or the local graduate chapter.

Advising fraternities and sororities is most often based on little or no professional preparation. The Council for the Advancement of Standards in Higher Education (CAS) has outlined specific criteria for advising college fraternal organizations (Council for the Advancement of Standards in Higher Education, 2009). However, it does not outline the required educational requirements or competencies. The Association of Fraternity/Sorority Advisors (AFA) has outlined several competencies (Association of Fraternity/Sorority Advisors, 2011). While these overarching standards from CAS and complementary AFA competencies for the profession of advising fraternities and sororities exist, they do not facilitate any programming to formally educate and certify advisors.

It is the opinion of the author that students receive a disservice when it is assumed an advisor is capable just because he/she has a masters degree related to higher education administration or has graduated from college. This assumption underlies the expectation that Kolb's (1984) Experiential Learning theory would come to fruition and leaves serendipity to chance. This notion holds the assumption that advisors will learn simply based on their experiences. Furthermore, based on the CAS standards for higher education administration graduate programs, advising is not among the required competencies that graduates must have. Therefore, graduate preparation will not prepare students to advise fraternities and sororities. Additionally, alumni/alumnae advisors receive little professional development or training. There is sometimes a guide or manual provided, and there maybe an orientation with a national staff member about expectations, but this does not support consistent quality advising. Ignorant chapter-based advisors are dangerous since they can reinforce negative traditions such as hazing and encourage further homogeneity of membership (Kimbrough, 2003; Nuwer, 1999). This phenomenon can become a significant liability and must be addressed.

Advising fraternities and sororities, in its current form, is extremely provincial and is literally "folksy." The majority of advisors draw from their undergraduate experience to inform their advising of chapters. Little evidence supports the notion that any student development or learning theory is intentionally applied in the advising of fraternity chapters (Sasso, 2008). Instead of advising, community standards have been developed in an attempt to legitimize interactions with students. This has led to greater bureaucracy and removed the focus on developmental outcomes of students. Programs with clear measureable outcomes should be focused and facilitated to support student learning and not used to establish more administrative protocol, procedure, and policy. They should not be utilized to replace interactions with students. What would better legitimize interactions with students is not needless bureaucratic community standards programs, but further education concerning how to advise fraternities and sororities.

There are bad advisors, not because they are inherently poor at facilitating their responsibilities, but because they have received no formal training. No forum for formal training currently exists that could support a structure to assist in creating fraternal advisor training or a certification process to mark successful completion. Therefore, a certification process should be established to train and educate fraternity and sorority advisors, on campus and within the chapter, to establish a consistent advising approach across all campuses. Too few advisors are knowledgeable of best practices in advising and of the vast diversity and complexity found within fraternities and sororities. Therefore, an advisor certification process should include content such as student development theory, learning theories, effective advising approaches, contemporary issues in higher education, history of fraternal organizations, and issues specific to fraternities and sororities such as alcohol, hazing, and academic achievement.

An advisor certification process would not serve as a panacea for the ills of advising fraternities and sororities, but it would help advisors navigate the complexity and ambiguity of their roles. Such a program would help to establish consistency and, if mandated for all advisors, would additionally further the fraternal movement and help to centralize the ideal that fraternal organizations are about the development of its members as students and eventually as lifelong members. Advisors are not the crux of the problems facing collegiate fraternal organizations, but they are contributing to it through a lack of education. Additionally, fraternity and sorority members as well as educators are part of it, too, for allowing this advising issue to continue. An advising certification for fraternities and sororities is merely a beginning, however.

Recommendation Two: Eliminate the Pledge System

One of the biggest challenges facing college fraternal organizations is the pledge system that most of them have. This system of new member education has become a burden on the fraternity/sorority community and faces many challenges, including hazing and alcohol misuse (Campo, Poulos, & Sipple, 2005). In fraternities, the pledge system has come to encourage an environment of hegemonic masculinity. In sororities, the pledge system has a lessened impact, given that not all sororities have a traditional pledge process, but those that do continue to perpetuate conformity as well (Allan & Madden, 2008). This is why it is strongly recommended that the traditional pledge system be eradicated.

Within male undergraduates, social desirability can be applied to the theory of hegemonic masculinity. Theorists also purport that hegemonic masculinity is not the most common form of male expression, but it is the most socially endorsed (Peralta, 2007). While not an empirically validated phenomenon, the theory states that men in specific competitive subcultures project and hold a favorable, culturally based, idealized version of themselves or others and subscribe to a dominant construction of masculinity (Connell, 1995).

These cultural norms within the practice of hegemonic masculinity include assertiveness, subordination of women, aggressiveness, and self-reliance (Connell, 1987; Connell & Messerschmidt, 2005). Within American society these cultural norms have been characterized as young, heterosexually active, economically successful, athletically inclined, and self-assured (Connell). These norms facilitate a demand characteristic that encourages conformity and institutionalizes these in-group norms with rites of passage (Kimmel, 2008). One specific group that has been specifically cited and identified to engage in hegemonic masculinity is the college fraternity (Peralta, 2007).

It has been theorized by Peralta (2007) and Wechsler, Nelson, and Weitzman (2000) that belonging to male-dominated or male-centered social institutions increases the likelihood men will engage in heavy episodic drinking (Locke & Mahalik, 2005). This is supported by McDonald's (1994) findings; marginalized men use alcohol to exert superiority over others who are prohibited from the same alcohol consumption, a practice of hegemonic masculinity. This phenomenon is demonstrated in the findings of the addictive organization framework by Arnold and Kuh (1992) in which pledges are restricted through alcohol consumption.

Additional findings are demonstrated specifically when men conform and engage in socially desirable behaviors according to the standards of hegemonic masculinity. This is especially in certain contexts involving alcohol as a form of gender expression (West, 2001). It has been found that men, especially those from a "blue-collar" socioeconomic background, consume beer as a compensatory masculinity (Hemmingsson, Lundberg, Diderichsen, & Allebeck, 1998; Janes & Ames, 1989; Kaminer & Dixon, 1995). This means that males respond to sex-role threat by exaggerating their masculinity.

Within sororities, issues of sex-role threat and alcohol are not significant issues as they are with fraternities. However, as aforementioned, hazing remains a challenge, typically dominating media reports concerning fraternity and sororities (Allan & Madden, 2008; Ellsworth, 2006; Nuwer, 1999). Within the research literature, hazing is typically defined as any forced task or activity that requires physical, mental, or emotional outcomes that endanger the physical safety of another person; produces mental or physical discomfort; causes embarrassment, fright, humiliation, or ridicule; or degrades an individual (Ellsworth, 2006; Nuwer, 1999; Sweet, 1999). Hazing within fraternities (Nuwer, 1999) and sororities (Kimbrough, 2000) with a pledge system remains a significant issue, including within African American fraternal organizations (Kimbrough, 2003). According to Kimbrough (2000), in 1999, dozens of African American fraternity or sorority hazing incidents filled headlines in state, local, and campus newspapers. Hazing traditionally is consistent with high levels of alcohol use by chapter (Nuwer, 1999). Hazing persists today because fraternity and sorority members hold it as a tradition (Nuwer, 1999; Sweet, 1999). For American undergraduates in fraternities and sororities, hazing is a "rite of passage" which established it as a tradition (Sweet, 1999). This rite of passage entitles the "survivor" to special recognition (Nuwer, 1999). There is little early research regarding hazing practices because Greek organizations are rooted in sworn secrecy amongst their membership (Leemon, 1972).

Drout & Corsoro (2003) analyzed situational responses to hazing. Their findings indicate that responsibility is based on level of leadership. Further, there are no gender differences between how fraternity and sorority members react when faced with hazing scenarios (Cokley et al., 2001; Drout & Corsoro, 2003). Thus, hazing and pledging activities are viewed similarly by fraternity/sorority members, except when asked to determine responsibility (Cokley et al.). Additionally, each chapter has an individual, unique culture and hazing practices vary from chapter to chapter (Ellsworth, 2006). Groupthink plays a significant role in these incidents (Allan & Madden, 2008; Sweet, 1999). It is also known that fraternities and sororities with higher levels of alcohol use also have higher levels of hazing (Allan & Madden, 2008; Nuwer, 1999). It has also been established that alcohol use is a much more frequent issue than hazing within fraternities (Nuwer, 1999; Sweet, 1999).

However, the pledge system does encourage conformity and increased alcohol use. It has been found that during pledging, expectations are established that are traditionally based on alcohol (Caudill et al., 2006; Thombs & Briddick, 2000). Further research indicates that chapter consumption expectations are strongly predictive of pledge consumption behavior, signifying strong social orientation of members (Trockel, Wall, Williams, & Reis, 2008). These expectations of alcohol within the fraternity and sorority culture potentially establish social desirability demands for members.

Danielson, Taylor, and Hartford (2001) concluded that the fraternity and sorority subculture is significantly different from the general student population in that drinking attitudes and behaviors are embedded in cultural aspects of fraternity members' lives, resulting in abnormal in-group social norms. Larimer, Irvine, Kilmer, and Marlatt (1997) concluded that becoming intoxicated and putting oneself at risk for academic or sexual consequences is an acceptable part of life in a fraternity or sorority. Binge drinking and unsafe sexual practices are reported as frequent occurrences among sorority and fraternity members (Elias, Bell, Eade, & Underwood, 1996; Kellogg, 1999; McCabe & Bowers, 1996; Tampke, 1990; Wechsler, Kuh, & Davenport, 1996). Further research also supports fraternity- and sorority-affiliated students as heavy alcohol abusers (Caudill et al., 2006; Presley, Meilman, & Cashin, 1996; Presley, Meilman, & Leichliter, 2002; Wechsler et al., 1996; Workman, 2001). In population comparisons, fraternity/sorority students consume more than students in volunteer organizations (Pace & McGrath, 2002), drink equivalent to or less than student athletes (Meilman, Leichliter, & Presley, 1999), and report more alcohol use and its tertiary effects than their non-affiliated counterparts (Eberhardt, Rice, & Smith, 2003; Wechsler et al., 1996).

These expectations, which facilitate demand characteristics that encourage conformity and homogeneity within chapters, have been found to vary by chapter (Kuh & Arnold, 1993). Members self-select into a heavy drinking culture where alcohol remains central to fraternity socialization in an environment that facilitates misuse (Trockel et al., 2008). This high level of conformity is potentially facilitated by a strong need for social approval. Need for social approval or social desirability is commonly thought of as the tendency of individuals to project favorable images of themselves during social interaction (Crowne & Marlowe, 1964). It has been found that young adults have high levels of need for social approval during their undergraduate experience (Bernardi & Guptill, 2008). According to Tinto (1993), students are constantly in a state of transition and are undergoing a series of developmental challenges. They must navigate college life and interface with new social and developmental dynamics (Guiffrida, 2006; Sessa, 2005; White et al., 2006).

During social adjustment fraternity/sorority members may have a high need for social approval since the social aspects of alcohol use by fraternity/sorority members are often influenced by additional individual factors (Gurie, 2002). This need for social approval has been found to be caused by several factors including peer acceptance and lack of self-concept (Chickering, 1969). Additionally, desire for popularity (Arnold & Kuh, 1992), fear of rejection (Hughes & Winston, 1987), and lack of self-worth and confidence (Kraft, 1979) are all potential causal factors, according to the research. Essentially, these causes are the desire to meet or exceed expectations, particularly of parents or leaders, and may increase alcohol use among fraternity and sorority members (Fairlie, DeJong, Stevenson, Lavigne, & Wood, 2010; Gurie, 2002; Cashin, Presley, & Meilman, 1998). All of these factors can positively or negatively impact behavior and attitudes, depending upon circumstances (Borsari & Carey, 1999).

In place of a pledge system with its companion process of hazing, fraternities and sororities should move towards total membership development. Several fraternities have established such as programs including Beta Theta Pi's Men of Principle Initiative, Sigma Phi Epsilon's Balanced Man Program, and Lambda Chi Alpha's True Brother Initiative. Tau Kappa Epsilon and Theta Chi have also recently developed similar programs. Initial outcomes from these programs demonstrate decreased insurance claims, higher grade point averages, increased membership retention, and tremendous decreases in hazing (Eberly, 2009). Additionally, sororities should move to establish similar branded and structured programs. Total membership programs are intentionally sequenced programming that seeks to engage a member over four years to provide rites of passage and personal development challenges that require commitment over a longer period of time. Total membership development programs replace the pledge system with an educational process as members do not have to their "earn" their letters.

In total membership development, new members are allowed to attend meetings, vote, and serve as full members. However, they traditionally cannot hold office until they have completed specific programming and undertaken sequenced rites of passage. Such an approach limits the opportunities for hazing and engages the members over the duration of their college experience. Additionally, such a program teaches brotherhood and sisterhood. With the pledge system, an individual learns to be a pledge and then learns to be a brother or sister after his/her initiation. Therefore, with the pledging semester and then the semester after initiation, it takes a full academic year to assimilate fully into the chapter. Total membership development allows for quicker assimilation into the chapter culture given that new members have full rights and can fully and equally participate in chapter activities, just as other chapter members do.

The pledge system was banned by NPHC organizations in 1990 (Kimbrough, 2000). However, it remains culturally intact with nothing to replace its existence (Kimbrough). Administrators should also consider banning pledging and encouraging the implementation of total membership development. By not encouraging the formation of chapters with traditional pledge systems, the national organizations would respond and begin to phase out and eliminate the pledge system. The pledge system was adapted from the early 20th century underclassmen caste system instituted by the Deans of Men (Caple, 1998). The idea of pledging emerged as early as 1919 at Ohio State University when organizations began to establish pledge clubs (Nuwer, 1999). Kimbrough (2003) and Nuwer state that hazing was incorporated as a part of the pledge process in the early 1900s through the 1920s. The underclassmen system became socially unacceptable during the 1960s as freshman stopped wearing "beanies" and *in loco parentis* unraveled. It remains to be seen why the pledge system continues when it was adapted from a social construct that no longer exists and, as aforementioned, only causes conformity, hazing, and encourages continued alcohol use. Clearly this antiquated form of socialization needs to be eradicated.

Recommendation Three: Eliminate Deferred Recruitment

It is the opinion of the author that fraternities and sororities, as they currently exist, are antithetical to the goals of the core teaching and learning mission of colleges and universities. Colleges and universities are ever more focused on this core mission given the increased demands by regional accreditors for accountability, increasing enrollments, stretching human and financial capital, and decreasing proportional state aid (Gregory, 2003). Therefore, fraternities and sororities should focus on *their* core mission, which should be the development of members through service-learning opportunities, leadership training, and facilitating greater connection to the cultural and extracurricular offerings of the host institution. That mission should not be exclusively based on the social development of members regulated to recruitment events, mixers, social exchanges, and raucous house parties.

A less litigious and administrative environment is necessary to facilitate an environment conducive to supporting fraternities and sororities. Members will need space to engage with their advisors and also develop as students from their fraternal experience. This means that institutions should create policies that support and enable Greek organizations to prosper and that are not restrictive. Much of the argument is that collegiate fraternal agreements are antithetical to the academic environment of the university campus and the current climate reflects this argument.

Currently, policies exist that restrict membership; they define how and when an undergraduate may affiliate. These policies are based on provincial logic and medieval assumptions which hold that fraternities and sororities negatively impact cognitive development and impact academics. Past and current research debunks this assumption by administrators.

Early studies found that Greek membership did not have a negative impact on academic performance (Baird, 1969; Crookston, 1960; Kaludis & Zatkin, 1966; Pike & Askew, 1990; Porta, 1991; Prusok & Walsh, 1964; Willingham, 1962). More recent research supports the notion that Greek membership impairs academic performance based upon standard grade point average measures (Kuh et al., 1996; McCabe & Bowers, 1996; Pascarella et al., 1996). However, additional research supports the notion that Greek affiliation has been found to have a negligible effect over time by students' senior year (Nelson, Halperin, Wasserman, Smith, & Graham, 2006). Fraternity and sorority members reported 1–10% lower cumulative GPAs versus non-Greek students by their senior year (Grubb, 2006).

The academic effect of Greek membership most heavily impacts first-year students (Nelson et al., 2006). During the recruitment and pledging semester, academic performance is lower than in other semesters (Nelson et al.). This is especially true for the semester in which a student affiliates and if they affiliate within their first year (Grubb, 2006). DeBard, Lake, and Binder (2006) found lower GPAs for first semester freshmen in fraternities and sororities; however, higher retention rates were found for students affiliated with fraternities and sororities compared to non-affiliated students. Those that deferred affiliation until at least their second semester had higher academic achievement.

Greeks and non-Greeks were found to spend the same amount of time towards their academics (Baier & Whipple, 1990). The individual fraternity and sorority chapter environment is an important factor in the scholastic achievement of membership (Carney, 1980b). It has been found that individual chapters vary greatly in the selection of potential academic achievers (Carney, 1980a). A chapter's academic success is dependent upon selectivity in membership recruitment (Shaffer, 1983). High achieving sororities and fraternities select better students as pledges, as measured by test data, than do the low achieving organizations (Carney, 1980a; Jelke, 2001). While academic performance may vary by chapter, the real academic value of fraternities and sororities is as a basis for retention (Carney, 1980b). Nelson et al. (2006) identified a positive relationship between Greek membership and retention.

The retention rates of those affiliated with Greek organizations are much higher than those of non-members after the first year (Santovec, 2004), and this is especially true for African Americans (Harper, 2007). These findings are consistent with those of Nelson et al. (2006).

Membership in a Greek community has been found to be an important component of social integration that affected students' persistence (Beil & Shope, 1990). Greek students have been found to have lower academic aptitude, as measured by standardized tests, than non-Greek students living in residence halls, but they still have higher retention and graduation rates (Carney, 1980a, 1980b).

There is no doubt that the research points to the notion that fraternal organizations do not impact cognitive development; however, it does reveal that membership has a negative impact on academic achievement during the first-semester of affiliation by first-semester freshmen. This is furthered by the phenomenon that academic achievement gain is made after initiation for this population (DeBard, Lake, & Binder, 2006). If this is truly the case, then the cultures of chapters must have a positive effect on members after they affiliate. Therefore, colleges and universities should allow for first-semester affiliation of traditional freshmen and transfer students for those chapters that have demonstrated satisfactory academic performance. Restricting membership only prohibits potential academic achievement of members by restricting access to academically successful chapters.

Recommendation Four: Diversity of Choice

It is the opinion of the author that offerings for fraternities and sororities are limited. There are too few chapters on most college and university campuses. Moreover, there is a lack of diversity of choice for prospective members. Several factors exist that impede the development of new chapters, offering few choices for students.

A polarization exists between large chapters and much substantially smaller ones. Often the chapters that currently exist are large and dominate the experience of the other chapters. This is especially true for fraternities, as their sizes are not regulated. In essence, the traditional fraternities operate on a capitalistic or free-market system of unregulated recruitment and membership intake. The sororities operate under a more communistic, if not draconian, procedure.

Traditional sororities have specific controls intact to cap the size of all chapters so that all remain equal. If a sorority chapter does not reach the total membership number, they are requested and allowed to continue to recruit new members. This is a fantastic example of equity; however, the sorority chapters also remain large. It is the opinion of the author that fraternity and sorority national organizations should encourage and support more chapters on their campus and reduce their size.

This notion to concurrently contract chapter size and expand choice may seem diametrically opposed to the current culture of collegiate fraternal organizations. However, the current climate is that the formation of new chapters is regulated through a gatekeeper, traditionally a campus administrator, or is dictated by campus politics in which both parties do not wish to seek new organizations and instead support stagnation. Both of these, the gatekeeper and the campus politics, are restrictive and debase the notion of the growth of fraternal organizations. Many campus administrators do not wish to support new chapters on their campuses because they are simply lazy; others are intimidated by the potential liability these organizations represent. Others are simply territorial and would like to facilitate a prospective plan based on their interpretations of the best way to form new chapters and require ridiculous amounts of paperwork and demands upon students and advisors, which results in a disinterest among students and national organizations.

Students facilitate the campus politics because they are scared that new organizations may upset the power differential that exists among the various chapters. Fraternity and sorority chapters have traditionally segregated and organized themselves into governing councils by special interest and differences. They are usually disinterested in growing the fraternity and sorority population because they feel that it may impact their membership levels. There is also fear that it may impact their popularity within their subculture, which cedes social status to alcohol use (Larimer et al., 1997).

However, this contraction of chapter size and expansion of choice would potentially increase the lure and improve the experience for students. Under this structure, fraternities and sororities would be each capped at a specific size based on the enrollment of the undergraduate population, and additional chapters would be allowed to form as chapter membership rolls are filled to the allowed total quota. Those campuses that allow for the existence of fraternities and sororities ought to consider embracing such a notion. Such a structure will help facilitate a paradigm shift of quality versus quantity. There will be competition for the best members, which may result in prestige for chapters based on membership and not alcohol. Additional chapters formed to accommodate interest from those not placed into chapters will invigorate and incite change within a fraternity and sorority community. New chapters will then offer diversity of choice to prospective members and further encourage selection of quality members. Competition may lead to ranking amongst the chapters; however, it will also encourage positive promotion of fraternities and sororities.

This proposed structure is borrowed from the African American and Latino fraternal organizations. These organizations, while not perfect, have embraced the idea of quality over quantity. While they do not traditionally accept students as members until they are a sophomore, they are smaller and their members cite this size as conducive to a more intimate experience (Kimbrough, 2003). This intimate experience consists of members supporting one another as they matriculate through and after college. Chapters become a more welcoming and supportive environment as members are more accountable due to their size. Smaller chapters are more manageable, and advisors and seniors are able to further focus on and develop new members. Additionally, due to the size, social desirability and conformity levels may decrease. Expression of identity is easier and processes of groupthink are not as likely to occur in smaller peer groups (Sweet, 1999). Additionally, within smaller chapters there are more opportunities to facilitate leadership development as a greater number of members must function to sustain and operate the organization. Most amazingly is that socialization through alcohol is not their focus. Instead, the chapter serves as a forum and supportive space for the advancement of individual identity, advancement of their members, and greater connection to the university.

It is recognizable that such a structure is a radical departure from the current social status composition ceded to alcohol for traditional fraternities and sororities. Potentially adapting the structure from the ethnic fraternities and sororities may result in stronger student development outcomes. Identity and lesser conformity amongst members may occur. Administratively they would be easier to manage given the smaller chapter sizes, resulting in the capacity to refocus some human capital to developing programmatic support structures to aid in the development of individual fraternity and sorority members. Students will potentially be the beneficiaries of a more intimate experience and greater opportunity for leadership involvement, and perhaps a more welcoming environment in which students can explore and better define them within the academic space of the university.

Conclusion

The issues of fraternities and sororities are systemic throughout the entirety of its support system as well as within the membership. Greek advisors are not properly trained, while administrators allow a pledge system to continue, but then restrict when and how members can affiliate. There is also a lack of diversity of choice among organizations. Yet, several umbrella organizations and leadership conferences exist to support the development of fraternity and sorority chapters. With all of this support, why does the research indicate that negative behaviors continue to occur? Hazing, sexual assault, alcohol misuse, and lack of response to programs continue to scourge fraternities and sororities (Larimer et al., 1999). The answer is that fraternities and sororities are slow to change and resistant to it. Their lack of response to programs demonstrates this phenomenon. Fraternities and sororities only trust etic and emic individuals, in that they only trust their own or those that are culturally neutral. This means that the change must come from within.

Tau Delta Phi fraternity member and former Vice President of the United States Hubert Humphrey stated, "This, then, is the test we must set for ourselves; not to march alone but to march in such a way that others will wish to join us." Others must lead the change from within and garner followers. Interventions from outside will not facilitate change—fraternity and sorority members must do it themselves. The undergraduates are not going to do it themselves and it is faulty thinking to train undergraduates as change agents when anything they change is undone after their graduation, rendering any gains unsustainable. Undergraduates must be educated and interventions must be designed, implemented, and facilitated by national staff members and campus-based professionals. These individuals, national staff members and campus-based professionals as fraternity and sorority members, must work together to facilitate change for undergraduates. It is the hope of the author that some of these implications are discussed further, refined, and implemented. While some may seem idealistic and not pragmatic, remember that this was also said of the progenitor of the fraternal organization, Phi Beta Kappa.

References

Allan, E., & Madden, M. (2008). *Hazing in view: College students at risk. Initial findings from the national study of student hazing*. Retrieved from http://www.hazingstudy.org.

Arnold, J. C. (1995). *Alcohol and the chosen few: Organizational reproduction in an addictive system*. (Doctoral dissertation, Indiana University, Bloomington). Retrieved from Dissertation.com.

Arnold, J. C., & Kuh, G. D. (1992). *Brotherhood and the bottle: A cultural analysis of the role of alcohol in fraternities*. Bloomington, IN: Center for the Study of the College Fraternity.

Association of Fraternity/Sorority Advisors. (2011). *Core competencies for excellence in the profession* (3rd ed.). Indianapolis, IN: Author.

Baer, J. S. (1994). Effects of a college residence on perceived norms for alcohol consumption: An examination of the first year in college. *Psychology of Addictive Behaviors, 8* (2), 43–50. doi: 10. 1037/0893–164X. 8. 1. 43.

Baier, J. L., & Whipple, E. G. (1990). Greek values and attitudes: A comparison within dependents. *NASPA Journal, 28* (1), 43–53.

Baird, L. (1969). The effects of college residence groups on students' self-concepts, goals, and achievements. *Personnel and Guidance Journal, 47,* 1015–1021.

Beil, C., & Shope, J. H. (1990, May). *No exit: Predicting student persistence*. Paper presented at the Annual Forum of the Association for Institutional Research, Louisville, KY.

Bernardi, R., & Guptill, S. (2008). Social desirability response bias, gender, and factors influencing organizational commitment: An international study. *Journal of Business Ethics, 81* (4), 797–809.

Borsari, B. E., & Carey, K. B. (1999). Understanding fraternity drinking: Five recurring themes in the literature, 1980–1998. *Journal of American College Health, 48* (1), 30–37.

Campo, S., Poulos, G., & Sipple, J. (2005). Prevalence and profiling: Hazing among college students and points of intervention. *American Journal of Health Behavior, 29* (2), 137–149.

Caple, R. B. (1998). *To mark the beginning: A social history of college student affairs.* Lanham, MD: University Press of America.

Carney, M. (1980a). *Persistence and graduation rates of Greek, independent, commuter and residence hall students: A nine semester study* (Office of Student Affairs Research, 1979–1980 Report No. 45). Norman, OK: University of Oklahoma.

Carney, M. (1980b). *Utilizing ACT data for predicting scholarship of fraternity and sorority pledge classes* (Office of Student Affairs Research, 1979–1980 Report No. 32). Norman, OK: University of Oklahoma.

Caron, S. L., Moskey, E. G., Hovey, C. A. (2004). Alcohol use among fraternity and sorority members: Looking at change over time. *Journal of Alcohol and Drug Education, 47* (3), 51–66.

Carter, C. A. & Kahnweiler, W. M. (2000). The efficacy of the social norms approach to substance abuse prevention applied to fraternity men. *Journal of American College Health, 49,* 66–71.

Cashin, J. R., Presley, C. A., & Meilman, P. W. (1998). Alcohol use in the Greek system: Follow the leader? *Journal of Studies on Alcohol, 59,* 63–70.

Caudill, B. D., Crosse, S. B., Campbell, B., Howard, J., Luckey, B. & Blane, H. T. (2006). Highrisk drinking among college fraternity members: A national perspective. *Journal of American College Health, 55* (3), 141–155. doi: 10. 3200/JACH. 55. 3. 141–155

Chickering, A. W. (1969). *Education and identity.* San Francisco: Jossey-Bass.

Cokley, K., Miller, K., Cunningham, D., Motoike, J., King, A., & Awad, G. (2001). Developing an instrument to assess college students' attitudes toward pledging and hazing in Greek letter organizations. *College Student Journal, 35* (3), 451–456.

Connell, R. W. (1987). *Gender and power.* Stanford, CA: Stanford University Press.

Connell, R. W. (1995). *Masculinities.* Los Angeles: University of California Press.

Connell, R. W., & Messerschmidt, J. W. (2005). Hegemonic masculinity: Rethinking the concept. *Gender and Society, 19* (6), 829–859.

Cornwell, L. (2010). Sororities' antics spur school alcohol efforts. *The Seattle Times.* Retrieved from http://seattle-times. nwsource. com/html/nationworld/2012271946_apussororitiesgonewild.html

Council for the Advancement of Standards in Higher Education. (2009). *CAS professional standards for higher education* (7th ed.). Washington, DC: Author.

Crookston, B. B. (1960). Academic performance of fraternity pledges. *Journal of College Student Personnel, 1,* 19–22.

Crosse, S. B. Ginexi, E. M. & Caudill, B. D. (2006). Examining the effects of a national alcohol-free fraternity housing policy. *The Journal of Primary Prevention, 27* (5), 477–495.

Crowne, D. P., & Marlowe, D. (1964). *The Approval Motive.* New York: John Wiley & Sons.

Danielson, C., Taylor, S., & Hartford, M. (2001). Examining the complex relationship between fraternity/sorority life and alcohol: A literature review. *NASPA Journal, 38* (3), 451–465.

DeBard, R., Lake, T., & Binder, R. (2006). Greeks and grades: The first-year experience. *NASPA Journal, 43* (1), 56–68.

Drout, C., & Corsoro, C. (2003). Attitudes toward fraternity hazing among fraternity members, sorority members, and non-Greek students. *Social Behavior & Personality: An International Journal, 31* (6), 535–543.

Eberhardt, D., Rice, N. D., & Smith, L. D. (2003). Effects of Greek membership on academic integrity, alcohol abuse, and risky sexual behavior at a small college. *NASPA Journal, 41* (1), 135–146.

Eberly, C. G. (2009, January 30). *A pilot program evaluation of the EDGE program for new members of Sigma Phi Epsilon fraternity.* Unpublished manuscript, Illinois Higher Education Center for Alcohol, Other Drugs, and Violence Prevention, Eastern Illinois University

Elias, J. W., Bell, R. W., Eade, R., & Underwood, T. (1996). "Alcohol myopia," expectations, social interests, and sorority pledge status. *Journal of Alcohol and Drug Education, 42* (1), 78–90.

Ellsworth, C. W. (2006). Definitions of hazing: Differences among selected student organizations. *Oracle: The Research Journal of the Association of Fraternity Advisors, 2* (1), 46–60.

Fairlie, A. M., DeJong, W., Stevenson, J. F., Lavigne, A. M., & Wood, M. D. (2010). Fraternity and sorority leaders and members: A comparison of alcohol use, attitudes, and policy awareness. *The American Journal of Drug and Alcohol Abuse, 36,* 187–193.

Gregory, D. (2003). The dilemma facing administration of fraternal organization in the millennium. In D. Gregory & Associates, *The Administration of Fraternal Organization on North American Campuses: A Pattern for the New Millennium* (pp. 3–25). Asheville, NC: College Administration Publications.

Grubb, F. (2006). Does going Greek impair undergraduate academic performance? A case study. *American Journal of Economics and Sociology, 65* (5), 1085–1110.

Guiffrida, D. (2006). Toward a cultural advancement of Tinto's theory. Review of Higher Education, 29 (4), 451–

Harper, S. (2007). The effects of sorority and fraternity membership on class participation and African American student engagement in predominantly White classroom environments. *College Student Affairs Journal, 27* (1), 94–115.

Gurie, J. R. (2002). The relationship between perceived leader behavior and alcohol consumption among university students who are members of social fraternities (Doctoral dissertation). Retrieved from ProQuest Dissertations and Theses Database (UMI No. 3042909).

Hemmingsson, T., Lundberg, I., Diderichsen, F., & Allebeck, P. (1998). Explanations of social class differences in alcoholism in young men. *Social Science and Medicine, 47* (10), 1399–1405.

Hokanson, K. A. (1992). *The changing status of fraternities at Northeastern, liberal arts colleges: Case studies of Bowdoin and Colby Colleges* (Doctoral dissertation, Harvard University). *Dissertation Abstracts International, 53,* 201.

Hughes, M., & Winston, R. (1987). Effects of fraternity membership on interpersonal values. *Journal of College Student Personnel,* 28, 405–411.

Janes, C. R., & Ames, G. (1989). Men, blue collar work, and drinking: Alcohol use in an industrial subculture. *Culture, Medicine and Psychiatry, 13,* 245–274.

Jelke, T. B. (2001). A cross-case analysis of Greek systems perceived to be high performing. *Dissertation Abstracts International, 6* (08), 2696. (UMI No. 3024170).

Kaludis, G., & Zatkin, K. (1966). Anatomy of a pledge class. *Journal of College Student Personnel, 7,* 282–284.

Kaminer, D., & Dixon, J. (1995). The reproduction of masculinity: A discourse analysis of men's drinking talk. *South African Journal of Psychology, 25,* 168–174.

Kaplin, W. A., & Lee. B. A. (2006). *The law of higher education* (4th ed.) San Francisco, CA: Jossey-Bass.

Kellogg, K. (1999). *Binge drinking on college campuses.* Washington, DC: George Washington University, Graduate School of Education. (ERIC Document Reproduction Service No. ED436110)

Kilmer R. J., Larimer, M. E., Parks, G. A., Dimeff, L. A., &Marlatt, G. A. (1999). Liability or risk management? evaluation of a Greek system alcohol policy. *Psychology of Addictive Behaviors, 4,* 269–278.

Kimbrough, W. (2000). Notes from underground: Despite a ban, pledging remains. *Black Issues in Higher Education, 17,* 88.

Kimbrough, W. (2003). *Black Greek 101: The culture, customs, and challenges of Black fraternities and sororities.* Cranbury, NJ: Rosemont.

Kimmel M. (2008). *Guyland: The perilous world where boys become men.* New York, NY: HarperCollins.

Kolb, D. A. (1984). *Experiential learning: Experience as the source of learning and development.* Englewood Cliffs, NJ: Prentice-Hall.

Kraft, D. P. (1979). Public drinking practices of college youths: Implications for prevention programs. In T. C. Harford & L. S. Gaines (Eds.), *Social drinking contexts* (Research Monograph No. 7, pp. 54–84). Rockville, MD: National Institute on Alcohol Abuse and Alcoholism.

Kuh, G. D., & Arnold, J. C. (1993). Liquid bonding: A cultural analysis of the role of alcohol in fraternity pledgeship. *Journal of College Student Development, 34,* 327–334.

Kuh, G. D., Pascarella, E. T., & Wechsler, H. (1996, February 13). The questionable value of fraternities. *Chronicle of Higher Education,* pp. 43–45. Retrieved Mar. 5, 2006 from LexisNexis Academic.

Larimer, M., Irvine, D., Kilmer, J., & Marlatt, G. (1997). College drinking and the fraternity/sorority system: Examining the role of perceived norms for high-risk behavior. *Journal of College Student Development, 38* (3), 587–598.

Larimer, M. M, Lydum, A. R., Anderson, B. K., & Turner, A. P. (1999). Male and female recipients of unwanted sexual contact in a college student sample: Prevalence rates, alcohol use, and depression symptoms. *Sex Roles, 40* (3/4), 295–308.

Larimer, M. E., Turner, A. P., Anderson, B. K., Fader, J. S., Kilmer, J. R., Palmer, R. S., & Cronce, J. M. (2001). Evaluating a brief alcohol intervention with fraternities. *Journal of Studies on Alcohol, 62,* 370–380.

Leemon, T. (1972). *Rites of passage in student culture.* New York: Teacher's College Press.

Locke, B., & Mahalik, J. (2005). Examining masculinity norms, problem drinking, and athletic involvement as predictors of sexual aggression in college men. *Journal of Counseling Psychology, 52* (3), 279–283. doi: 10.1037/0022–0167. 52. 3. 279

Maisel, J. P. (1990). Social fraternities and sororities are not conducive to the educational process. *NASPA Journal, 28* (2), 8–12.

Marcus, J. (2011). Schools for scandal: Can fraternities shed their sinister image? *Times Higher Education.* Retrieved from http://www.timeshighereducation. co. uk/story. asp? sectioncode=26&storycode=416566&c=1

McCabe, D. L., & Bowers, W. J. (1996). The relationship between student cheating and college fraternity or sorority membership. *NASPA Journal, 33* (3), 280–291.

McDonald, M. (1994). *Gender, drink, and drugs*. Providence, RI: Berg.

Meilman, P. W., Leichliter, J. S., & Presley, C. A. (1999). Greeks and athletes: Who drinks more? *Journal of American College Health, 47* (4), 187–190. doi: 10. 1080/07448489909595645

Nelson, S. M., Halperin, S., Wasserman, T. H., Smith, C., & Graham, P. (2006). Effects of fraternity/sorority membership and recruitment semester on GPA and retention. *Oracle: The Research Journal of the Association of Fraternity Advisors, 2* (1), 61–73.

Neuberger, C., & Hanson, G. (1997). The fraternity/sorority life self-study: A powerful process for change on campus. *NASPA Journal, 34,* 91–100.

Nuwer, H. (1999). *Wrongs of passage: Fraternities, sororities, hazing and binge drinking*. Bloomington: Indiana University Press.

Pace, D., & McGrath, P. B. (2002). A comparison of drinking behaviors of students in Greek organizations and students active in a campus volunteer organization. *NASPA Journal, 39* (1), 217–232.

Pascarella, E. T., Edison, M. I., & Whitt, E. J. (1996). Cognitive effects of fraternity/sorority affiliation during the first year of college. *NASPA Journal, 33* (3), 242–259.

Peralta, R. L. (2007). College alcohol use and the embodiment of hegemonic masculinity among European American men. *Sex Roles, 56,* 741–756.

Pike, G. R., & Askew, J. W. (1990). The impact of fraternity or sorority membership on academic involvement and learning outcomes. *NASPA Journal, 28* (1), 13–19.

Porta, A. D. (1991). Independents, actives, and pledges: A comparison of academic achievement. Unpublished manuscript, Murray State University, KY.

Presley, C. A., Meilman, P. W., & Cashin, J. R. (1996). *Alcohol and drugs on American college campuses: Use, consequences, and perceptions of the campus environment*. Carbondale, Ill. : The Core Institute.

Presley C. A., Meilman, P. W., & Leichliter, J. S. . (2002). College factors that influence drinking. *Journal of Studies on Alcohol, 63* (14), 82–90.

Prusok, R. E., & Walsh, W. B. (1964). College student residence and academic achievement. *The Journal of College Student Personnel, 5,* 180–184.

Robson, J. W. (1966). *The college fraternity and its modern role*. Menasha, WI: G. Banta.

Santovec, M. L. (2004). Fraternity recruitment delay doesn't affect academic success. *Recruitment and Retention in Higher Education, 18* (9), 1–2.

Sasso, P. A. (2008). From administrator to educator: Facilitating student learning in Greek affairs practice (Unpublished master's thesis). University of Rochester, Rochester, NY.

Sessa, F. M. (2005). The influence of perceived parenting on substance use during the transition to college: A comparison of male residential and commuter students. *Journal of College Student Development, 46* (1), 62–74.

Shaffer, R. H. (1983). Review of research in Greek affairs. In W. A. Bryan & R. A. Schwartz (Eds.), *The eighties: Challenges for fraternities and sororities* (pp. 6–30). Carbondale: Southern Illinois University Press.

Sweet, S. (1999). Understanding fraternity hazing: Insights from symbolic integrationist theory. *Journal of College Student Personnel, 40* (4), 355–364.

Tampke, D. R. (1990). Alcohol behavior, risk perception, and fraternity and sorority membership. *NASPA Journal, 28* (5), 71–77.

Thombs, D. L., & Briddick, W. C. (2000). Readiness to change among At-risk Greek student drinkers. *Journal of College Student Development, 41* (3), 313–322.

Tinto, V. (1993). *Leaving college: Rethinking the causes and cures of student attrition* (2nd ed.). Chicago: University of Chicago Press.

Tolliver, J. A. (1997). Administratively mandated change at Amherst College: Student reaction and its effect on student personnel administrators societies. *Dissertation Abstracts International,* DAI-A 58/09, p. 3444, Mar 1998.

Trockel, M., Wall, A., Williams, S., & Reis, J. (2008). When the party for some becomes a problem for others: The potential role of perceived second-hand consequences of drinking behavior in determining collective drinking norms. *The Journal of Psychology: Interdisciplinary and Applied, 142* (1), 57–69. doi: 10. 3200/JRLP. 142. 1. 57–70

Wall, A. (2005). *Alcohol prevention efforts within Illinois institutions of higher education: Assessing the state of prevention*. Charleston: Eastern Illinois University, College of Education and Professional Studies, Illinois Higher Education Center for Alcohol, Other Drug and Violence Prevention.

Wall, A. (2006). On-line alcohol health education curriculum evaluation: Harm reduction findings among fraternity and sorority members. *Oracle: The Research Journal of the Association of Fraternity Advisors, 2* (1), 29–45.

Wechsler, H., Kuh, G. D., & Davenport, A. (1996). Fraternities, sororities and binge drinking: Results from a national study of American colleges. *NASPA Journal, 33* (4), 260–279.

Wechsler, H., Nelson, T., & Weitzman, E. (2000). From knowledge to action: How Harvard's college alcohol study can help your campus design a campaign against student alcohol abuse. *Change, 32* (1), 39–43.

West, L. A. (2001). Negotiating masculinities in American drinking subcultures. *Journal of Men's Studies, 9,* 371–392.

White, H. R., McMorris, B. J., Catalono, R. F., Fleming, C. B., Haggerty, K. P., & Abbott, R. D. (2006). Increases in alcohol and marijuana use during the transition out of high school into emerging adulthood: The effects of leaving home, going to college, and high school protective factors. *Journal of Studies on Alcohol, 67* (6), 810–822.

Willingham, W. W. (1962). College performance of fraternity members and independent students. *Personnel and Guidance Journal, 41,* 29–31.

Workman, T. A. (2001). Finding the meaning of college drinking: An analysis of fraternity drinking stories. *Health Communications, 13* (4), 427–444. doi: 10. 1207/S15327027HC1304_05

Zacker, T. Y. (2001). An exploratory study of the institutional factors relating to the quality of social Greek letter societies (Doctoral dissertation). Retrieved from Dissertations & Theses: Full Text (Publication No. AAT 3037163).

CHAPTER SIX

Campus Conflicts

College Students' Perceptions of Heterosexism and Homophobia in Colleges and Universities

REGINA RAHIMI & DELORES D. LISTON

Introduction: Overview of the Study

The social, academic, and vocational landscape for young women and GLBQT youth remains hostile (Bradenburg, 1997; Quinn, 2002; Meyer, 2008). Sexism is still deeply in place and presents itself in a variety of ways, including sexual harassment, homophobic bullying, and even assault. We contend that sexual harassment as a gendered phenomenon is worthy of study, and we situate the phenomenon of bullying within the context of sexism. We believe that the sexist ideologies that persist in society serve to promote much of the aggression that takes place within all academic settings, including institutions of higher education. In studying P-12 educational experience, we found through our other research that sexual harassment and homophobic bullying are rampant in schools, and little is being done to educate students about the harmful consequences of such harassment. Given that students attending colleges and universities come from educational backgrounds (in their earlier schooling experiences) that have permitted such behaviors, it stands to reason that some of the same attitudes regarding harassment and bullying follow them into post-secondary schooling. Considering sexual harassment in college and university settings means not just conceiving such harassment as "quid pro quo" forms of sexual harassment on campus, whereby the professor abuses (his or her) power over a student and requests sexual favors for some preferential academic treatment. It also requires examination of the multiple ways in which sexual harassment and/or homophobic bullying exists on college and university campuses in and outside of the classroom setting.

This chapter explores the perceptions of college and university students regarding the prevalence of sexual harassment and gendered bullying, discusses suggestions for creating a safer environment for all students, and places the experiences of college/university students in the context of the larger educational systematic prevalence of sexual and gendered harassment, which we argue is formed and maintained through the tenet of sexism. Sexism forms the basis for both sexual harassment of young women (ways women are continuously subjected to harassment and objectification), and harassment based on sexual orientation and bullying (ways in which males and females who are presumed to be gay or lesbian are subjected to harassment and objectification).

We argue there seems to be, in some cases, an assault on feminist advancement; much conversation and attention has turned to the victimization of young heterosexual men, while the victimization of young women and GLBTQ youth is sidelined, even on the campuses of our post-secondary institutions. In our assessment of the research literature, we find that three main topic areas have dominated the research agenda and taken center stage in the popular discourse regarding sexual harassment: cyber harassment, bullying, and sexual orientation. While we concur that these are important topics, we do not believe that they should dominate the discourse as they do; rather they need to be incorporated into feminist analysis of the gendered power dynamics that promote sexual harassment in all forms. These topics hit "hot buttons" for sensationalizing media news outlets and obscure the view of the connections between sexism and harassment. We maintain that, like other aspects of the sexual harassment research agenda, these topics need to be re-integrated into the larger feminist discourse that recognizes cyber harassment, bullying, and sexual orientation as factors of the continuing gender discrimination and sexism against which feminists have been fighting for centuries.

As our research has shown, young women in schools are victimized by harassment at an alarming rate (Rahimi & Liston, 2012), and research has also demonstrated that the continued perpetuation of sexist ideology also contributes to the existence of homophobia and the harassment of GLBTQ youth. Among the recent research publications on sexual harassment stemming from (presumed) sexual orientation are Henning-Stout, James, and Macintosh, (2000); Hansen (2007); and Rivers (2011). These publications make it clear that heterosexism contributes significantly to peer sexual harassment. Sexual orientation is now, and has always been, a significant risk factor for sexual harassment. However, unless it is intended to be covered in "coded" language of "risky" and "problem" behaviors, this factor is commonly not listed among the risk factors. Further, the connections between sexism and harassment of GLBTQ youth, both in P-12 school settings and post-secondary educational experience, need to be fully incorporated into the analysis, since harassment of GLBTQ youth is not currently grounded in a perspective that highlights its nexus in heterosexism.

When it comes to the sexual harassment of young women and GLBTQ students, school personnel (including university faculty) are likely to remain deaf, dumb, and blind. Sexual harassment needs to be understood in context with gendered harassment. The interconnections between traditional gendered roles, heterosexism, and sexual harassment must be underlined; and the experiences of students in a variety of educational settings need to be examined.

Thus, in the research of school climate and sexual/gendered harassment, we should also consider the experiences of contemporary college and university students. In this chapter, we present a brief overview of sexual harassment concerns pertinent to higher education. These concerns are insufficient definitions of sexual harassment, frequency of incidents, and the multiplicity of forms of harassment, as well as the conditions on campus that promote or at least fail to protect from the harassment of young women and GLBTQ students in college and university settings.

The findings presented in this study demonstrate the existence of gendered harassment (especially the harassment of female and GLBTQ students) in academia. Emerging from a decade of research on name-calling and ostracism, moving in to sexual harassment at the P-12 level, our research has evolved into looking at how students in a variety of educational environments perceive sexual harassment. This study seeks to document the perceptions of, or experiences with, sexual harassment presented by students enrolled in post-secondary institutions. This research has been formed out of concern with the extent to which sexism creates an environment in academic settings in which the marginalization of young women and GLBQT students occurs.

Overview of the Literature

Historically, the image that comes to mind when considering sexual harassment in colleges and universities is the proverbial lecherous male professor seeking sexual favors from a female co-ed; perhaps our scenario goes so far as to imagine that the professor tells the student that if she has sex with him, she will get an A on her term paper. Certainly, this is a form of sexual harassment, and there is evidence that this scenario does in fact occur on college campuses (Bradenburg, 1997). However, this is certainly not the only scenario on college campuses that constitutes sexual harassment. Paludi, Nydegger, Desouza, Nydegger and Dicker (2006) report that incidents of sexual harassment among undergraduates by peers happen at an alarming rate, with some of the most frequent instances involving creating disturbances in women's residence halls and yelling, shouting, and whistling at women as they walk by (Paludi et al., 2006). Additionally, sexual harassment takes various forms: from "quid pro quo" in the case of the professor asking for sexual favors in return for an explicit mark, to numerous examples of "hostile environment" forms of sexual harassment (MacKinnon, 1979). As our participants confirm in this study, sexual harassment on campus can be found in examples of stalking, inappropriate gestures, name-calling, dating violence, rape, threat of sexual violence, ogling, whistling, and battering and hazing (Martin, 2008a).

In our previous research in P-12 settings, questions of what constitutes sexual harassment have been quite vague; yet these kinds of questions can be set aside somewhat in favor of acting on behalf of minors. Public school officials have a clearer mandate to intervene, whether or not the *victim* feels sexually harassed. Studies of sexual harassment in higher education enter more ambivalent waters, since young adults have the responsibility to make that determination. Nonetheless, research shows that many (if not most) college students do not hold clear definitions of sexual harassment, and do not know the policy of their college or university for addressing sexual harassment (Paludi et al., 2006). That finding has also been confirmed by the participants in our study. While many institutions subsume sexual harassment under policies related to bullying, alcohol abuse, hazing, or anti-discrimination policies, sexual harassment remains a "hidden" problem. Yet sexual harassment on college campuses is pervasive, and instances of the most serious forms of sexual violence also occur on campuses or at campus-sponsored events. Most studies estimate that 50–90% of college co-eds experience sexual harassment (Waits & Lundberg-Love, 2000; Hill & Silva 2005; Fisher, Daigle, & Cullen, 2010, Paludi et al., 2006). However, the behaviors associated with the harassment vary. About one third of college students report experiencing physical sexual harassment in college (Hill & Silva, 2005). Hill and Silva note that females experience grabbing, pinching, and sexual coercion, while males experience harassment related to sexual orientation. Mohler-Kuo, Dowdall, Koss and Wechsler (2004) suggest that one in 20 female college students are raped each year, with "acquaintance rape" among the most common. Fisher et al. (2010) found in their study, *The National College Women Sexual Victimization Study*, that of the female students reporting sexual assault, most knew or had seen the rapist. While most of the rapes reported in their study occurred off campus, many were nonetheless related to college functions. This clearly illustrates that an atmosphere of sexual harassment, violence, and inequity continues to plague contemporary college life.

There have been some studies that suggest there are victim characteristics that make it more likely for some to be harassed more than others. Paludi et al. (2006) present a list of those who seem to be more vulnerable to sexual harassment. This list should serve as an important reference for those in positions of educating the college community and designing policy information. According to Paludi et al., the most likely victims of sexual harassment on campus are as follows:

> Women of color, especially those with "token" status, students in small colleges or small academic departments where the number of faculty available to students is quite small, women students in male populated fields, e.g., engineering, students who are economically disadvantaged and work part time or fulltime while attending classes, lesbian women who may be harassed as part of homophobia, physically or emotionally disabled students, women students who work in dormitories as resident assistants, women who have been sexually abused, and inexperienced, unassertive, socially isolated women who may appear more vulnerable and appealing to those who would intimidate or coerce them into an exploitive relationship. Ethnic women and women of color are especially vulnerable to sexual harassment from their professors. (p. 106)

Sexual harassment and racial harassment were studied together, and the findings indicate that the impact is indeed additive (Buchanan, Bergman, Bruce, Woods, & Lichty, 2009). While this study does not explicitly address the role of race in instances of sexual harassment, other research supports the need to further examine this relationship. Further, our research reported in Rahimi and Liston (2012) indicates that race plays a significant role in incidents of sexual harassment.

Studies show that sexual harassment has many and varied negative impacts on victims. The costs of sexual harassment in higher education can be exponentially harmful, generating a cycle that has negative effects well into the future since victims may experience physical and emotional symptoms which can even derail their educational plans. Students report negative effects from sexual harassment ranging from mild to severe. "Sexual harassment can have devastating effects upon students, including diminished ambition and self-confidence, reduced ability to concentrate, sleeplessness, depression, and physical aches and ailments" (Cleary & Schmieler, 1994, para. 3).

Research with college students in several countries has documented the high cost of sexual harassment to individuals (e.g., Danksy & Kilpatrick, 1997; Hill & Silva, 2005; Lundberg-Love & Marmion, 2003; Quina, 1996). This research indicates that there are career-related, psychological, and physiological outcomes related to being sexually harassed. For example, women students have reported decreased morale, decreased satisfaction with their career goals, and lowered grades. Furthermore, women students have reported feelings of helplessness and powerlessness over their academic career, strong fear reactions, and decreased motivation.

Women college students have also reported headaches, sleep disturbances, eating disorders, and gastrointestinal disorders as common physical responses to sexual harassment (Lundberg-Love & Marmion, 2003; Thacker & Gohmann, 1996; Wasti, Bergman, Glomb, & Drasgow, 2000, Paludi et al., 2006).

Despite the prevalence of instances of sexual harassment and gendered harassment on campus, and given the emotional, physical, academic, and social consequences of harassment, much of the harassment goes unreported. In a study conducted by Cleary and Schmieler (1994), although most survey respondents claim that they would report sexual harassment if it happened to them, very few who recorded experiencing sexual harassment had reported the harassment to school officials. Similar findings were confirmed by our own research. Therefore, we suspect that sexual harassment on college and university campuses goes largely unreported.

> It is important to note that initiatives to stop sexual harassment entered the university (and U.S. society as a whole) with the advent of Title IX in the 1970s. Although overshadowed in colleges and universities by the requirements on athletics, Title IX provided the stimulus to develop policies to address sexual harassment. (For a more thorough review of literature related to the development of policy regarding sexual harassment, see Rahimi & Liston, 2012).

Despite the strides that have been made regarding eradicating harassment on campus, our research and others' have found that it continues to be a problem. It is important to examine how campuses educate on issues of harassment and how they repond to sexual harassment claims. Draugn, Elkins, and Roy (2002) identified characteristics of institutions where sexual harassment is most likely to occur: poor communication in reporting; no target programs for new faculty, sororities, or other groups; and encouragement of sexist-themed functions (p. 18). Recognizing these as areas of concern for universities can be a first step in strengthening campus initiatives to end sexual harassment.

Eyre (2000) conducted discourse analysis using one case of sexual harassment in a university community. Her findings indicate that dominant discourses related to academic freedom and jurisprudence have the effect of legitimizing sexual harassment on college campuses. Eyre (2000) notes: "It seems to me that sexual harassment policies and grievance procedures are consistently thwarted and that women's voices are undermined, distorted and silenced by those who hold powerful positions in the university community" (p. 293). The dominant discourses employed when talking about sexual harassment on college campuses tend to protect male faculty and male students, while undermining the positions of female faculty and students. The conversation shifted from sexual harassment (in this case hostile environment) to the professor's right of free speech and the juridical obligation of the university to prove misconduct on the part of the professor. It is not enough to just have sexual harassment policies in place; it is important to address the sexist ideology that prevails on campus and manifests itself even when cases of harassment have been illuminated.

Our Study

For this study, we chose to develop a mixed method research study. We developed an electronic survey instrument, employing both quantitative (Likert scale) and qualitative (open-ended) questions pertaining to the perceptions of sexual harassment on college campuses and in other social settings. This electronic survey was passed along through social networking sites (e.g.,

Facebook.com) by several college students, other university faculty, and family and friends of students and faculty. Forty-seven participants, currently enrolled in a college, university or other post-secondary institution, responded. The demographic profile of the participants was as follows: 60% of participants were juniors, 11% sophomores; 91% were female students, 83% were heterosexual, 8% were homosexual, 9% were bisexual; 75% percent identified themselves as Christian, 9% atheist; 75% identified themselves as White, 12% identified themselves as Black, 10% Hispanic, and 3% multiracial. Important questions were addressed by this study: How do young women/young men define sexual harassment? What behaviors do college/university students believe constitute sexual harassment? Do students at this level recognize a differentiation between sexual harassment and sexual bullying? How do young women/men define homophobic bullying? In what ways do schools help mediate any experiences with sexual harassment/homophobic bullying? How do college/university students perceive that school staff/students respond to sexually charged situations in classes and other areas of the school? Where do undergraduates report that instances of sexual harassment/homophobic bullying take place? How prevalent is cyber sexual harassment? To what extent have undergraduate students experienced harassment in their previous years of schooling?

Several findings emerged from the study that highlighted the degree to which sexual harassment and other forms of gendered harassment continue to plague the lives of young women and men on college campuses. Despite court sanctions and the threat of lawsuits (Stein, 2007), sexual harassment continues to be overlooked and tolerated on campus grounds. Many of the young women and men in our study cited specific instances involving gendered harassment. The existence of such hostile behaviors directed specifically at young women and GLBTQ youth underscores the fact that sexual harassment needs further examination in contemporary contexts. Additionally, many of the participants in our study seemed to suggest that little has been, or could be, done to counter sexual harassment and that there is little or no recourse for such harassment. Further, many of the participants expressed that they simply did not know where to go to report instances of harassment, so they have learned to "ignore" the behaviors, a response we have also seen from younger women in our earlier research.

The researchers in this study strongly believe that educators can and should play a vital role in helping reconstruct a positive discourse on sexuality for all students. We must revisit the conversation concerning sexual harassment and gendered harassment to make certain that university faculty, staff, and administration have an understanding of gendered harassment and can provide resources for dealing with discrimination and hostility on campus grounds. We also firmly believe that it is imperative that faculty in college and university settings not only acknowledge but actively seek to eliminate sexual harassment by intervening in instances of harassment. Inaction in response to sexual harassment only further solidifies the grounds undergirding sexual harassment and contributes to open hostility and violence on school campuses. We hope to continue to examine the prevalence of sexual harassment in schools and seek ways in which faculty and school staff can help to alleviate violence against all students.

Findings

When asked where they received information regarding sexual harassment, two thirds of the respondents indicated they learned about sexual harassment "in school"; however, they were unable to pinpoint exactly when (many of them said in middle or high school during a class).

From their responses, it is clear that there has not been a consistent educative experience regarding sexual harassment. Overwhelmingly, their responses indicated that the sexuality education they received was abstinence-based, heteronormative, and regulatory. The respondents indicated very few instances of education surrounding issues of sexual violence, experiences outside of a heteronormative context, or problems of sexual/gender inequality, despite an overwhelming response indicating such information would be/have been welcomed.

With regard to their experiences since enrolling in their post-secondary educational institution, the respondents in this study provided the following information. When asked if they ever witnessed sexual harassment on campus, half of the respondents answered yes. Some of the examples were as follows:

- "Verbal teasing of boys who were gay."

- "Classmates being yelled at walking down halls."

- "Too many instances to describe, particularly regarding members of the LGBT community."

- "Many of the African American males on campus look at other gay males and frown or make rude comments when a gay guy walks by."

- "Homophobia in classes with sexist clothing [T shirt slogans]."

- "Bullying, damaging property."

- "I have seen people picking on gay people."

- "There is a transgender student on campus now and the housing board would only give the student one week to find a roommate or he would have to be roomed with males even though the student has received operations."

- "Homophobia in classes."

- "A cross dressing student walked into the lunchroom a while back; immediately everyone got quiet, and you could hear the low laughing coming from multiple places in the cafeteria."

- "A group of girls making fun of a transgendered student's housing plight."

- "I am afraid of walking to my car after my night class."

- "I am small in height so I am very scared to go to certain places at night by myself. I carry pepper spray but no matter what I want to be in a well-lit area."

- "Just scared to walk to my car at night or scared to be in a room on campus late with people I don't know."

- "My ex-boyfriend attends college with me and he would get rough with me while walking to our cars."

- "My ex-boyfriend stalked me. We had to press charges against him."

- "I was walking by a group of people and one of the persons called me a dyke but I didn't pay any attention and just kept walking."

- "I get name-called on a regular basis, by multiple people. It's nothing I let get me down. It's just that I dress and look different from the black stereotype; people get upset that I dare to step out of the box that society has built for me."

- "I have been cat called on this campus more times in the 3 years that I have been here than I have my entire life."

- When asked if the college experience was the same for young men and young women, the respondents overwhelmingly noted that the experiences were in fact different, and all but six answered yes.

- "Women are typically the victims of any type of harassment."

- "Women have to be worried about walking to their cars or being out late at night. Men typically don't have to worry about those things."

- "I believe that people will accept women being lesbian or bisexual faster than men. It's almost o.k. to be a lesbian."

- "Young men take it as a time to get their wild side out of their system, while women use college as a way to figure out what they want out of life."

- "Young men are expected to act a certain way that young women are not, and if they do, they are looked down upon."

- "As young men, I feel like they are encouraged to go out and have sex with as many girls as they can. In this way, they are considered to be almost like Gods within their groups of friends. I almost feel like they go out looking for young women that will go with them easily so that these young men can add these girls to their list of girls they 'laid.' For young women, it is different. If they go out and sleep with as many guys as they can, they are labeled sluts and whores. Because of this, they may even be scared to report any sexual harassment they may have gone through. What is accepted among young men is not accepted among young women."

- "College experiences are the same as any other experience. The young men and women who look at homosexuals and harassment them [sic] have the same childish ways as anyone else."

- "If a woman wants to explore her sexuality in college, and kiss another woman, it is ok. It is harder for a man, so exploring myself in college is difficult."

- "There is still the disgusting notion that men are here for educations and women are here for husbands."

While there seems to be a sentiment among students that they would help out someone who is being harassed, there appear to be vague ideas about what campus resources were available to those being harassed or witnessing harassment. One participant mentioned that she ". . . would most likely take matters into my own hands because I don't have much faith in my university to do anything about it."

Quantitative Findings

Have you been privy to a formal discussion of sexual harassment since attending college?	62% answered **NO**
Have you ever been offered a formal class on sexual harassment during any educational experience (K-12 or post-secondary)?	80% answered **NO**
Have you ever had formal discussions regarding the harassment of homosexual, bisexual, transgendered youth during any educational experience (K-12 or post-secondary)?	80% answered **NO**
Have you ever witnessed sexual harassment on campus?	10% answered **YES**
Have you witnessed discrimination or harassment of GLBTQ students on campus?	21% answered **YES**
Have you observed sexual harassment at campus sponsored events?	6% answered **YES**
Have you experienced cyber sexual harassment since becoming a college student?	11% answered **YES**
Have you observed/experienced cyber sexual harassment of GLBTQ students?	3% answered **YES**
Are there fewer or more experiences of sexual harassment on college campus than on middle/high school campuses?	44% answered **MORE**
Have you experienced any of the following on your college/university campus?	Stalking 14% Dating Violence 14% Sexual Abuse 0% Sexual Harassment 0% Physical Abuse 7. 1% Name Calling 50% Fear of Walking on Campus 28. 6% Sexual Reference made to you or another 27% Fear of Being in a Particular Place on Campus 21%

As these results demonstrate, there is a clear need for more formal (and informal) discussions regarding issues of sexism, harassment, and homophobia. As most of the participants in this sample suggest, there are very few opportunities for students to address these issues in their educational experience, and this includes their college and university experience. Eighty percent of the participants in this study have received no education on the harassment of GLBTQ students, yet they also responded that such education would be welcomed. Additionally, the numbers reflect that there remain instances of harassment and discrimination of GLBTQ students at very high rates, as 21% of students in this survey alone reported observing such harassment, and 3% noted specific instances of cyber harassment of GLBTQ students. While the reporting of sexual harassment on campus appears to be low, with 10% of the participants witnessing sexual harassment on campus and 6% experiencing it online, we argue that these numbers still remain unacceptable. And further troubling is the rate of instances that occurred, according to the participants when they were asked about specific behaviors. Fourteen percent of the participants *experienced* stalking on their campus and 14% *experienced* dating violence. Looking at other examples of sexual harassment, 27% noted experience with having a sexual reference made to them or another while on campus, and clearly many students (arguably female students) still retain a great deal of fear of walking on campus. Lastly, name calling remains another form of harassment that continues to exist on campus, with 50% of participants experiencing it.

Conclusions

Just as we have argued in other work concerning sexual harassment in schools, the ideology and prevailing attitude that allows harassment to exist certainly does not exist in isolation on college and university campuses. Sexism is systematic and pervasive. As an institution, the university to some degree mirrors the social and cultural conditions in which it exists. However, this does not excuse the university from examination of the ways in which it prohibits social justice and allows the existence of sexual and homophobic harassment. The current "safeguards" that many institutions have in place, such as an explicit policy, do not address the sexist ideology that continues to serve as an undercurrent in the climate of contemporary academia. To address heterosexism, efforts against it must be systematic and campus-wide. As we have argued elsewhere, conversations of relevance to sexual harassment, bullying, sexual violence, homophobia, and gender inequity should begin in P-12 educational settings; but they should also remain a part of the curricular and social experiences of university and college students. Campus constituents should be engaged in ways in which to make the campus harassment- and bully-free. These conversations should not be relegated to the Gay Straight Alliances and Women's Organizations on campus, but rather they should become a more prevalent campus issue.

Martin (2008b) suggests an anti-violence, social justice pedagogy, perhaps involving interdisciplinary faculty who seek ways to incorporate its tenets into their own disciplines and course structures. Paludi, Denmark, and DeFour (2008) recommend requiring a course on the Psychology of Women as a means of eliminating campus violence. Providing more knowledge in the experiences of women can provide opportunity for more compassionate treatment of not just women, but of other marginalized groups as well. Sandler and Shoop (1996) suggest that institutions can require training in sexual harassment, make the issue prominent, and inform faculty; but making it an administrative priority is necessary. It cannot be an issue relegated to "student affairs" but rather should be seen as an important topic to all campus administration.

As we discuss contemporary colleges and universities, it is extremely important to examine the ways in which sexism, homophobia and heterosexism continue to plague the campus. We urge university faculty, administration, staff, and students to examine their own campus policy, atmosphere, and attitudes and call for a more active repudiation of the harassment of women and GLBQT students.

References

Bradenburg, J. (1997). *Confronting sexual harassment: What schools and colleges can do*. New York: Teachers College Press.

Buchanan, N. T., Bergman, M. E., Bruce, T. A., Woods, K. C., & Lichty, L. L. (2009). Unique and joint effects of sexual and racial harassment on students' well-being. *Basic and Applied Social Psychology, 31*, 267–285. doi: 10. 1080/01973530903058532

Cleary, J. S., & Schmieler, C. R. (1994). Sexual harassment of college students: Implications for campus health promotion. *Journal of American College Health, 43* (1), 78–95.

Dansky, B., & Kilpatrick, D. (1997). Effects of sexual harassment. In W. O'Donohue (Ed.), *Sexual harassment: Theory, research and practice* (pp. 152–174). Boston, MA: Allyn & Bacon.

Draugn, T., Elkins, B., & Roy, R. (2002). Allies in the struggle: Eradicating homophobia and heterosexism on campus. In E. Cramer (Ed.), *Addressing homophobia and heterosexism on college campuses* (pp. 9–20). Binghamton, NY: Harrington Park Press.

Eyre, L. (2000). The discursive framing of sexual harassment in a university community. *Gender and Education, 12* (3), 293–397.

Fisher, B., Daigle, L., & Cullen, F. (2010). *Unsafe in the ivory tower: The sexual victimization of college women*. Thousand Oaks, CA: Sage.

Hansen, A. L. (2007). School-based support for GLBT students: A review of three levels of research. *Psychology in the Schools, 44* (8), 839–848. Retrieved from EBSCOhost.

Henning-Stout, M., James, S., & McIntosh, S. (2000). Reducing harassment of lesbian, gay, bisexual, transgender and questioning youth in schools. *School Psychology Review, 29*, 180–191.

Hill, C., & Silva, E. (2005). *Drawing the line: Sexual harassment on campus*. Washington, DC. American Association of University Women.

Lundberg-Love, P. K. & Marmion, S. (2003). Sexual harassment in the private sector. In M. Paludi & C. Paludi (Eds.), *Academic and workplace sexual harassment: A handbook of cultural, social science, management, and legal perspectives* (pp. 77–101). Westport, CT: Praeger.

MacKinnon, C. (1979). *Sexual harassment of working women: A case of sex discrimination*. New Haven, CT: Yale University Press.

Martin, J. (2008a). Gendered violence on campus: Unpacking bullying, harassment and stalking. In M. Paludi (Ed.), *Understanding and preventing campus violence* (pp. 3–26). Westport, CT: Praeger.

Martin, J. (2008b) Anti-violence pedagogy: Strategies and resources. In M. Paludi (Ed.), *Understanding and preventing campus violence* (pp. 73–94). Westport, CT: Praeger.

Meyer, E. (2008). *Gender, bullying and harassment: Strategies to end sexism and homophobia in schools*. New York: Teachers College Press.

Mohler-Kuo, M., Dowdall, G. W., Koss, M., & Wechsler, H. (2004). Correlates of rape while intoxicated in a national sample of college women. *Journal of Studies on Alcohol, 65* (1), 37–45.

Paludi, M., Denmark, F., & DeFour, D. (2008). The psychology of women course as a catalyst for change for campus violence. In M. Paludi (Ed.), *Understanding and preventing campus violence* (pp. 103–112). Westport, CT: Praeger.

Paludi, M., Nydegger, R., Desouza, E., Nydegger, L., & Dicker, K. A. (2006). International perspectives on sexual harassment of college students: The sounds of silence. *Annals New York Academy of Sciences, 2087*, 103–120.

Quina, K. (1996). Sexual harassment and rape: A continuum of exploitation. In In M. Paludi (Ed.), *Sexual harassment on college campuses: Abusing the ivory power* (pp. 183–197). Albany: SUNY Press.

Quinn, B. (2002). Sexual harassment and masculinity: Power and meaning of girl watching. *Gender & Society, 16*, 386–402.

Rahimi, R., & Liston, D. (2012). *Pervasive vulnerabilities: Sexual harassment in schools*. New York, NY: Peter Lang.

Rivers, I. (2011). *Homophobic bullying: Research and theoretical perspectives.* New York: Oxford University Press.

Sandler, B., & Shoop, R. (1996). *Sexual harassment on campus: A guide for administration, faculty and students.* Boston: Allyn & Bacon.

Stein, N. (2007). Locating a secret problem: Sexual violence in elementary and secondary schools. In L. O'Toole, J. Schiffman, & M. Kiter Edwards (Eds.), *Gender violence: Interdisciplinary perspectives* (2nd ed; pp. 323–332). New York: New York University Press.

Thacker, A., & Gohmann, S. (1996). Emotional and psychological consequences of sexual harassment: A descriptive study. *Journal of Psychology, 130* (4), 429–446.

Waits, B. & Lundberg-Love, P. (2008). The impact of campus violence on college students. In M. Paludi (Ed.), *Understanding and preventing campus violence* (pp. 51–70). Westport, CT: Praeger.

Wasti, S. A., Bergman, M. E., Glomb, T. M., & Drasgow, F. (2000). Test of the cross-cultural generalizability of a model of sexual harassment. *Journal of Applied Psychology, 85,* 766–778.

CHAPTER SEVEN

Spirituality and Religion in Higher Education

Continued Relevance in the 21st Century

JULIE J. PARK & KRISTIN PAREDES-COLLINS

What role should spirituality and religion play in higher education? There is no one-size-fits-all answer to that question. The response is inevitably shaped by the eye of the beholder, or rather, the beholder's beliefs about what sort of support of religious and/or spiritual development, if any, is appropriate given the institutional context. Someone coming from a private Christian institution of higher education and someone coming from a public institution might have markedly different responses to such a question. Regardless of what initiatives institutions choose to sponsor, we believe that educators should, at a minimum, be prepared to recognize the relevance of spirituality and religion in students' lives. In this chapter we begin by providing some historical context for the increased interest in religion and spirituality in students' lives. We then discuss several reasons why educators should be prepared to recognize and respect the role of religion and spirituality in students' lives, including the relevance of religion and spirituality to mental health issues, supporting students of color, and cultivating a diverse democracy.

Before we launch our discussion of historical and contemporary issues influencing religion and spirituality in higher education, we would like to define how we are using such terms in this chapter. Although myriad definitions have been ascribed to the constructs, there is some agreement as to how to clarify differences between religion and spirituality: Religion involves an association with, and commitment to, an established set of customs and rituals; whereas spirituality is characterized by an individual pursuit of meaning, purpose, truth, and value, however elusive the quest may be (Astin, 2004; Chickering et al., 2006; Zinnbauer, Pargament, & Scott, 1999). A person can be distinctly spiritual and not religious, religious and not spiritual, neither, or both (Bryant, Choi, & Yasuno, 2003). According to Astin, Astin, and Lindholm (2011),

Spirituality has to do with the values that we hold most dear, our sense of who we are and where we come from, our beliefs about why we are here—the meaning and purpose that we see in our work and our life—and our sense of connectedness to each other and to the world around us. (p. 4)

These same authors define religiousness as "a devotion to, and practice of, some kind of faith tradition [that typically] involves membership in a community of fellow believers and participation in the rituals of the faith" (p. 82). Despite the distinctions between spirituality and religiosity, the two concepts are interconnected, as spirituality involves the internal pursuit of the sacred (e.g., the divine, concepts of God, and other entities that are transcendent)—a search that often occurs in a larger religious context, whether traditional or non-traditional in format.

Historical Context and Contemporary Growth

Old markers of religiosity on American campuses, such as mandatory chapel and prayers at school events, are gone at virtually all public institutions and most private institutions, with the exception of colleges and universities that continue to be religiously affiliated (Cherry et al., 2001). However, most early institutions were founded upon religious values, including those founded by denominational bodies for the purpose of training ministers and clergy; and overt expressions of religiosity were common at many public institutions well into the 20th century. As the American university began to embrace research as a primary function (Kerr, 2001), higher education underwent a major secularization process during the 20th century. Fostering religious devotion gave way to prioritizing scientific authority and, to some extent, religious skepticism (Marsden, 1994).

Higher education's embrace of modernity, with its emphasis on empiricism and objectivity, caused it to separate religious belief and scientific inquiry to the point where religion was, in essence, replaced by the pursuit of science in the academy (Smith, 2001). Postmodernism, with its rejection of universal truth and a single master narrative, seemed to be the final nail in the coffin of religious expression on college campuses. Ironically, postmodernism has, however, opened the door for a more diverse array of viewpoints to be considered in the academy (Love, 2000), allowing for a reconsideration of religious viewpoints and experiences as one perspective among many other standpoints.

Although postmodern forces within the academy have opened the door for the academy to consider the roles of religion and spirituality, they also complicate the way in which religion is discussed within higher education and society writ-large. Across numerous faith traditions worldwide, people hold differing perspectives on their religious beliefs, with some believing that all faiths are a way to the divine while others believe in absolute truth. Is it possible to accommodate both perspectives within higher education? Perhaps the inherent contradiction between the perspectives has contributed to the academy's apprehension to broadly acknowledge the role of spirituality and religion in the lives of students. However, despite the differences between perspectives, each pairs an inner awareness with an outward focus that can lead to a greater understanding of individual purpose, vocation, and meaning (Astin, 2004; Harris, Thoreson, & Lopez, 2007). Albeit challenging to accommodate multiple viewpoints on spirituality and religion into the higher education setting, we view it as a worthy effort.

The growth of racial diversity in higher education and higher education's role in a global society are two additional factors that have necessitated the recognition that religion and spirituality matter in many college students' lives. As we will discuss in greater detail, religiosity and spirituality is particularly high among communities of color; indeed, honoring religious beliefs, traditions, and values is part of honoring the whole student. Additionally, global forces have changed the way we think about U.S. higher education. No longer are we preparing students to be only citizens within their local communities; we are preparing global citizens who have to be prepared to be globally literate—part of which includes being able to understand the role that religion and spirituality continue to play in societies and governments outside of the U.S.

Thus, even though university-sanctioned religious activities may not be as prominent as they were a century ago, the post-modern climate of the university has made it possible for the study of religion and spirituality in higher education to experience somewhat of a revival (Bryant, 2004). Studies have emerged exploring the role of spirituality in the lives of college students (Astin et al., 2005), religious pluralism (Kazanjian & Laurence, 2000), well-being (Park & Millora, 2010), and campus ministry (Bramadat, 2002; Bryant, 2004; Kim, 2006; Magolda & Ebben Gross, 2009; Park, 2011), among other issues. In the academic community, various national symposiums and working groups of scholars have contributed to an increased interest in the exploration of religious and spiritual issues affecting higher education (Bryant & Schwartz, 2007).

In addition to the resurgence of the study of religion and spirituality in the context of higher education, students continue to assert their interest in exploring their beliefs and values in the collegiate setting (Hindman, 2002). In a comprehensive national study of spirituality, 80% of students noted their interest in spirituality, 76% engaged in the search for their life's purpose and meaning, 74% discussed issues of spirituality with friends, and 47% considered it essential or very important to seek opportunities for spiritual growth (Higher Education Research Institute of California, Los Angeles [HERI], 2007). Additionally, 79% of students believed in God, 69% prayed, 76% found that religious beliefs provided strength and comfort, and 40% of students considered it essential or very important to follow religious teachings in their daily life (HERI, 2007). Arguably, students are not interested in a life that is "splintered and fragmented into separate and seemingly unrelated parts: academic and social life, job and family, producing and being" (Hindman, 2002, p. 172). It appears that a sizeable portion of students desire for their college to allow personal—and in some cases communal—expressions of spirituality, as well as play a role in supporting the development of values and self-understanding. We believe that college should be a place for students to expand their minds intellectually, while also developing the interior aspects of their lives.

The benefits associated with spirituality and religion are numerous. An expanding collection of research has shown that spirituality is associated with college engagement (Kuh & Gonyea, 2005), service involvement (Chickering et al., 2006; Kuh & Gonyea, 2005), leadership skills (Yasuno, 2004), and identification of life purpose (Greenway, 2005). Providing students with more opportunities to connect with their "inner selves" enhances academic performance, psychological well-being, intellectual self-confidence, and satisfaction with college—all of which are important college outcomes (Astin et al., 2011). Encouraging students to grasp an understanding of their intrinsic value, their connection to others, and their ability to impact humankind through their actions could have an impact on their development as global citizens

(Chickering et al., 2006). In addition to the role that spirituality and religion play in the lives of students, Nash challenges the notion that the discussion of religion has no place in the academic setting: "Religion is such a fundamental part of human existence that students simply cannot understand the history or politics of most societies, including the United States, without a serious examination of religion's central role in producing both good and evil throughout the world throughout the last several millennia" (Nash, 1999, p. 4). In light of the breadth of research on the matter, we suggest that both public and private institutions of higher education would benefit from engaging their students in a discussion of spirituality, internal development, personal vocation, and the role of religion in society, both past and present.

The Roles of Religion and Spirituality in Supporting Students of Color

Culture represents a combination of deeply held values and belief systems, of which religion and spirituality are often cornerstones. Although race is a social construct, it has real ties to culture and thus religion and spirituality (Stewart & Lozano, 2009). For students of color, spirituality and religion are often particularly important constructs. Religious traditions, worship styles, and values often play an important role in people's understanding of their particular racial and ethnic cultural identity (Tisdell, 2003). Historically, race has often guided the manifestations of religion in society (Johnstone, 1997). For example, the development of the independent Black church emerged as a response to plantation worship services and the balcony segregation that occurred in White churches. W. E. B. Du Bois noted that the local Black church became the center of its members' social lives (as cited in Johnstone, 1997).

The connection between spirituality, religion, and culture has been widely identified. Examples can be drawn from Native American (Brooks, 2003), African American (Stewart, 2002; Strayhorn, 2011), Latino/a (Brandes, 1998), and Asian American cultures (Kim, 2006; Park, 2011). For instance, Native Americans often share a deep spiritual connection with all elements of the universe—in which everything has life, spiritual energy, and importance (Garrett & Garrett, 1994)—and many Chinese cultural values are connected to Buddhist and Confucian thought. Protestant churches are often the most prominent civic institutions in the Korean American community (Park, 2011). For Latino/as, particularly those of Mexican origin, celebration of the Dia de los Muertos (Day of the Dead) represents the intersection between race, culture, and spirituality (Stewart & Lozano, 2009). A combination of indigenous pre-Columbian rituals with Catholic tradition, celebrating Dia de los Muertos represents a time to honor deceased loved ones while also acknowledging a shared history of colonialism, oppression, and resistance. In addition to providing a forum for social support for African Americans, religious communities provide a medium to discuss issues of a political and social nature (Mays, Caldwell, & Jackson, 1996). Both Christianity and Islam played major roles in shaping the Civil Rights and Black Power movements.

Often attending college during the crossroads of racial identity development, many students of color draw particular meaning from religion and spirituality. For example, Stewart and Lozano (2009) note that celebrating Día de los Muertos can "serve to empower students as they recognize the importance of resistance, connect with their spiritual selves, and reaffirm the value of their cultural traditions." Evangelical Christian Korean American campus fellowships have quickly grown in popularity and prevalence across the country, outpacing growth in other campus fellowships at many institutions (Kim, 2006). Although these Korean American fellowships are often similar in style and theology to White evangelical groups, such groups allow Korean American students space to exercise leadership and majority status in institutions where they may experience marginalization as minorities. Several researchers have found that religion and spirituality are more central to the lives of Black students than their White counterparts (Blaine & Crocker, 1995; Chae, Kelly, Brown, & Bolden, 2004; Walker & Dixon, 2002).

Extending beyond their relevance for particular cultures, religion and spirituality also serve as important sources of comfort and solace for people of color. In relation to racial identity, many find spiritual beliefs as a source of strength and a refuge from racism that sustains them through racial identity development and "assist[s] them in deriving greater meaning from their racial ancestry or identity" (Wijeysesinghe, 2001, p. 143). Bowen-Reid and Harrell's (2002) work suggests that spirituality might mitigate the negative effects associated with racial discrimination and stress associated with racist experiences. Constantine, Miville, Warren, Gainor, and Lewis-Coles (2006) also found that Black students depend on spiritual or religious commitment or behaviors in times of adversity, stress, and when deciding on a future career path.

A great breadth of research has chronicled the common racial realities of campus life for students of color on Traditionally White Institutions (TWIs). Overwhelmingly, the research demonstrates that White students report higher levels of sense of belonging and more positive perceptions of campus climate than students of color (Ancis et al., 2000; Chavous, 2005; Johnson et al., 2007; Park, 2009). Minority students at highly selective TWIs report greater levels of stress associated with their racial and ethnic group status (Solberg & Villareal, 1997; Feagin & Sikes, 1995). Similarly, Rankin and Reason (2005) found that students of color were much more likely to describe the campus as being unfriendly, racist, and disrespectful, while White students perceived the climate to be exactly the opposite. Rankin and Reason found the perception of White students to be surprising, as nearly 40% of White students across ten campuses had observed race-based harassment on campus. According to Hurtado et al. (2008), "Subtle perceptions of a hostile climate [has] more of an impact on all areas of adjustment to college (social, academic, personal-emotional, and attachment to the institution) than actual behaviors" (p. 209). It is clear that students of color at TWIs perceive the campus racial climate to be more negative than their white peers. Religion and spirituality can be relevant tools to support resilience for students of color in college (Everett-Haynes & Deil-Amen, 2011); and in some cases religious institutions within the broader community (i.e., the Black church) can play a positive role in supporting and encouraging students of color as they persist through college. In light of this reality, we suggest that educators be acutely aware of the positive role that spirituality and religion can play in supporting students of color.

Mental Health: A Growing Concern

Religion and spirituality are also highly relevant in the college environment due to an increase in mental health and well-being concerns among the college-going population. In some cases, religious or spiritual struggle may be linked to emotional distress or other well-being issues for college students and, in other scenarios, students may turn to religion and/or spirituality to help them make sense of issues that challenge their well-being. Either way, we suggest that educators need to be prepared to support students as they make sense of their religiosity and/ or spirituality and to recognize that religious and/or spiritual communities can potentially play a positive role in supporting students' emotional and psychological well-being.

For students who grow up religious, college may be the first time they have to evaluate their belief systems and consider what they believe as adults independent of their parents or previous peer groups. The work of Marcia Baxter-Magolda and others show us how the college years are a vital time for students to develop "self-authorship" as they shift from relying on external formulas and pressures to the development of an internal voice that takes others' viewpoints into account when reacting to a situation or formulating an opinion (Baxter-Magolda, 2001). This developmental process is often triggered by provocative events that make an individual stand at a crossroads where he or she has the option of relying on old patterns of thinking or developing a more complex way of meaning-making.

Religion is just one of many spheres of life in which a student may experience challenges to their former way of thinking during college, but it may be one of the most impactful. For many students, religious background—or lack thereof—is not just a system of beliefs that influences one's worldview; it is also often tied to deeper social connections in one's family, community, cultural traditions, and sense of ethnic identity. Thus, evaluating religious beliefs and affiliations may be particularly stressful for students because doing so may have a potential ripple effect on a student's relationships and sense of self. Reflecting the potential impact of spiritual and religious struggle, Bryant and Astin (2008) found that spiritual struggle was significantly related to psychological distress during the college years, and Park and Millora (2010) found that religious struggle was negatively related to psychological well-being for students across racial/ethnic groups.

Some questioning about religious and spiritual values is a natural part of student development during the college years and may even be desirable to help students come to a more independent, internal definition of their beliefs. Still, educators should be aware that questioning religious and spiritual beliefs has the potential to cause significant emotional distress. Institutions can respond by preparing counseling center staff to be aware of such issues and also to educate residential life staff about options that students can turn to for support. Spiritual and/ or religious struggle may pose the greatest threat to a student's well-being when such struggling results in prolonged isolation, or if a student feels as though he or she lacks supportive options or people to process with.

Besides religion and spirituality having the potential to trigger emotional distress among students, these issues deserve educators' attention because of how they may function as a buffer or support system during times of stress. As we noted in the previous section, this dynamic is especially prevalent among students of color; and studies have found positive relationships between spirituality/religiosity and health for women of color (Musgrave, Allen, & Allen, 2002). Black students face numerous challenges to their well being at TWIs, including racial microaggressions and isolation for being a minority student. For many Black students in particular, religious involvement appears to work as a support system to help alleviate some of the stress and isolation that can come from being a minority student (Jang & Johnson, 2004; Strayhorn, 2011); religious values can also be a potent tool for coping in a difficult campus environment (Patton & McClure, 2009). Religious communities such as gospel choirs and campus fellowships can also be a positive source of support for students, helping them establish a sense of belonging and community on an otherwise alienating campus (Park, 2011; Strayhorn, 2011).

Educators should also maintain some awareness of religious communities because such communities may be the first place a student turns to report emotional distress, particularly in communities that are known for under-utilizing counseling services. Park and Millora (2010) note how many Asian American students may not feel comfortable accessing formal university counseling services due to cultural stigma—or they may simply be unaware that such services exist. However, these same students may turn to their small group within a campus fellowship for support while struggling with persistent high anxiety. Small groups and campus fellowships, most of which take place outside of university sponsorship or close oversight, are well-equipped to help support students during stressful, but low-risk, situations. They can also use religious values to frame pertinent messages around achievement and identity, i.e., "your self-worth is not defined by your grades." However, they are generally unequipped to support students through situations that require professional counseling. Because these groups are a place where some students turn during difficult times, it works in everyone's best interests for universities to build relationships with campus ministry staff and to help them become aware of the infrastructure that exists to support students' mental health concerns. In turn, campus ministry staff can become more aware of the resources within the university that they cannot only refer students to, but encourage them to use. Because professional counseling carries a certain stigma within certain communities of color and even religious traditions, having the endorsement of campus ministry staff or religious leaders from the local community may be particularly beneficial.

Connections to Social Justice and Engagement with Diversity

Finally, we advocate for institutions to recognize the roles of religion and spirituality in students' lives because systems of beliefs and values can serve as the foundation for commitments to social justice, community service, and engagement with diversity. Obviously, not all students are religious; but for those who are, religious beliefs and values may be a useful starting point to engage students in issues of social justice, service, and diversity who might not otherwise be interested. There are some students who need little coaxing to become involved in such activities, but other students may be initially more resistant or apathetic to these efforts. In some of the latter cases, students may see university-initiated efforts to promote such activities as something being imposed or even forced on them, i.e., a case of political correctness.

Some students may actually be initially resistant to engaging in issues of justice and diversity *because* of their religious values, and it is important for educators to understand the underlying foundations of their resistance. The work of Emerson and Smith (2000) has shown how colorblindness is the dominant mode for recognizing (or not recognizing) race among White evangelicals. White evangelicals are even more likely to oppose race-conscious social policies than Whites in general (Hinojosa & Park, 2004). This worldview is likely propagated by the fact that religion is the most segregated arena of American life, with fewer than 10% of U.S. churches being classified as racially heterogeneous. Thus, is it any surprise when a White student who grew up in a predominantly White town and attended an almost all-White church his or her entire life comes to college feeling at best bewildered, and at worst, outrightly hostile toward the idea that race has continuing significance in American society? On the one hand, the latter scenario is not uncommon in American universities in general; White students who grow up in predominantly White neighborhoods and high schools are less likely to engage in cross-racial interaction and engagement with diversity activities during the college years (Locks, Hurtado, Bowman, & Oseguera, 2008). However, its severity is compounded by the additional socialization that takes place in students' religious home communities, where ". . . religions can uphold legitimizing myths that explain and sustain problems such as inequality. . ." (Hunsberger & Jackson, 2005, p. 818).

Although religion can lead students to be more closed or skeptical in recognizing social inequality, it can also be a powerful motivation for social change. Gordon Allport summarized the paradoxical role of religion by stating: "There is something about religion that makes for prejudice and something about it that unmakes prejudice" (1966, p. 447). College is a unique time for students to be exposed to new ways of thinking. For those who remain religious and/or spiritual, college may be the first time when they are challenged to think about the implications of their faith traditions for issues of justice and equity. Interviewing evangelical college students at a large, public institution, Park found that very few had been encouraged to think of their faith as relevant to issues of justice and diversity prior to college, with the exception of Black students. Many students noted that, growing up, they held a colorblind attitude toward race relations and had not been exposed to issues related to poverty and inequality. However, through their involvement in a campus fellowship, students were challenged to think about such issues through the lens of their faith. Numerous participants noted that they would have never thought about these issues if not through their participation in the campus fellowship, and their faith gave them a framework to understand their responsibility to the world around them. Some would have never been exposed to such issues in the curricular realm, being science or engineering majors, but their co-curricular involvement in this religious community gave them an opportunity to think of their religious beliefs and values in a different light.

Thus, while many students do not draw on religion or spirituality as a source of motivation for engaging in social action during college, we note its relevance to students who might not otherwise engage in such issues if not for religious beliefs and values. A common maxim among student affairs educators is "meeting students where they are." Understanding how religion may shape a student's pre-college perspectives on the world is important to educators, both inside the classroom and outside of it; such understanding challenges students to comprehend the complexity of the world and their role in it. Furthermore, religion and spirituality may be particularly important for some students as they assess their beliefs, values, and convictions, asking the "big questions" about meaning and purpose.

Concluding Thoughts

In this essay we have advocated for colleges and universities to come to a greater understanding of how religion and spirituality are pertinent to many college students' lives, even in institutions that have no religious affiliation. Living in a global society spurs us to consider how our lives—economic, social, cultural, and political—are intertwined with people around the world, and part of global citizenship includes recognizing and respecting the deep role that religion and spirituality plays in people's lives. Simply stated, spirituality and religion matter for many college students. They matter for many students, both White and students of color, for emotional and psychological well-being—and for their connection to social justice and engagement with diversity. Further, as "spirituality acts as a catalyst for student development by providing students with a way to ask meaning-of-life questions often explored in the peer conversation" (Cady, 2007, p. 108), we believe that professionals in higher education should be prepared to recognize the spiritual side of students through the provision of resources, services, and, at the very least, through the acknowledgment that it matters.

That said, we have walked somewhat of a fine line between advocating for the recognition of religion and spirituality in the academy versus university endorsement of religion and spirituality. While we believe that it is critical for institutions of higher education to recognize the relevance of religion and spirituality in students' lives, we recognize that what universities actually "do" in regards to religion and spirituality will vary a great deal depending on institutional context. At a minimum, we believe that institutions should work to foster a positive climate for religious and spiritual expression by encouraging respectful discourse around religion. Many institutions, both public and private, have increased awareness of religious holidays outside of the Judeo-Christian tradition. However, we also recognize that it is not necessarily the responsibility of most institutions to sponsor direct religious programming, although they may build infrastructures to support religious/spiritual life staff and other initiatives such as interfaith dialogue or campus events that recognize major religious holidays.

Indeed, some of the most vibrant and active religious communities on campus are those that are not university-initiated or closely regulated. Perhaps it is something about giving students the choice and space to initiate their own communities that make them particularly meaningful experiences for student participants. Besides promoting religious and spiritual development, such groups also foster a "co-curriculum" of their own, as Magolda and Ebben Gross (2009) note, creating spaces that foster student learning and the exchange of ideas. One drawback of student-initiated religious communities is that they have the potential to be insular, preventing students from having meaningful experiences with other realms of campus life. When religious student organizations are racially homogeneous (as they often are) students are less likely to form interracial friendships during college (Park, 2010). However, an asset of religious community, at the risk of stating the obvious, is that it functions as a *community*, providing an arena outside of the classroom for sustained engagement and conversations that can happen in the context of meaningful, ongoing relationships. Students cycle in and out of classes after a semester, and students may leave their residential life communities for smaller off-campus sub-communities. Thus, co-curricular engagement that happens via community is an important part of campus life, providing a space for ongoing conversations and activism during the college years.

Through intentional actions, such as encouraging the development of student-initiated religious communities, providing resources and services for these communities to flourish, promoting interfaith dialogue, and building infrastructures to support religious/spiritual life staff and campus events recognizing major religious holidays, institutions can take great strides in acknowledging the wholeness of their student population. We recognize that acknowledging the important facet that religion and spirituality plays in the lives of many students and accommodating a variety of belief systems is a difficult task at most institutions. However, as spirituality is associated with college engagement (Kuh & Gonyea, 2005), service involvement (Astin, 2002; Chickering et al., 2006; Kuh & Gonyea, 2005), psychological well-being (Astin et al., 2011), leadership skills (Yasuno, 2004), personal vocation identification (Astin, 2004;

Greenway, 2005), and more, we submit that the benefit of acknowledging the significance of religion and spirituality really *does* matter.

References

Allport, G. W. (1966). The religious nature of prejudice. *Journal for the Scientific Study of Religion, 5* (3), 447–457.

Ancis, J. R., Sedlacek, W. E., & Mohr, J. (2000). Student perceptions of campus cultural climate by race. *Journal of Counseling & Development, 78* (2), 180–85.

Astin, A. (2004, Spring). Why spirituality deserves a central place in liberal education. *Liberal Education,* 34–41.

Astin, A. W. (2002, April). *Is spirituality a legitimate concern in higher education?* Keynote address presented at the Spirituality and Learning Conference, San Francisco, CA.

Astin, A., Astin, H., & Lindholm, J. (2011). *Cultivating the spirit: How college can enhance students' inner lives.* San Fransisco, CA: Jossey-Bass.

Astin, A. W., Astin, H. S., Lindholm, J. A. & Bryant, A. N. (2007). *The spiritual life of college students: A national study of college students' search for meaning and purpose.* Los Angeles: Higher Education Research Institute, UCLA. Retrieved from: http://spirituality. ucla.edu/docs/reports/Spiritual_Life_College_Students_Full_Report.pdf

Astin, A. W., Astin, H. S., Lindholm, J. A., Bryant, A. N., Szelényi, K., & Calderone, S. (2005). *The spiritual life of college students: A national study of college students' search for meaning and purpose.* Los Angeles: Higher Education Research Institute, UCLA.

Baxter Magolda, M. B. (2001). *Making their own way: Narratives for transforming higher education to promote self-development.* Sterling, VA: Stylus.

Blaine, B. & Crocker, J. (1995). Religiousness, race, and psychological well-being: Exploring social-psychological mediators. *Personality and Social Psychology Bulletin, 21,* 1031–1041.

Bowen-Reid, T. L., & Harrell, J. P. (2002). Racist experiences and health outcomes: An examination of spirituality as a buffer. *Journal of Black Psychology, 28,* 18–36.

Bramadat, P. (2000). *The church on the world's turf: An evangelical Christian group at a secular university.* New York: Oxford University Press.

Brandes, S. (1998). The Day of the Dead, Halloween, and the quest for Mexican national identity. *Journal of American Folklore, 111* (442), 359–380.

Brooks, J. (2003). *American Lazarus: Religion and the Rise of African-American and Native American Literatures.* New York: Oxford University Press.

Bryant, A. N. (2004). *Campus religious communities and the college experience.* Unpublished doctoral dissertation. University of California Los Angeles.

Bryant, A. N., & Astin, H. S. (2008). The correlates of spiritual struggle during the college years. *The Journal of Higher Education, 79* (1), 1–27.

Bryant, A., Choi, J., & Yasuno, M. (2003). Understanding the religious and spiritual dimensions of students' lives in the first year of college. *Journal of College Student Development, 44* (6), 723–745.

Bryant, A. N. & Schwartz, L. (2006). *Proceedings from the national institute on spirituality in higher education: Integrating spirituality into the campus curriculum and co-curricular.* Los Angeles: UCLA Higher Education Research Institute.

Cady, D. M. (2007). Spirituality and student development. In B. W. Speck & S. L. Hoppe (Eds.), *Searching for spirituality in higher education* (pp. 97-110). New York: Peter Lang Publishing.

Chae, M. H., Kelly, D. B., Brown, C. F., & Bolden, M. A. (2004). Relationship of ethnic identity and spiritual development: An exploratory study. *Counseling and Values, 49,* 15–26.

Chavous, T. (2005). An intergroup contact-theory framework for evaluating racial climate on predominantly white college campuses. *American Journal of Community Psychology, 36* (3/4), 239–257.

Cherry, C., DeBerg, B. A., & Porterfield, A. (2001). *Religion on campus.* Chapel Hill: The University of North Carolina Press.

Chickering, A., Dalton, J., & Stamm, L. (2006). *Encouraging authenticity and spirituality in higher education.* San Francisco, CA: Jossey-Bass.

Constantine, M. D., Miville, M. L., Warren, A. K., Gainor, K. A., & Lewis-Coles, M. E. L. (2006). Religion, spirituality, and career development in African American college students: A qualitative inquiry. *The Career Development Quarterly, 54,* 227–241.

Emerson, M. O., & Smith, C. (2000). *Divided by faith: Evangelical religion and the problem of race in America.* Oxford: Oxford University Press.

Everett-Haynes, L. & Deil-Amen, R. (2011). Converging realities and identities: A case study of resiliency among African American and Latino undergraduates. Paper presented at the American Educational Research Association annual conference. New Orleans, LA.

Feagin, J. R., & Sikes, M. P. (1995). How Black students cope with racism on White campuses. *Journal of Blacks in Higher Education, 8,* 91–97.

Garrett, J. T., & Garrett, M. W. (1994). The path of good medicine: Understanding and counseling native American Indians. *Journal of Multicultural Counseling & Development, 22* (3).

Greenway, K. (2005). Purpose in life: A pathway to academic engagement and success. *Dissertation Abstracts International, 66* (04A), 1292–1487. (UMI No. 3171374)

Harris, A., Thoreson, C., & Lopez, S. (2007). Integrating positive psychology into counseling: Why and (when appropriate) how. *Journal of Counseling and Development, 85,* 3–13.

Higher Education Research Institute of California, Los Angeles. (2007). The spiritual life of college students: A national study of college students' search for meaning and purpose. Retrieved June 15, 2009 from http://www. spirituality. ucla.edu/docs/reports/Spiritual_Life_ College_Students_Full_Report.pdf

Hindman, D. (2002). From splintered lives to whole persons: Facilitating spiritual development of college students, *Religious Education, 97* (2), 165–182.

Hinojosa, V. J, & Park, J. Z. (2004). Religion and the paradox of racial inequality attitudes. *Journal for the Scientific Study of Religion, 43* (2), 229–238.

Hunsberger, B., & Jackson, L. M. (2005). Religion, meaning, and prejudice. *Journal of Social Issues, 61* (4), 807–826.

Hurtado, S., Griffin, K. A., Arellano, L., & Cuellar, M. (2008). Assessing the value of climate assessments: Progress and future directions. *Journal of Diversity in Higher Education, 1* (4), 204–221.

Jang, S. & Johnson, B. R. (2004). Explaining effects of religious distress for African Americans. *Journal for the Scientific Study of Religion, 43* (2), 239–260.

Johnson, D., Soldner, M., Leonard, J., Alvarez, P., Inkelas, K., Rowan-Kenyon, H., & Longerbeam, S. (2007). Examining sense of belonging among first-year undergraduates from different racial/ethnic groups. *Journal of College Student Development, 48* (5), 525–542.

Johnstone, R. (1997). *Religion in society: A sociology of religion.* Upper Saddle River, NJ: Prentice-Hall, Inc.

Kazanjian, V. H. & Laurence, P. L. (Eds.). (2000). *Education as transformation: Religious pluralism, spirituality, and a new vision of higher education in America.* New York: Peter Lang.

Kerr, C. (2001). *The uses of the university* (5th ed.). Cambridge, MA: Harvard University Press.

Kim, R. (2006). *God's whiz kids: Korean American evangelicals on campus.* New York: New York University Press.

Kuh, G. D. & Gonyea, R. M. (2005). *Exploring the relationships between spirituality, liberal learning, and college student engagement. A special report prepared for the Teagle Foundation.* Bloomington, IN: Center for Postsecondary Research, Indiana University. Available at: http://www.teaglefoundation.org/learning/pdf/20050711_kuh_gonyea.pdf

Locks, A. M., Hurtado, S., Bowman, N. A., & Oseguera, L. (2008). Extending notions of campus climate and diversity to students' transitions to college. *Review of Higher Education, 31* (3), 257–285.

Love, P., & Talbot, D. (1999). Defining spiritual development: A missing consideration for student affairs. *NASPA Journal, 37* (1), 361–375.

Magolda, P. M. & Ebben Gross, K. (2009). *It's all about Jesus!: Faith as an oppositional subculture.* Sterling: Stylus Press.

Marsden, G. (1994). *The soul of the university: From Protestant establishment to established nonbelief.* New York: Oxford University Press.

Mays, V. M., Caldwell, C. H., & Jackson, J. S. (1996). Mental health symptoms and service utilization patterns of help-seeking among African American women. In H. W. Neighbors & J. S. Jackson (Eds.), *Mental health in Black America* (pp. 161–176). Thousand Oaks, CA: Sage.

Musgrave, C. F., Allen, C. E., & Allen, G. J. (2002). Spirituality and health for women of color. *American Journal of Public Health, 92* (4), 557–560.

Nash, R. J. (2001). *Religious pluralism in the academy: Opening the dialogue.* New York: Peter Lang Publishing.

Park, J. J. (2009). Are we satisfied? A look at student satisfaction with diversity at traditional White institutions. *The Review of Higher Education, 32,* 291–320.

Park, J. J. (2011). "I needed to get out of my Korean bubble": An ethnographic account of Korean American collegians juggling diversity in a religious context. *Anthropology & Education Quarterly, 42* (3), 193–212.

Park, J. J. & Millora, L. M. (2010). Psychological well-being for White, Black, Latino/a, and Asian American students: Considering spirituality and religion. *Journal of Student Affairs Research and Practice, 47* (4), 1–18.

Park, S. (2004). Korean American evangelical: A resolution of sociological ambivalence among Korean American college students. In T. Carnes and F. Yang (Eds.), *Asian American religions: The making and remaking of borders and boundaries.* New York, New York: New York University Press.

Patton, L. D., & McClure, M. L. (2009). Strength in the spirit: A qualitative examination of African American college women and the role of spirituality during college. *The Journal of Negro Education, 78* (1), 42–54.

Rankin, S. R., & Reason, R. D. (2005). Differing perceptions: How students of color and White students perceive campus climate for underrepresented groups. *Journal of College Student Development, 46* (1), 43–61.

Smith, C. (1998). *American evangelicalism: Embattled and thriving.* Chicago: University of Chicago Press.

Solberg, V. S., & Villareal, P. (1997). Examination of self-efficacy, social support, and stress aspredictors of psychological and physical distress among Hispanic college students. *Hispanic Journal of Behavioral Sciences, 19* (2), 182–201.

Stewart, D. L. (2002). The role of faith in the development of an integrated identity: A qualitative study of Black students at a White college. *Journal of College Student Development, 43* (4), 579–596.

Stewart, D. L., & Lozano, A. (2009). Difficult dialogues at the intersections of race, culture, and religion. *New Directions for Student Services 125,* 23–31.

Strayhorn, T. L. (2011). Singing in a foreign land: An exploratory study of gospel choir participation among African American undergraduates at a predominantly White institution. *Journal of College Student Development.*

Tisdell, E. (2003) *Exploring spirituality and culture in adult and higher education.* San Francisco: Jossey-Bass.

Walker, K. L., & Dixon, V. (2002). Spirituality and academic performance among African American college students. *Journal of Black Psychology, 28* (2), 107–121.

Wijeyesinghe, C. L. (2001). Racial identity in multiracial people: An alternative paradigm. In C. Wijeyesinghe & B. W. Jackson III (Eds.), *New perspectives on racial identity development: A theoretical and practical anthology* (pp. 129–152). New York: New York University Press.

Yasuno, M. (2004). Spirituality in action: Exploring spiritual dimensions of college student activists and their leadership for social change. *Dissertation Abstracts International, 66* (02), 521A. (UMI No. 3164335)

Zinnbauer, B. J., Pargament, K. I., & Scott, A. (1999). The emerging meanings of religiousness and spirituality: Problems and prospects, *Journal of Personality, 67* (6), 889–919.

CHAPTER EIGHT

The Impact of Athletics upon the Social Sustainability of the College Campus

AARON W. CLOPTON

Few elements of the extracurricular collegiate experience can claim to have as pervasive, and public, of an impact as intercollegiate athletics. The wealth of extant literature surrounding intercollegiate athletics often focuses on the pecuniary aspects of college sports, from alumni donations, to media exposure (Anderson & Birrer, 2011), to increased revenue streams from NCAA and conference membership (Getz & Siegfried, 2010). This essay will focus on the relationship between intercollegiate athletics and the overall sustainability of the university and the university campus. To do this, sustainability is looked upon through the triple-bottom line (e.g., O'Dwyer & Owen, 2005). Here, sustainable development and overall sustainability is only possible by taking into account the three pillars of sustainability: economic, environmental, and social. From an economic bottom line, the presence of college sport continues to escalate with fervor as median value expenditures of NCAA Division I athletics programs have risen steadily from $28.9 million in 2004 to $41.3 million in 2008 (Fulks, 2009). In fact, the NCAA has recently opted out of its 11–year, $6.2 billion contract with CBS for broadcasting its annual men's basketball tournament to sign a new 14–year, $10.86 billion agreement with CBS Sports and the Turner Broadcasting System (Johnson, 2010). Further, numerous studies have examined the intricate relationship between athletics success and monetary donations (e.g., Getz & Siegfried, 2010), yet the relationship is one that has proven to be mixed, or tenuous at best. Most, however, do find that highly successful intercollegiate sports and sporting programs elicit a significant increase in alumni donations, while football often had the largest, and most significant, impact on financial support (e.g., Baade & Sundberg, 1996; Daughtery & Stotlar, 2000; Sigelman & Brookheimer, 1994). The idea that athletics could motivate alumni to contribute more to the university is grounded in the premise of the power of external prestige. However, often the relationship between alumni and booster donations with athletics success is one of short-term impact, and many scholars suggest the athletics contributions merely take the place of, rather than exist in addition to, additional monetary support to the overall academic endowment. The influence of perceptions of external prestige has been observed at the university level with current students, where perceptions of prestige have positively impacted student loyalty and satisfaction (Alves & Raposo, 2010) and have been shown to be the strongest predictor of positive student attitudes (Sung & Yang, 2008). Even the Flutie Factor, where increased applications to a university are attributed in part to success in athletics, has its roots in this notion that athletics can shape perceptions of stakeholders in terms of academic quality. Among the assumptions of the Flutie Factor is that exposure to a college or university's successful athletic team(s) enhances prospective students' perceptions of that university as prestigious. Here, past research has examined intercollegiate athletics' ability to impact future generations of university students, as successful seasons—specifically, Bowl appearances for football and post-season tournament appearances for men's basketball programs—often lead to a significant increase in admission applications (e.g., Toma & Cross, 1998). However, the quality of the affected admission pool is contested (Mixon, Trevino, & Minto, 2004). While athletic success has been shown to attract students with higher SAT scores (McCormick & Tinsley, 1987), Smith (2008) discovered no significant relationship between success in basketball and numerous indicators of academic quality within the incoming freshmen class.

Still, as the "front porch" of colleges and universities today, the external community is frequently connected with the presence of a successful athletics program. For instance, athletic success has been credited with enhancing the public's perception of academic quality of those same institutions (Goidel & Hamilton, 2006; Lovaglia & Lucas, 2005). Toma (1999, p. 81) alludes to this ability as well, suggesting that athletics contribute to the "aura of importance to the campus."

Further, while monetary streams are one element of the athletics-academics dyad on a college campus, the contribution of college sport's "arms race" is another; and the most impactful in terms of environmental sustainability of the campus. The pursuit of the "arms race" was defined so by the mimetic isomorphism of intercollegiate athletics departments trying to bolster their athletic presence by investing in facility upgrades to out-build their counterparts and attract higher-profile coaches and student-athletes. Such a pursuit has led to spending on athletic facilities reaching $15.2 billion between 1995 and 2005 and an average of 20% of athletics spending in 2005 was tied to facility expansion and related debt (CollegeSports101).

Moreover, the focus of this essay is constrained to the impact of athletics upon the social fabric of the campus community, or the social sustainability of the campus. While encompassing similar concepts of social capital, social cohesion, social inclusion/exclusion, etc., social sustainability is a wide-ranging and a multi-dimensional concept aimed at exploring the social goals of sustainable development (Dempsey et al., 2011). It is also a concept specifically designed for the benefit of establishing sustainable communities, defined as "places where people want to live and work, now and in the future. They meet the diverse needs of existing and future residents, . . . contribute to a high quality of life . . . are safe and inclusive, and well planned, built, and run" (ODPM, 2006, p. 12). Here, the social dimension of the sustainable development of campuses would build upon traditional physical factors of development (i.e. facilities, accessibility, financial standings, etc.) with more non-physical factors such as sense of community, social cohesion, social networks, and active campus organizations. Interestingly, though, considerable barriers against community-building face the campus of today's large university, the host of big-time intercollegiate athletics programs. Many student affairs practitioners have felt that issues of disconnectedness and alienation between students exist as ever before (Spitzberg & Thorndike, 1992). And while increasing access to improve diversity within the fabric of today's campus community improves the experience of today's college student in many areas, the common bond amongst students has diminished to scant proportions—making the connecting of students on the periphery difficult (Boyer, 1990; Fugazzotto, 2012; Rovai, 2002). Further, still, because of the escalating dependence on extramural funding, the overall focus of faculty in larger universities has shifted from the interest and experiences of the general student body to chasing external agendas (Boyer, 1987, 1990). Thus, it is with these needs that student affairs administrators are charged with exhausting all avenues, and in and among all groups, to enhance the overall sense of community on campus (Levine & Cureton, 1998; Spitzberg & Thorndike, 1992).

Intercollegiate Athletics and Campus Community

Direct Connections with Athletics

On an individual level, direct participation in intercollegiate athletics as a student-athlete has exhibited mixed results regarding the student's campus experience, with no significant influence upon cognitive development (Pascarella, Bohr, Nora, & Terenzini, 1995; Terenzini, Pascarella, & Blimling, 1996), or time spent studying or attending class (Richards & Aries, 1999). Still, evidence supports the notion that student-athletes have been shown to display greater levels of academic engagement (Umbach, Palmer, Kuh, & Hannah, 2006), in addition to graduating at higher levels (Ferris, Finster, & McDonald, 2004). There also exist numerous studies assessing the relationship between sport participation as an athlete in college upon such outcomes as cognition (Pascarella, Bohr, Nora, & Terenzini, 1995) and college adjustment (Melendez, 2006). Conclusive evidence regarding the impact of sport participation upon one's academic and social integration remains tentative, however, as student-athletes have also failed to develop a long-term commitment to goals such as degree completion (Hyatt, 2003). Still, recent evidence indicates that student-athletes, in general, identify with the university at a significantly-greater level than their non-athlete counterparts (Clopton, 2008a). Such a finding is noteworthy, as university identity suggests athletics' potential to connect its participants with the overall campus community. This notion had been refuted in previous literature where significant division exists between perceptions and social worlds of students and student-athletes (Adler & Adler, 1991; Knapp, Rasmussen, & Barnhart, 2001).

In relation to these student-athletes and their social networks and trust perceptions, or social capital, Wolf-Wendel, Toma, & Morphew, (2001) found that athletes exhibited a strong sense of community, displaying such elements of community as sharing a common goal, engaging in intense and frequent interaction, and sharing adversity. This sense of community of student-athletes was also analyzed most recently by Clopton (2010), where student-athletes displayed significantly greater amounts of perceived sense of community within their college environment. This was, however, specific to the level of competition when the overall responses were disaggregated by level of competition. Athletes at the NCAA Divisions I and III reported higher amounts of sense of community than their non-athlete student counterparts. No differences were found at the NCAA Division II or NAIA levels (Clopton, in review). This ability to enhance community through athletics participation is even more notable as this is done in a markedly diverse population (Wolf-Wendel et al.) where diversity often weakens the sense of community within a group if not handled properly (Milem, 2003). Furthermore, current results are mixed on the division of race and athlete status in an intercollegiate athletic setting. While Brown et al. (2003) uncovered no problematic presence of racial or ethnic discrimination among White and African American athletes, African American athletes have reported being treated differently than their White counterparts (Singer, 2005). This treatment existed as a manifestation of racism within higher education and college sport programs in the United States. Such differences have also resonated across African American and White student-athlete interaction with faculty (Comeaux & Harrison, 2007) and within students' perceptions of African American athletes on campus (Harrison & Lawrence, 2004). Recently, Melendez (2008) noted that Black male student-athletes felt isolated, rejected, and distrustful of both their Black and White classmates and teammates. They also felt unfairly judged by the campus community which negatively influenced their educational experiences. Because of this, extant literature has examined the role that college athletics participation plays into the construction of the college social experiences of student-athletes. A tremendous amount of weight is placed upon athlete status in the social worlds of many members of underrepresented groups (e.g., Thompson, Neville, Weathers, Poston, & Atkinson, 1990). It is because of this, in large part, that recent research unveiled a significant difference between the role that race shapes the student-athlete experience on campus. Clopton (2011a) showed that white and black student-athletes report significantly different levels of social capital within the overall university context, yet this difference did not exist when examined within the team setting alone. Such a finding reiterated the potentially-divided campus in terms of treatment (Singer, 2005), faculty interaction (Comeaux & Harrison, 2007), and perceptions (Harrison & Lawrence, 2004). Distinct divisions have also been found in the perception of intercollegiate athletics, divisions that permeate all of higher education between athletes (Mahony, Riemer, Breeding, & Hums, 2006), athletes and non-athletes (Knapp, Rasmussen, & Barnhart, 2001), athletes and faculty (Engstrom, Sedlacek, & McEwen, 1995), and non-athletes and faculty (Trail & Chelladurai, 2000). A significant divide exists between faculty and the student body over the perceptions of goals, processes, and priorities of intercollegiate athletics programs (Trail & Chelladurai, 2000). It is also noteworthy that some faculty members have been found to harbor resentment and prejudicial attitudes towards athletes in both big-time college athletics (Engstrom, Sedlacek, & McEwen, 1995) and at lower divisions such as the NCAA Division II level (Baucom & Lantz, 2001). This may potentially exacerbate differences in culture surrounding today's student-athlete (Simons, Bosworth, Fujita, & Jensen, 2007) and could serve as a potential barrier to a campus climate connected through a sense of community (McDonald et al., 2002; Strange & Banning, 2001). This division in perceptions has also been found in attitudes of organizational justice (Mahony et al., 2006), purpose of sport (Finkenberg & Moode, 1996), social presence (Curry, Rehm, & Bernuth, 1997), and student-athlete culture (Nishimoto, 1997). Recently, while student-athletes were found to perceive a greater impact of athletics upon the campus community, athlete status also played a significant role in predicting one's perception of the place of athletics within the campus community (Clopton, 2008b). Such a division in perceptions has great potential to further divide today's campus community, one that already challenges institutions in creating a campus culture that is conducive to producing beneficial academic and social outcomes. It may be this division that contributes to previous findings where athletes have experienced negative stereotyping and prejudicial attitudes from their non-athlete counterparts (e.g., Engstrom & Sedlacek, 1991, 1993).

Indirect Connections with Athletics

Regarding the actual number of individuals connecting with intercollegiate athletics on campus, the overwhelming majority occur through the indirect consumption of college sport. Much of the work done in this area of study incorporates fan or team identity (i.e. the extent to which students identify with the athletics teams on campus) as the conduit of attachment and various aspects of athletics as the actual point of attachment to which campus stakeholders connect or identify. Individuals following a team can identify with numerous elements of the sport environment (Trail et al., 2003). Past research has indicated students as fans may feel a sense of attachment to their university (Van Leeuwen, Quick, & Daniel, 2002), the actual sport played by their school's particular team (Hill & Green, 2000), or the individual athletes on the team (Mahony, Nakazawa, Funk, James, & Gladden, 2002). Points of attachment and motives are interrelated in that, for example, the motives of aesthetics and drama are not significantly connected to organizational points of attachment, including team, coach, community, university, or players (Trail et al., 2003). Vicarious achievement, for example, has been particularly connected to most organizational points of attachment as fans at the NCAA Division I level are more likely to be motivated by vicarious achievement than at any other level (Robinson et al., 2005). Because of the unique level of competition played at most NCAA Division I institutions, most college students have never been scholarship athletes, have not had the opportunity to compete on comparable stages, or perform at that level of competition. Thus, by vicariously affiliating with their school's athletics teams these students can derive an extended sense of empowerment and an increase in self-esteem (Robinson et al., 2005). The presence of athletics on campus further impacts those students identifying as fans of the institution's athletics teams, displaying a significant correlation with both overall integration into the university and positive perception of the university (Wann & Robinson, 2002). This connection has also shown that those students connected with their university's athletics teams reported higher grade point averages and graduation rates (Schurr, Wittig, Ruble, & Henriksen, 1993). Most notable, even, was the impact that identifying with the athletics program maintained over the students' sense of community (Clopton, 2008a). In fact, the higher the maintenance of one's team identity, the greater the perceived sense of community on campus. Still, there was no control for university identity and no method for determining the extent to which athletics were perceived to have been connected to this sense of community (Clopton, 2008a). A similar finding resonated in later research, as Clopton and Finch (2010) showed a significant relationship between overall levels of social capital and students' connection with intercollegiate athletics. The results were limited, though, as the respondents' team identification was captured without the use of their overall university identification. This apparent methodological limitation carries a potentially significant impact as university identity is recognized as one of the main points of attachment in intercollegiate athletics (Trail et al., 2003). Thus, while intercollegiate athletics play a major role in shaping the social culture on a college campus in the United States (e.g., Beyer & Hannah, 2000), the value of this impact remains highly contested (Sperber, 2000). For instance, while team identification of college students enhances their perceived sense of community (Clopton, 2008a), questions regarding the value orientation of such a community and the actual benefits derived from this community remain as this team identification has also been found to detract from students' grade point average (Clopton, 2009). Still, the ability of athletics on a college campus to impact overall community and social networks among fans exists in accordance with the findings of previous research on sports fans, community, and social capital (e.g., Palmer & Thompson, 2007). While athletics on a college campus serves as a significant element in the construction of community, past literature also exists analyzing the directional impact of athletics upon the overall university community. In other words, while the presence of athletics on campus might be shown to impact certain features of the campus community, it might not necessarily be beneficial (Toma 1999, 2003). In fact, there seems to be a significant divide between the perceptions that students and student-athletes possess over the presence, worth, and impact of intercollegiate athletics upon higher education (Knapp, Rasmussen, & Barnhart, 2001). Further, like such organizations as fraternities and sororities, a sense of community enhanced by the presence of athletics (amongst either student-athletes or student followers) would be a negative contributor to the campus community if the values central to that group are antithetical to the overall institutional mission (Marsh & Kleitman, 2002). Interestingly, student-athletes have been found to garner higher levels of community than non-student-athletes (Clopton, 2010), yet this research has not examined whether that bonded sense of community unites the student body, rather than mere subgroups of student-athletes. Further research suggests a potential community-building property of sport, yet cautions against the actual community being reinforced where examples, such as the aforementioned Greek system, have been found to enhance a sense of community but detract from the values of the overall campus community like openness, inclusion, and social consciousness (e.g., Cheng, 2004; Marsh & Kleitman, 2002). Little research exists in examining the actual community that is created, or impacted, by the presence of athletics on campus. That is, the question remains whether pursuing the mission of big-time intercollegiate athletics is congruent with the overall mission of these same institutions (Sperber, 2000).

More recent research has brought to light further concern over the value-added potential of intercollegiate athletics over one's university identity as a point of attachment when examining students' social capital as a result. When looking above and beyond the contributions of one's university identity, team identity actually detracts from a college student's reported level of social capital (Clopton, 2011b). This finding was noteworthy on multiple levels, including running counter to the findings of past literature which has clearly indicated that team identity of students within a campus community has positively contributed to myriad social benefits, including integration into the university (Wann & Robinson, 2002), enhanced sense of community (Clopton, 2008a), and overall social capital (Clopton & Finch, 2010). While team identity has a role in many of these outcomes, it can be assumed that it is one's university identity that generates the ultimate impact into leveraging group identity into its derived benefits. Thus, to accurately assess the relationship between college students identifying with their school's athletics teams and their resultant levels of social capital, valid research must include this university identity. And it is this particular finding that sets forth a number of questions raised in the process. Mostly, this study suggested a much more stringent re-examination of the benefits derived from team identity on a college campus. In fact, maintaining a successful, high-profile college sports program has been credited with enhancing the overall public image of the university (Goidel & Hamilton, 2006) and enhancing the public's perceived academic prestige of the university (Lovaglia & Lucas, 2005). Its ability to improve the overall university identity of students is often asserted as one defense for investing in big-time intercollegiate athletics (Sperber, 2000). While identifying with athletics is a real and tangible connection to one aspect of the university, it could be that perhaps its impact may be more in line with the impact of other student programs on campus such as Greek organizations where bonding social capital and sense of community run high. But like Putnam's reference to the dark side of social capital, this bonded community within Greek organizations often reinforces outcomes that run counter to the mission of the overall university, including lacking an openness to diversity (Wells & Corts, 2008) and other antisocial behavior (Caudill et al., 2006). It is, perhaps, that the use of big-time intercollegiate athletics in the United States promotes the bonding among homogeneous networks which results in a significant connection with social capital levels (Clopton & Finch, 2010). However, this bonding social capital might create further divide, or even silos (Ardichvili, Page, & Wentling, 2003), across the campus that serve as barriers to bringing the campus together and promoting the overall campus community.

Furthermore, there is no relationship between athletics' ability to connect students and a student's overall adjustment into the college atmosphere—one aspect of bridging social capital. Past research has posited a positive relationship between team identity and university integration (Wann & Robinson, 2002) and sense of community (Clopton, 2008a); and myriad examples of anecdotal evidence support the assumption (e.g., Toma, 2003) that college sports—through providing a common bond and overall identity—can enhance the social integration, connections, and adjustment of its members. However, there has been no evidence that these connections are anything more than reinforcing a bonding social capital that fails to connect or integrate the college student fan into the broader social fabric of the university. It is this connection with the broader university community that diversifies one's social network and empowers one to "get ahead." It is also this network expansion that affords an individual social mobility, reinforcing Putnam's belief that it is the most important aspect to social capital. For it is the connection of loosely-based, diverse relationships that set apart the most successful communities, organizations, or campuses. Particularly at the university level, fans of spectator sports can range in a wide, disparate demography and these big-time athletics contests have shown the potential to bridge across these diverse identities (see Toma, 2003). This potential, however, might be an ephemeral expression of unity within these communities of sport. While future research in this direction is imperative, it is also essential that these institutions hosting sport—particularly spectator sport teams in any community context—re-examine the actually numerous avenues by which community members connect or identify with their teams. This connection should also be explored to uncover the extent to which there is a reinforcement of the overall community by bridging across diverse identities, or if there is an enclaving of demographies through the use of silos that prohibit the community from becoming unified. Such a finding would echo the long-held sentiment of the divided social worlds of athletics and the university. While students in the large university settings have varied interests that are as diverse as they themselves, not every student would be expected to have their social network enhanced by the presence of the athletics program. However, the budget of typical individual student programs pale in comparison to that of the typical college athletics department and, thus, athletics carries a unique responsibility of representing the student body.

All is not lost, however, regarding the current ability of athletics to contribute to the social sustainability of the college campus. Beyond that of the identity created upon the university itself, identifying with the athletics teams on campus actually enhanced the extent to which these students experience an emotional attachment and affective commitment to the university

(Clopton, in review). Because of this, there might be a measurable, almost palpable, byproduct of being a fan of the athletic teams of one's university that would lead to desired social and academic outcomes, such as turnover, (Meyer et al., 2002) and organizational support (Shore & Wayne, 1993). The connection between team identity and affective commitment to the university also confirms the assumptions on many college campuses regarding the promotion and enhancement of the collegiate experience through maintaining high-profile intercollegiate athletics teams. Because of their viability as a platform, athletics and university administrators must continue to revisit the extent to which intra-university promotion is a part of the athletic experience, through both the game-day experiences and in overall athletic marketing strategies.

However, while there is this sentiment that the athletics connection may parlay into deeper levels of commitment to the university, delineating the responses across level of athletics competition and level of team identity suggests another possible direction. The finding does seem to support the notion of the target similarity framework, though in opposition to the part of the accepted justification for college sport. Specifically, the target similarity framework requires that outcomes and antecedents connected with affective commitment be aligned with the target of commitment. In other words, if athletics of the university are perceived to be in line with the overall and academic missions of the university, then one's team identity would naturally be expected to enhance the affective commitment to the overall university. Research has revealed, though, that only at the NCAA Division I level, and among those students with a high-team identity, was team identity connected with affective commitment (Clopton, 2012). Among students reporting low or moderate levels of team identity at the NCAA Division I level and among all students at NCAA Division II and III levels, no connection existed between team identity and affective commitment. Such a finding is noteworthy as maintaining an athletics program or enhancing one's athletics program, often through the addition of football or through capital projects, is grounded in part upon the assumption that doing so contributes to the overall mission of the university. However, benefits from this connection are contingent upon the extent to which stakeholders—here, students—perceive that this connection exists. At the NCAA Division I level, athletics are high-profile and often fueled with a wealth of resources, and it was anticipated that students identifying with these athletic teams would—most naturally—experience an emotional or affective connection to the overall university through this identification. However, only those students with a strong team identity received any of this spillover from identifying with athletics to feeling additional emotional attachment or affective commitment to the university. The connection between those students most identified with the sports teams at the NCAA Division I level and their affective commitment to the university also appears to align with previous research where groups of high status result in greater affective commitment than that of the other lower status groups (Ellemers et al., 1999). Because of the intensity and public presence at the NCAA Division I level, it is assumed that identifying with the sports teams at this level would be most fashionable and conducive to a higher status.

Still, this finding suggests a significant limitation to the notion that athletics impacts the campus community. While a connection exists between team identity and sense of community (Clopton, 2008) and social capital (Clopton & Finch, 2010), no study has explored the actual extent to which those students identifying with the university's athletics teams received any of these potential beneficial outcomes. Further, this finding also seems to suggest that—perhaps—after the millions of dollars in athletics budget increases over the years, previously-assumed benefits that are derived from the presence of successful, high-profile athletics teams are only manifested in those students with a strong identification. This limitation also runs counter to the blanket assumption that athletics is a medium for uniting and drawing the student body together. Perhaps the student body drawn to athletics is much more limited in scope and heterogeneity than previously assumed.

Similarly, the lack of connection at either the NCAA Division II or III levels suggests there may be little, if any, pro-organizational benefit derived from the existence of athletics among the general student body. Scant research exists on team identification of students at these levels of competition and additional research efforts are strongly recommended before drawing significant conclusions from this finding. Another component to the findings at these levels is the makeup of students and student-athletes, as—particularly at the NCAA Division III level—the percentage of students-athletes in the overall student body is much higher than at the NCAA Division I level.

Some of this same disconnect occurs in the assumed relationship with athletics success and positive perceptions of prestige among the current student body. While previous studies have found evidence that big-time athletics may impact an outsider's views of an institution (Goidel & Hamilton, 2006), more recent research indicates more mixed evidence to suggest that college students (as internal stakeholders) believe that athletics affects outsiders' opinions of their universities (Clopton & Finch, in press). With this, there appears to be a stark difference in perception between those on the "inside" and those "outside" the university community. Of course, the notable aspect to this reality is that universities have multiple points of attachment (Robinson & Trail, 2005), which provide multiple stakeholders an opportunity to shape the "reality" of college athletics. That is, there still exists the potential to use athletics to shape the perceptions of external stakeholders, but a failure to deliver that as a reality when those external perceptions (from prospective students, for example) are not matched by the internal experience.

Notably, when using data from across the country, there is a conspicuous lack of significance of basketball and football success on a university's perceived academic and athletic prestige that seem to suggest that students believe that the general public does not connect big-time athletics and with the quality of the universities academics or athletics overall. However, Director's Cup points, a measure of overall athletic success, is a significant factor (Clopton & Finch, 2012). Success across the spectrum of sports may promote an image of overall excellence and balance, rather than being labeled a "football" or "basketball" school. Similar results were found in research looking at team identity and university identity (Clopton & Finch, 2010). This finding also suggests a reiteration of the presence of a disconnect between big-time athletics and the general student body on campus. When outsiders think about a university, whether the athletic team or the campus, they may see the university as one whole organism, with little delineation between academics and athletics. From the inside, students may more readily observe the differentiation between the academic life on campus and the athletic segment, whether this be athletic segregation in the classroom, separate dorm halls or cafeterias, or separate areas of campus where athletes are isolated from non-athletes.

When addressing the overall perceived external prestige of the university, the overall research now suggests that while numerous benefits are derived from identifying with athletic teams on campus, perhaps some of these may have less impact than previously believed when university identity is controlled for or when compared to outcomes more fully aligned with the direction of the overall university community (e.g., perceived academic prestige and perceived external prestige).

While current students may be affected by their insider view of campus life, it is important to note that perception may still be more important than reality for outside stakeholders, such as fans and potential students (Alves & Raposo, 2010; Kotler & Fox, 1995). Outsiders' views of the quality of the school have been shown to be influenced by successful athletic programs (Lovaglia & Lucas, 2005). Likewise, potential students take into account their brand image of the university, which is also impacted by athletic success or failure (Alves & Raposo). Because of this, several issues arise, including the risks involved with prospective students who have high perceived academic prestige because of successful athletics and may come to school and become a part of a group where athletics does not contribute to academic prestige. Universities may run the risk of luring students to their schools at the expense of potentially jading them later in their academic experience.

Another issue is the role of big-time spectator sports in the collegiate ideal (Toma, 1999). While athletics may yet play an important role in the selection process and social experience on campus, these results may suggest that students may not see big-time, high-profile sports as playing a vital role in an outsider's view of the institution or athletic program overall, or that perceptions of external prestige are particularly salient in their view of the collegiate ideal. From the results here, more questions are raised regarding Albert and Whetton's (1985) dual identity of an organization. The current data suggest no connection between the success of men's basketball and football—the two most high-profile athletics teams in NCAA competition—and perceptions of external academic prestige, which would fall into Albert and Whetton's normative identity of the university. This particular finding runs counter to Toma's (1999, 2003) call for the use of high-profile athletics to enhance members' perceptions of the collegiate ideal. However, where normative identity was the idealistic, pristine image of an organization, the utilitarian identity was more practical and business-like. When athletic prestige is attributed to the utilitarian identity of a university, all measures of athletics success were significantly connected. Such a relationship suggests that students are well aware of the place of athletics within their university and the role athletics has in the overall organization. Notably, however, it will be this awareness of the internal stakeholders that also limits the benefits of athletic success, in that while the academic prestige amongst outsiders can be enhanced through successful athletics (Lovaglia & Lucas, 2005), students do not make that connection.

In my opinion, it is these last two points that must concern higher education and athletics officials the most. If athletics are to continue to represent the college or university as its "front porch" then the front porch needs to be representative of the house upon which it stands. Else, we run the risk of developing a significant amount of "buyer's remorse" for college students and/or their parents as tuition-paying stakeholders who were influenced by the lure of prestige through intercollegiate athletics. While effective examples do exist of universities using successful athletics and championship platforms to convey messages of academics and scholarship, higher education administrators must be vigilant in their awareness of the extent to which intercollegiate athletics is used in developing the university's brand—this through both formal and informal modes of brand development.

In conclusion, the connection between team identification in college sport and beneficial outcomes in the overall academic and social experience—that is, the overall social sustainability—within the university remains tenuous. This indirect connection with a school's athletic teams has been shown to mediate the relationship between university identity and affective commitment. However, it appears that this contribution of team identity may only be limited to those students with a strong identification with the athletics teams in settings where those teams are highly-funded and maintain a high public profile. Further, when viewed on its own merits, the notion of team identity seems to contribute little to students' opportunity to adjust into the campus environment and actually detracts from quality social networks.

From a managerial perspective in higher education, the expectations and assumptions need to be revisited regarding the extent to which college sport is contributing to the overall experience of the general student body. Game day and event programming, marketing strategies, and on-campus promotion would all benefit from analyzing the extent to which the content targets general students and connects all stakeholders to the ideals and mission of the university. Such a move should manifest itself within overall strategic policies for minimizing the extent to which athletics departments are removed from the university culture and fail to capitalize on the unique ability of sport to capture the emotional attachment and affective commitment of its consumers.

References

Adler, P. A., & Adler, P. (1991). *Backboards and blackboards.* New York: Columbia University Press,

Albert, S., & Whetten, D. A. (1985). Organizational identity. In L. L. Cummings & B. M. Staw (Eds.). *Research in organizational behavior, 7,* 263–295. Greenwich, CT: JAI Press.

Alves, H., & Raposo, M. (2010). The influence of university image on student behavior. *International Journal of Educational Management, 24*(1), 73–85.

Anderson, K. S., & Birrer, G. E. (2011). Creating a sustainable competitive advantage: A resource-based analysis of the Gonzaga University men's basketball program. Journal of Sport Administration and Supervision, 3(1), 10–21.

Ardichvili, A., Page, P., & Wentling, T. (2003), Motivation and barriers to participation in virtual knowledge-sharing communities of practice. *Journal of Knowledge Management, 7* (1), 64–77.

Arpan, L.M., Raney, A. A., & Zivnuska, S. (2003). A cognitive approach to understanding university image. *Corporate Communications: An International Journal, 8*(2), 97–113.

Baade, R.A., & Sundberg, J.O. (1996). Fourth down and gold to go? Assessing the link between athletics and alumni giving. *Social Science Quarterly, 77(4),* 789–803.

Baucom, C., & Lantz, C. D. (2001). Faculty attitudes toward male division II student-athletes. *Journal of Sport Behavior, 24,* 265–276.

Beyer, J.M., & Hannah, D.R. (2000). The cultural significance of athletics in U.S. higher education. *Journal of Sport Management, 14(2),* 105–132.

Boyer, E.L. (1987). *College: The undergraduate experience in America.* New York: Harper and Row, Publishers.

Boyer, E.L. (1990). *Campus life: In search of community.* Princeton, NJ: Princeton University Press. The Carnegie Foundation for the Advancement of Teaching.

Brown, T. N., Jackson, J. S., Brown, K. T., Sellers, R. M., Keiper, S., & Manuel, W.J. (2003). "There's no race in the playing field": Perceptions of racial discrimination among white and black athletes. *Journal of Sport and Social Issues, 27*(2), 162–183.

Caudill, B.D., Crosse, S.B., Campbell, B., Howard, J., Luckey, B., & Blane, H.T. (2006). High-risk drinking among college fraternity members: A national perspective. *Journal of American College Health, 55*(3), 141–155.

Cheng, D.X. (2004). Students' sense of campus community: What it means, and what to do about it. *NASPA Journal, 41*(2), 216–234.

Clopton, A.W. (in review). An analysis of the potential of intercollegiate athletics as a medium for organizational commitment to the overall university. Manuscript submitted for publication.

Clopton, A.W. (2008a). College sports on campus: Uncovering the link between fan identification and sense of community. *International Journal of Sport Management, 9*(4), 343–362.

Clopton, A.W. (2008b). From message to messenger? Assessing the impact of athletics on a college campus. *Journal for the Study of Sports and Athletes in Education, 2*(3), 299–320.

Clopton, A.W. (2009). One for the Team: The Impact of Community upon Students as Fans and Academic and Social Integration. *Journal of Issues in Intercollegiate Athletics, Special Issue,* 24–61.

Clopton, A.W. (2010). The impact of intercollegiate athletic participation upon sense of community across multiple levels of competition. *International Journal of Sport Management, 12*(3), 440–456.

Clopton, A.W. (2011a) Examining racial differences in social capital development among college student-athletes. *Journal of African American Studies,15,* 58–73.

Clopton, A.W. (2011b). Social capital goes to college: Examining both the overall and bridging potential of intercollegiate athletics. Manuscript accepted for publication in the *Journal of Intercollegiate Sport, 4*(2), 84–100.

Clopton, A. W. (2012). An analysis of the potential of intercollegiate athletics as a medium for organizational commitment to the overall university. *International Journal of Sport Management, 4* (12), 363-384.

Clopton, A.W., & Bourke, B (in press). Perceptions of the impact of intercollegiate athletics along race and athlete status. Manuscript accepted for publication in the *College Student Affairs Journal.*

Clopton, A. W. & Finch, B. L. (2012). In search of the winning image: Assessing the impact of athletic success on perceptions of external prestige. *Journal of Issues in Intercollegiate Athletics,* 79-95.

Clopton, A.W., & Finch, B. L. (2010). Are college students 'bowling alone'? Examining the contribution of fan identification to the social capital of college students. *Journal of Sport Behavior, 33*(4), 333–366.

College Sports 101, (2009). A primer on money, athletics, and higher education in the 21st century. Report by the Knight Commission on Intercollegiate Athletics. Retrieved from http://www.knightcommission.org/index.php?option=com_content&view=article&id=344&Itemid=84.

Comeaux, E., & Harrison, C. K. (2007). Faculty and male student-athletes: Racial differences in the environmental predictors of academic achievement. *Race, Ethnicity, and Education, 10*(2), 199–214.

Curry, L. A., Rehm, M., & Bernuth, C. (1997). Participation in NCAA division I athletics: Self-perception differences in athletes and nonathletes. *College Student Journal, 31*(1), 96–103.

Daughtrey, C., & Stotlar, D. (2000). Donations: Are they affected by a football championship? *Sport Marketing Quarterly, 9*(4), 185–193.

Dempsey, N., Bramley, G., Power, S., & Brown, C. (2011). The social dimension of sustainable development: Defining urban social sustainability. *Sustainable Development, 19,* 289–300.

Ellemers, N., Kortekaas, P., & Ouwerkerk, J.W. (1999). Self-categorization, commitment to the group and group self-esteem as related but distinct aspects of social identity. *European Journal of Social Psychology, 29,* 371–389.

Engstrom, C. M., & Sedlacek, W. E. (1991). A study of prejudice toward college student-athletes. *Journal of Counseling and Development, 70,* 189–193.

Engstrom, C. M., & Sedlacek, W. E. (1993). Attitudes of residence hall students toward student-athletes: Implications for advising, training, and programming. *Journal of College and University Student Housing, 23,* 28–33.

Engstrom, C. M., Sedlacek, W. E., & McEwen, M. K. (1997). Faculty attitudes toward male revenue and nonrevenue student-athletes. *Journal of College Student Development, 36*(3), 217–227.

Ferris, E., Finster, M., McDonald, D. (2004). Academic fit of student-athletes: An analysis of NCAA Division I-A graduation rates. *Research in Higher Education, 45*(6), 555–575.

Finkelberg, M. E., & Moode, M. F. (1996). College students' perceptions of the purposes of sports. *Perceptual and Motor Skills, 82*(1), 19–22.

Fugazzotto, S.J. (2010). Physical space and the resource-based view of the college. *Innovation in Higher Education, 35,* 245–259.

Fulks, D. L. (2009). 2004–08 NCAA revenues and expenses of Division I intercollegiate athletics programs report. Retrieved from NCAA website: http://www.ncaapublications.com/ productdownloads/RE09.pdf.

Getz, M., & Siegfried, J. (2010). What does intercollegiate athletics do to or for our colleges and universities? Working Paper No. 10–W05, Vanderbilt Department of Economics. Retrieved from http://vanderbilt.edu/econ/wparchive/workpaper/vu10–w05.pdf.

Goidel, R. K., & Hamilton, J. M. (2006). Strengthening higher education through gridiron success? Public perceptions of the impact of national football championships on academic quality. *Social Science Quarterly, 87*(4), 851–862.

Harrison, C. K., & Lawrence, S. M. (2004). College students' perceptions, myths, and stereotypes about African American athleticism: A qualitative investigation. *Sport, Education, and Society, 9*(1), 33–52.

Hill, B., & Green, B. C. (2000). Repeat attendance as a function of involvement, loyalty, and the sportscape across three football contexts. *Sport Management Review, 3,* 145–162

Hyatt, R. (2003). Barriers to persistence among African-American intercollegiate athletes: A literature review of non-cognitive variables. *College Student Journal, 37,* 260–275.

Johnson, G. (2010). CBS, Turner break new ground in partnership. The NCAA News. Retrieved from NCAA website: http://www.ncaa.org/wps/portal/newsdetail?WCM _GLOBAL_CONTEXT=/wps/wcm/connect/

ncaa/NCAA/NCAA+News/NCAA+News+Online/2010/Asociation-wide/CBS%2C+Turner+break+new+ground+in+partnership

Knapp, T. J., Rasmussen, C., & Barnhart, R. K. (2001). What college students say about intercollegiate athletics: A survey of attitudes and beliefs. *College Student Journal, 35*(1), 96–100.

Kotler, P., & Fox, K. (1995). *Strategic Marketing for Educational Institutions*, 2nd ed. Englewood Cliffs, NJ: Prentice Hall.

Levine, A., & Cureton, J. (1998). Collegiate life: An obituary. *Change: The Magazine of Higher Learning, 30*(3), 12–17.

Lovaglia, M. J., & Lucas, J. W. (2005). High-visibility athletic programs and the prestige of public universities. *The Sport Journal, 8(1).*

Mahony, D. F., Nakazawa, M., Funk, D. C., James, J. D., Gladden, J. M. (2002). Motivational factors influencing behavior of J. League spectators. *Sport Management Review, 5,* 1–24.

Mahony, D. F., Riemer, H. A., Breeding, J. L., & Hums, M. A. (2006). Organizational justice in sport organizations: Perceptions of college athletes and other college students. *Journal of Sport Management, 20,* 159–188.

Marsh, H. W., & Kleitman, S. (2002). Extracurricular school activities: The good, the bad, the nonlinear. *Harvard Education Review, 72,* 464–514.

McCormick, R. E., & Tinsley, M. (1987). Athletics versus cademics? Evidence from SAT scores." *Journal of Political Economy, 95*(5), 1103–16.

McDonald, W. M., & Associates. (2002). *Creating campus community: In search of Ernest Boyer's legacy*. Jossey-Bass. San Francisco, CA.

Melendez, M. C. (2006). The influence of athletic participation on the college adjustment of freshmen and sophomore student athletes. *Journal of College Student Retention, 8,* 39–55.

Melendez, M. C. (2008). Black football players on a predominantly White college campus: Psychosocial and emotional realities of the Black college athlete experience. *Journal of Black Psychology, 34,* 423–451.

Meyer, J. P., Stanley, D. J., Herscovitch, L., & Topolnytsky, L. (2002). Affective, continuance, and normative commitment to the organization: A meta-analysis of antecedents, correlates, and consequences. *Journal of Vocational Behavior, 61,* 20–52.

Milem, J. (2003). The educational benefits of diversity: Evidence from multiple sectors. In Chang, M., Witt, D., Jones, J., & Hakuta, K. (Eds). *Compelling interest: Examining the evidence on racial dynamics in higher education*. Stanford, CA: Stanford University Press.

Mixon, F. G., Trevino, L. J., & Minto, T. C. (2004). Touchdowns and test scores: exploring the relationship between athletics and academics. *Applied Economics Letters, 11*(7), 421–424.

Nishimoto, P. A. (1997). Touchdowns and term papers: Telescoping the college student-athlete culture. *College Student Affairs Journal, 16*(2), 96–103.

O'Dwyer, B., & D. Owen (2005). Assurance Statement Practice in Environmental, Social and Sustainability Reporting: A Critical Evaluation. *The British Accounting Review,* 37, 205–229.

Office of the Deputy Prime Minister (ODPM). 2006. *UK Presidency: EU Ministerial Informal on Sustainable Communities Policy Papers*. ODPM: London.

Palmer, C. & Thompson, K. (2007). The paradoxes of football spectatorship: On-field and online expressions of social capital among the "Grog Squad." *Sociology of Sport Journal,* 24 (2), 187-205.

Pascarella, E. T., Bohr, L., Nora, A., & Terenzini, P. T. (1995). Intercollegiate athletic participation and freshmen-year cognitive outcomes. *The Journal of Higher Education,* 66, 369–387.

Putnam, R. D. (2000). *Bowling Alone: The collapse and revival of American community*. New York, NY: Simon and Schuster.

Richards, S., & Aries, E. (1999). The division III student-athlete: Academic performance, campus involvement, and growth. *Journal of College Student Development, 40*(3), 211– 218.

Robinson, M. J., & Trail, G. T. (2005). Relationships among spectator gender, motives, points of attachment, and sport preference. *Journal of Sport Management, 19,* 58–80.

Robinson, M. J., Trail, G. T., Dick, R. J., & Gillentine, A. J. (2005). Fans vs. spectators: An analysis of those who attend intercollegiate football games. *Sport Marketing Quarterly, 14,* 43–53.

Rovai, A. (2002). Building Sense of Community at a Distance. *The International Review Of Research In Open And Distance Learning, 3*(1), Article 3.1.6. Retrieved from http://www.irrodl.org/index.php/irrodl/article/view/79/152.

Schurr, K. T., Wittig, A. F., Ruble, V. E., & Henriksen, L. W. (1993). College graduation rates of student athletes and students attending college male basketball games: A case study. *Journal of Sport Behavior, 16,* 33–41.

Shore, L. M., & Wayne, S. J. (1993). Commitment and employee behavior: Comparison of affective and continuance commitment with perceived organizational support. *Journal of Applied Psychology, 78,* 774–780.

Sigelman, L., & Bookheimer, S. (1994) Is it whether you win or lose? Monetary contributions to big—time college athletic programs. *Social Science Quarterly, 12(1),* 347–359.

Simons, H. D., Bosworth, C., Fujita, S., & Jensen, M. (2007). The athlete stigma in higher education. *College Student Journal, 41*(2), 251–273.

Singer, J. N. (2005). Understanding racism through the eyes of African American male student-athletes. *Race, Ethnicity, and Education, 8*(4), 365–386.

Smith, R. (2008). Big-time college basketball and the advertising effect. *Journal of Sports Economics, 9*(4), 387–406.

Sperber, M. (2000). *Beer and circus: How big-time college sports is crippling undergraduate education.* New York: Henry Holt.

Spitzberg Jr., I. J., & Thorndike, V. V. (1992). *Creating community on college campuses.* State University of New York Press. Albany, New York.

Strange, C. C., & Banning, J. H. (2001). *Educating by design: Creating campus learning environments that work.* San Francisco: Jossey-Bass.

Sung, M., & Yang, S. U. (2008). Toward the model of university image: The influence of brand personality, external prestige, and reputation. *Journal of Public Relations Research, 20*(4), 357–376.

Terenzini, P. T., Pascarella, E. P., & Blimling, (1996). Students' out-of-class experiences and their influence on learning and cognitive Development: A literature review. *Journal of College Student Development, 37,* 149–162.

Thompson, C. E., Neville, H., Weathers, P. L., Poston, W. C., & Atkinson, D. R. (1990). Cultural mistrust and racism reaction among African-American students. *Journal of College Student Development, 31,* 162–168.

Toma, J. D. (1999). The collegiate ideal and the tools of external relations: The uses of high-profile intercollegiate athletics. *New Directions for Higher Education, 105,* 81–90.

Toma, J. D. (2003). *Football u: Spectator sports in the life of the American university.* The University of Michigan Press; Ann Arbor, Michigan.

Toma, J. D., & Cross, M. E. (1998). Intercollegiate athletics and student college choice: Exploring the impact of championship seasons on undergraduate applications. *Research in Higher Education, 39*(6), 633–646.

Trail, G., & Chelladurai, P. (2000). Perceptions of goals and processes of intercollegiate athletics: A case study. *Journal of Sport Management, 14,* 154–178.

Trail, G. T., Robinson, M. J., Dick, R. J., & Gillentine, A. J. (2003). Motives and points of attachment: Fans versus spectators in intercollegiate athletics. *Sport Marketing Quarterly, 12*(4), 217–227.

Umbach, P. D., Palmer, M. M., Kuh, G. D., & Hannah, S. J. (2006). Intercollegiate athletics and effective educational practices: Winning combination or losing effort? *Research in Higher Education, 47*(6), 709–733.

Van Leeuwen, L., Quick, S., & Daniel, K. (2002). The Sport Spectator Satisfaction Model: A conceptual framework for understanding the satisfaction of spectators. *Sport Management Review, 5,* 99–128.

Wann, D. L., & Robinson, T. N. III (2002). The relationship between sport team identification and integration into and perceptions of a university. *International Sports Journal, 6*(1), 36–44.

Wells, B., & Corts, D. P. (2008). Measuring of attitudes towards sorority and fraternity members: Indication of implicit, ingroup favoritism. *College Student Journal, 42*(3), 842–846.

Wolf-Wendel, L. E., Toma, J. D., Morphew, C. C. (2001). How much difference is too much difference? Perceptions of gay men and lesbians in intercollegiate athletics. *Journal of College Student Development, 42*(5), 465–479.

PART TWO

Faculty: Changing Roles in Today's World

CHAPTER NINE

First-Year Composition's Correlation with Undergraduate Education Aspirations

Culture Building and the Work of Good Teachers to Fight Minimalism (or Mediocrity?)

DAN BAUER

> We've lived with things abnormal for so long, we've gotten used to them and think them normal. Let us characterize slavery as all those things that keep us from being joyous.
> —Famed Old Testament theologian Walter Brueggemann

If we reflect on the roles of actual teaching and learning in academia, very few courses align across institutions in ubiquity. But within this elite cornucopia, surely first-year composition courses lead the trend toward unanimity—a course that in fact largely offers a microcosm of the very history of colleges and universities in this country. Certainly "process" pedagogy had a huge impact on composition course design and delivery beginning in the late 1970s and '80s (though probably less so in institutions with large populations of students in need of "remedial" courses, where too often drills in mechanical correctness still predominate, though discredited by research). Yet, despite whatever positive advancement has been made toward a more progressive and epistemologically richer practice inspired by the visionary influence of scholars like Donald Murray, James Berlin, Cynthia Selfe and countless others, still significant aspects of the course(s) have continued intact since the earliest development of higher education in the United States—and perhaps even further. In fact, beginning in 1971, Edward P. J. Corbett's influential *Classical Rhetoric for the Modern Student* (from the prestigious Oxford University Press) sought to take the course design back to much earlier roots. The most recent edition of the book, its fourth, was co-authored by Robert Connors, who at its debut in 1998 was part of the faculty at the University of New Hampshire—a veritable ground zero for esteemed composition scholarship and practice. And in the resulting wake that has followed, countless other composition scholars have likewise made links back to classical rhetoric, thereby compacting vast historical distance into an affinity. But with the exception of "process" pedagogy in which student idiosyncrasies garner much consideration, most of composition's history—including emphasis on classical ancestry—has focused on uniform methods, course content, and a teacher-centered emphasis. Course outcomes based on each individual student's intellectual growth receive scant attention. Likewise, only a few scholars have examined the context of faculty decision-making, which could lead to an embrace of a more sophisticated practice based in a much more robust concern for critical thinking rather than just completion of assignments and the course. Unfortunately, most of the first-year writing enterprises at many institutions have resulted in too many courses focused only on minimal achievements, without rich assessment and reflection on how the course(s) might impart more substantial leaps in student engagement and intellectual stamina. This chapter aims to explore paths to reversing those tragic and mediocre trends.

A case in point helps to illustrate this phenomenon. Over the past several years, my own institution has worked to revise our core curriculum in such a way that we distinguish ourselves from the other 34 schools in the University System of Georgia (USG), with the development of a unique core that still allows students to transfer between institutions but that also provides a "distinctive" divergence in a way befitting our public liberal arts mission. This hybrid model pays homage to the teaching and student-centered focus of private liberal arts colleges that has been adopted by the 26 public colleges and universities in 24 states and one Canadian province that comprise the Council of Public Liberal Arts Colleges (COPLAC). Both our old and new cores have five areas (consistent with the USG); the old core lumped first-year composition courses with entry-level math courses under a subheading designated as "basic skills." Of course, this ideology reinforces a notion that composition has little affinity with higher-order complex thinking. Rather, like handwriting, spelling, manners, tying one's shoes, and even rudimentary math functions, this conceptualization suggests that composition is seemingly the end result of rote learning and is a mere prerequisite or hoop to be navigated before one progresses to "real" academic work. Unfortunately, the newest revised core furthers this oversimplification. Now, with math courses removed to a different core area, the new subgroup identified as "communication skills" contains only the two first-year composition courses, with a painfully low-brow outcome more consistent with community colleges than with rigorous or prestigious private liberal arts institutions: "Students will be able to communicate clearly in oral and written English that meets conventional standards of correctness" (see http://catalog. gcsu.edu/ugrad/core-curriculum.htm). When in a public forum debuting the new core, I asked the chair of the faculty committee in charge of these revisions why no emphasis was placed upon characteristics of intellectual rigor such as synthesis of multiple disciplines or vantage points, depth or substance of inquiry, precision of language, resourcefulness of research, degree of perception, or any other similar high-level disposition, I was told, "There's no way to assess those concerns." Ouch. But really? And if so, how do we in this crude outcome assess whether or not a student text communicates "clearly"?

Don't institutions promise to do more than exhibit such low ambition? The very heart of research so rewarded in academia seemingly seeks to make possible what was previously impossible. But to continue to describe composition as merely "communication" suggests a tired, linear, two-part transaction. In fact, the prose in every chapter of this book likely has little to do with "communication" and much more to do with discovery, with solving difficult intellectual problems, and with complex understanding—not just developing vehicles of mere delivery to an audience (and I'm certain our generous editor exhibited a far more sophisticated desire than just conformity to "conventional standards of correctness"). I'd like to think that the intellectual seriousness that's good for us as writers and readers is also good for our students. But to be content with my institution's new core as written certainly suggests low expectations of both students and faculty. Furthermore, the conceptualization of writing as "communication" seems far too external, with too little room for emphasizing the need to expand the internal, intellectual benefits that accrue as a result of a rich composing process that arises out of an enterprise founded on the social construction of knowledge. Unfortunately, countless other institutions have strikingly similar outcomes statements that seem far more fitting for the 1930s than for the 21st century so mediated by technology, research, cultural studies, and accountability.

In her brilliant book *To Understand: New Horizons in Reading Comprehension*, Ellin Oliver Keene (2008) works to answer a haunting question posed by her husband in response to her dramatic excitement over occasional breakthrough deep learning among her fifth and sixth graders. He asked, "Why don't they do that *every day?*" (p. 20). In some candid soul-searching that follows, she makes a confession that certainly has accord with several of my most talented colleagues: "The truth is that they didn't think at high levels every day because I didn't expect them to" (p. 21). In the chapters that follow, Keene doesn't offer prescriptions nor does she oversimplify how teachers might accomplish more, but she does offer a laser-beam focus on how we as teachers might achieve "fervent learning" in our students. I would certainly ask the same thing with regard to first-year writing, particularly to department chairs who do little to highlight the learning of first-year students in introductory writing courses as central to the department's accomplishments. But in researching some of the most accomplished and visionary composition scholars and program directors, their university websites say very little about their tireless work to build first-year writing programs that unapologetically and boldly go far beyond concern with mere "communication" and instead center on instilling firm intellectual prowess in students. I speak of people like Chris Gallagher at Northeastern University, Richard E. Miller and Kurt Spellmeyer at Rutgers University, David Bartholomae and Anthony R. Petrosky at the University of Pittsburgh, Kathleen Blake Yancey at Florida State, Alfred Tatum at the University of Illinois at Chicago, Linda Christensen at Lewis and Clark College, Derek Owens at St. John's University in New York City, Glynda Hull at UC Berkeley, Jeffry Wilhelm at Boise State, or Thomas Newkirk and Donald Graves at the University of New Hampshire. Unfortunately, this list of "exceptions" to the rule contains so few names that one must wonder seriously about the gravity of our desire to achieve real accomplishments in first-year writing. But I do not consider desire for "fervent learning" as exceptional; I'd like to think it's something that all of us in academia *should* embrace; I'd like to think that what we truly value is reflected in what we assess, discuss, and put on university websites.

In the wake of dull recall inculcated by high-stakes tests at the pre-college level, and the ever-growing pattern of university administrators who opt to replace full-time tenure-bearing lines with part-time positions that lack health care and other benefits—as well as any hope of tenure, one must wonder: will teachers *ever* again feel they have any abundance of stability, rigor, and choices? Aside from the joys of success that teachers have with individual students, school dollars seemingly proliferate for a growing number of non-instructional outlays (my campus seems to have a contest to see if it can spend more dollars on golf carts that clog the sidewalks, on an overgrown retinue of time-consuming procedures that impose rigid bureaucracy, and a new controversial yet monstrously overpriced "wellness center" with an ugly flat roof straight out of the 1960s) and which will cost each student more than $300 in additional fees each semester for more than thirty years. Will teaching and learning ever eclipse athletics, simple branding, or publishing as the primary value of our institutions of "higher" education? As the revenue flow continues to buy goods other than teachers' acts of inspiration and dedication to students' encounters with burgeoning complex ideas, one must wonder about the joy that *could* reside in our educational institutions. Yet against this backdrop of the possible, one must also wonder if rather than choice and autonomy, teachers will continue to feel only pressure to conform to top-down mandates and less-than-ideal working conditions where intellectual rigor and nurture of students faces sacrifice to efficiency and simplistic number scores decontextualized from the complexity of the differentiated classroom where enthusiasm and curiosity should form the measure of educational excellence. In our current educational climate, do teachers and students feel more liberation and impassioned zeal for ideas, or do they instead languish in mediocrity and isolated drudgery that conforms to the kind of tragic enslavement encapsulated in this chapter's epigraph by theologian Walter Brueggemann?

Those of us who have devoted our lives to work in institutions, especially educational institutions, know well that a glaring disconnect can grow between what the institution says and what it actually does. Perhaps the role of any good teacher involves serving as an institutional conscience, or even a mirror, thereby revealing the institution's image as it actually should be viewed. Just as Oscar Wilde's fictional Dorian Gray's *real* image lurked in his closet and not in the strikingly beautiful façade he allowed the public to see, good writing teachers help their students to see beyond surfaces to recalcitrant, hidden, and not-so-obvious insights. In other words, on top of offering candid yet supportive commentary to all those papers that forever haunt our days, so perhaps must we offer our carefully honed powers of perception back to our employers. What price do our students and untenured or non-tenurable colleagues pay if those of us with the perks of tenure and stability opt not to speak truth to the powers that silence what the renowned paleontologist and gifted essayist Stephen Jay Gould termed "nasty little facts"?

During my last year of a five-year stint as leader of my institution's first-year writing program, 1101 students enrolled in 47 different sections of English 1101 (ah, what a fitting coincidence), my institution's required first-semester writing course and the only course in the entire "core" curriculum that requires at least a "C"—not just a passing grade—to satisfy graduation requirements. Another 117 students enrolled in five sections of English 1102 that term. While my institution prides itself on its title as "Georgia's public liberal arts university" class size for these sections seems anything but impressive, anything but "elite" anything but nurturing: since before 2003 the institution has had a "cap" of 22 yet a consistent average of 23. 4 students per section in both courses. Never mind that the best-known and most respected professional organization in the discipline, The National Council of Teachers of English (NCTE), sets 20 as an absolute maximum class size for a composition course (and 15 as an ideal for all writing classes and 15 as an absolute maximum for remedial courses). Never mind that the NCTE website quotes John C. Maxwell, a prolific author of a large number of books on leadership:

No football coach in his right mind would try to teach 150 players one hour per day and hope to win the game on Friday night. No, the team is limited to 40 or 50 highly motivated players, and the coach has three or four assistants to work on the many skills needed to play the game. The "student–teacher" ratio is maybe 15:1. But the English teacher—all alone—has 150 "players" of the game of composition (not to mention literature, language, and the teaching of other matters dropped into the English curriculum by unthinking enthusiasts).

In a similar tragic truth, 30 different faculty members taught those 52 sections. But of those 30 faculty members, only two are tenured or tenure-track faculty with terminal degrees (most semesters I was the only such full faculty member involved with teaching first-year composition, and during that semester, the fall of 2007, just one other "full" faculty colleague and I taught a total of just two sections, one each, or just under 4% of the total course load); approximately 90% of the sections were taught by graduate students, temporary instructors, or part-time instructors. Subtracting the two "full" faculty members from the first-year writing faculty of 30, one should note that in contrast to the 28 contingent composition faculty, just 17 "full" faculty members existed in English in the fall of 2007. In other words, nearly 61% of the faculty teaching English courses did so on a conditional and unstable basis. While my institution and many like it make bold claims about the kind of nourishing education offered, with regard to first-year composition, our performance seems more like fast-food than gourmet or even full-service fare. Unfortunately, this cost-cutting, low-quality Wal-Mart pattern represents the norm at public universities (top-tier "research" institutions like the USG's flagship University of Georgia would likely have an even smaller percentage of full tenure-track faculty involved in teaching first-year core composition). Those numbers have continued in a similar trend each semester since 2007.

So what? One could argue with good evidence that quality instruction happens because far fewer than 2% of students withdraw from the first-year writing courses. As a measure of the breadth of this success and persistence, I should note that during the semester in question, 62% of all my institution's students who enrolled in undergraduate English courses were enrolled in first-year composition courses. In contrast to the 1.1% withdrawal rate from composition courses, one non-composition instructor in English regularly had a withdrawal rate of 20–30% (imagine the implications if everyone had this same excessive withdrawal rate); this pattern became a major irritation for many of us because of the damage this instructor inflicted upon the psyches of the unlucky students enrolled in that instructor's courses. After much pleading by concerned faculty, an excellent former chair at least had the foresight to "ban" this instructor from teaching first-year writing courses. High rates of discontent likewise exist in other disciplines: 8.7% of students enrolled in first-year history courses withdrew during the same term, 14.1% of students did likewise from first-year math courses, 5.5% withdrew from first-year biology courses, 12% withdrew from first-year chemistry courses, and 7.2% withdrew from the introductory economics courses (though they are offered at the sophomore level). The mostly part-time contingent teachers of first-year writing courses, many of them first-time teachers, display enthusiasm, collegiality, and responsiveness to best-practices research emphasized in training and orientation sessions. We thus see substantiation of a good program, don't we?

This question exposes the *real* work of any decent assessment program, for its answer remains mixed and equivocal. Yes, some qualities of excellence emerge in the dedication and initiative of this lower-tier faculty who often agree to overfill their classes (often with the hope that such overextending will merit further employment in this uncertain environment without the perks of tenure, a decent salary, or even acknowledgment that this "work" represents the most visible "majority" of work accomplished by English "faculty"). Where this provisional faculty succeeds, the institution fails. Despite years of budget cuts, expenditures for non-instructional resources still flourish, yet visible commitment to quality instruction for the first-year writing program remains shaky at best. You see, like most institutions, my institution's actions suggest that merely finding instructors to "cover" the classes equals good practice. Notice how the language often used here to describe teaching reveals mediocrity and even contempt for the importance of composition to the liberal arts mission and as a foundation for intellectual achievement. And while this kind of minimalistic language can work its way unknowingly into utterances (and thus betray *real* allegiances or lack thereof), sometimes it also signals the difficult multi-tasking that even the best chairs do face at times. Probably the most talented chair I have ever worked for (now a provost at another institution) once spoke in a department faculty meeting of his difficulty finding enough adjuncts to teach first-year writing courses; he joked, "I only have two qualifications I must fulfill—a degree and a pulse, and I'm negotiable on the pulse." Of course, we all laughed and empathized with his plight, but his humor still reveals the seriousness placed (or not) on first-year writing.

One of my greatest professional honors is to work each day alongside the wisest, most generous, most accomplished colleague I'll likely ever know—the honorable Dr. John H. Lounsbury, one of our country's most unsung educational heroes (though my institution's College of Education bears his name in testament to his immense influence). As one of the four most important founders of the middle school concept (beginning in the 1950s), he understood the seminal role of these important years in the overall psychological, social, mental, and physical development of young adolescents. As a result of his tireless advocacy, junior highs slowly gave way to something different—to institutions not simply devoted to the inculcation of "subjects" but rather as organizations wholly dedicated to the multi-faceted developmentally responsive concerns for the needs of "the whole child." And as a result of the recognition of this crucial epoch in the lives of adolescents both in and out of school, he helped lead a fundamental revolution in teacher preparation. Armed with the full knowledge of the ways that school design and structure impacts healthy human development, he also helped cultivate a movement of teacher specialization in support of middle-level learners. Rather than training just "primary" and "secondary" teachers who by accident might end up teaching fourth through eighth graders as a second choice, he helped pioneer intentional programs where teacher candidates emerged fully prepared and devoted to this important age group in the "middle." Even Laura Bush recognizes the importance of this time in the lives of youth. While her husband's educational policies have dramatically transformed our schools into barren testing factories devoid of differentiation, nurture, or concern for individual needs (thereby doing profound damage to the overall quality of teaching, learning, curiosity, and activation of background knowledge necessary for real learning), Mrs. Bush has recently embarked on a "Middle School Matters" outreach (Stengle, 2011) specifically centered on some 11 elements of success. Set for implementation in 10–15 schools initially, the program even includes emphasis on generating family and community support. But most surprising in this positive step away from an obsession with tests as a sole measure of success is Mrs. Bush's keen understanding of the complex implications of this developmental stage; she commented, "We know now from research that a lot of kids who drop out in high school really drop out in middle school. They just leave in high school" (Stengle, 2011).

We know that first-year writing as a precise part of the overall first-year experience of college students occupies a nearly parallel decisive time of transition in the lives of young adults. Quite simply, not unlike middle school, a college or university's environment has far-ranging repercussions for the overall success and well-being of its students, particularly with regard to first-year writing programs, which foster habits of mind that can significantly foster and/or seriously hinder successive intellectual pursuits, depending on what I have come to label the degree of "intellectual ambition" inherent in each particular student's overall experience. Programs that divorce writing from thinking and instead conceptualize it as a mere "skill" do hefty damage at a time when a student's emergent intellectual character is most susceptible to influence. Furthermore, not unlike the old "junior high" model, many teachers of first-year writing don't arrive there intentionally. Rather, as an accident or second-choice they take jobs teaching such courses because top-tier tenure-track jobs are not available. Or they need assistantships to make graduate school affordable, but their teaching comes secondary to their own coursework (or as a means to "graduate" to some higher-esteemed position).

For our students, first-year writing programs also forge sentiments and behavior that go beyond cerebral proficiency (or the lack thereof). Similar to concerns raised across the nation, the state of Georgia has begun to pay close attention to completion rates and retention rates as a measure of excellence for its state institutions of higher education. In an extensive "predictive model" developed for my institution through a lengthy consultation with consultants Noel-Levitz, we found that the grade students earn in first-year writing forms one of the most accurate predictors of persistence by first-year students. We know, for example, that students who earn an "A" or "B" in first-year writing courses have an 86% chance of staying at the institution for a second year, but those who earn a "C" or "D" have a significantly lower persistence rate (74% and 76%, respectively). Those who earn an "F" or a "W" have a persistence rate of only 47% (Herr, 2005, p. 38). But my own experience of nearly 20 years in the profession suggests that while the grade indeed carries with it powerful implications, the overall depth and breadth of the learning experience also has important ramifications.

A yet unpublished qualitative assessment of my institution's first-year writing program over a three-year period has yielded substantial insights into the contexts that impact the learning processes fostered by the teachers in our program. One student in a section I taught offered an anonymous, impromptu reflection that illustrates my grandest hopes for what a successful course *could* achieve:

> This class did not teach me much about sentence structure or verb tenses. This class was more like a three-month-long brainstorming session. The fact that we were allowed to have huge discussions that hardly ever stayed on topic gave me more paper ideas than any other pre-writing activity I've ever tried. This happened because the discussions were about issues that were present in my life. Because I could relate to the topics, I found myself thinking about our class discussions as I was walking to Saga, climbing the stairs, or brushing my teeth.

This student's learning clearly extended beyond the classroom and beyond the 75 minutes allotted to each class period. While some might see this student seemingly critiquing "discussions that hardly ever stayed on topic" I would argue for an opposite reading. Indeed, this emergent design for discussion clearly fueled the intensity of rich intellectual engagement that had long-lasting effects upon this student, absorbing the student in reflection that embodies the kind of "fervent learning" envisioned by Ellin Oliver Keene. This student continued:

> Although the discussions were my favorite part of the class, I can't deny that the papers were also important. Because you expected so much of us, I worked harder on these four papers than I have worked on a paper in years. To be quite honest, I actually found this quite annoying. "Why on Earth do I care so much about a paper for a freshman English class" I'd mentally complain. The class would have been much easier if I hadn't cared.

I have no way of connecting this commentary with any specific student. The research design I chose for this assessment demanded this anonymity as an investment in hopes for candor of the most sincere kind. Finally, the student also made the following observation:

> Yet the reason I was so deeply concerned with my papers is because I knew my work would be appreciated. In our office conferences you offered compliments along with criticism and showed genuine concern for not only my paper, but also my ideas. Even the written comments on the paper conveyed this message. I wanted to work hard because I knew you would appreciate and recognize my efforts. This review process also helped me figure out some of my weaker writing habits. My most prominent habit of the semester was asking a unique and thought-provoking question and then leaving it unanswered. By recognizing this flaw, I have been able to strengthen not only my writing but also the quality of my ideas.

In a faculty development presentation on our campus in 2005, Ken Bain (2004) offered a commentary to accompany his book *What the Best College Teachers Do*. Based on countless interviews with countless college students on countless campuses, a large number of students did not have *any* teachers they would term as "excellent." In Bain's view, to have two to three outstanding teachers is luck of the highest order. His research suggests three important acts of successful teachers:

1. We put our students in a place where their existing mental models will not work. They must have an "expectation failure" (where they get surprised that the world is not as orderly as they think).

2. They have to care that their existing mental model will not work (and they have to get beyond just wanting an "A").

3. Emotional support must accompany the challenge we offer.

According to Bain, students who identified exemplary teachers shared one important common variable—the best teachers transformed how students thought about learning and what it means to learn. The students of truly excellent teachers learn if they experience paradigm shifts, and such learning would have sustained effects on how students thought, acted, and even felt.

Despite this rich understanding of writing's connection to thinking, we are still confronted with the overwhelming practice of minimalism with regard to first-year writing. And why does this expediency truly belie excellence? My institution's "Have" faculty (those with tenure, terminal degrees, recognition, small class size, single offices, visibility, autonomy, and agency) versus the "Have Not" composition faculty sadly embodies the kind of "house divided against itself [that] cannot stand" so eloquently described by Lincoln. Just as slavery and Jim Crow stood for too many years, so does the large class size and subcontracted composition workforce increasingly represent an "industry standard" in academia, made all the worse by the expedience of the ever-expanding for-profit sector of higher education. This horrible trend normalizes the kind of contempt for composition's importance that the very best composition programs eschew. In fact, when considering the demerits of this disturbing reality, one may profit by looking to the best book written on the assessment of college composition (both in terms of student writing and whole programs)—Bob Broad's 2003 Utah State University Press gem entitled *What We Really Value*. While my institution may *say* it values composition, Broad's rubric suggests that our actions (and likewise those of many other similar institutions) send a contradictory message.

Too many institutions may be more in the business of granting degrees instead of educating students in momentous and noteworthy ways. Arum and Roksa (2011) do not term limited educational attainment as a "crisis," but they do call attention to burgeoning costs, inequality of learning according to race, and a gap between principles espoused and actual practices: "The end result is that many students are only minimally improving their skills in critical thinking, complex reasoning, and writing" (p. 35). Indeed, these talents should flourish profusely in first-year writing courses, but most teachers of such courses often have only backgrounds in literature or creative writing, not in composition and rhetoric. In fact, in a recent book, Nowacek (2011) argues convincingly that writing programs must do more to facilitate knowledge transfer from one discipline to another. Contingent teachers often have only a singular background in English, with few resources for acquisition of multiple discursive perspectives. In their second-class institutional status, they often lack the "insider knowledge" of not only how to acquire such resources, but the substantial time commitment for doing so. And institutions, in their minimalist mindset of simply "covering" first-year writing sections, tend not to reward this potentially essential professional development. In Nowacek's fifth and final principle for the "recontextualization" utterly vital to a successful writing program, we hear,

> Increasingly in rhetoric and composition, meta-awareness has been seen as the lynchpin of transfer, the sine qua non. Wardle (2007), for example, has concluded that meta-awareness may be one of the most valuable and portable skills students develop in first-year composition. This emphasis on the role of metacognition in transfer resonates with the work on the role of reflection in writing instruction. Kathleen Blake Yancey (1992, 1996), for instance, has convincingly argued that without reflection, the writing portfolio is simply a folder of work; frequent and integrated reflection is a powerful way to facilitate metacognition, allowing students to critically engage with their prior work and knowledge within a new context. (p. 30)

Despite a rich heritage of public education pioneered by John Dewey and his insistence on rigor and his disciple William Heard Kilpatrick's emphasis on student-centered, active learning, Arum and Roksa (2011) report a disturbing trend in their expose of "limited learning" on campuses:

> Indeed while approximately 90 percent of college seniors say they have worked on projects and assignments with classmates inside and outside of the classroom, 50 percent have not written a twenty-page paper, only one-third have taken coursework that "very much" focused on applying or analyzing theories or concepts, and the vast majority spent less than fifteen hours a week studying. . . . Studies rarely gauge the content, depth, or actual learning that takes place in collaborative experiences, thus leaving open the question of whether in practice those experiences are as beneficial for mastering complex skills such as critical thinking, complex reasoning, and writing as they should be. (pp. 132–33)

Unfortunately, too many young teachers have been conditioned with media portrayals of heroic teaching that uncritically oversimplify the myriad subtleties inherent in fervent learning. Indeed, in his chapter, "Finding a Language for Difficulty" (one of his six "principles"), Thomas Newkirk (2009) resists "consistently upbeat success stories" where "the teacher never shows signs of despondency, frustration, anger, impatience, or disappointment" (p. 163). He reminds us, "In some school subcultures, it is even risky (or "being white") to appear to care too much about school performance. Boys, for example, frequently boast about who studied *least* for a test" (p. 164). In fact, as the chapter moves toward a conclusion, he lauds "smallness": "[I]t has always seemed to me that the great teachers are great not because they are constantly engineering revolutions in their classrooms—but because they are *alert* to the small changes, the small victories" (p. 172).

Good formative (not summative) assessment programs adjudicate between successful composition programs and all the rest. But the bulk of my institution's "assessment" of learning consists only of student opinion of instruction surveys (SOS). The instrument used only mentions tests—it does not ask students to evaluate the level of discourse generated by an instructor. Nor does it ask students to reflect on their growth as writers and/or thinkers. This dearth of comprehensive assessment strikes me as highly problematic; yet, like first-year writing programs, it has a high degree of ubiquity across campuses. Donald Graves's thoughtful collection of essays, *Testing Is Not Teaching: What Should Count in Education* (2002), yearns for "assessments that raise standards" though I'm certain that most administrators would argue that if used "correctly" a summative SOS could help to improve teaching and learning. Perhaps. But just as Graves's book title succinctly draws a powerful distinction, so I add a complementary corollary: Assessment is not Accumulation. Or contrary to the pervasive SOS as the "standard" for assessment of college and university teaching and learning, bad assessment *is* just mere accumulation, for it neglects and even obscures the complexity and even contradictions of learning (often through an overly simplistic Likert scale). It makes individuals unrecognizable and reduces them and their heteroglossic, disparate narratives to mere numbers that eliminate unique contexts and divergent experience.

Recently, in watching the conclusion of Simon Cowell's new myth-making show, *X Factor* (I must confess that I've never seen it or *American Idol* ever before and now I know I've not missed anything of value), I was appalled at the utter shallowness of commentary made both by contestants and judges. A few unsophisticated adjectives were repeated over and over; when awarded a $5 million recording contract and a championship, 19–year-old winner Melanie Amaro merely reflected that the journey had been "amazing." Scrupulously devoid of any shred of acumen, insight, perception, or critical analysis, she offered her audience nothing of intellectual worth—no sustained or ambitious attempt to understand deeply. While song has deep roots in poetry and the keen *awareness* inherent in that ardent genre of penetrating astuteness, *X Factor*'s concluding overview shows that those elaborate producers manufacture disguise, not wisdom. I hope the adolescents of a similar age in our first-year writing courses in sharp contrast come through their experiences conversely able to reflect fluently and astutely. I'd like to think that we offer them ample practice in critical thinking befitting our shared enterprise and professed high ideals.

My university has recently added new positions for an "assessment coordinator" in each college, but even though our Southern Association of Colleges and Schools (SACS) accreditation visit approaches quickly, still we have not yet developed any rigorous agenda of assessment, reflection, and long-range study of the efficacy of first-year composition (and by extension, critical thinking and literate practices). I'd like to think that, consistent with the title of this chapter, we have greater "aspirations" so that we indeed collectively model the kind of growth and development we *say* we value in students, or that we suggest we value in first-year writing. In conclusion, I offer here in a brief way the kind of things we should assess, consistent with the ideas presented thus far in this chapter. As a way to help ensure that we do not mislead "students into thinking writing is a generic skill that, once learned, becomes a 'one-size-fits-all' intellectual garb" (Beaufort, 2007, p. 10), we could help to build deep understanding in students of the necessarily intimate connection between writing and thinking with a formative assessment that helps to name the ideals of writing that arise out of a prosperous intellectual milieu. Those ambitious concerns that should guide instruction and curricular work include assessing the following:

- Fervency of learning (Keene, 2008)

- Intricacy of understanding that results

- Depth and breadth of synthesis modeled by the instructor

- Activation of previous learning that results in upgrades of mental models (Bain, 2004)

- Integration and transfer of knowledge across disciplines, including embedded reflection that leads to meta-awareness that leads in turn to interanimation of discourses and the regarding of one linguistic regime through the eyes of another (Nowacek, 2011)

- Emotional support

- Explicit instruction and feedback in the formulation of complex questions

- The possibility of resistance (rather than quashing it)

- Reflection and development of learning beyond the classroom

- Memory's use as not just a "storage unit" but as a foundation for sustained reasoning (Bain, 2004, p. 83).

Any decent first-year writing program should lead to ways to help the good teacher to become a more informed practitioner—where composition and rhetorical theory, textual ownership, and the emerging challenges of new writing and research environments meet the institutional values of best-practices composition pedagogy, assessment aimed at individual intellectual achievement, and long-term rigorous learning that extends beyond any single course. In his remarkable inter-locking cultural biography of four brilliant Catholic intellectual writers (Milledgeville's own Flannery O'Connor, Louisiana novelist Walker Percy, *Catholic Worker* founder Dorothy Day, and Kentucky monk Thomas Merton), Paul Elie (2003) writes: "More than he introduced Merton to particular books or writers, Columbia Professor and famed literary theorist Mark Van Doren emboldened Merton to read the way he read already: with his whole self, his whole life" (p. 80). I'd encourage us to continue to develop formative assessment processes that help us to allow our students get to a kind of writing and reading that embraces the whole learner, as well as exploration, vicarious experience, and complex understanding, NOT just recall that is so emphasized by the current fad culture of high-stakes testing so inherent in the hegemonic high schools from which our undergraduates venture to us in search of growth. The work of composition and the rightful assessment of composition programs should better help students access what they know and what they don't know, and to help continually push them off to that area of complexity—that area of "intellectual ambition" that area of not knowing—all the while affirming what they know and how they can use that existing knowledge to build deeper, more fervent understanding.

References

Arum, R., & Roksa, A. (2011). *Academically adrift: Limited learning on college campuses.* Chicago: University of Chicago Press.

Bain, K. (2004). *What the best college teachers do.* Cambridge: Harvard University Press.

Beaufort, A. (2007). *College writing and beyond: A new framework for university writing instruction.* Logan: Utah State University Press.

Broad, B. (2003). *What we really value: Beyond rubrics in teaching and assessing writing.* Logan, UT: Utah State University Press.

Corbett, E. P. J. & Connors, R. J. (1998). *Classical rhetoric for the modern student* (4th ed.). New York: Oxford University Press.

Elie, P. (2003). *The life you save may be your own: An American pilgrimage.* New York: Farrar, Straus, Giroux.

Graves, D. (2002). *Testing is not teaching: What should count in education.* Portsmouth, NH: Heinemann.

Herr, E. (2005). *Forecastplus for retention: Predictive modeling summary for Georgia College & State University.* Iowa City: Noel-Levitz.

Keene, E. O. (2008). *To understand: New horizons in reading comprehension.* Portsmouth, NH: Heinemann.

Newkirk, T. (2009). *Holding on to good ideas in a time of bad ones: Six literacy principles worth fighting for.* Portsmouth, NH: Heinemann.

Nowacek, R. (2011). *Agents of integration: Understanding transfer as a rhetorical act.* Carbondale: Southern Illinois University Press.

Stengle, J. (2011, February 8). 'Middle school matters': Laura Bush to announce education initiative to improve graduation rates. *The Huffington Post.* http://www.huffingtonpost.com/2011/02/08/bush-institute-middle-school-matters_n_820463.html

CHAPTER TEN

The New Literacy Agenda for Higher Education

Composition, Computers, and Academic Labor at U.S. Research Universities

ROBERT SAMUELS

This chapter examines how the changing economics and politics of higher education are affecting the integration of computers and writing into contemporary universities.[1] By analyzing a national study centered on the incorporation of new media in research universities, I develop a critical model for understanding the possibilities and problems of introducing multiple literacies into undergraduate programs. Central to this analysis of the ways that computer technologies are being utilized in U.S. universities is the connection between the teaching of writing and the new literacy agenda in higher education. Through an examination of the rhetoric of student-centered classrooms as it relates to the use of technology to teach composition skills, I show how the protection of the expertise and job security of writing faculty has often been ignored. Following this analysis of the loss of job protections in the new literacy agenda, I interpret Mark C. Taylor's Global Education Network (GEN) as an example of the problematic use of the student-centered pedagogies, the social constructionist rhetoric of information sharing, and the globalizing ideology of technological progress.

Much of this chapter is influenced by Cynthia Selfe's *Technology and Literacy in the Twenty-First Century* (1999), which represents an insightful investigation of the link between literacy and technology in new governmental and educational policies. Selfe begins her study by arguing that teachers need to be aware of a "new literacy agenda" shaping American public schools (xix). She also warns that teachers should keep in mind the continuing digital divides in our schools and the "importance of multiple literacies in our culture" (xx). As I do in my own work, Selfe seeks to avoid the current tendency to see the infusion of computer technology in education as either all bad or all good, and she motivates her readers to consider the interplay of governmental initiatives, contemporary educators, private sector businesses, and parents in the shaping of our nation's literacy agenda (xxii).

While Selfe focuses her analysis on K–12 public schools, I apply many of her concerns to the study of American research universities. This concentration on higher education is so essential because the new technology literacy agenda has often neglected to take into account how our universities and colleges have changed since the 1980s. As we shall see in my analysis of a national governmental report on introducing multiple technologies and literacies into research universities, the government, and the general public have not realized how the casualization of academic labor and the corporatization of research have worked to restructure the educational environments at most institutions of higher education (Nelson & Watt 1999; Noble 2002; Rhoades 1998). In order to integrate concerns for literacy with concerns for academic labor, I argue that any consideration of the ability of our research universities to adapt to our new information technologies must take into account the economic, institutional, and political forces shaping contemporary higher education.

Higher Education and the Information Literacy Debate

To clarify the stakes involved in the current push to have universities integrate new technologies and literacies into undergraduate instruction, I will now turn to a recent study conducted by the National Academy of Sciences.[2] In their national report, *Preparing for the Revolution: Information Technology and the Future of the Research University* (NAS 2002), the authors point out that as of fall 1998, doctorate-granting research universities in the U.S. enrolled over 4.24 million students (about 28% of total enrollment nationwide), and that these universities were also the recipients of over U.S. $10 billion in federal research funding in the Financial Year 1998 (about 88% of all federal research funding for higher education institutions) (8). Due to their high level of governmental funding, and their large number of both graduate and undergraduate students, the government sees these institutions as leading the way in developing the incorporation of new communication technologies into all aspects of higher education.

> Universities will have to function in a highly digital environment along with other organizations as almost every academic function will be affected, and sometimes displaced, by modern technology. The ways that universities manage their resources, relate to clients and providers, and conduct their affairs will have to be consistent not only with the nature of their own enterprise but also with the reality of "e-everything." As competitors appear, and in many cases provide more effective and less costly alternatives, universities will be forced to embrace new techniques themselves or outsource some of their functions.
>
> In any case, the panel believes that universities should strive to become learning organizations by systematically studying the learning process and re-examining their role in the digital age. This would involve encouraging experimentation with new paradigms of education, research, and service by harvesting the best ideas, implementing them on a sufficient scale to assess their impacts, and disseminating their fruitful results. (24)

Central to this governmental analysis of the role of technology in research universities is the argument that non-traditional, computer-based institutions of higher education will force "traditional" universities to either embrace new communication technologies or outsource many of their own activities (Noble 2002). Coupled with this call for research universities to become more efficient and competitive is the emphasis on having these traditional institutions provide research and experimentation concerning the proper role of new technologies in higher education.

The potential conflict in this national agenda is that research universities are being asked to embrace simultaneously both functional and critical models of literacy. In other terms, the government wants these institutions to affirm a modern rhetoric of technological progress and cost-effectiveness at the same time that these universities provide a critical venue to explore the positive and negative aspects of the postmodern information economy.[3] In fact, the government returns to a traditional understanding of the modern research university in order to call for a deployment of non-traditional, postmodern technologies, and literacies.[4]

Learning and scholarship do require some independence from society. The research university in particular provides a relatively cloistered environment in which people can deeply investigate fundamental problems in the natural sciences, social sciences, and humanities and can learn the art of analyzing difficult problems. But the rapid and substantial changes in store for the university—not only those related to information technology—require that academics work with the institution's many stakeholders to learn of their evolving needs, expectations, and perceptions of higher education (22).

On the one hand, the National Academy of Sciences turns to research universities to study the new information economy because these "modern" institutions are supposed to be independent from various social forces, and thus as the centers of value-free research, universities can provide a neutral and scientific understanding of technology and education. On the other hand, these same institutions are urged to give up their distance from society, and accept the new communication technologies and literacies in the greater postmodern culture. The problem with this mission is one of the fundamental problems facing all institutions of higher education: How do universities at the same time utilize new information technologies and remain critical of these same technologies (Selfe 1999)?

The variance between functional and critical literacies is rendered even more problematic by the way that this governmental report tends to affirm a false and misleading conception of our globalized world of higher education:

> We can now use powerful computers and networks to deliver educational services to any-one—any place, any time. Technology can create an open learning environment in which the student, no longer compelled to travel to a particular location in order to participate in a peda-gogical process involving tightly integrated studies based mostly on lectures or seminars by local experts, is evolving into an active and demanding consumer of educational services. (7)

We can tie this globalizing rhetoric of "anyone, at any place, and any time" to the way that many representations from businesses, politicians, and popular culture tend to deny the very real digital divides in our world. Often, the government invokes these claims of global access to higher education in order to hide important disparities in access and equality concerning technology and literacy (Selfe 1999). Within the context of this national study of the roles of technology in higher education, the rhetoric of globalization is combined in a contradictory fashion with a discourse of competition and uneven development. Thus, research universities are celebrated because they are removed from normal social concerns, but they are also cri-tiqued because they have not fully embraced the social rhetoric of globalized education.

At the heart of this contradictory representation of research universities is an unacknowl-edged debate over what types of values and literacies should determine the mission of our institutions of higher education (Gee 2003; Schroeder 2001). While the government wants to affirm the globalizing rhetoric of universal access to education, it also desires to place research universities in a privileged position. Our universities are therefore supposed to be both egalitarian and hierarchical, while they remain above society and central to the new social order.

These contradictory representations of research universities often work to conceal the growing corporatization (Rhoades 1998) of higher education behind a rhetoric of student-centered pedagogy and computer-mediated information sharing. For example, the following claim by this same national study calls for a radical restructuring of the teacher–student relationship:

> Yet we envision a future, enabled by information technology and driven by learner demand, in which two of the major (and taken-for-granted) ways of organizing undergraduate learning will recede in importance: the 55–minute classroom lecture and the common reading list. That digital future will challenge faculty to design technology-based experiences based primarily on interactive, collaborative learning. Although these new approaches will be quite different from traditional ones, they may be far more effective, particularly when provided through a media-rich environment. (25–26)

On one level, we can read this call to use technology to make undergraduate education more collaborative and learner-centered as a progressive affirmation of social constructivist pedagogy. However, this type of progressive claim can result in a downsizing of the expertise of teaching faculty. For example, the following argument clearly transforms the role of the teacher in higher education:

> Students may be more involved in the creation of learning environments, working shoulder to shoulder with the faculty just as they do when serving as research assistants. In that context, student and professor alike are apt to be experts, though in different domains. [. . .] The faculty member of the twenty-first century university could thus become more of a consultant or coach than a teacher, less concerned with transmitting intellectual content directly than with inspiring, motivating, and managing an active learning process. (26)

The logic of this kind of argument will become clearer later on in this chapter when I discuss labor issues concerning different for-profit and non-profit models of computer-mediated higher education. However, for now, I want to stress the ways that this seemingly benign call for student-based learning may secretly promote the possible end of public higher education.

After all, as this report highlights, public research universities have to compete with new modes of education and technology that are driven by cost-saving and consumer-oriented priorities. According to this study, the only thing that seems to help maintain the value and purpose of research universities for many students and parents is the prestige of particular degrees and the chance to study with expert faculty members (41). Yet, we must ask what happens in a system where all expertise is shared and the teacher becomes a coach and not an important source of valued information? Does not this model of the teacher as a facilitator or coach work to downgrade the importance of the teaching faculty, and does not the field of composition display some of the results of this type of transformation of the professoriate in higher education?[5] In other terms, does the affirmation of an educational structure based on distributive knowledge systems and student-centered pedagogy work to deflate the value of the faculty members?

I believe that we must explore the ways that research universities are participating in their own devaluation by downgrading the expertise of their own teachers. Making matters even worse, progressive faculty members are unintentionally aiding this process by affirming modes of pedagogy and literacy that work to downsize their own cultural and economic capital. Central to my argument here is the claim that if faculty members do not learn how to protect their own interests by claiming a significant intellectual role in the shaping of students' multiple literacies, the academic labor system will continue to deteriorate and the value of public universities will evaporate.

For educators in the field of composition, these transformations concerning the roles of faculty members in American universities should be very apparent. Yet, I have found that many people working in this field do not understand why there is such a high reliance on non-tenured faculty to teach writing. Furthermore, I do not know of any accounts in the field of composition that have been able to explain the relation between the increase in the under-employment of writing faculty since 1980 and the increase in our field's pedagogical concern for social justice and educational democracy. In other words, what is the connection between our desire to make our classrooms more democratic and just and the growing lack of democracy and justice for faculty teaching writing?

It is important to note that according to the 2000 American Historical Association study of tenure by academic fields, 85% of the faculty teaching in free-standing writing programs are not eligible for tenure and only 64% of composition instructors in English Departments are on tenure-track. The field of composition is therefore dominated by a casualized labor force that is often void of any academic rights protected by tenure. Instead of avoiding this labor issue, I believe we must show how educational effectiveness is tied to faculty justice and demonstrate that the future of higher education is dependent on our ability to reclaim the importance of having qualified and secure faculty teach in effective educational environments.

Returning to the National Academy of Sciences' study, we see how the integration of computers into contemporary society threatens to reshape the roles of students and faculty in research universities:

> The most dramatic impacts on university education are yet to come—when learning experiences are reconceptualized to capture the power of information technology. Although the classroom is unlikely to disappear, at least as a place where students and faculty can regularly come together, the traditional lecture format of a faculty member addressing a group of relatively passive students is threatened by powerful new tools such as the simulation of physical phenomena, gaming technology, telepresence, and teleimmersion (the ability of geographically dispersed sites to collaborate in real time). Sophisticated networks and software environments can be used to break the classroom loose from the constraints of place and time to make learning available any place, any time, and to any one. The outlines of what will be possible can even now be seen in the real-time collaboration and project-management tools that are becoming common in the corporate environment. (NAS 2002: 26–27)

This passage is structured by an important conflict that is prevalent in many accounts of how technology is affecting higher education. On one level, this argument affirms that the space and time of traditional classrooms and modes of pedagogy are being replaced by electronic models of distance education and communication. Yet, this same passage wants to hold onto the idea of traditional classrooms, and the value of having teachers and students meet together in the same physical space. One obvious solution to this conflict is to call for a blended or hybrid model of education where, for example, students meet once a week with their teachers in large lecture classes and then the other class meetings are held online. However, the initial problem with this solution is that this same passage makes the important argument that new technologies are also making students desire more interactive learning environments, and thus the current use of large lecture classes will not work in this new structure.

While this report does not make a direct call for smaller classrooms and more interactive pedagogical environments, it is clear that the only way we will be able to maintain the value of undergraduate education at research universities *and* adapt to the new technologies and learning styles of contemporary students is if universities combine their investments in technology with investments in smaller classes and thus more faculty members. In fact, there is only one place in this report that the government seems to indicate its awareness of this need to consider the role of faculty funding in new technology initiatives, and we can find this labor argument in the following passage:

> The research university will face particular challenges in this regard. Although rarely acknowledged, the research university relies heavily on cross-subsidies from low-cost, high-profit instruction in general education (e.g., large lecture courses) and low-cost professional training (such as in business administration and law) to support graduate training and research in the science and engineering fields. These high-profit programs are, not coincidentally, very attractive targets for technology-based, for-profit competitors. Their success in the higher-education marketplace could therefore undermine the current business model of the research university and imperil its core activities. This could be a politically explosive issue for some of the state universities as they try to maintain and increase public support from state legislatures. (40)

The first striking aspect of this passage is that it acknowledges that graduate and research programs are often funded out of the profits made by large undergraduate lecture classes. There is thus a counter-productive economic system at research universities that requires the wide use of educational environments that may work against our efforts to provide effective learning. Moreover, this type of mass production of education is precisely what for-profit virtual educational systems are supposed to do best (Noble 2002a). It is therefore imperative for research universities that want to maintain their role in undergraduate education to find ways of differentiating themselves from their electronic competitors by providing effective, interactive learning environments, and the use of large lecture classes is clearly working against this effort (Rose 1990). Furthermore, faculty members and university administrators are often working together to find ways to use technology to increase the use of large lecture classes and reduce the number of expert faculty teaching undergraduate courses. In other words, universities may be acting unknowingly to put themselves out of business by undermining their own value, and this act of devaluation often involves faculty denying their own expertise.

Rhetoric of Computers, Composition, and Higher Education

To further our critical understanding of the rhetoric behind many of the new technology literacy initiatives in higher education, we can examine Chris Werry's important article, "The Work of Education in the Age of ecollege" (2002). Werry's essay provides an effective framework for understanding the discourse of democratic sharing and student-centered pedagogy that is often employed in the promotion of computer-mediated instruction.

In his insightful analysis, Werry points out that there are four major positions that structure the debate concerning online education and other modes of computer-mediated instruction: administrative, corporate, resistant, and critical (136). Starting with the role played by (university) administrators in American universities, Werry claims that the central concerns of current traditional stakeholders are increased student enrollments, keeping up with technological advances, and cost management (136). From a current-traditional administrative perspective, the turn to new modes of technology and education delivery stems from a desire to control or reduce expensive overheads caused by "human resources, security and police, counseling and career services, facilities and management, health care and utilities" (136). In a totally online environment, many, if not all, of these labor-intensive functions of traditional institutions of higher education can be reduced or eliminated. Of course, this transformation of academic labor means unemployment or under-employment for many people now working at universities.

While no major universities have totally embraced this transition to online education, the National Academy of Sciences' study discussed above affirms that traditional universities are having to compete with new online universities, and many traditional institutions are moving toward an acceptance of the rhetoric and strategies of their electronic competitors. Werry posits that not only are non-online universities developing their own online courses and businesses, but these same institutions are adopting policies to shift funds from labor-intensive sectors, like tenured faculty, to technology-intensive systems of information delivery (136–137). This use of cost-cutting business models to transform the labor of education is in part derived from the growing connection between university administrators and corporations.

Werry points out that while administrators tend to speak a rhetoric of competition, rivalry, and progress, many corporate investors in higher education argue that the digitization of higher education will make these institutions "leaner, flatter, more flexible, and efficient" (137). In other words, corporations tend to circulate a modern rhetoric of technological and economic efficiency, cost-effectiveness, and flexibility (Johnson-Eilola 1997). In fact, administrators need to use these corporate principles in order to pursue their goals of being competitive and "doing more with less"; however, administrators tend to shy away from the globalizing anti-hierarchy rhetoric common among corporate sponsors of higher education.

Werry posits that in response to this linking of administrators and corporation in the quest for more computer-mediated education, many faculty members have taken on a more resistant rhetoric. Citing the work of Noble (2002) and Nelson and Watt (1999), Werry shows how some faculty are aware of the connection between online education and the casualization of academic labor; however, Werry also affirms that these resistant faculty members choose to simply reject all technology and do not consider ways of making the incorporation of computers into higher education work in a more fair and equitable manner (137–138). In contrast to the faculty who simply want to get rid of or control new technologies in education, Werry celebrates academics like Andrew Feenberg (199) and Tim Luke who present a critical engagement with computers and education (138). According to Werry, the critical users of new technology "advocate bottom-up, faculty-driven, craft-style forms of online education that carefully adapt existing teaching practices to new technological environments" (138). In this call for a blended model of electronic education, faculty retain the power over these new technologies; however, Werry does not indicate how the increase of faculty control over computer-mediated instruction will happen. In fact, everything that Werry describes in this new movement toward digitized higher education reveals that faculty will have less and less say in what technologies are purchased and how those technologies will be employed. For example, in his reference to Feenberg as a model for critical engagement, Werry relates the story of what happened when Feenberg's own institution, the California State University, engaged in a very expensive and controversial deal with several corporations in order to develop online education:

> Feenberg asked the chancellor what pedagogical model had guided the CETI project. Feenberg wrote that: "The chancellor looked at me as though I'd laid an egg, and said, 'We've got the engineering plan. It's up to you faculty to figure out what to do with it. ' And off he went: subject closed!" Feenberg was surprised by this response. (143)

Here, we see how faculty members and pedagogical factors are often excluded from consideration when major deals are being brokered between university administrators and corporate leaders. Thus, even if a teacher is critically engaged in the use of technology, this does not mean that his or her university will employ technology for pedagogical and critical purposes.

In response to this potential corporate and administrative takeover of technology and higher education, Werry proposes the following solution:

> In certain respects composition specialists are well positioned to engage administrators. Composition teachers are often involved in designing computer classrooms and purchasing software, and might be able to suggest open-source and free software alternatives to administrators. The emerging open-source courseware systems, email, bulletin boards, and instructional software [. . .] are typically free or inexpensive. This fact, if carefully used as part of an argument for a pedagogy-driven reallocation of funds (rather than an argument for mere cost cutting), could be used to help persuade administrators to invest in their use. (144)

I believe that Werry's proposed solution to these problems is a major part of the problem: faculty, like Werry, believe that the key to overcoming the power differentials at American universities is to just share more and provide better and cheaper models for effective pedagogy. Yet, this democratic ethic of sharing and service hides the fact that most composition faculty have little or no power in their institutions and that most universities are run by a series of competing power structures that are not always dedicated to improving pedagogy and education (Rhoades 1998: 173–209).

In terms of the position of composition faculty, Lisa Gerrard's argument made in 1993 still holds in 2003:

> As we well know, the practice of English, like that of other academic specialties, is built on competition and ranking. Thus, while we promote collaboration and democracy in our teaching, we are encouraged to be combative and hierarchical in other areas of our professional lives. As compositionists who use computers, we participate in a profession with contradictory values: one set for the classroom, another outside it. (23)

Gerrard here examines the central conflict between the social constructivist writing faculty who celebrate sharing, democracy, collaboration, and student-centered pedagogies and the current-traditional university that is structured by hierarchy and competition. Gerrard later extends this analysis by placing composition faculty within the larger structure of the university:

> As we interact with our colleagues, departments, and institutions, we participate in a profession that is built not on cooperation, democracy, and acceptance of divergent viewpoints, but

on competition, hierarchy, and divisiveness. English departments rank their faculty, putting theorists on top, other literary specialists beneath them, and composition faculty in the basement. (27)

Following Gerrard's lead, I believe that we must begin our analysis of how we want to use computers in our writing classes by first examining the roles played by power and economics in our institutional settings. Thus, we may find that our desire to be democratic in a non-democratic structure results in a situation where our best intentions are often being used against us.

My argument here is not that we should stop trying to make our classes democratic and collaborative; rather I claim that we need to integrate this rhetoric of democracy and sharing with a call to engage power structures in an open and forceful way. Therefore, we should not only argue for more equitable classrooms, but we also must fight for more equitable institutions, and I believe the key to this fight may entail the unionization of non-tenured faculty, who have everything to gain and often very little to lose. This drive for unionization of what is becoming the majority of faculty at our institutions of higher education has to be tied to a national effort to protect the intellectual property and expertise of all teaching faculty. Only through the foundation of a strong national union will disenfranchised faculty members be able to confront the growing power of administrators and corporations in higher education.

I am not arguing here that all administrators and corporate leaders are against improving education: rather, following Werry's analysis, we need to examine how administrative and corporate interests often have very different functions and priorities in comparison to many university teachers. One of the problems facing contemporary universities is that the more these institutions become involved in research and technology, the more their administrative staffs and costs grow, and in turn, the less power and influence faculty have over technology and education issues (Nelson & Watt 1999). In this context, it is simply naïve and self-defeating to call for more faculty sharing. In fact, Werry's call for more democracy and sharing on the part of the faculty is combined with his insightful analysis of how the rhetoric of technological progress is being used to convince people to participate in processes that are not at all progressive. For example, after discussing the ways many online education corporations use a rhetoric of community in order to assure faculty that these new computer-mediated modes of instruction share the same educational concerns as progressive teachers, Werry makes the following claim:

> *Community* becomes a way of managing some of the tensions inherent in systems that tend to reify educational practices. The discourse of community appears strategically drawn on to reassure educators—to quiet their fear of automation and displacement, and to show that the company understands that education entails issues of culture, communication, and socialization. (140)

As educators, we must become aware of how this rhetoric of community, democracy, and collaboration can be used for many diverse purposes. For example, Werry examines how *The Campus Pipeline*'s advertisements for outsourcing course delivery systems proclaims that the company's educational product generates: "a community dedicated to meeting individual needs. A business streamlined for maximum efficiency. And a campus that never closes" (cited in Werry 2002: 140). In this combination of the social constructionist rhetoric of community, the expressivist rhetoric of individual needs, and the modern rhetoric of efficiency, we see how postindustrial corporations integrate conflicting ideologies into a seamless structure. Interestingly, this combination of rhetorical strategies leaves out the profit motive, which is usually the central driving force for these educational corporations.

In analyzing the rhetoric of online education companies, Werry points to the ways that the pedagogical celebration of student-centered classrooms and democratic learning spaces is often placed within a system of economic exploitation:

> Many proponents of commercial online education stress the need to move from a traditional Fordist, mass production based model of education, to a more flexible, post-Fordist, "mass customization" model. This is sometimes allied with the language of constructivist, learner-centered approaches to education—language that stresses the importance of student-centered approaches in which knowledge is constructed within a community of learners. (139)

The key rhetorical term in Werry's analysis here is the notion of "flexibility" which is often used in academic circles as a code word for downsizing and casualizing the labor force (Readings 1996). By merging the rhetoric of flexible technologies with the discourse of flexible labor, contemporary institutions of higher education are often able to hide real economic transitions behind idealized cultural transformations. Thus, not only do faculty want to share and be democratic, but they also want to be flexible and student-centered. However, economic flexibility for administrators and corporations often means that one cannot make any permanent commitments to labor. Therefore, the rhetoric of flexibility is usually invoked when universities have to defend their high level of contingent faculty: according to this logic, the radical fluctuations in student enrollment and state funding make it necessary for universities to maintain great flexibility in their employment practices, and this often means a reduction of tenured or unionized faculty.

Since many progressive educators also call for the use of flexible and student-centered technology and educational structures, the rhetoric of these faculty members is easily used to justify the economic rhetoric of administrators and corporations. Werry shows his awareness of this manipulation of social constructivist rhetoric in the following passage:

> In some instances the connection between flexibility, mass customization, and constructivist pedagogy is thought through in a principled, sophisticated way. However, sometimes this focus on "student-centered" education seems merely a way of camouflaging shortcomings in models of online education. Some all-Internet courses offer no face-to-face interaction, and there is significant dissociation between different levels of the educational enterprise—between managers, advisors, system designers, content providers, technical assistants, and teachers. Further, the system is designed to be modular and scalable, so that teaching assistants and adjuncts can be slotted into courses as required (Irvine proposes that future models of online education will center on "reusable learning objects in customized modules with assessments for specific outcomes"). (140)

Werry argues here that in postmodern modes of communication and education, the stress on democratic discourses and student-centered media and pedagogical methods can work to hide the power of current-traditional authorities and modern systems of organization.

Central to this postmodern educational model is the emphasis on the student as reader/user/consumer of higher education. According to Werry, "[a]n impoverished notion of 'student-centered' education is often part of the argument that the technology will somehow democratize education and make student-centered learning happen by itself" (140). Not only do many rhetorical celebrations of student-centered pedagogies imply a false sense of democracy, but as revealed by the following statement from Andrew Rosenfield, CEO of Unext, endorsements of student users are often coupled with attacks on teachers: "lectures are dead. They are not a good way to learn [. . .] People want to learn what they need to know, not what professors want them to know. You can only do that on the Internet" (cited in Werry 2002: 140). Here, we see how central to the postmodern emphasis on student-centered individualism is an undermining of the authority of the teacher. Of course, progressive educators who proclaim the importance of student-centered classrooms also present a message that works against the authority of teacher-centered education. Thus, unknowingly, some educational theorists have played into the hands of political and corporate interests which want to do away with the expensive burden of having expert teachers in classrooms. In many ways, the extreme advocates of online education have unintentionally exposed the downgrading of teacher expertise that was going on already in American universities.

My argument here is not that we should return teachers to their rightful current-traditional place as masters, and students to their function as passive listeners; rather, I think that we need to integrate both current-traditional defenses of teacher expertise and progressive models of student-centered rhetoric. The problem is that many critical pedagogies present a polarized opposition that often works to rationalize the downsizing of faculty. Yet, very few enthusiasts of hypertextuality have questioned what this new pedagogical model will do to the employment of writing faculty and other teachers. In order to further clarify this connection among new computer technologies, the quality of university education, and the employment practices in higher education, I will end this chapter by examining Mark C. Taylor's (2001) call for a hypertextual and globalized university as presented in his book, *The Moment of Complexity: Emerging Network Culture*.

Hypertext Gone Bad

In this work, Taylor uses the notion of hypertext to argue for a new vision of higher education (234). Central to his argument is his claim that "in the future, the curriculum will look more like a constantly morphing hypertext than a fixed linear sequence of prepackaged courses" (234). Due to the changing nature of the way people access information in a postmodern, networked world, Taylor envisions a growing movement toward a totally online system of higher education where "[a]nyone anywhere in the world can, in principle, sit down around the same virtual table and learn together" (234). In this notion of a GEN, we find again the modern ideology of a universal system of knowledge and culture. Furthermore, by turning to the structure and logic of the hypertext, Taylor calls for the creation of a new mode of higher education patterned on the private ownership of a distributed network of interrelated information (262).

At first glance, Taylor's promotion of his GEN appears to be a progressive attempt to make higher education more responsive to our changing technological and social cultures. For instance, he begins his book by highlighting the movement from a Cold War environment based on political divisions to the postmodern globalized context of the World Wide Web, which according to Taylor is now centered on integration and the overcoming of all differences (23). Furthermore, in the first chapters of his book, Taylor concentrates on articulating the transition from the grid-oriented structure of modern society to the networked structure of postmodern culture. From his perspective, modern culture is dominated by centralized economic planning and top-down bureaucracy, while postmodern society has developed decentralized markets and bottom-up democracy (49). Moreover, Taylor posits that modern society is based on a productive economic system of manufacturing, while postmodern reproductive society is centered on "an information economy governed by new media" (66). This type of "progressive" historical narrative most often returns to a modern logic of linearity and universalized development in order to critique modern culture and celebrate contemporary society. The end result of this mode of theoretical narrativization is usually a globalized rhetoric where all social and technological changes are neutralized, naturalized, universalized, and rendered inevitable. In other words, all possibility for social change or cultural criticism is negated by the rhetorical moves that secretly posit that our particular economic, institutional, and literacy structures are natural, neutral, universal, and inevitable.

In terms of higher education, Taylor uses his notion of a global hypertext of knowledge to argue for a melding of business and educational interests. In a very revealing phrase, he states that "[i]n a networked culture, education is the currency of the realm" (234). He is quick to point out that he means that "[e]ducation, like money in the world of finance, is a currency that is also a commodity" (234). Here, we find the use of hypertextuality to argue that education equals money because they both circulate in the networked global economy. Once Taylor makes this argument, it is only a small step for him to claim that all educational pursuits should be run by private corporations. In fact, Taylor's "academic" book is also an infomercial for his own product: the GEN.

Central to this advertisement for globalized online education is his strong claim that "[t]he prospect of significant profits in the educational market is, of course, the result of new technologies for providing and promoting education" (235). Thus, according to Taylor's rhetoric of inevitable technological progress, the hypertextual nature of the World Wide Web and the development of a postindustrial, globalized economy have moved us to a new networked culture, which is creating pressures on all educational systems to shift from a modern industrial notion of knowledge delivery to a postmodern, postindustrial "education industry" (236). Furthermore, employing the rhetoric of globalized inevitability, Taylor proclaims: "Just as corporations that are unable to respond to the rapidly changing economic environment cannot remain competitive, so colleges and universities that are unwilling to adapt to the new education and economic landscape cannot survive" (236). In this model of universal and inevitable change, there is no space left for the public sphere or the protection of higher education from a completely business-oriented mentality. Furthermore, the radical fluctuations and disparities in today's global markets are concealed beneath a naïve celebration of contemporary business practices.

In order to gain support for his own educational product, Taylor posits that universities and colleges have turned to technology to help make them more competitive in the educational market, but these efforts have failed because the educational software programs that universities are purchasing do not come with support staffs, and the outsourcing of software development does not help the marketing of the schools' courses. Moreover, Taylor makes the important assessment that courseware developed by for-profit companies does not match each school's particular pedagogical needs (237–238). The solution, of course, is to turn to Taylor's own GEN, which will provide all of these services and will eliminate the messy conflict between not-for-profit public education institutions and for-profit businesses.

One of the reasons why hypertext plays such a prominent role in Taylor's GEN is that this connected and distributed system of knowledge storage and delivery mirrors his image of the networked, free market global economy. As a decentralized structure of linked nodes accessed by readers who are free to produce their own readings, hypertext represents the perfect model for postindustrial capitalism and postmodern education. In Taylor's own words, "[w]ith wired classrooms, the time and place of instruction are transformed: education becomes available anytime, anyplace in the world. Like networked global markets, education becomes a 24/7 business" (258). This globalized vision of education, technology, and the free market refuses to acknowledge all of the real social and economic differences that prevent much of the world's population from having any access to technology and higher education.

Another important blind spot in Taylor's argument is his claim that a hypertextual system of knowledge is necessary now because "[s]tudents are much more knowledgeable today about new media than most faculty members" (258). According to this logic, which is often presented by progressive teachers and advocates of student-centered pedagogies, contemporary faculty can only facilitate the education of students because students now know more about technology than the faculty. This argument that is supposed to celebrate the students often works to downgrade the teachers and is based on a misguided notion that students' uses of new media are equivalent to their critical understanding of these new technologies.

In the field of composition, and in higher education in general, this privileging of student knowledge has often worked to undermine the degrees, expertise, and experience of faculty members. Indeed, one of the factors contributing to the continual economic exploitation of faculty in the field of composition is the development by compositionists of a whole range of practices and belief systems centered on the idea that teachers of writing should make their classes student-centered, and that, in turn, faculty members should act as facilitators and not as experts who have a particular knowledge base to which students do not yet have access. Like Taylor's model of globalized education, many writing programs are structured by the combination of a few well-paid experts with tenure, and the employment of many graduate students and part-time faculty without the same credentials and expertise. Moreover, many universities are asking their faculty to place their course material on the web, so that all of a faculty member's expertise can be shared by the other teachers. In response to this rhetoric of democratic sharing, I would warn that once one has released all of one's intellectual property into a public arena, one's employment may no longer be needed. In fact, Taylor, whose global educational model is centered on the sharing of course material across the curriculum through the generation of a communal hypertext, openly admits that his networked courses will be monitored by "a pool of qualified teaching assistants from schools throughout the world" (263). He adds that it is inevitable that tenure will be eroded by the postindustrial educational system (265) and that any faculty member who complains about this loss of academic job security is just expressing "shortsighted self-interest" (239). One has to wonder if the fact that Taylor himself already has tenure plays into his willingness to give up on the system that has protected his own employment.

At one point in his chapter on the GEN, Taylor dismisses all academic criticisms of this perfect match between commerce, education, and technology by simply stating that faculty resistance to "distributed teaching and learning [. . .] is often expressed in lofty educational ideals" but the real problem is that many faculty members are highly suspicious of business and technology (239). After reading Taylor's employment model for higher education, is it any wonder that some faculty members are a little afraid of this perfect marriage between business and education? The problem with most faculty members is that they are too little concerned with the growing role that businesses are playing in shaping all aspects of higher education. For the recent history of the field of composition, and other areas of higher education, has shown that the development of progressive theories of education and culture have coincided with the increased exploitation of academic labor.

Not only do faculty members ignore the concrete material forces shaping higher education, but also students are usually taught in a way that downplays the role of economic exploitation in our society. For instance, the economics of higher education is most often a taboo subject in U.S. universities even though it shapes everything that goes on in our classrooms. Further-more, in higher education in America, there has been a trend to detach economic factors from our discussions of technology, writing, and pedagogy. For example, when I recently asked my fellow faculty members why they never discuss the constant downsizing and outsourcing of our faculty with their students, they returned to the modern argument that education must be neutral, objective, and disinterested. Yet our world is rarely any of these things, and our desire to shelter our students from these concrete economic realities only serves to render their educa-tion abstract and unreal.

I am not arguing here that teachers should spend all of their time discussing their personal economic problems with their students, but I do feel that we need to incorporate discussions of economics with all subjects that we cover with our students. For instance, when we examine any technological system, we need to ask who profits and who does not profit. Moreover, a careful analysis of the battle between critical and functional models of literacy in higher educa-tion can aid writing faculty in expanding their students' and colleagues' notions of composi-tion. By seeing writing as both an intellectual and pragmatic endeavor, we can help pave the way for the incorporation of new literacies into undergraduate education as we resist the types of destructive institutional policies I have examined in this chapter.

Notes

1. This chapter represents an extended version of a paper I delivered at the *2004 Computers and Writing Confer-ence* in Manoa, Hawaii, June 2004.
2. The National Academy of Sciences is a public, non-profit organization that supplies research to the U.S. na-tional government.
3. For a more detailed discussion of the battle between critical and functional literacies in higher education and the corporatization of research universities, see Edmundson (1997), Minsky (2000), Nelson and Watt (1999), and Noble (2002).
4. Throughout this chapter, I will use the term "postmodern" to refer to the contemporary stress on new media (Rifkin 2000), postindustrial economics (Baudrillard 1993), and a model of education that critiques the mod-ern stress on universal reason.
5. I focus on composition in this chapter because the field of writing has the most highly casualized labor force in American higher education.

This chapter originally appeared in Joe Lockard and Mark Pegrum (eds.), *Brave New Class-rooms: Democratic Education and the Internet* (New York: Peter Lang , 1999).

References

Gee, J. P. (2003). *What video games have to teach us about learning and literacy*. New York: Palgrave.
Gerrard, L. (1993). Computers and composition: Rethinking our values. *Computers and Composition, 10* (2), 23–34.
Johnson-Eilola, J. (1997). *Nostalgic angels*. Norwood, NJ: Ablex.

NAS (National Academy of Sciences) (US) (2002). *Preparing for the revolution: Information technology and the future of the research university.* Accessed November 5, 2005, at books. nap.edu/books/030908640X/html/3. html

Nelson, C., & Watt, S. (1999). *Academic keywords: A devil's dictionary for higher education.* New York: Routledge.

Noble, D. F. (2002a). *Digital diploma mills: The automation of higher education.* New York: Monthly Review Press.

Readings, W. (1996). *The university in ruins.* Cambridge, MA: Harvard University Press.

Rhoades, G. (1998). *Managed professionals: Unionized faculty and restructuring academic labor.* Albany, NY: SUNY Press.

Rose, M. (1990). *Lives on the boundary.* New York: Penguin.

Schroeder, C. (2001). *Re-inventing the university.* Logan, UT: University of Utah Press.

Selfe, C. L. (1999). *Technology and literacy in the twenty-first century: The importance of paying attention.* Carbondale, IL: Southern Illinois University Press.

Taylor, M. C. (2001). *The moment of complexity.* Chicago, IL: University of Chicago Press.

Werry, C. (2002). The work of education in the age of ecollege. *Computers and Composition, 19* (2), 127–149.

CHAPTER ELEVEN

Defining the "Faculty" and Getting It Right

MAYRA BESOSA & MARIA MAISTO

Although the public continues to be unaware that 75% of college faculty[1] in the United States are now employed in vastly under-supported temporary—or "contingent"—appointments that lack academic freedom protections, within the higher education community the casualization of the academic profession has been thoroughly documented and has increasingly become a focal point in discussions about the current state and future course of higher education. "Contingency" as we use the term in this essay, has become shorthand for the stratified, three-tier employment system in which tenure-stream faculty, full-time non-tenure-eligible faculty, and so-called part-time or adjunct non-tenure-eligible faculty now work. Where contingency is addressed in these discussions about the health of higher education, two dominant themes tend to emerge. On the one hand, the use and abuse of contingent faculty labor is recognized as a central component of the trend toward *corporate* postsecondary education, poignantly described twelve years ago by Stanley Aronowitz as "the knowledge factory"[2] and more recently by Benjamin Ginsberg as "the all-administrative university."[3] On the other hand, the move to an almost completely contingent academic workforce is now impossible to ignore as a critical piece of the puzzle of student learning. Alarm bells sound about students being "academically adrift"[4] even as more and more research[5] seeks to connect faculty working conditions to student learning outcomes.

In this essay, we explore how the roles and responsibilities of faculty are affected by the fact that the issue of contingent employment practices figures so prominently in these two national conversations (about corporatization and about student learning). The trend toward corporatization and an administration-focused culture in higher education—which in turn raises important questions about the appropriate roles of faculty unions and shared governance—is attributed to a multitude of interactive causes, but in any case it can only be understood within the context of the transformation of the workforce, both academic and non-academic, and the impact on wealth distribution of increasingly corporate-controlled political and judicial systems. The concern about student learning outcomes, while clearly an outgrowth of conflicts over K-12 education and of desperate attention by policymakers to workforce development during the worst economic crisis in the United States after the Depression, is also a manifestation of deep-rooted cultural divisions over who, among both students and faculty, does—and should—have access to the social, political, and economic power that higher education affords.

In the face of what is perceived by many observers to be a decades-long, multi-pronged assault on the soul of American higher education, it is safe to say that college and university faculty have been slow to respond with a coherent, collective voice. While individuals and groups, particularly faculty unions, have made compelling public arguments and taken collective action, it is only very recently that faculty at large seem to have realized the extent of the crisis and begun committing themselves to mounting a defense of the values that they had perhaps taken for granted for too long: access, equity, quality, academic freedom, intellectual inquiry, solidarity, democracy—in short, education as a public good. This renewed faculty commitment has clearly come about in traditional ways, through the rise of fields such as "critical university studies"[6] and in the form of increased faculty union activity (especially in the wake of assaults on public worker rights in Wisconsin and Ohio in 2011).

However, the commitment to education as a public good has also come about in non-traditional ways, most notably in the emergence of new coalitions like the Coalition on the Academic Workforce (CAW) and the Campaign for the Future of Higher Education (CFHE), both of which include union and non-union groups, disciplinary organizations, higher education-focused nonprofits, and even community organizations. CAW tends to focus on the academic workforce insofar as it affects educational quality, while CFHE targets the corporate values that have been dubbed "the new normal" in higher education. Both coalitions make the case for a reappraisal of faculty roles in and responsibility for quality higher education, which is identified by the Campaign in particular as a natural corrective to the misguided application of corporate values to higher education.[7]

While these coalitions show definitively that a movement toward more faculty activism in reaction to internal and external threats is under way, the emergence of New Faculty Majority (NFM), which is deeply involved with both CAW and CFHE (and which includes active union members and leaders as well as non-union-affiliated faculty and their allies within and outside of higher education), demonstrates the *pivotal* role of contingent faculty in (re)defining the faculty and "getting it right." Contingency, after all, has become, if not the locus of, then certainly the most obvious reflection of the intersecting crises of education, economics, and politics in the contemporary United States. If all faculty oppose and work to abolish contingency by adopting new ways of thinking and acting in regards to such contested academic values as tenure, academic freedom, and shared governance, we will have a profound effect on parallel crises in the non-academic "real world."

In other words, faculty can overcome the class structure of academic contingency—and all of the distorted values it promotes—by reconnecting with the premise that job security, due process, academic freedom, and shared governance are professional rights and responsibilities rather than privileges, foundational elements of the profession's social contract with the public to create and disseminate knowledge. In fact, as Neil Hamilton and Jerry Gaff argue in *The Fu-*

ture of the Professoriate: Academic Freedom, Peer Review, and Shared Governance, it is a requirement of the profession "to justify occupational control" by communicating effectively "the transcendent public good" that the profession serves.[8] Thus, the experience of faculty working together in union and non-union contexts, in coalitions and through a new dedication to shared governance and to foregrounding the commitment to learning that has always been at the heart of faculty work, shows that contingency will not be resisted through exclusionary attitudes and practices that merely replicate those misguided values, but rather through faculty unity and solidarity.

Finally, there is another reason unity and solidarity are an important goal for those working to re-establish higher education as a public right rather than a private privilege and to reconfigure college teaching and scholarship as a profession that specifically rejects elitism and stratification: from a strategic perspective, an approach centered on unity and solidarity is also more likely to encourage academic administrators to break ranks with the dominant managerial paradigm. This is because, first, it is (so far) still the case that high-level administrators may have begun their careers as faculty, even as faculty in contingent appointments, and have a visceral connection to that experience. Second (and counter-intuitively), it is actually on contingency that common ground with administrators is possible: after all, observers who focus on how tenured faculty, administrators, and contingent faculty regularly shift the blame for contingency onto each other often fail to notice the stunning fact that, in engaging in that blame game, all three groups are actually agreeing that contingency is a problem that needs to be solved.

In order to make our case that solidarity, through a more coherent definition of faculty identity, is a viable strategy, in this essay we draw on Mayra's experiences as a representative of the American Association of University Professors (AAUP) and the California Faculty Association (CFA) and Maria's experiences advocating for faculty equity outside the union context, since she works with New Faculty Majority, which is not a union, and in Ohio, where part-time faculty at public institutions are barred from access to collective bargaining. We note that, in protecting the integrity of the faculty, the goal of improving student learning is always central in both unionized and non-unionized faculty contexts; this is an assumption that we have realized can no longer go unstated, shocking as it may be to most faculty. We also draw on our experience with and research on shared governance. Our intention is to describe practices that can unite faculty—and administrators—across class divisions, in many contexts and using many tools, so that the definition of "faculty" can be properly realigned with its etymological origins as a locus of power, ability, means, and leadership in the creation of knowledge and the facilitation of learning.[9] Thus, we hope to collectively and effectively put our institutions back on the right track to providing an education that serves the common good.

After explaining how contingency plays a central role in two of the most prominent conversations about higher education today (the corporatization of higher education and the debate over student learning outcomes), we suggest three strategies for encouraging a more solid, and solidarity-infused, definition of faculty and getting it right for the purpose of advancing the common good. Those strategies are stabilizing the faculty through collective bargaining wherever possible; developing a stronger collective commitment from faculty, administration, students and communities to the *inherent* as well as instrumental values of scholarship and teaching at the heart of the profession and the institutional mission; and reaffirming the importance of shared governance as a critical exercise in, and lesson about, democratic values and practices.

Defining Contingency

In order to understand why the faculty needs to be redefined into a more solid, and solidarity-infused, entity, it is important to understand how "contingency" has figured in the contexts of 1) the emergence of corporatized higher education, which has in turn affected the development of faculty unions and shared governance; and 2) the debate over student learning outcomes.

Contingency and Corporatization

Economic crises can serve as opportunities to ram through regressive political agendas that, for example, ban unions and silence workers' voices, thereby facilitating the lowering of wages and the cutting of benefits in both private and public sectors. In the last several decades we have witnessed a drastic redistribution of wealth, and thus of political power and opportunity, upwards to the richest 10% of the population, which currently controls two-thirds of Americans' net worth. Political commentators Jim Hightower and Phillip Frazer describe the dismantling of the American middle-class as resulting from "a new normal of job insecurity" as big business shifts from a workforce of permanent employees to one in which "most jobs are temporary, scarce, low-paid, without benefits, and with no upward mobility."[10]

Twelve years ago, in his introduction to *The Knowledge Factory: Dismantling the Corporate University and Creating True Higher Learning*, Aronowitz argued that "far from the image of an ivory tower where, monk-like, scholars ponder the stars and other distant things, the universities tend to mirror the rest of society"[11] and Daniel Gilbert hits the mark when he states that "the defining feature of our age is the turning of the public good into private goods."[12] Corporatization empowers managers and executives over workers, for example, through the weakening or elimination of collective bargaining where it exists and, in higher education, of shared governance as well. Thus, today's academic workforce could be described as a shrinking core of faculty with status surrounded by a growing periphery of faculty hired *contingently* but who are really their peers.[13] The majority of graduates interested in academic careers are joining this peripheral workforce as our contingent colleagues. In addition, according to Jeffrey Williams, graduates enter the profession burdened with a substantial student debt—averaging $24,000 for an undergraduate degree, $25,000 for a master's, $52,000 for a doctorate, and $80,000 for a professional degree—that "binds. . . [them] for a significant part of their future work lives."[14]

It is widely known that the *new faculty majority*[15] comprises over 75% of the instructional faculty nationwide. Data collected by the U.S. Department of Education in fall 2009 and referenced in the *2010–11 AAUP Annual Report on the Economic Status of the Profession* demonstrate that between 1975 and 2009 the total of faculty members on part-time contingent appointments grew by over 280%. According to the report, between 2007 and 2009 alone,

> the numbers of full-time non-tenure-track faculty members and part-time faculty members each grew at least 6 percent. During the same period, tenured positions grew by only 2. 4 percent and tenure-track appointments increased by a minuscule 0. 3 percent. These increases in the number of faculty appointments have taken place against the background of an overall 12 percent increase in higher education enrollment in just those two years.[16]

Although understandable because of the sheer numbers of faculty on contingent appointments, a siege mentality or defensive attitude on the part of tenure-track faculty towards their non-tenure-track colleagues does not serve the profession. On the contrary, it enhances managerial and executive power and facilitates the eventual complete collapse of the tenure system from within, considering that tenure-track faculty themselves are increasingly marginalized by college and university administrations.

In his book *The Fall of the Faculty: The Rise of the All-Administrative University and Why It Matters*, Ginsberg traces changes in the nature of university administrations from the founding of the AAUP in 1915, when an alliance with the faculty by supporting tenure and shared governance served as a counterweight to interference by boards of trustees, to the present day, when, beyond choosing the chancellor or university president, boards have little direct involvement in university governance. Today's administrators are supported by an "army of professional staffers. . . [that] makes the administration 'relatively autonomous'. . . and marginalizes the faculty."[17] Citing 2006 data collected by the National Center for Educational Statistics, Ginsberg shows that between 1975 and 2005, while the average student to faculty ratio settled during this thirty-year period at 15 to 1, the student to administrators ratio dropped from 84 to 1 to 68 to 1, and the student to professional staff ratio from 50 to 1 to 21 to 1.[18] Changes in hiring practices reflect managerial priorities and impact the levels of institutional spending on instructional versus non-instructional costs. What management theories embraced by present-day administrators have in common, Ginsberg asserts bravely,

> is an effort to impose order and hierarchy on an institution. Even those theories that provide a place for employee involvement see this as a way of pacifying underlings with the appearance of consultation. Through their management speak, administrators are asserting that the university is an institution to be ruled by them. Shared governance, faculty power, tenure, and so forth have no place in management theory.[19]

Thus, in regard to faculty hiring, contingency is the preferred employment relations model in the corporate university. It is a prolonged assault on the collective faculty, on the academic profession. Faculty senates become complicit when they endorse or fail to challenge contingency (and heroic when they resist its pernicious effects on students and faculty).

If the explosion of contingency as the preferred hiring mechanism has failed to convince anyone that the corporate model has taken hold of higher education (nametags, customer service orientation, etc.), then one only has to look at new emphases on faculty productivity.[20] It is also no surprise that the response to this shift to a corporate managerial model has been a shift to an increasingly unionized labor force. Where faculty collective bargaining is legal, unions have been active. Ironically, assaults on worker rights in Wisconsin and Ohio seem to have contributed to a renewed sense among faculty that organizing is both necessary and honorable.

Yet, the battle to preserve unionization is not always won, as has been demonstrated in Wisconsin and was almost demonstrated in Ohio. Sometimes the threats are external, but, increasingly, they are internal—and again, center on the replication within faculty unions of the stratified culture that has eroded the effectiveness and unity of the faculty institutionally. Nowhere is this more apparent than in places like Washington state, where friction between unionized part-time and full-time faculty has reached toxic levels; Madison, Wisconsin, where the part-time union at Madison Area Technical College took legal action against its full-time faculty counterpart; and New York City, where CUNY Contingents Unite maintains steady pressure on the Professional Staff Congress to prioritize contingent faculty concerns more effectively. Indeed, NFM was formed in part out of contingent faculty concerns about a perceived lack of urgency among faculty unions regarding the terms and conditions of their employment, including directing resources to the most basic first steps in organizing, such as forming advocacy chapters.

In the face of internal and external challenges to unionization, shared governance might take on a more prominent role in preserving and promoting faculty involvement in decision-making on college campuses. If a tendency has existed, in the last couple of decades or so, for unions to play the more prominent role as the voice and force of faculty—particularly by supporting and complementing faculty senates[21]—then perhaps the new vulnerability of unions demonstrates a need for shared governance to take its turn as the more prominent voice and the force of faculty (and in the process to educate campuses about the proper and vital role of unions in securing faculty rights and responsibilities, thereby establishing an environment where shared governance can be more effective).

Just as faculty contingency is at the heart of the struggle over corporatization, however, so does it play a role in the evolution of shared governance as a mechanism for defining the ethos of both the faculty as a whole and the social enterprise of higher education. Contingency has affected, and been affected by, the relationship between unionization and shared governance. In places like Ohio, where part-time faculty at public institutions do not have access to collective bargaining, faculty senates are one of the primary avenues through which to effect change—as long as part-time faculty are given access to them, and as long as part-time faculty have the stamina to persist in working long hours for very slow progress on issues of concern. At the University of Akron, for example, it took two years for part-time faculty senators just to get a part-time faculty listserv up and running. Previous part-time faculty senators worked for years to secure such small gains as faculty parking permits and access to eligibility for health insurance (which was obviated for most adjuncts by the discovery that they would have to pay more for the insurance than they were bringing home in wages). With the ban on part-time faculty collective bargaining in Ohio still firmly in place, contingent faculty have turned to various iterations and outgrowths of shared governance, including formal participation and informal negotiations with sympathetic administrators.[22] It is important to note, then, that contingency figures prominently in discussions not only of the efficacy of shared governance but indeed of its very survival. Research supports the contention that tenure-line faculty are often resistant to contingent faculty participation in shared governance out of bias and fear that contingent faculty cannot adequately represent the faculty perspective or will not be able to make the same level of commitment to it (an echo of the criticism leveled at contingent faculty more generally with respect to their teaching). Administrative resistance to including contingent faculty in governance may be rooted in reluctance to share power more generally, and excluding contingent faculty means that fewer faculty are actually involved.

The problem, of course, is that by excluding the majority contingent faculty from shared governance, these bodies become discredited caricatures, oligarchic rather than democratic instruments. Thus, insofar as shared governance is meant to be a practical model for students and faculty of democratic institutions and processes that do not just benefit the institution but indeed strengthen democracy more generally, then contingency, as a system that reinforces bias, inequity, and disenfranchisement, undermines a fundamental intellectual and civic goal of higher education.

Contingency as a Factor in Learning Outcomes

The corporate mindset, in which concepts like "scale" and "productivity" dominate higher education, has been invigorated by corporate funders like the Lumina and Gates Foundations, which have developed their program areas with little to no faculty involvement, at least so far. Ostensibly focused on student learning outcomes and dubbed the "completion agenda" the programs supported by these funders have been criticized in particular by faculty who have observed, as Gary Rhoades does, that the completion agenda "is compromising the learning agenda" that it "offers no mechanisms for enhancing quality, reducing non-meritocratic social stratification, or building a new economy."[23] The completion agenda, according to these critiques, fails to understand or accept the critical role of faculty in the learning process.

Rhoades in particular notes the crucial role of contingency. He points out that an increasing number of studies[24] have attempted to document correlations between faculty working conditions and student learning conditions, usually finding that contingent employment as currently practiced in higher education is detrimental to its academic mission:

> Studies of student learning and success have yielded consistent evidence that the academic engagement of students by faculty (and other professionals) is fundamental. One proxy measure of the professional working conditions that facilitate student engagement is instructors' employment status. There is an inverse correlation between student success and the proportion of contingent faculty. The problem is that the working conditions of these faculty—not having offices, not knowing from one semester to the next whether they will remain employed, not knowing what they will be teaching more than a few days before classes start—undercut the opportunity for the "new faculty majority" (an empirical description and the name of a new advocacy organization) to engage students, and for students to engage them.[25]

Interestingly, even the self-studies produced by the most ambitious of the corporate-funded programs have yielded evidence of the folly of failing to attend to contingency.[26] Nevertheless, proponents of the completion agenda seem no more willing to address the elephant-in-the-room problem of contingency than anyone else in higher education.

It seems clear that the corporate approach to higher education has institutionalized an adversarial relationship between faculty and administration. It has discouraged collegiality and encouraged credentialism over education. It has promoted among students the belief that education is nothing more than a commodity to be bought and among faculty the conviction that tenure is a private reward rather than a social contract.[27] These attitudes are often evident in the nebulous definition(s) of faculty that abound in higher education and particularly in the ways that the definitional ambiguities are used to advance agendas that have less to do with educational quality than with the priorities of either administrators or tenured faculty over those of contingent faculty and students. Below we offer two examples of this tendency: one in a unionized and one in a non-unionized context.

Case Study #1 in the Need for a New Definition of Faculty: Cal State San Marcos

The AAUP 1940 *Statement of Principles on Academic Freedom and Tenure* identifies the members of the faculty as "teachers" and "investigators."[28]

The association defines the "faculty" as those appointed to primarily teach or conduct research at a professional level or to substantially participate in the processes of teaching and/or research—as in the case of librarians—whether in tenure-track or contingent appointments. Its 2003 *Policy Statement on Contingent Appointments and the Academic Profession* includes as members of the faculty serving contingently graduate student employees engaged in "independent teaching activities that are similar in nature to those of regular faculty" and postdoctoral fellows "employed off the tenure track for periods of time beyond what could reasonably be considered the extension and completion of their professional training."[29]

Throughout its history, the AAUP has consistently demonstrated the interconnectedness between "faculty" definition and function. Institutional definitions of "faculty" matter, as certain professional rights and responsibilities derive thereof. Conversely, when institutions deny faculty their professional rights and responsibilities, they undermine the ability of faculty to be defined as such—evident in the rapid unbundling of the academic profession taking place today. Thus, part of defining the faculty is protecting their professional right to participate in institutional governance. As of this writing, a joint AAUP Committee on Contingency and Governance is in the process of drafting a report on *Inclusion in Governance of Faculty Members Holding Contingent Appointments*. The report, whose first of eight recommendations on institutional policy is an inclusive definition of "faculty" thus argues for full integration of faculty serving contingently at all levels of governance, consistent with the association's long-standing position, articulated in the 1966 *Statement on Government of Colleges and Universities*, that

> agencies for faculty participation in the government of the college or the university should be established at every level where faculty responsibility is present. An agency should exist for the views of the whole faculty.[30]

The statement was jointly developed and adopted by the AAUP, the American Council on Education (ACE), and the Association of Governing Boards of Universities and Colleges (AGB). In 1978 the AAUP adopted a note to the report that specifically addresses institutions where faculty and administration collectively bargain:

> Where there is faculty collective bargaining, the parties should seek to ensure appropriate institutional governance structures, which will protect the right of all faculty to participate in institutional governance in accordance with the "Statement on Government."[31]

For Mayra's institution, the California State University, it was the state's Public Employment Relations Board (PERB) that in 1981 defined the "faculty" bargaining unit for the system. Finding that all instructional faculty "shared a substantial community of interests"[32] PERB placed all tenure and non-tenure track faculty, including chairs,[33] in the same bargaining unit along with coaches and librarians. Subsequently, PERB certified the California Faculty Association as the exclusive bargaining agent for the CSU faculty unit. The CFA is an active and supportive affiliate of the AAUP.

In the Cal State system, faculty in contingent appointments are classified as "temporary faculty" or "lecturers." Reflecting the 1981 PERB decision, the collective bargaining agreement (CBA) between the CSU Board of Trustees and the CFA defines "faculty unit employee" as

> a bargaining unit member who is a full-time faculty unit employee, part-time faculty unit employee, probationary faculty unit employee, tenured faculty unit employee, temporary fac-

ulty unit employee, coaching faculty unit employee, counselor faculty unit employee, faculty employee, or library faculty unit employee.[34]

In addition, the contract defines "department" as meaning "the faculty unit employees within an academic department or other equivalent administrative unit."[35] These contractual definitions, which reflect the 1981 PERB decision, facilitate enforcement of contract provisions that refer to "faculty unit employee" or "department" as inclusive of all faculty regardless of classification or rank—unless otherwise specified—such as the right to participate in the process of recommending candidates for department chair:

> Department chairs shall normally be selected from the list of tenured or probationary faculty employees recommended by the department for the assignment (CBA 20. 30).[36]

Unfortunately, senates—which serve at the pleasure of chancellors or presidents—tend not to be as egalitarian and inclusive as unions, which, under the National Labor Relations Act (NLRA), have the legal duty to fairly represent every employee in the bargaining unit, not just some,[37] and whose contracts with employers are legally binding.[38] In the Cal State system, where the scope of bargaining is limited by statute to terms and conditions of employment, the constitutions and bylaws of the statewide CSU Academic Senate and the twenty-three campus senates tend to circumvent the contractual definition of faculty and limit—if not outright prohibit—participation of non-tenure-track faculty in shared governance, even at its most basic: the department level.

Through its constitution, the CSU Academic Senate gives *carte blanche* to each of the twenty-three campus senates to define "faculty" for the purpose of electing representatives to the statewide senate:

> All members of the faculty at each campus shall be eligible to vote for campus representatives to serve in the Academic Senate. Each campus shall determine which members of the campus community are considered to be faculty.[39]

Clearly, this language needs to be challenged. It can be done on the basis of statutory, contractual, and AAUP definitions, and particularly on the CSU Academic Senate's own as implied in its 2004 resolution on *Service of Lecturer Faculty on Campus Academic Senates* whereby it encourages campus senate chairs,

> through discussions among themselves and with their local constituencies, to develop a common understanding of the current state of and best practices for enabling all CSU faculty to participate in campus shared governance process.[40]

Lukewarm encouragement from the statewide senate, however, has not compelled campus senates towards full faculty inclusiveness in governance. This is evident across the system, beginning with its inconsistent definitions of "faculty."

At Cal State San Marcos, the campus senate constitution excludes part-time lecturers ("temporary faculty") from senate membership by adding a qualifier to the term "faculty":

> Voting members of the Faculty shall consist of tenured and tenure-track persons holding faculty rank, library faculty, Student Services Professional-Academic Related faculty (hereafter,

SSP-AR), and full-time temporary faculty holding at least one-year appointments in academic departments. Faculty with the voting franchise shall be called eligible faculty.[41]

Unlike full-time lecturers, who can run for college and at-large senate seats and most standing committees, the part-timers—over 380 in headcount, as compared to around twenty-five full-timers[42]—have minimal representation. They are eligible to vote for only two seats, designated as theirs: one each for a part-time lecturer representative in senate and on the Faculty Affairs Committee (FAC).

After recent restructuring, the new College of Humanities, Arts, Behavioral and Social Sciences (CHABSS) inherited the former College of Arts and Sciences governance by-laws, which, in spite of affirming that

> College governance shall be consistent with the University and College Mission Statements, the Constitution of the Faculty, and the Memorandum of Understanding between the California Faculty Association and the Trustees of the California State University,

in fact undermine an inclusive definition of faculty by rendering the college faculty's voting franchise more exclusive than that of the senate: "The privilege of voting at Faculty meetings shall extend to all persons holding tenure-line appointments."[43] Thus, neither part- nor full-time lecturers are eligible to vote at CHABSS faculty meetings or to serve on any of the college's four standing committees.[44]

At the level of the departments—whose websites often list as "The Faculty" only the tenure-track—the degree of lecturer inclusion in "faculty" meetings and other activities varies. In regards to department elections, the administration has enforced the CBA provisions on the statutory grievance procedure introduced via the present contract, which include voting for faculty hearing panel members on the basis of a half vote for faculty appointed at below a 0.5 time base and a full vote for those at 0.5 or greater.[45] Although undoubtedly it was the best compromise that CFA could accept at the time, the bargaining into the contract in 2007 of this voting model is problematic: it sets a precedent that undermines what would otherwise be the default model of one person, one vote, suggesting that the weighting of votes is negotiable. In addition, although the provision preserves the contractual definition of "faculty" and applies the proportional vote on the basis of time base rather than track, because in reality a tenure-track appointment below half time would be extraordinary, the provision actually undermines the principle of equality built into the contractual definition of "faculty" that it reaffirms. This proportional model was reinforced when in 2009 it was adopted in a three-campus unfair labor practice settlement regarding the contractual procedure on department elections for the distribution of student evaluations and was also used for the statewide faculty furlough vote. It played a pivotal role in the events at Cal State San Marcos—to be described as part of this case study—regarding efforts by chapter officers to include lecturers in the "department" process for recommending candidates for chair (CBA 20. 30, quoted above). The vagueness of the contract language renders this—as we will see—highly divisive issue more likely to be successfully tackled on a campus-by-campus basis than, for example, via a statewide grievance.

In this light, it is not surprising then that only two of the twenty-three CSUs should have campus-wide chair selection policies that, albeit including lecturers, are quite dissimilar and coincide in not fully enfranchising lecturers as faculty. At San Jose State—where the campus policy predates the implementation of the statutory grievance procedure with its 0.5/1.0 voting model—the lecturer votes to recommend candidates for chair are pro-rated to their time bases (0.2, 0.4, . . . 1.0), reported separately, and informational only:

> The name or names of those receiving a majority vote of the regular (tenured and probationary) faculty shall be forwarded to the President via the College Dean as the nominee (s) of the department. A statement of the vote of all faculty, broken down into two categories—vote by regular faculty and by temporary faculty, including the actual number of votes cast in each category—will be forwarded to the President via the College Dean for information.[46]

At Cal State Long Beach—where the policy postdates the 0.5/1.0 voting model—only lecturers on three-year appointments—that is, having a minimum of six consecutive years of service in a department—with a time base of at least 0.5 are eligible to participate and cast a full vote.[47]

Effective in fall of 2012, lecturers at San Francisco State will be eligible to participate in department chair recommendations, casting votes pro-rated to their time bases during the term when the selection process is initiated. In recognizing that a "department" comprises "all faculty" and that the term "faculty" includes lecturers ("temporary faculty"), the San Francisco State policy sets some good precedent:

> Department faculty shall determine an electoral body comprised of all faculty. This electoral body shall vote by secret ballot. The results of this ballot, in a form determined by the department faculty, including a record of those who voted, will be forwarded to the dean as part of the report. The results may include numerical counts, and because the vote is pro-rated, rounded to the nearest whole number to protect the confidentiality of part-time faculty votes.

In the event that the dean does not support the department's recommendation, the policy calls for consultation, followed by mediation if the disagreement persists. If the president or designee disagrees with both the department and the dean's recommendations, then the department is to provide "alternative recommendations until a mutually acceptable candidate is identified."[48] Throughout, the process would engage all department faculty in joint decision-making.

In the fall term of this academic year at Cal State San Marcos, when the announcement of forthcoming spring department chair selection presented an opportunity to include lecturers, at a labor-management meeting the administration agreed with the CFA chapter officers present and requested a proposal on a lecturer vote. After much consideration of likely reactions from chairs, senate leaders and tenure-track faculty in general that would fuel faculty divisiveness during a time of a pending strike authorization vote, and in the absence of consensus among the chapter board members themselves in regard to recommending the default model of one person, one vote, the initial proposal for an interim procedure—agreed to by the administration—was that all department "faculty" would vote, with the concession, consistent with the contractual department vote on faculty hearing panel members, that "faculty" with less than a 0.5 time base would be entitled to a 0.5 vote and "faculty" with a 0.5 or greater time base would be entitled to a full vote, in other words, regardless of classification.

There was immediate pushback from tenure-track faculty members, in particular department chairs, who voiced their concern that "the lecturer vote" would change the outcome of "the tenure-track vote." Some faculty questioned the fairness of granting a 0.5 vote, for example, to lecturers teaching only one course at a 0.2 time base, and of granting eligibility to vote to new lecturers, especially those on their first semester of appointment. When the senate executive committee objected to not having been consulted in regards to the development of a campus-wide procedure to accommodate lecturers, at a meeting of the senate's Faculty Affairs Committee (FAC) the associate vice president for Faculty Affairs requested and obtained unanimous approval to "mandate" an interim procedure for use this spring only.[49] Faculty Affairs once again requested the chapter officers' assistance. Although, in order to placate dissenting faculty, the officers made additional concessions and modified the interim procedure so that (1) all tenure-track faculty are eligible for a full vote (regardless of time base), (2) lecturers with at least two semesters of service are eligible to vote, and (3) the results of the tenure-track and lecturer votes are reported to the deans separately (as under the San Jose model but in order to monitor any impact that "the lecturer vote" may have on "the tenure-track vote"), the modified procedure otherwise retains the original 0.5/1.0 vote for lecturers (to insist on contractual precedent), identifies lecturers as "lecturer faculty" (to insist on an inclusive definition) and directs the president's designee to, "[w]hen selecting the chair. . . take into consideration the total 'Recommend' votes cast by the department" (to avoid purely informational lecturer votes, as is the case in San Jose). However, members of senate exec mounted opposition to the modified proposal, claiming that the determination of who votes and in what proportion falls within the scope of shared governance rather than the contract. They scrambled to check with other campuses regarding their practices (finding CFA's proposal for San Marcos lecturers "extremely generous"), and to interpret the contract's references to "department" emphasizing instances where a "department recommendation" does not involve an all-faculty vote.

In an effort to maintain faculty unity as we approach the strike authorization vote, CFA is subsequently "not objecting" to a complete proportional vote as an interim compromise for this term only, as, referring the procedure back to FAC, senate's exec asked the committee to recommend an amendment adopting the San Jose and San Francisco voting model for lecturers. Thus, exec has conceded to lecturer participation in chair selection, albeit reduced. In addition, FAC, acting upon exec's referral, has drafted a *Resolution on the Interim Spring 2012 Procedure for Department Chair Selection*, whereby, led by the Chair, it has taken a principled position. Acknowledging the existing tension among the San Marcos faculty in regards to the issue, FAC recommends (1) a complete proportional vote, consistent with the San Francisco and San Jose chair selection procedures, for the purpose of spring 2012 only and (2) "in the spirit of shared governance further inclusive conversations among Unit 3 faculty employees on the consideration of *simple* versus *complete proportionality* regarding the issue of lecturer participation in the chair selection process" prior to the development of a permanent campus policy. Affirming the contractual definition of "faculty" that reflects the 1981 PERB decision to place all Cal State instructional faculty in the same bargaining unit, and concurring with and citing said decision, the committee "concludes that none of these differences merits splitting faculty along either tenured/non-tenured or full-time/part-time lines"[51]

> and will work diligently on behalf of all Unit 3 employees to address issues and concerns relative to the interim and permanent procedure for department chair selection, in concert with CFA representatives and the administration.[52]

In March 2012, senate exec accepted FAC's recommendation at a meeting where, it was reported, the overall tone was one of acceptance of lecturer participation, of diminished resistance. However, when the resolution was brought before the full senate for a vote, the debate shifted once more to one about lecturers participating at all, and senate ran out of time and quorum before a motion to vote. In light of the urgency of getting chair selection under way this spring in the departments where it is still pending, a lecturer who was present remarked in frustration, "senate doesn't act as though time is of the essence." Thus, as of this writing, there is still no ending to this somewhat tedious narrative.

As these developments demonstrate, in the CSU there is a general misunderstanding of the role of department faculty in recommending candidates for chair as a privilege and responsibility reserved for the tenure-track, as well as a misunderstanding of the role of chair. On the one hand, recommending candidates for chair is an exercise of both individual and collective academic freedom in making a professional judgment at a basic level of shared governance in which all department faculty should participate.[53] After all, the department chair "serves as the chief representative of the department within an institution."[54] On the other hand, it is a collective bargaining (or otherwise workplace democracy) issue: CSU department faculty, banding together as union workers, exercise their negotiated right to have a say on who their immediate supervisor will be. Department chairs are appointed by and "serve at the pleasure of the President." They "perform duties and carry out responsibilities assigned by the President."[55] As supervisors, department chairs make personnel recommendations to the next level of management (deans and/or associate deans), for example, regarding assignment of courses, professional leave impact on the department, and, more importantly, appointment and reappointment of lecturers. Not evaluated by peer review committees and only in special circumstances by academic administrators, for part-time lecturers, a chair's evaluation or recommendation not to reappoint carries disproportionate weight *vis-à-vis* their full-time lecturer colleagues.

Moving forward, prior to considering a permanent campus policy on department chairs, the San Marcos senate would do well to follow FAC's recommendations, rethink "shared" governance and the various institutional definitions of faculty, develop a better understanding of the faculty contract and collective bargaining, and be responsive when lecturers voice that it is their right and desire—as both fellow "faculty" and union members—to be included. The seemingly much-ado-about-nothing over a department recommendation that in the end the administration has the discretion to ignore brought to the surface unacknowledged prejudices and the opportunity to address them. It is evident that, after the initial shock and given time to consider tenure-track and lecturer colleagues' well-reasoned arguments, key campus faculty leaders are moving to a position of support for lecturer integration in governance at the department level and beyond; that is, there is willingness to accept what some colleagues have called "a c-change." Instead of brooding over the erosion of the initial proposal, one should celebrate the significant progress that the eroded proposal represents in terms of defining "the faculty." It is important to point out, although briefly due to space constraints, factors that aided in making progress: (1) a history of growing lecturer outspokenness and visibility and collaboration with tenure-track faculty on CSU campuses encouraged by the CFA, which integrates tenure and non-tenure track faculty as equals within its full governance structure; for example, this term at Cal State San Marcos the chapter board includes three lecturer officers (vice president, lecturer rep, faculty rights chair) and the senate's Faculty Affairs Committee three lecturer members (the part-time lecturer, School of Nursing and CFA reps); (2) the unprecedented commitment that the administration shared with chapter officers to enforce the right of lecturers, as members of the "faculty" and of "departments" to participate in the process of recommending candidates for chair; (3) the willingness—although with much trepidation—of chapter officers to take advantage of and follow through on an opportunity for change in spite of the risk involved; (4) the chapter officers' respect for shared governance and commitment to working with the academic senate; (5) the availability of AAUP statements that provide the principles and language upon which to build a platform for change.

* * *

Returning to Hightower and Frazer's description of the dismantling of the American middle-class as resulting from "a new normal of job insecurity" what the majority of the faculty in higher education has lost is the expectation of employment that recognizes their professional standing as university teachers/researchers and provides economic and job security.

The 1940 AAUP *Statement of Principles on Academic Freedom and Tenure* defines tenure as

> a means to certain ends; specifically: (1) freedom of teaching and research and of extramural activities, and (2) a sufficient degree of economic security to make the profession attractive to men and women of ability. Freedom and economic security, hence, tenure, are indispensable to the success of an institution in fulfilling its obligations to its students and to society.[56]

Since throughout its history the AAUP has not linked tenure with a particular faculty status, it can be granted at any professional rank or without rank.[57] In this light, the AAUP has more recently recommended that evaluation and appointment of faculty for contingent positions resemble those for the tenure track, while institutions transition "to a stable academic environment characterized by a predominantly tenure-line faculty."[58] In addition to creating new tenure-track positions, institutions may accomplish this through "conversion"; that is, by converting the status of faculty presently serving in contingent appointments to part- or full-time tenured or tenure-track.[59] To quote the 2010 *Report on Tenure and Teaching-Intensive Appointments*:

> The best practice for institutions of all types is to convert the status of contingent appointments to appointments eligible for tenure with only minor changes in job description.

Stabilization of the faculty workforce should be accomplished without negatively impacting current faculty and their students.[60] Throughout its various statements and reports, the AAUP has held on to its long-standing policy that, "with carefully circumscribed exceptions, all full-time appointments are of two kinds: probationary appointments and appointments with continuous tenure."[61] Until very recently, this long-standing policy has been invoked to deny the legitimacy of full-time appointments off the tenure track because they were in fact not probationary. In the case of part-time appointments at institutions where part-time tenure does not exist, the association recommends that, following the equivalent of a maximum probationary period of seven years, if reappointed, part-time faculty serving contingently be offered "appointment (s) with part-time continuing service."[62] But these two positions— on full- and on part-time appointments respectively—need not be mutually exclusive. If the AAUP recommends converting the status of faculty serving contingently—whether part- or full-time—to tenured or tenure-track, it follows that, in the absence of support for conversion, institutions could offer part- and full-time appointments with continuing service.

During the last twenty or thirty years, some faculty senates but especially unions that represent non-tenure track faculty have been taking incremental steps towards conversion or appointment with continuing service (whether full- or part-time) or their equivalents. The above-mentioned AAUP report provides examples of actual "Conversion Practices and Proposals" (Appendix A) as well as of "Forms of Stabilization Other than Tenure" (Appendix B), including automatic mechanisms for reemployment rights, time-based and seniority-based rights, and layoff and recall rights.

The following section will again focus on the lecturers in the California State University system. Unlike the American Federation of Teachers (AFT), which represents the UC lecturers or "nonsenate faculty" and the Regents of the University of California, the CFA and the CSU Board of Trustees have not thus far negotiated in their collective bargaining agreement lecturer eligibility for continuing appointments. However, the CSU-CFA agreement does provide terms and conditions of employment that significantly enhance economic and job security for the CSU lecturers and in various degrees recognize their professional standing. Following are examples worthy of note.[63]

Salary and Benefits

CSU lecturers are hired in ranges L (usually without a master's degree), A, B, C and D. Once in ranges B, C and D, they are on the same salary schedule as assistant, associate, and full professors, respectively; but, because they are not eligible for promotion, they move up within their range through negotiated 2. 65% service salary increases (SSIs) and may apply for a "range elevation" when they become eligible under their campus Range Elevation Policy, which establishes eligibility criteria. All faculty unit employees receive the general salary increases (GSIs) bargained in a given contract. Following passage of AB 211, CFA was able to bargain health benefits for lecturers who are appointed for at least one semester or two consecutive quarters at a 0.4 time base (6 weighted teaching units/WTUs). These benefits are provided through the California Public Employees' Retirement System (CalPERS) for the lecturers, eligible spouses or domestic partners, and children. Lecturers are enrolled in one of two mandatory retirement plans, Part-time, Seasonal, and Temporary Employees' Retirement Plan (PST) or CalPERS, where enrollment begins when a lecturer is employed at a minimum time base of 0.5 (7.5 WTUs) per term.

Due Process and Appointment Rights

CSU-CFA contract provisions are consistent with hiring standards articulated by the AAUP in *Recommended Institutional Regulations on Academic Freedom and Tenure*, which are designed to enable institutions "to protect academic freedom and tenure and to ensure academic due process"[64] which are equally applicable to institutions where there is collective bargaining (and contracts are legally binding) and where there is not (and institutional committees are charged with enforcement). CSU lecturers receive *appointment letters* that specify the terms and conditions of their employment, including beginning and ending dates of the appointment, classification, range, time base, and assignment. Part-time appointments may be (and generally are) issued on a conditional basis, while full-time appointments (1.0 time base)—excepting for coaches—may not be conditional and, thus, are subject to layoff procedures. Under the principle of *careful consideration*, a department has the contractual obligation to carefully consider lecturers who apply for subsequent employment or reappointment. At a minimum, the department chair or appropriate administrator must review a lecturer's *personnel action file* (PAF), a confidential file that contains pertinent information such as the curriculum vitae and the results of peer and student evaluations. In other words, a department's decision not to rehire or reappoint a lecturer may not be capricious or arbitrary. To quote arbitrator Adolph Koven:

The University should be able to show concrete evidence of how the decision not to retain him or her was reached and that the decision had a reasonable basis. . . [A] simple assertion by an administrator, standing alone, [cannot] be used to establish that "careful consideration" was given.[65]

After two semesters or three quarters in the same academic year in a department, a lecturer who is reappointed is entitled to a *similar assignment*, that is, a one-year appointment at the previous year's or *entitlement* time base. Because part-time appointments are conditional, entitlement time base might not be met, but, on the other hand, it may be exceeded, thereby resulting in a higher entitlement time base for a subsequent appointment. Following six consecutive years (a minimum of one semester or two quarters each) in the same department, except in cases of documented unsatisfactory performance or serious conduct problems, lecturers are offered an automatic *three-year appointment* at their current entitlement time base. Three-year appointments are renewable on the basis of satisfactory performance.

While lecturers on one-year appointments are evaluated on a yearly basis, lecturers on three-year appointments are evaluated at least once during the term of their appointments or more frequently upon their own request or that of the President/President's designee. While department chairs or appropriate administrators evaluate part-time lecturers, full-time lecturers undergo two levels of review: by a department peer review committee (PRC) and by an appropriate administrator. Implicit in the San Marcos senate's definition of "eligible faculty" is the idea that full-time status confers both certain privileges and responsibilities. If full-time status indeed renders non-tenure-track faculty more vested in institutional life to the benefit of student learning, then there should be in place automatic mechanisms to bring up part-timers to full-time status, to a level of employment that recognizes their professional standing as university teachers/researchers and provides economic and job security. In the CSU-CFA collective bargaining agreement that mechanism is the seniority-based *Preference for Available Work*. Below is the revised version, proposed by the CFA during the present round of bargaining (abridged):

> In the event that the department determines that a need exists to assign work to temporary faculty unit employees [or lecturers]. . . the work shall be offered to qualified temporary faculty unit employees [or lecturers] in the department who have performed satisfactorily according to the following preference for work order. . .
>
> First, offer work to. . . [lecturers] who are holding or are entitled to a three-year full-time appointment. . . up to a 1.0 time-base;
>
> 1. Next, offer work to. . . [lecturers] who are holding a continuing multi-year (not 3–year). . . full-time appointment;
>
> 2. Next, offer work to. . . [lecturers] who are holding or are entitled to a three-year part-time appointment. . . up to their time base entitlement;
>
> 3. Next, offer work to individuals whose names appear on the. . . [department recall list] up to the time-base entitlement of their most recent three-year appointment;[66]
>
> 4. Next, offer work to. . . [lecturers] who are entitled to a one-year appointment. . . or are holding a continuing multi-year (not three-year. . .) part-time appointment up to their time base entitlement;
>
> 5. Next, offer work to. . . [lecturers] who are holding or are entitled to a three-year part-time appointment up to a 1.0 time base;

6. Next, offer work to. . . [lecturers] who are holding or are entitled to a one-year part-time appointment up to a 1.0 time-base;

7. Next, offer work to any remaining. . . [lecturers] who were employed during the previous academic year;

8. Next, offer work to any remaining individuals who are entitled to careful consideration. . .

9. Last, offer work to any other qualified candidate.[67]

In brief, the *Preference for Available Work* aims to eliminate capricious or arbitrary hiring decisions and, when it is enforced, on the basis of seniority CSU lecturers are able to advance from conditional part-time, short-term status to unconditional full-time long-term status.

Vacancy Announcements
At San Marcos, the CFA Faculty Rights Committee is currently working to enforce a much ignored but important contract provision, that pertaining to the posting of vacancy announcements,

> Vacancy announcements of temporary employee positions shall be available on the campus where such vacancies may exist. Employees and the CFA shall be notified of the location where such vacancy announcements may be examined.[68]

Administrative practice has been to collect "applications" for potential vacancies through open department pools. Consequently, lecturers are not always notified of additional work available in their own departments (as implicit in the *Preference for Available Work*) or in other departments for which they may qualify, as in the case of a part-timer who explained, "Being a lecturer at CSU-SM is my main source of income, and I currently only teach 2 courses in Global Studies. . . I would be qualified to teach in poli sci, global business and ethnic (Middle East) studies."

Collective bargaining agreements, when effectively enforced (i.e., through joint labor-management efforts and the grievance procedure), can ensure stability for both the faculty and the institution in regards to terms and conditions of employment, professional standards, and shared governance (where it is subject to bargaining). However, these contract "rights" are rendered fragile and contingent status highly precarious when agreements expire and the parties engage in negotiations for a successor contract. In the present round of bargaining, the proposals by the CSU Chancellor's Office represent take-backs of the automatic mechanisms for reemployment rights, time-based and seniority-based rights, and layoff and recall rights that have become a national model in the struggle against contingency. As of this writing, the Chancellor's proposals would (1) limit the right to careful consideration to lecturers with a break in service of no more than 18 months; (2) render all lecturer appointments—including full-time—automatically conditional "unless otherwise stated in the official notification"; (3) make all initial three-year appointments dependent upon a special performance review (following six years of service with annual evaluations) and presidential discretion, and subsequent three-year appointments contingent dependent upon a positive recommendation from an appropriate administrator; and (4) eliminate the obligation in the *Preference for Available Work* to offer new or additional work to incumbent lecturers up to a 1.0 time base, enabling the administration to offer new or additional work instead to any other qualified candidate.[69] Contingency serves the corporate university well: administrative authority and discretion to hire off the tenure-track results in loss of faculty voice in both shared governance and in the unions that represent them, both of which rely on the strength of their membership. Not surprisingly, the California Faculty Association called for a strike vote in April of 2012.

Case Study #2 in the Need for a New Definition of Faculty: Ohio Community College

In Ohio, part-time faculty at public institutions do not have the right to bargain collectively. Lacking access to any kind of due process protections, the part-time faculty member featured in this case study has asked to remain anonymous.[70]

One well-known feature of life as a contingent faculty member is the experience of being hired at the last minute, sometimes days before (or even after) an academic term has begun. The practice has been justified by the reality of fluctuating enrollments. In collective bargaining contexts, faculty members are often somewhat protected from the insecurities of this system through guarantees of a certain percentage of their remuneration even when a class is cancelled.

For faculty who do not have access to collective bargaining, the dance of last minute hiring can be a nerve-wracking exercise, since the faculty member's ability to be "flexible" and "accommodating" can directly influence whether the hiring institution keeps the instructor on the list of people it is willing to rehire in the future. At the same time, most faculty members are concerned about having the time they need to prepare. They are often in a catch-22 situation, because if they know ahead of time what their assignment is, then they are expected to take uncompensated time to prepare. If they don't, and are hired at the last minute, then they are often in the position of scrambling to stay "a chapter ahead" of the class they are teaching.

At one community college in Ohio, a part-time instructor found himself approached days before the start of the semester to see if he was interested in taking over the teaching load of a (full-time non-tenure-track) colleague who had become unexpectedly ill. The situation was such that the originally assigned instructor would not know from week to week, for the first several weeks of class, whether she would be able to return. The part-timer was therefore being asked to take over his colleague's classes on a temporary basis. If the full-timer ended up not being able to return, then the part-timer would be hired on a full-time appointment, with full salary and benefits, on an "emergency temporary" basis.

The part-timer asked some questions to clarify the conditions in which he and his potential students would be operating. Whose syllabus would he be expected to use—his own or his colleague's? And what would his own status be while he was teaching his colleague's class? What would he be paid? Would he be expected to give his colleague the students' work to evaluate, evaluate it himself, or work with his colleague as a team teacher?

The part-timer was told that he would be classified as a "substitute" and paid at the substitute rate of pay, which was an hourly rate paid per actual hour in the classroom—no compensation for any time spent on class preparation, grading, or office hours, and not a per-credit hour rate like that of part-time faculty. The dean could not decide if he would teach his own syllabus or that of his colleague, nor how their responsibilities would be divided. The dean did say that if he ended up taking over the class, he would be upgraded to full-time non-tenure-track status and receive a pro-rated salary plus benefits. Meanwhile, he could continue to teach his own classes at the part-time, per-course rate.

In addition to pointing out the bewildering differences in pay and confusing set of responsibilities for himself, the adjunct pointed out that the students would be beginning the term not knowing who their permanent instructor would be and that this situation would be in place for several weeks before any final decision would be made. He observed that for the two developmental classes in particular, this situation was potentially quite harmful to the students who, he knew from experience and from existing studies, particularly need stability and depth in their interactions with faculty. He wondered out loud about alternatives, and the dean, in an attempt to persuade him, pleaded that if he did not take the classes they might have to cancel them. The instructor observed that since there was still a week to go before classes, cancelation might be fairer to the students than putting them in a class that would be staffed so precariously. The dean replied that the institution could not consider cancelling a fully enrolled class when all it needed was "a warm body in the classroom."

The adjunct declined the assignment, citing the economic cost to him and the almost certain damage to the students' educational experience.

In this short narrative one can see how the definition of faculty and the right of students to quality education was rendered absurd by the administrative prioritizing of enrollment figures, tuition dollars, and cost savings. One faculty member would, potentially, be a substitute, a part-time faculty member, and a full-time faculty member all in the course of one semester, with a corresponding difference in pay but not in his responsibilities to his students. Not only would the faculty member be negatively affected by the low pay and the insecurity of the situation, but the students would be walking into a disastrous academic situation practically guaranteed to undermine their educational progress.

Conclusion: Definitions Do Matter

The point of these case studies is to show that, in regard to a definition of faculty, "getting it right" is fundamental to restoring the academic profession by strengthening the faculty voice in collective bargaining and shared governance and preserving the integrity of the academic experience. Shared governance and collective bargaining are not mutually exclusive. Founded on the democratic principle of broad-based power sharing, shared governance and collective bargaining should be mutually supportive, not least because they model fundamental democratic principles. Similarly, advocating for professional working conditions for oneself is not, as too many people have tried to argue, "unprofessional" or "selfish" but rather the exact opposite; the fundamental premise underlying such efforts is that faculty working conditions are student learning conditions. Professionalism, as Hamilton and Gaff assert, is grounded in a conception of the social contract at the heart of faculty work and therefore requires, among other things, an "ethics of duty" and an "ethics of aspiration" that encourage all faculty members and groups to "hold each other accountable to meet the minimum standards of the profession, the discipline, and their institution."[71]

"Getting it right" involves consistent alignment of policies and practices with professional values and principles. "Getting it right" involves solidarity, hard work, vigilance, and the courage to challenge. With chair selection still pending, the authors hope that the Cal State San Marcos faculty are able to overcome class differences, share power, make "department" recommendations, and set precedent for meaningful faculty integration locally, on other campuses, and statewide, thereby offering faculty unions and senates nationwide a best practice to emulate. With collective bargaining for public institutions part-time faculty in Ohio still as elusive as representation on faculty senates at many institutions,[72] the authors hope that real attention to student learning processes and outcomes will reveal what faculty and students already know about the importance of faculty working conditions to student learning conditions. Definitions do matter indeed, when rights to fair employment and to quality education depend on them.

As we have approached it in this essay and as Ginsberg asserts in *The Fall of the Faculty: The Rise of the All-Administrative University and Why It Matters*, shared governance is about "the university . . . [being] capable of producing not only new knowledge but new visions of society." Administrative control, on the other hand, suggests that "the university can never be more than what Stanley Aronowitz has aptly termed a knowledge factory."[73] Gaff and Hamilton suggest that the transfer of control from the faculty to the administration and the "public renegotiat[ion of] the social contract toward a typical market relationship of consumer/service provider or employer/employee" is a result, in part, of

> . . . (1) changing market conditions undermining the precondition for the social contract for part or all of the profession, (2) failures of professionalism that undermine the public's trust in the social contract, or (3) failures of the profession to educate the public regarding the benefits of the social contract.[74]

Thus, practical strategies for encouraging a more solid, and solidarity-infused, definition of faculty must include mutually reinforcing activities: providing all faculty with the right of access to collective bargaining and shared governance, so that they can more effectively resist the effort to reduce them to "warm bodies in the classroom" and informing collective bargaining and shared governance with a constant awareness of and arguments for the connection between faculty working conditions and student learning conditions. Only when faculty, administrators, and students recognize this core truth will faculty truly be able to own their identities as professionals and as educators, to the benefit of higher education and ultimately for the common good.

Notes

1. This figure is based on analysis of 2007 IPEDS data by AAUP, which show that 15.1% of all faculty are full-time non-tenure track, 41.1% are part-time non-tenure track, and 19.4% are graduate student employees, for a total of 75.6% of faculty working without access to tenure. See http://www.aaup.org/NR/rdonlyres/6890A0F8–E43B-4B05–BEB4–C1A0720B1FC7/0/Fig1.pdf.

2. Aronowitz, Stanley, *The Knowledge Factory: Dismantling the Corporate University and Creating True Higher Learning*, Boston: Beacon Press, 2000.

3. Ginsberg, Benjamin, *The Fall of the Faculty: The Rise of the All-Administrative University and Why It Matters*, New York: Oxford University Press, 2011.

4. Arum, Richard, and Roska, Josipa, *Academically Adrift: Limited Learning on College Campuses*. Chicago: University of Chicago Press, 2010.

5. See Jacoby, Daniel, "The Effects of Part-time Faculty Employment on Community College Graduation Rates," *Journal of Higher Education,* 2006, 77 (6), 1081–1103.

6. See http://chronicle.com/article/An-Emerging-Field-Deconstructs/130791/

7. See the Campaign Principles in particular at http://futureofhighered.org/

8. Hamilton, Neil W. and Gaff, Jerry G., *The Future of the Professoriate: Academic Freedom, Peer Review and Shared Governance*. Washington, DC: AAC&U, 2009, p. 9.

9. http://www.etymonline.com/index. php? term=faculty

10. "The Hightower Lowdown" newsletter, February 2011.

11. Aronowitz, p. 11.

12. Gilbert, Daniel, "The Corporate University and the Public Intellectual" (working paper, *Work & Culture*, 2005/8, Working Group on Globalization and Culture, Yale University, http://laborculture. research. yale. edu//documents/gilbert_corporate_W&C.pdf).

13. In their "Introduction" to the book *Contingent Work: American Employment Relations in Transition* (Ithaca, NY: Cornell University Press, 1998), applying labor economist Dean Morse's analysis of labor market patterns, editors Kathleen Barker and Kathleen Christensen explain that beginning in the late 1900s, through successive waves of downsizing, firms have shifted to an employment relations model characterized by a growing highly skilled, technical or white-collar peripheral "just-in-time" or *contingent* workforce that, until recently, as "a relatively privileged set or workers has worked under a very different model of employment relations" (p. 2).

14. Williams, Jeffrey J., "Academic Freedom and Indentured Students" *Academe*, January–February 2012, pp. 12–13, citing data collected for 2008 by the National Center for Education Statistics.

15. Term coined by the National Coalition for Adjunct and Contingent Equity, http://www.newfacultymajority. info/national/.

16. *2010–11 Report on the Economic Status of the Profession*, AAUP: http://www.aaup.org/AAUP/comm/rep/Z/ecstatreport10–11/.

17. Ginsberg, p. 25.

18. Ibid., p. 26

19. Ibid., p. 208.

20. See Texas legislature activities and response, http://www.insidehighered.com/news/2011/11/14/study-finds-u-texas-faculty-are-productive, as well as *Winning by Degrees,* http://mckinseyonsociety.com/winning-by-degrees/.

21. Maitland, Christine, and Rhoades, Gary, "Unions and Faculty Governance" in *The NEA 2001 Almanac of Higher Education,* 27–33. Washingon, DC: NEA, 2001; Nelson, 2011, AFT/NEA joint pamphlet on unions and senates; Kezar, Adrianna, and, Sam, Cecilia, "Beyond Contracts Non-Tenure-Track Faculty and Campus Governance," in *The NEA 2001 Almanac of Higher Education,* 83–91. Washingon, DC: NEA, 2010, http://www.nea.org/assets/img/PubAlmanac/KezarSam_2010.pdf

22. http://www.aaup.org/AAUP/pubsres/academe/2010/JA/feat/mcgr.htm

23. http://www.aacu.org/liberaleducation/le-wi12/rhoades. cfm

24. http://www.insidehighered.com/news/2008/11/06/adjuncts

25. http://www.aacu.org/liberaleducation/le-wi12/rhoades. cfm

26. http://www.insidehighered.com/news/2011/02/10/five_years_of_achieving_the_dream_in_community_colleges

27. Hamilton and Gaff.

28. *AAUP Policy Documents and Reports* (tenth edition), "1940 Statement of Principles on Academic Freedom and Tenure with 1970 Interpretive Comments" pp. 3–11, http://www.aaup.org/AAUP/pubsres/policydocs/contents/1940statement.htm.

29. Ibid. "Contingent Appointments and the Academic Profession" p. 99, http://www.aaup.org/AAUP/pubsres/policydocs/contents/conting-stmt.htm.

30. Ibid. "Statement on Government of Colleges and Universities," p. 139.

31. Ibid. Note #5, p. 140.

32. PERB, "In the Matter of Unit Determination for Employees of the California State University and Colleges" September 22, 1981, http://www.perb. ca. gov/decisionbank/pdfs/0173h.pdf.

33. In considering whether or not to include chairs in the faculty bargaining unit, PERB "examined the evidence to determine whether department chairs exercise any of the enumerated supervisory functions. Second, and critical to the statutory direction. . . [it] examined the evidence to determine whether, in instances where it appears that the department chairs do exercise supervisory functions, they do so 'primarily in the interest of and on behalf of the members of the academic department'" (pp. 31–32). PERB concluded that ". . . department chairpersons exercise supervisory functions relevant to an employee's status but do so in a collegial format and that their inclusion in the unit with other faculty members will not pose conflicts of interest or divided loyalties" (p. 39).

34. Collective Bargaining Agreement between the California Faculty Association and the Board of Trustees of the California State University, Unit 3: Faculty, 2007–2010, Article 2. 13, http://www.calfac.org/resource/collective-bargaining-agreement-contract.

35. Ibid., Article 2. 12.

36. Ibid., Article 20. 30.

37. National Labor Relations Act, https: //www.nlrb. gov/national-labor-relations-act.

38. Although it is also true that many unions replicate the tiered faculty structures present in institutions, it is one of the advantages of unions that legal obligations can be invoked by contingent faculty seeking to reform their unions.

39. The Constitution of the Academic Senate of the California State University, http://www.calstate.edu/AcadSen/Records/About_the_Senate/2006_Constitution_Revised_Final.pdf.

40. Service of Lecturer Faculty on Campus Academic Senates, http://www.calstate.edu/AcadSen/Records/Resolutions/2003–2004/2674. shtml.

41. Constitution and By-Laws of the University Faculty and Academic Senate, http://www2. csusm.edu/academic_senate/GoverningDocs/ConstitutionApril2009.pdf.

42. Based on numbers provided by Faculty Affairs for fall 2011.

43. By-Laws for Governance of the College of Arts and Sciences, California State University, San Marcos, http://www.csusm.edu/coas/webdocs/bylaws.pdf.

44. Lecturers seeking reform have brought these matters to the attention of the new dean who, in conjunction with these lecturers, is considering the establishment of a Lecturers' Advisory Committee for the college.

45. Collective Bargaining Agreement between the California Faculty Association and the Board of Trustees of the California State University, Unit 3: Faculty, 2007–2010, Arts. 10.10 and 15.15, http://www.calfac.org/resource/collective-bargaining-agreement-contract, and Settlement Agreement: Grievance CFA No. 2006–212/CSU No. R03–2006–362 and Unfair Labor Practice Charge LACE-1032–H.

46. "Policy Recommendation: Departmental Voting Rights" http://www.sjsu.edu/senate/F02–4.pdf.

47. "Policies and Procedures for the Appointment and Review of Department Chairs" http://www.csulb.edu/divisions/aa/grad_undergrad/senate/documents/policy/2000/09/.

48. "Policy on Department Chairs and Equivalent Unit Directors" http://www.sfsu.edu/~senate/documents/policies/F11–145.html.

49. February 20, 2012, CSUSM FAC meeting.

50. 3561 (b); HEERA identifies what the scope of representation "shall not include" rather than what the scope of shared governance shall include, and states that "All matters not within the scope of representation are reserved to the employer and may not be subject to meeting and conferring, provided that nothing herein may be construed to limit the right of the employer to consult with any employees or employee organization [i.e. academic senates] on any matter outside the scope of representation (3562 (q) (2)." http://www.perb. ca. gov/laws/statutes. asp#ST3562_2, and Responsibilities of Academic Senates within a Collective Bargaining Context, CSU Academic Senate interpretive document, http://www2.csusm.edu/academic_senate/GoverningDocs/HEERA.pdf.

51. "Faculty Affairs Committee (FAC) Resolution on the Interim Spring 2012 Procedure for Department Chair Selection" Cal State San Marcos, March 5, 2012.

52. PERB, p. 22.

53. See *AAUP Policy Documents and Reports* (10th ed.), "Contingent Appointments and the Academic Profession" pp. 98–114, and the forthcoming AAUP *Report on Contingent Faculty Participation in Governance* and the *Statement on Government of Colleges and Universities*, pp. 135–140, http://www.aaup.org/AAUP/pubsres/policydocs/contents/conting-stmt.htm, http://www.aaup.org/AAUP/pubsres/policydocs/contents/governancestatement.htm.

54. *AAUP Policy Documents and Reports* (10th ed.), "Statement on Government of Colleges and Universities," p. 139.

55. Collective Bargaining Agreement between the California Faculty Association and the Board of Trustees of the California State University, Unit 3: Faculty, 2007–2010, Art. 20. 30–32, http://www.calfac.org/resource/collective-bargaining-agreement-contract.

56. *AAUP Policy Documents and Reports* (10th ed.), "1940 Statement of Principles on Academic Freedom and Tenure with 1970 Interpretive Comments," p. 3, http://www.aaup.org/AAUP/pubsres/policydocs/contents/1940statement.htm.

57. Ibid., "Contingent Appointments and the Academic Profession," p. 105, http://www.aaup.org/AAUP/pubsres/policydocs/contents/conting-stmt.htm.

58. Ibid., p. 108.

59. Ibid., p. 110.

60. *Bulletin of the American Association of University Professors*, Vol. 96 (2010), "Report on Tenure and Teaching-Intensive Appointments" p. 92, http://www.aaup.org/AAUP/comm/rep/teachertenure.htm.

61. *AAUP Policy Documents and Reports* (10th ed.), "Contingent Appointments and the Academic Profession" p. 104, http://www.aaup.org/AAUP/pubsres/policydocs/contents/conting-stmt.htm.

62. *Bulletin of the American Association of University Professors* 96 (2010), "Recommended Institutional Regulations on Academic Freedom and Tenure" p. 107, http://www.aaup.org/AAUP/pubsres/policydocs/contents/RIR.htm. R. I. R. 13 stipulates due process rights for part-time faculty appointments, while R. I. R. 14 addresses those for graduate student employees.

63. See the *CFA Lecturers' Handbook* (2007–10) developed by the statewide CFA Lecturers' Council, http://www.calfac.org/sites/main/files/file-attachments/lecturershandbook_sept2008_rev_1110_1.pdf, and the CSU-CFA Collective Bargaining Agreement (2007–10), http://www.calfac.org/resource/collective-bargaining-agreement-contract.

64. "Recommended Institutional Regulations on Academic Freedom and Tenure" http://www.aaup.org/AAUP/pubsres/policydocs/contents/RIR.htm.

65. Arbitrator Adolph Koven, "In the Matter of Betty Brooks, AAA Case No. 3–84–102, 1986," as quoted in the CFA Lecturers' Handbook (2007–10), p. 12, http://www.calfac.org/sites/main/files/file-attachments/lecturershandbook_sept2008_rev_1110_1.pdf.

66. These are lecturers on three-year appointments whose time-base is zero during the last year of their appointments or for whom there is no work available for a subsequent three-year appointment. They are placed on a department recall list for a period of three years.

67. CalState.edu, Labor Relations: Bargaining Updates, http://www.calstate.edu/LaborRel/Contracts_HTML/bargaining-proposals/2011/Art12–CFAProp.pdf.

68. Collective Bargaining Agreement between the California Faculty Association and the Board of Trustees of the California State University, Unit 3: Faculty, 2007–2010, Art. 12. 27, http://www.calfac.org/resource/collective-bargaining-agreement-contract.

69. The CSU and CFA bargaining proposals are posted side by side at http://www.calstate.edu/LaborRel/Contracts_HTML/bargaining_updates. shtml. Due to the nature of bargaining, proposals are subject to change.

70. Identifying information may have been changed in this account.

71. Hamilton and Gaff, p. 12.

72. According to the preliminary results of the Faculty Senate Leader Survey carried out by James G. Archibald at the Center for Higher Education at Ohio University, more than half of all institutions surveyed allow contingent faculty representation on faculty senates, and data were not collected regarding the degree of representation (numbers, voting privileges) that contingent faculty had at the institutions where contingent faculty do have representation.

73. Ginsberg, p. 3.

CHAPTER TWELVE

Researching for Justice

Using One's Role as Faculty Member to Fight for Equity in Higher Education

MARYBETH GASMAN

"You can't do research and also be an activist."
   —Dean, Ivy League institution

"I don't want to be a faculty member because you can't really have an impact. I want to make change; research can't do that."
   —Countless students, every college and university

The two quotes above are messages that I continually hear in academic settings. Interestingly, the very reason that I became a faculty member was to make change—to transform minds, to provide knowledge to larger audiences, to write a more inclusive and empowering history and to shape and reconstruct the future of the professoriate. The very thought of faculty members conducting dispassionate research from which they are "completely" detached doesn't make any sense to me and, in fact, runs counter to the way I am built. Perhaps this approach works for someone who has not felt oppression or been discriminated against, but there's a disconnect for someone like me who has had less than perfect experiences or has experienced circumstances in which others have endured extreme struggle.

In this chapter, I discuss my personal background and how it has shaped my research as I think all of us are fashioned by our identities whether we want to believe it or not (Lincoln, 2000). I also discuss the ways in which faculty members can use their role to make systemic change across their departments, schools, and institutions. In fostering this discussion, I draw from my personal experience and that of other faculty members and students. In addition, I discuss ways in which faculty members can instill a commitment to justice in their students— those who plan to pursue faculty and practitioner careers (hooks, 1994). Lastly, I discuss the possible negative ramifications of pursing a research agenda dedicated to justice.

Personal Background

I grew up in a family of ten children in a very rural area of the Upper Peninsula of Michigan. We were horribly poor. I often tell people, "We were so poor that when my mom made chipped beef on toast, there wasn't any beef." My mom did the best she could on about $7,000 a year. People often ask how ten children and their parents could survive on so little money—the answer—we grew and made everything. As a child, I learned how to can fruits, make jelly, wax vegetables for winter, cut sides of meat, and bake pies. Ironically, as an adult I don't eat meat and my husband is the cook in the house (enough is enough). As children, we entertained ourselves. We didn't have a television or any fancy games; we made up games. We shook apple trees for fun, flooded the backyard to make an ice rink during winter, played "kick the can" and rode the tractor for sport.

We had no idea that we were poor. Of course our parents knew, but we kids thought everyone lived this way. It wasn't until eighth grade when our house burned to the ground and we had to live in temporary housing in a nearby city (10,000 people—some city!) that we realized we were poor. I noticed what others had and the access that money gave people. It was then that I discovered that I was on free lunch and that my school uniforms had been worn by my brothers and sisters before I wore them. I wondered why my shirts weren't white and why my tights had holes in the knees. I didn't say much about my thoughts and feelings to anyone because I knew it would hurt my mom and dad.

My mom was lovely although she cried a lot. She tried her best to hide her tears but her struggle was hard. My father was an adequate husband. He was resentful and jealous of the accomplishments of others. He was bitter and this emotion resulted in very little love shown toward my mother. She did what she needed to raise her children and get through the madness that had her trapped in a life she had never envisioned. Perhaps what I admire most about my mom and why I am talking about her in an essay about researching for justice is that she spoke up and pushed back. In a provincial town where most people conformed and took part in hatred and bigotry, my mom did not.

Sadly, my father did. When I wrote that he was bitter earlier, I was referring to his hatred of others, be they Blacks, Latinos, or Asians. Native Americans were spared for some reason (more than likely, my mother says, because my father was actually part American Indian). I grew up hearing my father say nigger, spic, jap, and chink. But, I also grew up with a mother who told me that these words were wrong and hurtful. She washed our mouths out with soap if we ever repeated these words. I saw my older brothers endure the Zest or Dove bar many times. She told us that hatred of someone based on race, or color, or wealth was wrong. Of note, there were NO African Americans, Latinos, or Asians living in our town or within 150 miles from us at any point during my childhood (and even today—the town hasn't changed much). But, that didn't stop my father or many of the other residents of our town from hating these racial and ethnic groups. They were easy targets. Oh, they were fun to laugh at on *Sanford and Son* and *Chico and the Man,* but you wouldn't want "those people" as friends.

My father did anything he could to convince us that African Americans were bad and that we should always hold them suspect. "Martin Luther King was a rabble rouser and didn't really believe in peaceful protest." "Malcolm X was anti-American." "Blacks were dirty and lazy; they just wanted a handout." Ironically, my father was always trying to get government cheese. Many of my school teachers reinforced these stereotypical racist ideas. I learned nothing about

African American history and culture with the exception of slavery (and that was whisked over and romanticized and, of course, there was no blame to be had). I heard teachers say derogatory things about Blacks. My Catholic grade school had a slave auction and wasn't apologetic about it. As a small child, I didn't see a problem. I didn't even know what slavery was, let alone the horrors of Jim Crow. The local coffee shop was called "Little Black Sambos" and had a young African boy being chased by a tiger on the sign and on the menus. I thought Sambo was cute. The bakery had big fat cookie jars decorated like Black women. I dug my hand in for a cookie, never thinking twice about the image on the jar. I went to "Sambos" and the bakery with my father; my mother never took me to these places.

As my mom saw my father's influence on her children, she worked to counter it—ever so patiently. She told us not to listen to him. She confided in us—telling us how my dad blamed minorities for his lack of success, for his problems. She told us that she had grown up in Flint, Michigan, living next door to a Black family and that they were "exactly like you and me." When she married my father she had no idea that he held such racist views. Many times these views don't surface for years and by that time she had too many kids to make it on her own. She felt trapped. And as a result, she endured his hostile and shameful verbiage. Through our mother, some of us learned that prejudice is wrong and that we should speak up for others and confront injustice. Unfortunately, not all of my siblings learned this lesson—some of them harbor horrible thoughts and school their children in racist ideas. I no longer speak to these siblings—a choice I had to make when I had my own child.

Because of my mother, despite growing up in a racist and exclusionary environment, I chose to pursue a research agenda and scholarly life dedicated to issues of race. It makes sense to my mother. My father couldn't understand until very late in his life why his daughter would care so much about equity. In the spirit of true irony, my father had a stroke and we placed him in a nursing home near my sister in Tennessee. Unlike in the Upper Peninsula of Michigan, there are African Americans in Tennessee, and my father's roommate in the nursing home (he had a roommate because he couldn't afford a private room) was an African American man. Although disgusted and belligerent about the idea at first, my father grew to love the man and the man's family. They became close friends and when I would visit him, the two of them would be sitting in rocking chairs, laughing and sharing stories. A few months before my father died, he told me that he had been wrong about Blacks. He cried in my arms about the life of anger and hatred he had lived for over 80 years; he was proud of me for standing up against his racist beliefs. Sadly, he never acknowledged the work of my mother to push back against his influence over her children; he continued to resent her.

Given the example of my mother (and my father for that matter), my interest in race and equity might make sense. Despite not knowing anyone of another race or ethnicity (outside of Native Americans) until graduate school, I felt compelled to make a difference in the world. I idealistically believed (and still believe) that we should "be the change we want to see." I make no apologies for having this perspective. Yes, it might color my viewpoint—it might make a difference in what I choose to research. But, it doesn't mean that I will cover up findings to appease my ideology. It doesn't mean that I'll avoid asking questions that run counter to my hopes. I believe that it's entirely possible to pursue a research agenda steeped in a commitment to justice.

Making Change as a Faculty Member

Push with Your Research

I am a firm believer in doing research about which you are passionate and with which you can make a difference. For me, issues of race, class, and gender have been salient in my life. Growing up in poverty with a trapped mother and a racist father gives me a unique insight into these issues—not the only insight but an interesting one.

I chose to focus my research in three major areas. First, I do work related to the history of Black colleges, and while doing this research, I focus on uncovering examples and stories of agency or action on the part of African Americans. Sometimes this agency is positive and other times it is less than flattering. However, overall, my research gives a voice to African Americans because they are not merely depicted as victims in history. Yes, Blacks were the victims of brutal racism and apartheid; however, they also played a significant role in uplifting their own lives and shaping society at large. I never thought much about the idea of agency until I read James Anderson's (1988) book *The Education of Blacks in the South.*

In this book, Anderson details the efforts of Blacks in local communities to raise money for schools and libraries. Interestingly, those same schools and libraries eventually bore the names of wealthy White philanthropists and not those of African Americans. In some cases, Blacks raised half of the money for the buildings. When you read about these schools and libraries, you assume that their namesake paid for their establishment, and you miss the efforts of local Blacks completely—you miss the action and agency of these African Americans to shape and better their own existence.

My research draws upon Anderson's identification of agency and works to uncover the role of individual African Americans—students, faculty, and administrators—to craft and bolster African American higher education within the Black college setting. As I have moved along in my career, I've become aware of how historical incidents shape our actions in the current day, and as a result my research on Black colleges has taken on a more present-day manifestation. It is here that I have been able to shape policy and practice. For example, historical inquiry shows us that Black colleges have been much maligned by the media and scholars alike. A lack of understanding of these venerable institutions and a constant need to deny their individuality and treat them as a monolithic entity continue to permeate the media (Gasman, 2007). To counter this trend, I started to "educate" reporters every time they called me. As these reporters always begin with the same question—"Why do we still need Black colleges in an era of integration?"—I immediately stop them and spend a few minutes explaining the diversity among Black colleges. After almost 9 years of doing this with reporters, I can see a difference in the stories about Black colleges—with the exception of the *Atlanta Journal Constitution*, which doesn't seem to want to change. In fact, reporters will now often begin the conversation with, "now I know that not all Black colleges are alike. . ." when they call me. Although I am certainly not single-handedly responsible for changing the media's perspective, along with other researchers studying Black colleges, I have worked to counter the prevailing notions in the media. I do this by using empirical evidence to change the minds of those in the media, higher education, and policy arenas. One must not only conduct research but distribute it to various audiences and venues—those that have the potential to facilitate change.

It should be noted that I have also been critical of Black colleges when they invoke that criticism. Recently, for example, I wrote a controversial op-ed article that called for a new solution to the problems that Atlanta's Morris Brown College has been facing for decades. The institution has been limping along for years, asking alumni to pony up whenever there is a funding crisis. Although I have supported Morris Brown in the past, taking on the institution's critics, I think that the small college needs to reflect upon its future in creative ways and consider merging with one of the nearby Black colleges in the Atlanta University Center or becoming the junior college of the Center. It now faces insurmountable debt and has frustrated its loyal donors with its inability to find suitable leadership and financial assets despite considerable assistance. Holding on to an institution merely for the sake of holding on helps no one—especially the 100 African American students who are being led to believe that their degree from an unaccredited institution is valuable. Based on my historical knowledge, a good grasp of politics and policy, and my understanding of Black colleges, I decided to take a risk and recommend that the hopes and dreams of the former slaves who built Morris Brown College manifest in another form (Gasman, 2009).

The second area in which I do research is African American philanthropy. While I was conducting research related to Black colleges, I noticed that all of the philanthropic contributions discussed in the literature pertained to White philanthropy. African Americans and their efforts did not appear. Of course, one could assume that Blacks have not had and don't have access to wealth, but that would be a faulty assumption (Meizhu et al., 2006). Regardless of their access to money, African Americans have been philanthropic since the days of slavery. In fact, in the current day, African Americans are more philanthropic than the majority population in terms of the proportion of their discretionary income given to charity (Gasman & Sedgwick, 2005). My research in this area has sought to reshape the nation's views of African Americans. I want Blacks to be viewed as active participants in the betterment on our country and not as the mere recipients of philanthropy. Moreover, I want African Americans to view themselves as philanthropic because seeing one's impact on the world can be empowering.

My last area of research focuses on African American graduate students at elite, historically White institutions. This research interest grew out of my experience at the University of Pennsylvania, an elite, Ivy League institution with a dismal percentage of African American students (interestingly, Caribbeans and Africans are counted in this group). When I first arrived at Penn, I encountered a barrage of students who sought solace from their past experiences within my department. Faculty members, who have long since retired, drove them crazy. One young woman, who now teaches at another Ivy League institution, was told she was "dead in the water" upon admission—that she would never make it at Penn. Of course, when she graduated with distinction, she was a "phoenix rising from the ashes." Other African American students were discouraged from studying topics related to race. Classes revolved around White, Eurocentric ideas and rarely did anyone notice. Above all of that, admissions decisions were made with no commitment to bringing in a diverse class and as a result, I found myself looking out upon a sea of Whiteness in the classroom.

For me teaching a diverse student body and providing a nurturing and empowering community in which students can develop are essential (I have learned a lot from studying Black colleges). Although I will discuss the actions that I took to make change of a practical nature within my school below, I pursued research related to African American graduate students at elite institutions as well. Interestingly, there is little research in this area as faculty members tend to focus on undergraduates. However, the path to graduate school and graduate student experiences for African Americans at elite institutions is absolutely crucial to understanding the dearth of African American faculty at these same universities (Tierney & Salle, 2008).

I care deeply about the future make-up of the professoriate because I believe firmly in equity. I also believe that a diverse professoriate is the responsibility of all faculty and not just faculty of color. As such, I have focused much of my scholarly efforts on issues that will help bolster the future professoriate. Interestingly, my actions here are connected to my historical work on Black colleges. My dissertation was on an African American leader of a Black college named Charles Spurgeon Johnson. One of his goals was to change the face of the academy and to prepare future scholars and leaders. I decided to follow his lead. Of course, making a decision to change the status quo is not without its critics.

Push with Your Voice and Actions

Those who want to protect the status quo guard it with their lives. And taking on these individuals can mean coming to terms with your sense of integrity. Although I am fortunate to have, for the most part, good colleagues at Penn, there have been times during which I had to assert my perspective on equity in order to stop the extreme perpetuation of privilege.

One of my first efforts to make change at Penn related to admissions decisions. As mentioned, I was uncomfortable teaching an all-White class, and as such, I banded together with one of my White male colleagues to make much needed change. I knew that we would have more power working together. We conspired on ways to increase not only diversity in the applicant pool but how to push back against our senior colleagues who wanted to maintain the status quo. When the time came for the meeting in which admissions decisions were made, we pushed back at our colleague who had separated the candidates into acceptable and non-acceptable. Of course, the majority of the non-acceptable students were students of color. Together, we forced our colleagues to review each candidate in a holistic way, emphasizing the need for a diverse class and our commitment to access for more than merely White students from the Northeast. Our efforts started out slowly, with some success, but today, we have the most diverse programs in our school. Our cohorts are truly representative of the nation as a whole. Moreover, our faculty is now committed to enrolling a diverse class. We no longer have to push with such intensity.

Based on my knowledge of higher education and especially the experiences of African American students both within Black colleges and historically White institutions, I know that learning in an environment that embraces one's ideals and culture is beneficial. In addition, as someone who also wants to be part of an environment that cares about issues of race and tries to move forward in the ability to understand and manage these issues, I wanted to create an open conversation around race. With the help of the dean of students in my school, we started a Race in the Academy series that showcased research on race and also highlighted films and plays pertaining to race. Although the attendance was slow in the beginning, it picked up and students began to look forward to the events. They saw the gatherings as a safe space in which they could share their thoughts and frustrations. Of note, White students participated in these events as often as African Americans and saw them as a supplement to their classroom instruction. When the Race in the Academy series started there was some backlash from a few faculty and staff members who "didn't think race was a problem" or "wanted to see more talks on Whiteness because that is a race as well." We tried our best to embrace these faculty members and offer programs that met their needs too. Unlike some scholars, I believe that people who are resistant to change and the infusion of conversations around race should be included in discussions. The only way for learning to take place is through exposure. That said, with some faculty, we just could not change their minds.

Over time perhaps we have changed minds. Shortly after the launching of the Race in the Academy series, with the support of our dean at the time, we began a series of informal discussions about race among the faculty. We met once a month over breakfast and talked about issues of race in our research, teaching, and interactions with students and each other. Interestingly, different people showed up for the discussion every month. Sometimes those people who we knew were committed attended; we knew they were committed from student comments, from their research, and from their actions in the school. Other times those people who never spoke up in a meeting or never attended any race-related events showed up. They didn't talk, but they listened to the conversation. I think that just listening to others talk about the manifestations of race was helpful to those who live in fear of taking a risk. These monthly conversations about race and the Race in the Academy series bring the conversation to the surface and it bubbles up, and from time to time there is a breakthrough.

Recently, I feel that we had a breakthrough in terms of an individual's understanding of her own perpetuation of oppression. During a faculty meeting, we had a discussion about issues of race in the classroom, and one professor who is notorious for ignoring these issues, silencing others, and making deeply insensitive comments to students, spoke up. She said, in a trembling voice, something so important—"How do I know if I am one of the people making our African American students feel uncomfortable? I think I might be but how will I know unless someone tells me?" Interestingly, this professor is one of the most powerful faculty members in our school and commands immense respect externally and within the university—yet, she doesn't know how to manage her thoughts about race and doesn't know how to facilitate conversations around this issue in the classroom. She did, however, take the first step and admit her inability. Bringing issues of race (as well as class, gender, and sexuality—which is something we do) out into the open is vital and creates an environment in which people (eventually) feel comfortable asking for help, admitting fault, and expressing a desire to change. For those of us doing research related to race, it is crucial that we create these opportunities in our local environments. It's not JUST enough to do research—the research should engender change.

Push with Your Teaching

Perhaps the area in which a professor and researcher can have the most impact is in his or her teaching. Of course, this is a choice. One can merely present information and let students take from it what they want and move forward. Or, one can present information and ask probing questions to make students think—critically think. Or, one can teach with a particular ideological approach and ignore other perspectives. I want to make it clear that although I believe in discussing issues of race in the classroom, I do not believe in jamming an ideology down students' throats. I use the second approach I described above.

For example, in my History of American Higher Education course, I provide students with readings that speak to issues of race, class, gender, sexuality, ethnicity, and religion. Within these readings, I present many sides of each issue and a variety of perspectives. So, if I am teaching about the civil rights and student protests of the 1960s, I present readings from the right, left, and center. I want students to analyze these readings and understand the various perspectives. I want them to study the language—there is a difference between calling students "activists" and "radicals" for instance. Why are the different words used and how does the use of one word rather than the other color the reader's perspective?

In addition to presenting different perspectives, I try to push students to understand their role in the world and more specifically, in American history. So often, students think that they are powerless. Not true! I provide my students with many examples of how students have changed many aspects of academe as well as the larger society. One need look no further than the Black college students who sat at a lunch counters, in Greensboro, North Carolina, and endured ridicule and abuse in order to desegregate eating facilities (and so much more) (Branch, 1989). Students have had a great impact on the makeup of the faculty at many colleges and universities, pushing for greater diversity. They have also shaped the curricula, asking for offerings that represent their perspectives and serve their needs. Sometimes students doubt the ability of one person to make change. In response, I talk about those well known individuals who have led movements for change—Nelson Mandela, Martin Luther King, Jr., Cesar Chavez, among others. But, I also talk about those leaders, many people of color but also Whites, who have made change on a daily basis within their local communities, schools, and universities. The readings I provide to students focus on these people and their efforts. Of course, regardless of one's politics, all of my students now have a contemporary example of how one person can make a difference and make great change—Barack Obama—a person who started out making change in local communities and is now the leader of the United States. And, of note, students at colleges and universities across the country are partially responsible for Obama's success—students who many assumed were passive and lacked any inclination to step up and take responsibility for their country.

Although I only tell the students once that I want them to live their lives for something bigger than themselves, I secretly hope that my message will get through to them. I hope that they will choose to fight for justice in many areas—some do, some don't.

From time to time, students don't like my approach to teaching history. They are angered that I don't teach the traditional "White men and wars" curriculum. When I was younger, those students who disagreed with my approach got on my nerves—got under my skin. However, now I just let people know on the first day of class that my approach to teaching history is an inclusive approach. I let them know that I want each student to see himself or herself represented in the readings. And, I bluntly let students know that they might want to drop the class if they aren't comfortable with this approach. Rarely do people drop. Rumor has it that my class pushes people to think differently—that students leave feeling refreshed and energized about making change. They may not agree with everything I say, but they understand that "to be educated is to be conscientiously uncomfortable" (Peterkin, 2008, n. p.).

Concluding Thoughts

My identity has shaped the way that I approach scholarship, teaching, and service within the academy. Rather than merely pushing paper and pencil, I aim to push students, my colleagues, and the policies of the academy that exclude, oppress, and discriminate. I aim to push for change and progress regardless of the "sage" advice from older colleagues that researchers should be just that—researchers, keeping their noses out of activism. I urge future scholars to consider pushing back against the status quo. When you use empirical research to back up your opinions and perspectives, you can rest assured and feel confident that your actions are justified.

This chapter originally appeared in T. Elon Dancy II (ed.), *Managing Diversity: (Re)Visioning Equity on College Campuses* (New York: Peter Lang, 2010).

References

Anderson, J. (1988). *The education of Blacks in the South, 1860–1935.* Chapel Hill, NC: University of North Carolina Press.

Branch, T. (1989). *Parting the waters: America in the King years, 1954–1963.* New York: Simon & Schuster.

Gasman, M. (2007). Truth, generalizations, and stigmas: An analysis of the media's coverage of Morris Brown College and Black colleges overall. *Review of Black Political Economy, 34* (2), 111–135.

Gasman, M. (2009). Much ado about Morris Brown College. *Diverse Issues in Higher Education Blog.*

Gasman, M., & Sedgwick, K. (2005). *Uplifting a people: African American philanthropy and education.* New York: Peter Lang.

hooks, b. (1994). *Teaching to transgress.* New York: Routledge.

Lincoln, Y. S. (2000). The practices and politics of interpretation in N. K. Denzin & Y. S. Lincoln (Eds.) *The handbook of qualitative research.* Thousand Oaks, CA: Sage Publications.

Meizhu, L., Leondar-Wright, B., & Robles, B. (2006). *Color of wealth: The story behind the U.S. racial wealth divide.* New York: The New School.

Peterkin, D. (2008). Entry made on Teagle Foundation Blog.

Tierney, W. G., & Salle, M. (2008). Do organizational structures and strategies increase faculty diversity? A cultural analysis. *American Academic, 4* (1). 159–184.

PART THREE

Curriculum: Transmission and Transformation

CHAPTER THIRTEEN

Multiple Curricula in Higher Education

WILLIAM H. SCHUBERT

I recently completed 35 years as a professor of education at the University of Illinois at Chicago (UIC) and eight years as an elementary school teacher before that. For the past 43 years I have studied, researched, practiced, and pondered curriculum matters. My higher education background is in what is called the curriculum field, which grew out of educational foundations and educational psychology in the 1920s and 1930s. The first academic department of curriculum was founded by Hollis Caswell and colleagues at Teachers College, Columbia University, in 1935. The curriculum field emerged to facilitate curriculum development for the burgeoning numbers of students in comprehensive educational institutions in an attempt to meet their diverse needs. To satisfy such needs, many early curriculum scholars tried to situate the technical enterprise of curriculum development in the larger study of historical, philosophical, social, political, and economic contexts—intertwining curricular roots with those of the Foundations of Education. I draw these brief introductory comments from more elaborate historical work (Schubert, 1986, 2008, 2010b; Schubert, Lopez Schubert, Thomas, & Carroll, 2002; Marshall, Sears, Allen, Roberts, & Schubert, 2007).

By the 1970s many scholars on the periphery of the curriculum field (e.g., James B. Macdonald, Dwayne Huebner, Maxine Greene, Paul Klohr, Ross Mooney, Lawrence Cremin, and Herbert Kliebard) had become critical of curriculum development that facilitated governmental, corporate, and other ends. Combined with younger scholars, such as William Pinar, Janet Miller, Madeleine Grumet, Michael Apple, Alex Molnar, Henry Giroux, and George Willis, they precipitated a shift from focus on curriculum development to understanding of curriculum as a phenomenon of cultural, political, and inner dimensions of human life (both in and out of schools). This transformation, sometimes called reconceptualization, ushered curriculum theory into many different but interrelated discourse communities: historical, political, racial, gender-oriented, phenomenological, postmodern and poststructural, autobiographical, aesthetic, theological, institutional, and international perspectives (Pinar, Reynolds, Slattery, & Taubman, 1995). Thus, since the 1970s, curriculum studies is now about all levels of schooling, including higher education, and curriculum embodied in many spheres of educational life outside of school (Connelly, He, & Phillion, 2008; Malewski, 2009; Sandlin, Schultz, & Burdick, 2010; Sandlin, O'Malley, & Burdick, 2011). Alongside the growth of this scholarly field in which I have lived, a parallel study of curriculum in the field of higher or post-secondary education has occurred, treating some of the same issues (see for instance classic works in this realm: Kerr, 1963; Jencks & Riesman, 1968; Grant & Riesman, 1978; Rudolph, 1977; Bloom, 1987; Boyer, 1988; Levine, 1996; Cuban, 1999; Thelin, 2004).

Despite the import of this body of research on higher education curriculum, I suggest that it should be augmented by appropriating curriculum studies perspectives. Traditional studies in curriculum deal primarily with the intended curriculum of higher education, what it is and should or could be, and the contextual forces that shape it or impede its progress. I recommend here that these commendable contributions be complemented by work in the general field of curriculum studies, from which I derive the position that contextual forces can be seen as curricula in their own right. Some of these curricula, presented in the following, may be intended and others barely noticed as curricula that nonetheless shape the lives of students and faculty members in higher education. By combining extant curriculum literature in higher education with curriculum studies literature, I contend that a richer image of curriculum in higher education can be perceived. If perceived, it can become more fully embedded in the dialogue of curriculum decision-making bodies within academe and in analyses and interpretations about higher education institutions.

Having lived through much of the history of curriculum studies, I have become increasingly convinced that there is not only one curriculum, but many curricula. They have had too little attention in higher education and cast their influence simultaneously: intended, taught, hidden, null, experienced, learned, embodied, outside, tested, BIG,[1] and grassroots (Schubert, 2008, 2010a, b, c). The *intended curriculum* is found in policy statements of formal organizations, sometimes called the *overt curriculum* or *explicit curriculum*. The *taught curriculum* is what is actually offered to learners in the teacher-learner interchange, while *hidden curriculum* pertains to what is learned from the societal or organizational structures in teaching-learning situations. The *null curriculum* draws attention to what is not but could be taught. The *experienced curriculum* is the sum total of what learners encounter, and the *learned curriculum* is the subdimension of the experienced curriculum that is grasped, understood, demonstrated or applied. The *embodied curriculum* runs deeper than demonstrative learning in order to emphasize that which becomes part of the learner's personal perspective and thereby guides reflection, meaning, and action in the world. The *tested curriculum* remains a pale sample of that which is learned and embodied or when purchased from outside vendors; it may even bypass the experienced curriculum altogether. The *outside curriculum* focuses on the host of experiences and relationships that exist outside of schools or universities (e.g., homes, families, marriages, friendships, peer groups, clubs associations, gangs, hobbies, mass media of all kinds, churches, jobs, sports, the Web, and some dimensions of the extracurricular activities of educational institutions). Outside curricula shape us profoundly and are increasingly referred to as dimensions of *public pedagogy*. The *BIG curriculum* is curriculum of globalized propaganda—such a powerful form of hidden or outside curriculum that it necessitates separate attention. *Grass-*

roots curriculum is created through attempts of individuals and small coteries or communities to pursue opportunities to learn despite the BIG Curriculum or in resistance to it.

These fluid curricular venues have swirled around me throughout my life in academe, though it took a while for me to name them. I have noticed that curriculum committees in universities almost exclusively focus on the intended curriculum. In fact, after studying curriculum as a multifaceted theoretical area of study in my doctoral work guided by J. Harlan Shores at the University of Illinois at Urbana-Champaign (UIUC), I came to realize that the serious study of curriculum is interdisciplinary, trans-disciplinary, or counter-disciplinary—terms characterized well in Ming Fang He's (2010a, 2010b) curriculum inquiry today, though I did not have the words to express each of these at the time. What is clear is that the multiple curricula influencing the growth of any student in higher education need to be studied with all of the intellectual resources at our disposal.

In my first full-time university faculty appointment at UIC, where I have worked until retirement, I found myself on "curriculum committees" and thought such work would be right up my line; however, I soon realized that such committees too often were expected to do bean-counting about credits, sequences, prerequisites, course numbers, and other mundane matters. While perhaps a necessary part of bureaucratic life, it was hardly the place for the kind of theorizing I found in the work of James B. Macdonald, who was invited to speak in honor of my doctoral adviser, Harlan Shores, upon his retirement from UIUC. Macdonald's *Reschooling Society* (Macdonald, Wolfson, & Zaret, 1973) brought Ivan Illich's (1970) idea of *deschooling* to the U.S. curriculum field and appropriated it as a basis from which to reconstruct schooling for curriculum leaders in the Association for Supervision and Curriculum Development (ASCD), while his article *A Transcendental Developmental Ideology of Education* (Macdonald, 1974) introduced Paulo Freire's (1970) critical pedagogy to U.S. curriculum theorists.

Given the stark contrast between my sense of curriculum theory and the function of committees labeled *curriculum* in higher education, I wondered whether curriculum theorizing was as rare in higher education as I had known it to be in the public schools. Sadly, it seemed to me that, in its philosophical sense, curriculum studies might hardly exist outside of curriculum faculties in colleges of education. Sometimes I felt resigned to the idea that I could engage in curriculum theory only with my students and a few esteemed colleagues.

Over the years, as I grew through teaching experience, I increasingly realized that students themselves must be central to the curriculum I developed not just for them, but with them, ultimately concluding that in order for curriculum to be *for* students in a genuine sense, I must also embrace curricula that are *of* and *by* them (Schubert & Lopez Schubert, 1981). The point is simple though profoundly overlooked: we should know students before pronouncing definitively what they should study. Moreover, the best way to know them is to involve them in the design of their own curriculum, and to help them understand that curriculum should not be bestowed upon them but must be created consciously by them as they proactively shape their own becoming. Indeed, there is immense irony in the frequently heard professorial lament that graduates do not know how to self-direct their continued study when throughout their program they were expected simply to follow orders. Educational experience, I thought, must be derived through cultivation *of* students' experiential soil and consciously nurtured *by* their reflective participation. I have rarely seen this happen in universities, except sometimes in the one-to-one mentoring relationship. Needless to say, my interest in curriculum was not wrought by an interest in planning. It may be better to say it was kindled by a desire to subvert planning. Too much planning, I have witnessed, has been a flaccid proxy for getting (forgetting) to know students, a process captured by the banal non-word, *strategery*, used by comedian Will Ferrell on *Saturday Night Live* in his impersonation of George W. Bush when challenged to offer one word that summarized his platform.

From my elementary school teaching initially, and then from my university teaching, I concluded that my two best tools—the ones that helped me to invent or improvise the most meaningful experiences with students—were philosophy and imagination. I considered both as never-ending, always in the making—reminiscent of Alfred North Whitehead's (1926) image of *religion in the making*, and John Dewey's (1929) immensely inclusive image of educational inquiry:

> The sources of educational science are any portions of ascertained knowledge that enter into the heart, head, and hand of educators, and which, by entering in, render the performance of the educational function more enlightened, more humane, more truly educational than it was before. But there is no way to discover what is "more truly educational" except by the continuation of the educational act itself. The discovery is never made; it is *always making* (my italics, pp. 76–77).

Discovering the "more truly educational" for me at that time meant continuous philosophical inquiry into the meaning of Dewey's (1916) definition of education, which he characterized as "that reconstruction and reorganization of experience which adds to the meaning of experience and increases the ability to direct the course of subsequent experience" (p. 76) *in each lived situation*. Continuously monitoring this and adapting to student needs and interests has been for me an act of imaginative projection. Dewey (1934) addressed the idea first (wouldn't you know?) in *A Common Faith*:

> The connection between imagination and the harmonizing of the self is closer than is usually thought. The idea of a whole, whether of the whole personal being or of the world, is an imaginative, not literal idea. The limited world of our observation and reflection becomes the Universe through imaginative projection. It cannot be apprehended in knowledge or realized in reflection. Neither, observation, thought, nor practical activity can attain that complete unification of the self which is called a whole. The whole self is an ideal, an imaginative projection. (pp. 18–19)

Realization of the powerful and neglected place of imagination in teaching led me to build my doctoral dissertation around the idea of imaginative projection as a method of continuous curriculum invention, under the guidance of Harlan Shores (Schubert, 1975). Derived from Deweyan roots, the teaching of Louis Rubin (1984), another of my former professors, continued to influence the imagination behind my own practice through his *Artistry in Teaching*, which became a metaphorical inspiration for improvisational ways I would try to teach teachers, school leaders, and future curriculum scholars.

One of my early experiences at UIC was fruitful in helping me find curriculum theorizing in the university. I somehow became a member of the university-wide Curriculum Development Grants Committee, the purpose of which was to evaluate proposals for rather substantial funding from Amoco and other sources. David Weible, of the German Department, chaired the committee, and I guess I talked enough in the first couple of years to be selected to be chair in the third year of my participation. As I reviewed proposals from intelligent faculty members throughout the university, I saw the experience as an opportunity to study professors who were thinking of curriculum from a pristine position of having no formal exposure to the field of Curriculum Studies. I thought that perhaps I could categorize tenets of their perspectives relative to different schools of curriculum theory based on their proposals. Some faculty members couched their proposals in the technical and scientific language of Ralph Tyler's (1949) *Rationale*, others expressed political intrigue that reminded me of Decker Walker's (1971) *naturalistic model*, some saw curriculum as an inner-personal reconceptualization as developed by William Pinar and Madeleine Grumet (Pinar, 1975; Pinar & Grumet, 1976), who used the infinitive *currere* to depict the reflective autobiographical journey. Others saw curriculum revision as political or cultural, reminiscent of the early work of Paulo Freire (1970), Michael Apple (1979) and Henry Giroux (1979). So, I enticed Weible into joining me in doing a paper at the Annual Meeting of the American Educational Research Association on the implicit curriculum theories in proposals written by faculty members in higher education (Schubert & Weible, 1979). Doing this early project helped me see that categories of analysis and interpretation drawn from curriculum studies can illuminate higher education curriculum as well as that at other levels of education.

As I continued to reflect on curriculum of higher education over the years, I strove to enable students to have opportunities to pursue serious learning that was often not afforded by generic intended curriculum. I found that the most educationally valuable experiences often occurred outside the parameters of attempts to control students—allegedly for their own good. I am still convinced that the assumption that students do not know what they need should be substantially tempered; we must work *with* students to determine together what is needed. My experiences as a graduate student, elementary school teacher, and faculty member in higher education taught me that most of the best learning experiences evolve as surprises in the context of situational exigencies that cannot be predicted or even planned. Therefore, knowing that entities called *curriculum committees* will continue to abound at departmental, program, college, and university levels, my suggestion is that they broaden and deepen inquiry about how their work relates to the curricular venues noted above: intended, taught, null, hidden, experienced, embodied, tested, outside, BIG, and grassroots. In fact, as I reflect on my own curricular endeavors, I realize that I always resisted the intended, hidden, null, especially the tested, and much of the outside curricula, striving to create curricular resistance by protruding here and there as do wild grasses through cracks in roads for chariots adorned by those who contrive the BIG Curriculum that expands their own power and acquisition—*curriculum* being derived from the course of a chariot race, and gaudy chariots being symbols of Empire. Each of the multiple curricula is worth considering more elaborately vis-à-vis higher education, and I encourage those who develop curricular policies and practices in colleges and universities to consider them seriously. Asking "what's worthwhile?" and "who benefits?" in many different situations enriched my educational experience as professor. Thus, I urge those who develop curricular opportunities in higher education to be *wide-awake* (Greene, 1978) to multiple curricula shimmering in their midst.

Intended Curriculum

Most curriculum committee deliberation focuses on such matters as course or program revision, construction of new courses or programs, prerequisites, adequate sequences or clusters for majors or minors, course numbers and credit hours—all necessary if one is in the *business* of buying and selling understanding. Admittedly, we are partially in that business. At best, however, curriculum committees ask questions about the deeper value of education. I suggest that those on curriculum committees at least focus on what is worth knowing within their discipline. For reasons of disciplinary survival it takes even more courage to ask about the worth of their discipline or area of study itself, or to query who benefits and who may be hurt by the consequences of their work.

Taught Curriculum

A universally realized truism among college students is the tremendous variation among sections of courses with the same number and title. Although they have the same course outline and even similar syllabi and texts, they are often fundamentally different—almost with as much variation as any one section would have with another course title! This is what I sometimes call a metaphoric use of analysis of variance from quantitative methods. In any case, the taught curriculum can vary extensively from the intended curriculum. The central question is: Is such variance good or bad? It can be highly desirable when faculty members inspire students through emphasis on their strengths; however, it can be undesirable when a faculty member's interpretations of course content are prejudiced or convey misinformation. Thus, the answer is not as simple as the establishment of monitoring committees that identify diversity and then attempt to standardize practice to a mandated syllabus. While there are numerous effects of variation, questions need to be addressed that admit its existence and consider its relevance.

Null Curriculum

A subtle kind of curriculum was coined by Elliot Eisner (1979) as the *null curriculum*. It refers to the curriculum not taught. At first glance it would seem that this curriculum would have no effect, but a deeper look reveals that subjects not selected for the curriculum at any level skew the educational experience into myriad contortions and distortions. For instance, health and ecology or war and peace are among the largest problems facing human beings; nevertheless, majors from many fields of liberal arts and sciences or professional schools (e.g., engineering, education, architecture) may receive little if any emphasis in those areas. Similarly, medical students, social workers, educators, and others may receive little background in philosophy, poetry, and the arts, which may be central to building perspectives that guide their lives and illuminate their work. In elementary or secondary school, subjects not tested (the arts, health, philosophy, psychology) may be keys to well-being, but if the budget is cut, they are first to be discarded or are not offered at all. The correlate in higher education lies in the power of funding or accrediting agencies to support research, service, and programmatic endeavors. That which is given highest priority in national economies results in inflation of some academic areas and deflation of others. Curriculum committees in universities should develop serious study of such influences, not merely strategic plans that facilitate what the dominant power sources desire. Otherwise Jennifer Washburn's (2005) image of *University, Inc.* will reign supreme and we will see, as Frank Donoghue (2008) predicts, *The Last Professors*—products of university corruption by corporate mindedness.

Hidden Curriculum

I argue that socio-economic priorities that have created the ebb and flow of null curricula are perpetuated by hidden curricula as well. In considering the complexity of educational experience over 70 years ago, John Dewey (1938) referred to *collateral learning*—side effects of intended learning, often derived from its organizational structures. Just as military apologists have referred to injury or death as *collateral damage* in recent wars, the unintended and intended side effects of intended, taught, and null curricula can be deleterious. Thirty years after Dewey's use of *collateral learning*, Philip Jackson (1968) observed that life in classrooms has organizational practices that teach a great deal—submissiveness to authority, deferral of gratification, perception of oneself within pecking orders, and much more. The college and university correlates of such organizational effects were extended by E. R. Snyder (1970) in examples of how students learn to play games and gather *points* that lead to images of success.

Pioneering work by Paul Willis (1977) has shown through critical ethnography that secondary schools teach working class youth to learn to labor within social class constraints. Jean Anyon (1980) argued from critical evidence that rule following, giving *right* answers, keeping creatively busy but not rocking the boat, and manipulating the system are educational consequences that respectively derive from lower or working, middle, professional, and executive socio-economic class treatment in elementary schools. One could readily use these findings heuristically to explore class differences in colleges and universities that serve different socio-economic classes. Henry Giroux and David Purpel (1982) brought the emergent literature together and related it to structural dimensions of moral and spiritual messages. Michael Apple (1979) argued that educational institutions teach ideology by being the way they are—that curriculum is ideology and that ideology bespeaks power (Apple, 1982). Peter McLaren (1986, 1989), helped educators see the ritual performance in school life and the ways it reflected the societal culture in which it was situated, and moved on to show that the hidden curriculum is not so hidden; it is blatantly purveyed by globalized corporate interests that give little regard to borders, cultures, or societies (McLaren & Faramandpur, 2004). So, when Jean Anyon (2004) argues that educational reform cannot occur substantially without a complementary social movement, she is calling for radical possibilities that move into policy in the corporate sphere, which includes but is not confined to national politics or economics. Put another way, relative to racism, David Gillborn (2008) perceptively says that there is no longer a conspiracy of racial prejudice—instead, there is racist public policy right in front of our eyes. As I see it, the hidden curriculum has morphed into the BIG Curriculum (Schubert, 2006), which I take up later in this chapter. How can curriculum-making bodies and those who teach in universities attend more fully to hidden curriculum?

Experienced Curriculum

All of the curricula (intended, taught, null, hidden) are experienced simultaneously. Dominant curriculum studies literature from the 1940s through the 1970s (Schubert et al., 2002) was wont to broaden the purview of curriculum from subject matter to experience. Curriculum developers often qualified and reduced the magnitude of this new emphasis by contending that curriculum constitutes all the experience for which the school takes responsibility. I recall reading such qualification in my graduate studies, and wondering (based on my experience in schools) just what *responsibility* includes and excludes vis-à-vis lived experience. Ted Aoki (1993) pushed in a new direction from his phenomenological and postmodern cultural perspective, arguing for curriculum conceptualized as a landscape of multiplicity—interpreting curriculum as a lived phenomenon—replete with meta-narratives wherein one can come to know the faces of others, not merely faceless *othered* beings who received planned (should I say canned?) curriculum and instruction.

Learned, Embodied, and Lived Curricula

Here we return to the aforementioned characterization of education by Dewey (1916, p. 76) as a reconstruction of experience that adds meaning to and directs the courses of subsequent experience. To definitively call this the *learned curriculum* limits Dewey's purport. Learning is too cognitive, too cerebral. Consider Dwayne Huebner's (1966/1975) critique (trusting that you will forgive the male pronoun of the day):

> Think of it—there standing before the educator is a being partially hidden in the cloud of un-knowing. For centuries the poet has sung of his near infinitudes; the theologian has preached of his depravity and hinted at his participation in the divine; the philosopher has struggled to encompass him in his systems, only to have him repeatedly escape; the novelist and dramatist have captured his fleeting moments in never-to-be forgotten aesthetic forms, and the man [person] engaged in curriculum has the temerity to reduce this being to a single term—"learner." (p. 219)

So, how dare we sit in our colleges and require as truth the reigning intellectual prejudices of the day, lauding their superiority to conventional wisdoms held by students from their daily lives? Have we forgotten the spirit of questioning of Socrates, Lao-tse, or Galileo; or do we fear the ostracism, persecution, torture, and even death that can result from it?

To embody the questioning spirit of education at its finest is to live the questions (Tillett, 2011). Compatible with the Deweyan image of reconstructing meaning and experience, Lakoff and Johnson (1999) refer to the phenomenon as the *embodied mind* or *philosophy in the flesh*. Living the questions, asking what is worth knowing, doing, needing, being, becoming, overcoming, sharing, contributing, and wondering is taking up the mantle of cultivating one's own curriculum (Schubert & Lopez Schubert, 1981; Schubert, 2009b; Izuegbu, 2011).

Tested Curriculum

Much could be said about the testing fetish, the money maker for globalized power, and it should be said. However, the paltry character of tests and those who insist that they be relied upon is so obvious, the construct validity so inane, that in this chapter I utter little more than a joke about it; yet it is a joke with more punch than punch line, offered by none other than John Dewey. Dewey is said to have told the story in lectures on several occasions, which goes something like this:

> I like to compare (insert intelligence, achievement, or other standardized) testing with the way they weight hogs in Vermont. They catch a hog and tie it to a board, placing the board on a fulcrum (like a see-saw or teeter-totter). Next, they run around the country-side selecting rocks until they find one that equally balances with the hog. Then they guess the weight of the rock.

So much for construct validity; the embodied consequences of curricular experiences are so complex that they cannot be assessed by simplistic, isolated cognitive tasks. Rather, a holistic bodily aesthetic response is most appropriate, and certainly cannot be measured, as expressed by Emily Dickinson:

> If I read a book and it makes my whole body so cold that no fire can warm me, I know that is poetry. If I feel physically as if the top of my head were taken off, I know that is poetry. These are the only ways I know it. Is there any other way? (Bartlett, 2002, p. 547)

Outside Curricula

Curricula that shape us are surely not from educational institutions alone. In college and university life, Arum and Roksa (2011) marshal evidence to argue that institutional culture, social life, and employment too often limit the influence of academics. Writ large, these dimensions of college or university life amount to much more than life within higher education facilities. Institutional culture invokes the societal and global culture reflected in higher education. Social life includes family, friendships, marriages, peer groups, prejudices, folkways, mores, effects of class, race, gender, health, language, membership, ethnicity, belief or religion, and more. Employment reflects economics, vocation, job, avocation, possibilities, stress of unemployment, and balance of needs and interests. All of this evokes the question of who benefits from the kind and quality of life lived in places of higher education.

I have often written about the outside curricula (e.g., Schubert, 1981, 1986, 2008, 2010a, 2010b), and the categories under consideration surely apply to higher education. For instance, I call for using curriculum frames to analyze and interpret realms of experience outside of school, such as families, homes, peer groups, non-school organizations (e.g., sports teams, theatres, dance studios, churches, scouts, clubs, music groups, play groups, gangs), mass media (e.g., television, radio, video, videogames, popular books, magazines, and newspapers). One could analyze and interpret educative experience in these spheres of life through the Tyler (1949) Rational categories of purposes, learning experiences, organization (such as scope and sequence or environment), and evaluation. Or one could look through lenses that Joseph Schwab (1970) called "curricular commonplaces" to see consequences of interactions among teachers, learners, subject matter, and milieu as they fluidly evolve and devolve relative to situational exigencies. Or, one might study how any person in a given moment is shaped by interactions among his or her past, present, and possible (i.e., what Pinar and Grumet, 1976, called the regressive, progressive, analytic, synthetic autobiographical method of *currere*). Outside curricula, too, could be examined critically through lenses as they support or resist Paulo Freire's (1970) *banking* or *problem-posing* education, or in Michael Apple's (1999) parlance, as they perpetuate official or unofficial knowledge. Alternatively, from cultural studies and postmodern postures, outside curricula could be readily studied as a release of multiple counternarratives (Doll, 1993; Greene, 1995; Giroux, Lankshear, McLaren, & Peters, 1996). These inquiry postures simply illustrate that within curriculum studies there exists the wherewithal to study a considerable range of journeys (curricula) that shape our lives. Such journeys have been productively referred to as *public pedagogies* (Sandlin et al., 2010; Sandlin et al., 2011), and it is in the diversity of such work that curriculum-makers in higher education can come to know the multiple curricula that shape the students with whom they work. I have always thought it odd, and downright arrogant, for curriculum-makers to develop curricula for students they do not know.

BIG Curriculum

The BIG (all caps for reasons of extreme power) Curriculum is so overarching that it often goes unnoticed—as water for fish or air for a human, though, unlike air and water, it does not nourish life. All of the other curricula mentioned here are influenced, sometimes created, by the BIG Curriculum—the global corporate culture of propaganda that makes the rich richer and the rest live in servitude to BIG profit (Schubert, 2006). Have I stated it too blatantly? I do not think so. The BIG Curriculum is the most vicious hidden curriculum facing higher education (and all education) today. It is the curriculum that forces elementary and secondary schools to *teach by numbers* (Taubman, 2009), and higher education today sadly cowers down the same garden path cobbled with discourses of standards, tests, and accountability. For years David Harvey (2005, 2010) has warned of the problem of neoliberalism, and Pauline Lipman (2004) has shown concretely its instantiation in high-stakes tests, transforming schooling into a high- stakes enterprise spitting out policy mandates that enhance the global elite at the expense of the rest, especially the urban poor. Meanwhile, we (perhaps *the last professors*; Frank Donaghue, 2008) curl up in our *ruins* (Readings, 1996), criticize the testing fetish of elementary and secondary schools, turn around and ask what the SAT or GRE scores are for the next crop of university applicants so that we have a legal basis for rejection that the public is duped to deem plausible.

Caveats were sent about the globalized corporatization of universities by Page Smith (1990) as *killing the spirit* and Bruce Wilshire (1990) as precipitating *moral collapse* over two decades ago. It is naïve to doubt that we live under the aegis of a global Empire that has substantial origins in the United States (Chomsky, 2005; Vidal, 2004, Zinn, Konopacki, & Buhle, 2008) but by no means can be construed as merely national (Ellwood, 2010). In his last book, novelist Kurt Vonnegut (2005) decried being without a country, implying that nationalism is a ruse. In fact, nationalism and its corporatized elections seem to be a mere proxy for assuring a form of patriotism that controls today's masses. Noam Chomsky (1997, 2001) and Alex Molnar (2005) urge us to remember that from the Woodrow Wilson administration to the Great Depression, Edward Bernays (1928) and others, including noted columnist Walter Lippmann (1962), created popular opinion for a public they openly referred to as *the bewildered herd*. They insisted that public opinion had to be shaped, thereby producing a BIG Curriculum.

Indeed, there is much evidence today of the BIG Curriculum in stories by defectors from *corporatocracy* (Hiatt, 2007; Perkins, 2006; Klein, 2007) who could no longer participate in the shock and violence that rendered destruction of cultures for the gain of the few transnational moguls who govern Earth, the *de facto* movers and shakers who constitute what Chrystia Freeland (2011) calls *the global elite* [that] *is leaving you behind*. Consequences of such a power movement for universities are well-characterized by Jennifer Washburn (2005) in *University Inc.,* the cover of which sports a mortarboard graduation cap with a "sold" sign on it. Washburn begins by declaring ". . . the single greatest threat to the future of American higher education: the intrusion of a market ideology into the heart of academic life" (p. x), and concludes after 240 pages of evidence and argument by asserting, "the university is simply too important a public institution to be surrendered to the narrow dictates of the market" (p. 241). We are faced with the stark dilemma of what, if anything, we in higher education can do to overcome this threat to free inquiry.

Grassroots Resistance Curriculum

What can higher education do to preserve the ideals of university experience as a basis for democracy, freedom, and the cultivation of humanity? Must the *wretched of the Earth* (Fanon, 1963) continue to be wretched and even augmented to satisfy the gain of a few? Have those (once labeled *liberals*) who empathize with and seek to overcome human suffering almost disappeared or faced extinction, as Chris Hedges (2010) contends? Does such a conclusion support John Gray's (2002) contention that, while humans are highly inventive creatures, they are at base predatory and destructive? If this is so, what would be the point of continuing higher education? Or do those dastardly qualities fit only those who reach pinnacles of power? Is today's BIG Curriculum the instrument whereby the ultra-powerful have conquered and colonized the masses who seldom know the perpetrators of their plight and the surreptitious, stealthy, and covert devastation that fuels it, as can readily be gleaned from Perkins (2006), Klein (2007), Hiatt (2007), and others? Despite all of this, humans have a history of resisting oppression and even sustaining hope under tremendous oppression.

Education must be based in hope, as Paulo Freire (1970) emphasizes. Freire knew oppression from the inside, and yet he sustained hope. Without hope, there can be no education. Hope for Freire (2007) must be cultivated in critical epistemological curiosity and an outlook that dares to dream and to act on those dreams. Much turns on what we take to be human potential. Jeremy Rifkin (2009) marshals strong support for humans as basically empathic creatures, quite the contrary of John Gray's (2002) characterization of humans as a predatory plague on Earth. Rifkin's sense of human empathy heralds our capacity to cultivate humanity as Martha Nussbaum (1997) advocates in defense of giving new life to the humanities if we can only eschew the domination of a *for-profit* ethos (Nussbaum, 2010) that soaks us in a slime of globalized avarice and diminishes the value of the humanities which could lift us above the sardonic machinations of greedy barons of corporatocracy.

Dewey, with his conviction to eradicate dualistic thinking, would argue that humans are neither largely predatory nor wholly empathic, but rather we need to look more deeply and deal with the integration of these extremes. I agree. However, being full of contradictions, I also agree with Maxine Greene (1995) who, while she expresses profound intellectual debt to Dewey, senses a central flaw in his faith that all problems are soluble and, concomitantly, that all dualisms can be resolved by integration. From her pervasive forays into literature and the arts, existentialism, phenomenology, critical theory, and postmodernism, she points to a tragic side of human life, one insoluble and shrouded in mystery. For instance, she says:

> The central questions will continue to haunt us. How can we reconcile the multiple realities of human lives with shared commitment to communities infused once again with principles? How can we do it without regressing, without mythicizing? How, like Tarrou in *The Plague*, can we move ourselves and others to affirm that "on this earth there are pestilences and there are victims, and it's up to us, so far as possible, not to join forces with the pestilences (Camus, 1948, p. 229)? How can we, in every predicament take the victims' sides, so as to reduce the damage done?" (p. 197)

Toward this end, Henry Giroux (2007) exposes pestilences in higher education, naming devastating effects of universities enchained as agents for national security, marketers for corporate *factories*, and apologists for right-wing *unfreedom*. However, with concern for victims, he offers strategies for the academy to break the chains by making universities public spaces for addressing critical questions and the engaged action they invoke.

I see such questioning as the essence of higher education, something I encountered as an undergraduate student, continued as a young teacher, and appreciated as a doctoral student. While sometimes experienced in classes, such work was mostly pursued between and following classes. We need to ask: How can we ensure that pursuit of fundamental questions is held at the heart of higher education curriculum and deemed its most salient consequence? Ironically, this questioning spirit is seldom studied by higher education researchers, according to Pascarella and Terenzini (1991, 2005) in their massive reviews of some 5000 studies on student development in higher education. Astin, Astin, and Lindholm (2011) have attempted to fill this hole in the research with inquiry that speaks directly to the essence of questions that they argue should be the moving spirit of higher education curriculum:

> Who am I? What are my most deeply felt values? Do I have a mission or purpose in my life? Why am I in college? What kind of person do I want to become? What sort of world do I want to help create? (p. 1)

Arguably, such questions do not fit within the confines of discipline-centered curriculum. Understanding the need for focus on the inner lives of students, Parker Palmer and Arthur Zajonc (2010) call for renewal that involves integrated studies and engaged conversations among faculty and students as colleagues who strive to reclaim the highest calling in the traditions of academic life. Harkening back to Alfred North Whitehead (1929), who argued that the universities cannot justify their existence in knowledge creation or in its dissemination alone; rather, "the proper function of a university is the imaginative acquisition of knowledge. . . . A university is imaginative or it is nothing—at least nothing useful" (Whitehead, pp. 93–100, and Palmer & Zajonc, p. 57). It seems clear that such questions are not going to be facilitated by the corporatocracy, just as it would not fund inquiry into its own corruption.

So, where can we look for sources and exemplars that resist the BIG Curriculum? I have begun to find beneficial possibilities by turning to indigenous peoples who have been oppressed, suppressed, repressed, depressed, colonized, and compressed by the corporatocracy. Realizing that this source is not a panacea (nor are indigenous peoples necessarily pristine exemplars of human perfection in consonance with nature), I still argue that indigenous ideas and practices are both necessary to keep alive and substantially neglected. I suggest, first, the work of Linda Tuhiwai Smith (2001) on decolonization of research methodology derived from her work with Maori populations in New Zealand. It reminds me of precedents in curricula for the masses devised by Lao-Tse in China, the Trung sisters in Vietnam, Ki Hajar in Indonesia, Jose Marti in Cuba, Che Guevara throughout Latin America, M. J. Langeveld in Holland, Maria Montessori in Italy, Rabindranath Tagore in India, and Tsunesaburo Makiguchi in Japan. Most of those exemplars were advocates of peace and the rights of the people to have lives of freedom and quality built upon loving human relationships. A great deal of enlightening exploration has occurred among educational practices of indigenous populations worldwide. Higher education in America has a long way to go to learn from such work, such as that done by Lois Meyer and Benjamin Maldonado Alvarado (2010) who, along with Noam Chomsky, studied voices of indigenous resistance in North, Central, and South America; David Hansen (2007) has brought together ethical visions of education, ranging from the aforementioned Dewey, Freire, Montessori, and Makiguchi, to W. E. B. Du Bois, Jane Addams, Tao Xingshi, Rudolf Steiner, and Albert Schweitzer. Madhu Prakash and Gustavo Esteva (Esteva & Prakash, 1997; Prakash & Esteva, 1998) show that grassroots communities in Mexico and India engage in praxis that could rightly be called postmodern. Similarly, the neglected balance of heart, mind, body, and spirit in education is now uncovered by First Nation scholar Jo-ann Archibald (2008) through indigenous *storywork*, while Peter McLaren and Nathalia Jaramillo (2007) critique the curriculum of permanent warfare wrought by world Empire and its neo-liberal propaganda of citizenship, and they explicate a critical pedagogy for resisting such oppressions. In the United States, Joel Spring (2010) draws from his Native American ancestry to illuminate historical perspectives on Native Americans, African Americans, Mexican Americans, Puerto Ricans, and Asian Americans, emphasizing civil rights in the context of *deculturalization* of each of these populations and their resistance to concomitant inequities they have faced in increasingly globalized education and life (Spring, 2009). Clearly, germinal works by Howard Zinn (1995) and Ronald Takaki (1993) have provided portrayals of oppression and resistance to the BIG Curriculum without using that label. Focusing on Native American education, Sandy Grande (2004) offers *red pedagogy*, while William Watkins (2005) draws together colleagues who present educational implications of Black protest thought.

Returning to worldwide perspectives, I have found much potential in the writings of Daisaku Ikeda, a former student of Makiguchi, whose international, transnational, and counternational influence is known around the world, as illustrated in his lectures on the arts, culture, religion, and peace at prominent universities in many countries (Ikeda, 2010). His sixty-plus book-length published dialogues, from 1970 to the present, are masterfully engaging conversations between Ikeda and such intellectuals as Arnold Toynbee, Linus Pauling, Norman Cousins, Mikhail Gorbachev, Lokesh Chandra, Elise Boulding, Vincent Harding, and most recently, continuing his goal of bringing Eastern and Western perspectives together, through a dialogue with Chinese scholar Tu Weiming (Weiming & Ikeda, 2011). Additionally, Ikeda's (2010a) Soka schools attract considerable attention around the world, as does his 2011 Peace Proposal (Ikeda, 2011), which doubtless faces blockades from the corporatocracy because advocacy of peace challenges its conquest and power based on *perpetual war* (Vidal, 2004), which constitutes a nightmarish contradiction of college as the *perpetual dream* (Grant & Riesman, 1978). In between the machinations of the policies of nations and corporatocracy, however, works of Ming Fang He (2003), her colleagues and former students (He & Phillion, 2008) illustrate how dedicated human beings can work to counter macrocosmic oppression and greed through microcosmic relationships cultivated in movements in between cultures and fluid states of exile and being at home.

Nearly 80 years ago, John Dewey (1933) was prescient of the escalation of greed, to which he responded in a quasi-fictive essay published in the *New York Times*. He reported on a visit he allegedly made to Utopia, where inhabitants practiced the education and democratic community that he advocated. Seeing it in action, he almost did not recognize it and raised some of the same questions that are perennially raised about progressive education by neo-conservatives and neo-liberals. When Dewey appreciated the Utopian achievement before him, he questioned the Utopians about how they were able to accomplish such remarkable social practice. The Utopians told him that their biggest obstacle had been *acquisitiveness*. He revealed that the Utopians believed that the pattern which exists in economic society in our time affected the general habits of thought; that because personal acquisition and private possession were such dominant ideals in all fields, even if unconsciously so, they had taken position of the minds of educators to the extent that the idea of personal acquisition and possession controlled the whole educational system. (p. 7)

So enthralled was I with this short article by Dewey that I searched for compatible support for his perspective, and did so by also "visiting" the same Utopian society to construct a follow-up report. My book-length "report" (Schubert, 2009) contends that the Utopians overcome predatory tendencies, destruction, and suffering wrought by acquisitive societies through a will to create education that seeks justice from relationships of love. This kind of love is not mere sentimentality; it requires great strength to love what humans can become (King, 1963), and to act on that love to continuously revitalize ourselves. Love of this sort embraces mutual listening—a deep empathizing between teachers and students (Schultz, 2011). Such is reminiscent of the epilogue of James W. Garrison's (1997) study of *eros* and Dewey, wherein he poignantly observes:

> Moment to moment, as teachers move among their students, they are touching lives. Teachers, too, are poets and prophets. If they are wise, then they and their students will learn to care for each other, bestow value, and grow together. If teachers are foolish, no one will flourish. Of this, though, we may be sure: We become what we love. (p. 202)

As true for the relationship of teaching in higher education as at any other level, Dewey continued in a similar vein after his visit to Utopia, calling for primary emphasis on developing "the attitude which would give a sense of positive power" saying:

> This attitude. . . involved. . . elimination of fear, of embarrassment, of constraint, of self-consciousness; eliminated the conditions which created the feeling of failure and incapacity. Possibly it included the development of a confidence, of readiness to tackle difficulties, of actual eagerness to seek problems instead of dreading them and running away from them. It included a rather ardent faith in human capacity. It included a faith in the capacity of the environment to support worthwhile activities. . . . (p. 7)

I argue that we must act as if there is hope for higher education to be more than a mouthpiece for, and certifier of, acquisitive Empire. Faith in human capacity must be nurtured in the spirit of loving relationships as a necessary and neglected path (curriculum) to justice in higher education and in the world. With the perennial persistence of grassroots movements, we must emerge within the cracks of acquisitive power, examine the BIG Curriculum that strives to control higher education, and imaginatively create ever-evolving curricula of resistance.

Note

1. I have developed the term BIG Curriculum (Schubert, 2005) to refer to the massive media campaigns of educational dimensions of propaganda from the globalized corporate "government" that transcends, overpowers, and often rules national governments. I draw from Noam Chomsky's (1997, 2001, 2005) frequent reference to this phenomenon over the years; and to recent work on corporatocracy (Hiatt, 2007; Perkins, 2006), and the global elite (Freeland, 2011). I elaborate this curriculum construct more fully later in this chapter.

References

Anyon, J. (1980). Social class and the hidden curriculum of work. *Journal of Education, 162* (1), 67–92.

Anyon, J. (2004). *Radical possibilities: Public policy, urban education, and a new social movement.* New York: Routledge.

Aoki, T. T. (1993). Legitimating lived curriculum: Towards a curricular landscape of multiplicity. *Journal of Curriculum and Supervision, 8* (3), 255–268.

Apple, M. W. (1979). *Ideology and curriculum.* New York: Routledge.

Apple, M. W. (1982). *Education and power.* New York: Routledge.

Apple, M. W. (1999). *Official knowledge: Democratic education in a conservative age* (2nd ed.). New York: Routledge.

Archibald, J. (2008). *Indigenous storywork: Educating the heart, mind, body, and spirit.* Vancouver: University of British Columbia Press.

Arum, R., & Roksa, J. (2011). *Academically adrift: Limited learning on college campuses.* Chicago: University of Chicago Press.

Astin, A. W., Astin, H. S., & Lindholm, J. A. (2011). *Cultivating the spirit: How college can enhance students' inner lives.* San Francisco: Jossey-Bass.

Bartlett, J. (Ed.). (2002). *Bartlett's familiar quotations* (17th ed.). Boston: Little, Brown.

Bloom, A. (1987). *The closing of the American mind: How higher education has failed democracy and impoverished the souls of today's students.* New York: Simon & Schuster.

Boyer, E. L. (1988). *College: The undergraduate experience in America.* Princeton, NJ: Carnegie Foundation for the Advancement of Teaching.

Chomsky, N. (1997). *Media control: Spectacular achievements of propaganda.* New York: Seven Stories Press.

Chomsky, N. (2001). *Propaganda and the public mind.* Cambridge, MA: South End Press.

Chomsky, N. (2005). *Imperial ambitions.* New York: Metropolitan Books.

Connelly, F. M., He, M. F., & Phillion, J. A. (Eds.). (2008). *Handbook of curriculum and instruction.* Thousand Oaks, CA: Sage.

Cuban, L. (1999). *How scholars trumped teachers: Change without reform in university curriculum, teaching, and research, 1880–1990.* New York: Teachers College Press.

Dewey, J. (1916). *Democracy and education.* New York: Macmillan.

Dewey, J. (1929). *The sources of a science of education.* New York: Liveright.

Dewey, J. (1933, April 23). Dewey outlines utopian schools. *New York Times*, p. 7. Also in Boydston, J. A. (Ed.). (1989). *The later works (1925–1953) of John Dewey* (Vol. 9, pp. 136–140). Carbondale: Southern Illinois University Press.

Dewey, J. (1934). *A common faith.* New Haven, CT: Yale University Press.

Dewey, J. (1938). *Experience and education.* New York: Macmillan.

Doll, W. E., Jr. (1993). *A post-modern perspective on curriculum.* New York: Teachers College Press.

Donoghue, F. (2008). *The last professors: The corporate University and the fate of the humanities.* New York: Fordham University Press.

Eisner, E. W. (1979). *The educational imagination.* New York: Macmillan.

Ellwood, W. (2010). *The no nonsense guide to globalization.* Ottawa & Toronto: The New Internationalist & Between the Lines.

Esteva, G., & Prakash, M. S. (1997). *Grassroots postmodernism: Beyond human rights, the individual self, and the global economy.* New York: Peter Lang.

Fanon, F. (1963). *The wretched of the earth.* New York: Grove Press.

Freeland, C. (2011). The rise of the new global elite. *The Atlantic, 307* (1), 44–55.

Freire, P. (1970). *Pedagogy of the oppressed.* New York: Continuum.

Freire, P. (2007). *Daring to dream: Toward a pedagogy of the unfinished* (Organized and presented by Ana Maria Araujo Freire; Translated by Alexandre K. Oliveira). Boulder, CO: Paradigm.

Garrison, J. (1997). *Dewey and eros.* New York: Teachers College Press.

Giroux, H. A. (2007). *The university in chains.* Boulder, CO: Paradigm.

Giroux, H. A., Lankshear, C., McLaren, P., & Peters, M. (1996). *Counternarratives.* New York: Routledge.

Giroux, H. A., & Purpel, D. (Eds.). (1982). *The hidden curriculum and moral education.* Berkeley, CA: McCutchan.

Grande, S. (2004). *Red pedagogy: Native American social and political thought.* Lanham, MD: Rowman & Littlefield.

Grant, G., & Riesman, D. (1978). *The perpetual dream: Reform and experiment in the American College.* Chicago: University of Chicago Press.

Gray, J. (2002). *Straw dogs: Thoughts on humans and other animals.* London: Granta Books.

Greene, M. (1978). *Landscapes of learning.* New York: Teachers College Press.

Greene, M. (1995). *Releasing the imagination: Essays on education, the arts, and social change.* San Francisco, CA: Jossey-Bass.

Hansen, D. T. (Ed.). (2007). *Ethical visions of education: Philosophies in practice.* New York: Teachers College Press in association with the Boston Research Center for the 21st Century.

Harvey, D. (2005). *A brief history of neoliberalism.* Oxford: Oxford University Press.

Harvey, D. (2010). *The enigma of capital and the crisis of capitalism.* Oxford: Oxford University Press.

He, M. F. (2003). *A river forever flowing: Cross-cultural lives and identities in the multicultural landscape.* Greenwich, CT: Information Age Publishers.

He, M. F. (2010a). Exile pedagogy: Teaching in-between. In J. A. Sandlin, B. D. Schultz, & J. Burdick (Eds.), *Handbook of public pedagogy: Education and learning beyond schooling* (pp. 469–482). New York: Routledge.

He, M. F. (2010b). Curriculum inquiry. In C. Kridel (Ed.), *Encyclopedia of curriculum studies* (Vol. 1, pp. 213–217). Thousand Oaks, CA: Sage.

He, M. F., & Phillion, J. (Eds.). (2008). *Personal~passionate~participatory inquiry into social justice in education.* Charlotte, NC: Information Age.

Hedges, C. (2010). *Death of the liberal class.* New York: Nation Books.

Hiatt, S. (Ed.). (2007). *A game as old as empire: The secret world of economic hit men and the web of global corruption.* San Francisco: Berrett-Koehler.

Huebner, D. (1975). Curricular language and classroom meanings. In W. Pinar (Ed.), *Curriculum theorizing: The reconceptualists* (pp. 217–236). Berkeley, CA: McCutchan. (Reprinted from *Language and meaning*, pp. 8–26, by J. Macdonald & R. Leeper, Eds., 1966, Washington, DC: Association for Supervision and Curriculum Development.)

Ikeda, D. (2010). *A new humanism.* New York: I. B. Tauris.

Ikeda, D. (2011). *Toward a world of dignity for all: The triumph of the creative life.* Tokyo: The Soka Gakkai.

Illich, I. (1970). *Deschooling society.* New York: Harper & Row.

Izuegbu, V. (2011). *Students as designers of their own life curriculum.* Charlotte, NC: Information Age.

Jackson, P. W. (1968). *Life in classrooms.* New York: Holt, Rinehart, & Winston.

Jencks, C., & Riesman, D. (1968). *The academic revolution.* Garden City, NY: Doubleday.

Kerr, C. (1963). *The uses of the university.* Cambridge, MA: Harvard University Press.

King, M. L., Jr. (1963). *Strength to love.* Philadelphia: Fortress Press.

Klein, N. (2007). *The shock doctrine: The rise of disaster capitalism.* New York: Macmillan.

Lakoff, G., & Johnson, M. (1999). *Philosophy in the flesh: The embodied mind and its challenge to western thought.* New York: Basic Books.

Levine, L. W. (1996). *The opening of the American mind: Canons, culture, and history.* Boston: Beacon Press.

Lipman, P. (2004). *High stakes education: Inequality, globalization, and urban school reform.* New York: Routledge-Falmer.

Macdonald, J. B. (1974). A transcendental developmental ideology of education. In W. F. Pinar (Ed.), *Heightened consciousness, cultural revolution, and curriculum theory* (pp. 85–116). Berkeley, CA: McCutchan.

Macdonald, J. B., Wolfson, B., & Zaret, E. (1973). *Reschooling Society.* Washington, DC: Association for Supervision and Curriculum Development.

Malewski, E. (Ed.). (2009). *Curriculum studies handbook: The next moment.* New York: Routledge.

Marshall, J. D., Sears, J. T., Allen, L., Roberts, P., & Schubert, W. H. (2007). *Turning points in curriculum: A contemporary curriculum memoir* (2nd ed.). Columbus, OH: Prentice Hall.

McLaren, P. (1986). *Schooling as ritual performance.* Lanham, MD: Rowman & Littlefield.

McLaren, P. (1989). *Life in schools.* Boston, MA: Allyn & Bacon.

McLaren, P., & Faramandpur, R. (2004). *Teaching against global capitalism and the new imperialism: A critical pedagogy.* Lanham, MD: Rowman & Littlefield.

McLaren, P., & Jaramillo, N. (2007). *Pedagogy and praxis in the age of empire.* Rotterdam: Sense.

Meyer, L., & Alvarado, B. M. (Eds.). (2010). *New world of indigenous resistance.* San Francisco: City Lights Books.

Molnar, A. (2005). *School commercialism: From democratic ideal to market commodity.* New York: Routledge.

Nussbaum, M. (1997). *Cultivating humanity: A classical defense of reform in liberal education.* Cambridge, MA: Harvard University Press.

Nussbaum, M. (2010). *Not for profit: Why democracy needs the humanities.* Princeton, NJ: Princeton University Press.

Palmer, P. J., & Zajonc, A. (with Scribner, M.). (2010). *The heart of higher education: A call to renewal.* San Francisco: Jossey-Bass.

Pascarella, E. T., & Terenzini, P. T. (1991). *How college affects students.* San Francisco: Jossey-Bass.

Pascarella, E. T., & Terenzini, P. T. (2005). *How college affects students* (Vol. 2). San Francisco: Jossey-Bass.

Perkins, J. (2006). *Confessions of an economic hit man.* San Francisco: Berrett-Koehler.

Pinar, W. F. (1975). *Currere*: Toward reconceptualization. In W. Pinar (Ed.), *Curriculum theorizing: The reconceptualists* (pp. 396–414). Berkeley, CA: McCutchan.

Pinar, W. F., & Grumet, M. R. (1976). *Toward a poor curriculum*. Dubuque, IA: Kendall/Hunt.

Pinar, W. F., Reynolds, W. M., Slattery, P., & Taubman, P. M. (1995). *Understanding curriculum*. New York: Peter Lang.

Prakash, M. S., & Esteva, G. (1998). *Escaping education: Living as learning within grassroots cultures*. New York: Peter Lang.

Readings, B. (1996). *The university in ruins*. Cambridge, MA: Harvard University Press.

Rifkin, J. (2009). *The empathic civilization: The race to global consciousness in a world in crisis*. New York: Penguin.

Rubin, L. J. (1984). *Artistry in teaching*. New York: Random House.

Rudolph, F. (1977). *Curriculum: A history of the American undergraduate course of study*. San Francisco: Jossey-Bass.

Sandlin, J. A., O'Malley, M. P., & Burdick, J. (2011). Mapping the complexity of public pedagogy scholarship: 1894–2010. *Review of Educational Research, 81* (3), 338–375.

Sandlin, J. A., Schultz, B. D., & Burdick, J. (Eds.). (2010). *Handbook of public pedagogy: Education and learning beyond schooling*. New York: Routledge.

Schubert, W. H. (1975). *Imaginative projection: A method of curriculum invention* (Unpublished Ph.D. dissertation). University of Illinois, Urbana-Champaign.

Schubert, W. H. (1981). Knowledge about out-of-school curriculum. *Educational Forum, 45 (2)*, 185–99.

Schubert, W. H. (1986). *Curriculum: Perspective, paradigm, and possibility*. New York: Macmillan.

Schubert, W. H. (2006). Focus on the BIG CURRICULUM. *Journal of Curriculum and Pedagogy, 3* (1), 100–103.

Schubert, W. H. (2008). Curriculum inquiry. In F. M. Connelly, M. F. He, and J. Phillion, (Eds.), *Handbook of curriculum and instruction* (pp. 399–419). Thousand Oaks, CA: Sage.

Schubert, W. H. (2009). *Love, justice, and education: John Dewey and the utopians*. Charlotte, NC: Information Age.

Schubert, W. H. (2010a). Curriculum venues. In C. Kridel (Ed.), *Encyclopedia of curriculum studies* (Vol. 1, pp. 213–217). Thousand Oaks, CA: Sage.

Schubert, W. H. (2010b). Journeys of expansion and synopsis: Tensions in books that shaped curriculum inquiry, 1968–present. *Curriculum Inquiry, 40* (1), 17–94.

Schubert, W. H. (2010c). Outside curricula and public pedagogy. In J. A. Sandlin, B. D. Schultz, & J. Burdick. (Eds.), *Handbook of public pedagogy: Education and learning beyond schooling* (pp. 10–19). New York: Routledge.

Schubert, W. H., & Lopez Schubert, A. L. (1981). Toward curricula that are of, by, and therefore for students. *Journal of Curriculum Theorizing, 3* (1), 239–251.

Schubert, W. H., Lopez Schubert, A. L., Thomas, T. P., & Carroll, W. M. (2002). *Curriculum books: The first hundred years*. New York: Peter Lang.

Schultz, B. D. (Ed.). (2011). *Listening to and learning from students*. Charlotte, NC: Information Age.

Schwab, J. J. (1970). *The practical: A language for curriculum*. Washington, DC: National Education Association.

Smith, P. (1990). *Killing the spirit: Higher education in America*. New York: Viking.

Snyder, E. R. (1970). *The hidden curriculum*. New York: Knopf.

Spring, J. (2009). *Globalization of education*. New York: Routledge.

Spring, J. (2010). *Deculturalization and the struggle for equality: A brief history of the education of dominated cultures in the United States*. New York: McGraw-Hill.

Takaki, R. (1993). *A different mirror*. Boston: Little, Brown.

Taubman, P. M. (2009). *Teaching by numbers*. New York: Routledge.

Thelin, J. R. (2004). *A history of American higher education*. New York: Teachers College Press.

Tillett, W. (2011). *Living the questions* (Unpublished Ph. D. dissertation). University of Illinois at Chicago.

Tuhiwai Smith, L. (2001). *Decolonizing methodologies: Research and indigenous peoples*. London: Zed Books.

Tyler, R. W. (1949). *Basic principles of curriculum and instruction*. Chicago: University of Chicago Press.

Vidal, G. (2004). *Imperial America*. New York: Nation Books.

Vonnegut, K. (2005). *A man without a country*. New York: Seven Stories Press.

Walker, D. F. (1971). A naturalistic model for curriculum development. *School Review, 80* (1), 51–69.

Washburn, J. (2005). *University, Inc.: The corporate corruption of higher education*. New York: Basic Books.

Watkins, W. H. (Ed.). (2005). *Black protest thought and education*. New York: Peter Lang.

Weiming, T., & Ikeda, D. (2011). *New horizons in Eastern humanism: Buddhism, Confucianism, and the quest for global peace*. London: I. B. Tauris.

Whitehead, A. N. (1926). *Religion in the making*. New York: Macmillan.

Whitehead, A. N. (1929). *The aims of education and other essays*. New York: Macmillan.

Willis, P. (1977). *Learning to labour*. Lexington, MA: D. C. Heath.

Wilshire, B. (1990). *The moral collapse of the university*. Albany: State University of New York Press.

Zinn, H. (1995). *A people's history of the United States 1492–Present* (2nd ed.). New York: Harper Perennial.
Zinn, H., Konopacki, M., & Buhle, P. (2008). *A people's history of American empire*. New York: Harper Perennial.

CHAPTER FOURTEEN

Liberal Education

The Challenge of Consumerism, Careerism, and Commodification

CHRISTOPHER J. LUCAS

The only advantage of a classical brain is that it will enable you to despise the wealth it will prevent you from earning.
　　—Anonymous British mathematician

Admirers of American higher education are prone to claiming the nation's colleges and universities are the envy of their peers the world over (perhaps excepting Oxbridge and a very small handful of others). Public and private, non-profit and for-profit, secular and sectarian, elitist and populist, private liberal arts schools that serve the affluent, less-expensive, open-access flagship behemoths that aspire to offer something for everyone, former teacher-training colleges now refurbished as third- and fourth-tier regional state universities, industrial-looking urban institutions serving a predominantly "non-traditional" student clientele, two-year community colleges that mostly address the needs of first-generation attendees—in its endless variety and diversity, its openness and democratic spirit, postsecondary education in the United States, it is said, has no equal elsewhere.

A warrant for the claim of superiority is not necessarily obvious however. If dollars spent are a useful benchmark of quality, the United States reportedly expends more on education than any other nation, with roughly $186 billion of public funds going annually to higher education. And it remains noteworthy that American universities not only continue to attract upwards of two-thirds of all graduating high-school seniors yearly, they also take in large numbers of foreign students, especially at the graduate level. Most of the latter pay full freight, amounting to a multi-*billion*-dollar infusion into the American economy—this despite security concerns that until very recently made obtaining a visa to study in the United States a major challenge in the aftermath of 9/11. But once again, it is not entirely apparent just what it is that the rest of the world is supposedly admiring and why so many seek admission to the hallowed precincts of American academe.

Good public relations undoubtedly help: The glossy websites of most institutions of higher and not-so-higher education are typically chock full of news about endowments, statistics celebrating burgeoning enrollments, world-class cutting-edge research, and generous scholarship aid plus low-interest loans for deserving students. A stunning array of degree programs in every discipline imaginable attests to the variety of specializations offered at Ol'Siwash U. Harken to panegyric accounts of award-winning researchers and distinguished scholars, as well as inspired teachers and faculty mentors, all of them selflessly devoted to the welfare of their students. (The subliminal message, however hard to credit, is that Mr. Chips is alive and well even in the multiversity of modern times.) All told, it is alleged, never before have there been so many talented and committed faculty, so broadly dispersed, in institutions of so many different kinds.

The Halls of Ivy

Certainly first impressions are reassuring. Visit one of the celebrated Ivy League schools where the visitor is greeted by stately ivied buildings set out on vast expanses of verdant lawn; where tree-lined pathways are thronged with well-dressed students, while somewhere off in the distance sonorous chimes toll the hour. Campus aesthetics here cannot be trusted entirely nor relied on overmuch perhaps, but the unmistakable impression conveyed is one of seriousness of academic purpose and robust institutional health.[1]

Or maybe not. The peaceful calm that seems to prevail at places like Georgetown, Dartmouth, Stanford, and Wellesley may serve to minimize major internal strains and stresses within the larger system, tensions that have been simmering below the surface for the last several decades. Ivy League schools so far seem to have remained largely untouched by these forces for basic change, whereas the trends are more obvious in less prestigious institutions. At the heart of the matter is the much remarked-upon transformation of today's system of *higher* education into *mass* education, with all of the systemic adjustments and compromises thereby required. The advent on campus of a radical populism or egalitarianism is not necessarily an unalloyed evil. But neither is it all positive either. Think of easier access compared with the admission requirements of yesteryear, more forgiving grading standards, the emergence of a whole panoply of hand-holding student support services, insubstantial do-it-yourself programs of off-campus study, over-reliance on part-time adjunct faculty, overdependence on teaching assistants to deliver curricula at the larger schools, abandonment of foreign-language requirements and, finally, the whole infused with a pervasive sense of student entitlement: "I need that good grade in order to keep my scholarship!"

Radical Consumerism

In these opening years of the twenty-first century, the issues in higher education that prompted so much invective a scant decade or so—identity politics, cultural diversity, multiculturalism, institutional accountability, ballooning costs—have tended to give way in part to new—or in some cases, recycled—controversies. Looming as the most fundamental among them, arguably, has been the shift toward a form of radical consumerism. With it has come the rise of unrestrained careerism among a new generation of decidedly non-traditional collegians. In turn, neglect of "old-fashioned" liberal learning has been almost inevitable. The simultaneous intrusion of corporate values on campus goes a long way to help account for the apparent en-feeblement of the humanistic liberal arts as subjects of academic instruction and, more broadly, the prospect of the loss of a coherent, intelligible *idea* of higher learning as the lifelong pursuit of what the ancient Greeks termed "personal excellence." What is being lost, in other words, is something akin possibly to Cardinal John Henry Newman's mid-nineteenth-century inter-pretation of liberally trained intellect, an ideal buttressed by faith in the transformative power of liberal learning.

In any event, judging by the decreasing share of curricular "life space" for the humanities and humanistic social-science disciplines in today's colleges and universities, the decline of lib-eral learning as a presence in most institutions of higher learning already seems well advanced. Note current enrollments in business and agriculture schools and then compare them with student patronage of the arts and sciences.[2] Look to the imbalance as it existed three or more decades ago to see how much it has changed. The shift proves both instructive and profoundly disturbing. And the sound one hears in the background is the unmistakable throb of students voting with their feet.

Careerism in Academe

Time and time again, surveys demonstrate that parents and college-bound high school students have very little familiarity with the meaning or purpose of the liberal arts (beyond the possible benefit of learning how to be good conversationalists at social functions). Understandably, in an environment where the value of a liberal arts education is no longer taken for granted, fewer degrees are awarded in the liberal arts. In the United States today almost 60 percent of under-graduate degrees are in pre-professional and technical fields, with business degrees leading the way, accounting for some 20 percent of all degrees conferred. In contrast, in the early 1900s technical and pre-professional majors accounted for less than one-third of all undergraduate degrees awarded. The times, they are a-changing, and with a vengeance.

Meanwhile, as, journalist Jennifer Washburn puts it, a "foul wind" is blowing over the campuses of most of the nation's institutions of higher learning.[3] Its source, she claims, is the growing infusion of commercialism into the heart of academic life. Rutgers historian Jackson Lears similarly comments on the growing menace of market-driven managerial influence in colleges and universities: the impulse to subject universities to quantitative standards of ef-ficiency and productivity, to convert knowledge into a commodity, and to transform open sites of inquiry into corporate research laboratories and job-training centers.[4] Likewise for Washburn, in the absence of values capable of constraining unregulated markets careening out of control if left to their own devices, universities, she argues, are running the risk of becoming something close to appendages of corporate business and industry, no longer academic institu-tions as we have known them but citadels of unfettered commercialism.[5]

Corporate Transformation

It follows, naturally, in an environment where short-term practicality and utilitarian learning are valued above all else, that the humanities cannot command "market share" and so are apt to be marginalized or consigned to the curricular periphery. They do not disappear entirely, of course; they simply atrophy from neglect as subjects of instruction or migrate elsewhere beyond the boundaries of academe. Meanwhile, the mechanistic discourse that seems to be increasingly favored by collegiate administrators, and sometimes by academics themselves, attests to the growing ubiquity of a parlance that describes learning as a commodity, information as a "product" to be packaged and marketed, knowledge as something susceptible to being bundled into credits and delivered via an instructional "system" students as "consumers" or "human capital" awaiting batch "processing" and so on. David Kirp, of the University of Berkeley, takes note of what amounts to the same semantic assault:

> These dayspriorities are determined less by academic leaders than by multiple constituencies and managerial mandarins. The new vocabulary of customers and stakeholders, niche marketing and branding, and winner-take-all embodies this sea change in the higher education "industry."In this brave new world [every program] is a "revenue center" each party a "stakeholder" each student a customer, each professor an entrepreneur, and each institution a seeker after profit, whether in money capital or intellectual capital.[6]

For Lears, the single most egregious illustration of learning as commodity is higher education's preoccupation with the virtual classroom and the effort to substitute cyber-technology for live interaction between teacher and student. "Any use of computers that undermines face-to-face contact is potentially destructive to education" he insists. "Distance learning is to learning as phone sex is to sex: it may be better than no learning at all, but you wouldn't want to confuse it with the real thing."[7]

Faith in Education

All the while, students continue to pour into colleges, bringing with them strong consumerist attitudes and an expectation that college will serve to prepare them for the world of work. But does college truly lead to better jobs? The question is worth posing. Unhappily, the answer seems to be—not necessarily. After all, the more people go to college, the lower the scarcity value of the college degrees earned. Moreover, the mere possession of a diploma attesting to the claim that the holder is now educated is hardly sufficient to guarantee an applicant a good job, or any job, or even an interview for employment. Hence, little is to be gained by heaping calumny on entering students in their headlong quest for economic security, and for their hesitation about pursuing a liberal-arts degree. For better or worse, college has become the socializing mechanism of choice for parents and politicians of all stripes and ideologies. Students, well attuned and mindful of the oversupply of graduates competing for fewer desirable jobs, inevitably flock to career preparatory programs where they can ready themselves for "first-job placement."

As they enter, rational motives give way to faith in schooling as the most appropriate middle-class rite of passage into adulthood, and the chief means of preparing for one's economic role in society, even when its promise goes unfulfilled. But why should students have to endure the excoriations of the pundits for being narrowly obsessed with careers, and, if one accepts some of the recent reports, inept at writing, incompetent in mathematics, and moral barbarians as well? Students have to play the game, hope for the best, and look for a break, especially when the future payback on student loans bids fair to overwhelm their future earnings. A disinclination to pursue liberal learning in the midst of an uncertain economy, it must be said, is entirely understandable if not altogether justified.

Hard Questions

So the questions endure—questions so basic and fundamental one hesitates to dust them off for reconsideration. Is college actually the best place to equip oneself with the skills and knowledge needed for obtaining a job? If not, what does a college or university have to offer that is pertinent and worth the cost? Does everyone need to attend college? Should education stress practical learning or should it address the training of intellect? The queries are not new, of course. On the contrary, they are very old. "At present opinion is divided about the subjects of education" Aristotle observed over two millennia ago in his *Politics*.

> People do not take the same view about what should be learned by the young, either with a view of human excellence or a view to the best possible life; nor is it clear whether education should be directed mainly to the intellect or to moral character. . . whether the proper studies to be pursued are those that are useful to life, or those which make for excellence, or those that advance the bounds of knowledge. . . .

"Men do not all honor the same distinctive human excellence" he concluded, "and so naturally they differ about the proper training for it."[8]

And so the debate echoes down through the centuries. Toward what ends or goals ought education be directed? What curriculum best serves both the polity and the individual? In some imagined past when colleges were less democratic, more elitist, and clearer of purpose and priorities, monopolized as they were by a gentlemanly überclass, it might have been easier to design appropriate courses of study. Today answers elude us, or at least seem harder to come by, particularly when institutions of higher learning are expected to provide relevant, high-quality learning for nearly *all* comers.

Expectations Matter

What we do know is that schools are not doing that great a job with *lower* education, much less higher learning. According to recent reports, for instance, fully half of all high school seniors in one study could not identify in which century the Civil War took place or correctly date Columbus' voyages of discovery to within a half century, while the percentage of college seniors unable to answer the same question correctly was only slightly lower. A passage from Thomas Hughes' novel *Tom Brown's Schooldays*, for instance, has Squire Brown musing on sending his son to Thomas Arnold's Rugby.

> Shall I tell him to mind his work, and say he's sent to school to make himself a good scholar? Well, but he isn't sent to school for that. . . . I don't care a straw for Greek particles, or the digamma, no more does his mother. . . . If he'll only turn out a brave, helpful, truth-telling Englishman, and a gentleman, and a Christian, that's all I want" thought the Squire.[9]

Strip away the quaint allusions, and an article of faith remains, namely, belief in the efficacy of disciplined absorption in the liberal arts to strengthen character and instill basic values. Through mastery of the liberal disciplines—language, mathematics, music, grammar, logic—and exposure to great human models of literature and history, the point of education in an earlier day encompassed intellectual and moral development, not just bookish erudition. Admittedly, if ever such a time existed, it has long since passed. But the basic notion of an education aimed at fostering civic virtue, encouraging personal responsibility, and generating acquaintanceship with a broad array of subject matters is still with us, albeit in a noticeably attenuated form.

Do the liberal arts in fact produce specific qualities of mind and character, such as critical thinking and analysis, skill in formulating and criticizing abstractions, independence of thought, learning how to learn, self-control, leadership, emotional maturity, balanced judgment, or personal integration? Do liberally educated persons make for better citizens? Do the liberal arts enhance prospects for the enjoyment of a fuller, richer life? Is there any identifiable and practical "payoff" that would justify the time, energy, expense, and effort required to obtain a humane, liberal education? Challenging questions indeed, especially within a culture enamored of cost-benefit equations and a strict bottom-line mentality.

Education for Personal Liberation

Any truly convincing response must begin with a frank admission. If there is a contribution humanistic studies can make to desired outcomes of character, virtue and knowledge, the connection between the two is unlikely to be found to be direct or immediate. After all, as O. B. Hardison once remarked, one does not read *Macbeth* to learn about the evils of ambition and therefore become a better public servant. Likewise, reading Chaucer can be great fun, though it is doubtful whether there are any immediate lessons to be drawn from the *Canterbury Tales* other than those having to do so with the manners and mores of life in late medieval England.[10] The penumbral contribution of the liberating arts and humanities, it needs to be underscored, must be more subtle, more indirect, basically "associative" and *contextual* in character.

A bit of historical background may be helpful here. First, it should be kept in mind that liberal education was once permitted only to "free men" (Latin, *liberi*), and it had the dual connotation of being reserved for those who were free (as opposed to those who were slaves) and as the sort of learning conductive to the realization of personal, intellectual freedom, or "liberation" (from the Latin *liberare*, "to free"; *liber*, "free"; *liberalis*, "liberal"). In antiquity and long afterwards, "general" education (again, from the Latin, *generalis*, "of or pertaining to the whole, not particular or specialized") was used synonymously or interchangeably with "liberal" education to denote the same kind of learning experiences.

The liberal arts in their original sense, it may be worth adding, did not designate fixed fields of study so much as they referred to activities or techniques; they were conceived of, strictly speaking, as ways of *doing* things. This, in fact, was precisely what the word "arts" meant; as, for example, the means for engaging in rhetorical, logical, or grammatical analysis. Ancient writers categorized these liberal arts in slightly different ways, but the most common enumeration included grammar, logic, and rhetoric (the *trivium*), and music, geometry, arithmetic, and astronomy, or alternatively, philosophy (the *quadrivium*). The liberal arts were the means for achieving personal liberation, and, later, those studies that open up human knowledge and thereby liberate. A liberal-general education began with the study of the liberating arts.

When Graeco-Roman leaning first passed into the medieval world, the precedent of dividing the liberal arts into two parts, followed by Plato, Aristotle, Augustine, and others, was extended by the fifth-century writer Martianus Capella in his influential work *The Marriage of Philology and Mercury*. He specified grammar, rhetoric, and dialectic—the literary arts—as the *trivium*, and arithmetic, geometry, astronomy (and astrology), and the study of musical harmonies—the quantitative or mathematical arts—as the *quadrivium*.[11] Taken together, this combination of subjects, as H. I. Marrou has shown, constituted a "general" or "ordinary" education: *enkykliospaideia* ("recurring" hence "regular, "or "ordinary"; *paideia* connoted the *process* of education, the *means* through which it was conducted, and also, finally, its *end* or goal, the acquisition of "culture.") From a general education in the liberal arts (and hence a liberal education) issued the "cultured" individual, one who participates in and shares a literate culture.[12] The Romans later referred to much the same thing by the term *humanitas*, the condition or state of being fully human and sharing virtuous characteristics to the fullest possible extent.[13] The overarching goal of *enkykliospaideia* was the attainment of *arête*, the "virtue" or, better yet, the "distinctive excellence" that makes of a person the highest, finest, most exemplary form of human being possible—roughly, in modern terms, the fully "actualized" or "self-realized" individual. The word "form" is used here advisedly. "Be forever at work carving your own statue" urged one classical maxim—suggesting rather clearly that one shapes, molds, or fashions the raw, unhewn "stuff" or "substance" of the self and thereby creates a self-defined person. The German word *Bildung* also found use as a term to describe the process of "building" or making a self. The product of this act of self-definition or cultivation, once again, was participation in a shared "culture" (*paideia*).

Cognate with "liberal" as the type of education suited to the pursuit of *arête*, or "self-realized excellence" and the acquisition of culture was "liberality"—broad-mindedness—and "generous" implying compassion, tolerance, and humaneness. To be educated was to be "liberated" from bigotry, intolerance, and harshness. The educated person was "freed" from the bondage of ignorance, parochialism, and ethnocentrism. The original sense of "humanism" as a belief in the importance of liberation, or emancipation, and attaining one's true "humanity" was also closely bound up with this classical educational ideal.

In the medieval period, the study of the liberal arts was viewed as the necessary precondition for professional specialization. Through the study of the liberal arts, students were to acquire basic skills and facility in the use of an international language (namely, Latin) and proficiency in quantitative analysis. Thus, to speak of the study of grammar, logic, and rhetoric was but an antiquated way of referring to instruction in language, thinking, and speech. The study of arithmetic, geometry, harmonics in music, and so forth likewise was the means for achieving skills in quantitative analysis. Thinking precisely (qualitatively and quantitatively), writing correctly, and speaking clearly were the basic aims of university instruction.

Moreover, and contrary to later perceptions, university education was not always an elitist phenomenon, at least not in the sense of being restricted to members of the privileged social classes. In many ways, students were as internationally and socially heterogeneous a group as today's college students, and even less well prepared than their modern counterparts. Universities in any event appear to have afforded many less advantaged persons a route upward in terms of socioeconomic mobility. It is no accident that the liberal arts supplied the avenue over which the sons of Europe's poor made their way into high positions in church and state. Through practice in the liberal arts, they acquired skills as well as a first introduction to the knowledge and wisdom of their age. Much the same held true in the Renaissance period and in succeeding centuries.

Not until the eighteenth and nineteenth centuries did it become customary to define the liberally educated individual almost exclusively in terms of the books he had read and the extent to which he accepted the values of a socially restrictive, class-conscious, male-dominated society. As interpreted by the dons of Oxford and Cambridge and their latter-day American imitators, liberal education became rigidly defined by the canon of books and values it bequeathed to its students and the positions in society it provided for them. It was the commitment to social exclusivity and privilege for college graduates—deliberately so in Great Britain and derivatively so in North America—that differentiated a college education in the 1800s from the practices of the *artes liberales* in the Middle Ages. And while, upon occasion, the less advantaged did gain access to a collegiate education, they did so in smaller proportion than seems to have been the case formerly.

If this historical analysis holds, it would help explain why twentieth-century defenders of general education had to labor so assiduously to disassociate the concept from the elitist associations it inherited over the previous two centuries. In the eighteenth and nineteenth centuries the tendency was to identify a liberal or general education primarily with the study of theology, ethics, some rudimentary natural sciences, and the language and literature of Graeco-Roman antiquity. Education in the liberal arts (now expanded to encompass formal fields of study besides techniques for qualitative and quantitative reasoning) was variously defended on the grounds of mental training and moral discipline, conserving and transmitting a cultural heritage, sustaining high culture, and as a source of cultural unity or integration. In the twentieth century, in some quarters, the term "liberal" was retained as a prefix to describe education organized around basic disciplines, whereas "general" education, more broadly, was intended to connote learning experiences unrelated to vocational or professional preparation. By mid-century, general education as a term had come to refer loosely to almost any non-specialized, non-vocational learning.

Secondly, the fact of the matter is, there has hardly been a time when consensus was achieved over the content and organization of the undergraduate curriculum. Historians will look in vain to some former golden age when broad agreement prevailed about texts, organizational patterns, or undergirding assumptions and practices—which is to say, simply, that curricular issues have always been contentious, with very little about them commanding universal assent.

Nowadays the sweep of debate has been greatly magnified by the sheer scale upon which mass higher education is conducted. The urgency with which certain issues are prosecuted also may be said to have increased dramatically in comparison with the past. Yet when all is said and done, few if any of the elements of controversy are genuinely novel. They reduce, in some final analysis, to questions about purposes and goals; about conceptions of what the educated person is supposed to know and to be and to do (though some disputants will deny even this claim); about the worth of, and priorities among, different types of knowledge; about the meaning and function of the baccalaureate degree, and, for that matter, by extension, about the purpose of undergraduate collegiate experiences as a whole.

Harvard President Charles William Eliot's inaugural address of 1869 furnishes a convenient vantage point from which to gain a certain perspective on today's curricular debates. Throughout the first half of the nineteenth century, academic leaders had been locked in debate over the respective merits of a fixed curriculum built on classical learning as compared with a more flexible, open-ended course of studies incorporating modern subjects. At the time

Eliot assumed his new post, Harvard freshmen were still required to enroll for a rigidly prescribed curriculum, one including Latin, Greek, mathematics, French, elocution, and ethics. Victor Duray's *Historie Grecque* was required reading. Entering students were further compelled to familiarize themselves with at least twenty chapters of Gibbon's *Decline and Fall of the Roman Empire* and some 350 pages of a philosophic work entitled *The Philosophy of the Active and Moral Powers of Man* (1828) by the now-obscure Scottish philosopher Duglad Stewart.

Second-year students took physics, chemistry, German, elocution, and "themes." Juniors and seniors were allowed a limited number of elective choices, though the bulk of their studies was still prescribed. Surveying the scene as he found it upon his arrival, and taking note of the debates still swirling throughout the halls of academe, Eliot professed to discern no inherent conflict between defenders of the older classical conception of liberal learning and protagonists of curricular reform. "The endless controversies whether language, philosophy, mathematics, or science supplies the best mental training, whether general education should be chiefly literary or chiefly scientific, have no practical lesson for us today" he asserted. "This university recognizes no real antagonism between literature and science, and consents to no such narrow alternatives as mathematics or classics, science or metaphysics" he declared. "We would have them all, and at their best."[14]

The vexing question, of course, was precisely how to "have them all." Eliot's answer, in frank acknowledgment of the expansion of human knowledge and the growing impossibility of anyone's encompassing all that could be known, was an elective system permitting students for the first time to select from among alternative courses and programs of study.

Eliot's dethronement of the prescribed classical curriculum almost immediately provoked strong reactions. Critics denounced the elective system as impractical, a mischievous fad, an unworkable innovation, an academic fraud. President Noah Porter of Yale flatly denied students were capable of making intelligent and informed choices under an elective system. Andrew F. West of Princeton agreed, as did Charles Francis Adams, and countless others.

Thus the battle between proponents and opponents of a system of curricular choice in higher education was joined. It was a controversy that would arouse strong passions on both sides.[15] Nevertheless, one leading institution after another began to favor the adoption in some form of an elective principle. The larger state universities of the Midwest and West were the most enthusiastic in embracing the innovation, followed by some of the larger universities with private endowments. Least receptive were the old-time colleges of New England. By the 1890s Wisconsin and Michigan counted among the few major institutions still maintaining required freshman and sophomore courses. By 1896 Cornell was allowing a virtually unrestricted system of electives. The next year even Yale, then Wisconsin, permitted unlimited electives after the student's initial year of enrollment.

Gradually, as required courses were abandoned and elective courses of study became even more directly tied to occupational interests, the idea of acquaintance with *any* fixed body of knowledge, classical or otherwise, as the mark of an educated person began to disappear. Still left unanswered was the question as to whether all subjects of study should be weighted equally in value—bookkeeping no less than physics, civil engineering together with Greek poetry, theology and accountancy, metaphysics and domestic science. Increasingly, the tacit presumption was that no one discipline or field of study could be considered more or less important than any other. Each deserved its place within academe.

The corollary to curricular egalitarianism was the admission into collegiate courses of study of modern subjects heretofore excluded. This process of accretion had begun well before the midpoint of the nineteenth century, and it was to continue unabated thereafter. Modern languages first appeared as distinct fields for specialized study in the 1870s. In the decade following, modern philosophy, literature, and the fine arts won acceptance as academic studies. By the 1890s a variety of social sciences had appeared and were being enshrined in college curricula. Old barriers continued to tumble. By the late 1880s land grant colleges had expanded their offerings in animal husbandry, agronomy, veterinary medicine, horticulture, plant pathology, farm management, mechanical engineering, and "domestic sciences." Vocational and technical education across a nearly unrestricted spectrum were fast becoming legitimate, accepted aspects of American higher education.

Partly as a result, the distinction between professional and vocational education blurred. Universities, it was now apparent, would offer instruction for practically *all* careers for which some formal body of knowledge existed—not just divinity, law, or medicine, but also education, journalism, engineering, and other applied fields. With attendant specialization and departmentalization came fragmentation and the carving up of human knowledge into entirely separate disciplines or domains superintended by distinct, often contending, administrative units. This fragmentation of academic life simply underscored the growing conviction symbolized by the elective principle that not all educated people needed to command the same knowledge.

The problem, however, was to decide whether received notions of liberal learning and humanistic thought still had any relevance or applicability whatsoever in the modern age. By 1900, if not well before, the traditional notion that an educated person was distinguished by familiarity with a common body of thought and value was beginning to seem moribund. A felt loss of unity and coherence was widely remarked upon. The growing feeling among many writers at the turn of the century was that Eliot's elective system, begun three decades before, had borne bitter fruit. Not only had the college curriculum been fragmented beyond repair, matters had come to the point where specialization of interest and professionalism had threatened to replace entirely general learning and education of a liberal character altogether.

By the opening decade of the twentieth century, even the most ardent supporters of the idea of a fixed curriculum, uniform and prescribed for all, had to concede that the traditional scheme was no longer supportable. By the same token, there was widespread agreement that uncontrolled application of the elective principle—that all could freely chose whatever attracted their interest—offered no satisfactory alternative. Critics increasingly agreed that whatever gains were achieved by allowing students almost unlimited personal choices were overshadowed by a loss of coherence and intellectual integration. Eliot's bold scheme, it was said, had led to disintegration, to the taking of courses in isolation from one another, the whole lacking any overall unity or design. The typical course of study, it was now alleged, lacked organic unity, a system of connections and common tasks among disparate disciplines. If the old idea of a shared intellectual and moral "culture" or *paideia*, had been too narrowly circumscribed by classical learning, the alternative of a "cafeteria" approach to learning was too open-ended. As reaction to the "smorgasbord" curriculum set in, the consensus of opinion shifted toward seeking a better balance between elective anarchy and rigid curricular prescription.

The practical expedient that eventually won greatest acceptance among most institutions of higher learning was the "concentration and distribution" pattern. Seen as a sort of compromise between two extremes, students were required to "concentrate" their studies in a given field or discipline (the "major") while "distributing" or spreading their other choices across a range of subjects in the arts, humanities, and sciences. The academic major was intended to supply "depth" of content, while the distribution requirement supposedly supplied scope or breadth of subject matter. The former was to serve to prevent shallowness or superficiality; the latter was and is intended to ensure against excessive specialization.

The major advantage of balancing curricular breadth and depth in this way, advocates point out, is that it mandates exposure to those critical fields of knowledge a shortsighted or misguided student might otherwise seek to avoid. For all its imperfections, no better way has been found to balance out vocational/professional education against grounding in the humanistic liberal arts, the latter presumably conducive to the development of the well-rounded individual.

What of the future? Are the liberating arts and humanities relics of a pretechnocratic age destined in the years ahead to sink into oblivion? Sarah Lawrence College's Michelle Myers predicts confidently that society will always place a premium on an education whereby young people can come to know who they are, become knowledgeable in their chosen fields, and demand an environment that gives form and expression to values and ideals that make for good, just, and democratic human beings.[16] One can only hope she has it right.

Similar in spirit is a judgment recently forthcoming from Grant Cornwell and Eve Walsh Stoddard, of St. Lawrence University, writing in *Liberal Education*.[15] There is a compelling irony, they observe, in that precisely at the time when liberal education is coming under criticism for being insufficiently practical, its outcomes too amorphous to measure, its delivery too abstracted from career preparation, universities elsewhere throughout the world are revamping their educational systems in order to be more democratic, less elitist, and more inclusive. The old European model of narrow disciplinary tracking is being replaced by systems bearing the mark of American-style liberal-arts education: breadth and depth requirements, emphasis on writing and speaking skills across the disciplines, and greater attention to pedagogy.

Private institutions, it must be conceded, are being compelled to market their wares to a consumerist public more and more reluctant to pay a hefty price for something whose "value" is not tightly coupled with a high-paying job on graduation. Meanwhile, public colleges are controlled more and more by penurious legislatures concerned with cost cutting and economic efficiency. Nothing new there. But after pondering the issue at some length, Cornwell and Walsh conclude that, in a best-case scenario, liberal education *will* survive and continue to be about the development of the whole person, about cultivating multiple ways of knowing, promoting critical and creative thinking, and the developing of skills for lifelong learning. As such it will endure—possibly flourish—as long as academic institutions remain mindful that they are more than scholarly enclaves or mere job-training centers.

Notes

1.   David L. Kirp, "This Little Student Went to Market," in *Declining by Degrees, Higher Education at Risk*, ed. Richard H. Hershand John Merrow. (New York: Palgrave Macmillan, 2005), pp. 119–120.
2.   Richard H. Hersh, "Intentions and Perceptions: A National Survey of Public Attitudes Toward Liberal Arts Education" *Change* 29 (1997): 16–23
3.   Jennifer Washburn, *University Inc.: The Corporate Corruption of Higher Education* (New York: Perseus Books, 2005), p. xv.

4. Jackson Lears, "The Radicalism of the Liberal Arts Tradition" *Academe,* 89, no. 1 (2003): 1–5.

5. Note the discussions in Hersh, p. 2; Carol G. Schneider, "Liberal Education: Slipping Away?" in Hersh and Merrow, pp. 61–67; and R. G. Baldwin and V. L. Baker, "The Case of the Disappearing Liberal Arts College," *Inside Higher Education*, http://www.insidehighered.com/views/2009/07/09/baldwin.

6. Kirp, p. 114.

7. Lears, p. 3.

8. Aristotle, *Politics* (Chicago: University of Chicago Press; 1984).

9. Thomas Hughes, *Tom Brown's School–Days* (New York: Thomas Y. Crowell &Sons, 1890), pp. 70–71.

10. O. B. Hardison, *Toward Freedom and Dignity, The Humanities and the Idea of Humanity* (Baltimore: Johns Hopkins University Press, 1972), p. 57.

11. R. R. Bolgar, *The Classical Heritage and its Beneficiaries* (New York: Harper & Row, 1964), p. 36.

12. H. I. Marrou, *A History of Education in Antiquity* (New York: Mentor, 1964), pp. 243, 251, 288, 299.

13. H. I. Marrou, *A History of Education in Antiquity*, trans. George Lamb (New York: New American Library, 1964), p. 244.

14. Frederick Rudolph, *The American College and University* (New York: Vintage, 1962), pp. 282–287.

15. Michelle Myers, "Preparing Students for an Uncertain Future," *Liberal Education* 87, no. 3: 159.

16. Grant H. Cornwell and Eve Walsh Stoddard, *Liberal Education* 92 (Spring, 2006): 26.

CHAPTER FIFTEEN

The Debate over the College and University Curriculum

"The Artist Waits Upon Us"

MICHAEL SCOTT BIEZE & PHILO A. HUTCHESON

We love to hang artists works over the cultural hearth to show our good taste and aesthetic judgment, but heaven forbid we would ever invite the artists to the academic dinner table. The canon wars have produced ironies and strange bedfellows, but perhaps none as overlooked as the fact that the education of those responsible for the making of a large dimension of the canon, visual culture, is rarely ever directly addressed (except by Minnich, 1990). In all this talk about taste, exclusion, and marginalization, whatever happened to the artists themselves? For example, what would the artist Judy Chicago do with Lynne Cheney's or Elizabeth Minnich's place settings at her piece, *Dinner Party*? Judy Chicago's reworking of *The Last Supper* makes women "the honored guests" (Chicago, 1979, p. 11), their places set because of their contributions to knowledge, more specifically to gendered knowledge both visual and written. Her installation took the better part of the 1970s to complete and brings together symbolic and textual representations of hundreds of women of achievement from all times, from Sappho to Georgia O'Keeffe, to a celebratory banquet in order to reify their omitted, neglected or forgotten presence. The purpose of this chapter is to examine briefly how various thinkers on education would respond to the current curriculum of a mainstream fine arts school in higher education, the Corcoran College of Art and Design in Washington, D. C., an institution where artists' works are reviewed as well as created. This examination will highlight not only how fine arts schools represent important goals in college and university curriculum, but also will reveal some substantial flaws in the debates about curriculum. We will also argue for the inclusion of visual and performing arts in general education. But first our use of the term "mainstream fine arts school" needs to be defined, since "mainstream" colleges and universities also offer fine arts programs.

The range of ways in which artists are formally trained on the undergraduate level in this country is basically divided between a Bachelor of Fine Arts (BFA) degree achieved at a traditional university, or a BFA at a specialized school such as the Corcoran which, like most art schools, is affiliated with a museum. Universities have become the place for students who plan to continue into graduate programs for the purpose of becoming professors, that is, advanced degree teachers rather than full-time artists. At most universities the actual studio time is minimal until the student has completed two years of general distribution and core hours. Art schools, however, are a different story.

Most arts schools typically require very little, if anything, in the way of a core curriculum other than requirements in the fine arts (such as color theory). These schools are the modern version of the first formalized attempt at educating artists, namely the Académie Royale de Peintureet de Sculpture, organized to promote the ideals of Louis XIV. At the Académie Royale students continued the old guild system of master-pupil training, but were also offered electives in "anatomy, perspective and geometry, . . . literature, and in religious and ancient history" (Conisbee, 1981, p. 13). All of this was necessary because the best artists of the 1600s aspired to the highest aim of art, painting of history whose visual form finds direct parallels in the heroic narratives of writers such as Lynne Cheney. It is this type of training, repeated throughout Europe during the eighteenth century which, via the Royal Academy in London (founded in 1768), formed the basis of America's oldest art school and museum, the Pennsylvania Academy of the Fine Arts (founded in 1806). It was not until 1869 that the nation's first university program in the fine arts began at Yale, a time when the classical, prescribed curriculum was losing its hold on United States colleges (Stark & Lattuca, 1997, p. 430; Veysey, 1965). Fine arts programs entered the traditional structure of higher education on the eve of the great transformation toward the modern research university—with its specialization challenging general education, the shift toward an idea of academic freedom, and faculty empowerment in curriculum development (Veysey, 1965). Hence the importance of considering the curriculum at a fine arts school involves not only the use and meaning of artists in curricular arguments but also developments in curriculum from the late 1800s to the present.

There is a range of arts schools in terms of their offerings. For example, the Pennsylvania Academy of the Fine Arts represents the classical (i.e. figurative), studio-based (plaster casts and all) tradition; the addition of a liberal arts program was recent, occurring in 2008 (http://www.pafa.edu/About/History/1134/). One of the two bachelor's degree programs offered by the Pennsylvania Academy of Fine Arts is a Bachelor of Fine Arts from the University of Pennsylvania (http://www.pafa.edu/programs/Penn-BFA/52/)—make a note, add men to the formerly single-sex *Dinner Party* and seat Lynne Cheney next to Henry Louis Gates, Jr. to discuss the number of African American artists in *50 Hours* in recognition of Ivy League attempts to institute diversity. In contrast, other arts schools have long required liberal arts courses. For example, in 1997 the School of Visual Arts in New York required in its department of fine arts a minimum of 32 semester hours in the humanities and sciences, along with specified courses in Western Civilization (School of Visual Arts, 1997, p. 140). Now it declares:

> An arts education at SVA connects your hand to your eye and your mind to the world. Out of a matrix of learning in history, politics, literature, psychology, anatomy, biology and technology, you evolve as an artist. From Chaucer to William S. Burroughs, Stravinsky to the Ramones, Karl Marx to bell hooks, you get a cultural grounding that is at once classical and

contemporary, canonical and cutting-edge. (http://www.schoolofvisualarts.edu/ug/index. jsp? sid0=1&sid1=46)

Like most art schools in the late twentieth century, the School of Visual Arts has found itself surviving by primarily offering degrees which lead directly to careers, so we find in its program everything from clinical art therapy to computer graphics (place Booker T. Washington's setting here to recognize the utilitarian characteristics of art education).

The Corcoran College of Art and Design is somewhere in the middle in both its offerings and core requirements. The Corcoran offers seven bachelor's degrees in fine arts, in areas such as art studies and photography as well as professional areas such as graphic design and interior design (we address here only the bachelor's programs; the Corcoran also offers associate and graduate degrees). The academic requirements for all seven degrees include a minimum of two courses in art history, a course in drawing, two English composition courses, two humanities courses, a three-dimensional studies course, and a course on visual concepts (http:// www.corcoran.edu/degree-programs/undergraduate/freshman-foundation). Both humanities and arts courses will be discussed later. The question is, how does the structure and content of this typical fine arts school curriculum survive the educational theory-canon litmus test? To what extent do the requirements of the Corcoran address the structural arguments—typically derived from traditional arguments about higher education, from such people as Charles W. Eliot and Booker T. Washington, or John Henry Cardinal Newman, Alexander Meiklejohn, or Robert Maynard Hutchins? And, to what extent does the Corcoran curriculum address the arguments, highlighted in the 1990s and since then, by such people as Lynne Cheney, Dineesh D'Souza, Stanley Fish, Ellen Sedgewick, Henry Louis Gates, Jr., Gerald Graff, and Elizabeth Minnich? While much of that debate has had political overtones, and it has also had extended consideration of the challenges of content (Gaff & Ratcliff, 1996), the question of content may be more complex than the debaters have acknowledged.

Thinkers on the structure of higher education have focused on cultural (used in this context as culture as art) issues without ever including any discussion of how the university should treat the education of those very makers of culture, that is, the poets, artists, and musicians who become the voices these thinkers resurrect for their respective arguments. Among the few thinkers on education who might provisionally support the structure of traditional art school training are Charles W. Eliot and Booker T. Washington.

Potential Advocates of the Structure

Students at the Corcoran College of Art and Design, as is the case for many art schools, have relatively few required courses. Concentration in one area of expertise is encouraged; hence we can consider the curriculum as a structure of courses built by the university and the student. The Corcoran fulfills all three tenets of Eliot's transforming ideal for Harvard (Eliot, 1898/1969): a great range of choices, the opportunity to specialize in one area, and placing the responsibility of personal growth and discipline on the shoulders of the student. For example, students in the Fine Art program "work independently across multiple disciplines and media" (http://www.corcoran.edu/degree-programs/undergraduate/bfa-fine-art), in complete agreement with Eliot's belief that a student is capable of selecting his or her own course of study. The only area of discrepancy is in the entrance requirements. Eliot believed that "two foreign languages and the elements of algebra and geometry" were the only courses "indispensable" in the pursuit of higher education (Eliot, 1898/1969, p. 135), whereas the Corcoran specifically requires only an essay or a portfolio in order to show the applicant's ability and which "should demonstrate creative imagination, the potential for artistic growth, and the applicant's areas of artistic interest" (http://www.corcoran.edu/admissions/application-requirements/portfolio-requirements-babfa-applicants). Nevertheless, Eliot's "free university" is as close as any early educator will come to a fine arts program, advancing the notion that an elective system will link with an individual's "peculiar skill, faculty, or aptitude" to produce a higher degree of achievement than a uniform curriculum could offer (Eliot, 1898/1969, p. 134). When he wrote this essay in the late 1890s Eliot made it clear that "all the studies which are allowed to count toward the A.B. at Harvard are liberal or pure, no technical or professional studies being admissible" (Eliot, 1898/1969, p. 139). However, in a later 1903 article in which he praised the arts and imagination, he would reverse himself, stating that

> we have lately become convinced that accurate work with carpenter's tools, or lathe, or hammer and anvil, or violin, or piano, or pencil, or crayon, or camel's-hair brush trains well the same nerves and ganglia with which we do what is ordinarily called thinking (Eliot, 1903, p. 3807).

Obviously, however, Harvard's curriculum never grew to include the lathe or the crayon, the University now offering only art degrees in the history of art and architecture (http://isites.harvard.edu/icb/icb. do? keyword=k69286&tabgroupid=icb.tabgroup106995,2012).

In contrast, historically Tuskegee Institute also emphasized both inclination and individual skills over a "unified knowledge" program, but of course its interest has always been utilitarian. Booker T. Washington's industrial education program at Tuskegee did not offer any art. Nor has that curriculum changed much, since even today Tuskegee offers only eight art courses, whose emphasis is on "proficiency in basic art skills" (http://www.tuskegee.edu/sites/www/Uploads/files/Academics/Course_CatalogBulletin.pdf, p. 270). As in everything concerning Washington, he is a very complex man to describe, so his exact feelings are difficult to ascertain. On a personal level, he reached out to African Americans to support artists like Henry O. Tanner by writing articles in publications such as the *Colored American* (Harlan, 1976, p. 141; Bieze, 2008). In addition, he thoroughly supported his daughter Portia's music studies both here and abroad in Germany. Yet publicly he often used art as a symbol of misplaced luxury to contrast with industrial education, as in an 1898 article in which he stated that "'one of the saddest sights I ever saw was the placing of a three hundred dollar rosewood piano in a country school located in the midst of the Black Belt'" (as cited in Harlan, 1975, p. 366).

It is Washington's emphasis on practical craft which potentially aligns him with art school philosophy and separates him from most educational thinkers, especially those in the general education camp. Unlike John Henry Cardinal Newman, Alexander Meiklejohn, or Robert Maynard Hutchins, Washington's emphasis was always on skills, Plato's *techne*, rather than abstract or conceptual knowledge (Plato's Forms).

Structure Critics

Early general education proponents would dismiss the curriculum of the Corcoran College of Art and Design School of Art on two main points: first, the technical emphasis, and second, the lack of "unified knowledge" (as they define it). The curriculum is thus a body of knowledge constructed by the institution, a body of knowledge that all students ought to have. For example, Meiklejohn makes the typical "unified knowledge" statement that "the technical school intends to furnish training which. . . is not intellectual but practical" (Meiklejohn, 1916, p. 35). This same age-old *techne*, anti-craft bias is found in all of these thinkers. Newman (1873/1982) and Hutchins (1936/1995) would immediately dismiss the art school program as an intellectually centerless void, crafting the objects which cast the illusionistic shadow shows on the cave wall. The best that Corcoran could hope for is being called a professional school. Moreover, Newman would argue that his Universal Knowledge places him in an even better position than the artist to judge works of art, since "it is. . . [the]man who has been trained to think upon one subject [who]. . . will never be a good judge even in that one: whereas the enlargement of his circle gives him increased knowledge" (Newman, 1873/1982, p. 131).

On the unified knowledge side, the Newman and Hutchins arguments call to mind Plato's famous laureled banishment of the artists from his Republic. For Platonists, art is both sensory and imitative (*mimesis*), plus manual (*techne*), and therefore both morally suspect and intellectually inferior. Art is a copy of a higher reality. Since truth and beauty can only reside in the Forms, the physical object of art, like the industrial and manual pursuits of Washington, cannot qualify as knowledge. Iris Murdoch brought this together by stating that in Plato's religious fundamentalism "art is dangerous chiefly because it apes the spiritual and subtly disguises and trivializes it" proliferating ideas which are appropriated from Reason itself, creating "a pernicious caricature of the Form" (Murdoch, 1977, pp. 65–67).

Cardinal Newman would certainly find nothing redeeming in the Corcoran's plan to educate artists. His "cultivation of the mind" is a Platonist world of first principles in direct opposition to the "unreal" world of the senses, where the ignorant are "dazzled by mere phenomena, instead of perceiving things as they are" (Newman, 1873/1982, p. xliii). Furthermore, as far as Newman is concerned, knowledge is an end itself, not a means to some other use. Newman's belief found a correlation in the late nineteenth-century cry of "art for art's sake" the early modernist quest for the pure conception not sullied by utility or social purpose. In contrast, the purpose of the Corcoran's Freshman Foundation program is "to introduce [the student] to the essential elements of visual thinking and critical understandings that underpin [the student's] creative process" (http://www.corcoran.edu/degree-programs/undergraduate/freshman-foundation) (Corcoran, 2012). Since according to the Corcoran, art is both sensory based and ultimately utilitarian to the degree that an end product is sought, it fails on both counts. While Newman might excuse the fact that religion 'is notat the center of this training, since art also falls under the "province of judgment" to establish the strength of an argument (Newman, 1873/1982, p. 132), he could never accept the visual world as the basis for that judgment. When he wrote that one might aspire to "careful judgment of the arts and sciences upon the right models" (Newman, 1873/1982, p. 151), he probably did not have nudes in mind. Remember, gentle reader, that this lower education is for "the profession of an artist, not the commission of an Apostle" (Newman, 1873/1982, p. 155). Nevertheless, these distinctions of judgment and education do not stop him from continuously making visual judgments such as St. Paul's character is the "most graceful in form, and its most beautiful hues" (Newman, 1873/1982, p. 154), or that the branches of knowledge are like the "selection and juxtaposition" of colors (Newman, 1873/1982, p. 75). Newman does not seem to have anything against art. In fact, he seems quite moved by paintings and buildings. He just 'would not consider them knowledge—unless of course we brought back his beloved Gothic Perpendicular Style (Newman, 1873/1982, p. 61), or Sir Christopher Wren to run the art school (Newman, 1873/1982, p. 43).

Newman may tuck the artists away in Plato's Cave, but Robert Hutchins locks them in the dungeon. While Hutchins extols the virtues of general education, it is an education of the written text and not the visual image (Hutchins, 1936/1995). The only thing lower may be the realm reserved for the football team (e.g., see Hutchins, "Gate Receipts and Glory," *The Saturday Evening Post*, Dec. 3, 1938). Hutchins' objections to schools such as the Corcoran are explicit. Not only are empiricism and utility at odds with "*the* higher learning" (emphasis added), but also instruction in the fine arts has "little or no effect upon the mind itself" (Hutchins, 1936/1995, p. 86). Even worse, one's imagination can "tyrannize" an undisciplined mind (Hutchins, 1936/1995, p. 106). In other words, the Corcoran doesn't even qualify to call itself capable of higher learning, and as Plato as well as Newman and Hutchins warned, it is potentially dangerous. Hutchins might excuse the lack of philosophy as the core, but like Newman, he could never accept, in his terms, "unqualified empiricism" as the core of what surely would degenerate into a fragmentation of truth without the connecting force of metaphysics. In his words, "without theology or metaphysics a university cannot exist" (Hutchins, 1936/1995, p. 99). He would see a few writing courses and a smattering of humanities as folly. The only part of the Corcoran curriculum[1] which might appeal to Hutchins are the numerous courses in classical art history and art theory, but one can only imagine what he would think of offerings such as AH4280—African-American Art: Harlem Renaissance or AH6375—Arts of the Caribbean and its Diaspora. At the dinner party serve Newman and Hutchins Greek salads (tastefully arranged for the Cardinal Newman).

Political and Content Debates

Since the early 1980s a renewed debate about the curriculum, and especially general education, has arisen. Professors and intellectuals argue about the curriculum's content, and much of the debate has exhibited political commitments and expectations. The content of the minimal course requirements in the liberal arts at the Corcoran College of Art and Design would be objectionable to thinkers on both the Right and the Left, although for different reasons. The loudest criticisms would certainly come from writers in the 1980s and early 1990s such as Dineesh D'Souza and Lynne Cheney; their voices echo in the present.

One look at the course offerings in the Corcoran catalog is enough to know that it is time to take cover from the charges of D'Souza (1991) and Cheney (1988, 1989) of specialization and postmodernist fragmentation of higher education, both of which they claim ignore the Western classics. One does not find Shakespeare or Milton among the English offerings at the Corcoran, but rather AS 3230—The Beat Generation, AS3340—Innovators of Modern Literature, and AS3345—Cyborgs, Gods, and Dwarves. Nor does one find Plato in the philosophy section, butAS3750—Ladakh: Ancient culture—modern times. Finally, there are no course offerings in the catalog on American Democracy as D'Souza andCheny argued for, but students can sign up for AS3210—Political Washington or AS3350—Post Colonial Cultures.

D'Souza would find the lack of any "core curriculum" standards or uniformity a problem, most likely calling them a "diluted" curriculum because of the emphasis on gender and diversity issues in the humanities offerings (D'Souza, 1991, p. 52). Cheney's complaints would be more specific. Placed against her *50 Hours*, a statement of the ideal undergraduate curriculum, the Corcoran curriculum fails to offer her brand of core ideological coherence or encouragement of democratic ideals. Cheney specifically cites the audacious fulfillment of the humanities requirements at a university in the West "with courses in interior design" as an example of the decline of higher education (1989, pp. 12–13). Whether or not an intensive art history requirement like the Corcoran's ultimately prepares a student to answer questions concerning culture better than the Civilization courses in Cheney's *50 Hours* is debatable. At the least, Cheney completely disregards the reports done by national and state art organizations that have requested that "those majoring in science and the humanities disciplines. . . should study one or more of the arts in the course of acquiring a liberal education" (Working Group on the Arts in Higher Education, 1988, p. 8).

As for Cheney's use of artists, one must seriously wonder why she selects such an arbitrary list of artists for her program, singling out someone such as Gauguin for the introduction of *50 Hours* (1989, p. 11). Who, here, indeed is the hero? Do the students in her class discuss how Gauguin projected Western patriarchical misogynist fantasies on Tahitian women, or how he abandoned his wife and children and died from syphilis (Eisenman, 1994)? So much of her content is sanitized and recast to fit an ideology, avoiding the problematic issues completely. Instead of her notion of diversity, a version of what Stanley Fish calls the "and Alice Walker" syndrome of simply adding women and people and color (Fish, 1992, p. 259), the Corcoran offers full semesters on topics such as AH4370—The Sacred Arts of the African Diaspora and AH3201—Arts of South and Southeast Asia. Cheney may be right in her attack on specialization, given that art schools do not offer a little bit of everything from the cultural menu. Instead, schools like the Corcoran attempt to prepare a student by unifying a skill base with a highly specific concentration in visual history. Since she likes a little bit of everything, serve Cheney the minestrone—mostly broth with a few imported spices to taste.

The postmodernists can be just as political and purist as Cheney and D'Souza. Cheney and D'Souza may love the great man ideal (see, for example, Cheney 1989, p. 23), but at least the artist exists. On the Left, well, its proponents simply make the artists or authors disappear, or make them bit players whose identity is either unnecessary, or a product of sexual proclivity, or the Left subsumes culture under the new hegemony of literary criticism. While the Left attacks the Right as being politically totalitarian, hierarchical, asymmetrical, and purist, it is frequently just as guilty of exclusionary essentialism. Culture is decoded to mean only literature.

It is particularly interesting to watch the Left use the art vocabulary, easing in terms such as asymmetry, image, vision, taste, and aesthetic. The Left also name-drops artists, and seems to be just as capable as the Right of making arguments work for its needs. The Right may have its Core, a transcendent deity or philosophy, but so does the Left: literary criticism. The Left can be as sweeping as the Right in believing that its ideological plan applies to content in other disciplines. It too is guilty of reading history in dangerous ways. For example, the "academic outing" of Michelangelo and Leonardo da Vinci by Ellen Sedgewick is simply unnecessary (Sedgewick, 1992, p. 151). No one knows whether or not they were gay. This highlights the point that the notion of venturing into multiple disciplines or fields with grand generalizations is dangerous. In other words, she's moved too far afield. Literary criticism has in this case, to use Newman's lament, moved outside its discipline and begun to believe its decrees explain all the other disciplines. With apologies to Yeats, the Left might believe that the canon "falls apart, the center cannot hold," but it has replaced that center with literary theory. As one last example of the Left's elitism, consider this question: which schools enter their canon debates? Answer: Harvard, Yale, Chicago, and Stanford. Yet, which schools produce most of this nation's artists: the Art Institute of Chicago, the Corcoran, the Pennsylvania Academy, and their likes. So it is ironic that those writers most interested in revising the cultural canon define culture as literature, have curious things to say about artists, and never mention art schools. Even a keenly sensitive and insightful thinker such as Henry Louis Gates shifts the culture debate constantly back to literature. His contention that teaching the literary canon "is the teaching of values" as well as the "teaching of *aesthetic* and political order" (emphasis added), along with several other statements makes it clear he is aware of the visual problems in the canon (Gates, 1992, p. 35). His 1998 film on black Americans highlights his interest in the visual. We could not agree more about the importance of the visual, but it is perplexing why he simply would not select any number of black artists to demonstrate how the same hierarchy and politics exist in the visual as well as the verbal. Practically every art school in America now requires a survey in art outside of the Western tradition and offers many courses in African American art.

Of the writers defined as canon revisionists, Elizabeth Minnich is the most eloquent and knowledgeable on the subject of art, and Gerald Graff the writer whom art historians are bound to quote. The questions Minnich raises are fundamentally in line with the types of issues confronting students at schools such as the Corcoran. Both her analysis of the flaws in what passes for knowledge (faulty generalizations, circular reasoning, mystified concepts, and partial knowledge), and the difficulty in where to place these new ideas (mainstream or separate canons), are being hotly debated in the art world. For an example of the problems with the canon, the *Arts Journal* (one of the College Art Association's journals) "canon issue" was filled with statements such as:

> In the end I think we need to recognize that the canon is not a yardstick for determining enduring timeless masterpieces, but an agent of power, the power to decide whose culture and whose views will set agendas for the rest of us. Any efforts to reshape or replace the art history survey will have to accept, eventually, that any canon is contingent and constructed. Moreover, we need to make canonicity and its power implications a part of the course, kept not behind the scenes, but out in the open, in both curriculum committees and lecture halls. (Graham, 1995, p. 30)

Its language is remarkably close to Minnich's in the first part, and it is not surprising that another article in the *Arts Journal* issue quotes both her and Henry Giroux (Dietrich & Smith-Hurd, 1995). The closing part of the quotation sounds like Graff because it is Graham's paraphrased citation of Graff's "teach the conflicts" (Graff, 1992, p. 57). To understand just how controversial the question of whether to mainstream or not (i.e., how to respond to the contingent and constructed nature of the canon, the conflicts) has become in the arts, consider the problem which divided women in the arts a decade ago. When the National Women's Museum in Washington, D.C., opened, it created two camps: those who felt that finally women had a forum in which to present their work, and those who felt it signaled a surrender, meaning that women had failed to make it in the real art world (i.e. men's art world). This debate continued. Georgia O'Keeffe, one of only two women artists represented at the *Dinner Party*, resented being categorized as a woman artist (Adams, 1996).

One of the Corcoran's art history survey courses approaches these canon questions in ways similar to Graff and Minnich. In Part II of the Corcoran's art history survey, "Emphasis is placed on development of style in each culture prior to and after contact with the Western world" including "cross-cultural exchange of artistic ideas" (AH1010—Art History II, http:// corcboard. corcoran.edu/iqweb/Visitor/CrsCatal. asp). Serve Graff some nouvelle cuisine at the dinner party, preferably with traditionally conflicting tastes.

Minnich is the only writer on the canon debate who directly examined an art curriculum. Her description of the work of feminist art historians such as Linda Nochlin and Ann Sutherland Harris, her criticism of the major survey text in art history, and her curricula descriptions are all grounded in art historical method. She attacks the major art history survey text used in higher education but kindly never mentions the author by name (H. W. Janson). Her hypothetical "course in the art of North Carolina" is a sound argument in the methodology of art history against the traditional way in which survey courses in art history have not only canonized certain works of art while marginalizing others (the art of women and African Americans, for example), but also made it seem "ridiculous" to even include them in the discussion (Minnich, 1990, p. 42). Until the 1990s American students in higher education were subtly told the great narrative of art through the filters of the Italian Renaissance, a seamless tale of cultures floundering between each salutary classical revival until Platonic light replaces darkness, harmony triumphs over discord. Minnich would be an excellent spokesperson to defend the Corcoran curriculum against the charge of incoherence. There is, in Minnich's word's, "faulty" and "circular reasoning" operating when a self-contained set of masterpieces (from the Italian Renaissance and subsequent classical revivals) is presented as a neutral, objective, apolitical paradigm, as H. W. Janson does (Minnich, 1990, pp. 83–87; Janson, 1997). Moreover, she argues, it is a form of a "Closet Platonism" (pp. 87–88) argument since an ethical dimension is implied by this paradigm, a "good" by which all others are rendered subjective, political, and threatening to the status quo.

Conclusion

In closing, here is a possible reason for this role, especially as taken on by criticsof the curriculum in the United States. The United States has been since its beginning a country of "the word" with our historic ethos being based upon the Protestant independence of textual exegesis coupled with its aniconic nature. When witches were tried by Harvard-educated men in the 1690s, they were often commanded, "Now stand up, and Name your Text"—meaning the Lord's or devil's *book and word* (Brown, 1988, p. 21). The only *images* in Salem were voodoo dolls—work of the devil. We see the domination of the word in the shift from Newman to the secularized, evangelical spirit of Hutchins, to the recent canon debates. While everyone talks about taste and culture, it is unequivocally literary or word culture. Images only seem to matter in our cultural psyche when they veer toward pornography, and then they are chastised with moral text. This is not to indict these thinkers as elitist or even exceptional, but simply to highlight their participation in the American cultural tradition. For example, when this country's first internationally recognized art movement, Abstract Expressionism, began in the late 1940s, it was reviled for its lack of narrative text. When Jackson Pollock was featured in the August 8, 1949 issue of *Life* magazine with the title "Is he the greatest living painter in the United States?" he was not embraced, but described as drooling, dribbling, doodling, and scrawling enamel on canvas ("Jackson Pollock" 1949, p. 45). His art was not representational; there was not a narrative to read. The article tells us that his neighbors "amuse themselves by trying to decide what his paintings are about. His grocer bought one which he identified as an aerial view of Siberia" (p. 42). Scanning the handful of listed artists in the texts on curriculum, all of them are narrative artists with readable images in the very traditional sense. Their art is representational, pictures which tell seemingly easy stories, images which serve as supplemental illustrations for texts. Furthermore, the history of art itself in this country is often based on the idea of a visual analogue for the written word (Mitchell, 1994, pp. 84–85), with the beginnings of the discipline in United States higher education usually located with Charles Eliot Norton's new position as "Lecturer on the History of the Fine Arts as Connected with Literature" at Harvard in 1874 (Preziosi, 1989, p. 9; Minor, 1994, pp. 20–21).

In the end it is difficult to hold the Corcoran College of Art and Design up to such standards since the canon debaters past and present understand art not as independent knowledge, but rather as an illustration of knowledge, despite the apparent ease with which they use art and artists to buttress their arguments. For this reason, we should not find it surprising that even a book such as Minnich's *Transforming Knowledge*, unusual in that it actually deals with visual issues intelligently, has the wrong sphinx on the cover of the paperback edition. Her references are to the sphinx of the Greek oracle, not the Egyptian sphinx on the book's cover. Serve Minnich flan for dessert; unfortunately, the caramel is not fully baked.

Over the past century, a variety of educators have debated the meaning and structure of a thorough college education. Regardless of the ideological or theoretical perspective of the educator, however, the artist is consistently kept away from the academic dinner table—ignored, or developed without attention to the context of visual art itself, or bound by the traditions of text. In view of the contributions of visual artists, often used for illustrative purposes in arguments about the college and university curriculum, it would seem to be a straightforward matter to bring the artists to the dinner party as part of the requirements for the baccalaureate degree. It would be less straightforward, however, to recognize the marginal, perhaps even anti-canonical, nature of the artist. The artist still waits upon the table of the undergraduate curriculum and its authors.

Note

1. All courses are found on the Corcoran's web site, at http://corcboard. corcoran.edu/iqweb/Visitor/CrsCatal. asp; for ease of reading, we do not use this citation after each example of a course at the Corcoran.

References

Adams, L. S. (1996). *The methodologies of art.* New York: HarperCollins.

Bieze, M. (2008). *Booker T. Washington and the art of self-representation.* New York: Peter Lang.

Brown, D. (1988). *A guide to the Salem witchcraft hysteria of 1692.* Worcester MA: Mercantile Printing Company.

Cheney, L. (1988). *Humanities in America: A report to the president, the congress, and the American people.* Washington, DC: National Endowment for the Humanities.

Cheney, L. (1989). *50 hours: A core curriculum for college students.* Washington, DC: National Endowment for the Humanities.

Chicago, J. (1979). *The dinner party.* Garden City, NY: Anchor Press/Doubleday.

Conisbee, P. (1981). *Painting in eighteenth-century France.* Oxford: Phaidon Press.

Dietrich, L., & Smith-Hurd, D. (1995). Feminist approaches to the survey. *Art Journal, 54,* 44–47.

D'Souza, D. (1991, March). Illiberal education. *The Atlantic Monthly,* 51–79.

Eisenman, S. (1994). *Nineteenth century art: A critical history.* London: Thames and Hudson.

Eliot, C. W. (1903). A new definition of the cultivated man. *The world's work,* 3806–3811.

Eliot, C. W. (1969). Liberty in education. *Educational reform: Essays and addresses* (pp. 125–148). New York: Arno Press. (Original work published 1898)

Fish, S. (1992). The common touch, or, one size fits all. In D. Gless & B. H. Smith (Eds.), *The politics of liberal education* (pp. 241–266). Durham, NC: Duke University Press.

Gaff, J. G., & Ratcliff, J. L. (1996). *Handbook of the undergraduate curriculum: A comprehensive guide to purposes, structures, practices, and change.* San Francisco: Jossey-Bass.

Gates, H. L. (1992). *Loose canons: Notes on the canon wars.* New York: Oxford University Press.

Graff, G. (1992). Teach the conflicts. In D. Gless & B. H. Smith (Eds.), *The politics of liberal education* (pp. 57–74). Durham, NC: Duke University Press.

Graham, M. (1995). The future of art history survey and the undoing of the survey. *Art Journal, 54,* 30–34.

Harlan, L. (Ed.). (1975). *The Booker T. Washington papers* (Vol. 4). Urbana: University of Illinois Press.

Harlan, L. (Ed.). (1976). *The Booker T. Washington papers* (Vol. 5). Urbana: University of Illinois Press.

Hutchins, R. M. (1995). *The higher learning in America.* New Brunswick, NJ: Transaction Publishers. (Original work published 1936)

"Jackson Pollock: Is he the greatest living painter in the United States?" (1949, August 8). *Life, 27,* 42–45.

Janson, H. W. (1997). *History of art* (5th rev. ed.). New York: Prentice Hall.

Meiklejohn, A. (1916). The aim of the liberal college. In M. G. Fulton (Ed.), *College life: Its conditions and problems.* New York: Macmillan.

Minnich, E. (1990). *Transforming knowledge.* Philadelphia, PA: Temple University Press.

Minor, V. H. (1994). *Art history's history.* Englewood Cliffs, NJ: Prentice Hall.

Mitchell, W. J. T. (1994). *Picture theory: Essays on verbal and visual representation.* Chicago: University of Chicago Press.

Murdoch, I. (1977). *The fire & the sun: Why Plato banished the artists.* Oxford: Oxford University Press.

Newman, J. H. (1982). *The idea of a university.* Notre Dame, IN: University of Notre Dame Press. (Original work published 1873)

Preziosi, D. (1989). *Rethinking art history: Meditations on coy science.* New Haven, CT: Yale University Press.

School of Visual Arts. (1997). *Fifty reasons to be here: 50th anniversary* [1998–99 catalog]. New York: Author.

Sedgewick, E. (1992). Pedagogy in the context of an antihomophobic project. In D. Gless & B. Herrnstein Smith (Eds.), *The politics of liberal education* (pp. 145–162). Durham, NC: Duke University Press.

Stark, J. S., & Lattuca, L. R. (1997). *Shaping the college curriculum: Academic plans in action.* Needham Heights, MA: Allyn& Bacon.

Veysey, L. (1965). *The emergence of the American university.* Chicago: University of Chicago Press.

Working Group on the Arts in Higher Education. (1988). *Thearts, liberal education and the undergraduate curriculum.* (1988). Reston, VA: Author.

CHAPTER SIXTEEN

Community Service Learning and Higher Education

The Need for a Prerequisite to Thoughtful Service

ERIC C. SHEFFIELD

I am a hearty supporter of the community service learning (CSL) pedagogy—one firmly rooted in the progressive notions of education championed by such scholars and practitioners as John Dewey, William H. Kilpatrick, and more recently, Janet Eyler and Dwight Giles. CSL, when implemented in accordance with a clear philosophical understanding is, I believe, limitless in its potential for success at every level and in every subject area of higher education.

However, CSL is also a pedagogy that has lost its philosophical grounding, particularly when it comes to the notion of thoughtful community service. Nearly anything and everything counts as CSL these days; so long as students are interacting with a community population who has a need (regardless of the nature of the need and regardless of the nature of the "service"), one can call it CSL and likely receive service-learning grant monies and kudos from the department chair, dean, and even the university president. Missouri State University's (home to Missouri's Campus Compact) recently retired president, Dr. Michael Nietzel, has, I think, put the matter succinctly in saying that "what matters most about our community service efforts is that it is thoughtful community service."

CSL: The briefer course

I begin this discussion with a very brief description of CSL for those readers who may be unfamiliar with it. CSL is a pedagogy wherein students apply knowledge and skills learned in a university course of study (for our present purposes, though, the same might also be said of P-12 classwork) to community problems that they (with instructor guidance) find both socially important and academically appropriate to the community problem and its possible solutions. In so doing, course-based content knowledge and understanding can be expanded and deepened, a disposition to, and capacity for, reflective thinking grown, interaction among disparate community "strangers" encouraged, and service, as an essential democratic practice, duly incorporated into the regular modus operandi (habit) of the CSL participants. Though the CSL pedagogy looks simple enough, it is not and its complicated structure makes CSL, though incredibly worthwhile, difficult to practice successfully. This is especially so at colleges and universities in which the typical semester course lasts no more than several months—certainly not enough time to either understand CSL nor practice it with much, if any, real understanding. In fact, as I will ultimately argue here, I believe that CSL programs at traditional, "semester-schedule" colleges and universities would be wise to develop a course on the theoretical structure of CSL that emphasizes how and why service-learning can be educationally sound. Alternatively, I would suggest that CSL courses be sufficiently long (two semesters, at the very least) to provide the time needed to explore the nature of CSL as a pedagogy that is, above and beyond anything else that it might be, a transformative pedagogy of reflection.

Thoughtful Community Service: A Philosophical Shortcoming

Unfortunately, many CSL projects fail to reach their full potential because its sophisticated theoretical underpinnings are ignored and consequently its practice is poorly implemented. The misunderstanding and/or ignorance regarding the philosophical basis of CSL is particularly dangerous in colleges of education where we hope to encourage potentially powerful transformative pedagogies and yet often fail to teach their underlying structures. This lack of theoretical understanding on the part of pre-service teachers spreads, rather than contains, the very disease that might well destroy CSL's potential as a sound pedagogy: bad practice based on bad, or incomplete, theory. Those of us in colleges of education who champion critical pedagogy might do well to first understand those underlying theories ourselves and then clearly and thoroughly "teach" them to our students. The need for a full semester course extension and/or the development of a full semester course that exclusively examines CSL's complicated theoretical structure can be seen by closely examining one of its numerous components: reflection—that which makes service "thoughtful."

Janet Eyler expresses quite clearly the central importance of reflection to a service-learning project when she argues that

> Reflection is the hyphen in service-learning; it is the process that helps students connect what they observe and experience in the community with their academic study. In a reflective service-learning class, students are engaged in worthwhile activity in the community, observe, make sense of their observations, ask new questions, relate what they are observing to what they are studying in class, form theories and plans of action, and try out their ideas. (2001, p. 35).

CSL advocates like Eyler have long understood that reflection is *the* component that transforms the interaction of academics and service into a deep and abiding understanding of both (Chickering 1977, pp. 12–18; Honnet and Poulsen 1989; Mintz and Hesser 1997; Sheffield 2011). As Eyler says, "In practice it is critical reflection that provides the transformative link between the action of serving and the ideas and understanding of learning" (Eyler, Giles and Schmiede 1996, p. 14). Clearly, understanding reflection, and practicing it accordingly, is essential to successful CSL particularly at colleges and universities.

What happens all too often in CSL projects, however, is a failure to *understand* that reflection is paramount to success and, at the same time, a disinclination to teach reflective theory or even to incorporate structured reflective practice into the project design (Eyler 2001; Duley 1981; Boud, Keough, and Walker 1985; Eyler, Giles and Schmiede 1996; Toole and Toole 1995; Maybach 1994; Sheffield 2011). This disconnection between understanding and practice on this matter has a two fold cause. Firstly, as Boud, Keough, and Walker argue,

> The activity of reflection is so familiar that, as teachers or trainers, we often overlook it in formal learning settings, and make assumptions about the fact that not only is it occurring, but it is occurring effectively for everyone in the group. It is easy to neglect as it is something which we cannot directly observe and which is unique to each learner. (1985, p. 8)

Secondly, because humans come into the world able to reflect on a limited, instinctual level, educators often assume our students simply do it both regularly and successfully:

> The basic reflective and puzzling techniques that help us make sense of everyday life form the core of the very same techniques that enable students to derive meaningful learning from the experience of service; [however,] it is the critical questioning of why things are and the attempt to fully understand the root causes of observable events and behaviors [that must be taught]. This depth of critical reflection grows out of the instinctual reflective process but must be cultivated purposefully as a habit of the mind. (Eyler, Giles, and Schmiede 1996, p. 14)

If CSL practice is to be successful, reflection (as well as the various other components) must be clearly understood, modeled, taught, and practiced. In the case of university/college students (particularly future/practicing public school teachers), the complicated structure of reflective thought has to be examined in detail if it is to be successfully incorporated into a CSL project. That examination can be initially undertaken by looking at the theoretical structure provided by John Dewey.

The Features of Deweyan Reflection

Dewey argued that thinking could be understood in several different ways. It is first discernible as conscious thought that, try as one might, cannot be stopped. It is this type of thought that William James described as the "flights and perchings" of consciousness (1892, p. 27). Thought is also found in fancy and imagination. "Story-making" falls into this second category and is characterized not by the quest for knowledge or problem solution, but as an emotive expression that has as its goal an interesting plot or surprising climax. A third kind of thought Dewey called "belief." Belief is the type of thought that is built up through "tradition, instruction, [and] imitation" (1933, p. 7). Belief is based on "prejudgments" not on examinations of evidence. Finally, Dewey talked of formal, scientific thinking. It is this formal, problem-oriented thought that he called "reflective thought." Reflective thought is "active, persistent, and careful consideration of any belief or supposed form of knowledge in the light of the grounds that support it and the further conclusions to which it tends" (1933, p. 5). It is reflective thinking that Dewey was most concerned with, and it is reflective thinking that brings CSL projects and academic, classroom skills together to create learning.

Dewey theorized that reflective thought has specific features that can be understood by disentangling them conceptually from the actual process:

So much for the general features of a reflective experience. They are (i) perplexity, confusion, doubt, due to the fact that one is implicated in an incomplete situation whose full character is not yet determined; (ii) a conjectural anticipation—a tentative interpretation of the given elements, attributing to them a tendency to effect certain consequences; (iii) a careful survey (examination, inspection, exploration, analysis) of all attainable consideration which will define and clarify the problem in hand; (iv) a consequent elaboration of the tentative hypothesis to make it more precise and more consistent, because squaring with a wider range of facts; (v) taking one stand upon the projected hypothesis as a plan of action which is applied to the existing state of affairs: doing something overtly to bring about the anticipated result, and thereby testing the hypothesis. (1944, p. 153)

It is essential to point out here that Dewey's conceptual outline of reflection is not a regulated, four- or five-step program or stop-and-go cycle that leads to reflective perfection. Numerous writers who support CSL particularly, and experiential learning generally, seem to forget that Dewey's discussion is a means to understand what is, in reality, an intricate process (Fry and Kolb 1979, pp. 79–92). Additionally, contemporary scholars point out that the above understanding of reflection is dangerously reductionist (Moore 1990, p. 278; Sheffield 2011, p. 111). To "view" the process is to see complicated meanderings from problem, to hypothesis, to past experience, to testing, and back and forth. That means that individual students may be at different reflective "places" doing somewhat different things, at different times. Though this makes a teacher's work even more complicated, it is indeed the nature of reflective thought.

"Felt Problems" as Catalysts to Reflection

In Dewey's construction, reflective thought comes about because an experience causes a "state of doubt, hesitation, perplexity, mental difficulty" in individual students (1933, p. 12). In reflective practice and, therefore, in CSL, student interest and purpose are essential. This becomes acutely clear when one examines how reflective thought is initiated. Reflective thought begins only when a truly felt problem (one vitally important enough to cause perplexing uneasiness) is "discovered" "found" "stumbled upon" or "led to." If a problem does not come out of student experience, if it is fabricated by another, or is not genuinely felt by the student, there will be no catalyst to reflection. And without reflection, no contextual connections are made between classroom learning and the experience itself, i.e., learning/growth does not occur.

For CSL practice to be successful, the emotive nature of problems, both as catalysts and aims of reflection, must be understood as well. The realization of a problem comes about as a "feeling" that something is amiss. In an article defending Dewey's view of emotion in problem discovery, Robert Sherman reminds his readers that

The fact of the matter is that we do have such feelings. (Though we may suppress them and not recognize that they are a motive to thought.) We are *surprised* or *intrigued* or *revolted* or *elated* by experiences. We *like* the recommendations that one essayist has, or *dislike* the proposals put forward by some legislator. Our "guts" are tense, our heads ache, we pace the floor, and our voices rise. These all are indications that we have an "interest" in the matters at hand. Alas, instead of using these as a motive to thought, to exploit the interests, we suppress the feelings; we believe they are in competition with thought and always should be judged the loser. (Sherman 1985, p. 7)

This affective character of the reflective process is precisely what Dewey meant when he described the initiating stage of thought as "a felt difficulty":

The difficulty may be *felt* with sufficient definiteness as to set the mind at once speculating upon its probable solution, or an undefined *uneasiness* and *shock* may come first, leading only later to definite attempt to find out what is the matter. (Dewey 1997, p. 72)

CSL participants must understand that projects, to be successful, can come only from a direct emotional attachment to the service problem. In this way, the service itself, through reflective connection to academic study, can accomplish educationally sound aims. Without that emotional attachment, there is no problem to be solved and no context for the application of academic, course-acquired knowledge and skill.

Not only does the affective realization of a problem initiate thought, it also necessarily drives the entire reflective process. Because the initiator of thought is a perplexity, or incompleteness in experience, the goal of reflection is the closing of that uneasiness, a reconstruction of the experience that brings wholeness to it once again. As Dewey argued, "The two limits of every unit of thinking are a perplexed, troubled, or confused situation at the beginning and a cleared-up, unified, resolved situation at the close" (Dewey, 1997, p. 106).

In bringing academic skills learned in a university course to the service project, purposeful activity in the form of knowledge and skills are brought to a genuinely felt problem in a student's experience. In this way, the particular knowledge and skills are practiced, honed, and critiqued for success and adjustment within the service project activity. The service project experience and academic learning are bound together intimately through reflection by asking and answering such questions as "what can be done together, using the knowledge/skills learned in this course of study, to solve this important community problem?" The result can be the reinforcement in experience of academic learning as well as the formation of participatory, democratic habits.

The Mediation of a "Felt Problem"

As an emotional, affective activity, problem detection is no more a reflective feature than the instinctual, involuntary reactions of beasts. If humans simply felt and immediately reacted, they would be as other creatures on earth, that is, acting simply on instinct. However, the second, third, and fourth of Dewey's "features of reflective thought" replace instinctual reaction with thoughtful mediation:

To be genuinely thoughtful, we must be willing to sustain and protract that state of doubt which is the stimulus to thorough inquiry, so as not to accept an idea or make positive assertion of a belief until justifying reasons have been found. (1997, p. 16)

This reflective patience is a crucial feature of reflection; and it is essential that students as well as other community members participating in a CSL project understand its importance to the reflective process. The mediating feature of reflection is where reasoning proper occurs and where answers to the question, "What can we do to solve this community problem?" are initially considered. Avoidance of snap, or unreasoned, or reactionary attempts to solve problems is, in fact, the hallmark of good reflective thinking.

While mediating a problem, plans for problem solution are turned over in the mind, discussed, and hypotheses are formed:

The object of thinking is to help reach a conclusion, to project a possible termination on the basis of what is already given. Certain other facts about thinking accompany this feature. Since the situation in which thinking occurs is a doubtful one, thinking is a process of inquiry, of looking into things, of investigating. (Dewey 1944, p. 152)

The ultimate goal of problem mediation is to develop a hypothesis that, once applied, will result in a reconstruction of the problematic situation to make it complete and satisfying once again. That is, mediation as a reflective feature provides the time and consideration to develop academic solutions that can be applied to the community problem.

Reflection After Mediation: Hypothesis Testing

Testing hypotheses involves two important steps. Initially, hypotheses are formulated and go through a "mental testing." Through this mental testing, possible consequences are considered for each plan; and those that are found lacking in one way or another are discarded. Once one hypothesis, or plan, is chosen, it must go through a second, decisive stage of testing. This second stage of testing the hypothesis is accomplished through application to the project problem and makes experience both the means and aim of CSL education. That is, to be educative, CSL must begin and end with student experience. If it does not, then the purposeful nature of student interest will not drive learning. This process necessitates that hypotheses or ideas about how best to solve a felt problem be tested in experience. In describing this feature of reflection, Dewey explained that the

> concluding and conclusive step is some kind of experimental corroboration, or verification, of the conjectural idea. Reasoning shows that if the idea be adopted, certain consequences follow. So far the conclusion is hypothetical or conditional. If we look and find the characteristic traits called for by rival alternatives to be lacking, the tendency to believe, to accept, is almost irresistible. If it is found that the experimental results agree with the theoretical, or rationally deduced, results, and if there is reason to believe that only the conditions in question would yield such results, the confirmation is so strong as to induce a conclusion. (1933, p. 114)

In the particular case of CSL, reasoned "guesses" about how to transform the community problem are applied and then evaluated for their success or failure. The community problem is then reevaluated and the process continues until reconstruction brings back the initially lost equilibrium. The hypothesis-testing feature of reflective thought shows those involved in the project exactly how their hypotheses worked out. Learning in and by experience occurs in testing these reasoned hypotheses, and academic skills learned in theory become experientially real—including lessons learned about reflection itself.

Reflection: A Continual Component of Service-Learning Projects

As Eyler argues and Dewey implies, reflection must be a continual component of any CSL project. Reflection, as explained by Dewey, is an unending cycling from experience to mediation to testing to experience that cannot be ignored before, during, or after a service project. Eyler, Giles, and Schmiede make clear that "reflection should maintain an especially coherent continuity over the course of each [service] event or experience. Continuous reflection includes reflection before the experience, during the experience and after the experience" (1996, p. 17). James and Pamela Toole write that "although the literal definition of reflection means 'looking backward,' reflection occurs at every phase of the CSL cycle: reflection to prepare for service, reflection during action, and reflection upon action" (1995, p. 102). Exactly how reflection can and should be maintained before, during, and after service projects is a crucial issue to the success of service-learning—one that often is ignored or left only for post-service activities.

Reflection Before Practice: "Preflection"

According to Diane Falk, "preflection" is the reflective preparation that occurs before the actual service project begins (1995, p. 23). Keogh, Boud, and Walker point out that during preflection "students start to explore what is required of them, what are the demands of the field setting and the resources which they themselves have to bring" (1985, p. 9). Preflection provides the opportunity for students to imagine what the experience will be like and to express concerns related to the project (Falk 1995, p. 23). It is a concept that reminds CSL educators that reflection must be continual and adds to Dewey's analysis of reflection by indicating the preparation needed, both emotionally and cognitively, to engage in problem-solving service.

However, preparatory reflection as described above is missing an essential Deweyan element: student involvement in project choice. As I argued above, for students to involve themselves in a project whole-heartedly and with purpose and, therefore interest, the project absolutely must come out of the felt interests of the students. The feeling of a crucial community problem is the catalyst to reflection and, therefore, must genuinely be "felt" for substantial learning to occur. That felt interest must be part of the "preflective" stage of project reflection. Combining Deweyan felt interest with the preparatory character of preflection makes it a complete and helpful notion to reflective theory and, therefore, to service-learning practice. As James and Pamela Toole make clear:

> Reflection *before* service may seem a contradiction, but we commonly reflect on and use prior knowledge and experience when we plan and design any project. In preparing for service work, students recollect, propose, hypothesize, build models, predict and make judgments. Students reflect when they choose a service project (*What do we wish were different in our community?*); when they clarify project goals and action plans (*What do we want to see happen?*); and when they prepare for the service itself (*How do we feel about participating in this project?*) (1985, p. 105).

Dewey was also adamant that reflection, as described here, does not imply leaving students—even university students—to their own means, hoping that they stumble upon a problem of interest (1938, p. 71). Instead, the preflective/affective stage of reflection entails a reformulation of the professor's role that is far from traditional. Instead of being a purveyor of already established knowledge or a teller of problems, a university professor working under the CSL pedagogy must be a guide who leads students to realize problematic situations. The leading of students to problems in experience is not an easy task. The CSL instructor might use traditional modes of teaching (the reading of great works and contemporary literature, for example) as well as more non-traditional practices, such as going into one's community to see firsthand what is happening. In either case, the problem must be owned by the participants for the project to evolve successfully.

In addition to project choice and interest, preflection must be a time for project preparation. Once students discover a problem, the reflective process is in full swing. The process will naturally incorporate previous experience and, more importantly, indicate lack of previous experience. This will be particularly true when students meet community "strangers"—those fellow citizens who have firsthand knowledge of the "felt" problem (Radest 1993). The preflective stage, as is pointed out above, must include expressions of emotions and clarifying of assumptions about the problem and about those citizens who regularly experience that problem. It will involve some guessing as to outcomes, roles, and further problems. Preflection will, in short, be the catalyst or, as Dewey says, "The steadying and guiding factor" for the project (1997, p. 72).

Reflection During Service

Reflection is an ongoing process and though "preflection" is essential to project implementation, much, if not most, reflective thought in service-learning occurs during the project work. Reflection during the project drives academic learning as the hypotheses developed for solving the project problem are tested, adjusted through further data gathering, re-applied, and re-tested. Reflection provides the opportunity for learning by bringing the service problem and the university together in the context of the project. Applying classroom learning in the project context "teaches" academic understanding well beyond traditional classroom settings because the students use classroom-constructed knowledge and skills to solve real problems. Students, side by side with community members who have a stake in the service problem, make project decisions. Students operating in the project context create knowledge and sharpen academic skills as they attempt to solve present and future community problems. The project context also leads to better reflective skills as students make project decisions and test those decisions for success or failure.

Reflection, as understood in this discussion, will unite students and community members, classroom learning and experience only if it is structured with both cognitive and affective goals in mind. Boud, Keough and Walker argue that

> reflection as we have described it is pursued with intent. It is not idle meanderings or day-dreaming, but purposive activity directed towards a goal. This is not to say that it may not be helpful to have periods of reverie and mediation associated with conscious reflection, but in themselves these activities are not what we are referring to when we discuss goal-directed critical reflection. (p. 11)

The reflective process is a complex one in which both feelings and cognition are closely interrelated and interactive. Negative feelings, particularly about oneself, can form major barriers towards learning. They can distort perceptions, lead to false interpretations of events, and can undermine the will to persist. Positive feelings and emotions can greatly enhance the learning process; they can keep the learner on the task and can provide a stimulus for new learning. The affective dimension has to be taken into account when we are engaged in our own learning activities, and when we are assisting others in this process (1985, p. 11).

I want to emphasize one additional aspect of reflection that is often forgotten or misunderstood in CSL projects: reflection has a public side as well as the commonly understood private side. Reflection is certainly private in that it comes out of personal experience, involves personal thought, and ends in personal action. Yet, as a process whose end goal is the solution of a public (in the case of CSL) as well as a personally felt problem, it must involve reflective dialogue with those who find themselves most intimately connected to the particular community problem. That is, it must involve a communal application of the problem solution. Reflection is in these ways a community activity. It is only through reflective public discussion—dialogue among all community members affected by the problem—that individuals in a community can connect or reconnect with one another in cooperative and more insightful ways to meet the project problem with viable, democratic solutions. This public aspect of reflection is in some ways synonymous with Amy Gutmann's conception of reasonable public dialogue/debate and, as such, celebrates critical public disagreement as well as public agreement so long as the debate is reflective, inclusive and nonrepressive (1987, pp. 7–23). It is also public reflection that can foster the important community action component that advocates of CSL believe can become a regular participatory habit of students who work within service-learning pedagogy. Unfortunately, the public aspect of reflection is often ignored in CSL projects (Maybach 1994). There simply is not space here to give a full accounting of why CSL projects so often lack essential public dialogue. Suffice it to say, it is a complicated issue more often related to the concept of service being relied upon rather than the concept of reflection . Indeed, it is another clear indication that a prerequisite course on CSL theory is necessary.

Post-Project Reflection: A Continuation, Not a Culmination

Reflection means "looking back" so it is most commonly practiced when projects are over. As James and Pamela Toole remark, "In the aftermath of a project, students therefore need to formally reflect in order to evaluate the project, assess their own development, look for generalizations to guide future decision making and find 'new applications' for what they have learned" (1995, p. 107). In the case of American universities, reflection more often than not is seen as an end to the particular project and as a culmination of a semester course. Certainly it is crucial that reflective discourse carry into the post-project period. However, viewing post-project reflection as the final act in the project context is clearly a misunderstanding of Deweyan reflective features. Instead of the project ending when the CSL course ends, reflective practice (when understood correctly) requires that the project problem be re-examined by all stakeholders together. In this way, democratic interaction and evaluation are practiced and encouraged, and project success is evaluated through continuing reflection.

Reflective post-project examination will determine the successes and failures of the problem solutions. The post-project evaluation will also indicate future and related problems with the project context or similar contexts. Project activities must, therefore, be constructed and implemented based on the idea that the project is over only when a satisfactory reconstruction of, or solution to, the problem has been achieved. Until that time, the project will continue in new and different ways, with new and different insights, and perhaps new and different students. Post-project reflection is simply another case of stepping back from the situation to see the degree to which project activities have solved the initial problem. It is a time for bringing together both project impact and learning with an eye to future similar experiences. As to time constraints, it is post-project reflection that also calls for courses to be tailored to the longer period of time needed to understand CSL, carry out a project, and evaluate that project.

On an individual basis, Deweyan reflective theory asks each student involved in the project to continue reflecting on the problem after the project is completed. In like fashion, effective CSL pedagogy asks that students take both the general reflective skills and the knowledge of the particular community problem with them to other, future community destinations. In this way, reflective thinking, generally, and the problem situation, particularly, will enhance their lives after the particular project is completed. CSL, when done well, will create continuity through opening new and related experiences from those of the past, and in so doing, will insure continued student growth.

Unfortunately, as indicated above, reflection is often the weakest aspect of a CSL project when it should, in fact, be the strongest. At times reflection and celebration have seemingly become one in the same as reflection is reduced to simply some "fun" activities that allow students to look back with (albeit) well-deserved pride and joy at what their service project has accomplished (Learn and Serve Florida 2002). Celebration can be an important aspect of any service-learning project, but it is not necessarily reflective. Additionally, I agree with Rahima Wade that there is a common and understandable tendency among CSL advocates to engage in more action-oriented cheerleading than in open-minded critical reflection on our practices (1997, p. 13). Evidence of this can be found in simply looking to the numerous volumes that have been published listing reflective activities (rather than examining its meaning) (Hiott, Lyday and Winecoff 1998; Honnett and Poulsen 1989; Casey et al. 2006; Root, Billig, and Callahan, 2005; Chi 2000; Meyer and Sandel 2001; Bowden, Billig and Holland 2008). Suggested activities in these volumes are wide and varied in structure. Group discussion, role-playing, writing, acting, presenting, and debating activities all might lead to good reflective practice.

These kinds of activities, however, do not, in and of themselves, satisfy the reflective requirement suggested here for CSL education. The success of each such activity will be found in whether or not it leads the student to reflect in a manner that is similar to that described by Dewey. Does the activity lead students to see a problem in their experience? Does the activity make students step back from a problem to plan a solution? Does the activity get students to apply their academic learning to possible solutions? Does the activity lead students to test that plan in the problem situation? Does the activity bring students to a reevaluation of the problem situation and those similar to it? Does the activity involve dialogue among all stakeholders? Does the activity encourage further reflection? Regardless of what the reflective activity specifically entails, if it is not structured in such a way to answer the above questions in the affirmative, then it is not reflective in nature and should probably be eliminated from a CSL project. Of course, and this is the crucial point, the evaluation of the activity cannot be accomplished by anyone who does not understand the underlying structure of reflective thought.

Service-Learning Theory: Sound Practice Through Sound Understanding

As I hope I have made clear, the reflective process is a far cry from a purely instinctual process that college and university professors can rightly assume our students understand and practice well—though certainly some do better than others. Because reflection is an essential component to a viable CSL project, I believe that its underlying structure must be thoroughly examined by students so that sound theory, rather than vagaries and ignorance, direct practice. I believe just as strongly, and for much the same reason, that understanding the history of CSL, the concept of service, experiential learning theory, and the democratic demands on CSL, are equally paramount to its success as a transformative pedagogy and should, in fact, be the core concepts around which a prerequisite course for CSL students (and future teachers) is developed (see Sheffield 2011). In this way, we might be much more confident that the rather complicated CSL pedagogy will truly "sink-in" with our students.

Of course, it is one thing to abstractly discuss and then assert the need for yet another course, and quite another to actively defend that need by actually developing the course and trying it out. Leaving the discussion in that shadowy realm of "what if" is precisely the kind of inaction that leads practitioners to doubt and even dismiss foundational thinking of the sort found here and is certainly antithetical to the reflection called for in a CSL project. I am, it seems to me, duty bound to at least briefly outline a course that examines CSL history, theory, and practice and will use the remainder of this discussion to do just that.

Community Service Learning 101: Pedagogical Theory and Practice

As you look over this course outline, I ask that you keep the following in mind. First, I have only implemented the course in a limited way: several years ago I taught what my university calls an intersession course on CSL pedagogy. In that course, a limited number of students for a limited period of time examined the CSL pedagogy theoretically and then used that understanding to construct a hypothetical CSL project. Since that time, intersession courses have been increasingly restricted as a result of the contemporary university economic "situation." Secondly, I teach in a college of education and so although this is a course that would be a prerequisite elective for other university-wide courses that carry the CSL "tag" it would also fit well into a college of education curriculum in which future teachers would have the opportunity to study its theoretical and practical structure and incorporate it into their future public school classrooms.

Thirdly, since that intersession course I have published a book that was written in part to be a text for exactly the kind of course I describe here; my apologies to the reader if I champion it as a core for each of the course components. Fourthly, and unfortunately, the current trend in teaching teachers (pre-service and practicing) is to restrict elective hours and in their stead require content area "methods" courses *ad nauseum*, thereby limiting such a course's availability (in terms of credit hours) in an undergraduate or graduate course of study. Finally, I am not an administrator and so I use the "101" course number somewhat in jest. This course would in fact be far beyond simply an introductory course—its nature is that of a higher-level foundations/epistemology/philosophy of education course and its course title would certainly have to reflect that degree of depth.

A typical university semester course runs approximately 16 weeks and, at least initially, I would simply divide the course into equal sections to cover the history of CSL, the concept of service, experiential learning theory, reflection, community theory, and CSL as a form of democratic education. I would also build in a course-ending "mini" service project so that we could apply our theoretical work in a very Deweyan, hypothesis-testing manner to see how we did and as a way to pull the different theoretical discussions together to form a complete picture of the CSL pedagogy. Much of this course would be built around reading and discussion and, as such, I would make the course similar to a graduate-level seminar (as I did with the above-mentioned intersession course). This format would give us about two weeks on each topic, additional time for a mini project, and importantly, some unstructured time to adjust to the particular needs of the students (some sections, I imagine, will need more time working out the nature of service, for example, and so course/time adjustments will be needed).

Because I believe that understanding the history of an idea is essential to understanding its contemporary state of affairs, I would spend some time tracing through the very interesting educational events/movements that brought CSL to where it is today. Admittedly, there are few histories of CSL (in fact, none that I know of that could be described as comprehensive). Thus, studying its historical evolution would be a matter of pulling pieces from various texts together to give a clear picture of its development as a pedagogy. Service, experiential learning, and reflection are the core educational concepts that drive CSL's practice and, as such, each must be closely examined for understanding. There exists a myriad of possible texts that could be called on for that purpose (see the suggested readings below).

Additionally, I believe there is great value in examining the educational aims that CSL can/cannot accomplish. The emphasis of more contemporary research in CSL is in fact directed toward the examination of "outcomes" and there are endless studies that might be utilized in that area. Finally, CSL must answer the demand that it be a viable form of democratic education. Accordingly, an analysis of what a democratic form of education must entail and then an examination of CSL as such is crucial to understanding and defending its practice within our system of P-12 schools, colleges, and universities.

The following is a suggested list of possible readings for each section of the Service-Learning 101 course of study:

The History of CSL Education

For the history section, I suggest a packet of readings that contains:

ACTION. 1972. *High School Student Volunteers*. Washington, D.C. : National Center for Service Learning.

Conderman, B., and B. Patryla. 1996. Service Learning: The Past, Present, and the Promise. *Kappa Delta Pi Record* 32 (4): 122–125.

Giles, D., and J. Eyler. 1994. The Theoretical Roots of Service-Learning in John Dewey: Toward a Theory of Service-Learning. *Michigan Journal of Community Service Learning* 1 (Fall): 77–85.

Hepburn, M. 1997. Service Learning in Civic Education: A Concept with Long, Sturdy Roots. *Theory Into Practice* 36 (3): 136–142.

Hill, D. 1997. *Death of a Dream: Service Learning 1994–2010: An Historical Analysis by One of the Dreamers*. Stanford, CA: Service Learning 2000 Center, Stanford University.

James, W. 1910. *The Moral Equivalent of War*. International Conciliation, no. 27. New York: Carnegie Endowment for International Peace.

Sheffield, E. 2011. A Brief History of an Educational Idea. In *Strong Community Service Learning: Philosophical Perspectives*, 19–40. New York: Peter Lang.

And, selected portions of

Hanna, P. 1936. *Youth Serves the Community*. New York: D. Appleton-Century Company.

Stanton, T., D. Giles, and N. Cruz, N., eds. 1999. *Service-Learning: A Movement's Pioneers Reflect on Its Origins, Practice, and Future*. San Francisco: Jossey-Bass.

A few alternatives:

Adams, A., and S. Reynolds. 1981. The Long Conversation: Tracing the Roots of the Past. *Journal of Experiential Education* 4 (1): 21–28.

Cooley, R., and G. House. 1930. *School Acres: An Adventure in Rural Education*. New Haven, CT: Yale University Press.

Eberly, D. *National Service: A Promise to Keep*. 1988. Rochester, NY: J. Alden Books.

Hatcher, J. 1997. The Moral Dimensions of John Dewey's Philosophy: Implications for Undergraduate Education. *The Michigan Journal of Community Service Learning* 4 (Fall): 50–58.

Kilpatrick, W. H. 1922. *The Project Method: The Use of the Purposeful Act in the Educative Process*. New York: Teachers College, Columbia University.

Merrill, P. H. 1981. *Roosevelt's Forest Army: A History of the Civilian Conservation Corps, 1933–1942*. Montpelier, VT: P. H. Merrill.

Pollock, S. 1997. *Three Decades of Service-Learning in Higher Education (1966–1996): The Contested Emergence of an Organizational Field*. Stanford, CA: Stanford University Press.

Service

I would probably stick with one text here:

Radest, H. 1993. *Community Service: Encounter with Strangers*. Westport, CT: Praeger.

Some alternatives:

Bellah, R., et al. 1985. *Habits of the Heart*. Berkeley, CA: University of California Press.

Coles, R. 1993. *The Call of Service*. Boston, MA: Houghton Mifflin Company.

Dass, R. 1992. *Compassion in Action: Setting Out on the Path of Service*. New York: Bell Tower.

Sheffield, E. 2005. Service in Service-Learning: The Need for Philosophical Understanding. *The High School Journal* 89 (1): 46–53.

Sheffield, E. 2011. Service: Self and Stranger. In *Strong Community Service Learning: Philosophical Perspectives*, 71–90 New York: Peter Lang.

Tocqueville, A. *Democracy in America*. 1956. New York: The New American Library. (Orig. pub. 1835.)

Experiential Learning

Though there exist numerous resources on experiential education (including *The Journal of Experiential Education*), I would rely mostly on portions of the following:

Bacon, F. 1901. *Advancement of Learning*. New York: P. F. Collier and Son. (Orig. pub. 1605.)

Chickering, A. W. 1977. *Experience and Learning: An Introduction to Experiential Learning*. New Rochelle, NY: Change Magazine Press.

Dewey, J. 1931. *The Way out of Educational Confusion*. Westport, CT: Greenwood Press.

Kolb, D. 1984. *Experiential Learning: Experience as the Source of Learning and Development*. Englewood Cliffs, NJ: Prentice-Hall.

Sheffield, E. 2011. Epistemology. In *Strong Community Service Learning: Philosophical Perspectives*, 91–106 New York: Peter Lang.

There are, of course, many other texts/articles that would work equally well, including these additional Dewey titles:

Dewey, J. 1938. *Experience and Education*. New York: Macmillan.

Dewey, J. 1944. *Democracy and Education: An Introduction to the Philosophy of Education*. New York: Macmillan. (Orig. pub. 1916.)

Dewey, J. 1966. *Lectures in the Philosophy of Education 1899*. New York: Random House.

Reflection

There is no doubt that I would use Dewey's treatment of reflection found in

Dewey, J. 1933. *How We Think: A Restatement of the Relation of Reflective Thinking to the Educative Process*. Boston: D. C. Heath and Company.

Additionally, I might use any of the articles mentioned in the above discussion of reflection and listed here in the references list. Also:

Sheffield, E. 2005. Reflection and Service-Learning in Higher Education: Some Philosophical Underpinnings to Transforming Service into Learning. In *Perspectives on American Education*, ed. T. Deering, 29–50. Dubuque, IA: Kendall Hunt Publishing.

Sheffield, E. 2011. Reflection: Binding Together Community, Service, and Learning. In *Strong Community Service Learning: Philosophical Perspectives*, 107–124. New York: Peter Lang.

Educational Aims/Outcomes

As I mention above, the preponderance of CSL research, particularly of late, is oriented to discovering what CSL can and cannot accomplish with reference to academic, civic, and community transformation. Rather than list the extensive possibilities here, I will simply suggest looking at the appendix to my book, *Strong Community Service Learning: Philosophical Perspectives* (New York: Peter Lang, 2011). There you will find several pages of research to use as a start—outcomes research continues to grow by proverbial leaps and bounds.

CSL as a Form of Democratic Education

I would pull from the following texts/articles on democratic forms of education:

Boyte, H. C. 1989. *Commonwealth: A Return to Citizen Politics*. New York: Collier Macmillan.

Dewey, J. 1944. *Democracy and Education: An Introduction to the Philosophy of Education*. New York: Macmillan. (Orig. pub. 1916.)

Gutmann, A. 1987. *Democratic Education*. Princeton, NJ: Princeton University Press.

Harkavy, I., and L. Benson. 1998. De-Platonizing and Democratizing Education as the Bases of Service Learning. *New Directions for Teaching and Learning* 73 (Spring): 11–15.

Lisman, C. D. 1980. *Toward a Civil Society*. Westport, CT: Greenwood Publishing.

Putnam, R. 1995. Bowling Alone: America's Declining Social Capital. *Journal of Democracy* 6 (1): 65–78.

Sheffield, E. 2004. Service-Learning as a Democratic, Public Affair: Some Necessary Philosophical Ingredients. *The Journal of Public Affairs* 9 (1): 1–15.

Sheffield, E. 2007. Root Metaphors, Paradigm Shifts, and Democratically Shared Values: Community Service-Learning as a Bridge-Building Endeavor. *Philosophical Studies in Education* 38: 105–117.

Sheffield, E. 2011. Democratic Education: Weak Community Service Learning. In *Strong Community Service Learning: Philosophical Perspectives*, 125–136 New York: Peter Lang.

Sheffield, E. 2011. Community: A Rose by Any Other Name. In *Strong Community Service Learning: Philosophical Perspectives*, 55–70. New York: Peter Lang.

Sheffield, E. 2011. Toward Strong Community Service Learning. In *Strong Community Service Learning: Philosophical Perspectives*, 137–148. New York: Peter Lang.

Conclusion

As an advocate of CSL pedagogy, I am concerned about its future—a future that I believe depends on the degree to which we examine and understand its practice as firmly grounded in reasonable foundational thinking. Misunderstanding and ignorance of that foundation lead (as is usually the case) to bad practice; and bad practice might well lead to the demise of service-learning. I suggest that to insure sound practice based on sound understanding requires colleges and universities that utilize CSL to require a course on its theory and practice—a prerequisite for anyone wanting to participate in a course that carries the service learning "tag." Alternatively, initial CSL coursework might be extended to at least two semesters so that an examination of CSL theory could take place as part of the coursework. In either case, the above course outline is provided simply as a starting point for what I believe can be a valuable, rigorous, and, ultimately, an essential part of protecting and growing the service-learning pedagogy of reflection—a sophisticated pedagogy that can lead to sophisticated construction of socially important knowledge.

References

Boud, D, R. Keough, and D. Walker. 1985. What Is Reflection in Learning? In *Reflection: Turning Experience into Learning*, ed. David Boud, Rosemary Keough, and David Walker, 7–17. London: Kogan Page.

Bowden, A., Shelley H. Billig and Barbara A. Holland. 2008. *Scholarship for Sustaining Service-Learning and Civic Engagement*. Charlotte: Information Age.

Casey, Karen McKnight, Georgia Davidson, Shelley Billig, and Nicole Springer, eds. 2006. *Advancing Knowledge in Service-Learning: Research to Transform the Field*. Charlotte, NC: New Age.

Chi, B. 2000. *Service-Learning as "Citizenship Education": The Promise and the Puzzles*. Washington, DC: Corporation for National Service.

Chickering, A. W. 1977. *Experience and Learning: An Introduction to Experiential Learning*. New Rochelle, NY: Change Magazine Press.

Dewey, J. 1933. *How We Think: A Restatement of the Relation of Reflective Thinking to the Educative Process*. Boston: D. C. Heath.

Dewey, J. 1938. *Experience and Education*. New York: Macmillan.

Dewey, J. 1944. *Democracy and Education: An Introduction to the Philosophy of Education*. New York: Macmillan. (Orig. pub. 1916.)

Dewey, J. 1997. *How We Think*. Ontario Canada: Dover Publications. (Orig. pub. 1910.)

Duley, J. 1981. Field Experience Education. *The Modern American College*, ed. Arthur Chickering. San Francisco, CA: Jossey-Bass, 1981.

Eyler, J. 2001. Creating Your Reflection Map. *New Directions for Higher Education* 114 (Summer): 35–42.

Eyler, J., D. Giles Jr., and A. Schmiede. 1996. *A Practitioner's Guide to Reflection in Service-Learning*. Nashville, TN: Vanderbilt University.

Fry, Ronald and David Kolb. "Experiential Learning Theory and Learning Experiences in Liberal Arts Education." *New Directions for Experiential Learning* 6 (Fall 1979): 79–92.

Falk, D. 1995. Preflection: A Strategy for Enhancing Reflection. *NSEE Quarterly* 13 (Winter): 21–23.

Gutmann, A. 1987. *Democratic Education*. Princeton, NJ: Princeton University Press.

Hiott, B. C., W. J. Lyday, and H. L. Winecoff. 1998. *Service Learning Handbook for Teacher Educators and Practitioners*. Columbia: University of South Carolina.

Honnet, E. P. and S. J. Poulsen. 1989. *Principles of Good Practice in Combining Service and Learning*. Racine, WI: Johnson Foundation.

James, W. 1892. *Psychology: The Briefer Course*. Reprint, Notre Dame, IN: University of Notre Dame, 1985.

Learn and Serve Florida, *2002 Request for Proposals*. Florida Learn and Serve.

Maybach, C. E. 1994. *Second Year Evaluation of Three Components of Colorado Campus Compact*. Denver, CO: Colorado Campus Compact.

Meyer, S, and K. Sandel. 2001. *Research on Service-Learning and Teen Pregnancy and Risk Behavior Prevention: Bibliography*. Denver, CO: RMC Research Corporation.

Mintz, S. D. and G. Hesser. 1997. *Principles of Good Practice in Service-Learning in Service Learning in Higher Education: Concepts and Practices*, ed. Barbara Jacoby. San Francisco: Jossey-Bass.

Moore, D. T. 1990. Experiential Education as Critical Discourse. In *Combining Service and Learning: A Resource Book for Community and Public Service*, ed. Jane C. Kendall, 273–283. Raleigh, NC: National Society for Internships and Experiential Education.

Radest, H. 1993. *Community Service: Encounter with Strangers*. Westport, CT: Praeger.

Root, S., Shelley H. Billig, and Jane Callahan, eds. 2005. *Improving Service-Learning Practice: Research on Models to Enhance Impacts*. Charlotte, NC: New Age.

Sheffield, E. C. 2011. *Strong Community Service Learning: Philosophical Perspectives*. New York: Peter Lang.

Sherman, R. R. 1985. Philosophy with Guts. *Journal of Thought* 20 (Summer): 3–11

Toole, J., and P. Toole. 1995. Reflection as a Tool for Turning Service Experiences into Learning Experiences. In *Enriching the Curriculum through Service Learning*, ed. James Toole. San Francisco: Jossey Bass.

Wade, R. 1997. *Community Service Learning*. New York: State University of New York Press.

CHAPTER SEVENTEEN

The Changing Hidden Curriculum

A Personal Recollection

ERIC MARGOLIS

Throughout my school years we were taught and practiced "duck and cover" in case of nuclear attack. I was in 9th grade when the Cuban Missile Crisis had everyone wondering if nuclear war was imminent; we were old enough to know that New York City would be ground zero and that hiding under our desks or going down to the basement would not save us. I was in 11th grade English class, perhaps discussing *A Separate Peace* by John Knowles, when the school loudspeakers came on with what sounded like random shouting. Finally, a voice broke through and announced that President Kennedy had been shot in Dallas. We were in a state of shock, many cried, school was dismissed. For two days nearly everyone in the country was glued to the television, we saw Jack Ruby shoot Lee Harvey Oswald. What was happening to our country? I took 11th grade biology from Anne Schwerner. Her son Michael was one of the civil rights activists registering Blacks to vote in Mississippi. Michael Schwerner, James Chaney, and Andrew Goodman disappeared on June 21, 1964 and their bodies were not discovered for two months. I attended the memorial service at a temple in New Rochelle. We stood outside because there were so many mourners. In 1965 Malcolm X was assassinated in front of a huge crowd in Harlem; about two weeks later we watched TV in horror once again as Alabama State Troopers beat civil rights workers on a bridge in Selma, Alabama. The next day, quietly and away from the cameras, the first 3500 marines arrived in Vietnam as the United States began to take over the fight from the French. Civil rights and the war dominated my school years—as it did others of my generation.

I started college in 1965 at the State University of New York, New Paltz. Tuition was around $100.00 a quarter and the hidden curricula in higher education could scarcely have been more different than it is today. In those days the need for growth in Higher Education in the United States was spurred by the cold war and the desire to "beat the Russians." Within a span of ten years the Soviets launched the first artificial satellite in Earth's orbit (*Sputnik* in 1957), the first animal in space (a dog in 1960), and the first human spaceman (Yuri Gagarin in 1961). Other things were happening. The GI Bill had proved successful in enrolling returning service men and women in college; their children, born from 1946 onward, were the "baby boom" and were reaching college age. In other words, higher education was a growth industry defined as a social benefit. As later, the U.S. worried about its post-war place in the world and growing competition from the Communist "bloc;" the country wanted rocket scientists, engineers, and physicists, but also wanted to produce educated people fluent in foreign languages, history, foreign relations, sociology and anthropology who could serve as essential parts of the state ideological apparatus (Althusser, 1971). The United States clearly saw the need to project soft as well as hard power. Soft power like the Peace Corps and the "green revolution" worked hand in glove with the maintenance of a massive military presence in the countries defeated in World War II, Japan and Germany, but also Korea, the Philippines, and so on. Military and technological development in atomic weapons and rocketry continued at increasing levels in the projection of hard power.

During my four years in college, the State University of New York grew at an amazing pace, all supported by taxpayer funding. The Republican governor, Nelson Rockefeller, "was the driving force in turning the State University of New York into the largest system of public higher education in the United States. Under his governorship it grew from 29 campuses and 38,000 full-time students to 72 campuses and 232,000 full-time students" (State of New York, *Public Papers of Nelson A. Rockefeller*, Fifty-third Governor of the State of New York, vol. 15, 1973 Albany, NY: State of New York, 1973, p. 1380).[1]

The space race and global cold war competition underlay one (not so) hidden curriculum; there were others that were much harder to see. A holdover from past practices was the notion that colleges and universities were to act *in loco parentis*; that is, to act in the place of the parent. In real life this meant students, boys and girls as they were considered at the time, lived in sex segregated dormitories and were forbidden to visit one another's rooms except for an occasional Sunday visit when the halls were patrolled and curious rules enforced (doors open, three feet on the floor at all times. . .). Girls had to be in the dormitory by 11:00 pm on weekdays (maybe midnight on weekends), and no alcohol was permitted. A great amount of time and effort was invested by both sides of the morality play; the administration had systems of monitors to make sure the rules were obeyed, "boys and girls" developed elaborate ways to beat the system so they could have sex, signing each other in and out, meeting in the woods, getting motel rooms off campus. A similar struggle went on over alcohol. The legal age to drink in New York was 18 at the time, and shops in town were only too glad to sell to anyone with a driver's license—of course this meant the 18-year-old in the group would buy for everyone. Numerous schemes to smuggle booze into the dorms were successful. Simultaneously, and seemingly nationwide, college students discovered marijuana. This was something college and university administrators were not prepared for and it put them in a bind. On the one hand, *in loco parentis* suggested the duty to protect the students; on the other hand, this was not simple university rule breaking but rather federal rule breaking. Most college towns became, in effect, youth ghettos, places where the usual practices of law enforcement were suspended.

Another hidden curriculum was course requirements. At New Paltz, and many other colleges and universities, the entire freshman and sophomore years consisted of required classes that were considered foundational. Math, philosophy (mostly Greek), three terms of a foreign language, introduction to psychology (I was planning to major in psychology; rats and T mazes pushed me to sociology), introduction to sociology, three terms of history—if I remember correctly they were U.S., World, and one you could choose. I took African history taught by a Nigerian professor. Three terms of literature—U.S. and World again, I think, and my choice of Asian literature. In any case it had been decided long ago that students' brains had to be furnished with certain information and trained in certain ways of thinking—like a muscle that needed to be exercised. Only after the first two years were we allowed to pursue "elective" courses in our major. We received report cards, but there was no way for students to evaluate either courses or faculty.

Perhaps the most important "hidden" curriculum is right up there in the name "State University." Buildings were built and owned by the state and paid for by willing taxpayers. The parents of the baby boomers, who had lived through the Depression and fought World War II, believed in education as a social benefit. They wanted their children to have the opportunities for higher education that before had been generally available only to the upper classes.[2] The universities cooperated with the state and federal governments in myriad ways, from small grants to subsidies for massive projects like the Lawrence Livermore National Laboratory founded by the University of California in 1962 and funded by the Department of Energy. One visible presence on nearly every campus was the Reserve Officers Training Corps (ROTC), with an ancient heritage going back to the Morrill Act of 1862 that created the land-grant colleges and required military training as an element of the curriculum. Students receive a stipend or scholarship and take elective classes in military tactics. ROTC units were (and are today) often visible marching or practicing on the college or university training fields.

In an earlier anthology (Margolis 2001), my co-authors and I emphasized what Michael Apple called the "strong form of the hidden curriculum" which reproduced race, gender, and social class inequalities (Apple and King 1977).[3] In the introduction we also discussed various ways that curricula can be hidden. In the case of the curricula discussed above, they were hidden in plain sight:

> In Edgar Allan Poe's short story, "The Purloined Letter" a seasoned investigator has been called upon by the French police to lend his intuitive skills to solving a mystery. He asks the police about their search for critical clues: "I presume you looked to the mirrors, between the boards and the plates, and you probed the beds and the bed-clothes, as well as the curtains and carpets?" To which they reply: "Certainly; we opened every package and parcel; we not only opened every book, but we turned over every leaf in each volume. . . We also measured the thickness of every book-cover, with the most accurate admeasurement, and applied to each the most jealous scrutiny of the microscope. . ." The investigator continues: "You explored the floors beneath the carpets? And the paper on the walls? You looked into the cellars?" To which the police again affirm, "We did." "Well then" speculates the investigator, "perhaps the mystery is a little too plain."[4] In this sense some of the hidden curriculum is intentionally hidden in plain sight, precisely so that it will remain undetected (Margolis, Soldatenko, Acker, and Gair 2001).

In essence, while these elements of the hidden curriculum were well known to political decision makers, administration, and faculty they remained hidden to students as "just the way school was." Students worked to subvert these structures, but did not confront them directly. This was soon to change. All that was hidden was revealed, challenged, and changed.

Cracks began to appear as tectonic plates shifted. If you were old enough at 18 to go to Vietnam, why couldn't you vote? Why was your girlfriend or boyfriend not able to visit your room? Why did you have to take a string of "meaningless" coursework when the world outside the ivory tower seemed to be going up in flames? Why were there so few Blacks, Puerto Ricans, or Chicanos on campus? Why were there no classes on civil rights, Black history, women's studies, or American involvement in foreign wars? Why did students not have the right to demonstrate on campus? TV and the glossy magazine photographs in *Time* and *Life* were central in spreading the war in Vietnam, brutality against the civil rights movement, and highlighted a growing student movement. In a remarkable short period of time many of the elements of the hidden curricula would be brought into the full glare of the media, challenged, and changed.

One of the first breakouts from the hidden curriculum of the university as an ivory tower (isolated and insulated from political life) took place as early as 1960 when four freshmen from the historically black land-grant university, North Carolina Agricultural and Technical State University in Greensboro, sat down at the "white's only" lunch counter in Woolworth's, ordered cups of coffee, and refused to leave when ordered to do so. They stayed all day and the following day. The number of students "sitting-in" reached 20 or more; it was up to 60 the next day. The students were attacked by whites who poured ketchup and other food on them, and sometimes beat them physically. Nevertheless, the movement spread rapidly to other cities and other segregated corporations. Eventually, financial pressure, the power of non-violent resistance, and national television coverage forced many national corporations to end Jim Crow practices.

In the same year that the sit-ins began in earnest, The Sharon Statement was written by a group of young conservative activists. The name was drawn from the name of William F. Buckley's estate in Sharon, Connecticut, and the statement was the founding document for Young Americans for Freedom (YAF). Articulating what they termed "transcendent values" the statement supported individualism ("God-given free will"), small government, the market economy, and most intensely the existential threat of "international Communism" arguing that the "United States should stress victory over, rather than co-existence with this menace."[5]

In 1962 a meeting was held at Port Huron, Michigan. Attendees were mostly student activists from the left; many were from the labor and civil rights movement, including Tom Hayden, who was a secretary for Students for a Democratic Society (SDS). The manifesto written at that meeting came to be called the Port Huron Statement. It rallied against alienation and the emphasized need for political activism in support of civil rights and against the cold War ideology that produced fear of nuclear annihilation.[6] It was addressed primarily at apathetic, middle-class, white, and privileged youths, many of whom were, or would soon become, college students. SDS stood for "A free university in a free society." A central argument was that "the American political system is not the democratic model of which its glorifiers speak. In actuality it frustrates democracy by confusing the individual citizen, paralyzing policy discussion, and consolidating the irresponsible power of military and business interests."[7]

The Sharon Statement and the Port Huron Statement set the internal political battles in the United States well into the 21st century. Battles took place on campuses as well as in the general body politic (Klatch 1999).

What had begun as ideological doctrine from both left and right soon morphed into practice. The 1964/65 free speech movement (FSM) at the University of California Berkeley galvanized and politicized students across the country, and baffled school administrators. Like the "sit-ins" the student movement also started as a small-scale event and rapidly grew into a national movement for student power that eventually exposed and then eliminated the *in loco parentis* curriculum. In October 1964 a Berkeley dean announced that students could no longer set up tables to advocate or collect money for "outside" political organizations other than the national Democratic or Republican parties. Jack Weinberg, a former graduate student, was sitting at the table supporting CORE (The Congress of Racial Equality). When Jack failed to show his ID card to the campus police he was arrested and put in a police car. Thousands of students spontaneously surrounded the police car in which Weinberg was detained, and the car did not move for 32 hours. As he continued his one man sit-in, speaker after speaker stood on top of the police car to advocate for free speech. The most famous speech was made on the Sproul Hall steps on December 2, 1964 by a student activist and civil rights worker, Mario Savio:

> There's a time when the operation of the machine becomes so odious—makes you so sick at heart—that you can't take part. You can't even passively take part. And you've got to put your bodies upon the gears and upon the wheels, upon the levers, upon all the apparatus, and you've got to make it stop. And you've got to indicate to the people who run it, to the people who own it, that unless you're free, the machine will be prevented from working at all.[8]

In the next stage of the developing demonstration thousands of students occupied Sproul Hall; they sat-in in shifts and attended classes, including newly organized "teach-ins" where free speech, civil rights, and the beginning of the Vietnam War were openly discussed. On December 4th almost 800 students in Sproul Hall were arrested, but most were released on their own recognizance. The University chose to file more serious charges against those whom they perceived as "leaders." In response, Cal students basically shut down the University and the administration backed down. Political organizing was "allowed;" the FSM and branches of SDS spread to other campuses and many of the old *in loco parentis* rules fell. College students came into their own as "adults" free to express opinions, eventually evaluating their courses and professors, living in co-ed dorms, and so on.

American involvement in the Vietnam War increased steadily, and television brought it into every living room and dormitory. On the right the war was perceived as an essential battle against the Communist menace. On the left the war was seen as an imperialist adventure that served the interests of the Military Industrial Complex that a Republican President and hero of World War II, Dwight Eisenhower, had warned against in his farewell address. Ike was concerned that revolving doors and tight relationships between Congress, the military, and huge defense contractors would create a permanent wartime state.[9]

Two of the reasons the Vietnam War became a flashpoint on campus were first the draft, and second the concern that instead of being "free" the university was increasingly entangled with the military industrial complex—not only in huge investments like the Lawrence Livermore National Laboratory, but in myriad small grants to individual professors and campus laboratories. The role of the hidden curriculum of relations between a university supposedly dedicated to the open pursuit of knowledge, and a university that many saw as an arm of a permanent wartime state, became highly visible and increasingly contentious.

As the war escalated the draft became the most obvious element of the once hidden curriculum. From the beginning college students had been given draft deferments. This separated middle-class males from their working-class brethren and caused many to go to college who might not have otherwise. In 1966 the government went one step too far by requiring students to take an achievement type test called the "student draft deferment test." Presumably the intent was to separate "worthy" students from those who were escaping the draft. On campuses across the country there was massive resistance to the very concept; many refused to take the exam and many picketed the testing sites. The "test" was only offered once. But it opened a window on the relationship between the university and the military. Sacred cows like ROTC came to be questioned, and in many cases were moved off campus.

The Hidden Curricula Change

There is neither space here, nor need, to write about the turbulent history of the 1960s and early 70s. Instead, I will turn to the direct effect of the political battles on hidden curricula in the university. It has been said that the right won the political war while the left won the cultural war. In university politics there is much truth in this observation. Hippies and leftist students brought sex, drugs, and rock and roll on campus and organized anti-war, civil rights, and student power marches, demonstrations, and human be-ins. But Ronald Reagan was elected Governor of California, at least partly by promising to clean up "the mess at Berkeley." Clark Kerr, as Chancellor of the California system, sought to protect protesting students from being expelled, and was fired for being "too lenient" by the conservative board of regents.[10] Nonetheless, there would be no return to a university acting as surrogate parents and policing student morality. Nor would the nexus of university research with the military be interrupted; instead it grew and strengthened.

Required coursework, general education requirements, had long been stakes in a struggle between "traditionalists" who believed certain courses were essential scaffolding for a higher education degree and "progressives" who thought students should have freedom of choice to decide on their educational interests. Famously, the University of Chicago and Columbia University had the most rigorous core requirements while Cornell and Brown led in open enrolment and student-driven courses. In undergraduate education the number of required core courses tended to shrink as an agreement was reached between those who saw school as a path to employment and those who saw higher education as a place for intellectual experimentation and advocated for freedom of choice. While their goals were disparate, they agreed that two years of required credit hours was too much.[11]

As the old hidden agendas and practices were exposed by new generations of scholars, and by students no longer content to simply follow along, it became essential for the University to find new ways to hide many elements of the curriculum once again. Accusations of racism, classism, and sexism and a long history of discriminatory practices by faculty "good old boy" networks were dealt with by two developments: affirmative action in student recruitment and faculty hiring and the development of interdisciplinary studies, such as ethnic and women's studies programs.

Beginning in 1961 the term "affirmative action" began to be used in programs designed, among other things, to open educational opportunities for students of color and to increase the presence of women on campus.[12] Admissions in most colleges and universities had been truly a hidden process in which SAT or other test scores were used, but there was ample room for individual faculty and admission committees to make selections based on unspoken criteria. In the Ivy Leagues and other prestigious institutions "legacy" admissions were (and are) common; i.e., students whose parents had attended the same institution were far more likely to be admitted. Even if not discriminatory on purpose, these policies had the effect of producing incoming classes homogeneous in terms of race, social class, and gender. Students of color and those from blue-collar backgrounds, older students, or students who were the first in their family to attend college, faced barriers to admission as well as to success in attaining degrees. Certain majors—engineering, math, and the non-biological sciences—tended to have gendered hidden curricula: a perceived hostility that marginalized women.[13] Universities set up offices of affirmative action that monitored admissions procedures and outcomes. The goal was to eliminate barriers to under-represented groups and make admissions policies transparent.

Affirmative action programs produced a counter-narrative among conservative faculty and students that students of color or women would not have been admitted "on their own academic merits." Affirmative action was seen as "reverse discrimination" in which more qualified white males were denied admission to provide room for the underqualified in the name of political correctness. Alternately, it was said by some that well-qualified women and students of color would suffer from the stigma of being perceived as "affirmative action" cases (Bloom 1987; Rodriguez [1982] 1983; Steal 1991; Sykes 1988). Both sides recognized that mostly hidden admissions and hiring practices shaped the faculty and student body—indeed the university itself. This battle has been fought in scholarship and in the courts for more than half a century with opposing sides having been largely determined by the Sharon and Port Huron ideological statements.

Simultaneously, efforts from inside and outside the university created whole new departments and programs with their own formal and hidden curricula. Women's studies, Black studies, Chicano studies, and Asian/Pacific Islander studies programs struggled to be established— often with pressure on university administrations from community action groups. The names of ethnic studies programs changed as political word usage change; e.g., Black studies became African American Studies (and now at ASU, African and African American Studies; Chicana/o Studies was re-branded Transborder Studies[14]). More or less at the same time, existing course work in history, the social sciences, and humanities began to change the formal curriculum to include untold (hidden) stories of workers, women, immigrants, and minority groups. Alongside these developments grew a conservative whispering campaign and eventually a literature that these programs were "crap courses" that they were anti-male, anti-white people—in essence that they had created their own hidden curriculum of discriminatory practices (Bloom 1987; Sykes 1988; Steal 1991). In an interesting analysis of the development of Chicano Studies programs, Michael Soldatenko pointed out that what actually happened was that the new programs were disciplined by the academy. Programs sought to become departments, faculty held each other up to "rigorous" tenure and promotion policies, for example downgrading publications in "Chicano" journals in favor of mainstream disciplinary journals in the social sciences or humanities (Soldatenko 1998, 1999).

Often, instead of disestablishing good old boy networks, parallel good old girl and ethnic studies networks were developed. The hidden curriculum of race and gender had become far less visible, but it did not disappear. Nonetheless, the routinization of these new academic disciplines took much of the fury out of civil rights attacks on the academy.

The anti-war movements that sprang from the war in Vietnam and later Cambodia were perhaps an even bigger threat to hidden curricula that connected the "multiversity" to the growing military industrial congressional complex. As the war raged on there were repeated calls to move ROTC off campus and many universities did just that, e.g., Harvard in 1969 and Stanford in 1971. (Even when the war ended, the anti-ROTC policy continued in objection to the "don't ask, don't tell" policy for gays in the military that President Clinton instituted in 1993.) It had been the practice for recruiters from each branch of the armed services to come to campuses and set up tables to promote their branch and induce college students to enlist. Demonstrators blocked the tables, chanted anti-war slogans, and in some cases sprayed blood on the recruiters. They became a flash point. Student demonstrators also confronted the draft directly—chanting "hell no, we won't go" and burning their draft cards.

The long-term solution to this, both for the government and for academia, was the so-called "All Volunteer Army." Nixon had promised to end the draft in his 1968 campaign and five years later this became a reality. The brute fact that middle-class college students no longer had to fear being drafted was a brilliant strategy in reducing opposition to wars the U.S. entered into. In effect it depoliticized the campus. While the "Shock and Awe" attack on Iraq did provoke widespread anti-war demonstrations, they had neither the impact nor the holding power of the Vietnam protests.[15] As the hidden curriculum of links between colleges/universities and the military became less and less visible once again, no campuses were shut down; no administration building occupied. After 40 years, in 2011 Harvard welcomed back ROTC.[16]

The morality of military support for university research had been controversial at least since World War II and the development of the atomic bomb. The SDS call for "a free university in a free society" implied opposition to secret research projects. The very notion of "science" requires open publishing of results so that they can be "replicated" and tested. Secret science is an oxymoron. Similarly, there was awareness and much criticism of the CIA sponsorship of social science research in the Cold War, counter-insurgency, and wars of national liberation, as well as domestic spying programs in the U.S. like COINTELPRO. Many academics learned through the Freedom of Information Act and the multi-volume "Church Report" that they had been the subject of warrantless surveillance by the FBI and CIA (United States Senate Select Committee to Study Governmental Operations with Respect to Intelligence Activities).[17] In the recent wars in the Mid-east and Central Asia the U.S. army recruited U.S. academics—anthropologists and other social scientists—into what they termed "the Human Terrain System." They were to be "embedded" with Army units to "recruit, train, deploy, and support an embedded operationally focused socio-cultural capability; conduct operationally relevant socio-cultural research and analysis; develop and maintain a socio-cultural knowledge base, in order to enable operational decision-making, enhance operational effectiveness, and preserve and share socio-cultural institutional knowledge."[18] Much university research is now privately funded by large electronics, pharmaceutical, and other corporations with patent and intellectual property rights negotiated between the university administration and the funding corporation. In increasingly common practice, open publication of research findings is becoming tightly controlled as "trade secrets."

Above and beyond the ongoing relations between academia and the Military Industrial Complex, the single most important change in the hidden curriculum in higher education was a change in the publically perceived mission of the institution. Where education during the cold war era was seen as a broad social benefit and state colleges and universities perceived as public goods, a college education came to be defined as a personal benefit. In good or bad economic times state legislatures began to cut back on their contributions to higher education. Pell Grants, based on need, were increasingly replaced by a system of government-backed loans. Pell Grants, which do not have to be repaid, are capped at $5,500 for the 2011 school year. The cost of tuition has been rising steadily. According to the College Board:

> Public four-year colleges charge, on average, $7,605 per year in tuition and fees for in-state students. The average surcharge for full-time out-of-state students at these institutions is $11, 990. Private nonprofit four-year colleges charge, on average, $27,293 per year in tuition and fees. Tuition is only a portion of college costs; on top of that one must add costs such as living expenses, texts, and supplies. Thus, there is an increasing gap between what the Pell Grant might cover and the cost of college, a gap increasingly covered by loans; some are direct federally financed low-interest loans, others like the Federal Family Education Loan Program are made by private banks but backed by the government.[19] According to the *Atlantic*, student loans have grown by 511% since 1999.[20]

In a modern version of the GI Bill, universities increasingly saw their mission as a higher sort of vocational education; and students were expected to reap individual rewards by getting advanced degrees. However, unlike the GIs, many went deeply into debt to attain those degrees. According to *Forbes*:

> . . . one out of every 10 students who graduated from four-year colleges and universities in 2008 (the most recent year for which data is available) owed $40,000 or more in loans, according to the Institute for College Access and Success. Overall more than two-thirds (67%) of students earning degrees from those institutions carried loan debt, owing an average $23,200.[21]

One of my Education students (who will remain anonymous) wrote this, summarizing the desperation of students, especially those in the low-wage "helping" professions like teaching and social work:

> 1 semester of doctoral tuition at ASU=$5,000. My yearly salary as a high school teacher—less than $40,000. The possibility that I will get to mentor a student teacher for the Spring semester that will cover the cost of 6 credit hours—priceless! (fingers crossed)

With debts piling up, students were basically eliminated as a threat to the status quo; they were unlikely to be demonstrating against wars, or for civil or any other rights. As students and their parents assumed a much greater share of the educational cost, students began to see themselves as consumers of a service—eroding "pedagogical authority" and contributing to grade inflation.[22] In some ways challenging the notion that the "professor was always right" helped balance the hidden curricula of the ivory tower, but as with anyone who is paying for a service, student/consumers expected not only to be served "education" but also to be entertained in ways that George Ritzer and others termed McDonaldization. In the McUniversity students ". . . see themselves as consumers of education in much the same way as they are consumers in the mall (including the cybermall)" (Ritzer 2002, p. 19). Ritzer termed McUniversities "cathedrals of consumption." He argued (as Max Weber would have) that they are also rational bureaucratic structures that simultaneously produce disenchantment (Ritzer 2002, p. 20). To counter disenchantment, McUniversities create three kinds of spectacle:

> 1. The creation of simulations—"elaborate fakes, designed to amaze and delight consumers"—because "the real, the authentic, is difficult to work with."

2. "Implosion" which "involves the elimination of boundaries between extant phenomena so that they collapse in on one another." His example is the way that theme parks and malls became one and the same in places like The Mall of America—in "The New American University" dormitories have become country clubs (discussed below).

3. "The manipulation of time and space." Time compression means that things that used to take weeks, say writing a research paper, can be done in an evening (nothing in that statement implies quality.) A final component of McDonaldization is "edutainment":

. . . classes taught by closed circuit television or online make it possible for students across the country to take courses at a given university. These courses can be taken. . . at the leisure of the student. And universities pour funds into building immense facilities such as stadiums and athletic centers with the attention of attracting students. (Ritzer 2002, pp. 20, 21)

McDonaldization of Higher Education: The New American University as a Case in Point

Full disclosure: I am an Associate Professor at Arizona State University (ASU), and have been teaching here since 1995; I speak from experience and the experiences of my colleagues and students. In 2002 Michael M. Crow took over as president of Arizona State University (ASU) and immediately set about employing the "shock doctrine" borrowed from business designed to disrupt the hidden curricula of university culture.[23] Curiously, when many businesses are moving to diffuse models that employ distributed web-like structures and social media, ASU and the Arizona Board of Regents chose to impose a command and control structure reminiscent of the old factory system. Using a variety of means, Crow sought to disrupt and eliminate cultural practices including faculty governance (already weakened to "shared governance") and the structure of discipline-based departments, and replace the traditional diffused and loosely coupled power with a top-down control model. He circulated a pamphlet to deans and department heads produced by a private management firm, Dallas-based Pritchett & Associates, titled *High-Velocity Cultural Change: A Handbook for Managers.* The opening lines read:

Your approach to changing the culture should be highly out of character for the organization. Choose methods that stand in stark contrast to standard operating procedures. From the very outset you must free yourself from the existing culture and conceive a plan of action that starts to liberate the organization from its past. (Pritchett and Pound 1993, p. 3)

High velocity destruction of university culture and replacing it with a command and control hierarchy were essential to McDonaldize what had been a mid-level state university, albeit one with Research One status. ASU was re-branded "The New American University." Soon after he arrived, Crow, who held degrees in Public Policy and Public Administration (Science and Technology Policy), called the entire faculty of the College of Education (COE) to a meeting. I remember it like it was yesterday, because I knew from that moment on that the COE's days were numbered—especially my program, Educational Leadership and Policy Studies (ELPS). The ASU program was one of the top ten graduate programs in public universities in the field. Our faculty included three Regents Professors, Mary Lee Smith, Gene V. Glass, and David Berliner, and a number of other highly accomplished policy researchers including Alex Molnar, Terrence Wiley, and Teresa McCarty. These scholars were internationally known in educational policy research, and perhaps more importantly as public intellectuals. They were also at odds with many of the policies being promoted by the Arizona State Department of Education, especially the development of unregulated charter schools, English-only instruction, and the development of and the use of "high stakes" tests as both graduation requirements for K-12 students and as a way of evaluating teacher "merit." As a generalization, the COE faculty saw attacks on public education as a policy of right-wing politicians, of which Arizona has no shortage.

The meeting was held in a lecture hall, faculty seated in the "student" desks and Crow standing at the podium on a raised dais. One of the more junior faculty asked president Crow what his position as a policy analyst was on some of these issues. Red faced and obviously angry, Crow came down from the dais and shouted directly at Glass and Berliner, who were seated next to each other. I am paraphrasing, but the gist was that "Policy analysts do not take positions. Their job is to collect data for the real decision makers to use in setting policy." The faculty remained mutely embarrassed while Crow's angry tirade went on for some time. The adversarial relationship between ASU's COE and the conservative officials at the State Department of Education was clearly more than a sore point for Crow. Moreover, he clearly intended to do something about it.

Berliner's book *The Manufactured Crisis* (Berliner and Biddle 1995) exposed and debunked the right-wing attack on public schools. Alex Molnar's work excoriated the effect of business on public schools (Molnar 2001). Through The Education Policy Research Unit (EPRU), Alex and his colleagues quickly and directly attacked misinformation distributed by right-wing think tanks; Gene Glass had created one of the first online, peer-reviewed scholarly journals in education, *Education Policy Analysis Archives* (http://epaa.asu.edu/ojs/), which freely distributed a good deal of policy analysis similarly countering attacks on public schools and disproving many of the claims by those who advocated market-based school reforms like vouchers and charter schools. Glass and Berliner had each published peer-reviewed papers showing that so-called charter schools operated to increase racial and social class segregation. And Smith was examining the Arizona school controversies as "political spectacle" (Smith, Miller-Kahn, Heinecke, and Jarvis 2004). At the time, Thomas "Tom" Horne had recently replaced Lisa Graham Keegan as the State Superintendent of Public Instruction for Arizona.

In 1995 Keegan had laid plans to develop a test required for students to graduate high school, and the following year the legislature established AIMS, the Arizona Instrument to Measure Standards. In 1999, the first official year of the test, nine out of ten sophomores failed the math exam.[24] As one of the foremost statisticians in educational research, Glass testified in court that, even if the curriculum and the examination questions were in alignment, there was no scientific basis for where to set the "cut point" for passing or failure. It was purely a political decision whether 60, 70, or 80 percent of students "passed" the exam.

Both Keegan and Horne pushed extremely conservative agendas mandating English Only instruction, advocated for school vouchers or tax refunds for parents sending their children to private (including religious) schools, and eventually banning Ethnic Studies in K-12 schools. The adversarial relationship between Educational Policy Studies at ASU and the State Department of Education was, in my opinion, a factor motivating Crow's anger, which at the time seemed both out of control and inappropriate for his first meeting with more than 100 faculty members of one of the largest and most successful colleges of Education in the nation.

The college got a new dean and was reorganized and re-branded as "The Mary Lou Fulton Institute and Graduate School of Education" but the 4000+ undergraduates in the Teacher Preparation Program were placed under a different dean. This was done in two back-to-back half-hour meetings called by the Provost—they took place at the exact moment of the Obama inauguration. In the Tuesday, January 20, 2009, meetings, the faculty were given the new Organization Chart, and after a brief descriptive presentation (no questions), faculty were asked to leave through the back door so staff could file in through the front door.

Mary Lou Fulton and Graduate School of Education staff were told that they would each meet with their supervisor within the next few hours and would receive an envelope. Some were told to empty their desks and go home immediately; others, with more seniority, were expected to stay at their posts through October. I cannot even write about the shock and tears of people who had just been summarily fired, almost all women, some of whom I had worked with at the university for fifteen years.

This "reorganization" essentially left the graduate programs without financial support beyond grant overhead funds. The new dean dressed very well and assured us that everything would be fine. But I noticed that the new programs had not received any of the "magic" words like "sustainability," "global," "embedded," or even "student success" (discussed below). I took this as a strong indication that the enterprise was doomed from the start. I had stopped going to faculty meetings, considering them a waste of time and a sham democratic process, but as cynical as I was, I was not prepared for a text from one of my junior colleagues who wrote from a meeting "What does 'disestablished' mean?" I did not have the heart to text back. The Mary Lou Fulton College of Education (MLF) was "disestablished" in May 2010 by the Arizona Board of Regents. The memo read in part: "The faculty in the Mary Lou Fulton Institute and Graduate School of Education *will be reassigned to the appropriate academic unit that best fits their expertise*" (emphasis added).[25] In its place a MLF "Teachers College" was established. Seemingly little or no thought had been given to approximately 400 graduate students in the "pipeline." The new dean left abruptly in mid-term, December 2010.

I was able to move my tenure line to the Hugh Downs School of Human Communication; many older faculty, including those named above as public intellectuals, retired; some of the best and brightest moved to other, more hospitable, universities. Many faculty from Psychology in Education, especially the program in Measurement and Statistics and Methodological Studies (MSMS), went to "Family Dynamics" and a rather large group found themselves outside of any program but became affiliated with a newly branded "School of Social Transformation." Then an even more telling set of demands took place. In a widely circulated memo from the Provost dated August 12, 2010, it was announced that

> Faculty from the MLF Institute that have been reassigned to other departments continue to have teaching responsibilities in the Mary Lou Fulton Teachers College. They cannot take on teaching assignments at this time. . . [but] **will be dependent on the needs of the Mary Lou Fulton College to deliver the programs under their responsibility** (bold face in the original).

This communique solved the immediate problem of what to do with the graduate students still needing classes, committee members, and chairs. But it accomplished a far more important administrative goal of defining faculty as "employees" to be reassigned as needed or desired. In my own case, even though I was a full-time faculty member in Communication, I was required to teach "my full load" in the Teachers College. At one point, when I was teaching

Communication classes, my chair received a "bill" from the Teachers College for $4,000 per course—I presume to cover a TA's salary.

Re-branding and Weakening the Power of the Disciplines

George Ritzer (1996) used the organization of fast food industries as exemplary of new management systems that demanded "efficiency," "calculability," "predictability," and "control." McDonaldization also included reliance on "shadow labor" (Lambert 2011). In the fast food industry this means tasks such as picking up and "fixing" your food and bussing your table. Lately it has meant "checking" yourself out at the supermarket.

In "The New American University" shadow work has meant that students go online to do everything from registering and scheduling their classes and paying their bills, to creating their "Program of Study" and even, for graduate students, scheduling the room for their oral defense. For faculty "shadow work" includes preparing an online Faculty Activity Report (FAR) for annual review, managing benefits and time and leave statements, filing grades, and so on. Shadow work eliminated many staff positions including departmental secretaries, administrative assistants, and business managers. Mass firings of administrative staff with institutional memory aided in the "culture shock" intended to break up existing social relationships.

McDonaldization accelerated already ongoing processes of replacing tenure and tenure-track faculty with adjuncts who were paid by the course and received little if any benefits. As I wrote in an earlier review of Dennis Hayes and Robin Wynyard's anthology on the McDonaldization of Higher Education (Margolis 2004, p. 368):

> Where not so long ago professors "owned" the tools of scholarship, controlled the labor process, and certified the quality of our product, the process of McDonaldization has torn this relation asunder. Rapidly increasing student faculty ratios, mass classes, and the use of low-wage teaching assistants and adjunct faculty have changed the job of professor. (Hayes and Wynyard 2002, p. 64 ff.)

One of the most visible results of the practices McDonaldization set in motion has been "re-branding." While still Arizona State University, in almost every case it was simultaneously referred to as "The New American University" and was planned to become the largest university in the United States—which it has achieved. In fall of 2010 ASU had more than 58,000 students.[26] Under the slogan "One University in Many Places" (which faculty and students quickly turned into "one university all over the place"), ASU East campus was re-branded the "Polytechnic" campus. The school of art and the school of design were merged into the "Herberger Institute for Design and the Arts." The ASU College of Liberal Arts and Sciences (CLAS), reflecting its own changes, describes itself thus:

> Just as ASU is positioning itself as a model of the New American University, the college is redefining liberal arts education for the 21st century. Along with such traditional core departments as chemistry, English, physics and psychology, the college has created a number of transdisciplinary schools that facilitate the creation of new knowledge across disciplinary boundaries. Among these are the schools of Earth and Space Exploration, Human Evolution and Social Change, International Letters and Cultures, and Social and Family Dynamics.[27]

Within CLAS, the School of Justice Studies, which had taken 25 years to build a nationally recognized name and reputation, was rebranded as "Justice and Social Inquiry." Most of the ethnic studies programs and women and gender studies were downgraded and incorporated in the new "School of Social Transformation" that modestly proclaims "Together we create new knowledge that challenges conventional thinking and transforms the world."[28] Meanwhile, Chicana/o Studies became ASU's "School of Transborder Studies." The CLAS at ASU is currently composed of the following:

Earth and Space Exploration

Geographical Sciences and Urban Planning

Historical, Philosophical and Religious Studies

Human Communication

Human Evolution and Social Change

International Letters and Cultures

Life Sciences

Mathematical and Statistical Sciences

Politics and Global Studies

Social and Family Dynamics

Social Transformation

Transborder Studies

Departments:

Aerospace Studies

Chemistry and Biochemistry

English

Military Science

Physics

Psychology

Speech and Hearing Science

Programs:

American Indian Studies

Jewish Studies

Naval Science[29]

This is not simply about name changing, which might simply be amusingly pretentious. It is about disrupting the power of academic departments and their connections to larger disciplines and professional organizations. While there are sociologists in Communication, Justice and Social Inquiry, and so on, there is no department of sociology and thus no direct connection with the American Sociological Association which might interject itself in matters of promotion and tenure or research ethics. Anthropology is in a similar situation, re-branded "the ASU School of Human Evolution & Social Change." Similar dis-integration occurred in other schools and colleges. The Ira A. Fulton School of Engineering restructured its departments such as Computer Science, Electrical, Mechanical, and Aerospace Engineering into five new units. Initially, the faculty were given the mandate to identify new names that included none of the original departmental terms in their titles. After a brief softening (anecdotally, at least partially resulting from funding agency confusion about the applicability of faculty from the new departments to apply for funding) a series of generic titles similar to the other "reorganizations" were developed, also with little resemblance to their professional associations and organizations:

School of Biological and Health Systems Engineering

School of Computing, Informatics, and Decision Systems Engineering

School of Electrical, Computer and Energy Engineering

School for Engineering of Matter, Transport and Energy

School of Sustainable Engineering and the Built Environment[30]

The importance of disciplines in the development of science cannot be overestimated. When Stephen Toulmin wrote his 1972 rejoinder to Kuhn's *Structure of Scientific Revolutions* (Kuhn 1970) he argued that

> what was fundamental to the development of "human understanding" was not "paradigms" subject to radical transformation in "crisis" times, but rather "disciplines"—that is, the stable institutions of the continuing scientific community which are predicated upon assumptions as to how knowledge was to be gained (e.g., physiological processes are to be explained in chemical terms). Thus, Toulmin concentrated on explaining how social institutions develop procedures for understanding, how they change those procedures, evaluate their efficacy and present the understanding gathered from them. (Toulmin 1972) (Cited in Margolis, 1976, p. 26)

The position of "The New American University" is thus antithetical and hostile to the notion that the professoriate consisted of independent intellectuals, whose work was best judged by disciplines of like-minded scholars familiar with the presuppositions and standards of truth. Instead, professors are seen as employees of the university as corporation, and the officers of that corporation should be free to hire or fire, as well as to determine their working conditions.

Multidisciplinarity, has taken place slowly over decades as the arts and sciences developed new fields—psychopharmacology, behavioral genetics, justice studies and so on—created out of new knowledge and which developed their own "courts of reason" (Toulmin 1972). However, the creation of "made-up" disciplines like "social transformation" or "Language, Literacies and Technology" have quite the opposite effect by degrading independent researchers guided by disciplinary standards into mere employees. Moreover, future graduates may have a difficult time "selling" their degrees in traditional university settings.

Centralizing the Tenure Process

Another clear example of the centralizing of command and control structures took place in matters of promotion and tenure. It has always been the case that the last and deciding stage in the tenure and promotion process took place in the president's office. Except in unusual circumstances, recommendations from the scholar's department, college, or school, and the university tenure and promotion committee were accepted by the provost and president. But as the new president of Arizona State University, or just to show that there was a new sheriff in town, Dr. Crow made a number of decisions overriding tradition. In some cases tenure was awarded but not promotion, in other cases promotion but not tenure—which produced the odd effect of having an untenured professor eligible for a sabbatical. Several lawsuits resulted.

The University as Spectacle

Most colleges and universities have created themselves as "spectacle" whether through centuries of tradition like the Harvard-Yale football rivalry, or slightly more recent Texas A&M's bonfires. There are well-known "school colors" and mascots. Semi-professional college sports teams are consumption offered as spectacle and recreation. Nevertheless, in re-creating itself as "The" New American University, ASU has done more to manufacture itself as spectacle than most. Much of the new spectacle consists of re-branding and commercialism. There has been much concern expressed that ASU was perceived as a "party school" and not as a serious institution, and the new words expressed attempts to counter the image.

Faculty and students alike have mocked the "Word Salad" at "The New American University" because it consists of odd slogans like "We embrace complexity" that seem like they were written by Madison Avenue—they sound pretty but are generally empty of content—something like IBM's current advertisement about "engines of a smarter planet"[31]—as if there were dumb planets—or universities that embraced simplicity. On the ASU website the reader is told that "Eight design aspirations guide ASU's transformation." With the exception of perhaps number six, discussed earlier, this is a kind of magical thinking; either free-floating signifiers empty of content, or simply a publicist's restatement of what every university strives for:

01. Leverage Our Place
ASU embraces its cultural, socioeconomic and, physical setting.

02. Transform Society
ASU catalyzes social change by being connected to social needs.

03. Value Entrepreneurship
ASU uses its knowledge and encourages innovation.

04. Conduct Use-Inspired Research
ASU research has purpose and impact.

05. Enable Student Success
ASU is committed to the success of each unique student.

06. Fuse Intellectual Disciplines
ASU creates knowledge by transcending academic disciplines.

07. Be Socially Embedded
ASU connects with communities through mutually beneficial partnerships.

08. Engage Globally
ASU engages with people and issues locally, nationally and internationally.[32]

Yet another spectacle of McDonaldization is what is termed "Residential Life." Freshmen are generally required to live on campus as part of the ASU "experience" and there are a variety of choices in cost, amenities, and lifestyle. (It is also the case that while tuition for all three Arizona Universities is set by the Board of Regents, fees including dorm rents, meal tickets, and so on are not.)

Living on campus gives you access to a new world of opportunities in a dynamic university environment. The residential experience is designed to promote your academic and personal success and to help you make the most of your first year as a Sun Devil. Student housing at the Tempe campus is divided into neighborhoods, each offering its residents a variety of academic support services, study lounges and wireless connectivity, co-curricular programming and dining options.[33]

There are also "residential colleges" for example the Mary Lou Fulton Teachers College: "All first-time incoming freshman education majors are required to live in the Residential College unless they are exempt by University Housing." As part of the residential college experience one is promised dinner with the dean, ice cream socials, tutoring, peer mentoring etc.[34] It simultaneously creates a panoptical world in which the student is endlessly observed and must engage in impression management (Goffman [1959] 1971, pp. 203ff) and emotional labor (Hochschild 1983).

As another example of Ritzer's notion of "implosion" as a hallmark of McDonaldization in higher education, just this month (November 2011) another block of older student housing was bulldozed to make way for what is being described as "Tempe's most exclusive student housing community. . . . huge apartments and townhouses, leather-style sectional sofa, hardwood-style flooring, etc." The complex will include a fitness center, computer center and a "resort-style" pool.[35] While the term "exclusive" is unfortunate and suggests the publicist never learned American history,[36] this is intended for older and/or married students. If the new housing follows the pattern, the ground floor will be rented as retail space. Thus the dorm and the resort hotel have merged.

Conclusion

Actually there is no way to conclude or adequately summarize what is an ongoing process. McDonaldization has proceeded faster and more completely in England because, as many of the chapters in the *McDonaldization of Higher Education* indicate, their system is much more centralized than higher education in the U.S. (Hayes and Wynyard 2002).

Nevertheless, the process is bound to accelerate here due to a combination of forces including the ongoing economic crisis that is leading many states to reduce funding for state colleges and universities; competition with private for-profit universities specializing in "have it your way" schedules, simulation, and the manipulation of time and space through computerized instruction; increasing tuition and other costs of living that reinforce the student as consumer-of-a-service view; and the demand for "edutainment."

Will "The New American University" become a model? Perhaps. But there is an internal contradiction in the "re-branding" which, as with all products, is intended to set ASU apart from similar products. It must remain unique and have a reasonable cost if it is to meet its 100,000 student goal. Moreover, it is unlikely that neologisms like the school of "social transformation" will catch on and may not even have much shelf life here. There have been several other units here that were given spectacular names, had a few years in the sun, and then quietly disappeared.

Given the diffuse nature of higher education in the U.S., and its already strong hierarchical structure, the McDonaldized University will likely occupy the same kind of niche as the food franchise. The Ivy Leagues and similar "highly selective" universities (Stanford, the "Seven

Sisters". . .) will remain at the top. High quality and selective state universities—Wisconsin–Madison, Berkeley, Michigan–Ann Arbor—may adopt some elements of McDonaldization but have little reason to re-brand themselves. Small high quality liberal arts colleges like the so-called "little three" in New England, the Claremont colleges, Bard and so on already offer real individual instruction and mentoring and have no need for the simulacrum created through McDonaldization.

Many of the old elements of the hidden curricula have quietly returned. Ties with the military, especially in Research One universities, are if anything much stronger than they were in the 1960s. There are top-secret facilities at ASU like the former "Air Force Research Lab" near the polytechnic campus where public/private partnerships are planned.[37] There is also a semi-public Army/ASU project to create flexible screens for battlefield use.[38] It is not unrelated that Criminal Justice is one of the fastest growing fields and where job opportunities are available; and ASU offers majors ranging from the BS to the Ph.D.[39] Also many of the research grants solicited focus on developing new technologies for Homeland Security.[40]

Although the old gender-segregated dorms will not return, "choice" has allowed some elements to be re-instated. In one of ASU's dormitory neighborhoods, the building is co-educational—but the fourth floor is for women only. All buildings on campus are non-smoking and alcohol can only be served in the University Club. Nevertheless, binge drinking is a major problem, and there have been alcohol-related student deaths.

Fear of terrorism and school shootings have replaced fear of atomic attack. In place of duck and cover drills, ASU has basically developed a militarized police force that patrols the campus on every type of vehicle from foot patrols to Segways. When we arrived in 1995, the police "headquarters" was a modular building and the campus police were unarmed. Today they carry hand guns and what I presume is pepper spray. All three Arizona universities have armed police with assault rifles.[41] There have been several bills in the legislature to allow faculty and students to carry concealed weapons on campus but, although the last one passed, the governor vetoed it. The new campus police headquarters is a large building defined by a bar-like façade, and they have 141 personnel, many of whom no doubt spend hours monitoring surveillance cameras.[42] Security video cameras are all over campus; surveillance is the new *in loco parentis*, I suppose. Regardless of how one feels about the direction taken by this evolution of higher education, it would be an interesting exercise to assess the effectiveness of the "The New American University" and what alternatives might be possible in fulfilling the significant educational mandate given by Arizona's founders. Section six of Article 11 of the Arizona Constitution outlines this charge (italics added for emphasis):

Text of Section 6:

Admission of students of both sexes to state educational institutions; tuition; common school system.

The university and all other state educational institutions shall be open to students of both sexes, and the instruction furnished shall be as nearly free as possible. The legislature shall provide for a system of common schools by which a free school shall be established and maintained in every school district for at least six months in each year, which school shall be open to all pupils between the ages of six and twenty-one years.[43]

Notes

1. Cf. http://en. wikipedia.org/wiki/Nelson_A. _Rockefeller#Education
2. There were of course exceptions like the City University of New York, Hunter College and The University of Chicago that had helped many immigrant children get higher educations. But nothing like the massive expansion of public universities that began with the GI Bill.
3. There is no doubt that the strong form was dominant in the 60s and early 70s. Even in the state universities there were few students of color. The gendering process visible in dorm life continued as women were tracked into traditional occupations—teaching and nursing for example (at New Paltz art education was a popular choice). Everyone knew that in general "state universities" were for the middle classes and upwardly mobile as opposed to the Ivy Leagues, the Seven Sisters or Stanford.
4. Taken from the online version at http://bau2. uibk. ac. at/sg/poe/works/p_letter.html
5. The full text is available online: http://www2. fiu.edu/~yaf/sharon.html
6. Full text at http://www.h-net.org/~hst306/documents/huron.html
7. Ibid.
8. A video of the speech is online at http://www.youtube.com/watch? v=u5o_0ZYA5HM
9. The text of Eisenhower's Farewell address can be read here: http://www.h-net.org/~hst306/documents/indust. html, and seen on BBC TV here: http://www.youtube.com/watch? v=nUXtyIQjubU
10. Clark Kerr's influential 1963 book detailed the successes and troubling influences of the emerging "multiversity" that included undergraduate and graduate teaching, professional schools like medicine and law, as well as being the most important center for research and development. Cf. Kerr, Clark. [1963] 2001. *The Uses of the University: The Godkin Lectures on the Essentials of Free Government and the Duties of the Citizen.* Reprint, Cambridge, MA: Harvard University Press. A decade later, Talcott Parsons & Platt's *The American University* explained how the structure of the university, with its disparate functions including undergraduate and graduate education, professional schools like law and medicine, and research grew and were indispensable. Parsons, Talcott, and Gerald M. Platt. 1973. *The American University.* Cambridge, MA: Harvard University Press.
11. http://en. wikipedia.org/wiki/General_education_requirements
12. "The term "affirmative action" was first used in the United States. It first appeared in Executive Order 10925, which was signed by President John F. Kennedy on March 6, 1961, and it was used to refer to measures to achieve non-discrimination. In 1965, President Lyndon B. Johnson issued Executive Order 11246, which required federal contractors to take "affirmative action" to hire without regard to race, religion and national origin. In 1968, gender was added to the anti-discrimination list. . . . In 2003, a Supreme Court decision concerning affirmative action in universities allowed educational institutions to consider race as a factor in admitting students, but ruled that strict point systems are unconstitutional." http://en. wikipedia.org/wiki/ Affirmative_action
13. See chapters in Margolis, Eric. 2001. *The Hidden Curriculum in Higher Education.* New York: Routledge.
14. http://sts. asu.edu/
15. *BBC News World Edition*, "Millions join global anti-war protests," February 17, 2003, http://news. bbc. co. uk/2/hi/europe/2765215. stm (retrieved November 12, 2011); *Frontline*, "Operation Iraqi Freedom: A chronology of the six-week invasion of Iraq, drawn from the FRONTLINE documentary" PBS, http://www.pbs. org/wgbh/pages/frontline/shows/invasion/cron/ (retrieved November 25, 2011)
16. http://news. harvard.edu/gazette/story/2011/03/harvard-welcomes-back-rotc/
17. http://en. wikipedia.org/wiki/Church_Committee. See also full report: Church, Frank, John G. Tower, et al. 1975. *Covert Action in Chile 1963–1973.* Washington, DC: U.S. Government Printing Office 63–372.
18. http://en. wikipedia.org/wiki/Human_Terrain_System
19. http://en. wikipedia.org/wiki/Federal_Family_Education_Loan_Program; http://en. wikipedia.org/wiki/Federal_Direct_Student_Loan_Program
20. http://www.theatlantic.com/business/archive/2011/08/chart-of-the-day-student-loans-have-grown-511–since-1999/243821/
21. http://www.forbes.com/2010/08/01/student-loan-financial-aid-opinions-colleges-10–debt.html
22. Grade inflation was also boosted by formal student course evaluations and informal online "rate your professor" sites.
23. A list of Dr. Crow's relations with elements of the U.S. government can be found in his biography on *Wikipedia.* http://en. wikipedia.org/wiki/Michael_M. _Crow
24. http://www.azcentral.com/arizonarepublic/news/articles/0516aimslawsuit0516.html
25. https: //provost. asu.edu/files/shared/capc/April%202010/UAC%20and%20CAPC%20Acad%20Re-org.pdf
26. http://en. wikipedia.org/wiki/List_of_United_States_university_campuses_by_enrollment
27. http://clas. asu.edu/about

28. It is interesting that after "Justice Studies" formed itself when a group of sociologists left Sociology, it took decades to have the name—hence the legitimacy of the degree—recognized. Many of these new brands will have the same problem placing graduate students from programs that, no matter how novel and transdisciplinary, have no established meaning in academia; http://sst. clas. asu.edu
29. http://clas. asu.edu/academicunits
30. http://engineering. asu.edu/schools/
31. https: //www.ibm.com/engines
32. http://newamericanuniversity. asu.edu/design-aspirations/
33. http://www.asu.edu/housing/
34. http://education. asu.edu/content/residential-colleges
35. http://vistadelsol.com/
36. "Exclusive" in American history meant no Blacks, no Jews, and no Mexicans allowed—depending on what part of the country in which the exclusive housing or country club was located.
37. http://www.azcentral.com/community/mesa/articles/2010/11/21/20101121asu-mesa-gateway-research-lab. html
38. http://www.asu.edu/feature/includes/spring05/readmore/flexdisplay.html
39. http://ccj. asu.edu/degree-programs
40. http://asunews. asu.edu/20080228_homelandsecurity
41. http://www.azcentral.com/arizonarepublic/local/articles/0305asuguns0305.html
42. http://cfo. asu.edu/police
43. http://ballotpedia.org/wiki/index. php/Article_11%2C_Arizona_Constitution

References

Althusser, Louis, 1971. Ideology and Ideological State Apparatuses: Notes Towards an Investigation," Pp. 127-186, in *Lenin and Philosophy*, New York: Monthly Review Press.

Apple, M. W., and Nancy R. King. 1977. What Do Schools Teach? *Curriculum Inquiry* 6: 341–358.

Berliner, David, and Bruce J. Biddle. 1995. *The Manufactured Crisis: Myths, Fraud, and the Attack on America's Public Schools*. Reading, MA: Addison Wesley.

Bloom, Allan. 1987. *The Closing of the American Mind*. New York: Simon and Schuster.

Goffman, Erving. [1959] 1971. *The Presentation of Self in Everyday Life*. Reprint, London: Penguin Books.

Hayes, Dennis, and Robin Wynyard. 2002. *The McDonaldization of Higher Education*. Westport, CT: Greenwood Press.

Hochschild, Arlie. 1983. *The Managed Heart: Commercialization of human feeling*. Berkeley: University of California Press.

Klatch, Rebecca E. 1999. *A Generation Divided: The new left, the right, and the 1960s*. Berkeley: University of California Press.

Kuhn, Thomas S. 1970. *The Structure of Scientific Revolutions*. Chicago: University of Chicago Press.

Lambert, Craig. 2011. Our Unpaid, Extra Shadow Work. *New York Times*, October 29, p. SR 12.

Margolis, Eric. 1976. Paradigms, Disciplines and Human Understanding. In *Forms and Formulations of Education*, ed. E. Rose, 16–44. Lincoln: University of Nebraska Press.

———. 2001. *The Hidden Curriculum in Higher Education*. New York: Routledge.

———. 2004. Review of *The McDonaldization of Higher Education*, edited by Dennis Hayes and Robin Wynyard. *The Journal of Higher Education* 75: 368–370.

Margolis, Eric, Michael Soldatenko, Sandra Acker, and Marina Gair. 2001. Peekaboo: Hiding and Outing the Curriculum. In *The Hidden Curriculum in Higher Education*, ed. E. Margolis, 1–19. New York: Routledge.

Molnar, Alex. 2001. *Giving Kids the Business: The Commercialization of America's Schools*. Boulder, CO: Westview Press.

Parsons, Talcott, and Gerald M. Platt. 1973. *The American University*. Cambridge, MA: Harvard University Press.

Pritchett, Price, and Ron Pound. 1993. High-Velocity Culture Change: A Handbook for Managers." Dallas, Texas: Pritchell & Associates.

Ritzer, George. 2002. Enchanting McUniversity: Toward a Spectacularly Irrational University Quotidian. In *The McDonaldization of Higher Education*, ed. D. Hayes and R. Wynyard, 19–32. Westport CT. : Bergin & Garvey.

Ritzer, George. 1996. *The McDonaldization of Society*. Thousand Oaks, CA: Pine Forge Press.

Rodriguez, Richard. [1982] 1983. *Hunger of Memory: The Education of Richard Rodriguez*. Toronto: Bantam Books.

Smith, Mary Lee, Linda Miller-Kahn, Walter Heinecke, and Patricia Jarvis. 2004. *Political spectacle and the fate of of American schools*. New York: RoutledgeFalmer.

Soldatenko, Michael. 1998. The Origins of Academic Chicano Studies 1967–1970: The Emergence of Empirical and Perspectivist Chicano Studies. *Latino Studies Journal* 9 (2): 3–25.

———. 1999. Empirical Chicano Studies: The Formation of Academic Chicano Studies, 1970–1975. *Latino Studies Journal* 10 (3): 67–96.

Steal, Shelby. 1991. *The Content of Our Character: A New Vision of Race in America*. New York: Harper Perennial.

Sykes, Charles J. 1988. *Profscam: Professors and the Demise of Higher Education*. Washington, DC: Regnery Gateway.

Toulmin, Stephen. 1972. *Human Understanding: The Collective Use and Evolution of Concepts*. Princeton, NJ: Princeton University Press.

PART FOUR

Administration: Negotiating the Labyrinth

CHAPTER EIGHTEEN

Leading from the Middle

Embracing the Role of Department Chair

JAY PAREDES SCRIBNER

> A basic truth of management—if not of life—is that nearly everything looks like a failure in the middle.
> —R. M. Kanter (1997)

As uninspiring as the above quote might seem, for a department chair or department chair-to-be, it is quite apropos. I appreciate Rosabeth Moss Kanter's comment above (and all of her writings) because when you're "in the middle" it's often difficult to feel successful even when progress is being made. As a current department chair and having served in the role at two different universities, my sense of what a department chair does has evolved with my experience. Certainly the role is one of leadership. But it is a role that requires one to share leadership with others to get things done. It's a leadership role that requires much more negotiation, convincing, and cajoling than it does directing and managing. The "middling role" of departmental leadership requires the chair to negotiate simultaneously and on myriad issues with different groups of people (e.g., faculty students, and administrators), different organizational levels (department, college, and university), and constituents in different contexts (internal to the university and external). In addition to negotiating, the role also involves buffering, integrating and adapting to pressures beyond the department and emanating from a multitude of origins.

But while the imperative for the "middle manager" in positions like the department chair may be to negotiate and work toward consensus, it does create somewhat of a paradox. That is to say, when a department chair tries to make everyone happy all the time the result is, more often than not, not much. A major challenge (if not truism) facing department chairs is the tension embodied in the *rugged individualist* mindset instilled in faculty members by their own institutions versus the need to also attend to matters that serve the "greater good" of the department and university. Tensions also manifest when chairs attempt to navigate between cultures of research and scholarship on the one hand, and teaching and learning on the other. The latter tensions have been heightened in recent years as universities are being held increasingly accountable to demonstrate their relevance to the external community in a way that directly challenges not only cultures of research and scholarship, but also teaching and service.

But make no mistake, serving colleagues, colleges, and one's university as department chair is an invigorating and rewarding experience. This short essay aims to bring attention to aspects of the department chair role and the tensions facing its occupant that are glossed over by quaint catch phrases such as "Department Chair, first among equals" that are at best of little use and at worst misguided. I attempt to pass along some of the major themes I keep present during my day-to-day practice as a department chair. These themes are not new, and I try to connect them with some examples of literature that I have found helpful over the years.

A Brief Review of the Literature: Some "Big Picture" Ideas

The literature on the role of the department chair in higher education is replete with advice about all sorts of relevant topics (see for example, Bolman & Gallos, 2011; Carroll & Wolverton, 2004; Gmelch, 2004). They range from studies about the behaviors, beliefs, and activities of successful department chairs, to administrative dimensions such as human resource management, development, and support. Recent scholarly and professional literature supports the fact that today's department chairs are dealing with fiscal challenges just as their predecessors have in the past, but with a twist. Today's fiscal challenges are coupled with and exacerbated by increased competition for students from "for profits" and non-profits alike and unprecedented (and permanent) decreases in state financial support for public higher education.

The literature also advises department chairs on the traditional topics of leadership and management. In an environment of unpredictable resources, there is growing pressure to be "mission driven" to have a "strategic vision" and to be able to account for the productivity of the department and individual faculty members—in other words, to have a direction and to demonstrate the department's worth. Like it or not, department chairs are operating in an environment of accountability and being measured by standards that not only reflect traditional measures of academic success, but new measures (and sets of values) more economic and social in nature.

With all the dimensions of leadership that I could focus on, I will instead just focus on a few central themes. With the cognitive demands and multifaceted nature of "leading from the middle" in complex organizations like universities, it helps to categorize and tame the knowledge we do have into guiding principles that we can rely on during our daily professional practice. As a successful CEO I know likes to say, even in the best of circumstances we can only access a fraction of our knowledge base at any given moment. So we need strategies to 1) draw upon that knowledge and experience when the situation demands and 2) stay focused on what really matters in our work. Research on professional learning backs this informal observation. The hot action of practice more often than not forces us to rely on the same truncated set of knowledge and solutions in spite of the limitless and ever changing source of challenges to organizations (Eraut, 1994). In response to these human limitations I try to always keep the following three categories in mind: fostering a culture of continuous improvement, distributing leadership to staff and faculty, and building trust.

The Continuously Improving Department

Edgar Schein, in his classic book *Organizational Culture and Leadership* (1992), encouraged us to consider the leader's role in developing organizational culture as well as culture's influence on leadership. He also argued eloquently for those inclined to bring about organizational change to consider not only culture but also the point in an organization's life cycle at which that culture exists. At the risk of oversimplifying Schein's point, older more entrenched organizations often have more deeply rooted cultures (agriculture being the origin of the culture metaphor). Given that most academic organizations have rather entrenched and developed cultures—defined by both the broader institution and the unique cultural dimensions of the department—my argument is not to say that leadership is constrained, but rather that one must be well attuned to organizational culture and history to lead effectively.

In my experience department leadership centers on the need to foster an organizational culture that embodies continuous improvement. The dichotomy represented by the rugged individualist versus the organizationally minded colleague is a tension that needs to be continually managed (and respected). On the one hand, the lifeblood of the university is the faculty member's research program. To be successful, faculty must be single-minded (even in their collaborative activities) to compete for external funding and to produce scholarship that enacts the university's mission, serves the broader community, and meets the standard of performance set down by the college and department. On the other hand, organizational work doesn't get done on its own. Programs need to be developed, managed, and revised. Advisory boards should be created and utilized. Students need to be advised, and so on.

In departments I've been associated with we address this tension by always keeping focused on the one aspect of our work that drives all else—students. From this perspective we never forget that all our work (research, teaching, or service) one way or another derives from the fact that we must address the learning needs of our students. As department chair it's my job to show why this is so and why it behooves us to reflect this understanding in our work. As we work with students, they sustain other aspects of our work. To that end, I have found the most effective way to bring this point home is to focus on creating robust programs, healthy class sizes, and appropriate faculty advising loads. In my field, demands (both from within and external to the department) pressure us to make decisions that threaten this balance. Universities tend to see professional schools as cash cows and encourage large graduate programs of master's and doctoral students. This approach is misguided. What departments need to be healthy is the right mix of students. In most professional fields the demand for our degrees lies mostly at the master's level and thus our programs should represent relatively larger numbers of entry-level graduate students. With doctoral students come much heavier advising loads, and any faculty member with a large doctoral advising load would admit that the larger the doctoral advising load the less able one is to leverage dissertation research into published scholarship. Astonishingly, this is a habit that has been hard to break in my field.

Leadership as an Organizational Quality

Another departmental leadership principle I try to keep present is to remember that leadership is an organizational quality, not an authority bestowed on any one person by virtue of the position they hold. As Ogawa and Bossert (1995) so aptly described, leadership is a quality, an attribute, that flows through organizations. And individuals are the medium through which leadership flows. People occupy roles that reflect a sense of responsibility, accounting, and authority for decision-making, but leadership is not bestowed upon them. It is exercised. Thus, leadership exists only when it is exercised. The ability to recognize the opportunity to exercise one's leadership capacity is what defines who is a leader at a given point in time. . . and that leader could be any one in the organization. Burns (1978) described this phenomenon when reflecting on the role of context in creating opportunities for leadership and how a changing context can both create and undo leaders.

Abstract as the notions above may seem, I have found that thinking of leadership as an organizational quality and remembering the role of context in leadership have helped me to 1) stay grounded in my role as chair, 2) never forget that I am surrounded by incredible knowledge, skill, and creative talent (much beyond what myself have), and 3) tap into the leadership of others when the shifting context demands leadership that I can't provide. I try to turn these abstract notions into practical action by never underestimating people's desire to contribute to the organizational good. The tension embodied in the individual-community dichotomy is worsened when chairs assume their colleagues would rather close the door, work on their research, and prepare for class. In fact, I've almost never encountered a situation in which someone turned down the chance to develop an important policy, or lead any number of continuous improvement activities.

The Conflict-Trust Paradox

Finally, I believe the single most necessary ingredient to the prolonged success for any department is the willingness of department chairs and faculty alike to continually engage in those activities that build trust among colleagues (Bolman & Gallos, 2011; Starkey & Stone-Briggs, 2009). In my experience, engaging in difficult conversations without fear of reprisal and advocating and defending the department to the external environment are key to ensure that obstacles do not short-circuit efforts at organizational improvement. The literature bears this out: the most important elements to building the level of trust needed to sustain continuous improvement and a positive culture include 1) conversations that lead to positive change by focusing on issues (not personalities) and that assume good intentions (but acknowledge varied value sets) (Miller, 2002) and 2) buffering and adapting to external pressure the department when the situation demands it (Schein, 1992).

Conversations that resolve conflict in organizations are paramount and require collaboration that is built on trust. In this symbiotic pattern the building of trust among a group requires that conversations address meaningful topics that require resolution. It is within this space that conflict becomes a precious natural resource of the organization (Kanter, Stein, & Jick, 1992). Conversations—be they about organizational mission, direction, scarce resources, etc. —that instill trust need to value differences of opinion and leverage these differences for the betterment of the organization. They need to nurture and reinforce transparency. And they must focus on setting mutually meaningful priorities and directions. Another dimension to trust building is to always operate with a commitment to listening and understanding and to instill that commitment in others. Mutual respect in action requires a commitment to listening, to airing concerns publically and properly with a focus on the issues, and to gathering as many facts as necessary before making decisions (Gunsalus, 2006).

My faculty colleagues and I have spent substantial energy developing a sound department culture based on trust and the assumption of good intentions by making the act of seeking out areas of improvement an organizational norm, not an exception. We actively seek out those tensions. Then we strategize and prioritize our responses to these challenges and put our strategies into action. As a group we have developed this through hard work, sustained focus, determination, and an awareness that the fruits of change don't ripen overnight. There's nothing magical or easy about it. It's a habit that needs to be developed. The distinguishing factor between departments that improve and adapt and those that don't is that the former make and implement important group decisions and the latter do not.

To illustrate how these conversations might play out, one of the challenges in higher education is the phenomenon of academic silos. Silos are great for storing things like feed grain, but in academic departments they isolate and balkanize. The actual challenge is to respect and encourage program identity, but not at the expense of department identity, interdisciplinary work, and, dare I say, efficiency. More often than not the typical department culture consists of a "contrived collegiality" (Hargreaves, 1990) that defines the interactions among faculty in and across the program areas. Unfortunately, this "elephant" has been present in the room during much of the time I've been a faculty member or department chair. And it has limited collaborative opportunities and thus handicapped potential. For a department chair one of the ongoing, never-ending challenges is to break down silos where they exist while also recognizing difference among degree programs and scholarly focus. I've spent a lot of time working with colleagues to (re)conceptualize how we think of ourselves as a department, how we ought to think of ourselves, and how our work within and between program areas should change (or not). This dialogic process aims at surfacing people's fears, frustrations, and hopes regarding what we were and what we want to become. In fact, we should always remember that one of the most popular strategies for addressing conflict in organizations is to avoid it. As Jeffrey Miller (2002) argued, a negative implication of avoiding conflict is, paradoxically, to create additional counterproductive stress in the organization that leads to rumor mongering, power tripping, information hoarding and so on are disastrous for organizational health. Thus, this process of engaging in difficult conversations should have no end; what changes over time is the intensity of the dialogue that ebbs and flows as issues are dealt with, as personnel changes, and as the environment brings and retracts stressors. This dialogic process has helped us to identify those issues that are solely the purview of program areas and those issues that the entire department should worry about (e.g., policies and practices surrounding tenure and promotion, student progress, doctoral education, and any number of policy-related issues). Struggling to understand and define our community allows us to know what we must worry about together and where we celebrate our distinctive interests—identifying what was common and distinct among us has actually made the department more cohesive.

Another key theme in this conflict-trust paradox is the buffering and adapting role that department chairs can play to help protect faculty from external demands that may keep them from focusing on their core activities of research and teaching, or at times, to integrate external demands into departmental functions (Schneider & Somers, 2006). A common external demand these days is the pressure to partner with external stakeholders. In my field, partnerships are seen as a mechanism to increase credibility with key external stakeholders. I have spent a lot of time and energy developing and sustaining partnerships over the years. Partnerships with natural competitors (i.e., other universities) have actually increased enrollments and strengthened programs. Partnerships have increased grant opportunities for faculty and strengthened our pool of adjuncts. The limited space here cannot do justice to the power of partnerships as a source of organizational learning and adaption or to the power of collaboration as a strategy to maximize positive organizational impact on the community. In short, the process of vetting, engaging with, and assessing partnerships with external entities is itself an exercise in continuous improvement.

Another aspect of departmental leadership that is critical for building trust is the embrace of diversity in all its forms. In so doing, we harness the energy and full capacity of our precious human resources that can lead to true innovation and a culture of risk taking that pays huge dividends in myriad ways in the future. Embracing diversity is an investment in organizational health and vitality. My life and work experiences have helped me learn to continuously seek to understand what I don't know, and frankly may not even see. As department chair, my role is not merely to celebrate or value diversity, but to engage it, to make the department as diverse as possible and to harness the power of diversity as a learning tool for faculty and students. Our own faculty are critical players in diversifying departments across all sorts of dimensions. Faculty culture must be open to diverse ways of thinking, teaching, producing scholarship, and being. As department chairs, our commitment to diversity manifests in various ways. We must recruit, hire, and mentor with the fortitude that it takes to challenge sometimes strong but hidden undercurrents to maintain a status quo. But as department chairs we also need to recognize that we have allies in these efforts all around us in our colleagues, university diversity officers, and others.

Closing Thoughts

A brief word on department management. Where the aspects of leadership that I discuss above are rather obvious contributors to trust building and continuous improvement, there remains another often overlooked piece that is vital to department health. So many good intentions within departments have fallen prey to insufficient information, unclear policies, and other types of organizational missteps and oversights that I am convinced having a solid grip on management is critical and one of the greatest challenges facing a department chair. Effective administration and management are a fundamental part of any department chair's work, particularly in times such as these with pressure to produce more with less.

Frankly, leadership, mutual trust, and cultures of continuous improvement cannot be sustained long enough to make a difference if critical, or even mundane, administrative tasks are not taken care of. For example, as the person ultimately responsible for the department budget and its impact on faculty and students, the department chair must take that responsibility seriously. Whether or not you lean on staff for these management activities, ultimately the use (and misuse) of resources is your responsibility. I have focused my attention on 1) reducing unnecessary work for faculty by streamlining processes, 2) communicating what work is necessary and important for the department, 3) ensuring that program and fiscal data are accurate, up-to-date, and accessible, and 4) working with faculty to strengthen those policies that relate to core department functions. These efforts have served us well in challenging environments. Having sound data that illustrates faculty productivity and growing student enrollments has enabled departments to make a strong case for resources and avoid significant budget cuts. Further, strong and convincing data allows for sound decisions about where to spend our efforts. For instance, clear data can inform at what levels enrollments should be maintained or what programs merit additional faculty.

In sum, the challenges to departmental leadership are numerous. "Wicked problems" will never cease to rear their ugly heads. What I have shared here are my strategies for addressing the challenges of "leading from the middle" in a way that allows you to remain energized by the continuous stream of challenges. Leading from the middle, as department chairs do, necessitates an attitude that allows you to embrace that fact that each and every day a wicked problem, headache, whatever you choose to call it, will be waiting at your door. And if it isn't you should be actively seeking it out yourself!

Note

The author would like to thank Dr. Karen L. Sanzo, Dr. Joe DeVitis, and Jennifer Giblin for their helpful comments on earlier drafts of this chapter.

References

Bolman, L., & Gallos, J. (2011). *Reframing academic leadership*. San Francisco: Jossey-Bass.

Burns, J. M. (1978). *Leadership*. New York: Harper & Row.

Carroll, J. B. & Wolverton, M. (2004). Who becomes a department chair? In W. H. Gmelch & John H. Schuh (Eds.), *The life cycle of a department chair* (pp. 3–10). San Francisco: Jossey-Bass.

Eraut, M. (1994). *Developing professional knowledge and competence*. London: Falmer Press.

Gmelch, W. H. & Madden, V. D. (2004). *Chairing an academic department* (2nd ed.). Madison, WI: Atwood Publishing.

Gunsalus, C. K. (2006). *The college administrator's survival guide*. Cambridge, MA: Harvard University Press.

Hargreaves, A. (1990). Paths of professional development: Contrived collegiality, collaborative culture, and the case of peer coaching. *Teaching and Teacher Education, 6* (3), 227–241.

Kanter, R. M. (1997). *On the frontiers of management*. Harvard, MA: Harvard Business School Publishing.

Kanter, R. M., Stein, B. A., & Jick, T. D. (1992). *The challenge of organizational change: How companies experience it and leaders guide it*. New York: Free Press.

Miller, J. (2002). *The anxious organization: Why smart companies do dumb things*. Tempe, AZ: Facts on Demand Press.

Ogawa, R., & Bossert, S. (1995). Leadership as an organizational quality. *Educational Administration Quarterly, 48* (1), 224–243.

Schein, E. H. (1992). *Organizational culture and leadership*. San Francisco: Jossey-Bass.

Schneider, M., & Somers, M. (2006). Organizations as complex adaptive systems: Implications of complexity theory for leadership research. *The Leadership Quarterly, 17* (4), 351–365.

Starkey, C. B., & Stone-Briggs, A. (2009). Conflict and working relationships: Strategies for success. *The Department Chair, 20* (2), 12–14.

CHAPTER NINETEEN

Supervision, Suicide, Strategic Planning, and Shenanigans

Life of a Small College Dean

SCOTT C. BROWN & STEPHEN C. LEAVITT

Have you ever thought about putting students on "double secret probation" (as did the dean in *Animal House*)? Have you ever wondered about the life of a dean? How to become one? From Dean Wormer in *Animal House* to Dean Pelton in the sitcom *Community*, Dean Pritchard in *Old School* to even Dean Rooney from *Ferris Bueller's Day Off*, there are not many flattering portrayals of the dean position. But that is okay—we have the best jobs in the world. Being a dean is one of the most exciting roles on campus. We may be working on issues that can be solved in three minutes or three years, or whipsaw from a 30,000 foot conversation to three inches in an instant. We get to be hard-wired into all aspects of campus from matriculation to graduation and beyond. Here, two deans from different backgrounds will give a gimlet-eyed snapshot of being a dean at a small college, including an overview of the chief student affairs officer's portfolio, relationships, being a leader, tips on how to make the move to the deanery, and lessons learned that can help anyone new to the dean job.

The Dean's Portfolio

Being a dean at a liberal arts college has some particular characteristics that will be highlighted in the chapter. The authors came to their positions from different paths. Scott has a student affairs background, coming up through the ranks, so he is familiar with the student affairs literature as well as having considerable hands-on experience; Steve was faculty in the department of anthropology before shifting over to administration. It is our hope that these different perspectives add to this overall assessment of being a dean.

A dean is the personification of educational leadership. Deans must leverage nearly every student affairs professional's knowledge and skill to serve the institution most effectively. Additionally, much of the dean's job involves helping subordinates perform at their very best level. It is important to understand the specific skills required as a manager.

As a small community, a liberal arts college offers the dean an opportunity to think about the unique values of a broad education and to help shape priorities for the direction of the college. It is important to think about the unique "culture" of your institution, and to frame your priorities in terms of that culture.

The dean's portfolio can cover many things such as personnel, managing key relationships, politics, crisis management/legal issues, diversity, and strategic planning managing (Tederman, 1997; Westfall, 2006). All these are important, but relationships in particular are critical to the position of dean.

Relationships

The dean must be able to connect with almost every campus constituency, each with specific needs and interests. This means internal constituencies (students, faculty, your direct reports, other administrative offices), external constituencies (parents, alumni/ae, Board of Trustees, Alumni Council, local elected and emergency personnel), the president and other senior colleagues (e.g., admissions, communications, administration/finance, development, and provosts). A dean must manage all of these relationships effectively (Ellis, 2009).

Looking at this list, one can easily be struck by the wide range of people the dean must be able to interact with effectively. Interpersonal skills are important. But what exactly do "interpersonal skills" mean? Are they an attribute of personality or can they be learned? One thing that every dean will say is that skills clearly do develop over time—the longer you have been a dean, the better your skills are. So it makes sense to think about articulating those skills, pointing out what works well with different constituencies.

One skill—probably the most basic and important—is to listen carefully and authentically to whoever you are interacting with. This sounds like a cliché, and it can be, but truly listening is an important skill that can be cultivated. As an anthropologist, Steve learned specifically about skills required for interviewing (see Leavy, 2011). One aspect is to genuinely hear what the interviewees are saying, and to convey that you are hearing them. Repeat back what they have said, starting with "Let me be sure I understand what you are saying. . ." Another key to conveying that you are listening is to ask questions, ask for more details, ask for specifics, ask them to "start at the beginning." These skills are especially important for being a dean, as the dean has to be able to relate effectively; for example, to genuinely hear concerns expressed by parents. The dean may also often have to "get to the bottom" of situations, such as investigations, or ferret out what problems a student may be having at any given time. Being able to listen effectively is therefore an important skill.

Another is the capacity to see things from the point of view of others. This can be often glossed over as "having empathy" but it involves more than that. It involves understanding the overall context for the communication. Each person has basic understandings, cultural "schemas" that define how one interprets a situation (Quinn & Strauss, 1998). It is important for the dean to understand it and to know something of the way people are interpreting events. One striking fact, for example, is that today's students understand "adulthood" as something that one attains at the age of twenty-seven or twenty-eight. This leads them to regard their parents differently from what we might expect if, say, they believed "true" adulthood started at eighteen. Parents themselves, famous for their involvement with students' lives, are calling the dean in part because their son or daughter may be exaggerating a situation to get their parents' attention. All of this, the cultural understandings and the environmental context, needs to be appreciated by the dean.

The issue of different frames of reference based on basic understandings becomes especially important when the dean reviews the different *types* of relationships one has with various constituencies. Much of the dean's time and energy is spent working with those that report to him or her, the directors and deans on the staff. Developing mentoring skills is an art that takes considerable practice. It is important to allow direct reports considerable independence, while at the same time correcting their errors and reinforcing their standards. There is also considerable value in reminding the direct reports of their importance and in giving positive feedback, even if it seems obvious, and therefore unnecessary, that they are doing a good job. The best situation is one where the direct report comes up with initiatives that fit with your overall objectives but are his/her own ideas.

The relationship with members of the Board of Trustees is very important, though very different. Here one learns that the overall positioning of the institution is an important consideration, and it is important to think about the institution from the point of view of a board member. The trustee is often an alumnus/a of the institution, and has distinct memories of how the school used to be. Trustees are also often leaders in their own right, and are used to calling the shots. Trustees view their roles as a board member as one of looking after the best interests of the institution, and of making sure that it is operating well. And the trustee is a financial contributor. The dean therefore must often walk a fine line between reporting only the good news, and engaging board members in very real issues that require their feedback. It is key to convey that you know what you are doing and have the institution's best interest in mind. Plan in advance how you would like to have a board committee meeting go. Set the topics of conversation so that they can feel like they are contributing, but also make sure to keep in mind that they are looking for deficiencies, and you are there to reassure them. This relationship is a complicated and very important one.

Finally, it is also important to remember that being a dean is a prominent position on the campus. People will know who you are. And they expect a certain comportment that may at first be unfamiliar. Steve remembers how campus safety officers at first regarded him as distant and cold; when he looked into it to find the evidence, it was simply that he had been used to being a faculty and largely ignoring campus safety. He had therefore failed to acknowledge them with a wave or a smile when walking on campus. The officers, recognizing the head of their campus section, expected the dean always to acknowledge them. The situation (and reputation) was easily rectified by the dean's simply making an effort to always acknowledge people who work for him. Someone who is new to being a dean may easily forget this feature of the dean's relationships.

Being a Leader

One thing to recognize is that as a dean you are a leader, and as a leader you are expected to lead. This may sound obvious, but it is important to remember. It is easy to forget the degree to which your constituents look to you for guidance. This means that you should spend some time thinking about your priorities as the leader of an important department or division at the college. Think about the issues your school faces. Then think about *your* approach to dealing with those issues. Articulate that approach to yourself. Identify its characteristics. For example, Steve, in coming from the field of anthropology, appreciated the importance of one-on-one interactions toward helping improve behavior in students. He also understood that everyone operates according to cultural assumptions. He then identified the "type" of student drawn to his college. He would quickly quip that those students were the "cool" people in high school, those who were athletes, those who were engaged, and those who were the "beautiful people" on the campus. From this he assumed that those students, in particular, were concerned about their self-image and looked to their peers to guide them—even to a greater extent than most college students. You could see it in the similar way they dressed, in their fashion sense.

What is the importance of all of this? Steve recognized that they, more than many students, would follow the example of their own leaders. This led him to focus, for example, on having the very best resident assistant (RA) program he could, because he understood that the RAs serve as critical role models at his college. He cultivated relationships with student leaders and was sure to convey to them his vision for what the ideal college would look like, hoping that they in turn would convey that to their peers, and that those peers would then try to emulate that model. He also shifted the focus of residential life toward a greater one-on-one emphasis, hiring enough residence directors to be sure that he had good supervision of the RA staff and also developed strong relationships with the students.

This is a fairly concrete model for how to think about his program, and it needed to be articulated to his staff. The staff could then pick up that direct relationships were important in their daily tasks, that those they supervised should value that as well. So the keys here are to articulate to yourself the characteristics of your particular vision, and then to convey that vision to all of your staff. The unique qualities of the leader will easily be transmitted down through all dimensions of your operation. Think of the impact of the distinctive philosophy of the late Steve Jobs, one leader, on the entire approach of Apple Computer. You can convey a similar distinctive philosophy to those who work under you.

Preparing for the Move: Pathway to the Deanery

Moving towards a dean position requires an intentional consideration of where to spend your discretionary time, no matter from what part of the institution you come. Make it easy for a search and selection committee to strongly make the case that you could do the position they are searching for. Some key strategies that will improve your chances:

Assess where you are today. This is an important starting point and can help ascertain where you are relatively strong, and those areas in which you need improvement. Think also about your priorities and your vision, and spend some time articulating them to yourself, so you can convey them in a job application.

Cultivate mentors. Most people will serve as a resource to you, but you have to manage these relationships. Being a dean requires a lot of hands-on knowledge which takes time to learn, so it is important to glean what you can from more experienced colleagues.

Diversify your portfolio. Don't get pigeonholed unless you like that hole. Constantly seek out collateral assignments in areas that will expand your scope, particularly if it is of a larger divisional or institutional nature. These can include doing a mini-internship in another area

(Dean of Faculty, Administration), chairing division-wide committees, or volunteering to be on search committees.

Be the one to volunteer to take on extra tasks. People in leadership positions are "can-do" people. They do not shy away from things that may be difficult. By volunteering to take on extra tasks, you convey that kind of persona. And often those tasks can be educational in themselves, so they are worth the effort.

Keep abreast of professional and related literature. A dean should be plugged in, as new research, laws, or trends can come to the fore quickly. Deans should have a range of periodicals, scholarly materials, websites and related materials outside of higher education that they monitor. Additionally, they should encourage staff to share pertinent info with them as well.

Get involved professionally. Professional organizations can be an easy way to gain exposure, network, and develop skills that the generalist requires. Major student affairs organizations have commissions and knowledge communities related to various functions and general administration. Most welcome any volunteers.

Study your dean, ask questions. What keeps your dean up at night? Read communications that come from that office and ask yourself, why is this coming out? What is the intention of this communiqué?

Advance your degree. There was a time when having a master's degree with significant work experience would be plenty to secure. While this is still true depending on the institution, a doctorate is an opportunity to deeply study core issues of higher education.

Lessons Learned

Life accepts lessons from the School of Hard Knocks. These are a few, hard-won lessons that can be helpful to you as an aspiring or new dean.

Use multiple frames. As Bolman and Deal (2008) argue, organizational leadership requires the capacity to utilize multiple frames of reference to suit the particular context or objective: "structural" (organizing teams to get results); "human resource" (building positive interpersonal and group dynamics); "political" (building coalitions, dealing with internal and external politics); and "symbolic" (giving purpose and meaning to work, and building team spirit through ritual, ceremony, and story). All of those you interact with are influenced by scripts for how that interaction is supposed to go. So, for example, if you organize a retreat, it is important to think about the "frame" that people expect with retreats. They are looking to bond as a community and to develop some specific "big picture" objectives moving forward. It therefore makes little sense to organize a retreat around sharing how individual departments operate—it may be useful, but it does not fit well with the "retreat frame" that people bring to the situation.

Cultivate an information network. In this position, you will naturally have many formal and informal ways of receiving information. This is not merely gossip but will allow you as a person with decision-making power to be more understanding of the entire institutional eco-system and how one action may affect others. Think of yourself as a major node in a neurosystem that includes students, faculty, townsfolk, alums, and parents.

Learn from experience. One of the exhilarating, exhausting, and anxiety-provoking aspects of being a dean is the range of issues—crises—you have to deal with. Each year some significant issue, whether it be H1N1, a racial incident, a student death, a public embarrassment, may come across your desk, and the challenge is to develop the skills to deal with that wide range of issues. Much like a doctor who works at a hospital, the dean must use his or her experience to know how to respond. And as with a doctor, nothing replaces that experience. It is therefore important in dealing with a crisis to assemble a team of people to brainstorm on the crisis, to identify paths of actions, and to look ahead at possible repercussions. Then, following every incident, it is helpful to review what worked and what did not, so that you can most effectively use that experience in dealing with crises in the future.

Understand your faculty. Student affairs divisions are extremely important to the educational mission. However, the faculty are at the heart of any institution. At most institutions, particularly smaller liberal arts colleges, it is critical that student affairs deans be acutely aware of the best ways to extend and enhance the classroom experience in ways that are easiest for the faculty. The teaching environment is critically important to faculty. Faculty, to student affairs professionals, seem an odd breed. They seem to have a great deal of freedom to act in any way they want, they seem to be oblivious to the standards set by their supervisors. And they seem to think the world revolves around them! It is important to remember that faculty are highly skilled, highly educated people who have chosen to forego extra money to become professors. They do not want to work for a "boss." Many prefer the relatively unstructured life of a faculty member, so they work hard to preserve that. Faculty initiatives therefore often have to be decided by consensus. Faculty often talk about how they "have no time" to do anything other than their job. And to a harried student affairs professional, they seem to work very little at first glance. But one critical thing to understand is that all faculty, in addition to developing and preparing for all of their classes, have long-standing projects, such as an article or a book, sitting over their heads. They will have to see structured interactions with student affairs as a part of their job, and therefore necessary. All of this regarding faculty means you will have to adopt a "paving over footpaths" approach that creates opportunities and interventions to work with faculty that flow naturally from the ways their lives are currently configured (Brown & Roseborough, 2007).

Create a personal advisory board. A dean position will often disallow having frank conversations with many people, and though you will be a strong leader, you should know whom you might turn to and for what. This can be anyone from a mentor to colleagues at similar institutions in another division. It is a place where you feel comfortable puzzling through some questions. Most, if not all, are generous, honest, and have accrued much wisdom. As noted above, it is especially important to tap advisors when facing some kind of crisis. Many minds are better than one in sorting out all of the issues that need to be addressed.

Think in terms of the "culture" of your institution. Colleges have features that cause them to build up distinct cultural environments over time. Like cultures, they often develop policies and practices with very little communication with other institutions. And the turnover of students every four years means that the culture of the school can change relatively quickly, becoming more distinct. When pursuing change, it is essential to recognize the basic parameters of the institution. For example, in some schools faculty have a direct say in all school policies, in others they don't know "student affairs" from "student activities." Some schools are top-down, recognizing student voices only as an afterthought; at others, students define school policy. These characteristics, distinct at your school, are worth considering in enacting change.

Simplify, simplify, and simplify. The great coach Vince Lombardi was famous for paring down his offensive strategy for a given context to a small number of things that they did well and executed flawlessly. Cut out extraneous things. For example, Scott funnels everything to his email, and does what he can to keep his email at zero.

Control your calendar. Know your biorhythms. If there is a certain time of day or night when you are fresh—then protect it. Control your calendar when you can to actually get work done.

Be prepared to move quickly. A crisis, in any form, can scuttle your day's activities. It is very easy to fall behind on your day-to-day chores. This often means you have to "call an audible" and quickly connect with key players in resolving the crisis. Good decisions need to be made quickly, with as much circumspection as possible.

Know when to hold 'em, know when to fold 'em. Your role as a dean is to help set the strategic direction and support your president. That means providing sage advice to help inform institutional decision making. Sometimes that will mean being more insistent if you know a particular direction is the best way to resolve an issue. However, it is also critical to know how, when you provide feedback that is not incorporated, to move forward and support the decision publicly. Something may be a good idea, but the time is not right, or you may not be the right champion for it.

Be friendly but not familiar. In this role, there is the reality that you have influence or control of another person's livelihood. This is a great responsibility. Counter to what probably helped you get to this position, walk and do not run into relationships. We also realize our friendship can be a burden to subordinates, as they are constantly thinking of you as a dean and that you are possibly evaluating them.

Enlarge your sphere of influence. There are a number of ways that you can be an asset to your campus, thus enlarging the ways you can influence others in a positive fashion. You should be able to assess your situation within the campus context, understand the political landscape for student affairs, make strategic alliances, align with campus priorities, and implement a strategy (Brown & Porterfield, 2008; Strenger, 2009).

"Cross a street and cut a ribbon." A colleague of ours explicitly uses every opportunity when she meets with key constituencies to educate them on the role of student affairs. Get a sense of how you can be helpful, and create partners. Knowing how to efficiently "work" a room at an event is important—you must be visible and engaged with many other attendees, but also able to leave briskly so you may attend other events.

Take care of yourself. Steve makes it a priority to play the piano during lunch. Scott protects his lunch hour and forces himself to exercise every day. All those Toll House pies take their toll! If you are comfortable, exercise in the school facility—it is also a way for you to humanize yourself, and we have met students and community members that we would have never known otherwise. Whatever works for you, build something into your schedule to refresh your mind and spirit.

Leave the place better than you found it. As a senior officer of the institution, you must resolve any conflict that will put the institution in a good place. This often means considering the impact of your decisions many years down the road. It is up to you to help navigate many, often competing, stakeholders and priorities.

Conclusion

We believe work in higher education is the "secular sacred." People do not do this work for the money or the glamour. We get to work comprehensively with students at the most developmentally dynamic part of their lives. As student affairs professionals, we are "educational decathletes" who must know how and when to lead, manage, advise, teach, and counsel. We believe higher education work is truly a love made visible and higher education professionals, regardless of background, are called by the same sense of purpose, which galvanizes our work on our campuses.

References

Bolman, L. G., & Deal, T. E. (2008). *Reframing organizations: artistry, choice, and leadership* (4th ed.). San Francisco: Jossey-Bass.

Brown, S. C., & Porterfield, K. (2008). Not taught in graduate school: Increasing student affairs' sphere of influence. In M. Weaver (Ed.), *Transformative learning support models in higher education* (pp. 165–180). Abington, UK: Facet Publishing.

Brown, S. C., & Roseborough, J. (2007). They're just not that into you: Working with disinterested faculty. *NACE Journal*, Winter, 28–32.

Ellis, S. (2009). Developing effective relationships on campus and in the community. In G. S. McLellon, J. Strenger & Associates (Eds.), *The handbook of student affairs administration* (3rd ed.) (pp. 447–462). San Francisco: Jossey-Bass.

Leavy, P. (2011) *Oral history: Understanding qualitative research*. Oxford: Oxford University Press.

Quinn, N., & Strauss, C. (1998). *A cognitive theory of cultural meaning*. Cambridge: Cambridge University Press.

Strenger, J. (2009). Political environment of the student affairs administration. In G. S. McLellon, J. Strenger & Associates (Eds.), *The handbook of student affairs administration* (3rd ed.) (pp. 425–446). San Francisco: Jossey-Bass.

Tederman, J. (1997). *Advice from the dean: A personal perspective on the philosophy, roles, and approaches of a dean at a small, private, liberal arts college*. NASPA Monograph Series. Washington, DC: National Association of Student Personnel Administrators.

Westfall, S. B. (Ed.). (2006). Charting the territory: The small college dean. *New Directions in Student Services, 2006* (116), 5–13.

CHAPTER TWENTY

The Multi-Faceted Journey of a Community College President

DEBORAH L. FLOYD

Introduction

This descriptive and interpretive chapter attempts to characterize the multi-faceted dimensions of the community college presidency. It will spotlight many of the rewarding opportunities to make a difference—and some surprises along the way. Predictable pleasures will be presented, as will threats, challenges, twists, and turns that are integral parts of this amazing leadership journey. This essay offers the author's personal reflections on choosing a presidency, preparing for the job, doing the work of a community college president, and exiting the job with dignity and grace. (Those lessons are grounded in years of experience, observation, reflection, and a review of the literature.)

In anticipation of a wave of vacancies at all levels of leadership, especially the presidency, the American Association of Community Colleges (AACC) in 2003 launched a Leading Forward Project that resulted in the identification of six competencies necessary for successful community college leadership: organizational strategy; resource management; communication; collaboration; community college advocacy; and professionalism (AACC, 2005). This AACC framework has served as a useful guide for professional in-service, grow-your-own leadership, and graduate programs (Hassan, Dellow, & Jackson, 2009; McNair, 2009; Sinady, Floyd, & Mulder, 2010), and has guided research on the work of community college presidents (Eddy, 2010; McNair, Duree, & Ebbers, 2011).

The six AACC leadership competencies provide a practical framework for understanding community college leadership, especially the advocacy role of presidents. Successful community college presidents know that "an effective community college leader understands, commits to, and advocates for the mission, vision and goals of the community college" (AACC, 2005, p. 5). In fact, competencies in organizational strategies, resource management, communications, collaboration, and professionalism all work in tandem as a community college president advocates for the mission, vision, and goals of the college.

While the AACC competencies are a useful framework for understanding community college leadership, the role of president is even more complex, multi-dimensional, changing, and stressful, as described by Beckman (2011), Eddy (2010), Floyd, Maslin-Ostrowski, and Hrabak (2010), McNair, Duree, and Ebbers (2011), Pierce (2012), and Vaughan (2000). Intricacies associated with new media, board relations, shifting stakeholder expectations, and limited resources to address broad missions have all added to the challenges and complexity of the community college president's role (Maslin-Ostrowski, Floyd & Hrabak, 2011; O'Banion, 2009). But what truly grounds the work of a community college president is a passionate resolve to advance the mission of the college and the joys of knowing one's leadership has truly made a difference in the lives of many stakeholders.

Flag Bearer and Chief Advocate

First and foremost, the role of a community college president is to serve as the flag bearer and chief advocate for the institutional mission. While community college missions vary somewhat, almost all include a commitment to communities and workforce development, student learning and success, and education for diverse populations. Community college presidents must model the way of service to their area communities by ensuring that the institutional commitment to their communities is honored through all college programs. Community college service areas are as diverse as the people living and working in the communities they serve. Of the 1,167 community colleges in the United States, more than half serve rural communities, small towns, or fringe areas of mid-sized cities (AACC, 2012a, 2012b).

Understandably, the majority of community college student enrollments are in colleges located in large and mid-sized cities and towns where the community challenges are often different from those in more intimate and smaller communities. Community college presidents must effectively lead and adapt to the uniqueness of their college's setting and the communities served by their college. Whether serving large, medium, or small colleges, or rural, urban or suburban areas, community college presidents are expected to serve their communities and be the *face and voice* of the college everywhere and always. Presidents are the public face of the college to internal and external communities and all stakeholders—a role that also requires skill in dealing with diverse personality issues (Weill, 2009).

Workforce Partner and Community Advocate

An essential mission for community colleges is to lead in the preparation of the nation's workforce (Boggs, 2010). This commitment to workforce education is increasingly being broadened beyond geographic borders to online delivery of courses, and delivery of programs in the United States and abroad, as the definition of community is expanded. Presidents are often the agent that brings together new businesses with job training programs and the funding to support those programs.

Community colleges provide both academic/for-credit, and non-credit workforce programs, with no particular pecking order. Community colleges are also called upon to offer short-term skills training, often outside the traditional college credit structure. Students in truck driving or mechanics programs studying for a certificate, for example, are treated as valuable to the college as students in business administration pursuing an associate degree with plans to transfer to a four-year institution. Increasingly, community colleges are providing workforce baccalaureate degree programs in fields that lead directly to jobs locally. It is, in fact, local workforce needs that are driving the community college baccalaureate movement (Walker, 2005). Presidents must become adept at working with local and state business partners and legislators to support the continuous shift in college mission and program delivery, which includes the commitment to workforce development as regional economic conditions shift and may include expanding college offerings beyond traditional associate degrees (Floyd & Walker, 2009; Skolnik & Floyd, 2005).

Student Advocate

Effectively serving a diverse student body is also an important mission of community colleges and thus, important to the work of presidents. Collectively, community colleges enroll almost half of all U.S. undergraduate students and serve large numbers of first-time freshmen, people of color, and persons from diverse socioeconomic backgrounds. The average age of community college students is 28 years old, with 39% of students 21 years of age or younger, and 15% of students 40 years or older. Forty-two percent are first-generation college students; 13% are single parents (AACC, 2012a). Community colleges are challenged to provide services and programs, such as developmental education, counseling, and academic advisement, to this diverse student demographic to ensure all students have opportunities to succeed and graduate.

Recently, these "people's colleges" (Cohen & Brawer, 2008, p. 5) have been propelled into the forefront of President Obama's College Completion Agenda, the American Graduation Initiative, a challenge that is not easy, given the diverse student population served (White House, 2009). "Public colleges and universities are now called upon to address low graduation rates by their state legislatures, and both public and private institutions feel pressure by regional accrediting associations to improve retention" (DeAngelo, Franke, Hurtado, Pryor, & Tran, 2011, p. 3). Thus, the mission to ensure student success (and demonstrate the value of the education that students receive) is one that must be embraced by contemporary community college presidents.

At the end of the day, the priority of promoting and ensuring student success is set by the community college president. Unlike private or large public colleges and universities that may increase admissions standards in order to impact student graduation rates, for open-admission community colleges "the focus needs to be squarely on creating the conditions for success for all students who begin college" (DeAngelo et al., 2011, p. 4). The implication for the community college president is he/she must always keep his/her eye on the prize of student success for all students, those pursuing for-credit and non-credit programs in both workforce and transfer education. Presidents must lead the development of programs, services, and course offerings and schedules that are responsive to the fiscal and academic needs of their students in order to promote student retention through to completion.

Doing the Job of the President: Personal Considerations

The role of a community college president is complex, demanding, and rewarding. Doing the job with excellence requires political, managerial, communications, and interpersonal skills and talents that challenge even the most seasoned leaders. Presidents are always on stage on campus, in their local communities, and beyond. They are ultimately responsible for personnel, fiscal and physical plant management, and the overall health of the college. Exhaustive time and energy is dedicated to faculty and staff relations, working with internal leaders, board relations at various levels, resource development and fund raising, the physical plant, accreditation and academic leadership, media and image relations, legislative affairs, and most of all ensuring that students and the communities are served well by the college. The buck stops with the president, although presidents don't always feel that way because disgruntled constituents often contact board members, the media, governors, and others if they have issues or complaints. As president, you are ultimately responsible for every aspect of the internal and external management of the institution and that. . . .

Personal questions and issues to consider when beginning and executing the job of a community college president include the following:

How will you enter the job? Listen and learn. Think before doing. A good president is not a storm trooper, even if you were hired to clean up after a crisis or years of neglect. A good president is a good listener. Listening is about gathering information, identifying the problem and the source of the problem, focusing on being objective as early decisions and actions are made, and being patient through this early learning process.

Do you have the right people on your team at the right time, and if not, how will you get the right people in place? Collins (2005) offers sage, research-backed advice that you must begin with getting the right people on the bus and in the right seats before you can go anywhere with your organization. Internally, having the right people on your team is a huge key to presidential success. Getting that team in place is often not easy, especially for presidents who follow long-term leaders or those serving in small political communities. Putting your team in place is challenging because it requires terminating people, moving people, and almost always includes conflict. It simply does not always feel good. People are entrenched in organizational culture and when you make changes, you are dismantling established systems so beware of moving too quickly as the pace of change is important.

Do you have a vision and a "can do" attitude? You need a vision, a mission, and a plan for your presidency. You need to *work* that vision, mission, and plan. You need to lead others toward working that vision, mission, and plan. To do so, it is best to have a *can do* attitude and help create and sustain a positive *can do* college culture. Others will look to you for believability and passion. Not only are you the number one cheerleader for the college, you must be the one to teach others to be successful. My advice to my graduate students applies just as much to potential executives: plan your work, and work your plan.

Are you ethically grounded? Know what you stand for because you will be tested. "Presidents should not be surprised to find themselves caught in a crisis" (Maslin-Ostrowksi & Floyd, 2012, p. 296), and when they do, they need to be able to use their ethical standards to help them decide how to manage that crisis. "What matters most is being clear about professional values and boundaries, especially during difficult times" (Maslin-Ostrowski & Floyd, 2012, p. 296).

How will you balance day-to-day management challenges and your ultimate accountability? Presidents must ensure that the day-to-day management functions run smoothly without appearing to micro-manage the college, but when something goes wrong, the president is ultimately accountable. Thus, a team of loyal and competent deans, vice presidents, and provosts is essential to your success as a president. With this team in place, internal management and personnel issues will be less likely to distract from external demands of working with boards, communities, and legislators. But keep in mind there are no guarantees that you won't have distractions, even if you have the right people in the right places. Find ways to listen and learn and get to the truth. Listening to those who honestly tell you what you *need* to hear, not necessarily what you *want* to hear is essential to successful leadership.

What will you do to ensure your visibility? The job is a 24/7 commitment; you must be able to work long hours effectively. Stakeholders expect the president to be present everywhere—at every event. Presidents are expected to be on campus, in the community, and legislatively active yet with limited time to do everything and be everywhere. As a former community college president, I vividly remember the many competing demands of my position; having to represent the college during legislative sessions while soliciting donors and maintaining campus visibility to faculty, staff, and students. My predecessor was a local, long-term, founding president who spent most of his final years focusing on internal college matters. The challenge I faced, therefore, was dealing with expectations for internal visibility while working tirelessly to raise funds, support, and resources externally. Learn to manage your calendar, don't let it manage you.

How will you handle the personal scrutiny? As mentioned earlier, presidents are the flag bearer and face of the institution. This is true regardless of the type of institution. As a community college president in rural Appalachia, this was clearly one of the biggest surprises to me during my tenure as a president. While I expected scrutiny, I was surprised that how I dressed, what I said or did not say to neighbors, how I interacted with stakeholders, and ways that I related to the media were all heavily scrutinized. I learned to carefully select my words, slow down when I grocery shopped, and make positive eye contact with all people in the community.

How will you deal with rumors? One of the realities of the presidency is that there will be rumors about the president and the college; some will be positive and others negative. The slightest error in word choice in a casual setting is often exaggerated through rumors. Rumor management, therefore, is an important presidential skill. Rumors and rumblings can be minimized by skillful presidents who are present and visible, especially when a piece of bad news (such as budget cuts) is to be delivered. Keep in mind that for some presidents, regardless of your finesse in rumor management, everything will be exaggerated in the rumor mill, even stories about your personal life and past.

How will you answer to your diverse stakeholders? You will have many bosses ranging from faculty and staff, the board, the governor, legislators, students, parents, business partners, and donors. Community college presidents must be skillful in reporting out to all stakeholders. As much as open communication is important, knowing what to share with whom, and when, is a critical skill. Of course what you can share is sometimes bounded by legal constraints (often an advantage), and at other times bounded by the trustworthiness of your audience. Learning how to manage your communications must be a top priority of your presidency, and very early on.

Does criticism hurt you? Develop a thick skin, and quickly, because you will be criticized. That is simply a part of the job. Learn to learn from criticism and don't take it to heart. Remember that often the critics are focusing on the role of the president, not you personally, although the arrows may feel very personal when they penetrate.

Do you take press coverage to heart? Don't believe your own press—good or bad. Newspapers, television, and new media will cover the college and your leadership with self-proclaimed balance that will include good news and news you may not agree with or like. When attacked, decide when and how to effectively manage media relations. This does not mean retaliation or revenge, it means focusing on respect, for the college and yourself. Equally important, don't let the good news go to your head, especially positive news about you personally. Effectively manage communications, correspondence, and the media by learning impromptu speaking skills, having several speeches ready for a variety of audiences, and delegating correspondence responses.

How will you ensure faculty members are included in shared governance and decision-making processes? Even if you are working your plan, plans don't always go right. You won't always have the confidence of your faculty. As a president, you need to establish systems and oversee processes that clearly articulate the role of faculty in decision-making and how you will interface with them. Strategic systems that ensure that faculty are engaged in planning, and key decision-making processes are integral to presidential success. Inclusion in shared governance is especially important for long-term presidents as they often get comfortable with their decision-making and may become more directive over time. There are times, however, that no matter what you do to include faculty, the president becomes the target of their wrath. This may be especially true during challenging fiscal times and collective bargaining negotiations.

How will you cultivate and maintain positive board relations? Board of trustees positions are political and either elected by constituents or appointed by a political figure, such as the governor. They change regularly, and will likely change during your presidency. The board that hired you one year may not be the one that has the power to fire you the next. Be true to your ethical standards with a board. Insist that the board adopt a policy governance model (Carver & Carver, 1994) for leadership and encourage routine board training, perhaps through the Association of Community College Trustees, Association of Governing Boards, or International Policy Governance Association.

Those who decide to pursue community college presidencies know that process requires a careful self-examination of the skill set required to perform on the job with a level of commitment and excellence unlike any you may have ever needed to use thus far in your career. Aside from exemplary leadership and management skills, it requires a thick skin, stamina, finesse, balance, and a daily dose of renewed energy grounded in your passion as well as moral aptitude. To thine own self be true.

So You Want to Be a Community College President: Points to Consider

Choosing the right presidency can be as important as choosing to be in the presidency. When choosing the career path of the community college presidency, you need to consider whether you want to live in a small fishbowl or a larger one because all presidents live in fishbowls. You will lose your privacy and be under scrutiny constantly. Much like an elected political figure, what you wear, whom you associate with, what you attend and do not attend, and what you say or do not say will be evaluated and judged. Most presidents, especially women, even think twice about a casual trip to the grocery store in sloppy clothes, instead opting for more carefully selected attire for even short errands in the community. Students, faculty, staff, donors, parents, and others often recognize you! You are always the president and a local celebrity.

A large number of presidential positions are in smaller colleges in small towns or rural areas. Be aware that in some ways, the smaller the college, the tougher the job. Small college presidents have fewer specialized staff for jobs such as public relations, governmental affairs, community relations, and fund raising, which leaves the bulk of the pressure for performance on the president who must wear many hats. These colleges often have a tougher time getting on state lists for funding projects and are located in tight-knit communities often with intrusive community media and community expectations. Large college presidents have the same duties to effectively lead and manage the college with larger specialized resources, but often are saddled with the complexities of multiple campuses or centers and the challenges associated with large, complex organizations. If you have options, pick your setting wisely. When selecting a college, keep in mind that the governance of the institution impacts the role of the community college president. In many ways, the job of presidents who report to a state system chancellor or a college district chancellor are quite different from that of presidents who report directly to a governing board. Working directly with a board brings a set of time-consuming and often stressful challenges that are well-documented in O'Banion's (2009) research on community college rogue trustees. Much time and attention are necessary to inform, engage, support, and be responsive to a governing board that has the power to hire and fire the president. Thus, presidents reporting directly to governing boards must carefully manage time devoted to internal campus and college issues and challenges, external community expectations and opportunities, and the ever-shifting demands of a governing board. Similarly, presidents with local advisory boards often treat those boards as if they were governing boards since these boards often advise a governing board or chancellor about hiring or firing the president and serve in advocacy roles for the college.

In systems with presidents who report to chancellors, who in turn report to governing boards, the role of a community college president with regard to board relations is often less demanding, but not without its stressors. In fact, a community college president reporting to a chancellor may find the position uncomfortable or unstable at times since the communication line is between the president and the chancellor directly, and only and indirectly and secondarily, to a board that ultimately may determine your fate.

Community colleges, whether small, medium, or large, rural, urban, or suburban, multi- or single-campus, all have in common a commitment to their local communities. When assessing your readiness for the job, consider the college's community service area and setting, its mission and your fit with organizational culture, its governance structure, and whether you want to lead in community building both internally and externally. Still interested in the job? The following are questions to help guide you in your readiness for the position.

Preparing for the Job

Aspiring community college presidents should realistically assess their readiness for the job and consider their areas of strength and weakness. Presidential hopefuls need to consider the challenges of making some very difficult decisions, the context and setting of the college, their preparation, and many other factors, advises Beckman (2011), an experienced community college search consultant. Building on Beckman's (2011) seasoned advice, the following questions should be addressed when considering readiness for a community college presidency:

Do you have a doctoral degree? Most presidencies require a doctorate and prefer one in higher education or a related field. If you don't have a doctoral degree or if you want additional training, several organizations provide excellent workshops and institutes for presidential leadership training. Ask a community college president to mentor you or seek internships so you can learn about the job.

Do you have the knowledge and experience to be successful as a community college president? To get the job, you don't have to demonstrate experience in all areas such as student affairs, business affairs, workforce development, instruction, and resource development, but you should have enough experience in these areas to be effective and know how to surround yourself with experts in these areas. "When you rise, you rise within a silo" but you need to think of a presidency as the horizontal position where you are responsible for all areas of your institution (Beckman, 2011).

Do you have enough experience in high-level administrative positions to know how to make some extraordinarily difficult decisions, often in isolation, and live with those decisions? Most stakeholders don't know what decisions you are making daily in areas such as personnel, community politics, and board relations. It is lonely at the top.

Do you have the support of your family, partner, children, and spouse? The presidency takes a lot of time, so if you have to take care of children, parents, a spouse or partner, or others that will distract from the demands of the job, you should rethink your timing of a presidency. You need to have a spouse willing to attend events with you and understand your long work hours. Pick your timing wisely, personally and professionally. Successful community college presidents pick the right time and right presidency to fit where they are in life.

Do you like to work alone or do you enjoy working with people and around people? If you enjoy working alone, don't consider a presidency because the job requires a substantial amount of time building internal and external relationships and working with diverse stakeholders.

Are you physically and mentally ready for the job? Vaughan's (2000) research on community college presidents weathering challenges of the job yielded advice that is very true for today's presidents: take care of yourself physically and emotionally. The job is taxing and can be dangerous to your health if you don't lead a healthy lifestyle. Schedule time to exercise every week, don't drink too much alcohol, eat nutritious and balanced meals, make time for your family, and do what it takes to ensure your personal life is healthy and balanced.

Is your resume appropriate for the job and does your application address the criteria advertised? Beckman (2011) warns candidates for community college presidencies to ensure that their resumes and application documents address the specific job skills advertised for specific presidencies. If you provide too much information and you are not clear about how you meet the advertised job requirements, your application risks being excluded early in the process.

Are your interview skills polished? If you make it to the interview stage, you should research the college and ensure that your responses are polished and genuinely reflect your potential as the new president. When possible, seek the advice of interview coaches and mentors.

Do you fit in with the college for which you are applying? It is important to ask why the presidency is available at this time and under what circumstances the former president exited. Whom will you follow if you are selected as president? Following a long-term or beloved president will surely bring challenges of leading a college through change and will result in resistance of your leadership, in spite of the good intentions of those professing they want change. Following a president who was fired should be a "red flag," and you should realistically assess the situation and determine if you will be a successful leader, or not, and follow a similar fate.

Be honest with yourself about your timing and readiness for the presidency. Pick your timing wisely, personally, and professionally. There is too much at stake for your career, and the lives of the stakeholders of the community college itself, to waste your time and theirs on an application process for an executive leadership position for which you are not prepared and ready to accept. If you are serious about the community college presidential career path, take all the time you need to go through those questions like a checklist until you can answer them all satisfactorily, even if it takes years. It is only worth pursuing if you are serious about executing the job to the best of your abilities.

Leaving the Job

As a community college president, or any leader for that matter, it's necessary to know when to leave and how to leave. Do not stay too long—you are not the president for life! You are privileged to hold a position for a period of time. Leave gracefully and celebrate your tenure and the accomplishments of the college.

Job departure requires knowing when to leave, planning the transition, ensuring that processes and workflow are maintained, supporting the search process, and bowing out with grace and dignity. It is a time to look back and acknowledge the successes and failures, trials, tribulations, and moments of great joy and pride. As outgoing presidents prepare to transition out of their roles, it is not only the college who faces a transition.

Outgoing community college presidents no longer retire into oblivion. "Career transitions are life markers and can be pivotal to what happens to the individual in the immediate and long-term future" (Maslin-Ostrowski & Floyd, 2012, p. 293). New windows of opportunity abound, in the private and public sector, in higher education and elsewhere. Once a president begins to daydream about leaving, it's time to fantasize about where he or she would like to be going next. Another preparation phase is ahead. How well one prepares to bow out depends on the answers to the following questions:

How will I know when I am ready to move on? Many presidents find that a significant crisis drives their decision to leave (Maslin-Ostrowski & Floyd, 2012). There is no need to wait for a dramatic crisis to make the decision to exit, however. Others look to their goals and plans and determine their exit based upon having reached certain accomplishments and being able to reflect on them (Mulder, 2001). Maintaining an awareness of one's role as placeholder is key to coming to this decision. One thing seems certain, leaving on your own terms is always better than leaving on others' terms. Knowing when to leave makes the transition smoother for all parties involved.

What do you want to be remembered for when you leave? Make your mark and always remember why you accepted the job: to make a difference. Keep your eye on the prize—the mission, vision, values, and goals of the college—and have a vision, mission, plan, and agenda to match. Work to include others in your vision through strategic planning and fundraising, so that they share your goals and help work toward meeting them. Never ever forget that the reason the college exists is for the students and communities.

What do I want to do next? "Extensive anecdotal evidence indicates that a growing number of community college presidents are joining university graduate programs concentrating on community college leadership" (Floyd & Vigil Laden, 2007, p. 914). Pierce (2012) offers that outgoing presidents have an opportunity to reinvent themselves, as officers of professional associations or search corporations, teaching and research faculty, and independent consultants. Only you can answer to your next calling, but staying true to your passions is a sure way to find your new direction.

Am I prepared to go? The preparation for your exit is both material and immaterial. Besides honing skills valuable for the next career stage, presidents need to make a tremendous mental shift from being somebody important, to perhaps being someone less so who is no longer at the center of their university or college, no longer in the know about what is going on around them (Floyd & Vigil Laden, 2007). It is important to consider the mental and emotional shift that will come with the transition out of the community college presidency and the understanding that it will take work to successfully navigate that shift.

Will the building fall over if I am not leaning against the wall? Hopefully not, and if you have worked hard to fulfill the mission of your college, then certainly not. Even after a crisis, the institution will remain standing. Part of the responsibilities of your exit, however, includes making sure that coffers are adequately stocked and people are in place to continue where you leave off.

What have I accomplished? Leave an exit report. Document the condition of the college when you arrived, what you accomplished, and the state of the college now. Draft two versions, one for your internal leadership and board and an executive summary for the public. The report should be balanced, not aggrandized, and should address the challenges in a professional way.

How do I say goodbye? When you leave, make it clean cut and let the next person lead. This is both an ethical imperative and for the maintenance of your own sanity. Don't look over your shoulder and don't look back; it's not good for the college, you, or your stakeholders. Intentionally shape your memories in a positive light rather than dwell on any negative experiences. You will never complete the job—there is no ending. You can't do it all. You are merely guiding the college along one step of a longer journey.

How do I exit with grace? Exiting the presidency is a rite of passage, as explained by Mulder (2001). "Recognizing when something is over and then being able to leave without regret may well be the result of being fully present" (Mulder, 2001, p. 241). It is a time for growth, planning, farewells, gratitude, and celebration. Exiting gracefully is exiting with no regrets (Mulder, 2001). Your legacy will be best remembered if you leave gracefully and let your replacement lead without interference.

Most presidents no longer retire at age 65; rather they retire into something else, increasingly a university graduate professorship (Floyd & Vigil Laden, 2007). So think about what you want to do next. Is the life of an academic on the horizon, or perhaps a higher education consultant? Regardless of the vision, the main focus should be on making a graceful exit. This is not the time to burn bridges, take revenge, or even simply vent pent up anger and steam. It is a time to exit gracefully. It is a time to prepare yourself and your college for the transition. Gather your resources and stay true to your ethics and passion. Leaving your legacy includes doing right by your organization, and by your stakeholders.

Unsolicited Advice: What I Know Now That I Wish I Knew Then

Hindsight, as the saying goes, is always 20/20. As a former community college president, the lessons learned offered below aim to provide an insider's look at the presidency and ways in which you can make your tenure as community college president as successful as possible. Some of these lessons were easier to learn than others. How quickly you learn to adapt to the unique challenges of the community college presidency is up to your focus, determination, and combination of skills, talents, and experiences.

The following list is complementary to the prior narrative about the preparation for, execution of, and departure from the community college presidency. It is inclusive of a potpourri of lessons, some of which I picked up on the job, others that I wish I had learned much earlier in my career. It is not meant to be exhaustive.

Do your homework when negotiating a contract and don't overcompensate yourself. It is tempting to accept a presidency paying a handsome salary with benefits such as a house, annuity, entertainment allowance, and a car. Pay attention to how your compensation package compares to others in similar college settings. If your compensation is higher than the average, you can expect scrutiny and criticism. If your package is lower than average, your value may be questioned. Make sure to include in your pre-job contract negotiation "a safety net for your departure" (Maslin-Ostrowski & Floyd, 2012, p. 297).

Build alliances. One never knows who is connected to whom. Getting the job often requires connections. Keeping the job depends on alliances, friends, and connections as well. You will have plenty of friends when you enter the presidency and serve. You will need friends as you exit the job.

Find trusting confidantes, but select those people very wisely. Do not lean on your staff or board for personal advice. Always remember that you are the president and their advice will be couched in that relationship. Living in a community's fishbowl can be lonely and stressful. Ensure you have a network and support group you trust.

To lead is to be wounded, but how you deal with being wounded ultimately helps define your success or failure. You need to learn to trust your feelings, listen internally, and find trusted people to talk to, circles of friends, about your experiences and feelings, openly, honestly, and deeply (Ackerman & Maslin-Ostrowksi, 2002).

Find a mentor and be a mentor. Mentors can be useful with providing access to resources and assistance in areas unfamiliar to them. By maintaining a presence with national professional associations, community college presidents increase opportunities to connect with potential mentors and experts and find opportunities to mentor others.

Learn the pedagogy of leadership and management. Participate in leadership development programs offered by organizations such as the American Association of Community College's President's Academy and Harvard University's Institutes on Educational Leadership.

Create a toolbox for unexpected public appearances. I kept four things in my office as a personal toolbox: a blue blazer on the back of my office door, a strand of pearls in my desk drawer, makeup in an accessible bag for touch ups, and flash cards with talking points about the college. This toolbox was essential for my confidence and preparation for impromptu photographs, speeches, or media interviews.

Donate to the college. Presidents are expected to raise money, including funds for buildings, scholarships, and endowments. They should model the way for others and give back some of what they earn as president. In doing so, others will follow, but don't ask faculty, staff, and your community to donate money if you have not done so yourself.

Your role is a servant leader. Leaders serve by empowering others, our students, faculty and staff, board members, business partners, and community members to both lead and follow in a shared vision (Wheeler, 2012). To lead is to serve all of our stakeholders with an eye on the prize for student success, and in turn institutional effectiveness and regional economic health.

Follow your passion and use it to stay motivated. While there is a lot of personal satisfaction in the work of the presidency, it is a lonely satisfaction. You have to be self-motivated and be able to appreciate positive milestones amidst a sea of challenges.

Pray. Regardless of your spiritual or religious perspective, a leap of faith (in God, people, yourself, whatever works for you) is in order to give you the courage to take on the community college presidency and all of its wonderful rewards and challenges.

In Conclusion

The community college presidency is a unique, multi-faceted leadership role with amazing opportunities to make a difference. Community college presidents embark on a mission to prepare millions of students to improve their lives by achieving gainful employment in fields demanding an able workforce, navigating career transitions, and developing life skills. By working toward the goal of workforce development, community college presidents strengthen their regional economies and transform public policy. It is a tremendously rewarding job with innumerable opportunities to make a difference in the lives of others and develop one's own leadership skills.

Regardless of how well you feel you have prepared yourself to take on a community college presidency, you should expect to make mistakes, as all leaders do. If a president truly leads and takes necessary risks, then the president will make mistakes, and that's to be expected. It is important to be able to learn from mistakes. As with all leaders, community college presidents need to acknowledge their mistakes and grow from them.

The best advice I can offer to hopeful new community college presidents can be summarized in the following. Look to the future, keep your eye on the prize, learn from the past rather than dwell on it, and don't be afraid to take the plunge. When you do, go in with knowledge of the real expectations and potential challenges, and be prepared to do the job well. When you leave, and your exit is inevitable, leave with dignity, pride, grace, and good memories of a legacy worth sharing in your next phase of life.

References

Ackerman, R. H., & Maslin-Ostrowski. P. (2002). *The wounded leader: How real leadership emerges intimes of crisis.* San Francisco, CA: Jossey-Bass.

American Association of Community Colleges (AACC). (2005). *Competencies for communitycollege leaders.* Retrieved fromhttp://www.aacc. nche.edu/Resources/comptencies/Documents/competencesforleaders.pdf

American Association of Community Colleges (AACC). (2012a). *American Association of Community Colleges 2012 fact sheet.* Washington, DC: Author. Retrieved from http://www.aacc. nche.edu

American Association of Community Colleges (AACC). (2012b). *Institutional characteristics of communitycolleges.* Retrieved fromhttp://www.aacc. nche.edu/acoutcc/Trends/Pages/instcharacteristics/aspx

Beckman, B. (2011, April). *Are you ready to be a president?* Presentation at the Annual Convention of the American Association of Community Colleges, New Orleans, LA.

Boggs, G. R. (2010, October). *Democracy's colleges: The evolution of the community college in America.* Prepared for the White House Summit on Community Colleges, Washington, DC.

Carver, J., & Carver, M. (1994). *A new vision for board leadership: Governing the community college.* Washington, DC: Association of Community College Trustees.

Cohen, A. M, & Brawer, F. B. (2008). *The American community college* (5th ed.). San Francisco, CA: Jossey-Bass.

Collins, J. (2005). *Good to great and the social sectors: A monograph to accompany Good to Great.* New York, NY: HarperCollins.

DeAngelo, L., Franke, R., Hurtado, S., Pryor, J. H., & Tran, S. (2011). *Completing college: Assessing graduation rates at four-year institutions.* Los Angeles: Higher Education Research Institute, UCLA.

Eddy, P. L. (2010). *Community college leadership: A multidimensional model for leading change.* Sterling, VA: Stylus.

Floyd, D. L., Maslin-Ostrowski, P., & Hrabak, M. L. (2010). Beyond the headlines: Wounding and the community college president. *New Directions for Community Colleges, 2010* (149), 65–73.

Floyd, D. L., & Vigil Laden, B. (2007). Transferring leadership skills: When community college presidents become university professors. *Community College Journal of Research and Practice, 31* (11), 913–932.

Floyd, D. L., & Walker, K. P. (2009). The community college baccalaureate: Putting the pieces together. *Community College Journal of Research and Practice, 33* (2), 90–124.

Hassan, A. M., Dellow, D. A., & Jackson, R. J. (2009). The AACC leadership competencies: Parallel views from the top. *Community College Journal of Research and Practice, 34* (1–2), 180–198.

Maslin-Ostrowski, P., & Floyd, D. L. (2012). When the time comes for the community college president to step aside: Daunting realities of leading. *Community College Journal of Research and Practice, 36* (4), 291–299.

Maslin-Ostrowski, P., Floyd, D. L., & Hrabak, M. L. (2011). Daunting realities of leading complicated by the new media: Wounding and community college presidents. *Community College Journal of Research and Practice, 35* (1), 29–32.

McNair, D. E. (2009). Preparing community college leaders: The AACC core competencies for effective leadership & doctoral education. *Community College Journal of Research and Practice, 34* (1–2), 199–217.

McNair, D. E., Duree, C. A., & Ebbers, L. (2011). If I knew then what I know now: Using leadership competencies developed by the American Association of Community Colleges to prepare community college presidents. *Community College Review, 39* (1), 3–25.

Mulder, A. E. (2001). Rites of passage: On grand entrances and graceful exits. *Community College Journal of Research and Practice, 25* (3), 239–241.

O'Banion, T. (2009). *The rogue trustee: The elephant in the room.* Phoenix, AZ: The League for Innovation in Community Colleges.

Pierce, S. R. (2012). *On being presidential: A guide for college and university leaders.* San Francisco, CA: Jossey-Bass.

Sinady, C., Floyd, D. L., & Mulder, A. E. (2010). The AACC competencies and Ph.D. completion project: Practical implications. *Community College Journal of Research and Practice, 34* (1–2), 218–226.

Skolnik, M. L., & Floyd, D. L. (2005). Community college baccalaureate: Toward an agenda for policy and research. In D. L. Floyd, M. L. Skolnik, & K. P. Walker (Eds.), *The community college baccalaureate: Emerging Trends & Policy Issues* (pp. 191–198). Sterling, VA: Stylus.

Vaughan, G. B. (2000). *Balancing the presidential seesaw: Case studies in community college leadership.* Washington, DC: Community College Press.

Walker, K. P. (2005). History, rationale, and community college baccalaureate association. In D. L. Floyd, M. L. Skolnik, & K. P. Walker (Eds.), *The community college baccalaureate: Emerging Trends & Policy Issues* (pp. 9–24). Sterling, VA: Stylus.

Weill, L. V. (Ed.). (2009). *Out in front: The college president as the face of the institution.* The ACE Series on Higher Education. Lanham, MD: Rowman & Littlefield Education, American Council on Education.

Wheeler, D. (2012). *Servant leadership for higher education: Principles and practices.* San Francisco, CA: Jossey-Bass.

White House. (2009). *American Graduation Initiative fact sheet.* Retrieved from http://www.whitehouse.gov/the_press_office/Excerpts-of-the-Presidents-remarks-in-Warren-Michigan-and-fact-sheet-on-the-American-Graduation-Initiative/

CHAPTER TWENTY-ONE

Hermeneutical Adeptness and Presidential Leadership

Navigating the Contemporary Higher Education Landscape

DOROTHY LELAND

> You must read, you must persevere, you must sit up nights, you must inquire, and exert the utmost power of your mind. If one way does not lead to the desired meaning, take another; if obstacles arise, then still another; until, if your strength holds out, you will find that clear which at first looked dark.
> —Giovanni Bocaccio

Presidential leadership in the contemporary public university takes place in a complex semantic landscape.[1] One can think of this landscape as the topography created by competing organizational frameworks that inform how diverse interests understand and judge presidential actions. Not surprisingly, effective presidential leadership often entails a kind of hermeneutical adeptness—an ability and proclivity to attend to the meanings that may be ascribed to the president's actions by multiple institutional stakeholders: faculty, students, staff, alumni, athletic boosters, elected officials, community members, and governing boards.

A compelling example of how diverse interests understand and judge presidential actions, and how powerfully the forces generated by such judgments can play out, is the case of Gene R. Nichol, erstwhile president of the College of William & Mary. In October 2005, not long after assuming the office of president, Nichol announced that an eighteen-inch-tall brass cross would no longer remain on permanent display in the state-supported college's Wren Chapel, though it would still be available on request for Christian services and other events. Nichol's reason for removing the cross was to make Wren Chapel a more welcoming place for non-Christians. Though Nichol had his supporters among those who saw his action as an endorsement of religious pluralism and tolerance, he was criticized, even vilified, by conservative students, alumni, bloggers, media commentators, and state legislators, who interpreted his action as an example of left-wing political correctness trampling on cultural tradition. The backlash was so strong that in March 2007 an unidentified donor withdrew a $12,000,000 pledge to William & Mary due to his displeasure over the removal of the cross (Fain, 2007).

Nichol survived the Wren Chapel incident, but his ultimate fate is a vivid reminder that the various interests that understand and judge presidential actions are embedded in networks of power. Throughout his presidency Nichol would continue to make a number of principled decisions that grated against the sense of propriety of powerful external constituencies. His popularity with faculty and students and acknowledged successes in many areas were insufficient to shield him from the ensuing backlashes, and in the end his leadership was destabilized. Amid a final storm of outrage—this time over a controversial campus art show—and under pressure from conservative state legislators, William & Mary's Board of Visitors voted to not extend Nichol's contract beyond June of 2008, resulting in Nichol's abrupt resignation. The divided reactions to Nichol's departure are pithily summed up in an article from *The Chronicle of Higher Education*: "Hundreds of students and faculty members held a candlelight vigil outside Mr. Nichol's home hours after his resignation was announced. Meanwhile, some alumni and conservative commentators praised the board's action" (Fain, 2008, p. A1).

The history of Nichol's presidency illustrates the perils of principled decisionmaking given the countervailing forces and power dynamics that buffet the contemporary public university. A president who angers powerful alumni, political leaders, donors, athletic boosters, governing boards, faculty, staff, or students risks a tenure clouded by controversy so intense that his or her ability to lead is severely diminished. And the opportunities for igniting a firestorm of controversy that can destabilize presidential leadership are plentiful. Today, in a nation where the role of civil discourse and reasoned debate are diminished, where technology has radically altered the intensity and speed of public reaction, where public confidence in higher education has declined, and where the resources needed to deliver instruction and conduct non-funded research increasingly depend on the goodwill of politicians and donors, it is little wonder that presidential leadership sometimes suffers from a pall of timidity.

But timidity is not a desirable leadership trait for the contemporary university president who must lead institutional transformations under extraordinarily difficult circumstances. Our institutions are under deep financial stress and call upon higher education leaders to be inventive fiscal managers who can navigate the waters of reduced state support without damaging the core academic enterprise. The depth of a prolonged economic recession has made people fearful about their future and angry at the inability of political leaders to provide hope and solutions, and our campuses have again become sites of contest in broader economic and ideological struggles. Faced with deep structural budget deficits, lawmakers have rationalized huge budget cuts to public higher education by inflating flaws—real and imagined—and pointing fingers of blame at the academy itself. As cries for accountability have grown shriller, the weight of bureaucratic control on our colleges and universities has grown heavier.

In this complex and volatile environment, presidential leadership requires a finely tuned sensitivity to the competing expectations and power dynamics that constrain the contemporary public university. As Bolman and Deal (1991) famously asserted near the close of the last century, "an increasingly complex and turbulent organizational world demands greater cognitive complexity: effective managers need to understand multiple frames [perspectives] and know how to use them in practice. . . to be fully effective as both managers and leaders" (pp. 528–529). Birnbaum (1992) echoed this thesis in a study that identified four organizational cultures in higher education, arguing that the ability to simultaneously use the multiple interpretive frames that structure these cultures is a key to leadership effectiveness. Indeed, since the 1990s leadership theory in higher education has produced a number of studies that attempt to identify the complex cognitive maps that university presidents must use to effectively lead their institutions.

In this essay I adapt elements of frame theory as developed by Bolman and Deal, Birnbaum, and others to explore some prevalent tensions and sites of discord and struggle faced by the contemporary public university president. My focus is on viewing potential "flash points" in the life of a university president as manifestations of the often conflicting, contradictory, or otherwise discordant values and expectations embedded in the multiple organizational frames that a president must navigate. I draw from my own experience as a university president and use examples from the experience of others in an effort to illustrate and illuminate the hermeneutical adeptness that I believe is a key competency for presidential effectiveness.

Bureaucratic, Collegial, Political, and Symbolic Frames Revisited

At its best the literature on organizational frames in higher education leadership theory points to the pluralistic and often chaotic nature of the organizational context in which a university president must manage and lead. This organizational context invariably includes bureaucratic, collegial, political, and symbolic dimensions, though not always in an equal mix and perpetually subject to shifts over time.

As identified in the literature, the bureaucratic frame corresponds to an institution's decision-making hierarchy and the policies, procedures, and rules that regulate the institution and its actors (Baldridge & Higher Education Research Institute, 1978; Bolman & Deal, 1997; Edelstein, 1997). It is structured by expectations related to delineated lines of formal authority and organizational effectiveness through specialization, control, and coordination. Such expectations are manifested, for example, when members of an institution's governing board—often grounded in the models of managerial authority used in the business world—become frustrated with the pace of decision making on a college or university campus and fault the president for not getting results. Similarly, state and federal calls for higher education reform often reveal expectations inherent in the bureaucratic frame; for instance, that greater or better managerial control will yield desired results, most often results related to efficiency, accountability, and such easily quantifiable educational outcomes as degree productivity, retention, graduation, and post-graduation employment.

The collegial frame, in contrast, is rooted historically in the ideal of the university as a collegium or community of scholars. This ideal was embodied imperfectly in the early colonial colleges (which, like today's colleges, had lead administrators and lay governing boards) and manifests itself in the contemporary American university through the involvement of faculty and other internal stakeholders in decision-making processes. The expectation of meaningful faculty participation in managing the academic and educational affairs of the institution is particularly strong in contemporary American colleges and universities and has been institutionalized through formally recognized faculty governance bodies; institutional, state, and national faculty governance watchdog organizations; and even, in some cases, faculty representation on governing boards.

Although faculty governance bodies are typically part of the bureaucratic structure of American universities, with delegated authority based on expertise, the collegial dimension of organizational culture often has broader significance. It is linked to core values related to faculty autonomy and freedom from coercive influences on faculty intellectual work and academic decision making. As universities have increased in size, complexity, and managerial layers, faculty have experienced a loss of autonomy and control over the academic life of their institutions. Managerial intervention has created a host of new academic regulations and process, ranging from the use of course management systems to the mandatory inclusion of specific information on course syllabi in order to satisfy the risk-management instincts of university counsel. Curricular initiatives and mandates handed down by states, governing boards, and presidents—for example, time-to-degree requirements, completion of a state history course as a graduation requirement, pressure to replace face-to-face learning with online courses—can be experienced as egregious acts of meddling into the rightful domain of faculty control. Benjamin Ginsberg's polemic, *The Fall of the Faculty* (2011), attributes most of the ills that beset American higher education to the proliferation of professional administrators and the corresponding marginalization of faculty in academic and curricular decisions. In Ginsberg's view, American higher education suffers from administrative blight as cadres of career managers have asserted control over faculty in the academic arena and sucked up resources to support misdirected programmatic initiatives.

On a deeper structural, and less polemical, level, the strains and tensions between bureaucratic and collegial frames often play themselves out in a highly politicized and ideologically tinged environment, particularly in public higher education. It is common for state budget offices to demand that plans for harsh—and unreasonably inflated—budget cuts be produced for public scrutiny in a timeframe that precludes meaningful internal consultation. State governing and coordinating boards routinely hand down mandates that seem alien or even antithetical to the academic enterprise, often in the name of efficiency, risk management, and accountability; and university presidents, consistent with their delegated authority and responsibility, must—often reluctantly—implement these mandates. In unionized campus environments, presidents and other senior administrators can become entangled in contentious, rule-bound contract negotiations that polarize the institution through overheated rhetoric. Frequently pulled into non-academic realms of engagement and influence by the heavy burden of external demands related to off-campus fundraising and governmental relations, contemporary presidents risk being positioned as outsiders to the academic enterprise they are charged to lead.

Expectations related to consultation and shared decision making are not limited to faculties. Students and sometimes staff share these expectations, some of which have been institutionalized through formally recognized student-government and staff-assembly bodies. Student participation in the affairs of the university has a strong tradition in many smaller liberal arts colleges, but even in comprehensive and research universities the voice of the student has begun to carry a new kind of weight in the wake of the widespread application of commercial models under which higher education is viewed as a commodity and students as consumers who pay a fee for goods and services. As J. E. Groccia (1997) explains, students as customers perceive themselves to have specific entitlements to express their needs, expectations, and satisfaction with respect to the goods and services they have purchased. Even in the absence of the student-as-consumer mindset, sharp increases in student tuition and fees have understandably provoked greater student interest in the benefits to students of institutional expenditures, an interest that, in some states, has manifested itself as organized advocacy efforts by students for representation (or increased representation) on governing boards.

While expectations related to shared decision making, consultation, and participatory processes are strong forces in many contemporary colleges and universities, the constituencies that share such expectations are often divided by differences in circumstance, role, interest, values, and ideology. The contemporary American university, as Baldridge (1971) noted, is "fractured by conflicts along lines of disciplines, faculty subgroups, student subcultures, splits between administrators and faculties and rifts between professional schools" (p. 52). Students may view themselves as customers or consumers, but many faculty sharply disagree and challenge the student's ability to make informed judgment on matters related to academic quality. In a research university environment that emphasizes funded research expenditures and technology transfer, faculty in the humanities and arts may feel that their work is underappreciated and undervalued. Issues of voice, compensation, access to resources, and prestige are frequent sites of contention between ladder rank and temporary faculty. Staff who lack the delegated decision-making authority enjoyed by faculty governance bodies can feel disenfranchised by decisions that impact their work. Conservative student groups rail against the perceived hegemony of liberal control over curriculum, speakers, and programs, while religious, ethnic, and sexual minorities struggle for representation and place. When divides between campus constituency groups are rooted in sharp differences of ideology and strongly held values, campuses can become sites of discord thatreflectbroader social and political struggles.

As originally introduced by Baldridge (1971), the political frame conceives of the university as a political system composed ofcompeting interest groups that are managed through coalition building, negotiation, and compromise when conflict inevitably and routinely arises. This initial conception was expanded (Baldridge & Higher Education Research Institute, 1978; Bolman & Deal, 1997; Riley & Baldridge, 1977) to include external factors, issues related to power and resources (Hardy, 1990; Millett & Harcleroad, 1984), and the broader state and national political context (Pusser, 2003). For my purposes here, the political frameincludes both micro-political and macro-political elements that often intersect in important ways. Campus debates over curricula and programs related to ethnic studies, gender studies, and multiculturalism grew out of broader social and political movements. More recently, turmoil on university campuses has reflected, and sometimes sharpened and refined, national debates over immigration, globalism, higher educationfunding, and social and economic justice issues related to the nation's growing wealth gap.

The policies established by governing boards can have profound impacts on universities and their students, faculty, and staff, including policies that emerge on the cusp of broader political issues that get played out through reigning alignments of power. For example, the national debate on immigration reform has differentially affected public university campuses across the nation based on differing alignments of power and ideology. The push by conservative groups to limit access to public benefits for undocumented residents has focused, in part, on access to public higher education, including access to state financial aid, in-state tuition, and even, in the extreme, access to public university classrooms under any circumstances. In California, a favorable political alignment enabled leaders of the state's public higher education institutions to join legislative leaders and advocacy groups to secure passage of AB 130, a law which grants undocumented students access to state financial aid (McGreevy & York, 2011, p. A1). The situation is far different in Georgia, one of only four states that currently bars in-state tuition for undocumented students.

When the governing board of the University System of Georgia was pressured by powerful legislators to ban undocumented students from its classrooms, a number of board members saw merit in one of the points of argument—that undocumented students should not take up seats in classrooms to the exclusion of qualified Georgia citizens. The board struck a compromiseof sorts by adopting a policy that bans undocumented students only from its most competitive, selective institutions while leaving them free to enroll in institutions that admit all qualified applicants. Although the board perceived this as a rational response to a state public-policy priority (providing higher education access to every qualified Georgia citizen), others perceived the action as caving in to political influence, as an abdication of the board's constitutional granted autonomy that will result in further disenfranchising a vulnerable segment of the population (Diamond, 2011, p. A1). The action ignited protests that continue to this day.

The final campus organizational dimension that I will touch on here is the symbolic frame. This frame corresponds, roughly, to those aspects of organizational life that are propelled by an institution's mythology—canonical stories; ceremonial events and objects; and deeply held beliefs, values, and perceptions about the institution. We have already encountered this organizational dimension in the Wren Chapel saga where the act of removing across in the name of religious diversity and inclusion ran headlong into the iconic role that the cross had played in William & Mary's history. Claudia Limbert, the former president of Mississippi University for Women, encountered a bitter backlash from alumni when she advocated considering new, less gender-specific names for a school that for decades had been co-educational. For many alumnae from the school's female-only days—some with very powerful connections within the state—Limbert's act was tantamount to an act of sacrilege against the proud past of the institution (Salter, 2009). Similarly, when a disgruntled University of Alabama football fan poisoned a grove of 130–year-old oak trees near the campus of football rival Auburn, it was clear from the aftermath that these oak trees held considerable symbolic significance for Auburn fans (Boone, 2011). Located at historic Toomer's Corner, an area where fans have traditionally celebrated Auburn victories with spontaneous eruptions of jubilation and camaraderie, the trees constituteda sacred grove within the human landscape of Auburn University.

The symbolic dimension of organizational life most often plays itself out less dramatically. Consider the case of the Ghost of George. A university president, after working diligently to establish strong lines of consultation with her faculty, was unable to understand why the faculty continued to reflexively assume that the administration was preparing to act autocratically. Enlightenment finally came when the president confided her perplexity to a group of senior, long-serving, and well-respected faculty members who took it upon themselves to describe for her the autocratic rule of George, a long-departed chief academic officer who also served a term as interim president.[2] Over timeGeorge hadbecome the symbolic embodiment of top-down bureaucratic management and punitive actions. As the senior faculty explained, his ghost still lurked in the hallways where faculty members informally exchange information and speculation, routinely emerging when gossip preceded clear and effective communication on the part of the administration. The Ghost of George invoked the fear that "bad action" from the administration was about to occur.

As an organizational frame, the symbolic dimension may seem to pale in comparison to bureaucratic, political, and collegial organizational dimensions, but in fact it permeates each of these. On its broadest level, it is the realm of sense making and sense giving crystalized into potent narratives; institutional life as it is understood and interpreted through iconic events and objects; and the sometimes discordant—but often emotionally charged—meanings that processes, persons, actions, objects, and events have for various groups. Presidents ignore this dimension at their peril.

Concluding Thoughts on Presidential Leadership

You got to know when to hold 'em, know when to fold 'em,
Know when to walk away and know when to run.
—Kenny Rogers, "The Gambler"

I opened this essay with the assertion that effective presidential leadership often entails hermeneutical adeptness—the ability to navigate through a complex semantic landscape. The institutional landscape is semantic not because it is composed of words, although words are indeed found there, but because it is fraught with complex layers of organizational signification and shaped by multiple and sometimes discordant interpretive frames. And while the bureaucratic, collegial, political, and symbolic frames sketched here do not represent this complexity with the situational nuance needed to navigate specific institutional environments, they provide useful guideposts for university presidents who must manage and lead their institutions through extraordinarily challenging times.

Today's public university president faces the consequences of a sustained erosion of state investment in higher education that has created serious strains on the ability of institutions to deliver on commitments to quality, access, and affordability. Fueled in part by sharply rising tuition costs, public confidence in public higher education has declined while state and federal scrutiny has become more burdensome. Policy think tanks urge market-based reengineering of higher education and call for greater transparency and accountability through the adoption of management approaches drawn from business. Inside our institutions, faculty and staff are fearful and uncertain about their future—the changing nature and circumstances of their work; the fate of their research or programmatic initiatives; the (mis)alignment of institutional change with their core values, interests, and priorities; encroachments on academic freedom and autonomy; the stagnation of compensation and wages; and a host of other issues that touch their personal and professional lives.

To respond to such challenges, the contemporary university president must be a principled, innovative, and bold thinker who also has the capacity to manage change in a complex and often volatile organizational environment. Presidents must be principled in order to avoid taking the path of least resistance simply because it is there, to resist flying on the winds of change simply because change is in the air, and to forestall self-serving tendencies or temptations. Although principled decision and action can be a source of conflict and discord, it also lends presidential leadership its integrity and helps to ensure that decision and action are guided by the core academic and institutional values that the president was hired to steward.

The contemporary university president must also be innovative and comfortable moving beyond familiar strategies and paradigms. For example, the fiscal challenges facing public higher education simply cannot be managed for the long-term using strategies that have worked in the past for the short term. During successive years of budget cuts, many public university presidents employed predictable strategies for coping—not filling vacant positions, hiring more temporary faculty, deferring salary increases, furloughing faculty and staff, streamlining "back office" operations, sharp tuition and fee increases, etc. But many of these same presidents acknowledge that such strategies are inadequate for securing the longer-term financial sustainability of public higher education, and that innovative solutions are required if public interests in educational quality, student access, and student affordability are to be preserved (Lederman, 2011).

Presidential leadership in the contemporary university also requires boldness if only because principled and innovative decision making and change will encounter resistance. The university presidency is a rough and tumble job. Boldness is required to shake up internal institutional alignments that have become dysfunctional, for rejecting unreasonable demands of powerful constituencies, for truth-telling when the truth is unsettling. Presidents, unlike most other institutional employees, are public figures, subject to the heaps of scorn and blame that sometimes befall political leaders and others in the public eye.

But principle, innovation, and boldness alone are not enough if the university president is to succeed in advancing a leadership agenda; they also must be guided by the kind of organizational savvy I have called hermeneutical adeptness. Presidents must become students of their organizations, in continual learning mode, as they seek a sophisticated and nuanced understanding of prevailing organizational frames and the dynamics of power and influence that can impede or assist in the implementation of their agendas. This includes becoming students of signs and signals that things are "out of whack" and could, without serious attention, destabilize the president's leadership. For example, presidents who measure their effectiveness in terms of the bureaucratic framework all too frequently rationalize faculty "no-confidence" votes as an expression of the resistance of an entrenched organizational culture opposed to necessary innovation and change (Schmidt, 2009). While there may be some truth to that perception, such a reading also misjudges the power of the faculty voice in higher education. Presidents who find ways to convince faculty to support, or at least not resist, change agendas are much more likely to, in the end, succeed.

The bureaucratic frame contains numerous pitfalls for university presidents who often must operate within its parameters. The delegation of authority within bureaucratic organizational structures, with graded levels of authority and control, leaves presidents vulnerable when managers turn a deaf ear to appropriate constituency demands, fail to consult or communicate effectively, act in ways that are inconsistent with core academic and institutional values, exert control over information that needs leadership attention, or behave illegally or immorally. Under the latter circumstances in particular, the symbolic dimension of the institution's organizational culture can have a powerful impact on the president's ability to lead. On a symbolic level, presidents are often positioned as the embodiment of institutional ideals and self-images: they represent the institution's pride, reputation, and integrity. When institutional actions and events tarnish this image an onslaught of emotionally charged reaction predictably ensues. Quick and appropriate corrective management actions may not be sufficient to overcome the palpable and deeply felt sense of outrage and betrayal.

The preferential treatment of politically connected students in the admissions process at the University of Illinois provides an instructive example. In 2009, a *Chicago Tribune* article alleged that prospective students with known connections to influential politicians and members of the institution's governing board were routinely placed on a "clout list" during the admissions process and that applicants on this list were admitted at a much higher rate than other applicants (Cohen, St. Clair, & Malone, 2009a). What the *Tribune* called the "clout list" in fact consisted of a red stripe applied to the files of Category 1 applicants—those who had influential connections.

A subsequent investigation launched by Illinois's governor determined that substantial abuses in the admissions process at the Urbana-Champaign campus had occurred, forcing the resignation of the campus chancellor and several governing board members, including the chairman, who were directly implicated in the scandal. While the president of the three-campus University of Illinois system reportedly had no knowledge of the politically tainted admissions process, the cries of outrage that erupted from the university, state, and beyond were so loud that he eventually stepped down (Cohen, St. Clair, & Malone, 2009b). President White was unable to effectively lead the University of Illinois beyond the scandal because he was its leadership face—a face symbolically stained by the political corruption of others at the highest levels, scarred by the affront to the institution's academic integrity, and seen as a visible reminder of the egregious violation of academic honor.

Finally, there are numerous examples of the destabilization of presidential leadership that occurs when presidents flaunt, ignore, or misunderstand key organizational dynamics and relations of power. Consider the following recent and compelling story.

On November 28, 2011, the governing board of the Oregon University System (OUS) voted unanimously to terminate without cause the contract of Dr. Richard Lariviere, President of the University of Oregon (Graves, 2011). The action met with loud boos from the assembled crowd, many of whom had testified before the OUS Board praising Lariviere's leadership accomplishments. Based on their testimony, these supporters would surely agree that Richard Lariviere's efforts on behalf of Oregon's flagship public university were principled, innovative, and bold. His expressed and admirable goal was to "rebuild our broken system of governance and funding in Oregon higher education" (Lariviere, 2011), and his proposals for doing so represented significant departures from business as usual in the Oregon University System. He advocated for the University of Oregon's independence from the state governing board and proposed a plan for eventual financial independence from the state. The plan called for permanently funding the University of Oregon through a $160,000,000 endowment, with the state generating half the amount via bond sales and the University of Oregon generating the other half via private donations (Lariviere, 2010, p. A23).

But in advancing this leadership agenda, Lariviere bucked critical alignments of power and bureaucratic control. For example, he took his proposals directly to the state legislature after the OUS Board had rejected them, a direct affront to the Board's statutory authority. Also, he opted out of a cost-containment strategy agreed to by the governor and the Oregon University System when he used banked tuition revenue to provide raises to a number of administrators and faculty—an action that reportedly complicated ongoing union contract negotiations at the state level and left parties to the agreement—including the governor, the presidents of other Oregon public universities, the OUS Chancellor, and members of the OUS Board—feeling betrayed.

Lariviere's supporters contend that he was fired because his innovative proposals were a threat to the established state higher-education bureaucracy and its alignment with the governor (Berdahl, 2011). Others, including Oregon's governor, argue that Lariviere was fired not for his ideas but rather for repeated violations of OUS Board policy, his dismissal of management directives, and his failure to act as a team player (Kitzhaber, 2011). Still others maintain that Lariviere's undoing was a result of political naiveté (Jaquiss, 2011). Regardless of who is right in this matter, Lariviere's termination left the University of Oregon without its leader. It left a campus that was once filled with hope for its future torn with anger and despair. And it left the ultimate fate of his leadership initiatives uncertain.

Lariviere's plight is a cautionary tale for presidents of other flagship universities who seek greater independence from state funding and control: they must steer their way through state-political and bureaucratic landscapes with hermeneutical adeptness to reasonably hope to accomplish their objectives. On a broader level, the story reveals an epic, possibly tragic, clash of the organizational frames that a president routinely encounters. Lariviere's ringing defense of academic quality and its link to freedom from bureaucratic meddling clearly resonates within the collegial frame. Thus the strong support from faculty. But from the perspective of the bureaucratic frame, his defiance of OUS Board priorities and direction emerges with equal clarity as a form of insubordination, an unwillingness to follow established rules and authorities. Politically, the interests of the state in the coordination of policy and funding across Oregon's public higher education sector was put to test by Lariviere's proposal for an independent University of Oregon, and the alignment of the OUS Board and governor around statewide coordination proved to be an enormous and, ultimately, fatal obstacle to success. The symbolic frame is most clearly visible in the canonical narratives that have begun to unfold in the aftermath of Lariviere's dismissal, with depictions of heroism and sacrifice on the part of Oregon's fallen president—narratives that are likely to hold, at least for a time, a potent cluster of leadership hopes and expectation that the university's future presidents must surely navigate.[3]

Notes

I acknowledge, with appreciation, the research and editorial assistance of Donald A. Barclay, a scholar in his own right, who elected to lend a hand to his overburdened chancellor.

1. The phrase "university president" is used here to designate a college or university CEO. The term "chancellor" is a less common alternative designation. Although the focus of this essay is on presidential leadership in public higher education, aspects of this analysis will apply to private institutions.
2. "George" is a fictionalized name used to protect the identity of the maligned former provost and his ghost.
3. Canonical narratives are not necessarily false, and I leave it to others to determine whether Lariviere failed to grasp and pursue alternative tactics that could have led to success. It could be that no path would have been viable and that the president, in allegiance to his principles and with great boldness, chose to fall on his sword.

References

Baldridge, J. V. (1971). *Power and conflict in the university: Research in the sociology of complex organizations*. New York: John Wiley.

Baldridge, J. V., & Higher Education Research Institute (Los Angeles, Calif.). (1978). *Policy making and effective leadership : A national study of academic management*. San Francisco: Jossey-Bass.

Berdahl, R. (2011, November 30). UO President's downfall was his pursuit of excellence. *Register-Guard*. Retrieved from http://www.registerguard.com/web/opinion/27247002–47/university-state-lariviere-board-oregon.html. csp

Birnbaum, R. (1992). *How academic leadership works: Understanding success and failure in the college presidency*. San Francisco: Jossey-Bass.

Bolman, L. G., & Deal, T. E. (1991). *Reframing organizations: Artistry, choice, and leadership*. San Francisco: Jossey-Bass.

Bolman, L. G., & Deal, T. E. (1997). *Reframing organizations: Artistry, choice, and leadership*. San Francisco: Jossey-Bass.

Boone, C. (2011, February 18). Auburn tree-killing the talk of Alabama. *Atlanta Journal-Constitution.* Retrieved from http://www.ajc.com/sports/auburn-tree-killing-the-841586.html

Cohen, J. S., St. Clair, S., & Malone, T. (2009a, May 29). Clout goes to college. *Chicago Tribune.* Retrieved from http://www.chicagotribune.com/news/watchdog/college/chi-070529u-of-i-clout, 0,5173000. story

Cohen, J. S., St. Clair, S., & Malone, T. (2009b, September 24). University of Illinois President B. Joseph White resigns. *Chicago Tribune.* Retrieved from http://www.chicagotribune.com/news/chi-u-of-i-white-resign-24–sep24, 0,161068. story

Diamond, L. (2011, August 18). AJC exclusive illegal immigration colleges ask proof of legal residency; 1 student barred; effect on enrollment unclear. *Atlanta Journal-Constitution,* pp. A1. Retrieved from http://infoweb. newsbank.com/iw-search/we/InfoWeb?p_product=AWNB&p_theme=aggregated5&p_action=doc&p_docid=13933053D92B2168&p_docnum=5&p_queryname=1

Edelstein, M. G. (1997). Academic governance: The art of herding cats. In J. Martin, & J. E. Samels (Eds.), *First among equals: The role of the chief academic officer* (pp. 58–78). Baltimore, MD: Johns Hopkins University Press.

Fain, P. (2007, March 9). College loses donation after removing cross. *Chronicle of Higher Education,* pp. A35. Retrieved from http://chronicle.com/article/College-Loses-Donation-After/15522/

Fain, P. (2008, February 22). William andMary's president exits on his own terms. *Chronicle of Higher Education,* pp. A1. Retrieved from http://chronicle.com/article/WilliamMarys-President/4375/

Ginsberg, B. (2011). *The fall of the faculty: The rise of the all-administrative university and why it matters.* Oxford: Oxford University Press.

Graves, B. (2011, November 29). University of Oregon rally pushes for independent boardafter firing of President Richard Lariviere. *Oregonian.* Retrieved from http://www.oregonlive.com/education/index. ssf/2011/11/university_of_oregon_rally_pus.html

Groccia, J. E. (1997). The student as customer versus the student as learner. *About Campus, 2* (2), 31–32.

Hardy, C. (1990). "Hard" decisions and "tough" choices: The business approach to university decline. *Higher Education, 20* (3), 301–321.

Jaquiss, N. (2011, November 30). Flunk a duck: U of O President Richard Lariviere may be brilliant—But he failed politics 101. *Willamette Week.* Retrieved from http://wweek.com/portland/article-18266–flunk_a_duck.html

Kitzhaber, J. (2011, November 26). Gov. John Kitzhaber's statement on University of Oregon President Richard Lariviere. *Oregonian.* Retrieved from http://www.oregonlive.com/education/index. ssf/2011/11/gov_john_kitzhabers_statement.html

Lariviere, R. W. (2010, November 23). Saving public universities, starting with my own. *Wall Street Journal.* Retrieved from http://proquest. umi.com/pqdweb? index=3&did=2194945351&SrchMode=1&sid=1&Fmt=3&VInst=PROD&VType=PQD&RQT=309&VName=PQD&TS=1325811027&clientId=48051

Lariviere, R. W. (2011). *Statement of University of Oregon President Richard W. Lariviere to the Oregon State Board of Higher Education.* Retrieved January 5, 2012, from http://newpartnership. uoregon.edu/blog/2011/12/02/statement-from-richard-larivieres-statement-to-ous-board/

Lederman, D. (2011, March 4). Perspectives on the downturn: A survey of presidents. *Inside Higher Ed.* Retrieved from http://www.insidehighered.com/news/survey/perspectives-downturn-survey-presidents#ixzz1iKHW2l3h

McGreevy, P., & York, A. (2011, October 9). Brown signs California Dream Act funding bill: Illegal immigrants who qualify can get state aid to attend publiccolleges. *Los Angeles Times,* pp. A1. Retrieved from http://proquest. umi.com/pqdweb? index=2&did=2479787341&SrchMode=1&sid=3&Fmt=3&VInst=PROD&VType=PQD&RQT=309&VName=PQD&TS=1325802644&clientId=48051

Millett, J. D., &Harcleroad, F. F. (1984). *Conflict in higher education: State government coordination versus institutional independence.* San Francisco: Jossey-Bass.

Pusser, B. (2003). Beyond Baldridge: Extending the political model of higher education organization and governance. *Educational Policy, 17* (1), 121–140.

Riley, G. L., & Baldridge, J. V. (1977). *Governing academic organizations: New problems, new perspectives.* Berkeley, CA: McCutchan.

Salter, S. (2009, August 12). MUW name change faces capitol battle. *Greenwood Commonwealth.* Retrieved from http://infoweb. newsbank.com/iw-search/we/InfoWeb? p_product=AWNB&p_theme=aggregated5&p_action=doc&p_docid=12A0FDA51B1F8AE0&p_docnum=9&p_queryname=1

Schmidt, P. (2009, June 12). How to fire your president: Voting "no confidence" with confidence. *Chronicle of Higher Education.* Retrieved from http://chronicle.com/article/How-to-Fire-Your-President-/47315

PART FIVE

Social Forces: Mirror Images and Transfigurations

CHAPTER TWENTY-TWO

An Economy of Higher Education

BENJAMIN BAEZ

What the bourgeoisie, therefore, produces, above all, is its own grave-diggers.[1]

Introduction: Economics

It has become a truism in the field of higher education to say that decreasing public financial support (especially since the 1980s) by federal and state governments has led colleges and universities to seek alternative sources of funding, which requires of them specifically to engage in market-like behavior, such as raising tuition, utilizing enrollment management, deferring the costs of services to students, engaging in fund-raising, marketing themselves and their services, and promoting the commercialization of knowledge via aggressive pursuits of intellectual property.[2] Those of us on the left are prone to critique such activities, referring to them derisively as forms of "academic capitalism."[3] Such arguments, theoretically acute and empirically valid as they are, nevertheless require an economic view of higher education, which I find paradoxical since subtending such arguments seems to be a sense that economics as an all-encompassing logic for thinking about higher education is somehow inappropriate.

Still, the fact that higher education may be thought about in economic terms is not surprising, for over the last 40 years, policymakers and bureaucrats all over the world have looked to the discipline of economics as a major, if not the sole, source of wisdom about how our society should run. As Steve Keen argues, "The world has been remade in the economist's image."[4] Keen questions such a privileging, arguing that economics has not made the world a better place to live; indeed, the predominant form of economic theory (i.e., the neoclassical school) has led to great inequality, instability, and inefficiency: income gaps are getting wider, and economic meltdowns and crises seem the norm.[5] Yet, because the global economy today looks more like the textbook ideal (e.g., barriers to trade have been reduced, government regulations of capital flows have been liberalized, etc.), economists have advised that the best way to allocate resources is an unfettered market.[6]

Keen argues that neoclassical economics, in particular, is inferior to the other sciences because of the "irrational tenacity with which it holds to its core beliefs in the face of either contrary factual evidence or theoretical techniques that establish fundamental inconsistencies in its intellectual apparatus."[7] Specifically, neoclassical economics holds on to the classical notion of *homo economicus*, or "economic man" concerned only with furthering his own needs. I agree with Keen about this irrational tenacity but will suggest that it is not unique to economics, for all institutions claiming scientific expertise must, by definition, maintain tenacity for their theories.

For now, let me just say that neoclassical economics, for which I will give a brief account later, is the predominant school of economics.[8] Recently, as Keen's work suggests, critics have mounted an attack on mainstream economists, taking aim at, as a recent article in *The Chronicle of Higher Education* states, the ideology of "free-market fundamentalism" that has dominated economics for some time now. This attack questions the logic of (neoclassical) economics' core tenets: the market is the most efficient way to allocate resources, people generally make rational decisions when buying goods and services, and government regulations are to be minimized because they risk undermining purer market forces and can lead to corruption. Yet, this ideology, according to the *Chronicle* article, has been accepted by presidential administrations from both political parties in the U.S., and it is most often associated with prestigious academic departments in the Ivy League, Stanford University, and the University of Chicago.[9]

The rejection of *homo economicus* is at the root of much of the critiques of economics. Mark Osteen and Martha Woodmansee argue that there is irony in the fact that economists' belief in the self-interested, rational agent is rarely applied to themselves; that is, they ask, how is the positing of such ideas in the economists' self-interest?[10] I will be concerned in this chapter with the self-interest of economists in putting forth such ideas, but I don't believe that the problem can be located by focusing on economists' motives, as the *Chronicle* article does. There is a tendency in critiques of neoclassical economics to blame economists. Interestingly, in this *Chronicle* article, N. Gregory Mankiw, a professor of economics at Harvard University, took exception to the assertion that economists were ideologically motivated, indicating that because economics does not lend itself to settled conclusions, it is a method, not a doctrine.[11] I agree that the issue here is not ideology per se, but not for the same reasons that Mankiw gives. Still, such attacks on economists seem misguided to me, for if my premises are correct, there are no legitimate epistemological grounds from which to do so. These attacks, after all, presuppose an economic claim that is not ideological, and I've been influenced too much by critical theorists to accept that.

I will, therefore, not offer here a psychology of the economist, which seems to me to be the case when critiques are leveled at neoclassical economists: their motives are put into question. Doing so seems to me to be another kind of individualizing of social phenomenon, which, ironically, is what most critics say is wrong with neoclassical economics. I will focus on the economist, not as a psychological being but as an academic one. With regard to the economics of higher education, there is a tendency to focus on government funding and overall financing of higher education, or on the economic impact of a higher education. In this paper, however, I will focus on a particular kind of economy in higher education: the production of the academic expert. If you will, I will try to locate *homo economicus* within *homo academicus*. My task in this chapter, following Pierre Bourdieu, is to offer a way to "trap *Homo Academicus*, supreme classifier among classifiers, in the net of his own classifications"[12] classifications that will come to haunt the very institution that created him.

In the next section, I offer a (very) brief account of the prevailing ideas about the economics of higher education. Then I focus more specifically on neoclassical economics. Next, I offer a sociology of higher education, focusing predominantly on the legitimization of the social scientist and the power she yields in the world. Finally, I end with a critique of economics that focuses less on the validity of its claims about the field of higher education than on the ways it dictates how such a field is to be understood and affirmed.

The Economics of Higher Education in the U.S., In Brief

In the U.S., the federal government's overall aid to institutions of higher education exceeds $100 billion and much of that is in student aid, though student aid is increasingly coming only in the form of loans, leaving students with extensive debt after they graduate.[13] The states still play the largest role in higher education, but this will be affected by escalating demands on their budgets, among other things.[14] Indeed, the recessions hitting most states lead to fewer funds for institutions of higher education, but also the politics of state funding require that a state allocate its funds among other competing institutions: corrections, K-12 education, and healthcare. As a result of this, students and their families have to shoulder a greater burden of college expenses. It appears, therefore, that the philosophy of funding for higher education has changed. Higher education is no longer seen as a public good by policymakers but as a private good, justifying their categorization of expenditures for higher education as discretionary, and leaving the burden for its costs on the so-called consumer.

While college costs are being shifted to the student and her family, states are also insisting that institutions of higher education, especially public ones, which they can control, produce a highly educated and skilled workforce to ensure future economic growth.[15] This insistence comes across in calls for "more efficiency" "more productivity" "more accountability" and these calls lead to the kind of logic underlying Texas Governor Rick Perry's 7–point plan, which at the time of my writing this chapter, Governor Rick Scott wanted to implement in Florida.[16] The 2006 Spellings Report furthers this logic, stating, for example, that "in this consumer-driven environment, students increasingly care little about the distinctions that sometimes preoccupy the academic establishment, from whether a college is nonprofit or offers classes online. They care about results."[17] In order to receive funding at all, according to the logic of such initiatives, colleges and universities must "prove" the benefits they generate for the economy with their graduates, public service, and research.

On top of all this, as Simon Marginson argues with regard to American public universities, they have come under pressure by two models. On the one hand, there is the model of the private research university, which is sustained by stellar reputations, selectivity, high price, and national/global leadership in a "winner take all" market; and, on the other hand, there is the model of the for-profit, vocational institutions, which have become the fastest growing sector in American higher education and are siphoning off students.[18] Both of these models are heavily subsidized by, predominantly, the federal government via student aid.

What is happening in the federal and state governments in the U.S. is largely what shapes the logic of the discourse on the economics of higher education, but there is also a sense in which what is happening in the U.S. is a global phenomenon. The undermining of the nation-state as a result of global cultural and economic exchanges facilitates the forces of privatization, shedding doubt on the roles of institutions of higher education as public trusts. Public and private funding of higher education, if in the past focusing on altruistic or "national" concerns, now seems tied to economic prosperity, especially in the global marketplace.

Conventional wisdom has it that current funding patterns and the forces of global capitalism lead to "academic capitalism" but it may also be true that a new economic logic shapes those patterns and forces. That is, the traditional model of public funding for ostensibly state and national objectives has been replaced by another kind of model of "public funding" one generally promoting consumerism for students, entrepreneurship for faculty, commercialization for knowledge, and privatization for services.

Ironically, such "academic capitalism" is shielded from the vagaries of the market, for the promise of profits allows universities to invest vast amounts of money in such activities, even if such profits fail to materialize. For example, very few universities generate revenues from commercially sponsored research, despite huge investments in it.[19] F. King Alexander explains that since the 1980s, universities have sought to acquire greater wealth in order to generate more fiscal capacity. In this environment, their primary objective is "prestige maximization" in which academic and financial standards are defined by the relative status and ranking with other institutions. Institutions have to outspend each other, inflating educational expenditures to the highest common denominator and creating an educational expenditure "cold war" among institutions, now defined not by the intrinsic worth of any particular goal but by comparison with other institutions.[20]

The "economics of higher education" therefore, might be understood within larger economic and political forces, which are made possible by, but now also make possible, the (1) major shifts in government spending, which have pushed institutions of higher education to pursue alternative sources of revenue; (2) globalization of the economy, which has put a premium on products and processes derived from scientific innovation; and (3) evolution of government policies, which have enabled "academic capitalism."[21] The culture of public higher education, if one can speak of it this way, is one now driven less by a notion of itself as a public trust than by financial incentive.

Others have written extensively about all this, so I will say little more about the economics of higher education, as commonly understood. I would like to focus here on how the logic of economics structures thought in higher education. I am reminded of the debates over college costs that periodically come about, especially when the federal government tries to do something about it. In one such instance in 1998, the federally sponsored National Commission on the Costs of Higher Education ("Commission") issued a report, *Straight Talk About College Costs and Prices*, which informed us that higher education is a "life-long investment" and that the public anxiety about college prices is very real and worthy of attention.[22] The report explained the complexity of college costs. For example, "tuition" or the "sticker price" does not include education-related costs borne by students, such as books, laboratory fees, and living expenses. Furthermore, many students receive financial aid, so that what they actually pay is unlikely to be related to the tuition charged.

I don't want to spend too much time on the content of this report, as much as on the language it uses in reducing a college education to the language of economics, and particularly neoclassical economics. Breaking down the concept of "cost" the report also distinguished between expenditures institutions incur to provide education ("costs") and expenses that students and their families face ("prices"). The report also analyzes "cost drivers" or the factors believed to lead to rising tuition (e.g., institutional aid to the student, cost of student services, etc.). There was also a discussion regarding the "expectations about quality" leading to increased costs (e.g., things like facilities to attract students, supporting new disciplines, and, in short, prestige maximization).

Language like this leads to unquestioned neoclassical claims by even those advocating greater financial support for underserved populations. For example, Thomas Kane focused on how financial aid policies constrain the "investment decisions of low-income families."[23] He argues that if "there is an economic rationale for public intervention in higher education, it is to ensure that all families have access to the resources to finance worthwhile investments on their own."[24] The language of neoclassical economics, therefore, can serve all kinds of debates on the left and the right and even encompasses what can even count as economic wisdom. When Robert Toutkoushian offers a "lay" understanding of the economics of higher education in a higher-education program's magazine, he refers to the concerns of economics as being about how decision makers want to make the best out of their situation, and how they can do so while assessing the constraints that limit their ability to reach their ultimate goals. The primary economic model, he argues, is a free and competitive market.[25] "Economics" here is taken to be neoclassical economics, presumptively without need to reference other kinds of economic theories.[26]

So, the prevailing logic is that the economics of higher education is structured by neoclassical economics, either as the basis of the logic of the scholars who support its use in thinking about higher education, or as the basis for the critique of those who oppose its use. But what exactly is neoclassical economics, and why has it come to mean "economics?" This question leads me next to a (very) brief discussion of neoclassical economics and its predominance in economic thought.

Neoclassical Economics: *Homo Economicus*

In this discussion, I will avoid the technicalities of the tenets of the school of neoclassical economics (e.g., marginal utility, Pareto efficiency, equilibrium, etc.) and focus instead on its overall philosophical presuppositions. The purported premise of neoclassical economics harks back to Adam Smith's famous metaphor that a self-motivated individual is led by an "invisible hand" to promote society's welfare; that is, the self-centered behavior of individuals necessarily entails cooperation leading to the highest possible level of welfare for society as a whole.[27] Smith's logic is explicitly espoused, but it seems that Jeremy Bentham's philosophy of utilitarianism actually undergirds neoclassical economics. For Bentham, humans are products of innate drives to seek pleasure and avoid pain; all behavior is rooted in these drives. Society is a fiction; only individuals exist, and what can said to be in the interest of society is simply the sum of the interests of the individuals that make up society.[28] Given this, it is always best to leave individuals alone. Bentham serves not only to justify a philosophy of an unfettered market, but he also proposed that pleasure and pain can be objectively measured, allowing economists to erect complex mathematical models of human behavior that not only address individual behavior but society itself.[29]

Bentham notwithstanding, the classical economists were not advocating individual freedom for its own sake; indeed, Smith and others were concerned with the negative effects of such freedom and advocated for it only with regard to the market. But the neoclassical view stripped away from inquiry any moral questions. In this view, all questions of value are determined "in the market" as a result of supposedly subjective calculations.[30] Objective social relations were thus replaced by individual subjectivities. Constructed via these theories, according to John Duprè and Regina Gagnier, was an economic man, "a rational maximizer of utility derived from consumption of material goods, for whom the society at which economic man aims is indeed the ideal." *Homo economicus* was thus born from this. So successful is *homo economicus* that rational choice is now seen to govern all kinds of actions, economic and otherwise.[31]

For well over 100 years, *homo economicus* has figured mainstream economics, standing for self-interest, egoism, competition, and pleasure-seeking; *homo economicus*, "reared in the Cartesian nursery, nourished by a diet long on atomism and short on empathy, has generally been treated as a rather transparent agent."[32] We see ourselves in him, for regardless of his materiality, he carries the Western humanist dream of a conscious, knowing, unified, and rational individual, a master of his fate.[33]

How has *homo economicus* gained such prominence in economic thought? Economics as such began in the eighteenth century, when it was realized that there were such things as economic mechanisms to study, and especially with the writings of Adam Smith. Economics as a field of study has concerned itself mainly with understanding how a capitalist system works.[34] The economy was conceived of a large number of independent firms and households, whose interactions with each other consisted of voluntary exchanges of goods and services. Smith and others, to a large extent, thus came to see the economy as a self-regulating system.[35] Economic agents were also conceived as well-informed, rational, and self-interested, with firms seeking to maximize profits and households seeking wealth or whatever best satisfied their preferences.[36] The classical economists did not care much about consumers, being more interested in production and the factors that influenced the supply of goods. In the 1870s, a "neoclassical" economics focused on individual choice and exchange after the writings of William Stanley Jevons, Carl Menger, and Leon Walras, who were influenced by utilitarianism and who posited that social policy can and should be determined by calculating the alternatives for the total happiness of individuals.[37] Such logic began to dominate economic thinking. Then came the Great Depression following the stock market crash of 1929, which provided the setting for the most serious challenge to neoclassical economics to date.[38] Enter John Maynard Keynes, who challenged the logic of self-correcting mechanisms in the market, and who also convincingly argued that governments should intervene to stabilize the economy until the self-correcting mechanism could take hold.[39] His economic theory was influential through the post-war period and into the 1970s. In the 1970s and 1980s, Keynesian economics was seriously challenged because it was inadequate for explaining inflation and unemployment, and because economists became enamored of microeconomics. Despite Keynes influence, his work did not shake the foundations of neoclassical theories, and economics divided itself into (a) microeconomics, concerned with individuals, firms, and industries, and (b) macroeconomics, concerned with aggregate demand and the performance of the economy as a whole. And since the 1930s, neoclassical economics has been becoming more and more mathematically complex, which enables modern economics to gain many new theoretical and scientific insights.[40]

This new microeconomics drew upon new techniques that assumed that each economic agent acts upon the same, consistent economic model, fully deploying the information available; economic fluctuations are understood primarily as the consequence of responses to shocks by optimizing and efficient economic agents who can neutralize systematic government intervention by anticipating its intended impact.[41] Thus, such intervention is bound to fail. These techniques and logic ratchet up the levels of mathematical and statistical techniques required of economists and instantiates rational expectations into areas of economics not traditionally concerned with them; it pushes economics further down the road of esoteric modeling in which mathematical and statistical techniques prevail over conceptual advance.[42] The technological explosion of information processing further makes possible the explosion of econometric studies.[43] At any rate, today, although the distinction between micro- and macroeconomics has vestiges in economic thought, for the most part macroeconomics has been subsumed into microeconomics.[44]

The subsuming of much of economic thought into microeconomics is made possible by the privileging of economic formalism, which purports to derive its practice, and hence its authority, from the nature of the object under scrutiny and the nature of the subject performing the analysis. According to Howard Horowitz, such formalism devises measures that correspond to the activity it studies; this analysis purportedly is conducted by (and measures the effects of) rational selves, able to comprehend fully the reasons for and consequences of economic activity.[45]

This formalism in neoclassical economics, and especially the preposterous assumptions about *homo economicus* that sustains it, of course, lead to scathing critiques. According to Daniel Hausman, many of economics' premises are platitudes, such as individuals can rank alternatives or individuals choose what they prefer; others are simplifications, such as commodities are infinitely divisible or individuals have perfect information. On such platitudes and simplifications, he argues, economists have erected a "mathematically sophisticated theoretical edifice, whose conclusions, although certainly not necessarily erroneous, are nevertheless often off the mark."[46] The most serious critiques question the notion of *homo economicus*, with his Crusoe-like existence, arguing that neoclassical economics ignores how social institutions dictate behavior and influence choices.[47]

More recently, the critiques of neoclassical economics focus on how it overreaches itself. During the past 40 years, some neoclassical economists have tried to extend economic logic beyond economic questions, indicating that rational choice works in the realm of culture, guiding things like religion, gift giving, suicide, substance abuse, marriage, reproduction, and whatever else.[48] Ben Fine argues that economics is "colonizing" the other social sciences, extending its methods as never before to analytical terrain that had previously been seen as lying outside its scope. An economics of optimizing individuals is now deployed to address all that is cultural, facilitating the flow of the so-called economic approach to previously non-economic subject matter.[49] The rationale for this extension of economic logic beyond the realm of the economy is exemplified by the work of Gary Becker, a Nobel prize-winning economist at the University of Chicago.[50] I will critique Becker's notion of human capital in the concluding section of this chapter. For now, let me point out that it is only because of the power economics has gained as a way of knowing that such overreach is possible, and a theory of why this might be the case is the focus of my next section.

Homo Economicus=Homo Academicus

In the introduction to this chapter, I suggested an economy of the academic expert, one who is produced by universities and through which they put out theories of the world, some of which come to question the very existence of their institutions. Institutions of higher education are vulnerable to economic logic but, in a sense, such logic gains power only because it comes from those very institutions. In this section, I would like us to think about the production of academic experts. Economics is a well-established social science (probably the social science many physical scientists would counts as real science), and as such it was integral to the making of Western modernity.[51] These sciences articulated ideals and maps of the new social order, legitimized the role of the state, offered it objective knowledge with which to govern the population, and provided strategies for defining identities and constituting norms.[52] The social sciences as a whole were instrumental in promoting theories of individual freedom and self-reliance that were keys to the burgeoning capitalism and state, as well as to the economic science that already legitimated these other sciences (particularly psychology). Thus, as Thomas Popkewitz explains, the social sciences cannot be separated from the development of organized capitalism and the welfare state. The project of creating self-governing, morally directed individuals, Popkewitz argues, was largely conceptualized by the emerging social sciences, especially psychology, which conjured up a consciousness committed to hard work and democratic principles.[53]

All scientific theories for Pierre Bourdieu have particular authority in politics because of what he calls their "theory effects."[54] With regard to our problematic, this means that by expressing in coherent and empiricallyvalid discourse that which is supposedly implicit (such as the costs of higher education), economics transforms the representation of the social world (for instance, to one that sees education as human capital), and consequently, transforms the social world itself, to the extent it renders possible practices that conform to this transformed representation (such as the conversion of education from a public to a private good via government funding). Economics, as a social science, does not simply give us a view of the world; it brings into existence what it declares.

What gives economics the power to produce what it says? This power comes from the university as the institution with the authority over the legitimate production of knowledge. In particular, what sustains the power of economics are (1) the conventional legitimacy accorded to science's pursuit of knowledge and truth, a legitimacy ensured by its use for capitalist and bureaucratic interests in governing an economy and a population; (2) its institutionalization in universities, which since the 1800s have had the sole conventional legitimacy to pursue knowledge and truth; and (3) the conventions associated with scholarly expertise and professional autonomy. As Randall Collins explains, for "objective" knowledge of the social world to develop, two things had to happen: First, societies had to become rationalized; second, there had to emerge an institutional apparatus for the support of intellectual specialists.[55] This apparatus received its foundations in the Middle Ages with the rise of universities in cities such as Paris, Bologna, and Oxford.[56] These early universities were religiously affiliated, and so a further requirement for the rise of the sciences was the secularization of the universities. Today, economists are anchored primarily in universities, but after they attain their credentials they also occupy a range of other institutions (e.g., state agencies, private foundations, think tanks, private corporations, and so forth).

The university's installation as an institution for the pursuit of knowledge thus created a new kind of subjectivity: the academic expert, one who saw her identity in terms of the pursuit of knowledge, and who developed an ethic around such an identity. The university gave rise to *homo academicus*. Pierre Bourdieu argues that the structure of the university reflects the structure of power relations in a society, while its processes of selection and indoctrination reproduce those structures.[57] The whole system of higher education is hierarchical, and as such reproduce the hierarchies of power and privilege in a society. So that with regard to the overall system in the U.S., the Ivy League universities sit at the top, and the community colleges sit at the bottom, and, accordingly, their graduates will be similarly placed in society. Within particular institutions, those fields closest to economic and political power (e.g., economics, law, medicine, etc.) similarly guarantee cultural privilege masked as legitimate academic classifications.

Thus, as Bourdieu argues, the progression of academic disciplines corresponds to the substitution of an academic necessity (e.g., divisions within knowledge) that is socially arbitrary for a social necessity (e.g., professional status) that is academically arbitrary; academic knowledge tends to gain social recognition, and thus social efficacy, as it increases (or is recognized by others as increasing) its scientific value. Thus, such knowledge and its producers can only receive their social authority from the outside, "in the form of delegated authority able to use socially grounded academic necessity to legitimate its arbitrary social values."[58] So, with regard to economics, academic classifications are needed by capitalist and bureaucratic interests, for the capitalist needs a theory of scarcity and free will in order to give his interests legitimacy, and the bureaucrat needs the same in order to allocate resources and thus justify her social role.

Following Marginson, the autonomy of the university makes possible its cultures and value, its academic and intellectual legitimacy, the forms and hierarchies it takes, and their conversion into forms of social advantage not only for those within it but also for those on the outside who "need" it in the form of its degrees or the knowledge it produces. University autonomy, then, is not really about self-government; it is about the ability to structure lives, and thus is why the system is structured into hierarchies, overall and within its specific units.[59]

The political practices of scientists, however, are masked by the ideology of the intellectual and moral legitimacy in their expertise. But, as H. Jamous and B. Peloille argue, such legitimacy is the historic product of a struggle which divides those who try to control the processes of production underlying the system by putting forward particular definitions of those activities, and by the tendency of those who control the system to exclude or subordinate those who could redefine those productions.[60] Thus, the demarcations associated with debates over knowledge in economics are premised on the notion of a "pure research function" and this is expressed in the fact that prestige is distributed throughout the learning professions according to the qualities of the esoteric value of what is taught, the consequent difficulties involved in attaining it, and the audience to whom it is communicated. In other words, if the audience is the scientific community, as it would be for economic researchers, then esoteric knowledge is more prestigious than if the audience was simply businessmen. This is why econometrics, with its highly sophisticated models, is becoming so dominant in economic journals—its logic is decipherable only by other such-skilled economists. Changes to this system, by the way, do not take place by assuming a self-regulating system, but by sudden jolts, when the principles of the dominant legitimacy are questioned, as Keynes did to the prevailing economic logic in the 1930s.[61]

Despite all the rhetoric associated with economics as providing objective knowledge and benefitting society, it should be granted that the social forces discussed above converged to ensure such beliefs. Economics, as much as it is a way of knowing the world, is also a practice of professional legitimization. Randall Collins argues that knowledge that brings professional privilege is inevitably knowledge embellished by its status image.[62] That the facts of economics-might be truer than others is less relevant than its success in winning over converts.[63]

In the case of the emerging social sciences, the need for massive resources opened them to cooptation by those who control the resources, and the latter will almost always support experts who deliver something of value to them.[64] Similarly, following Dorothy Nelkin, the authority of neoclassical economics rests on assumptions about the rationality of its discourses, one deemed rational because of the "objective" data gathered through complex and almost indecipherable mathematical formulas and diagrams of which only other economists make sense. Its "scientific" claims are thus regarded as means by which to de-politicize economic issues, and policy makers "find that it is efficient and comfortable to define [economic] decisions as technical rather than political."[65] So, in this sense, economic claims are actually the most important means of de-politicizing (and thus removing from government and public oversight) economic conditions. With regard to economics, this is particularly problematic because it often involves claims about an ideological being—*homo economicus*—now deemed an empirical and historical one, and such claims only reflect the political and economic interests of economic elites and the bureaucrats in their pockets.

That neoclassical economics insists on untenable assumptions about abstract individuals and firms, and a tenacious belief in an unfettered market, furthers the interests of transnationally exchanged capital, and this is exactly why it is a predominant form of economics and why it is creeping into the logic of the other sciences. That such notions are almost universally acknowledged to be fictions is beside the point. For as Bourdieu argues, academics espousing the "canon" devote considerable time to the production of works whose social intentions are more or less cleverly denied but which offer privileges, often economically fruitful, of social power in so much as they canonize legitimate heritage.[66] From this perspective, such works are not about empirical validity but about social legitimacy.

The critiques of neoclassical economics as a weak science, of neoclassical economists as ideologically motivated, and of neoclassical economics as colonizing other fields of study, might be correct but miss the point that what is really at issue is not whether neoclassical economics can put forth empirically valid definitions of the social world; at stake is a struggle over the professional status of a science. This status must be countered in the case of neoclassical economics, not by offering different philosophies of economics, but by questioning the ideological presumptions and conventional practices that make the authority of economic knowledge possible, particularly those granting universities the legitimacy to put forth ostensibly objective scientific knowledge about the social world, and the transnational capitalist practices that ensure a scientific need for their legitimacy. It is only by challenging the political practices that guarantee the authority of any scientific discourse to govern our lives so completely that we can open up these political practices to question.

The university, conventionally authorized to put forth legitimate scientific knowledge about the world, now authorizes neoclassical economists to put forth legitimate claims about the nature of the economy and heaven knows what else. Of course, this comes to haunt those very universities, for now authorized by them are experts who attempt to reduce what the university is to their formalistic and thus problematic logic, a logic that in reducing what the university is to its costs and investments actually makes it vulnerable to governmental and capitalistic interests, who can then claim scientific "data" with which to direct its actions to their purposes. So, coming back to the government initiatives like the 7–point plan in Texas and the Spellings Report, we are seeing that such initiatives for accountability, efficiency, and evidence-based data are only partly ideological; they are also technical, for their econometric logic is made possible by economists trained to reduce all things to technicalities and espouse theories about their worth accordingly. Indeed, we might look to accreditation, the ratcheting up of tenure requirements, the concerns with learning outcomes, and so on, as providing the kind of quantifiable reductionism that economists need in order to espouse their claims and to gain social power because they can do so. Economists now seem to have authority to capture all kinds of cultural practices within their logic.

So, we must be leery about the fact that as social theorists we might be complicit in the deployment of economic logic to describe all kinds of cultural practices, and especially what defines an "educated" person, as such language has become a privileged way of understanding the world.[67] Economic language is bound to privilege neoclassical ideas, since those are the most predominant at this point in our history. And one of the most disturbing illustrations of this is the almost wholesale appropriation of the theory of human capital in education, an argument with which I conclude this chapter.

The Economism of Educational Thought: "Grave Digging"

I want to focus this concluding section on one deployment of economic terminology in the field of education: the notion of "human capital" which is thrown about so uncritically that it masks how we can become complicit in questioning our own existence. With regard to the field of education, the notion of human capital is particularly problematic, for its history reflects an attempt by neoclassical economists to make claims about education and its monetary worth, and so it was specifically for justifying particular kinds of educational expenditures that the notion was first deployed by economists.[68]

"Human capital" first coined by neoclassical economist Theodore Schultz and then after operationalized by Gary Becker, isa micro-level view of human action, in which human activity is characterized as the "rational choices" of entrepreneurial individuals who see everything they do in terms of maximizing their self-investments (embodied in knowledge and skills) in order to maximize their economic capital; for it is by investing in themselves that individuals can take advantage of the range of opportunities available to them.[69] This logic, clearly premised on the existence of *homo economicus*, has become a powerful scheme for thinking about education, and higher education in particular.[70] Jerome Karabel and A. H. Halsey are correct that human capital theories appeal to pro-capitalist ideologies that workers are holders of capital (as embodied in their skills and knowledge), and that they have the capacity to invest in themselves. So, "in a single bold conceptual stroke the wage-earner, who has no property and controls neither the process nor the product of his labor, is transformed into a capitalist."[71] Such economism, Bourdieu explains, amounts to nothing more than ethnocentrism, for its principles derive from capitalism and recognizes no other form of interests than that which capitalism has produced.[72]

This theory, however, tends to work against the field of higher education, even though it purportedly justifies it, for its logic works like this: individuals are free and rational and only make decisions that will further their economic interests; they will need to invest in higher education but will also judge their institutions only in accordance with whether they actually gain economically. Institutions of higher education serve no other purpose than promoting the opportunities for self-investments, and they need not be funded if they cannot prove they do so. Human capital ideas are thus surreptitious and insidious, with their problematic origins in neoclassical economics overlooked. Their uncritical use fails to recognize that "skills" have been constructed as part of physical, capital-like processes, and that the "return" on those skills is not taking place in a perfectly working labor market.[73] Yet, human capital, presupposed to be well proven in economics and thus authoritatively valid, is simply taken as given in its deployment in other areas of thought.

This notion has serious social consequences, for nothing will make sense outside of an overriding economic rationality. The commitments to higher education will make no sense without a "cash nexus" to appropriate a term Marx used. So, educational scholars, if they take seriously the notion of higher education as a public good, and institutions of higher education as public trusts, and even if politically motivated to promote access, need to be very careful about bringing in such concepts into their analyses. For these concepts cannot account for something called "public" that is not actually a private investment meant to further the economic interests of would-be capitalists, who will easily dispense with their colleges or universities if expected "profits" don't materialize, just as they might do with their stocks.[74]

Am I saying, then, that all economic ideas are bad? No. Such language grants legitimacy to claims about economic inequality. I want only to say that they are dangerous, for bringing economic concepts into the analyses of social and cultural phenomena, even if intended to further democratic goals, inadvertently "put us in danger." Modern economics is dominated by neoclassical logic, so economic theories, given how powerful economic discourse is in shaping reality, should not be allowed to become so easily translatable into other fields, for with such translations come the kinds of controls that not only further social inequality but also shut out other avenues for thought, and for imagining what we are, what we can be, and what our world might look like. Such economics only limits democratic possibilities, not furthers them.

Neoclassical views on higher education have not proven themselves to offer the kinds of self-reflections that scientists believe themselves to have when they further knowledge. To the extent that theories like human capital reconstitute human life as entirely economic, we lose our ability to reflect upon ourselves except with such logic. Rather than blindly bringing in economic concepts, therefore, we must examine the productive functions of knowledge and the institutions that grant them legitimacy. I thus end with a call for education scholars to find completely new ways of rationalizing higher education, and they should start by resisting the economic logic that pervades so much today across our social milieu, even though the imperatives of late capitalism appear to compel it.

Notes

1. Karl Marx and Max Engels, *The Communist Manifesto* (New York: Washington Square Press, 1964), 78–79.
2. See Sheila Slaughter and Gary Rhoades, *Academic Capitalism and the New Economy: Markets, State, and Higher Education* (Baltimore: The Johns Hopkins University Press, 2004).

3. Sheila Slaughter and Larry Leslie, in particular, define academic capitalism as "institutional and faculty competition for moneys, whether these are from external grants and contracts, endowment funds, university-industry partnerships, institutional investment in professors' spinoff companies, or student tuition and fees." See Sheila Slaughter and Larry L. Leslie, *Academic Capitalism: Politics, Policies, and the Entrepreneurial University* (Baltimore: The Johns Hopkins University Press, 1997), 11.

4. Steve Keen, *Debunking Economics: The Naked Emperor of the Social Sciences* (London: Zed Books, 2004), xiii.

5. Ibid., xiv.

6. Ibid., 2.

7. Ibid., 158.

8. John Duprè and Regina Gagnier, "The Ends of Economics," in *The New Economic Criticism: Studies at the Intersection of Literature and Economics*, eds. Martha Woodmansee and Mark Osteen (London: Routledge, 1999), 175–187, 176.

9. Dan Berret, "Economists Push for a Broader Range of Viewpoints in Their Fields" *Chronicle of Higher Education* 58, no. 18 (2011), http://chronicle.com/article/Economists-Push-for-a-Broader/130094 (retrieved January 13, 2011).

10. Mark Osteen and Martha Woodmansee, "Taking Account of the New Economic Criticism: An Historical Introduction" in *The New Economic Criticism: Studies at the Intersection of Literature and Economics*, eds. Martha Woodmansee and Mark Osteen (London: Routledge, 1999), 3–50, 22.

11. Berret, "Economists Push for a Broader Range of Viewpoints."

12. Pierre Bourdieu, *Homo Academicus*, trans. Peter Collier (Stanford: Stanford University Press, 1988), xi.

13. Michael Mumper et al., "The Federal Government and Higher Education," in *American Higher Education in the Twenty-First Century: Social, Political, and Economic Challenges*, 3rd ed., eds. Philip G. Altbach, Patricial J. Gumport, and Robert O. Berdahl (Baltimore: The Johns Hopkins University Press, 2011), 113–138, 113, 134.

14. Aims C. McGuinness, Jr., "The States and Higher Education" in *American Higher Education in the Twenty-First Century: Social, Political, and Economic Challenges*, 3rd ed., eds. Philip G. Altbach, Patricia J. Gumport, and Robert O. Berdahl (Baltimore: The Johns Hopkins University Press, 2011), 139–169, 139–140.

15. F. King Alexander, "The Changing Face of Accountability: Monitoring and Assessing Institutional Performance in Higher Education" *Journal of Higher Education* 71 (2000): 411–430.

16. For the Texas 7–point plan, see http://texashighered.com/7–solutions (retrieved January 1, 2012).

17. The Secretary of Education's Commission on the Future of Higher Education, *A Test of Leadership: Charting the Future of U.S. Higher Education* (Washington, DC: The Department of Education, 2006), xi.

18. Simon Marginson, "Putting the 'Public' Back into the Public University" *Thesis Eleven* 84 (2006): 44–59, 44–45.

19. See Slaughter and Leslie, *Academic Capitalism*, 203.

20. F. King Alexander, "The Silent Crisis: The Relative Fiscal Capacity of Public Universities to Compete for Faculty" *The Review of Higher Education* 24, no. 2 (2001): 112–129, 117–118.

21. cf. Melissa Anderson, "The Complex Relations Between the Academy and Industry: Views from the Literature" *The Journal of Higher Education* 72, no. 2 (2001): 226–246.

22. National Commission on the Cost of Higher Education, *Straight Talk About College Costs and Prices* (Washington, DC: American Council on Education, 1998), http://www.eric. ed. gov/PDFS/ED416762.pdf (retrieved January 15, 2012).

23. Thomas J. Kane, *The Price of Admission: Rethinking How Americans Pay for College* (Washington, DC: Brookings Institute Press, 1999), 90.

24. Ibid.

25. Rob Toutkoushian, "Common Criticisms of the Economics of Higher Education," *The Report* (Athens: The University of Georgia, Autumn 2010), 15; cf. William R. Doyle, "The Political Economy of Redistribution Through Higher Education Subsidies" in *Higher Education: Handbook of Theory and Research*, ed. John Smart (New York: Springer, 2007), Vol. XXII, 335–409, 336.

26. There are other, albeit marginalized, theories of economics: neo-institutional economics, Marxist economics, Post-Keynesian economics, evolutionary economics, etc.

27. See Keen, *Debunking Economics*, 24; cf. Gerald F. Gaus, "Public and Private Interests in Liberal Political Economy, Old and New, in Public and Private," in *Social Life*, eds. Stanley I. Benn and Gerald F. Gaus (London: Croom Helm, 1983), 183–221, 183.

28. Keen, *Debunking Economics*, 26.

29. Ibid.

30. Jack Amariglio and David F. Ruccio, "Literary/Cultural Economics, Economic Discourse, and the Question of Marxism," in *The New Economic Criticism: Studies at the Intersection of Literature and Economics*, eds. Martha Woodmansee and Mark Osteen (London: Routledge, 1999), 381–400, 392.

31. Duprè and Gagnier, "The Ends of Economics" 184.

32. Susan F. Feiner, "A Portrait of *Homo Economicus* as a Young Man," in *The New Economic Criticism: Studies at the Intersection of Literature and Economics*, eds. Martha Woodmansee and Mark Osteen (London: Routledge, 1999), 193–209, 193.

33. Ibid., 194.

34. "Economics"since the work of Lionel Robbins in the 1930s has now come to mean the study of human behavior as a relationship between ends and scarce means that have alternative uses. See Keen, *Debunking Economics*, 9.

35. Daniel M. Hausman, ed., *Introduction to the Philosophy of Economics: An Anthology*, 3rd ed. (Cambridge: Cambridge University Press, 2008), 23.

36. Ibid.

37. Ibid., 26.

38. Karl Marx, of course, offered the most serious attack on the logic of classical economics.

39. cf. Hausman, "Introduction to The Philosophy of Economics" 28.

40. E. K. Hunt and Howard J. Sherman, *Economics: An Introduction to Traditional and Radical Views*, 4th ed. (New York: Harper & Row, 1981), 169.

41. Ben Fine, "A Question of Economics: Is it Colonizing the Social Sciences," *Economy and Society* 28, no. 3 (1999): 403–425, 408.

42. Ibid., 409.

43. Ibid., 412.

44. Ibid.

45. Howard Horowitz, "The Toggling Sensibility: Formalism, Self-Consciousness, and the Improvement of Economics" in *The New Economic Criticism: Studies at the Intersection of Literature and Economics*, eds. Martha Woodmansee and Mark Osteen (London: Routledge, 1999), 150–174, 150.

46. Hausman, "Introduction to The Philosophy of Economics" 1.

47. Daniel Defoe's *Robinson Crusoe* promotes the idea of *homo economicus* because of the rather primitive simplicity of his life on an island as the sole producer and consumer of goods and services, not cluttered with social relations, family, government, and so on, a metaphor which seems to confirm the essentialism of choice under conditions of externally-imposed scarcity. See M. Neil Browne and J. Kevin Quinn, "Dominant Economic Metaphors and the Postmodern Subversion of the Subject" in *The New Economic Criticism: Studies at the Intersection of Literature and Economics*, eds. Martha Woodmansee and Mark Osteen (London: Routledge, 1999), 131–149, 134. For a critique of the logic of choice as a whole, cf. Andrew Bard Schmookler, *The Illusion of Choice: How the Market Economy Shapes Our Destiny* (Albany: State University of New York Press, 1993), 10–15.

48. Amariglio and Ruccio, "Literary/Cultural Economics" 387.

49. Fine, "A Question of Economics" 404.

50. See Gary S. Becker, *The Economic Approach to Human Behavior* (Chicago: The University of Chicago Press, 1976); Gary S. Becker and Guity Nashat Becker, *The Economics of Life: From Baseball to Affirmative Action to Immigration: How Real-World Issues Affect Our Everyday Life* (New York: McGraw-Hill, 1997).

51. I have made similar claims about science more generally; cf. Benjamin Baez and Deron Boyles, *The Politics of Inquiry: Education Research and the "Culture of Science"* (Albany: State University of New York Press, 2009).

52. Steven Seidman, introduction to *The Postmodern Turn: New Perspectives on Social Theory*, ed. Steven Seidman (United Kingdom: Cambridge University Press, 1994), 1–23, 3.

53. Thomas S. Popkewitz, "A Changing Terrain of Knowledge and Power: A Social Epistemology of Educational Research" *Educational Researcher* 26, no. 9 (1997): 18–29, 19.

54. Pierre Bourdieu, *Language and Symbolic Power*, ed. John B. Thompson, trans. Gino Raymond and Matthew Adamson (Cambridge: Harvard University Press, 1991), 133.

55. Randall Collins, *Four Sociological Traditions* (United Kingdom: Oxford University Press), 5.

56. Ibid., 8–9.

57. Bourdieu, *Homo Academicus*, 41.

58. Ibid., 64.

59. Marginson, "Putting 'Public' Back into the Public University" 47.

60. H. Jamous and B. Peloille, "Changes in the French University-Hospital System," in *Professions and Professionalization*, ed. John A. Jackson (Cambridge, UK: Cambridge University Press, 1970), 111–152, 138.

61. Ibid., 142.

62. Randall Collins, "Changing Conceptions in the Sociology of the Professions," in *The Formation of Professions: Knowledge, State and Strategy*, eds. Rolf Torstendahl and Michael Burrage (Newbury Park: Sage, 1990), 11–23, 19.

63. Charles Derber, William A. Schwartz, and Yale Magrass, *Power in the Highest Degree: Professionals and the Rise of a New Mandarin Order* (United Kingdom: Oxford University Press, 1990), 16.

64. Edward T. Silva and Sheila Slaughter, "Prometheus Bound: The Limits of Social Science Professionalization in the Progressive Period," *Theory and Society* 9, no. 6 (1980): 781–819, 805.

65. Dorothy Nelkin, "The Political Impact of Technical Expertise" *Social Studies of Science* 5, no. 1 (1975): 35–54, 36.

66. Bourdieu, *Homo Academicus*, 101–102.

67. Amy Koritz and Douglas Koritz, "Symbolic Economics: Adventures in the Metaphorical Marketplace" in *The New Economic Criticism: Studies at the Intersection of Literature and Economics*, eds. Martha Woodmansee and Mark Osteen (London: Routledge, 1999), 408–419, 408–409.

68. I have made similar arguments about the uses of "cultural capital" and "social capital" in education; cf. Glenda Musoba and Benjamin Baez, "The Cultural Capital of 'Cultural Capital,'" in *Higher Education: Handbook of Theory and Research*, ed. John Smart (Bronx: Agathon Press, 2009), 151–182.

69. Theodore W. Schultz, "Investment in Human Capital," in *Power and Ideology in Education*, eds. Jerome Karabel and A. H. Halsey (Oxford: Oxford University Press, 1977), 313–324, 314.

70. See Gary S. Becker, *Human Capital: A Theoretical and Empirical Analysis with Special Reference to Education*, 3rd ed. (Chicago: The University of Chicago Press, 1993).

71. Jerome Karabel and A. H. Halsey, eds., *Introduction to Power and Ideology in Education* (Oxford: Oxford University Press, 1977), 1–86, 13.

72. Pierre Bourdieu, *The Logic of Practice*, trans. Richard Nice (Stanford: Stanford University Press, 1990), 113.

73. Fine, "A Question of Economics," 413.

74. For examples of such uses in higher education, see Laura W. Perna and Marvin A. Titus, "The Relationship Between Parental Involvement as Social Capital and College Enrollment: An Examination of Racial/Ethnic Group Differences," *The Journal of Higher Education* 76, no. 5 (2005): 485–518; cf. James S. Coleman, "Social Capital in the Creation of Human Capital," *The American Journal of Sociology* 94 (1988): S95–S120.

CHAPTER TWENTY-THREE

The Privatization of Higher Education

JEFFREY S. PITTMAN & DANA D. BURNETT

The current and anticipated future financial model for higher education appears bleak. In light of the tuition-driven new realities of higher education funding, colleges and universities alike are seeking new revenue sources. While tuition is the primary source of revenue to offset increased costs at present, the rapid growth of higher learning's annual cost increases and resultant tuition hikes cannot continue forever. Consequently, institutions are seeking new and enhanced revenue streams from multiple sources. Fund-raising is a key area of focus, but due to the existing economic challenges of our times, the majority of charities, churches, other faith-based organizations, and philanthropic entities have heightened their financial development strategies and tactics. It seems that solicitations are coming from every quasi-worthy group. Higher education institutions are increasingly becoming more prudent in the way that they manage their existing endowments in order to garner the most income possible, while simultaneously attempting to shelter the endowment's total value from downward risk.

Anything and everything is now being reviewed and considered in an effort to find and develop additional institutional revenue, especially in areas connected to campus services and student life. Higher learning is increasingly adopting a highly entrepreneurial perspective when it comes to finding diverse sources of income. The trend of using privatized services that began in earnest in the 1990s is now booming in part due to the economic downturn.

The Mission of Higher Education

The mission of higher education in the United States has evolved slowly during the past 375 years. When the Puritans founded Harvard College in 1636, the mission of the colonial college was clear: to produce "a learned clergy and a lettered people" (Rudolph, 1962, p. 6). How this was to be accomplished was left to the college. The Yale Report of 1828 confirmed that "the discipline and furniture of the mind" were at that time seen as the predominant reasons for higher education and would continue to be so for at least the first half of the nineteenth century (Hofstadter & Smith, 1961, p. 252).

The Morrill Act of 1862 gave rise to colleges in each state and a more practical educational curriculum. This act also ushered in an era of federal support for nineteenth- and twentieth-century higher education and the use of colleges and universities as instruments of public policy. A college education as a public good was still a relevant concept when the Servicemen's Readjustment Act (GI Bill) injected significant financial support into mid-twentieth century higher education, greatly expanding the proportion of the U.S. citizenry who earned a baccalaureate degree. The mission of higher education as a vehicle of public policy was confirmed again in 1958 when, in reaction to the space race, the federal financial aid program was enacted to provide access to all who could benefit from a college degree (National Defense Education Act of 1958).

The mission of public U.S. higher education has changed rapidly and altered significantly during the last two decades. Priest, St. John, and Boon (2006) conclude that, in the twenty-first century, the privatization of public colleges and universities is evidence that state and national governments have come to view higher education more as a private than a public good.

> The privatization of public colleges and universities is inexorably linked to shifts in public policy both in the United States and globally. Declines in state funding and in federal need-based grants, along with the emergence of federal loans, have been the root cause. (p. 3)

Have these changes resulted in unintended alterations in the mission of public colleges and universities? A quick sampling of institutional mission statements as contained in college catalogs may lead us to conclude that stated institutional missions have not changed appreciably, or at all, in the past two decades. It is likely that these statements include language that refers to

- educating citizens for democratic engagement,
- supporting local and regional communities,
- preserving knowledge and making it available to the community,
- advancing knowledge through research,
- developing the arts and humanities,
- broadening access to ensure a diverse democracy,
- developing the intellectual talents of students, and
- creating leaders for various areas of the public sector. (Kezar, 2004)

But is the academy ignoring the impact on mission within the current financial realities that have led to privatization? New sources of funding to support the academic enterprise can be found, but at what cost to institutional mission? If a donor wants to donate funds for an academic or non-academic program that the faculty do not support, and if the funds are accepted, does this affect institutional mission? On a more mundane level, if commuter students and faculty cannot find a place to park because a lucrative, non-academic program has reserved a large proportion of available spaces, how does this impact institutional mission? If the athletic program at a Bowl Championship Series (BCS) public institution becomes a competitor for the increased tuition dollars needed to replace vanishing support from the state, how is institutional mission, as described above by Kezar, transformed?

Organizational evolution is not too different, conceptually, from that which occurs to the flora and fauna of our planet. As organisms (or academic institutions) experience and are influenced by the environment in which they exist, those that can adapt (change) will survive. Those that cannot adapt (change) will eventually perish. As the context of nineteenth-century higher education changed, the classical curriculum was replaced by courses of study that contained vestiges of the classical mode of study, but also featured electives and more pragmatic means of transferring knowledge. The curriculum described in the Yale Report of 1828 did not survive intact, because it was not adaptable and thus was unable to meet the needs of latter nineteenth-century stakeholders. Perhaps some of the contributions to the public good as defined above by Kezar (2004) are no longer needed, or are or will be provided by another entity. Given the current evolution of public institutions of higher education from public support to privatization, it is not at all certain which, if any, of these functions serving the public good will prevail as the fittest of our colleges and universities adapt to survive in the current economic environment.

Some would say that the tail is wagging the dog. This argument ignores the pressure to change the way we manage the academic enterprise and ignores the reality that there is a process of natural selection that explains the outcomes of organizational change in higher education. The result is highly predictable: the fittest organizations will survive.

Campus Services in the Twentieth and Twenty-First Century

Throughout the twentieth century, colleges provided funding and operational oversight for all aspects of campus life. Of course, academic units were under the direct purview of the college administration and faculty. During this time period, colleges also planned, organized, managed, and operated campus support services, including functions such as constructing facilities; maintaining buildings; purchasing, preparing, and serving food; and selling books (Duryea, 1997; Matthews, 1997).

The reduction in government financial support in recent years from the generous levels of the 1950s caused college administrators to seek out partnership arrangements with the business community, particularly in nonacademic areas. A common example of this trend often occurs with college bookstores. Rather than investing institutional dollars to acquire bookstore inventory, many institutions negotiate a contract with a retail bookstore and school supply company to provide the inventory and staffing in an on-campus location. In such situations, the actual bookstore facility may or may not be owned by the institution. In return for the privilege of doing business on the college campus, the retail book companies guarantee a set annual payment to the institution and, perhaps, even a percentage of sales (Wertz, 1997a). Even this outsourcing may be evolving as more students find on-line alternatives that are less expensive than shopping their on-campus, privatized book store.

Another example of outsourcing is campus facility maintenance. Rather than employing a staff of housekeepers, a higher education institution might hire a local company to clean campus facilities. Another prevalent example in today's higher education world is the replacement of a campus-operated food service department by a food service operation managed by a national provider such as ARAMARK, Chartwells, or Sodexho (Hustoles & McClain, 1998; Wertz, 1997b).

In recent years, privatization has been expanded to embrace areas beyond the traditional business affairs units of an institution to include operations such as career and personal counseling departments, childcare centers, information technology, and institutional marketing (Burnett & Collins, 2010; Jacobson, 2001; Kennedy, 2000).

Benefits of Privatization to Higher Education

There are many potentially beneficial factors that appeal to college and university administrators who look favorably on privatization (Byrne, 1998; Kirp, 2002; Wertz, 1997b). Among the most frequently mentioned privatization benefits are the following:

- Financial contribution
- Improved cash flow
- Reduced cash outlays for capital projects
- Guaranteed revenue for revenue-generating services
- Facility issues
- Inventory buyout
- Management change
- Focus on core mission and values
- Lessening college administrator stress
- Fewer employee problems
- Campus support for privatization of a particular service
- Improved customer service (Byrne, 1998; Pittman, 2003)

In the finance area, improved and/or guaranteed cash flow is one of the most attractive features of an outsourcing arrangement. From an operating perspective, in the typical privatization arrangement the service provider assumes responsibility for paying all labor costs and acquiring new inventory. In addition, the general contractual agreement stipulates that the for-profit service provider is responsible for any physical plant changes as well as the acquisition of any needed equipment or furnishings related to the service (Byrne, 1998; Wertz, 1997a; Wright, 1998). Consequently, the for-profit service company assumes payment accountability for those costs, relieving the university's coffers from bearing that burden. In addition to the cost of labor and other expenses, such an arrangement also relieves many other burdensome administrative tasks from the university. For example, personnel records, payroll checks, benefit program administration, and purchasing of goods and supplies used in the privatized service unit are no longer directly managed or supported by university departments. The administration of these activities becomes the duty of the for-profit company. The transfer of financial activities related to expense items alleviates significant direct and indirect costs from the postsecondary school that chooses to privatize a service activity. This financial relief is seen in both administrative (nonprofit) campus service areas as well as in the auxiliary (revenue-generating) service units (Wertz, 1997b; Wright, 1998). The auxiliary areas, however, are frequent bene-factors of additional advantage—guaranteed revenue. Bookstore and food service contracts, among other auxiliary support provider arrangements, typically include fixed remuneration to a college for the privilege of operating a for-profit service on campus. In many cases, there is a minimum revenue guarantee plus commission potential to the school based on the service's sales-garnering success (Byrne, 1998).

A second benefit widely touted by privatization experts is the cost savings realized from on-campus facility renovation (Biddison & Hier, 1996; Wertz, 1997b). Instead of an institu-tion directly funding costly bookstore construction or a renovation project, a contract arrange-ment with a for-profit bookstore company could be a solution to meeting the facility need. The for-profit company would be expected to pay for construction of a new bookstore or the remodeling costs of an existing store as part of its contract offer to the college. In addition, in future years of the contract, the privatized service provider typically assumes responsibility to pay the cost of general facility upkeep. The bookstore contractor would make arrangements with the university's physical plant department or a university-approved outside physical plant contractor for any painting, electrical work, minor structural modifications, or other facility maintenance needs for buildings or building areas occupied by the non-university campus service contractor.

The third rationale widely asserted as a benefit of privatization is inventory buyout. In self-operation mode, a campus service would utilize university funds and, depending on their affiliation arrangement with the college or university, the assistance of university support staff to operate the campus service. In other words, in the case of a campus-run bookstore or food service operation, the store's inventory would be acquired using university funds; and the in-ventory's acquisition, payment of invoices, and other accounting functions would be handled by support staff in the bookstore or from other university administrative support departments. A privatization agreement, on the other hand, normally requires the for-profit campus service provider to buy-out the bookstore, food service operation, or other campus service's existing in-ventory from the higher education institution at the time the contract is implemented. There-after, the private contractor is financially responsible for inventory acquisition. In addition, the purchasing function, accounts payable duties, and general accounting for the service become the obligation of the for-profit company. The university's administrative support departments are no longer obliged to perform the work previously associated with the campus-operated ser-vice. The transfer of inventory provides cash-flow benefits as well as labor savings through staff time and energy, which can be reassigned to other university tasks or staffing can be lowered to generate direct cost savings (Byrne, 1998; Kennedy, 2000; Wertz, 1997b, 1997c).

A fourth benefit of outsourcing a campus service is management change. This concept covers two aspects of management: a reduction in the existing college administrator's direct level of service oversight and the presupposed expertise of managers assigned to the privatized campus service by the outsource service provider. Obviously, college executives expect a reduc-tion in the oversight of day-to-day operations with which college staff members were tasked formerly. If there were no lessening of management attention, privatization efforts would not attract the support of college administrators. The decrease of management duties formerly required of college auxiliary directors provides at least three benefits. First, the college auxiliary director and/or chief business officer can focus more attention on the institution's core mission and values. Second, the campus employees should have less direct involvement and concern over the business operation of a specific campus service unit, once the unit is privatized. Logic holds that this unburdening of operational concerns should provide for lower stress levels for the formerly tasked campus administrator. Thus, the administrator should be relieved of a substantial amount of personal stress, making the individual more effective in the remaining aspects of her or his position. Finally, with the transfer of direct supervision of college employees or of non-college employees of the privatized company to the privatized company's manager, it is assumed that college administrators will have fewer employee problems. Although this is a reasonable expectation, any significant problem on campus always has the potential for direct impact on the institution and the particular administrative division regardless of whether the campus service is privatized or not (Byrne, 1998).

Another benefit of outsourcing is the campus community's strong preference for utilizing an established branded or well-known private enterprise (Matthews, 1997; Wertz, 1997a). The campus may already offer a particular service; however, the campus community may demand the initiation of a particular privatized service on campus that will provide a greater perceived quality than the current campus service. Consumer demands and, particularly, student satisfaction with campus services play a primary role in the privatization efforts of some campus support services. For example, in the food service area, the campus community may be quite pleased with the general food offerings available in the college cafeteria. However, there may also be a large outcry from students for a nationally branded food concept, such as Starbucks, Pizza Hut, or Burger King. Even though the pizza and similar products served by the campus' own dining service may be as appealing and even more nutritious than the products offered by Pizza Hut, students might still demand a Pizza Hut franchise on campus. In such scenarios, campus service administrators are compelled by market forces, including a branded food purveyor's national advertising and students' consumer expectations, to negotiate a contract to operate a Pizza Hut or similar enterprise on campus (Pittman & Gray, 2006).

Improved customer service to the campus community can be an additional benefit of privatization. This expectation comes about due to the narrowly focused expertise that for-profit ventures can bring to a service operation. It is assumed that privatized services will be far more focused on excellent products and customer service in their particular market niche. Certainly, this is the presumption when one compares the focus of a specific campus service operating unit to the broad management view of a college division administrator who manages numerous service units in unaligned fields, such as photocopy departments, food service, and mail centers, or even counseling centers and athletic programs (DeLoughry, 1993; Kennedy, 2000; Nicklin, 1997).

Increasing numbers of college students do not live on campus. Contemporary students are generally older than their college-age predecessors, and increasing numbers of students attend school only part time. Nevertheless, student integration is still necessary in order to enhance academic success. For part-time or commuting students, positive feelings about the campus and their place in the campus community are often dependent on the availability of campus services (Levine & Cureton, 1998; Matthews, 1997).

The community component of a campus environment and the service levels provided by campus services play an even more important role than simply helping to keep students on campus happy and enrolled. These on-campus businesses provide employment and needed financial support for contemporary students of all ages (Binard, 1998; Johnson & McCatty, 1998).

Student Employment and Training

For years, college students have relied on campus employment to help them meet their financial needs. This is no less true today and for the foreseeable future. Basic business skills, management proficiency, and life experience can be learned and practiced far easier in campus service departments than in any other area of the campus, including the classroom. "Leadership development requires an environment where a student can learn and experience leadership by putting it into practice. Auxiliary services are the leading contributors providing this experience" (Binard, 1998, p. 13).

College students have much more time for learning outside the classroom than the required time spent in traditional classroom endeavors. Consequently, total life experience is important in student educational growth. In order to be a true place of learning, the campus environment should be the first place to provide these out-of-classroom opportunities.

Students as Consumers

During the last half of the twentieth century, significant changes occurred in the profile of the American college student (Levine & Cureton, 1998; Matthews, 1997). According to Levine and Cureton (1998), contemporary students want

> their college nearby and operating at the hours most useful to them, preferably around the clock. They want convenience; easy, accessible parking (in the classroom would not be at all bad); no lines; and polite, helpful, and efficient staff service. They also want high-quality education but are eager for low costs. For the most part, they are willing to comparison shop, placing a premium on time and money. They do not want to pay for activities and programs they do not use. In short, students are increasingly bringing to higher education exactly the same consumer expectations they have for every other commercial enterprise with which they deal. Their focus is on convenience, quality, service, and cost. (p. 50) . . . It is easier for undergraduates to perceive themselves as consumers rather than as members of a community. (p. 53)

Today, students' consumer attitudes and actions determine the success or failure, and certainly the effectiveness, of campus services. An understanding of student characteristics is fundamental to any decision related to service privatization (Pittman, 2005). Students have exhibited such strong consumer behavior in recent years that it is changing campus life. The shift has been so dramatic that students' attitudes have now permeated the perspectives of senior administrative staff and faculty. "Perhaps it is not such a bad thing (some administrators quietly say) to turn the student world commercial, the faculty cosmos entrepreneurial, and the administrative universe corporate, to let markets shape student life, faculty time, and administrative style" (Matthews, 1997, p. 232).

The Experience Economy

Pine and Gilmore (1998) provide a clear picture of privatization's use in colleges and universities in an article published in the *Harvard Business Review* entitled, "Welcome to the Experience Economy":

How do economies change? The entire history of economic progress can be recapitulated in the four-stage evolution of the birthday cake. As a vestige of the agrarian economy, mothers made birthday cakes from scratch, mixing farm commodities (flour, sugar, butter, and eggs) that together cost mere dimes. As the goods-based industrial economy advanced, moms paid a dollar or two to Betty Crocker for premixed ingredients. Later, when the service economy took hold, busy parents ordered cakes from the bakery or grocery store, which, at $10 or $15, cost ten times as much as the packaged ingredients. Now, in the time-starved 1990s, parents neither make the birthday cake nor even throw the party. Instead, they spend $100 or more to "outsource" the entire event to Chuck E. Cheese's, the Discovery Zone, the Mining Company, or some other business that stages a memorable event for the kids—and often throws in the cake for free. (p. 97)

The experience economy idea directly relates to service outsourcing. In the example above, the birthday party happens in all three scenarios. However, the outsourced party at Chuck E. Cheese's provides a more professional, albeit more costly experience. While higher education has not yet fully embraced the experience economy concept, there are numerous campus examples that easily lend themselves to the experience economy idea as espoused by Pine and Gilmore (1998). Food courts on campus, theme houses in student housing, and college sporting events are just three examples. "An experience occurs when a company intentionally uses services as the stage, and goods as props, to engage individual customers in a way that creates a memorable event. Commodities are fungible, goods tangible, services intangible, and experiences memorable" (Pine & Gilmore, 1998, p. 98).

If Pine and Gilmore (1998) are correct in their assessment that the U.S. is indeed moving to an experience economy model, then the privatization of campus service will flourish as never before. Outside companies/experts will be needed to provide the memorable "experiences" that students of the future will demand.

On many campuses, even instruction has been privatized to a large extent. Adjunct faculty are private contractors who often teach at more than one institution simultaneously. If this outsourced academic function is properly assessed, it can be an effective means for dealing with escalating costs of providing instruction. But if decisions to outsource such basic functions as teaching are not made deliberately, like any other privatized function, there will be an impact on overall faculty productivity in teaching, research, and service as well as student advising and the development of future scholars. Outsourcing can solve financial challenges, but it may result in unintended consequences.

Whether it is fast-paced or only a gradual occurrence, change is a constant in modern society. Jack Welch, former CEO of General Electric, uses a wonderful analogy about the subject in many of his speeches. "Change is like a steamroller moving at five m.p.h. You can easily walk ahead of it, but if you stop, it'll run you over" (Scherrens, 1999, p. 39).

Fazal Rizvi, professor of educational policy studies at the University of Illinois at Urbana-Champaign, advises that universities must "re-imagine the manner in which they are funded, relate to their clients, and manage their resources" (Rizvi, 2006, p. 65). Institutional leaders who struggle to find resources to fund the essential activities that support the educational mission have been forced to re-imagine assumptions about institutional funding in a rapidly changing fiscal environment—often with little input from students who will be the users of about-to-be privatized services and faculty who are responsible for the academic programs that may be impacted by the unintended consequences of outsourcing. Because the change process often happens relentlessly, it is critical that faculty, students, and administrative leaders, who are responsible for the well-being of their institutions, keep their focus on their vision for the institution's future, while constantly scanning their environment for change, and assessing the effectiveness and overall consequences of new ways of doing things.

In a recent editorial for *Change*, titled " Doing Things Differently" (July 2010), editor Margaret Miller advises us that, when it comes to dealing with issues impacting higher education, ". . . we need to keep in mind two things: there are no silver bullets, and there are no Lone Rangers" (p. 4). It takes the full involvement of all campus leaders, each of whom plays a critical role when deciding how to respond to external pressures, economic and otherwise. The broad perspectives of faculty, students, and administrators together can influence natural institutional evolution and ensure that decisions are made which preserve institutional practices that must not change—and also presage those changes that are advantageous to the academic enterprise. Outsourcing isn't a silver bullet; but if the benefits of privatization are understood by all campus leaders, and if the results are assessed properly, it can provide the revenue needed to operate essential institutional programs.

The bald eagle has been an emblem symbolizing the strength of our nation since the eighteenth century. The mighty, robust bearing of this powerful creature projects an enduring, invincible quality that our Founding Fathers hoped would become our national destiny. During the twentieth century, changes in the bird's environment caused by hunting, habitat destruction, and pesticide poisoning resulted in its near demise; and the bird was listed for protection under the Endangered Species Act. Its recovery has been dramatic and successful, but only due to the swift recognition that the root cause of the decline of the species was due to dramatic changes in the environment.

The twenty-first century environment of higher education has also changed dramatically and at an accelerating pace, affecting the academy's ability to retain its once seemingly invincible status of preeminence. There is no Endangered Species Act for institutions of higher education to provide restoration of the environment that nurtured their standing during the peak period of the last century. The economics of the last century which coddled the nation's colleges and universities by providing a seemingly limitless amount of financial resources is no more. Instead, the solution is for our institutions to change their business models or face extinction. Decisions about how to respond to a rapidly changing environment so as to preserve fundamental programs and services should involve a broad cross-section of institutional leadership. We can learn to fly in a new environment only with the advice and consent of all campus leaders. Outsourcing can be a viable response in a challenging economic environment, but decisions to privatize must be carefully analyzed from all possible perspectives; and then, once implemented, the results of these decisions must be scrupulously and constantly assessed. Our institutions can soar once again, but only with significant changes in our ways and means.

References

Biddison, G. B., & Hier, T. C. (1996, May/June). When your dorms become their business. *Trusteeship*, 19–23.

Binard, K. (1998, June). Auxiliary services and student leadership development. *Campus Services Administration*, 12–13.

Burnett, D., & Collins, N. D. (2010). Higher education for our time. *Journal of Computing in Higher Education*, 22 (3), 192–198.

Byrne, T. (1998, July/August). To lease or not: Why campus administrators privatize college stores, and what you should know about it. *The College Store*, 48–52.

DeLoughry, T. J. (1993, January 13). More colleges eye outside companies to run their computer operations. The *Chronicle of Higher Education*, 39, 19, A19–A20.

Duryea, E. D. (1997). The historical emergence of American academic organization. In T. I. K. Youn &P. B. Murphy (Eds.), *Organizational Studies in Higher Education* (pp. 10–15). New York: Garland.

Hofstadter, R., & Smith, W. (1961). *American higher education: A documentary history*. Chicago: University of Chicago Press.

Hustoles, T. P., & McClain, J. R. (1998). The challenge: Outsourcing to cut costs and improve services while maintaining labor peace. Unpublished manuscript.

Jacobson, J. (2001, February 8). City Colleges of Chicago will farm out its financial operations. *The Chronicle of Higher Education*, 1–2.

Johnson, B. R., & McCatty, P. A. (1998, October). Security's amazing recovery. Security Management, 30–38.

Kennedy, M. (2000). Public schools, private profits. *American School and University*, 72 (6), 14–22.

Kezar, A. (2004). Obtaining integrity? : Reviewing and examining the charter between higher education and society. *The Review of Higher Education*, 27 (4), 429–459.

Kirp, D. L. (2002). Higher Ed Inc.: Avoiding the Perils of Outsourcing. *The Chronicle of Higher Education*, 48 (27), B13.

Levine, A., & Cureton, J. S. (1998). *When hopeand fear collide: A portrait of today's college student*. San Francisco: Jossey-Bass.

Matthews, A. (1997). *Bright college years: Inside the American campus today*. New York: Simon & Schuster.

Miller, M. A. (2010). Editorial: Doing Things Differently. *Change*, 42 (4), 4–5.

National Defense Education Act. Retrieved from http://www.govtrack. us/congress/bill. xpd? bill=h109–4734

Nicklin, J. L. (1997). Universities seek to cut costs by "outsourcing" more operations. *The Chronicle of Higher Education*, 44 (13), A35–A37.

Pine, J. B., II, & Gilmore, J. H. (1998, July/August). Welcome to the experience economy. *Harvard Business Review*, 76 (4), 97–105.

Pittman, J. S. (2003). *Privatize or self-operate: Decision-making in campus services management* (unpublished doctoral dissertation). Old Dominion University, Norfolk, VA. Retrieved fromhttp://odu. worldcat.org/title/privatize–or–self–operate–decision–making–in–campus–services–management/oclc/57761565&referer=brief_results

Pittman, J. S. (2005, October). Understanding campus culture: A key to operating successful auxiliary services. *College Services*.

Pittman, J. S., & Gray, M. (2006, April). Trends in contracted campus services. *College Planning and Management*.

Priest, D. M, , St. John, E. P., & Boon, R. D. (2006). Introduction. In D. M. Priest & E. P. St. John (Eds.), *Privatization and public universities* (pp. 1–7). Bloomington: Indiana University Press.

Rizvi, F. (2006). The ideology of privatization in higher education: A global perspective. In D. M. Priest & E. P. St. John (Eds.), *Privatization and public universities* (pp. 65–84). Bloomington: Indiana University Press.

Rudolph, F. (1962). *The American college and university: A history*. New York: Knopf.

Scherrens, M. W. (1999, July). Maximizing service provider relationships. *Business Officer*, 38–45

Wertz, R. D. (1997a, Winter). Big business on campus: Examining the bottom line. *Educational Record*, 78 (1), 19–24.

Wertz, R. D. (1997b). *Outsourcing and privatization of campus services*. Staunton, VA: National Association of College Auxiliary Services.

Wertz, R. D. (1997c). *Privatization survey summary*. Staunton, VA: National Association of College Auxiliary Services.

Wright, S. W. (1998, March 23). Public colleges, private contracts: Outsourcing is on the upswing—but what's the true bottom line. *Community College Week*, 10 (17), 6–7.

CHAPTER TWENTY-FOUR

How Did We Get to This Situation?

The Immiseration of the Modern University in a Globalizing Context

JOHN SMYTH

> Within the capitalist system all methods for raising the social productivity of labour. . . become a means of domination and exploitation. . . they distort the worker into a fragment. . . they degrade him [her] to the level of an appendage of a machine, they destroy the actual content of his [her] labour by turning it into a torment, they alienate from him [her] the intellectual potentialities of the labour process. . . (Marx, 1867/1986, p. 799)

I will start with an anecdote which I think is highly relevant and revealing. Almost two decades ago, I brought into existence what I thought was a fairly unique and controversial edited collection entitled *Academic Work: The Changing Labour Process in Higher Education* (Smyth, 1995a), published jointly by the Society for Research into Higher Education in the UK and the Open University Press. There can be no doubt about the pedigree of the international contributors I managed to cajole into this project—they were the "who's who" among the international scholars and commentators on higher education, among them Simon Marginson, Jan Currie, Roger Woock, and Anna Yeatman (Australia); Sheila Slaughter, Larry Leslie, William Tierney, Wes Shumar, Clyde Barrow, and Robert Rhoads (USA); Howard Buchbinder (Canada); and Henry Miller and Richard Winter (UK). Many of them went on to publish significant works in higher education and either continue careers in that area, or start careers in that area. The book was a sharp (one could say "blistering") critique of what was being "done to" higher education around the world at the time, along with a clarion call for us to collectively wake up to what was happening before it was too late. The book has not exactly been a blockbuster—it sold a few copies, and I can see that over the years it has received 61 Google Scholar citations—hardly earth-shattering, considering the topic and the quality of the contributors! So, what has gone on here? How come we have been so reticent to speak out?

Why have we not been outraged by what was happening to higher education then, and what has become an international disgrace since then?

To pursue these questions, along with my title to this chapter, I want to do three things. First, it may be helpful if I rehearse some of the key arguments from my *Academic Work* that animated me to bring this book into existence in the first place. Second, along the way, I want to bring these arguments into conversation with the contemporary situation in higher education in Australia—a country that has gleefully embraced the managerialist/marketized/corporatist turn. And, thirdly, I shall conclude with some brief comments on what this might mean for higher education more generally. But first I need to do a little scene-setting to lay out the issues as many of us are experiencing them in higher education, regardless of domicile.

Contours of the Problem

Regardless of where we are located around the world, there are four generalised features that could be said to constitute the immiseration of the university that most of us affiliated with universities will readily recognize.

Managerialism is possibly one of the most irritating of these, comprising as it does, the view that institutions of higher learning can be run and administered by those who have no intrinsic knowledge, experience of, or commitment to universities as cultural institutions, and that, as a matter of fact, universities are no different in substance from breweries or supermarkets—i.e., all that is required is the application of a set of generic management skills that operate regardless. Added to this is the view that managerialism is about the right to know, and that this is invested exclusively in universities in a class designated as "managers."

Privatization refers, in the general usage of that term, to the divesting of publicly owned entities to the private sector where they are considered to rightfully belong. More specifically, privatization denotes an ideology of market relations around the idea that everything has a monetary use value which consumers are prepared to pay, and activities should be organized accordingly.

Corporatisation infers that the preferred way for higher education institutions to be organized is like competitive entities in a "market" in which a failure to attract resources brings with it the penalty of atrophy that will lead to eventual demise.

Domestication, as the names suggests, involves a taming of something otherwise considered to be wild or feral and training it to be more amenable or hospitable. In the case of higher education, that can be taken to mean that the untidy process of engaging in a battle over ideas is somewhat quaint and old-fashioned, and no longer has a place in the mean, sleek, trimmed-down and hyper-efficient corporatized and marketized world of the new higher education orthodoxy.

Something about the Genesis

My prefacing argument in *Academic Work* could not have been more direct and prescient in relation to these contours. Forthrightly expressed, my grave fear was that our collective failure to engage theoretically and politically with what was happening to our work as academics in universities, and metaphorically burying our heads in our laboratories hoping the threat would go away, would bring about our complete undoing. That is what has largely come to pass as we have sat idly by and allowed a toxic mix of market ideology and corporate managerialism to infect the academy. At the time, I put it like this:

> Most of what is happening is going ahead largely unexamined, and certainly unopposed, and it is not that academics are unaware of these changes, for they clearly are—such changes impact daily on the quality of their work. . . That we devote so little time to analysing what it is we do, and how others are increasingly coming to shape that work, must be one of the great unexplained educational issues of our times. . . [The fact of the matter is] that many of the extensive changes being visited upon universities around the world are occurring in contexts which themselves are far from subject to intense and rigorous intellectual analysis and scrutiny. (Smyth, 1995a, p. 1)

I went on to argue, quite passionately, that my fundamental purpose in bringing about the publication of *Academic Work* (even though it was far from being my primary area of academic scholarship) was

> . . . to bring the issue of academic work [and what was being "done to" universities] out of the closet and subject it to the kind of discussion, analysis and debate it so desperately deserves. Unless we do this, a decade or so down the road, we are going to look back and find that many of the uneasy feelings we had about what is happening to our work would have come to pass, and that the situation is irretrievable. (Smyth, 1995a, p. 2)

My basic thesis, pursued in several papers I wrote in the early 1990s on globalization and higher education (Smyth, 1989, 1990, 1991, 1994, 1995a), and pursued subsequently (Hunt & Smyth, 1998; Smyth & Hattam, 2000), was that to understand what was happening to the reform of higher education in Australia—reforms that have continued uninterrupted ever since—we need to look to the wider international restructuring of capitalism and how higher education has become caught up in those changes. My argument, in short, was that higher education policy amounted to "a form of settlement or temporary historical compromise in an endeavour to resolve Australia's economic vulnerability" (Smyth, 1994, p. 66). At the time, Australia was going through an intense process of economic restructuring due to a high level of dependency on foreign capital inflow and escalating foreign ownership of strategic Australian resources—all of which required a re-working of capital/labour relations and a "high-tech" response to the rapid de-industrialization brought on by the flight of manufacturing industries to low labour cost countries.

The "temporary settlements" that occurred, and which I will speak about in more detail shortly, took four basic forms:

1. the shift of higher education from a public good to a private good;

2. deregulation and pedagogy for profit;

3. the instrumentalisation of knowledge and the proletarianisation of educated labour; and

4. gender and labour market segmentation in higher education.

These reforms were regarded at the time as being appropriate responses within higher education and the economy more generally, "away from a social agenda towards individualist market-oriented modes of responding to broad international economic forces" (Smyth, 1994, p. 66). Accompanying all of this was the unprecedented shift in Australia from an elite system of higher education that catered for only a small minority of the population, to a mass system of higher education available to a much broader group. As I observed at the time, these economistic views were "portrayed as having a gloss of credibility about them" but even more remarkable "was that such significant reforms drew so little response from the higher education sector" (p. 66). My theorising of this was that, "rather than seeing these reforms as threatening" increasing numbers of "managers" within higher education regarded these reforms as opportunities that enabled them to serve their own interests. In other words, what the reforms did was "license" or legitimate tendencies and pre-dispositions that some people within higher education had long held, and provided them with the opportunity to take advantage of the circumstances. Nowhere was this more apparent than in the quality and accountability arrangements that were starting to be inflicted upon higher education in a hitherto unseen way. What I was, in effect, arguing was that the reforms to higher education provided respectability and license to do from "within" what could not have been achieved through a full frontal invasion of the academy from outside. This is not to suggest that what occurred politically *outside* of higher education was benign or innocent—it was far from that! Rather, what occurred was that local political interests hitched themselves to what I call the international fundamentalist economic agenda of the powerful "international predator organisations"—the IMF, World Bank, WTO and the OECD—who were ideologically warehousing a seemingly irrefutable set of ideas (Smyth & Shacklock, 1998); and that arrangement provided respectability from "up there" and "from afar." The explanation for what was happening locally to entities like higher education—at least from the university mandarins—was the mantra "we are simply following international trends and best practice."

Let us return now to the expressions that these "settlements" took in the global re-arrangement of economic forces afflicting Australia. But just before I do that, I should explain a little of what I take the notion of "settlement" to mean. Seddon (1990) captured this nicely when she said that a settlement is a political heuristic device for explaining the re-worked political relationships that occur during periods of social fluidity when complex and contradictory changes occur:

> These political relationships appear as a distinctive framework for public policy, a characteristic pattern of social forms (i.e. institutions, relationships, individuals, ideas) and the boundaries that delineate them. Settlements are contested and contradictory, but persist for a time, giving a period of history a particular qualitative character. Ultimately they break down into a crisis: a period when social forces struggle to redefine the social order. In this time of economic, political, social, ideological and cultural restructuring, conflict is intense as familiar social arrangements are questioned, debated and fought over until a new balance of social forces emerges and is consolidated as a new settlement—a new pattern of social forms and boundaries. (pp. 134–135)

By linking the necessity for economic restructuring that Australia had become caught up in as a result of the global rearrangement of capitalism to the need for an enhanced educational skills base, it was possible to usher in a highly interventionist and hierarchical mode of educational policy making in Australia by "creating a whipping horse out of the higher education system" (Smyth, 1994, p. 39). Rather than analysing what was occurring to the economy in terms of "the penetration of the economy by the TNCs [transnational corporations] and the net outflow of national capital in terms of the contribution of such forces" (O'Malley, 1989, p. 11), what occurred, instead, was that the education system was "blamed. . . for its economic shortcomings and [the] alleged inability [of the economy] to compete on world markets" (Smyth, 1994, p. 47).

Let me now turn to some specifics of what this four-element temporary settlement looked like.

(A) The slide from higher education as a "public good" to a "private good"

It is important that I not over-romanticise and convey the impression that somehow Australia slipped at some point from having a passion for a wider public benefit accruing from higher education to one of suddenly seeing it as being for narrow sectional interests. In policy terms, there never was a "golden era." What did occur around the beginning of the 1990s in the process of Australia moving to what it termed a "unified national system of higher education" was the growing infatuation with a "human capital" view of higher education to satisfy the national economic agenda—and that was done largely by introducing various aspects of a "user pays" philosophy in which the individual vocational desires of consumers were closely linked to the national interest. Policy documents at the time, and since, have been replete with reference to the importance of links between higher education and training and economic growth—the appearance of the word "training" was a very deliberate inflection. There was a constant exhortation that higher education be more "flexible"—meaning more accommodating to the needs of industry—and for there to be closer links of all kinds between higher education and industry—what is taught as well as how. In addition, the research agenda of universities, it was argued, ought to be consistent with the needs and interests of industry. It has advanced to the point now in Australia that it is almost a "no-brainer" that the sole purpose of higher education is to contribute to the economic strength and vitality of the nation through direct forms of vocationalism. In the "demand-driven funding model" to commence in Australia in 2012, all universities will compete directly for undergraduate students, and universities will virtually have to stand or fall based on their capacity to secure market share in terms of attracting students. There can be little doubt that Australia has virtually given up on any pretence that higher education has much to do with intrinsic value beyond that which has a direct economic use value. What has occurred is a slippage into a form of language that naturalises, in a common sense way, what ought to be the emphases—efficiency, accountability, excellence, international competitiveness, world class standards, etc.—all of which are expected to be accepted unproblematically and without challenging the efficacy of what accompanies these economic imperatives.

(B) De-regulation and the pedagogy for profit

Underlying all of this is the most insidious influence of all—the totally unproblematic acceptance that universities ought to operate *per se* according to the principles of stand-alone cost centres. In its crudest form, this translates into an unregulated rush to "get bums on seats"—meaning, fee-paying students, domestic or international, at any price! This also often means oversubscribing the number of students that can reasonably be accommodated and properly supported in universities, placing unbearable and unsustainable strains on overloaded infrastructure and facilities in a context in which the funds often do not follow the students. There is often extensive cross-subsidisation of activities in which "cash cow" activities such as teaching are used to fund more costly activities like research—all in a context in which often well over 50% of total resources are taken off the top for the managerial and corporatist agenda of universities, most of which contributes little or nothing to supporting core activities of teaching and research. This untrammelled pursuit of the dollar leads to a gross distortion and corruption of purpose in which the ideology of the corporate sector has been permitted unwarranted and unfettered access. Australia has a foreign international student fee-making industry that annually garners in excess of $AUD 15 billion, rivalled only by Australian exports of coal and minerals to China. As I have summarised it elsewhere, this is "the epitomy of the final commodification of education" (Smyth, 1994, p. 53).

(C) Instrumentalism of knowledge and the proletarianisation of educated labour

The other trend that began emerging in the early 1990s, not unrelated to the other tendencies already mentioned, and for related reasons, was the proclivity for global shifts in economic power to produce a "new orthodoxy" which Burgess (1989) claimed was a "search for scape-goats and quick fix solutions" (p. 23). Put another way, education was being promulgated as the new tool of economic reform in which "what remains hidden from view are the ideological judgements" (Smyth, 1994, p. 53) about the kind of adjustments needed in the labour process. In the case of higher education, this "adjustment" meant the rapid escalation in the casualisation of the workforce—in effect, a wholesale shift to something almost akin to the insecure piece-rate system that had characterised earlier periods of industrialisation. This pronounced labour market segmentation—of a small core of tenured faculty engaged in teaching and research, and a large reserve army of lowly paid and highly insecure teaching staff—was rationalised on the grounds of the need to be nimble and be able to quickly adjust to changing conditions of international capitalism. Again, this kind of reform was regarded as an unproblematic response to a pragmatic problem—the supposed need to adjust to international competition or be "put out of the game." The only problem with this approach, in hindsight, is that its very short-termism has completely undermined any long-term workforce planning; and Australia, as a result, is faced with a depleted academic workforce which is leaving it far removed from the notion of the self-proclaimed "clever country."

According to Meisenhelder (1983), speaking of higher education in the U.S. and who I invoked at the time, the emerging problem was that academic faculty were being unwittingly duped and further incorporated into a process of proletarisation that was already well under-way. I concurred (Smyth, 1994, p. 58) that faculty were "paying dearly" for what Meisenhelder termed "the rewards that come with the acceptance of the self-deceptive set of beliefs and norms inherent in the counter-factual definition of themselves as professionals" (p. 298). In other words, faculty were becoming implicated in their own demise by being bought off with the subtle "purchase of employee loyalty [that comes with] granting some of its employees professional status and its attendant privileges" (p. 300). They thought they were being given professional freedom, something always prized by lowly paid academics, but in reality they were becoming even more beholden to management by, for instance, being co-opted into "individual [career] mobility" by "enter[ing] into competition (rather than cooperation) with their fellow faculty" (p. 300). The emerging upshot of this, which sounds remarkably contemporary in its ring, is that faculty

> are more or less powerless employees of bureaucratic institutions. . . . evaluated, ranked, and rewarded according to an increasingly rationalized set of pseudo-scientific procedures and artificially precise, even mathematical criteria. . . (p. 299)

In a further prescient resonance (that sounds remarkably like a business-as-usual call), Meisenhelder (1983) put it most sharply when he said:

> Faculty are delegated tasks rather than power and authority in crucial areas of institutional life. . . Management defines the institution's priorities and ensures that employees are judged according to the standards derived from those goals. (p. 299)

The way I described the watershed period I was writing about in the early 1990s in Australian higher education was that what we had emerging was a "new technology of control" (Smyth, 1994, p. 59) in which the "enemy [was] from within" (p. 59)—meaning that a process of co-option was increasingly underway in which some faculty were being "bought off" through, for example, being anointed with the title of "professor" without the necessary scholarly track record, and with an increasing tendency for senior positions to be managerial rather than academic. One final word from Meisenhelder (1983) on this:

> Although relative to many other workers faculty still exercise some control over the temporal and spatial resources with which they work, this discretion is diminishing and may soon be limited to questions surrounding how to exercise assigned tasks. (p. 304)

Even that freedom may have been ephemeral as early as the1980s in the US, with "rules stipulating "office hours" "student contact hours" and/or days on campus" (p. 304).

Any reworking of capital-labour relations as dramatic and fundamental as what lay behind the structural adjustments of higher education I have described thus far was bound to bring with it some dramatic re-alignments of internal labour relations—some of which I have just described, but others that have quite a different inflection, as I will discuss now.

(D) gender and labour market segmentation in higher education

While my thesis about the genesis of how we got into this situation has been around notions of structural adjustment within international capitalism that produced a new form of "settlement" that has accommodated higher education through human capital approaches, it was inevitable that this was going to lead to equity issues. As I argued at the time, drawing on Freeland (1986), while the primary struggle was between labour and capital and the way "capital accumulation [constitutes] the broad parameters within which the struggle over the social relations of production. . . and consumption take place" there can be no escaping the fact that "this conflict is pre-figured by the gender-based struggle centred on domestic use value production and consumption" (p. 213). To put this another way, the crisis gets to be re-configured around two sites—the market and the household—and while these are often "frequently divorced in analysis. . . in reality [they are] interdependent" (p. 213). As I argued:

> What the interaction of these two sites does, ideologically and practically, is act as a mediator in the creation of an educated labour market in higher education, one. . . a "primary" market (which is predominantly male), and which is fundamentally and qualitatively different from a "secondary" market (largely female). (Smyth, 1994, p. 60)

The essence of my claim, which seems largely to have come to pass, was that we were heading for a dual higher education labour force that would operate on the basis of two principles: (i) "proletarianisation"—the separation of the conceptualization from the execution of the work, and along with it the capacity to see the inter-connectivity in academic work and regard the work holistically, as discussed above; and (ii) "segmentation"—in which rewards and incentives would become the driving force in further demarcating the boundaries between different types of academic labour. Yeatman (1988) argued, in this regard, that the "selectively economistic" (p. 39) line being taken in the watershed Australian higher education reforms of the early 1990s, were not only "gender blind" but were pre-disposed to ways that would further exacerbate existing advantage, in four ways. First, in allowing market forces to do their ugly deforming work, this would further entrench the already advantaged, mostly males, and further exclude marginalised groups, such as women. Second, apparently commonsense notions of workforce mobility that have appeal in difficult economic times might work for those who have the capacity to be mobile, but not for those who have "domestic and parenting responsibilities"—leading to even further "gender stratification of academic staffing" (p. 40). Third, notions of economies of specialization were seen by Yeatman (1988) as further solidifying women into the "intensive and mass teaching areas of the social sciences and humanities" (p. 40)—which are also the cheapest to provision, a point not lost on MacIntyre (2010) in his charting of the history of the social sciences in Australia in his aptly titled book *The Poor Relation*. According to Yeatman, as a result of the Australian higher education reforms, women were destined to find themselves positioned, yet again, "on the wrong side of the new binarism" (p. 41). Fourth and finally, there was the "gender-based mythology about what counts as productive work" (p. 41), with Jackson (1991) anticipating that women were to suffer again from "job tunneling" and "shearing" as their skills were appropriated and made "invisible" doing in academic work what Offe (1985) termed "shit jobs" that "anybody can do" (p. 40). All of these trajectories were predicted at the time, and each has largely come to pass in higher education in Australia and elsewhere, for that matter.

What, Then, Has Transpired?

It is almost old hat to use the language, but Australia has allowed itself to be seduced and subjected to a relentless and unremitting ideological dose of "economic rationalism" (Pusey, 1991)—the local idiom for deregulation, privatisation, and marketization—that has been going on now for over thirty years, at both a policy and practice level; and higher education has been one of the parts of the public sector most eager to embrace this set of ideas. This is rather odd, really, because we would have thought that, of all entities, higher education would have been fiercely analytical and protective of anything that smacked of infringing freedoms and would have wanted to maintain some considerable distance from something as seemingly smutty as the marketplace and exploitation in the pursuit of profit. Equally surprising is the overall embrace within what lies behind higher education reforms, i.e., of the notion of *homo economicus*—the view that people are animated by naked fiscal self-interest and that somehow this ought to be the defining idea in a knowledge-creating institution like a public university. As it turns out, Quiggin (2010) has argued that continuing to embrace market-based solutions, when all of the contemporary evidence points to their dismal failure as regulators of anything, is akin to allowing a dead set of ideas to stalk us—hence, his description of the market ideology as "zombie economics"! If they ever had any relevance, their time has well gone, as we can see from the overwhelming interventions of governments round the world to prop up disintegrating economies who have allowed their pro-market economies to engage in profligate activities of unfettered greed.

Once of the problems in engaging in a critique of something as pervasive and apparently seemingly common sense as neo-liberalism (another name for the ensemble of deregulation, privatisation, and marketization) is that these ideas have become so insinuated into, or embedded in, our discourses and our lives that it almost seems silly to be critiquing them—which is what makes them so insidious.

As numerous commentators have noted (see, among them, Campbell, 2000; Coady, 2000; Cooper, Hinkson, & Sharp, 2002; Currie & Newson, 1998; James, 2000; Readings, 1996; Slaughter & Rhoades, 2004; Tierney, 2006; Tudiver, 1999; Turk, 2000), including most recently Blackmore, Brennan and Zipin (2010), what has fundamentally changed in universities is the "mode of governance" in relation to academic work. As Blackmore et al. (2010) put it, for much of the twentieth century universities enjoyed "a degree of relative autonomy" in relation to "political-economic concerns" (p. 1), but that has been severely eroded over the past three decades as governments have moved aggressively to "reposition" higher education in response to the kind of globalising forces I have already described. What has eventuated is the active encouragement—almost to the point of being mandatory—of notions like the "enterprise university" (Marginson & Considine, 2000), the "corporate university" (Giroux & Myrsiades, 2001), or what Aronowitz (2000) labelled "the knowledge factory." Within these new regimes there are a myriad of micro-technologies that add up to an explosion of an "audit culture" (Power, 1994, 2003; Strathern, 2000), comprising what can only be seen as a "dramatic renormalisation" (Blackmore et al., 2010, p. 2) of academic work. We see this manifested in the proliferation of control mechanisms, among them, an attenuated list including

- league tables of various kinds
- performance indicators
- quality, accountability, and ranking and assessment measurements
- compliance standards and frameworks
- demand-driven funding
- competitive research grant mechanisms
- risk management strategies
- strategies of image and impression management.

What these corrupt, fake, "interloper" (Adorno, 1974, p. 23) technologies do, as I have argued extensively elsewhere (Smyth, 2010), is eat away and corrode trust and respect, which are the cornerstones of relational institutions such as schools and universities. As I put it:

> . . . [this] over-exaggerated emphasis on checking, monitoring, and control . . . [for that is what they are] through arbitrarily determined performance indicators, and the process of converting [what ought to be] educational leaders into clerks, may not in any way contribute to advancing the real substance of education. . . which is fundamentally about the formation of intellect. . . . (Smyth, 2010, p. 171)

Stephen Ball, of the Institute of Education, University of London, writing about these issues, invokes the notion of "performativity" to describe what he regards as being "done to" universities. He defines performativity as

> . . . a technology, a culture of regulation, or a system of 'terror', in Lyotard's words, that employs judgements, comparisons and displays as a means of control, attrition and change (Ball, 2000, p. 1).

According to Ball (2000), "who controls the fields of judgement is crucial" and "accountability and competition are the lingua franca of this new *discourse of power*. . ." (p. 1, emphasis in original). Ball goes on to describe how the "research assessment exercise" (RAE) that was deployed in the UK was used to redefine academic identities—the same strategies that have been introduced into Australia in 2010 under the seemingly inoffensive title "Excellence in Research for Australia" (ERA), which I will turn to in more detail shortly.

Persisting with Ball (2000) for a moment longer, he says that this "new mode of regulation" brings with it both a "structure" and a "flow" comprising ". . . the data base, the appraisal meeting, the annual review, report writing and promotion applications, inspections, [and] peer reviews. . ." (p. 2). These "performativities" are "continuous" "eventful" and "spectacular" but the way they work is

> . . . not so much the possible certainty of always being seen that is the issue, as in the panopticon [but rather] the uncertainty and instability of being judged in different ways, by different agents; the "bringing off" of performances—the flow of changing demands, expectations and indicators that make us continually accountable and constantly recorded. . . . (p. 2)

What this does, Ball (2000) says, is to construct a "recipe for ontological insecurity: "Are we doing enough? Are we doing the right thing? How will we measure up?" (p. 3). This leads us into "a perverse form of response/resistance. . . that I will call *fabrication*" (p. 5). In other words, we go along with it and, in the process, become complicit in constructing a persona that looks convincing, but which is actually a facsimile. Ball's (2000) example is informative:

> . . . in my role as Chair of our School Research and Development Committee, I regularly review the School's publications data base and "meet with" those colleagues whose publications look like they might fall short of the measures and requirements of the national Research Assessment Exercise. These meetings both offer support and entreat the person to greater efforts. The interplay of collegial and disciplinary aspects in all this are very murky indeed. (p. 6)

Where this leaves us, he argues, is in a "schizophrenic" state in which we suffer a considerable loss of self-respect. In the end, we become implicated in a new set of "social relations" (Ball, 2000, p. 5) in which we perpetuate the inauthenticity by "splitting" our personal and institutional identities and going along with the façade.

Clever Country? — Or Dumbing Australia Down?

In the words of former Prime Minister Bob Hawke during the 1990 election campaign, Australia was going to insulate itself from the vicissitudes and uncertainties of international economic crises, by becoming "the clever country" through promoting research and innovation—an idea that still persists rhetorically in the minds of politicians. This fantasy ranks up there with Hawke's rhetorical proclamation in 1987 that "by 1990 no Australian child will be living in poverty." Two decades on, and in the context of recent federal government initiatives in higher education, it is interesting to re-visit the "clever country" proclamation and ask if it stacks up in the current context of reforms to Australian universities.

What Australia has done most recently through the federal government's "Excellence in Research for Australia" (ERA), which commenced in 2010, is to attempt to bludgeon universities with a very blunt instrument into accepting a neo-liberal ideology of a fake set of market conditions that rank and rate universities against one another according to measured research performance, resulting in a hierarchy, and rewarding "performers" with large amounts of cash, and arguing that "under-performers" will somehow lift themselves up by their bootstraps. The way this works is that universities are, among other things, required to submit their repositories of research publications, which are then used as the basis for both peer review (along with various metrics including citations and quantitative measures of research grants). All academic disciplines in universities (known as "units of evaluation"), on the basis of this, are accorded a descending order ranking from 5 (well above world standard), 4 (above world standard), 3 (at world standard), 2 (below world standard), 1 (well below world standard), and "not assessed" because of the low volume of outputs.

In parallel, the first round of the ERA by the Australian government in 2010 (which reached back over the six-year period 2003 to 2008), using a bevy of 700 experts, produced a rank ordering of all 19,000 journals in which academics published, and accorded all these journals an individual descending order ranking on a four-point scale: A*, A, B, C. When institutional publications were aligned with this hierarchy, this was supposed to lead to a process in which the quality of research could be assessed by means of a series of metrics. All universities in Australia were required, as part of the ERA, to submit their repositories of research outputs to be assessed against these arbitrary benchmarks. The 330,000 published pieces were then peer reviewed by an army of 50,000 assessors, along with other indicators drawn by government from databases, such as success in winning research grants. This was a process of epic proportions in which the bulk of the costs were borne by universities themselves, but they had no choice.

The journal-ranking process generated such outrage and a rancour among academics in Australia because of its inherent unfairness, inaccuracy, and the fact that it was being used by university research managers to bully academics into publishing in particular journals and ignoring others, that the Minister was eventually forced to back down and abandon it. In typical political fashion, without seeming to have capitulated, waxing eloquently all the while about the need for "refinements" and for the sector to maintain "rigour and comparability" the Minister proclaimed with a straight face that "the exercise has been an overwhelming success in meeting its objective of providing institutions, researchers, industry and students with a sound, evidence-based means of identifying areas of strength and potential, as well as where we need to do better" (Carr, 2011)—notwithstanding that the ERA centrepiece—the prescriptive A*, A, B and C journal rankings—had been completely jettisoned.

Forever watchful of any opportunity to create further hierarchies and league tables that constitute ever-expanding fake forms of competition that are gleefully picked over by a complicit media, in the latest twist of the ERA for 2012 (covering the years 2005 to 2010), the government is forcing universities to corral their research outputs ever more narrowly into what are being called designated "Fields of Research Codes" (FORs) in order to promote more vigorous competition between universities and academic disciplines. The problem with all of these measures that are supposed to demonstrate research quality and impact is that they totally miss the point. As an Australian Vice Chancellor is reported to have said, "Narrow measures of research performance are of limited value when the global imperative is finding interdisciplinary answers to macro problems. . ." (Rowbotham, 2011, p. 23). The problem, as articulated by this Vice Chancellor, is that while research measurement criteria can be developed and implemented, the consequence is "failing to tackle the harder challenge of finding ways to assess what really matters: impact and innovation" (p. 23). Instead, the argument is endlessly diverted onto "small things. . . [like] fields of research codes. . . [and] journal rankings" (p. 23), while the most important thing of all, whether the research "makes a difference" goes unattended.

In yet another illustration of gross stupidity, and the futility of driving a system that is supposed to be about the innovative pursuit of inquiry into important questions by using something as ineffectual as competition on an athletic field, a paper on the allocation of medical research grants in Australia, reported in the *British Medical Journal* (Graves, Barnett, & Clarke, 2011), indicated just how stupid we really are. According to the senior author, Nichols Graves, the 2983 research grant applications submitted to the National Health and Medical Research Council in Australia in 2009 "cost a total of $AUD 47. 9 million—or $ AUD 17,744 each—to prepare. Of this, 85 per cent of the cost was borne by applicants who spent on average 22 days preparing the application; 9 per cent was spent on the peer review process, and 5 per cent in administrative costs. . . [The total cost was]. . . 180 years of researcher time" (Hare, 2011c, p. 23) in which less than one in five applications were successful. Little wonder that suggestions are being made that a "lottery" would be more cost effective and certainly less damaging to morale. These figures are for the medical sciences only (the situation is replicated in the physical and social sciences). It is hard, with examples like these, not to see the logic in Quiggin's (1995) rhetorical headline applying to contemporary higher education—"The clever country: not so smart then even less so now."

To draw this rather depressing account to something of a conclusion, it seems that successive Australian governments, including the current one, have turned into an art form the capacity to inoculate themselves against unpleasant facts, preferring instead to dismiss them merely as the bleatings of a self-interested profession. Notwithstanding this obdurate position, by any account the evidence is incontrovertible that over thirty years of relentlessly assaulting higher education with policies of neo-liberalism has been a dismal failure. For example, the harsh realities revealed recently, include that

> two in five academics under the age of 30 plan to leave Australian higher education within the next five to ten years because of high levels of dissatisfaction caused by lack of job security [McDonald's are said to have less sessional staff], poor pay and mountains of paperwork and red tape. (Hare, 2011b, p. 23)

The most recent report into the state of Australian higher education (Bexley, James & Arkoudis, 2011), and from which the above media report was drawn, makes exceedingly glum reading, with the senior author reported as saying:

> . . . Academics love the intellectual stimulation of their work. . . [but] there is widespread dissatisfaction because of. . . poor management and overwhelming layers of bureaucracy. . . [There is] constant accountability. . . [and] surveillance and the message [that] you need to be scrutinised: that there is something wrong. (Hare, 2011a, p. 27)

The inescapable prognosis as captured in the tone of this review into the current health of the Australian academy, and reinforced by others about the imminent flight of academic faculty (see Petersen, 2011), is one in which the inhabitants feel the overwhelming burden of "excessive and unmanageable workloads and anxieties of not feeling in control or on top of one's load and the relentless pressure to do more faster" (Hare, 2011a, p. 27).

What I have described in this chapter gives all the appearances of being the "perfect storm" in relation to higher education. Perhaps the wider implications are that *this is* the new orthodoxy of higher education: develop an insecure and fearful workforce; force it to compete against one another for spurious rewards and the resources necessary for it to do its work; relentlessly bombard it with meaningless regimes of accountability; and wrap it all up in a mantra about national productivity, international competitiveness, world's best practices, and taxpayer transparency—and maybe Marx's immiseration prediction will just have come true! Just maybe Marginson (2010) is correct and national and international university rankings are "here to stay" (p. 32)—and we should give up the pretence that academe is about the pursuit of "big ideas" and simply resign ourselves to participating in the "knowledge economy world cup."

References

Adorno, T. (1974). *Minima moralia: Reflections from damaged life*. London: Verso.

Aronowitz, S. (2000). *The knowledge factory: dismantling the corporate university and creating true higher learning*. Boston: Beacon Press.

Ball, S. (2000). Performativities and fabrications in the education economy: Towards the performative society. *Australian educational researcher, 27* (2), 1–24.

Bexley, E., James, R., & Arkoudis, S. (2011). *The australian academic profession in transition*. Commissioned report prepared for the Department of Education, Employment and Workplace Relations. Melbourne: Centre for the Study of Higher Education, The University of Melbourne.

Blackmore, J., Brennan, M., & Zippin, L. (2010). Repositioning university governance and academic work: An overview. In J. Blackmore, M. Brennan, & L. Zippin (Eds.), *Re-positioning university governance and academic work* (pp. 1–16). Rotterdam, The Netherlands: Sense.

Burgess, J. (1989). Productivity: A worker problem? *Journal of Australian political economy, 24,* 23–38.

Campbell, J. (2000). *Dry rot in the ivory tower*. Lanham, MD: University Press of America.

Carr, K. (2011). Improvements to excellence in research for Australia—Ministerial statement to the Senate Economics Legislation Committee [Press release].

Coady, T. (Ed.). (2000). *Why universities matter*. Sydney: Allen & Unwin.

Cooper, S., Hinkson, J., & Sharp, G. (Eds.). (2002). *Scholars and entrepreneurs: The universities in crisis*. North Carlton, VIC: Arena.

Currie, J., & Newson, J. (Eds.). (1998). *Universities and globalization: Critical perspectives*. Thousand Oaks, CA: Sage.

Freeland, J. (1986). Australia: The search for a new educational settlement. In R. Sharp (Ed.), *Capitalist crisis and schooling: Comparative studies in the politics of education* (pp. 212–236). Melbourne: Macmillan.

Giroux, H., & Myrsiades, K. (Eds.). (2001). *Beyond the corporate university: Culture and pedagogy in the new millennium*. Lanham, MD: Rowman & Littlefield.

Graves, N., Barnett, A., & Clarke, P. (2011). Funding grant proposals for scientific researcher: Retrospective analysis of scores by members of grant review panels. *British Medical Journal, 343,* 1–8.

Hare, J. (2011a, 21 September). Academe faces looming crisis. *The Australian (Higher Education),* 27.

Hare, J. (2011b, 21 September). Harried, underpaid staff plan to flee the sector. *The Australian (Higher Education)*, 23.

Hare, J. (2011c, 28 September). Procurement of research grants a costly, time-consuming lottery. *The Australian (Higher Education)*, p. 23.

Hunt, I., & Smyth, J. (Eds.). (1998). *The ethos of the university: West and beyond*. Adelaide: Centre for Applied Philosophy/The Flinders Institute for the Study of Teaching, Flinders University of South Australia.

Jackson, N. (1991). *Skills formation and gender relations: The politics of who knows what*. Geelong, VIC: Deakin University Press.

James, P. (Ed.). (2000). *Burning down the house: The bonfire of the universities*. North Carlton, VIC: Arena.

MacIntyre, S. (2010). *The poor relation: The history of the social sciences in Australia*. Melbourne: Melbourne University Press.

Marginson, S., & Considine, M. (2000). *The enterprise university: Power, governance and reinvention in Australia*. Cambridge: Cambridge University Press.

Marginson, S. (2010). How universities have been positioned as teams in a knowledge economy world cup. In J. Blackmore, M. Brennan & L. Zippin (Eds.), *Re-positioning university governance and academic work* (pp. 17–33). Rotterdam, The Netherlands: Sense.

Marx, K. (1986). *Capital: A critique of political economy, volume 1*. Harmondsworth: Penguin. (Original work published 1867)

Meisenhelder, T. (1983). The ideology of professionalism in higher education. *Journal of Education, 165* (3), 295–307.

O'Malley, P. (1989). Editorial: Social justice and the client state. *Social Justice, 16* (3), 4–14.

Offe, C. (1985). *Disorganised capitalism: contemporary transformations of work and politics*. Cambridge: Polity Press.

Petersen, E. (2011). Staying or going? Australian early career researchers' narratives of academic work, exit options and coping strategies. *Australian Universities' Review, 53* (2), 34–42.

Power, M. (1994). The audit society. In A. Hopwood & P. Miller (Eds.), *Accounting as social institutional practice* (pp. 299–316). Cambridge: Cambridge University Press.

Power, M. (2003). Evaluating the audit explosion. *Law and Policy, 25* (3), 186–202.

Pusey, M. (1991). *Economic rationalism in Canberra: A nation-building state changes its mind*. Cambridge: Cambridge University Press,

Quiggin, J. (1995). The clever country: Not so smart then even less now. *Sydney Morning Herald*.

Quiggin, J. (2010). *Zombie economics: How dead ideas still walk among us*. Princeton, NJ: Princeton University Press.

Readings, B. (1996). *The university in ruins*. Cambridge, MA: Harvard University Press.

Rowbotham, J. (2011, 5 October). VC strikes a blow for research with impact. *The Australian (Higher Education)*, p. 23.

Seddon, T. (1990). On education and context: Insights from the first Monash University forum on the VCE. *Australian Journal of Education, 34* (2), 131–136.

Slaughter, S., & Rhoades, G. (2004). *Academic capitalism and the new economy*. Baltimore: Johns Hopkins University Press.

Smyth, J. (1989). Collegiality as a counter discourse to corporate management into higher education. *Journal of Tertiary Educational Administration, 11* (2), 143–155.

Smyth, J. (1990). Higher educational policy reform in Australia in the context of the "client state" (Unpublished Master of Policy and Law thesis). LaTrobe University, Melbourne.

Smyth, J. (1991). Theories of the state and recent policy reform in Australian higher education. *Discourse, 11* (2), 48–69.

Smyth, J. (1994). A policy analysis of higher education reforms in Australia in the context of globalisation. *Melbourne Studies in Education, 35*, 39–72.

Smyth, J. (1995a). *Academic work: The changing labour process in higher education*. Buckingham, England: Open University Press.

Smyth, J. (1995b). Higher education policy reform in Australia: An expansive analysis. In J. Mauch & P. Sabloff (Eds.), *Reform and change in higher education: International perspectives* (pp. 51–82). New York: Garland.

Smyth, J. (2010). The politics of derision, distrust and deficit: The damaging consequences for youth and communities put at a disadvantage. In E. Samier & M. Schmidt (Eds.), *Trust and betrayal in educational administration and leadership* (pp. 169–183). New York: Routledge.

Smyth, J., & Hattam, R. (2000). Intellectual as hustler: Researching against the grain of the market. *British Educational Research Journal, 26* (2), 157–175.

Smyth, J., & Shacklock, G. (1998). *Re-making teaching: Ideology, policy and practice*. London: Routledge.

Strathern, M. (2000). *Audit cultures: Anthropological studies in accountability, ethics and the academy*. London: Routledge.

Tierney, W. (2006). *Trust and the public good: Examining the cultural conditions of academic work*. New York: Peter Lang.

Tudiver, N. (1999). *Universities for sale: Resisting corporate control over Canadian higher education*. Toronto: James Lorimer.

Turk, J. (Ed.). (2000). *The corporate campus: Commercialization and the dangers to Canada's colleges and universities*. Toronto: James Lorimer.

Yeatman, A. (1988). The Green paper on higher education: Remarks concerning its implications for participation and equity for women as staff and students. *Australian Universities' Review, 31* (1), 39–41.

CHAPTER TWENTY-FIVE

Danger U

How Conservative Attacks on Higher Education Undermine Academic Freedom, Science, and Social Progress

AARON COOLEY

> Where did this idea come from that everybody deserves free education, free medical care, free whatever? It comes from Moscow, from Russia. It comes straight out of the pit of hell. And it's cleverly disguised as having a tender heart. It's not a tender heart. It's ripping the heart out of this country.[1]
> —Debbie Riddle, Texas State Representative

> To those of you who received honors, awards, and distinctions, I say, well done. And to the C students I say, you, too, can be President of the United States. [*Laughter*] A Yale degree is worth a lot, as I often remind Dick Cheney—[*laughter*]—who studied here but left a little early. So now we know: If you graduate from Yale, you become President; if you drop out, you get to be Vice President. [*Laughter*][2]
> —George W. Bush, President

Each of these epigraphs effectively illustrates the common jabs that conservatives take at higher education in America. The first is a frontal attack that aggressively tears down education as a type of socialist entitlement linked to other programs that allegedly restrict liberty. The second comment is meant to humorously undermine the value of education even when received from one of the country's elite institutions, such as Yale. In both cases, the underlying points are that education is a private good that the public should not bother investing in and that one should not take it or the liberal professors that work at such institutions seriously. Unfortunately, these comments and the ideas that support them cannot be easily dismissed as meaningless exaggerations or off-the-cuff statements, because they reveal the conservative agenda to limit access to higher education for students by lowering its quality, reducing its public support, and moving to privatize as many parts of it as possible. These strategies should, of course, be familiar to political observers who have seen the conservative restoration pursue similar paths in other policy arenas. Higher education, though, impacts many other policy areas, making these attacks particularly harmful. As such, this chapter focuses on academic freedom, science, and social progress and how conservatives have attacked the professors, students, and general idea of higher education. Through these discussions of specific incidents as well as their policy and philosophical implications, the peril in which higher educational institutions operate will be demonstrated and the potential loss of these institutions as sources of political dissent and progressive change will emerge. I conclude with a call for renewed activism and vigor in the fight to preserve the critical role higher education plays in our democratic political system.

Academic Freedom: The Only Kind of Freedom Conservatives Don't Like

One of the guiding myths of higher education is the notion that the protection of academic freedom is vital to its success. Of course, like most myths, this is based in what a social group wants to think and not what really exists. Unfortunately, there are far too many instances when higher education institutions and their governing authorities have not stood up for those students and faculty who have chosen to dissent from prevailing opinions on controversial issues. Comparatively, there are only a few positive counterexamples that support free speech and academic freedom, such as the overturning of the speaker ban at the University of North Carolina[3] or the eventual support for Mario Savia at the University of California at Berkeley.[4]

However, in recent decades, the culture wars have taken a strong hold on higher education, and conservatives have sought to attack higher education—none more aggressively than David Horowitz. According to Horowitz's autobiography, *Radical Son: A Generational Odyssey*, he came to his conservative views later in life, having been raised by Marxists. He makes a lot of having grown out of his liberal beliefs upon advancing in age and wisdom, that fits with the general conservative slogan of "Show me a young Conservative and I'll show you someone with no heart. Show me an old Liberal and I'll show you someone with no brains" which is often speciously sourced to Winston Churchill. This ideology suggests that there is something adult, or grown up, about letting the poor suffer without a shred of empathy. In this vein of conservative activism, Horowitz has turned into higher education's fieriest critic in terms of liberal bias. He has written several books over the last decade attacking higher education and its professors including *The Politics of Bad Faith: The Radical Assault on America's Future*, *The Professors: The 101 Most Dangerous Academics in America*, and *Indoctrination U: The Left's War Against Academic Freedom*.[5] Each of these volumes follows a similar theme of how the left is irresponsible and reckless with ideas and that its ideas harm the country. The form of the texts varies, with *The Professors* being the most aggressive in specifically naming college professors who Horowitz deems as having views that put America in peril. Of course, he mostly picks on disciplines known for their historic and substantial lack of power in controlling the nation's economic policy and political institutions such as communication studies, literature, and education. He, of course, neglects the truly dangerous professors in terms of the harm that has resulted from their advice to presidents and corporations, like certain faculty members in economics (the notion of which was brilliantly highlighted and skewered in Charles Ferguson's Oscar-winning documentary *Inside Job*).[6]

The consequences of Horowitz's efforts in *The Professors* are particularly strange in that he succeeded in targeting professors for scorn and ridicule for researching and publishing in fields which they were hired to be experts in for their institutions. One of the most public examples of fallout from his attacks in recent years was a possible invitation to speak at a National Communication Association meeting. Among the professors who expressed their outrage were ones he had targeted, including Dana Cloud at the University of Texas at Austin. Professor Cloud was distressed because Horowitz's attacks had led to harassment by third parties:

> Cloud said that in other ways, Horowitz's attacks have been significant. People who read the book or his Web site regularly send letters to university officials asking for her to be fired. Personally, she has received—mostly via e-mail—"physical threats, threats of removing my daughter from my custody, threats of sexual assaults, horrible disgusting gendered things" she said. That Horowitz doesn't send these isn't the point, she said. "He builds a climate and culture that emboldens people" and as a result, shouldn't be seen as a defender of academic freedom, but as its enemy.[7]

The last point is the trickiest because Cloud is quite right in her view that Horowitz is not a supporter of academic freedom. In fact, he uses the banner of academic freedom not to advance discussions over critical issues of the day, but to attack those individuals committed to that type of work through shoddy research and the manipulation of out of context comments, as detailed in a *Facts Count: An Analysis of David Horowitz's* The Professors: The 101 Most Dangerous Academics in America.[8] Unfortunately for the professors attacked, the nation's anti-intellectual elements were easily appealed to and Horowitz was able to profit from the attention, with more speaking engagements before conservative audiences around the country.

So, why has Horowitz pursued this strategy and why is it central to this section of the chapter? Namely, because his attacks and his Orwellian-named Academic Bill of Rights[9] have had sway with policymakers and legislatures around the country where some have passed resolutions supporting it. More generally, his efforts contribute to the environment in conservative political culture that sees higher education as liberally biased, which provides a predicate for the findings of research from colleges and universities that contradict their political ideology and views on specific policy issues to be dismissed.

Further, those professors who speak up for unpopular views can be punished with mixed protection from the courts under the *Garcetti* precedent.[10] The holding in this case, although not directly applying the right to free speech to college and university professors, has been interpreted by lower courts as providing possibly little protection for higher education faculty when they speak out about matters that are within the scope of their employment. This could be a cumbersome standard when it comes to the research agendas of faculty and their attempts to influence the policy debates as public intellectuals. There are several cases making their way through the courts regarding the extent of the case that will shed further light on the legal rights of faculty members when they voice unpopular opinions. The hope, however, from Horowitz and the conservatives who support his perspective is not to foster further conversations about the controversial issues, but to silence liberal views through intimidation and censorship based on public outrage.

A particularly indicative example occurred when Dr. Timothy J. L. Chandler, a candidate for provost of Kennesaw State University, had accepted the position. A local newspaper discovered that he had written an article many years previously that referenced Marx.[11] Although the University president and other constituencies supported Chandler, he decided to withdraw from the position and remain at Kent State in Ohio. He asserted he was not a Marxist, but given the atmosphere it would have been difficult to succeed in the position. The upshot is that the third party commentary was able to reinforce stereotypes of academics as closet Marxists who cannot be trusted.

Another instance of this effect is the pressure asserted by independent groups in the labor protests in Wisconsin in 2011. In this case, a University of Wisconsin professor, William Cronon, had requests for his email records from conservative groups looking for anything to embarrass or incriminate him in activities with the protests.[12] Similar requests were then made by conservatives in Michigan.[13] These instances were meant to pressure lesser known professors from joining such protest efforts.

Further, these instances fit with other ones that demonstrate a bias towards silence and prohibiting dissent in controversial political environments where substantial amounts of research money are at stake. A recent example is noteworthy. At Louisiana State University, Dr. Ivor Van Hebben did not have his contract renewed in his view because of his criticism of the Army Corps of Engineers.[14] According to Dr. Van Hebben, this criticism made LSU uncomfortable when seeking additional research funds from the Corps.

This leads to the final element in the lessening of academic freedom in higher education, which is the ever increasing level of contingent and adjunct faculty who dare not speak out for fear of losing their present or next term contract. Here the protections are even weaker as these contracts are written in such a manner that no justification is needed for nonrenewal and no presumption for future employment exists. This makes such faculty extremely wary of expressing almost any view of any kind—be it controversial or innocuous. As this new contingent faculty majority expands, fewer and fewer faculty will feel comfortable criticizing everything from the strength of levies to drinking water to the state of higher education for fear of being replaced by a more compliant non-agitator the following semester on grounds that they were grumbling to a superior. A prohibition against such grumbling is now policy at community colleges in San Antonio.[15]

Science May Only Be Supported When It Matches Ideology

In the last few years, there have been several instances that illustrate that conservative forces have put forth efforts to undermine science—often by directly attacking professors whose research agendas possibly conflict with their deeply held views. What is particularly disheartening about this development is that it is a significant step back from reasonableness and reliance on rationality and toward non-scientific and non-empirical understandings of technical issues. The greatest critics of higher education here are certain members of the media and advocacy organizations, but in some cases the criticisms come from within the academy. Not surprisingly, these criticisms center on two main issues: science and religion and climate change. The first has been played out over decades since the Scopes trial,[16] but it came to the fore in the *Kitzmiller v. Dover Area School District*[17] case in Pennsylvania about the teaching of intelligent design in high school. The second area involves the attacks on climate change over the past decade culminating in the so-called "Climategate" scandal [18] and wrongly accusing several university researchers of misconduct. In each case, the overall thesis is supported because of the reliance upon ideology over analysis of empirical evidence.

In the *Kitzmiller* case, a new slate of school board members decided to expand the science curriculum by mandating that the high schools begin using a new educational resource entitled

Of Pandas and People.[19] The text described the origins of life from the perspective of intelligent design. The use of the text and teaching of intelligent design was challenged in court. During the trial, several examples of the text being repackaged creationism, which had been previously found to be unconstitutional in *Edwards v. Aguillard*,[20] showcased the desire to promote a non-scientific understanding of human origins. The federal judge in the case, John Jones, found that the teaching of intelligent design was unconstitutional and it promoted religious views in the public school curriculum. The importance of this case is not in its direct attacks from conservatives on science professors in higher education, but in the general undermining of the principles of science for political purposes. All scientists only believe in theories as far as the theory stands up to testing from many researchers in many places over time. Instances like this one illustrate how people with little or no scientific training attempt to erode the fabric and continuum of science education in the country. The results of this attack land squarely at the feet of college science professors who must try to overcome some students' misplaced sense of justification in challenging evolutionary theory.[21] However, the greater effect of efforts in the creationism/intelligent design movement is the way this undermining carries over from a fairly abstract and theoretical debate about the origins of life to a public environment that questions scientific evidence on the basis of misinformation and ideology.

This effect was clearly demonstrated in this section's second example, "Climategate." In this incident from 2009, conservative anti-climate change groups and associated blogs obtained and published thousands of emails and documents that they felt called into question decades of research and empirical evidence. In reality, the information from East Anglia University did nothing of the sort. This did not stop conservative forces and media organizations, spearheaded by FoxNews, from running non-stop coverage of the incident without providing the appropriate context or presenting any significant dissenting views about the importance of the information. These attacks fed the trope widely believed by conservatives that climate science is not science, but actually liberal propaganda meant to restrain economic growth.[22] What is remarkable about this narrative is how utterly baseless it is and how simply repeating it over and over convinces viewers to be skeptical about the research of scientists working at colleges and universities. As the events unfolded, there were many investigations and analyses of the data. They consistently found that there had been no misconduct by the researchers and that there was no hidden agenda or evidence that contradicts the established scientific consensus supporting the notion of climate change. In fact, numerous independent scientists and even some mainstream media outlets began to question the relentless campaign waged by the right as a severe overreaction. As the coverage began to run its course, the oil industry funded a study to reanalyze the data.

When the report was released in 2011, which supported the original contention that global warming is continuing to happen, there was not nearly the same widespread coverage that the initial story had warranted from the conservative media outlets. One can imagine that this lack of coverage was due to the evidence not fitting the ideology of the news outlets and therefore being pushed down the list of important stories of the day such as coverage of the re-introduction of McDonald's McRib.[23] Here again, the effect is a reduction in the legitimacy of science and the institutions of higher education that advance it.

Essentially, the conservative attacks upon science are attacks on higher education, as these are the sites where science is advanced, college students receive further instruction in science, and teachers who educated students in K-12 settings learn the best methods for communicating science to younger students. However, as these attacks gain in terms of credibility, intensity, and consistency, the tasks of educating students about science becomes more difficult. As it stands, the two examples from this section regarding evolution and climate change are ideas that Americans on average believe in less than the populations of most other advanced industrial countries.[24] This campaign against science has at least two important effects. The first is practical in terms of reducing the country's ability to produce science-based advancements and related careers. The second is the further deterioration of reasonableness in policy debates that impact every aspect of political and private life. If empirical and evidentiary-based judgments can be overturned in the minds of many people by repetition of false information via media outlets, then the crisis in our democratic process will grow evermore.

Social Progress Is Only Desirable if the Free Market Leads the Way

Anti-intellectualism has long been a staple of American culture, but in recent decades higher education has come increasingly under fire from the right for indoctrinating impressionable students at colleges and universities. Ironically, as this critique has become more widespread and widely held, the country has become more politically conservative along with the growth of conservatively branded media outlets. Of course, the critique that students are being indoctrinated in liberal beliefs by elitist college professors is far from accurate. To be sure, college professors at elite institutions and most liberal arts faculties do have more registered Democrats than Republicans.[25] A host of explanations account for this statistic, like the comparison of what type of personalities enter the academy compared to business, but the overriding attack from the right on higher education obscures a much more complicated picture. The first major rebuttal to this attack of elite liberal indoctrination is that most college students do not attend elite institutions or take a completely non-vocational liberal arts degree. As such, students who are attending schools to receive a criminal justice associate's degree from a rural community college in Kansas are unlikely to be taught by a slate of liberal professors. In point of fact, these students are also less likely to be influenced if they do have a liberal adjunct instructor for their one or two elective courses. Given this reality, the right should not be able to get away with attacks on higher education as being overly liberal, but the previous discussion about the media system which perpetuates such ideas carries over to this area as well.

What is particularly odd is that, when it comes to the influencing of public policy from higher educational institutions, the right is much more effective. In particular, schools of business, departments of economics, and colleges of law often have more conservatives than other divisions of the academy. Needless to say, these disciplines often get seats at the table in elite policymaking circles at the federal and state level. There are, undoubtedly, somewhat similar circumstances among liberals, but the difference is the comfort of the right to nominate individuals with rather extreme views for high level posts such as the Supreme Court (Justice Scalia) or Defense Department (Paul Wolfowitz). Even more examples can be drawn from the Council of Economic Advisors and Treasury Department, which have a revolving door between elite business schools, financial firms, and positions in government that are charged with regulating the banking and financial sectors that caused the recent economic crisis. The most recent counterexample of the left not being able to successfully shepherd a left-leaning member of the academy to a post would be the Obama Administration deciding not to nominate

Elizabeth Warren to be the head of the newly created Consumer Financial Protection Bureau.[26] She was criticized from the right as being an out of touch liberal elite professor from Harvard University. This purely deceptive attack worked, even though it was baseless as she attended public colleges for undergraduate and law school and sought to protect the economic interests of the middle and working classes. Nonetheless, this contrast is indicative of how the right is able to undermine certain professors who focus on social justice while concomitantly drawing from the conservative ranks to influence major aspects of public policy. Yet, as disturbing as this trend is, it is not the only one that seeks to undermine social progress. The second of these strategies centers on changing the focus of the types of research that are being carried out in higher education. Conservatives have long fanned the flames of the culture wars on university campuses. However, the latest battles have moved from the often abstract rethinking of literary canons and inclusion of multiculturalism in the curriculum to more concrete adjustments such as limiting the scope and funding of law school clinics to sue environmental polluters.[27] Instances, like this one, starkly demonstrate the ways in which conservative legislators and policymakers view the role of colleges and universities. They see them as engines of entrepreneurism and sources of job growth, and, if the programs do not further that goal, they may be eliminated. This task of conservative reform of higher education has been helped along by the economic crisis and recession of the last few years in which colleges and universities have cut programs, eliminated research centers, and restricted internal research funds. The result is less and less research that documents parts of society about which some groups believe deserve limited public knowledge. In the future, it may be more difficult to find funding sources even from private philanthropic organizations to collect data about the country's most vulnerable and disenfranchised individuals.

In addition to this problem of funding is the change in higher education to a reliance on adjunct faculty members. These contingent faculty members are even less likely to carry out extended research programs given their own vulnerability without tenure protections and without the time to devote to researching controversial or unpopular subjects. Organizations such as The New Faculty Majority[28] have sought to raise this concern to tenured members of the academy, but the efforts and prospects to remedy the situation are bleak given the financial strain, limited interests of other parties, and the retreat from shared governance at most state universities.

The last aspect of how conservatives mount attacks on higher education that limit social progress is in the area of undermining established elements of the social welfare state. The work of conservative media outlets to relentlessly erode the foundations of such programs by attaching them to liberalism via conservative think tank reports changes the public policy conversation from independent evaluations about the merits of Social Security and Medicare to an ideological discussion. These attacks on liberalism are also assaults on reason, which have real policy implications. A prime example here is from the recent debate on health care where numerous evaluations from health care policy experts from higher education were drowned out of the debate by baseless and senseless allegations that the law created so-called "death panels." The theme here again is one of rationality, empiricism, and evidence versus ideology and rhetoric. It says something rather negative about our public debates that higher education no longer is able to influence and distribute the kinds of research that push our society towards a fuller and more robust democracy and instead they must constantly fight to be relevant in the present day. This is related to the left's search for relevant public intellectuals. The work of Noam Chomsky and Cornel West has had a substantial public impact, but the continued assault from the right has chipped away at their resonance to equate them to any other talking head on a cable news show.

In sum, the right has successfully muted the impact of critical voices from the left in higher education through an active campaign to marginalize their voices while at the same time claiming that higher education has a liberal bias. The result of the continued attacks via repetition and misrepresentation is that a portion of the public is misinformed about crucial issues in public debate, and no manner of complex research from presumably liberal college professors will change their deeply held views.[29] Undoing this campaign via satire in the form of *The Daily Show*[30] or *The Colbert Report*[31] is as effective as more legitimate groups such as Media Matters[32] in countering the narrative of a liberal professoriate out to ruin the country. In sum, overcoming these attacks will continue to be difficult especially in the lean economic times of the present, but the noble ideals of higher education are worth the fight.

Conclusion

Overall, the attacks from the conservative movement on academic freedom, science, and social progress have sought to diminish the role that higher education plays in teaching the rest of the country about aspects of our society and systems around the world that powerful interests do not want the masses to think about or focus their attention upon. The questions that then arise are troublesome to the status quo for the policy priorities foisted upon the public as important. As voices of dissent from higher education are drowned out and their research about marginalized populations becomes further pushed to the side, these attacks will have succeeded. However, agitators and activist academics can respond. For example, even with the faults of the Occupy Wall Street movement, it has succeeded in bringing economic inequality to the fore of the public debate in a period when the country had been focused on debt ceiling fights. Although the Occupy movement was taken down in many places via police crackdowns and the remaining elements drowned out by the Republican primary, one of its legacies is in the potential for revolution that still exists in the country to advance the cause of social justice through political action. As these forces continue to mount, each member of our broad higher education community from online adjunct community college instructors to tenured professors at elite universities must continue to advance our common interest in the hallmarks of higher education that unite us: rationality, observation, and evidence. Otherwise, higher education may continue in the future, but it will be something unrecognizable to our present eyes and something that the right will no longer need to attack.

Notes

1. See Alan Smithee, State Rep. Debbie Riddle says "I Want You. . . OUT! United States for United Statesians" http://www.freepresshouston.com/featured/state-rep-debbie-riddle-says-i-want-you-out-united-states-for-united-statesians/
2. See George W. Bush, George W. Bush: Commencement Address at Yale University in New Haven, Connecticut, http://www.presidency. ucsb.edu/ws/index. php? pid=45895#ixzz1jUBc9sa7
3. See http://www.northcarolinahistory.org/commentary/187/entry/
4. See http://www.savio.org/
5. See http://www.horowitzfreedomcenter.org/
6. See http://www.sonyclassics.com/insidejob/

7. See http://www.insidehighered.com/news/2008/02/19/horowitz
8. See http://cdn. publicinterestnetwork.org/assets/woUsLGhMMPR98xFTxvDWyw/Facts_Count-Report.pdf
9. See http://www.insidehighered.com/news/2006/01/09/resolutions
10. See Garcetti v. Ceballos, 547 U.S. 410 (2006)
11. See http://www.insidehighered.com/news/2011/03/18/provost_designee_withdraws_at_kennesaw_state_amid_controversy_over_journal_citation_of_marx#ixzz1jUEBXjBE
12. Seehttp://chronicle.com/article/Wisconsin-GOP-Seeks-E-Mails-of/126911/
13. See http://chronicle.com/article/Michigan-Think-Tank-Asks-3/126922/
14. See http://www.nola.com/news/index. ssf/2009/04/ivor_van_heerden_who_pointed_f.html
15. Seehttp://www.insidehighered.com/news/2011/11/04/faculty-alamo-colleges-gird-battle-tenure#ixzz1jUDZC86s
16. See http://law2. umkc.edu/faculty/projects/ftrials/scopes/evolut.htm
17. See http://www.pamd. uscourts. gov/kitzmiller/kitzmiller_342.pdf
18. See http://www.factcheck.org/2009/12/Climategate/
19. See http://ncse.com/creationism/analysis/critique-pandas-people
20. See http://www.law. cornell.edu/supct/html/historics/USSC_CR_0482_0578_ZD.html
21. See http://news. nationalgeographic.com/news/2006/08/060810–evolution.html
22. See http://www.foxnews.com/story/0,2933,591415,00.html
23. See http://www.thedailyshow.com/watch/wed-october-26–2011/weathering-fights
24. See http://www.usnews.com/opinion/blogs/energy-intelligence/2011/08/26/fewer-americans-see-climate-change-a-threat-caused-by-humans
25. See http://www.studentsforacademicfreedom.org/news/1898/lackdiversity.html
26. See http://content. usatoday.com/communities/theoval/post/2011/07/obama-passes-over-creator-of-consumer-bureau/1
27. See http://www.abajournal.com/magazine/article/taking_their_pains_to_the_clinic/
28. See http://www.newfacultymajority. info/national/
29. See http://www.huffingtonpost.com/2011/11/21/fox-news-viewers-less-informed-people-fairleigh-dickinson_n_1106305.html
30. See http://www.thedailyshow.com/
31. See http://www.colbertnation.com/
32. See http://mediamatters.org/

CHAPTER TWENTY-SIX

Trends in Higher Education

Legal and Ethical Issues

THOMAS M. LOVETT

A basic tenet of the U.S. Social Security system is that those who have paid into the system have to be alive to win. Death terminates recipient benefits, no matter how much has been paid in. With a twist, the same logic applies to history. Survivors write the history of an event or an era. As scholars, great faith is placed in the preserved words of those who lived long enough to put stylus to clay or quill to parchment. Whoever said that hindsight is 20/20 failed to consider the distortions associated with such vision. Looking back from today, finding an economist who predicted the financial crisis of 2008 is simply a matter of searching a relevant database. Believing the accuracy of such an economist in 2007 would have been another matter. The same can be said for political pundits, legal sages, and those who face the folly of writing an essay on legal trends in higher education. Addressing what has happened in and to higher education in the past two decades and finding legal scholars who published the truth about what was then the future is a matter of history and, of course, of being alive to reap the blessings of that past work. Seeking trends for the next decade reminds one of visions of the crystal orb that clears sight and sound, letting the viewer enjoy tomorrow's sunrise today. That said, let's look into the all-knowing orb and, in the same glance, consider a mirrored reflection from over our shoulders.

Bifurcating higher education trends into short term and long term may be artificial but is still useful. Short-term trends are linked to yesterday and are somewhat easier to tease out of the smoke. Detailing long-term trends, like long weather forecasting, is a bit more complex. In the short run, compliance with governmental mandates, diminishing financial resources and options for addressing budgetary shortfalls, and the changing role of institutional administration capture the meat of prevailing issues. These, along with a potpourri of associated and continuing trends, will make for interesting times for, and within, our campuses. Within this potpourri are governance and governing board issues, including conflict of interests and board management; the relationship between changes in technology and instructional costs; international issues, including technology transfer, identifying and managing risks, and international transactions; on campus threat assessment and safety concerns; high risk students and student activities; federal investigations and increasing federal scrutiny via legislated mandates; and, for public institutions, the continued privatization of our campus with the associated financial and control issues. As for longer-term trends, some of which represent a maturing of short-term trends, one must consider continued regulation of higher education, including faculty academic freedom concerns in light of state and federal mandates and institutional ability to respond to issues; compliance requirements; increased use of technology, including assessing online learning in our current learning paradigms, access to information issues, outsourcing of technology (how many senior administrators understand the issues of cloud computing?), and next-generation intellectual property concerns; changing roles of key administrators and faculty, particularly in the areas of risk management; preventative assessment of legal liabilities; decreasing buying power of budgets as the "new normal"; and a basket of possibly lesser issues such as increasing demands for accountability and transparency, continued globalization and internationalization of higher education as engendered by the rise of India's and China's economic clout; dependence on public/private partnerships as a means to manage costs; ever-increasing governmental scrutiny, including IRS audits; employment law concerns as institutional workforces become more knowledgeable of individual rights and employment law processes; and changes in faculty tenure-track processes due to financial constraints and the need to balance resources. Had enough with trends? Not really? Administrators and faculty leadership must balance which risks can be eliminated, which may be set aside, and which must be addressed with the demands to stay competitive within their respective professions while scanning current news for threads on trends overlooked or previously misdiagnosed and dancing on the spinning top of ethics and legal issues—all to protect our student, faculties, staff, and institutions. For a beginning, let's consider short-term trends, which are easier to spot and easier to digest.

First: Compliance and Recordkeeping

Any essay of trends or key legal issues has to start with a disclaimer, actually three rather significant ones. First, this essay is of limited space and not intended to be all-inclusive or all-encompassing. This is not a treatise as used in the legal profession, nor is it intended to be a patently scholarly work. For a detailed compendium of higher education law, consider Kaplin and Lee's *The Law of Higher Education: A Comprehensive Guide to Legal Implications of Administrative Decision-Making* (4th ed., Jossey-Bass, 2006) or Joseph W. Ambash's *Federal Record-Keeping and Reporting Requirements for Independent and Public Colleges and Universities* (3rd ed., National Association of College and University Attorneys, 2005). To the contrary, this essay is a beginning guide intended to spur thought and lead to further reading. Second, this is an essay and only an essay. For details on the various legal trends noted herein, sound advice would be to have a conversation with one's campus legal counsel or consult more in-depth, detailed works such as the two noted above, among others. Third, this essay, unless otherwise specified, addresses only federal laws. The array of state laws is too broad for the scope or purpose of an essay and would be of limited merit to all except those operating within the specific state under discussion. Those in the other 49 states plus the District of Columbia would have to wade through marginally applicable material and would be, for the most part, bored. The same can be said for efforts to bifurcate legal issues into those impacting public institutions and those impacting not-for-profit (private or independent) institutions and, more recently, those issues focused on the for-profit sector of institutions. An effort has been made to note if a trend is more likely to impact one sector of institutions as opposed to another; however, this can be dangerous, as demonstrated by the number of public institutions that have adopted all or some of the provisions of the Sarbanes-Oxley Act of 2002 (SOX) (Pub. L. 107–204, 116 Stat. 745, enacted July 30, 2002) as guidance for good business practices when, in fact, SOX was intended and enacted to apply to publicly traded, for-profit business entities, not higher education institutions and certainly not public colleges and universities. That said; let's step off into the Serbonian Bog.

The key legal issues and trends that have been with us can be grouped into five categories: those issues and trends involving students, including student financial aid, educational, medical, admissions, and disciplinary records and files; personnel issues, including affirmative action information, faculty tenure and promotion concerns, reassignment of personnel, and an aging cadre of faculty and staff mixed with dwindling resources; mandated business reporting of compliance to grants and sponsored research, unrelated business income (UBIT) and instructional technology; campus law enforcement reporting and records, including campus security, hazing reports, such as specific records, including the Drug Free Schools and Communities Act; and the legal issues relating to accrediting bodies and voluntary sports associations, such as the National Collegiate Athletic Association (NCAA). Granted, the offered list is neither small nor exhaustive and, even these categories can all be categorized under the general headings of compliance issues and trends.

The Family Educational Rights and Privacy Act (FERPA) (34 C. F. R. 99. 1 et seq.) governs access to student educational records maintained by educational institutions and mandates how and which information may or may not be disclosed, whether with or without the consent of the student about whom those records are maintained. Within certain prescribed instances, FERPA prohibits the release, without consent, of a student's educational records. The key is that each institution should review its guidelines and procedures for compliance with FERPA and, although not mandated, engage actively in relevant continuing education for institutional personnel. At worse, violation of FERPA could subject an institution to the loss of federal financial aid and grant funds, albeit unlikely based on the Act's enforcement record. The Act does not provide that an individual may bring suit alleging violation of FERPA; that is, Congress, in passing FERPA, did not create a private right of action for an institution's violation of FERPA. This was clarified in the U.S. Supreme Court's decision in *Gonzaga University v. Doe* (536 U.S. 273, 2002). However, time lost and personnel costs in addressing a Department of Education complaint and the adverse publicity associated therewith merit significant attention to FERPA compliance. The same can be said for the federal requirements mandating publication of crime reporting, falling under the popular names of the Clery Act, the Student Right to Know Act, or the Crime Awareness and Campus Security Act of 1990 (20 U.S. Code§ 1092 (f); 34 C. F. R. 668. 46). Enforcement is through the Department of Education and institutional access to federal funds is at stake. If anything, the trend in recent years is increasing protection of student privacy and increasing disclosure of crime statistics to allow students and their parents to make educated choices involving the selection of colleges and universities and the provision of campus specific information so as to allow students the opportunity to take measures to better protect their safety and well-being.

Similar to student records, management of employee records has evolved and is the focus of federal attention. For example, the Fair Labor Standards Act (FLSA) (29 U.S. Code Chapter 8§206 et seq.) mandates that institutions must maintain certain records about all employees, including payroll records. The FLSA has distinct record maintenance provisions and considers higher education institutions to be no different than other covered employers, a concept that remains alien on some of our campuses. For example, a recurring issue is the treatment of assistant coaches as being exempt or non-exempt employees for purposes of the overtime provisions of the FLSA and the consequences for getting the classification wrong. Campuses could do well to designate personnel with oversight authority for FLSA compliance, as well as the Equal Pay Act (EPA) (29 U.S. Code Chapter 8 § 206 (d)), affirmative action programs under Title VII of the 1964 Civil Rights Act (Title VII) (42 U.S. Code Chapter 21), and other such mandates (for example, Executive Order 11246 [E. O. 11246, September 24, 1965]).

Compliance and maintenance of records in human resources and employee/student worker/faculty matters has been and will increasingly be a concern for institutions, and compliance is painted with a broad brush to include Occupational Safety and Health Administration (OSHA) (29 U.S. Code Chapter 15)and the Americans with Disabilities Act of 1990 (ADA) (42 U.S. Code Chapter 14 and amendments of 2008 under Pub. L. 110–325) issues for employees, record retention issues in faculty tenure and promotion and peer review, personnel records relating to Title VII and, with an aging and diversification of the "workforce" defending Age Discrimination in Employment Act of 1967 (ADEA) (29 U.S. Code Chapter 14) and Equal Pay Act (op. cit.) charges. For most institutions, unrelated business income tax (UBIT) is a fact of life, providing welcome, albeit many times sporadic, supplemental income to bolster dollar-starved budgets; however, with UBIT comes the necessity to generate and maintain tax records and face the occasional IRS audit.

The new reality of doing more with less focuses on the need to augment departmental budgets with grant funds. Once seen as a way to promote research and community involvement, the pursuit of grant resources has increased on many campuses, not merely as a means for junior faculty to build tenure and promotion portfolios but as needed supplemental resources. Oversight and recordkeeping associated with grant dollars has received increased focus and will continue to do so.

Consumer quality assurance concerns are increasing due to pressure by students and their families, by governing bodies and boards, and by benefactors. No longer is a college education seen as the "given" element in the pursuit of a higher standard of living, however that may be interpreted. As costs have increased and student debt load has reached the point of being worthy of national news coverage, the need to consider the worth of a degree in a cost/benefit analysis continues to increase. Likewise, federal oversight will continue and sharpen in such areas as student financial assistance, movement toward academic progress and graduation rates, the ability of students to attain meaningful employment within a reasonable time after graduation, and institutional relationships with lending institutions. Federal oversight translates into federal audits. Quality assurance, once the domain of accrediting agencies and commissions, now has a distinctive federal flavor.

Added to the quality assurance soup is the increasing dependence by institutions and students on online education and the surfacing issues of state regulation and control of online course offerings by out-of-state institutions to in-state students. Disguised by state agencies as concerns about quality assurance, the seminal issue may revolve around protection of turf. On-line course offerings that cross state borders incorporate all the legal issues associated with the decade-old legal issues of doing business in foreign jurisdictions, such as across state borders, and have morphed into e-commerce and Internet sales issues. An institution that would not have considered crossing into another state to deliver face-to-face classes without approval of the higher education commission of the host state dismissively considers the place of residence of students enrolled in online classes.

Intercollegiate athletics has to be considered in a discussion of trends with legal implications. Other athletic associations notwithstanding, the most significant factor is the NCAA which still talks the talk of student-athletes and the merits of amateur collegiate athletic programs, never mind if the talk matches the walk in theory or as practiced. Somewhere in the mix of student-athlete recruitment, academic progress and eligibility, booster and sponsor support, school and team spirit and pride, and fan identification with respective athletic programs, the quagmire of legal issues continues to grow—and especially so as NCAA Division II schools are pressured by fans, alumni, significant contributors, and their own trustees/regents/curators to seek Division I/IA designation. During this era of dwindling institutional resources, the amount of money necessary to make a divisional move, coupled with a limited pool of potential Division I capable student-athletes, provides multiple opportunities for conflicts of interests, collusion and undue influence, and personal agendas—any of which welcome an NCAA investigation, potential civil legal liability, and endless institutional personnel hours and associated legal expense addressing athletic association infractions and rules violations.

Second: Budget Cuts and Management of Resources

The budget cuts and management of resources category is a mix of legal and managerial issues (perhaps the two cannot be cleanly or practically separated). The newest buzz phrase, like a sound bite, is "new normal" that is, doing more with less and less and less. Granted, institutions have tried to offset the loss of external funds by increasing student tuition and adding student fees; but the market can bear only so much and students begin to make other choices, including migrating to state four-year institutions or from four-year institutions to two-year and technical colleges to attending less than full-time to not attending at all. Institutions also attempt to address dwindling resources by passing increasing insurance costs and retirement contribution expenses to employees and by offering the occasional early retirement incentive program, along with the associated Older Worker Benefit Protection Act of 1990 (OWBPA) (Pub. L. 101–433, 104 Stat. 978), collective bargaining agreements, and Age Discrimination in Employment Act (op. cit.) issues.

The aging cadre of faculty and staff presents a unique dilemma. Simply stated, the more senior faculty and staff cost more in terms of salaries and benefits and have more insurance claims; however, they also represent much of an institution's memory and are a vital link to alumni and other important constituent populations. Maintaining an older employee group is more expensive than having planned, retirement-induced turnover; however, without institutional benefits, many older faculty and staff simply cannot afford to retire, thereby remaining in the positions, happy and productive, or not. Promotional opportunities for new hires consequently are limited. Weighed at the bottom line, a department of tenured, full professors is expensive. Administrative nudging to increase productivity or to retire can run afoul of the Age Discrimination in Employment Act and, in some cases, can result in Americans with Disabilities Act claims. As the percentage of institutional budgets increasingly moves to cover personnel costs, faculty/staff management issues continue to focus on such concerns as the ability to offer competitive salaries and the retention of key personnel; consolidation of personnel positions; the shelving of vacancies; the impact of leaving positions unfilled; the retraining and retooling of current personnel; and the angst and strife associated with weathering more and more budget cuts and potential layoffs. Parsing pure management issues and pure legal issues and trends is difficult. Senior personnel generally are more aware of their rights, whether via collective bargaining agreements, employment contracts, personnel manuals, or state and federal discrimination laws. A managerial misstep may have significant legal consequences, if not the associated morale issues. Missteps are expensive, not merely in legal costs to defend claims of illegal employment actions, but in the personnel time, personal angst, and internal turmoil associated with such disputes.

With diminishing budgets comes a secondary reality, not so unique to private institutions but a new reality for public colleges and universities. The role of the institutional administration has changed. An academic dean or the administrative counterpart, such as a dean of student life, has by necessity become more focused on fundraising and alumni development and on the seeking of grants. Senior administrators increasingly must demonstrate the value of their respective administrative units by documenting the value of work done and by fundraising accomplished, thereby seeking to justify programs and staffing levels. Such a competitive-edge business model imposed on higher education may be alien to some administrators, particularly for senior administrators who gained administrative positions having progressed through the faculty ranks.

Third: A Potpourri of Trends from Yesterday into Today

A trend is a lesser trend if it can be dealt with at some other time than today. In higher education administration and for counsel representing colleges and universities, the crisis of the day demands our time, resources, focus, and energy. Lesser issues tend to be shelved until each in its turn becomes the crisis of the day for its appointed day. Several lesser trends have emerged and appear to be continuing. These relate to governance matters, international ventures, home campus threat assessment and high risk student activities, federal investigations, and the changing public perception of higher education.

Governing board management issues are legendary—both in terms of information flow to and from board members and the need to encourage board members to do their jobs diligently and effectively. Absentee board members are problematic in that being absent from meetings or a lack of attention to due diligence duties does not relieve such board members from appointed or legislated obligations, responsibilities, or expectations. Associated therewith is a cluster of conflict of interest concerns at all levels, but especially with faculty and board members. Granted, most states have legislated disclosure of economic interests for those state employees who earn above a certain minimum compensation, are elected or appointed to office, or who otherwise have been deemed by the state legislature to pose a risk of self-dealing and conflict of interest. Awareness of potential conflict of interest issues arises particularly in contract management, land acquisition, or personnel appointment and promotion matters plus untold other instances of self-dealing. The next two trends with legal overtones, changes in technology and crossing international borders, are related. Technological changes are not new. Education has moved from the slate and chalk board to the iPhone and downloadable lectures, available to students anywhere at any time, shaping a market that once was focused on the recruitment of international students to U.S. campuses to now seeking international students online and offering courses with U.S. and native instructors teaching for U.S. institutions in the international students' home countries. For example, China has become a ready and profitable market for U.S. institutions. Consequently, campuses are more aware of the finer legal points of international transactions; student and faculty exchanges; technology sharing, especially as relates to intellectual property; and visa concerns for both U.S. scholars teaching overseas and international scholars hired to teach and conduct research on U.S. campuses. Having a resident expert knowledgeable of U.S. Immigration and Customs Enforcement (ICE), Department of Homeland Security issues, and U.S. regulations concerning technology transfers has become the norm.

Threat assessment and the associated safety concerns continue. Campus violence inflicted by disgruntled faculty, students, and staff has joined ranks within safety, management, and public relations issues. What senior administrator has not read a headline decrying another campus shooting and not (at least for a fleeting instant) thought, "Thank goodness, that was not my campus"? Balancing threat assessment in the unique environment of a college campus requires weighing privacy issues, such as access to faculty and staff computer usage and emails, with the concerns by faculty (and the American Association of University Professors) about the erosion of academic freedom and the right of open inquiry inherent in the life of a campus. Whether monitoring cyber activity, staffing surveillance cameras, or mandating building access ID badges, the issue highlights the historical isolation of a campus from the rough-and-tumble world versus the real and present danger of physical bodily harm to those within the campus community. Few campuses monitor access to their grounds and buildings, especially as campuses endeavor to establish links with the surrounding communities. Particularly for public institutions, once purely campus buildings where access could be legally limited now become quasi-public buildings and forums where, thereby, at least some level of institutional control is abridged.

Even with the non-campus community public population removed from the equation, campuses, especially public institutions, must balance First Amendment freedom of speech and freedom of assembly limitations with the need to maintain campus safety. This comes to a head when addressing high risk student activities. Protocols for responding to sexual violence on campus must include consideration of the requirements for Title IX, Education Amendments of 1992 (20 U.S. C. § 1681–1688; 34 C. F. R. part 106) for coordinators; the design of campus training programs; development of grievance procedures and student codes; and the implications of the Department of Education "Dear Colleague" letters on existing campus policies (for example, the Department of Education "Dear Colleague" letter of April 4, 2011 for responding to and reporting of campus sexual violence). Parents, the public, and governing board members may have cloudy recollections of their youthful undergraduate days and are morally shocked to read headlines declaring what happens when 1000 (or more) bright and creative late adolescent males and females, with considerable free time and limited supervision, are housed in close quarters, say within an apartment complex or high-rise residence hall.

Increasing federal and state scrutiny, along with the occasional governmental investigation, constitute reality. Diminished public support, evidenced by less philanthropic participation and, for the state institutions, cuts in appropriations, is also reality. The value of higher education is questioned, being increasingly seen as a private, rather than a public, good. This is not news. Anyone who has been involved in higher education during the past three to four decades can recall television news programs decrying that, based on the then cost of tuition and rate of inflation, the cost of a college education would be beyond the means of most U.S. citizens within the then foreseeable future. That predicted future may be now.

What about the Future?

The legal trends on the horizon incorporate unique problems. For purposes of this essay, the trends are collected into five clusters, not necessarily insular. These clusters are the regulation of higher education; the use of technology; roles of key administrators; budgets; and a mixed cluster encompassing accountability and transparency, globalization and internationalization, and public/private partnerships. Alas, these are similar to the legal issues campuses wrestled with yesterday and are wrestling with today. Let's look over the horizon at the five clusters.

First: Regulation of Higher Education

Listed as a short-term trend, regulation by federal and state interests, as well as by accrediting bodies and athletic associations, offers no indication of abating. To the contrary, attention to regulatory matters will doubtlessly increase. Regulation may not be the seminal issue, however. The impact of regulation on the traditional concept of faculty academic freedom and an institution's ability to respond to regulatory issues will be problematic. For example, for federal Title IV financial aid purposes, institutions are required to indicate "last date of attendance or participation" for students earning a grade of F, U, or NC. Faculty members are being required to indicate such dates when entering grades for these students. Realistically, who other than faculty stands in a better position to know when a student stopped attending class or stopped participating in an online class? In the pure sense, asking or requiring faculty to perform this function is not an imposition upon faculty academic freedom; however, faculty may well see this task as demeaning and an erosion of their prerogatives, mistaken as they might be.

Compliance issues arise not only with student grants and loans, but also with crime reporting (for example, are residence hall custodial or resident advisor staff now considered part of the group of employees who are required to report crimes? (Title IX, op. cit.); employee background checks (invasion of privacy or sound, necessary human management practice and for which positions?); and health insurance and employee benefit plans (for example, notice of reportable events under the Employee Retirement Income Security Act (Pub. L. 93–406, 88 Stat. 829).

Waiting on the sidelines are the issues touching textbooks as faculty move away from the traditional hardcopy textbook to the digital media and the inherent issue of copyright protection. For public institutions, are faculty-produced textbooks in pending collision with state conflict of interest and ethics laws? As a general statement, state ethics acts mandate that a state employee cannot benefit personally as a consequence of her/his position. Granted, most state ethics laws are misunderstood and, at this time, enforcement is focused more on the high profile employees and elected officials, not faculty. To save money for students, will institutions ask faculty to produce textbooks for their respective courses, then sell the textbooks to the enrolled students, and not allow the faculty members to benefit from their work?

Second: Use of Technology

Problematic as the assessment of student learning in the current learning paradigm may be, as more students elect and more institutions offer online courses, the issues will compound. With the current push toward placing a dollar value on course credits and interpreting the cost of a higher education, not in terms of a potential for a higher quality of life but in terms of job placement and employment potential, institutions are struggling, and will be struggling, to meet federally mandated performance demands, accrediting agency benchmarking, and governing board expectations. With increased use of technology, faculty as the literal head of the class may become secondary to the technological medium and the ability to monitor learning as assessed by exams, tests, and quizzes becomes more abundant. This trend offers legal issues for those institutions needing faculty to retool to meet tomorrow's technology demands. Nudging a tenured, full professor to master new teaching tools is a challenge undertaken only by the strong-hearted administrator. Even more troubling are the issues that arise if, or when, the senior faculty member balks. The currently accepted concepts of tenure, collective bargaining agreements, job descriptions, and faculty workloads will have to be addressed. Equally, what does an institution do with a senior faculty member who simply cannot adjust to the demands of changing technology? Budget constraints may not allow for "other assignments" and involuntary termination is a legal quagmire.

On the other side of technology concerns are control of records access and retention of records, invasion of privacy, defamation of character issues associated with social media, wireless access, outsourcing of technology such as cloud computing, and international data access. Of unique interest are the websites that allow students to rate professors, offering student comments and publicly "sharing" information about identified professors and classes seemingly without even nominal editorial control by the website owners.

In the technology mix are issues of freedom of information (FOI) and access to institutional records, particularly for public institutions. Using state public records acts, external organizations can request program-specific institutional documents, such as course syllabi and documents related to student training programs (i.e.; internships and practica). Previously, institutions, in responding to FOI requests, used the cost of producing such requested documents as a means to discourage records requests, as most, if not all, state-legislated FOI acts provided that the costs may be passed along to the requesting party. As more institutions turn to electronic storage, the use of cost-to-produce as a FOI request deterrent will vanish. Granted, institutions may be reluctant to release course and program-specific documents since, once released, they have no control over the methodology used by external interests to evaluate courses and programs. For example, law schools can become defensive about job placement data. Other professional schools understandably are concerned if their programs will be next to hear demands about career prospects (cf., October 18, 2011 *Chronicle of Higher Education*, Academe Today article "Crisis of Confidence in Law Schools" by Katherine Mangan).

As computers increasingly talk with and design programs without human intervention, a new next generation of intellectual property issues will arise. For example, who owns a computer program designed by a computer? At first blush, absent a sponsored research contract provision or institutional intellectual property policy to the contrary, the owner would be the party who *owns* the computer program that created the subsequent program, using the same legal logic that the party who owns an organism, say livestock, owns the progeny of that organism. In the same bundle of issues, what happens when faculty develop iPhone and iPad mobile apps that would, under existing institutional policies, be owned by the institution? As a practical matter, most institutions have little interest in the commercialization of mobile apps and allow faculty to deposit the apps where they want in their own names, particularly as such apps are free to access and use.

Third: Changing Roles of Key Administrators and Faculty

Risk management is like insurance. Insurance is a terrible buy until coverage is needed; then it becomes a most worthy investment. The same can be said for risk management. Faculty, staff, and students do not want to be bothered with risk management, regardless of the risk, but are willing, along with other constituents and the media, to blame senior administrators for failing to provide for risk management—again, whatever the risk. How many campuses actively plan for floods, yet how many have experienced significant flooding in the past decade? Heaven forbid, but how many campuses will experience a significant act of violence, yet woe unto the president or senior vice president who has not prepared her campus for them. Institutional legal counsel, especially in-house counsel, along with faculty and student leadership, will be expected to participate in risk management planning, preparation, and practice drills.

As to legal counsel, campuses will be well advised to use knowledgeable legal counsel, i.e., those who specialize in the representation of higher education institutions, to plan and implement preventative legal education that assists campus units (especially student financial aid offices, the registrar's office, human resources, campus police/public safety, student activities, physical plant, computer services, housing and residence life, health services, academic departments, alumni relations, fundraising/philanthropy, and athletics) to develop systems, protocols, and procedures to address federal and applicable state legislation. Knowledgeable legal counsel is valuable in addressing the public relations and media interests of risk management. For example, several states (Arizona SB 1070, Georgia HB 87, and Alabama HB 56, among others) have legislation mandating certain actions for those providing services to "illegal" aliens. How this will play out on higher education campuses is yet to be determined, pending numerous cases challenging the constitutionality of such state action; however, the accompanying legal and public relations implications are significant.

Fourth: Decreasing Budgets

The new normal appears to be diminishing public support for higher education, whether that support comes from state or federal funds or from philanthropy. Those funds available will probably have significant regulations and restrictions attached to the disposition and reporting of their usage. Along with shrinking resources, institutions will have to make organizational and personnel decisions that can have significant contractual implementations, whether early retirement incentive programs for senior faculty and staff; outright elimination of programs, majors, and departments; or merger of internal organizations, functions, and duties. In some cases, merger, as a tool to survival, may mean closing of campuses, continued movement to distance and Internet-based course offerings, and consolidation of ventures with other institutions. How long will it be before budget pressures will result in state mandates on program offerings? How many engineering, education, business, law, nursing, or whatever programs does any given state need or can afford? How many academic programs could be offered regionally, instead of at the state level? As governing boards realize the diminishing returns of passing costs on to students in the form of additional fees and tuition and begin to consider measures to address fading resources, alternatives must be considered, such as the impact on institutional and program accreditation, disposition of faculty and staff, maintenance of buildings and grounds, and the reality of shrinking growth. All of those possibilities have significant regulatory and legal implications, including contractual obligations. Reflecting tighter budgets, faculty roles and workloads may change. For example, will institutions be willing to refocus faculty release time to put an increased emphasis on teaching (and tuition generation) to the point of amending agreed upon contract terms (cf., *The Chronicle of Higher Education*, Academe Today, October 16, 2011 article, "Back in the Classroom" by Robin Wilson)?

More public/private partnerships will emerge to reflect efforts to address the need for resources. With increased commercialization of institutions, some institutional control will be waived. This may be in the form of privately funded research or outsourcing of certain core functions as administrators, boards, and departments seek other ways to garner fiscal resources. Inherent in such partnerships are technology transfer and intellectual property issues; continued government scrutiny, particularly in the form of IRS audits; more employment law issues, especially as institutional personnel are increasingly knowledgeable about employment law and employee rights; and changes in the faculty tenure-track process as financial constraints and the need for flexibility result in fewer tenure-track positions and an increased use of adjuncts.

Increased globalization and internationalization of higher education will continue to be driven by competition and by the need for resources. Cultural and social issues aside, the international treaty and U.S. law implications of taking U.S. higher education into the international market will require, at a minimum, assessment of student and faculty safety and travel issues, concerns relating to technology transfer and intellectual property rights, real property access and ownership management, and awareness of foreign (in-country) legal requirements.

Fifth and Last: Demands for Accountability and Transparency

Removing a legislative act from the books, that is, making it no longer a law to be enforced, is harder than getting the particular law enacted in the first place. Institutions will face cumulative demands for accountability and for transparency in the coming years as existing legislation is either enforced more efficiently with new tools (aka, electronic access to institutional records) or laws are modified to address specific issues, such as the amendments to the Americans with Disabilities Act (ADA Amendments Acts of 2008 and 2009) or the reporting changes to the Clery Act Amendments of 2010. This is not to suggest that the original acts were bad, deficient, or in any other way ill conceived. Instead, adjustments are likely as acts are tested between institutional practices and the expectations of those who shepherded the acts through the various legislative bodies plus the legality of implementation as interpreted by the judicial system. Some adjustments are in reaction to tragic events and understandable in that context, such as the amendments to the Clery Act following the tragic murders at Virginia

Tech, while some are a mere reflections of regional political reactions, such as the increasing number of state legislative acts requiring verification of the citizenship of students enrolled in public higher education institutions or receiving state educational assistance. Whether via modification of current legislation or enactment of new laws, the number and scope of laws that will mandate accountability by institutions will continue to grow, as will the burden and cost of such compliance. Rarely does a legislative body provide the funds necessary to meet the demands of its enactments.

In the mix of increased accountability and transparency, as constituents and institutional personnel become better educated about personal rights, institutions (particularly public institutions) will see an increase in freedom of information act filings, compliance oversight of open meetings laws, and adherence to procurement policies and protocols. At the state level, as awareness of state ethics act requirements becomes more widely known and as state administrative, political, and legislative bodies shrink the loopholes in their respective ethics acts, institutions will be forced to be more proactive to do a better job of educating employees and governing boards, and to be more responsive in investigating internally, or in cooperation with state or federal agencies, alleged violations. Such issues should not be surprising as the public and elected bodies seek to ensure that the value of the education received is comparable to the dollar spent, whether that dollar comes from the pockets of individuals in the form of tuition or via public and private coffers.

Ferreting out issues not yet faced is an exercise in assisting our institutions as to how best not to become a defendant and, if named as a defendant, how to ensure that the other side does not win. Institutional resources are not limitless. Looking over the hill, deciding which risks can be eliminated, which may be set aside, and which must be addressed requires a high level of diligence, staying current within our respective professions and fields, and scanning the current environment for news and trends on other campuses. Fostering sound institutional ethics and managing a changing array of legal matters demands dedication, allocation of resources, and administrative skill and energy—a dance that necessitates protecting our institutions while educating those students entrusted to us and fulfilling the missions within which our institutions were created.

Bibliography

Books

Kaplin, W A., & Lee, B. A. (2006). *The law and higher education: A comprehensive guide to legal implications of administrative decision-making* (4th ed.). San Francisco: Jossey-Bass.

Ambash, J. W. (2003). *Federal record-keeping and reporting requirements for independent and public colleges and universities* (3rd ed.). Washington, DC: National Association of College and University Attorneys.

Federal Legislation/Regulations/Guidance

Age Discrimination in Employment Act of 1967, 29 U.S. Code, Chapter 14, §621, et seq.

Americans with Disabilities Act of 1990, 42 U.S. Code, Chapter 126, and amendments of 2008, 110 P. L.

Crime Awareness and Campus Security Act of 1990, 20 U. S Code, §1092 (f), 34 C. F. R. 668. 46.

Department of Education Office for Civil Rights, Dear Colleague Letter: Sexual Violence, April 4, 2011.

Equal Pay Act, 29C. F. R. §162. 1 et seq. ; 29 U. S Code §206 (d).

Employee Retirement Income Security Act of 1994, Pub. L. 93–406, 88 Stat. 829.

Executive Order 11246, September 24, 1965, 30 C. F. R. 12319, 12935, 3 C. F. R., 1964–1965 Comp., p. 339.

Family Educational Rights and Privacy Act, 34 C. F. R. 99. 1 *et seq.*

Fair Labor Standards Act, 29 U.S. Code, Chapter 8 §206 *et seq.*
Occupational Safety and Health Administration, 29 U.S. Code, Chapter 15 §651et seq.
Older Worker Benefit Protection Act of 1990, Pub. L. 101–433; 104 Stat. 978.
Sarbanes-Oxley Act of 2002, Pub. L. 107–204, 116 Stat. 745.
Title VII of the 1964 Civil Rights Act, 42 U.S. Code, Chapter 21.
Title IX, Education Amendments of 1992, 20 U. SCode§1681–1688; 34 C. F. R, part 106.

State Legislation Referencing Immigration

Arizona Senate Bill 1070, Support Our Law Enforcement and Safe Neighborhoods Act, signed August 23, 2010.
Georgia HB 87, Georgia Illegal Immigration Reform and Enforcement Act of 2011.
Alabama HB 56, Beason-Hammon Alabama Taxpayer and Citizen Protection Act, Sect. 32–6–9 amended, passed June 2011.

Chronicle of Higher Education *Articles*

"Crisis of Confidence in Law Schools" by Katherine Mangan, "Academe Today" 10/18/2011.
"Back in the Classroom" by Robin Wilson, "Academe Today" 10/16/2011.
Federal Case
Gonzaga University v. Doe, 536U.S. 273 (2002), addressing private cause of action for institutional violation of FERPA; that is, Congress, by passing FERPA, did not create a right which is enforceable under 42 U. SCode §1983.

CHAPTER TWENTY-SEVEN

Historically Black Colleges and Universities and Philanthropy

MARYBETH GASMAN

From their arrival on the shores of the United States, African Americans have yearned for knowledge and viewed education as the key to their freedom. These enslaved people pursued various forms of education despite laws, in southern states, barring them from learning to read and write (Anderson, 1988). In the North, free Blacks pursued education at three colleges for African Americans: Lincoln and Cheyney Universities in Pennsylvania and Wilberforce University in Ohio. With the end of the Civil War, the daunting task of educating over four million African Americans was shouldered by both the federal government, through the Freedman's Bureau, and many northern church missionaries. As early as 1865, the Freedmen's Bureau began establishing HBCUs, resulting in mainly male staff and teachers with military backgrounds. During the post-Civil War period, most HBCUs were so in name only; these institutions generally provided primary and secondary education (Anderson, 1988).

As noted, religious missionary organizations—some affiliated with northern White denominations such as the Baptists and Congregationalists and some with Black churches such as the African Methodist Episcopal—were actively working with the Freedmen's Bureau. One of the most prominent White organizations was the American Missionary Association, but there were many others as well. White northern missionary societies founded HBCUs such as Dillard University in New Orleans, Louisiana, and Morehouse College in Atlanta, Georgia. The benevolence of these missionary philanthropists was tinged with self-interest and often racism. The missionaries' goals in establishing these colleges were to Christianize the freedmen (i.e., convert formerly-enslaved people to their brand of Christianity) and to rid the country of the "menace" of uneducated African Americans (Anderson, 1988). In fact, this notion of a "Black menace" was at the center of White hatred toward African Americans, and had been one of the chief justifications for perpetuating the slave system prior to the Civil War. Among the colleges founded by Black denominations were Morris Brown College in Atlanta, Georgia, Paul Quinn College in Dallas, Texas, and Allen University in Columbia, South Carolina. Unique among American colleges, these institutions were founded *by* African Americans *for* African Americans (Anderson, 1988). Because these institutions relied on less support from Whites and more support from Black churches, they were able to design their own curricula; however, they also were more vulnerable to economic instability. To this day, these institutions remain unstable—often losing accreditation and experiencing frequent financial issues. Without a strong foundation of philanthropic support, built up over time, it is difficult to sustain a healthy institution.

During the post-Reconstruction period, many Southern Whites disagreed with and protested the education of Blacks in the liberal arts—it was seen as "impractical." Perhaps what they really feared was the political and economic advancement of Blacks. According to Raymond Wolters (1975), many Southern Whites thought that any education beyond elementary schooling would not only lead Blacks to more dissatisfaction with their inferior status, but would also make them less submissive, less respectful, and less willing to work. Instead of liberal arts education, Southern Whites advocated instruction in trade skills that would bring wealth to the South and further the goal of segregation.

In this spirit, in 1882, the Slater Fund was created and became the impetus for industrial education for ex-slaves in the United States. John Slater, who inherited his uncle's textile properties, donated one million dollars to be used for uplifting the former slaves through a Christian-oriented education. In his letter establishing the fund, Slater (1950) wrote,

> the disabilities formerly suffered by these people and their singular patience and fidelity in the great crisis of the nation established a just claim on the sympathy and good will of humane and patriotic men. I cannot but feel the compassion that is due in view of their prevailing ignorance which exists by no fault of their own. (p. 7)

Clearly, Slater felt some compassion for the Black people and their lack of education. Like the missionary philanthropists, he believed that they were capable of learning. However, Slater wanted to educate them in a way that would create a Southern economy on which industrialists could capitalize. Philanthropists like Slater supported training in manual labor skills, including cooking, cleaning, farming, etc. Some of these philanthropists clearly had other motives besides the advancement of Blacks in mind. For example, William Baldwin, the General Manager of J. P. Morgan's Southern Railroad Company and an important contributor to Southern Black education, saw Blacks as an important piece of the economic puzzle in the South. According to Henry Bullock (1967), one of Baldwin's primary motivations was his need for thousands of Black railroad workers. Slater, Baldwin, and other Northern industrialists differed from the missionary philanthropists in that their power came from their ownership of essential resources rather than from grassroots support.

In addition to Slater and Baldwin, the captains of industry who supported industrial education included Andrew Carnegie, John D. Rockefeller, Julius Rosenwald, and John Foster Peabody. Like Slater, these philanthropists professed a deep commitment to Christian benevolence. However, it is easy to see that their philanthropic activity dovetailed neatly with their desire to control industrial enterprises nationwide (Anderson, 1988; Watkins, 2001). The organization making the largest contribution to Black education was the General Education Board (GEB), a conglomeration of northern White philanthropists, established by John D. Rockefeller, Sr., but spearheaded by John D. Rockefeller, Jr. Between 1903 and 1964, the GEB gave over $63,000,000 to Black colleges, an impressive figure, but nonetheless only a fraction of what they gave to White institutions (Anderson, 1988). The board was a conglomeration of major industrial philanthropists and some lesser known individuals: George Foster Peabody, a banker; Frederick T. Gates, a former minister and Rockefeller's chief philanthropic advisor; Wallace Buttrick, a former Baptist preacher; William Baldwin, Jr., a railroad entrepreneur; Robert C. Ogden, manager of the Wanamaker's Department Store in New York; J. L. M. Curry, a moderate Southern educator; and several others. Because of the tremendous financial backing and the influence of its members, the GEB gained a virtual monopoly on education and philanthropy for Southern Blacks. The GEB was primarily concerned with the prosperity of the South's agricultural economy and the role of Blacks in this prosperity. When the GEB members looked at the South, they saw "a superb climate, an abundance of fertile soil, and no end of labor" (Chernow, 2004, p. 486). It wanted to provide Blacks with skills, morals, and enough education to keep them in the South as the laboring class.

The motives of the GEB and other industrial philanthropists have been characterized by some historians as benevolent and by others as self-serving and reactionary. Christopher Jencks and David Reisman (1968), as well as Merle Curti and Roderick Nash (1965), depict the Northern philanthropists as pragmatic contributors who supported Black education for genuinely philanthropic reasons. These historians generally accepted the Northern industrialists' own explanations for their support of industrial education—that support of anything more forward would have incurred white supremacist vengeance. Raymond Fosdick (1962), a member of the GEB, gave this type of apology when he wrote:

> the Board was aware from the start of the dangers inherent in a Northern institution working in the highly charged emotional atmosphere of a biracial South. . . . A single misstep could be disastrous. . . . Consequently its role was marked with caution and modesty. . . . That the philosophy of Buttrick [former head of the General Education Board] and his contemporaries was based on the idea of gradualism cannot be denied. But his was the thinking of the time. . . . Their strategy was strongly pragmatic. To raise the level of education in the South. . . it was necessary to work through the race in power. Sixty years ago there was no alternative to this approach; there was no public opinion to support any other cause. (p. 323)

In contrast, Edward Berman (1983) and several other historians note that the industrialists wanted to focus their resources on a small group of "safe" Southern Blacks in order to perpetuate an educational structure that repressed the social and economic advancement of all but a selected few. The GEB's use of its financial resources to gain power over institutions parallels Rockefeller's monopolistic business strategies in his other enterprises.

Regardless of their personal motivations, the funding system that these industrial moguls created showed a strong tendency to control Black education for their benefit and to produce graduates who were skilled in the trades that served the industrialists' enterprises (commonly known as industrial education) (Anderson, 1988; Watkins, 2001). Above all, the educational institutions they supported were extremely careful not to upset the segregationist power structure that ruled the South by the 1890s. Black colleges such as Tuskegee and Hampton were showcases of industrial education. It was here that students learned how to shoe horses, make dresses, cook, and clean under the leadership of individuals like Samuel Chapman Armstrong (Hampton) and Booker T. Washington (Tuskegee).

The philanthropists' support of industrial education was in direct conflict with many Black intellectuals who favored a liberal arts curriculum. Institutions such as Fisk, Dillard, Howard, Spelman, and Morehouse were more focused on the liberal arts curriculum favored by W. E. B. Du Bois than on Booker T. Washington's emphasis on advancement through labor and self-sufficiency. Whatever the philosophical disagreements may have been between Washington and Du Bois, the two educational giants did share a goal of educating African Americans and uplifting their race. Their differing approaches might be summarized as follows: Washington favored educating Blacks in the industrial arts so they might become self-sufficient as individuals, whereas Du Bois wanted to create a Black intellectual elite (the "talented tenth") to lead the race as a whole toward self-determination (Lewis, 1994).

With the passage of the second Morrill Act in 1890, the federal government again took an interest in Black education, establishing public Black colleges. This act stipulated that those states practicing segregation in their public colleges and universities would forfeit federal funding unless they established agricultural and mechanical institutions for the Black population (Gasman, 2007; Thompson, 1973). Determined to maintain a segregated system of education, southern and border states established public Black colleges. In practice, none of these institutions were equal to their White counterparts with regard to facilities and resources. Through the 1890 Morrill Act, 17 Black institutions were funded. Six of these were actually newly established colleges, resulting directly from the federal government's funds. However, rather than spending the additional state funds needed in order to establish separate, fully functioning, Black public institutions, most southern states chose to allot the monies from the Morrill Act to colleges that were already included in the state budget; in a few cases they annexed private institutions, changing the colleges' status to public. The curricula at all of these land grant institutions funded through the 1890 Morrill Act focused on agricultural and mechanical arts, the English language, math, and the physical and natural sciences (Christy & Williamson, 1992).

Beginning around 1915, there was a shift in the attitude of the industrial philanthropists, who started to turn their attention to those Black colleges that emphasized the liberal arts. Realizing that industrial education could exist side by side with a more academic curriculum, the philanthropists opted to spread their money (and therefore their influence) throughout the educational system (Anderson, 1988). These actions followed a pattern that the philanthropists had established in their funding of other types of educational institutions. For example, a study of medical schools conducted by GEB member Abraham Flexner in 1910 led to funding policies that favored a few elite institutions and squeezed out the "inferior" schools. Similarly, the GEB hoped to develop one or two private Black colleges to the point that they would set new standards and force the inferior colleges to disappear or convert to secondary schools (Anderson, 1988; Fosdick, 1962).

Another factor that led to this shift in interest was the realization that the industrial jobs for which Blacks were being trained were unavailable to them. Reports showed that racial discrimination was displacing Blacks from the Southern workplace. To investigate these reports, the Rosenwald Fund, a philanthropic organization founded by Sears and Roebuck tycoon Julius Rosenwald, hired the young Charles S. Johnson to conduct a sociological study. The Rosenwald Fund began by advocating a status quo position on race relations in the South. However, under the leadership of Edwin Embree, who was closely aligned with Charles Johnson, it pushed for racial integration.

According to Anderson (1988), Johnson's findings confirmed that the "rampant displacement of black workers from even the lowest rung of the industrial ladder posed anew the question of what could be accomplished by the industrial education of black youth" (p. 227). These findings provided yet another reason for the philanthropists to shift their support to Black collegiate education.

The pervasive influence of industrial philanthropy in the early twentieth century created a conservative environment on many Black college campuses—one that would seemingly tolerate only those administrators (typically White men) who accommodated segregation. But attention from the industrial philanthropists was not necessarily welcomed by institutions such as Fisk University, where rebellions ensued against autocratic presidents who were assumed by students to be puppets of the philanthropists (Anderson, 1988). In spite of these conflicts, industrial philanthropists provided major support for private Black colleges up until the late 1930s.

At this time, the industrial philanthropists turned their attention elsewhere, providing only minimal funding to HBCUs. Meanwhile, in the late 1930s and early 1940s two of the largest supporters of Black higher education—the General Education Board and the Julius Rosenwald Fund—were turning their attention to other projects. Their contributions to Black colleges, as well as those of other large philanthropic organizations, waned. Some foundations were liquidated; others turned their attention to special ventures in Black affairs such as Gunnar Myrdal's (1944) *American Dilemma*. Still others were directing money toward White education (Hoving, 1944). In addition, philanthropists were calling for more support from the Black community itself—individual alumni, organizational, and church-related. According to James P. Brawley (1982), president of Clark College, foundations and corporations were asking, "How much do your alumni give?"and "Where are your alumni and what are they doing?" Although many alumni gave what they could, most did not have any extra income. The majority of alumni at this point were teachers and college professors at Black schools, being paid one-fourth what their White counterparts received (Johnson, 1937). Meanwhile, Black colleges were faced with students who could not afford to pay tuition and church boards that were reluctant to increase their contributions (most churches supported more than one institution and did not have enough money to spread large donations among multiple institutions). These factors combined to produce near-impossible financial hurdles for Black colleges, putting them in debt and unable to keep up with operating costs. Without the support of the foundations and affiliated churches, Black colleges needed to broaden their search for funds, and therefore the task of fundraising for individual colleges could not be left to the president alone.

Black colleges were in dire financial trouble. According to financial data published by the United States Office of Education in 1943, between 1930 and 1943 the overall income of Black colleges decreased 15 percent and income from private gifts decreased 50 percent (Gasman, 2007). Among the nation's White colleges and universities, the situation was similarly dismal. According to a study conducted by John Price Jones, which reported the results of forty-six White colleges' fundraising efforts, these institutions received $77,867,380 in gifts and bequests in 1930, but less than half as much in 1935 (Gasman, 2007). As a result of the financial difficulties felt throughout the nation, between 1930 and 1940 several of the better known small Black colleges closed their doors, including Roger Williams, Mary Allen, Walden, and Howe Institute. Some of the more nationally known Black colleges were merging in order to survive. Under the guidance of John Hope, Atlanta University had become the graduate university of the Atlanta University Center (which included Spelman, Morehouse, and Atlanta University). Likewise, New Orleans and Straight Colleges merged to form Dillard University. Other, once-private institutions had their grounds and facilities taken over by state governments in an effort to survive. These "new" state institutions included Fort Valley State, North Carolina College, and Jackson State University (MS) (Gasman, 2007).

In response, Frederick D. Patterson, then president of the Tuskegee Institute, suggested that the nation's private Black colleges join together in their fundraising efforts. After much frustration with the fundraising situation, Patterson began to correspond with a cadre of Black college presidents about the challenges of raising money and possible solutions to these problems. The majority of college presidents wrote back to him detailing their similarly bleak financial situations and providing anecdotes about the difficulty of approaching foundations for funds. Patterson realized from his correspondence that Black college presidents were competing for the same small pool of funds—everyone was soliciting the same organizations and the same donors (Gasman, 2007). In fact, in his autobiography, Frederick D. Patterson noted,

> I can recall bumping into some of the presidents of other black colleges in the offices of the General Education Board. Our meeting wasn't intentional; it was just happenstance. They were going for their interests, and I was going for mine. There was no secret about who was donating what: reports were usually available indicating the gifts a particular foundation had made to various colleges. (Patterson, 2002, p. 123)

Oddly, many of the college presidents who responded to Patterson thought he was assessing their situation so as to make fundraising connections for them with major philanthropists, something that Booker T. Washington had done in the past as president of Tuskegee. The presidents were most likely under this impression because Tuskegee was considered one of the philanthropists' favored institutions and was thought to be the least likely to have financial problems (Patterson, 1981).

As a result of Patterson's efforts, in 1944, the presidents of 29 Black colleges created the United Negro College Fund (UNCF). The UNCF began solely as a fundraising organization but eventually took on advocacy and educational roles as well (Gasman, 2007).

Until the *Brown v. Board of Education* decision in 1954, both public and private Black colleges in the South remained segregated by law and were the only educational option for African Americans. Although most colleges and universities did not experience the same violent fallout from the *Brown* decision as southern public schools, they were greatly affected by the decision. The Supreme Court's landmark ruling meant that HBCUs would be placed in competition with White institutions in their efforts to recruit Black students. With the triumph of the idea of integration, many began to call HBCUs into question and label them vestiges of segregation (Gasman, 2007). However, desegregation proved slow, with many public HBCUs maintaining their racial make-up well into the current day. After the *Brown* decision, private HBCUs, which have always been willing to accept students from all backgrounds if the law would allow, struggled to defend issues of quality in an atmosphere that labeled anything all-Black inferior (Gasman, 2007). Many Black colleges also suffered from "brain drain" as predominately White institutions in the North and some in the South made efforts to attract high-achieving Black students once racial diversity became valued within higher education (Gasman, 2007).

The Black college of the 1960s was a much different place than that of the 1920s. The leadership switched from White to Black, and because Blacks had more control over funding, there was greater tolerance for dissent and Black self-determination among the student population. On many public and private Black college campuses throughout the South, students were staging sit-ins and protesting against segregation and its manifestations throughout the region. Most prominent were the four students from North Carolina A & T who refused to leave a segregated Woolworth lunch counter in 1960. In some cases, large foundations such as the Ford Foundation sponsored the student activism at Black colleges. They tended to support the students' non-violent protests rather than the more radical actions of the Black Power movement (Gasman, 2007).

During the 1960s the federal government took a greater interest in Black colleges. In an attempt to provide clarity, the 1965 Higher Education Act defined a Black college as ". . . any. . . college or university that was established prior to 1964, whose principal mission was, and is, the education of black Americans" (Higher Education Act, 1965). The recognition of the uniqueness of Black colleges implied in this definition has led to increased federal funding for these institutions.

Another federal intervention on behalf of Black colleges took place in 1980 when President Jimmy Carter signed Executive Order 12232, which established a national program to alleviate the effects of discriminatory treatment and to strengthen and expand Black colleges to provide quality education. Since this time, every United States president has renewed the commitment to Black colleges set forth by Carter through this program.

The history of HBCUs continues to shape these institutions in meaningful and positive ways; however, this history also confines HBCUs from time to time. Often when outsiders are only familiar with the history of HBCUs, they fail to see what is currently happening, including these institutions' service to diverse constituencies, their enormous track record in the sciences, and their continuing and crucial role in educating those African Americans who eventually occupy the Black middle class.

In the twenty-first century, foundations and corporations continue to support Black colleges. However, they are most inclined to support efforts focused on increasing degree attainment and student success. Foundations such as Lumina, Kresge, Walmart, and Gates are interested in increasing the retention and graduation rates at Black colleges and link their grant funding to accountability measures around these issues. In addition, foundations are focused on data-driven decisions. Frustrated with the lack of progress at Black colleges despite foundation support, these major foundations are looking for a return on investment with their support of Black colleges. Of note, throughout most of their history, Black colleges have been supported at much lower levels by foundations than their White counterparts. Given the inequity in funding over time, it is not surprising that many Black colleges have not been able to thrive and meet their full potential. Although philanthropy is essential to the future of Black colleges, it can also confine them, and has historically, to a life as struggling institutions on the higher education landscape.

References

Anderson, J. A. (1988). *The education of Blacks in the South, 1865–1930*. Chapel Hill, NC: University of North Carolina Press.

Berman, E. (1983). *The influence of the Carnegie, Ford, and Rockefeller Foundations on American foreign policy*. Albany: State University of New York University.

Brawley, J. P. (1982). *Interview by Marcia Goodson, March 1982* [Transcript]. UNCF Oral History (No. 1331), 59.

Bullock, H. A. (1967). *A history of Negro education in the South from 1619 to the present.* Cambridge, MA: Harvard University Press.

Chernow, R. (2004). *Titan: The life of John D. Rockefeller.* New York: Vintage.

Christy, R., & Williamson, R. (1992). *A century of service: Land grant colleges and universities, 1890–1990.* New Brunswick, NJ: Transaction Press.

Curti, M., & Nash, R. (1965). *Philanthropy in the shaping of higher education.* New Brunswick, NJ: Rutgers University Press.

Fosdick, R. (1962). *Adventures in giving: The story of the General Education Board.* New York: Harper & Row.

Gasman, M. (2007). *Envisioning Black colleges: A history of the United Negro College Fund.* Baltimore, MD: Johns Hopkins University Press.

Higher Education Act, 20 U.S. C. § 1002 (1965).

Hoving, W. (1944). Hoving, Walter to Contributors of the United Negro College Fund Campaign, memo, December 1944. Messers Rockefeller (III2G, box 94, folder 665). Rockefeller Archive Center, Sleepy Hollow, New York.

Jencks, C., & Reisman, D. (1968). *The academic revolution.* New Brunswick, NJ: Transaction Press.

Johnson, C. S. (1937). *The Negro college graduate.* Chapel Hill: University of North Carolina Press.

Lewis, D. L. (1994). *W. E. B. Du Bois: A biography.* New York: Henry Holt.

Myrdal, G. (1944). *An American dilemma: The Negro problem and modern democracy.* New Brunswick, NJ: Transaction Press.

Patterson, F. D. (1981). *Interview by Marcia Goodson, March 1981* [Transcript]. UNCF Oral History (No. 1332).

Patterson, F. D. (2002). *Chronicles of faith: The autobiography of Frederick D. Patterson.* Tuscaloosa, AL: University of Alabama Press.

Slater, J. (1950). Southern Educational Foundation promotional materials. Rockefeller Archive Center, Sleepy Hollow, New York.

Thompson, D. (1973). *Private Black colleges at the crossroads.* New York: Greenwood Press.

Watkins, W. (2001). *The White architects of Black education: Ideology and power in America, 1865–1954.* New York: Teachers College Press.

Wolters, R. (1975). *The new Negro on campus: Black college rebellions of the 1920s.* Princeton, NJ: Princeton University Press.

CHAPTER TWENTY-EIGHT

For-Profit Models of Higher Education

Current Issues on the Proprietary Front

WILLIAM L. NUCKOLS

The modern proprietary institution's influence spans from Main Street to Wall Street, from the classroom to Capitol Hill. For many, for-profit colleges are the gateways to training for a more successful career and a better life (Sperling & Tucker, 1997). Others consider them corporate diploma mills, where a worthless degree can be had by anyone who is able to pay the tuition (Associated Press, 2008). In spite of the differing opinions, the proprietary institution is changing the face of higher education.

What are "proprietary colleges" or "for-profit institutions of higher education"? Proprietary institutions of higher education are private, for-profit institutions owned by individuals, closely held corporations, or shareholders of large publicly traded corporations. These for-profit schools are funded by student tuition that is most often subsidized by the federal government. The proprietary institutions of higher education offer job skills training, certificate programs, undergraduate, and graduate degrees in a limited curriculum with a rapid turnaround for new course offerings. Proprietary schools usually provide a shorter program time commitment than their nonprofit or public counterparts (usually due to the limited liberal arts requirements), for a more timely completion of degree requirements, enabling students to move quickly into employment scenarios. The for-profit schools often combine distance education with flexible course sessions to accommodate working students' schedules and lifestyles. Most successful proprietary schools hold accreditation from a regional or a national accrediting body. While they tend to be described by their similarities, for-profit institutions are incredibly diverse and often share few characteristics (Kinser, 2006c).

Through the utilization of large marketing campaigns and intense recruiting practices, proprietary schools are often viewed as competition for public and nonprofit institutions of higher education. Reviewing the development of proprietary colleges, it is suggested that the institutions have filled voids in the higher education arena that were not being addressed by other institutions. By filling the gaps left by traditional higher education models, proprietary colleges have become influential in the way higher education operates today.

How did the modern proprietary institution gain such influence on the traditional college education model? Throughout the history of higher education, the for-profit college has been influential on some level. In the late 1800s, there were approximately 250 for-profit business colleges in the United States, spanning every major city in the nation (Kinser, 2006a). Of the proprietary colleges in existence today, over 100 can trace their origins back over 100 years (Kinser, 2006b). One of the oldest is Bryant and Stratton, dating back to 1854 (Kinser, 2003, 2006a). While most for-profit schools prior to the 1970s were non-degree granting, government legislation allowed the proprietary institutions of that decade to reach a more equal playing field as traditional colleges (Floyd, 2005).

From the 1970s to the present, more federal assistance for students became available through the 1972 reauthorization of the Higher Education Act (Kinser, 2006a, 2006c). Accreditation policies were also impacted when proprietary schools began to receive accreditation through regional accrediting bodies, like their nonprofit and public counterparts (Kinser, 2005; VanDyne, 1974). Federal regulations through the Higher Education Act reauthorized in 1992 recognized and attempted to address the increasing default rates of student borrowers and the high-pressure recruitment practices at many proprietary institutions (Kinser, 2006a, 2006c). These issues still permeate the subject today.

The Publicly Traded Model

As early as the 1960s, shares of proprietary colleges were publicly traded (Kinser, 2007). The rise of the publicly traded institution continued until the economic recession of 1972–73. During that time, profits slipped as the federal government increased investigations for fraudulent practices in the federal financial aid program in the for-profit sector (Kinser, 2007).

With the 1980s came the "pure play" model of the corporate investment proprietary institution. These schools earned that name because they were formed with education as their only business, led by the National Education Corporation. The pure plays were able to rise in the 1980s partially due to a thriving economy and relaxed federal regulations (Kinser, 2007). That era of reduced regulation allowed 10–12 pure play institutions to grow quickly. As fast as the pure play colleges grew, they rapidly fell due to allegations of student loan fraud (again), adverse issues with the Securities Exchange Commission, shareholder lawsuits, tumbling stock values, and ultimately bankruptcy (Kinser, 2007). As the curtains fell on the pure play for-profits, the "Wall Street Era" emerged.

The 1990s saw the creation of the for-profit degree-granting stand-alone college model (Kinser, 2007). Of these publicly traded corporations, the largest market share and market value is held by the Apollo Group, whose primary asset is the University of Phoenix (Kinser, 2006c, 2007; Noone, 2004). Although Phoenix is the largest of the corporate-owned for-profit institutions, none are replicas of a single business or educational model (Kinser, 2006c, 2007). Since Phoenix is the largest of its kind, it is often the subject of praise, controversy, and some occasional boasting (Noone, 2004). Phoenix's president takes great pride in the belief that students who have little chance of admission or survival in a traditional university system are proving to be successful graduates through a more flexible and less mainstream curriculum (Noone, 2004).

Sperling and Tucker (1997) set the tone for the University of Phoenix's educational model. With a mission of educating America's workforce, the initial focus was on the development of the workplace and the skills necessary for life-long improvement. The worker needs to stay in tune with rapid workplace changes in the new knowledge sector of the service industry. By developing programs that cater to employees who are on the rise in their careers, Phoenix created the necessary tools to meet public demand. Accordingly, most of the Wall Street for-profits followed suit, mainly offering degrees in career oriented fields such as: Computer Science, Business, Health, and Engineering Technology (Kinser, 2007).

Success at the University of Phoenix is measured as it is in the business world, by *profitability* (Noone, 2004). High profits from a rapid increase in student enrollment are key indicators of a successful institution, so long as it is properly managed (Berg, 2005). This business management strategy as applied to institutions of higher education has a proven track record of success, even in the traditional university setting (Mangan, 1999). Proper management comes from maintaining a narrowly focused business mission and operating with total adherence to the mission (Noone, 2004). The institution's working student desires convenience in the form of course availability and degree programs, and access to their college. By offering the students what they want, when they want it, the convenience pays off in dividends to the corporation.

As relative newcomers to the higher education field, the Wall Street for-profits are accountable to several parties. Like traditional colleges and universities, the school is accountable to its faculty and students as well as to the various educational regulatory agencies. As publicly traded corporations, they are also regulated by the Securities Exchange Commission (Noone, 2004). The president of the University of Phoenix views the heavy regulation as a positive that keeps them on their toes (Noone, 2004). In spite of the regulation, that institution claims to keep the student as its primary focus; the student is the consumer of scheduling convenience and curriculum design (Noone, 2004).

The primary tool for rapid growth and convenience is through distance education (Kinser, 2007). While distance education is not a new phenomenon in higher education, it is paramount in discussions of accessibility. With the movement toward electronic education comes higher student enrollment and exceptional growth in profitability (Kinser, 2006c). Between 1996 and 2003, Phoenix added 39,000 new students by expanding its physical campuses into communities nationwide. During that same timeframe, it added 70,000 new students through its online division (Kinser, 2006c). Distance education allows the proprietary institution to reach students virtually anywhere that has a phone line (Sperling & Tucker, 1997). Online education has also allowed institutions to operate across state and national boundaries without having to meet the licensing requirements of each state government entity and to reach across the regional accreditation systems. This flexibility and accessibility have changed the path of higher education in the United States in a relatively brief historical period.

Accreditation and Other Issues

The primary key to the success of an institution of higher education is the ability to offer financial aid to its students. Congress gave students at for-profit colleges access to federal financial aid under Title IV with its reauthorization of the Higher Education Act in 1972 (Floyd, 2005). A primary requirement for an institution to qualify under Title IV is that it must be accredited.

Accrediting agencies are private educational associations. These groups develop evaluation criteria and perform peer reviews to determine whether the criteria are met. Any institution that meets the criteria of an agency is considered accredited by that agency. The United States Department of Education (USDOE), through the Secretary of Education, publishes a list of nationally recognized accrediting agencies that are determined to be reliable authorities on educational quality issues (USDOE, 2012).

There is no central authority exercising national control over postsecondary education in the United States. States have some degrees of control over higher educational institutions, but generally, colleges are given considerable autonomy (USDOE, 2012). The accreditation system serves to establish institutional standards, help students to locate acceptable institutions, assist universities in determining the acceptability of transfer credits, and to involve faculty and staff in institutional evaluation and planning. The agencies can establish criteria for self-improvements to weak programs, thus raising educational standards among institutions.

According to the U.S. Department of Education, the procedure for accreditation begins with the accrediting agency establishing a set of standards. Once an institution identifies the agency it wishes to be accredited by, it begins a period of self-study. This self-evaluation allows the college to measure its performance against the accrediting agency's standards. The self-study is followed by an on-site evaluation performed by a team selected by the agency to determine if the standards are met. If all standards are met, the agency grants accreditation and publishes the institution in the agency's official publication. Once accredited, there is constant monitoring by the agency and scheduled reevaluation.

National vs. Regional

There are six regional accrediting bodies. In addition to these regional accreditors, there are over 90 national and specialized accrediting agencies. A specialized accreditation agency pertains to an individual program within an institution. Most large-scale traditional colleges may hold regional accreditation as well as several specialized accreditations (Kelly, 2001). Most traditional colleges and universities and approximately 10% of all proprietary institutions are regionally accredited (Kelly, 2001).

Most degree-granting for-profit colleges hold national accreditations. The two most popular national accrediting bodies are Accrediting Commission of Career Schools and Colleges of Technology (ACCSCT) and the Accrediting Council for Independent Colleges and Schools (ACICS) (Floyd, 2005; Kelly, 2001). The primary reason for the majority of private, for-profit institutions seeking of national accreditation is that new programs can be introduced more rapidly (Floyd, 2005). In addition to fast changes to curriculum, there are usually fewer courses necessary for general education degree requirements. National accreditation also carries a simpler decision-making process (Floyd, 2005). Finally, the national accreditation boards place less emphasis on college faculty degrees and credentials (Floyd, 2005). In the name of flexibility and being able to operate on a small-business "shoe-string" budget, the advantages of national accreditation can outweigh the disadvantages, initially.

National accreditation, for all of the surface advantages, contains many negative issues. The primary issue is that few if any credits from a nationally accredited institution are transferable to a regionally accredited college (Floyd, 2005). Since many for-profit degrees are sought for job training and advancement, many employers have displayed an unwillingness to reimburse tuition spent at a nationally accredited school (Floyd, 2005). The students who find themselves with an associate's degree from a nationally accredited institution may be disappointed when they try to transfer those credits to a regionally accredited four-year institution to no avail.

Regional accreditation allows more flexibility to the student, making regionally accredited for-profit institutions highly sought after by students. The increase in student advantages has made the large publicly traded proprietary institutions view regional accreditation as a good business decision (Floyd, 2005; Kinser, 2003). In addition to the students' benefits of greater transferability of credits and possible employer reimbursement of tuition, there are advantages to the institution as well. Many states tend to waive license renewal requirements for regionally accredited colleges (Floyd, 2005). As the for-profit sector expands into regional accreditation, Floyd (2005) recommends that regional accrediting boards become better trained in the ways of the proprietary institutions.

The greater advantages associated with regional accreditation may cause regional publicly traded proprietary schools to gain more respect among the working degree seekers. As the credibility of these institutions increases, the regionally accredited for-profit begins to compete with the traditional institutions on a greater level (Kinser, 2007). The for-profit can "cherry pick" students from the traditional schools by offering more flexibility, fewer general education requirements, and more class scheduling options (Kinser, 2007). However, the regional accreditation of for-profits also leaves some issues lingering.

An unresolved issue resulting from the regional accrediting of multi-campus proprietary institutions is the concept of branch campuses located out of the region from where the accreditation is granted (Kinser, 2007). Since regional accreditation is sought by the corporate owners to lend legitimacy to the institution, the possibility of "accreditation shopping" for the most flexible regional accreditation board surfaces (Kinser, 2007). This issue is warranted, as several proprietary schools seek the accreditation of the North Central Association of Colleges and Schools, since that board is more lenient on schools with extensive distance learning and non-traditional educational models (Kinser, 2003).

In recent years, the entire accreditation system has fallen under attack. In 2006, the Commission on the Future of Higher Education proposed overthrowing the current accreditation system in favor of a central national accreditation board (Bollag & Selingo, 2006). That proposal met with heavy resistance, and was cut from the Commission's final proposal (Bollag, 2006). The primary objections to the current regional system are due to the non-transferability of credits from a nationally accredited institution to a regionally accredited school (Miller, 2007). As a result of the issues between the accrediting bodies, many refer to the regional system as a historical artifact, in need of an overhaul (Bollag & Selingo, 2006). The supporters of the overhaul believe that the existing system has outlived its usefulness (Bollag & Selingo, 2006). The proposed national system would operate with literacy at the core of institutional approval. This system would serve the public, rather than the institutions (Bollag & Selingo, 2006). However, many think that the regional system has made marked improvement in recent years, measuring learning assessment over faculty pedigree (Bollag & Selingo, 2006). Opponents of the proposed overhaul fear that diversity will be sacrificed and the institutions will be less responsive to local economies (Bollag & Selingo, 2006).

Issues of Transparency

Since the Securities Exchange Commission regulates the publicly traded Wall Street-era proprietary institutions, the proposal of an accreditation overhaul from the Commission on the Future of Higher Education could devastate their operations. In addition to one national accreditation body, the proposal also calls for greater transparency and disclosure of the colleges' information (Bollag & Selingo, 2006). The transparency clause is designed to allow students and parents more information for the decision-making process. For the shareholder institutions, the release of certain vital information could risk corporate confidentiality and cause an adverse effect on stock valuation (Bollag, 2006). The disclosure of all strong and weak points of a school could allow one competing school to be privy to its adversary's shortcomings, no matter how minor. These shortcomings could be exploited in the marketing and recruitment process (Bollag, 2006; Kinser, 2007). Any adverse news released unnecessarily could also spark a government investigation. A possibility of an investigation by the government could cause a rapid drop in stock value (Kinser, 2007). While transparency and disclosure are noble policies when discussing institutions of higher education, for publicly traded corporations they can be highly detrimental.

The 90/10 Rule

In order for an institution to be eligible to offer federal student aid, the school must carry a valid accreditation. The legislation does not designate whether national or regional accreditation is preferable. Once an institution is accredited and able to offer federal financial aid, the Department of Education performs occasional audits of the college's financial aid documentation to insure accuracy and in an attempt to prevent fraud (Floyd, 2005). Absent the ability to offer students this financial aid, obtaining and retaining students are severely difficult.

The issue of federal financial aid in the proprietary institution carries another obstacle not encountered in the nonprofit or public colleges. In 1992, Congress enacted the "90/10 rule" (Miller, 2005). The rule requires at least 10% of the institution's gross revenue to come from avenues other than federal student loan programs. The rule came about as a result of widespread fraud by for-profit colleges, where each student represents profit (Miller, 2005). Opponents of the rule blame the state departments of education and the regional accreditation agencies for ineffective administration and enforcement. While efforts have mounted to overturn the 90/10 rule, today it is still in force.

Increasing Student Debt

Over the last four decades, the percentage of Americans between the ages of 18 and 24 who have attained some form of higher education has increased by more than 11% (Cunningham & Santiago, 2008). During this increase in college enrollment, the federal loan volume has increased by 800% (Cunningham & Santiago, 2008). This dramatic increase in student loans has created great discussion on the causes and effects of student debt.

The increase in accumulated student debt while attending college is an issue faced by most students and graduates of the higher education system. While admission to traditional colleges is based on specific academic criteria, sometimes the admitted student may be prevented from attending due to a lack of funding. The various forms of available financial aid make the possibility of financing a college education more accessible for Under Title IV of the Higher Education Act, federal student aid was initially created to assist those who may not otherwise be able to attend college due to financial constraints (Gladieux, King, & Corrigan, 2005). Since then, the evolution has gone from assistance for those less fortunate, to relieving a cost burden to those students who would have attended college without government assistance. Add to this evolution the introduction of private lenders and the ultimate focus leans more on borrowing money and less on grants and scholarships (Gladieux et al., 2005; Holtschneider, 2008).

The problem of increasing student debt may not be as simple as drastic increases in tuition and other costs of higher education. Some think that the issue partially lies with the aggressive business practices of the private student lending companies and institutions that push federal student loans as an easy method to afford a college education (Greiner, 2007). The Iowa College Student Aid Commission suggests that a major portion of the problem lies in the discrepancy between the rate of growth of tuition and fees and the growth of scholarships and grants. As the student aid model shifted from grants, scholarships, and other need-based awards to loans, the students' long-term focus must include efforts to address accumulated student debt. The availability of loan instruments combined with the ever-rising costs of higher education created a greater focus on the topic of student debt. Without some type of reform to the current student loan system, current and future generation students may be entering the workforce with a debt that may never be paid in full.

Student Debt and Its Impact on Higher Education

Since the mortgage industry's collapse in August 2007, which led to the recession of 2008–2009, lending of any form has taken center stage of many discussions. The federal student loan program and private entities lending to students are no exception. With so many searching for a method to finance their postsecondary and postgraduate education, the student loan industry has been compared to the "wild west" (Holtschneider, 2008). While student loans are designed to enable students to wisely invest in their futures, many student borrowers lack the financial knowledge to adequately manage the responsibility.

Concern over rising debt obligations leads some students to seek alternatives to borrowing. Students often view the debt accumulated during their college years as a deterrent to using the student loan process (Cunningham & Santiago, 2008). Students deciding not to borrow enroll in less expensive (and often less prestigious) colleges or work and attend school on a part-time basis. Current research shows that such debt-avoiding strategies place students at a greater risk of non-completion, or at least compromising their school performance due to a division between work and studies (Burdman, 2005).

The Non-Borrowing Student

According to Cunningham and Santiago (2008), there are three basic types of students who will not borrow their way through their higher education courses. The basic categories of non-borrowing students are students who will make a specific effort to attend less expensive institutions or change their attendance pattern, those with access to other financial resources (current income or parent/ family support), and students from certain ethnic/racial backgrounds with cultural perspectives that discourage debt. In the 2003–2004 academic year, student loans were obtained by 12% of students in the community college system. When compared with the 45% of students in public four-year institutions and 73% of those in for-profit colleges in that same year who borrowed, the research shows that students in community colleges have much less need or desire to borrow (Cunningham & Santiago, 2008). Cochrane and Shireman (2008) claim that over one million students in the community college system are not participating in the federal loan program. This is most likely due to the part-time nature of community college attendance or the likelihood that the students hold some form of employment during their college career.

Students with alternative resources such as family support or employment generally do not borrow (Cunningham & Santiago, 2008). Many in this classification are older students, entering college with different needs than the traditional college student. Students over age 30 with full-time employment are less likely to borrow at all institutional types except for-profits (Cunningham & Santiago, 2008). These students are often financially independent and can draw college expenses from existing assets (Cunningham & Santiago, 2008).

Certain races and ethnicities are discouraged to borrow by cultural influence (Cunningham & Santiago, 2008). Hispanic and Asian students are less likely to take on student loans than their White and Black counterparts (Cunningham & Santiago, 2008). In their research, Cunningham and Santiago (2008) discovered that particularly Latino students were reluctant to borrow for college because of the obligation to pay back the note even if they do not complete their course of study. They choose to operate on a "pay-as-you-go" standard and believe that a quality education can be earned regardless of the institution. As a result of this mindset towards higher education, more than half of Latino students attend college on a part-time basis (Cunningham & Santiago, 2008).

Since students with an aversion to borrowing often have remaining financial needs, they resort to other methods to fill in the financial gaps. As mentioned earlier, many will enroll on a part-time basis and work to cover the costs. Others will offset their living expenses by remaining at home with their parents and attend full-time. Of the students who choose to work their way through college, other factors must be considered.

King (1999) addresses the issues related to the working college student. In her study, she creates two specific categories of students: students who work and employees who study (King, 1999). While the differentiation appears minor, it is important to explain the goals and intentions of the student. While the statistics are dated (1995–1996), according to the U.S. Department of Education, eight out of ten students work while enrolled in undergraduate studies (USDOE, 1998). Of every ten undergraduate students, nearly four are full-time employees (USDOE, 1998). Approximately two-thirds of the working students describe themselves as "students who work" while the remaining third claim membership to the "employees who study" category (King, 1999).

When looking at the effect that working hours can have on the students' grade point average, there is a direct correlation (USDOE, 1998). Regardless of which of the categories the students associate themselves with, as the hours worked increase, grade point average decreases (USDOE, 1998). This is only trumped in the employees who work category, with those working hours over 25 per week actually displaying an increase in grade point average (USDOE, 1998). This is most likely due to the level of maturity of the employee, and the ability to balance multiple obligations (family, job, expenses, etc.). Of the employees who study, nearly 80% work more than 35 hours per week and fewer than 20% were full time students (King, 1999). Of the students who work, most work 25 hours per week and attend school full-time (King, 1999).

While employment is good for students to build experience, professionalism, and other levels of maturity, employment during the college years can adversely affect scholastic performance, persistence, and degree completion (Saunders, 1997). The students who work perform an average of 25 hours per week of employment while maintaining their course loads (King, 1999). The efforts to develop a balance between this level of employment and the traditional college experience prove difficult. As a result, they are not enjoying the well-rounded college experience that is advertised on the recruitment websites, and are making minimal progress towards their degree completion (King, 1999). While many of the working students stay employed because of the enjoyment of the job, others work to pay for other priorities like clothing or automobiles. Many work to pay for the basic essentials and to avoid borrowing (King, 1999).

The Borrowing Student

Mariott (2007) conducted a questionnaire in an attempt to gain greater perspective on students' attitude toward debt accumulation. The instrument includes a 1–5 measure, with strong debt aversion at one end of the spectrum and a tolerant attitude at the other (Mariott, 2007). While this study is limited in that it only focuses on first-year business students in the United Kingdom, the results do show an aversion to debt, even if the students must work during the semester to offset the need for borrowing (Mariott, 2007).

Of the students who do choose to borrow some or all of their higher education costs and expenses, the amount borrowed or placed on credit is increasing. In 2009 the average annual cost for tuition, room, and board at a public four-year institution was $14,333 (Kuzma, Kuzma, & Thiewes, 2010). That same year, the total amount borrowed by students and paid to institutions of higher education increased by 25% (Kuzma et al., 2010). Over the past ten years, debt levels for graduating seniors (upon the completion of their degrees) increased from $9,250 to over $20,000 (Combe, 2009). Nearly 67 percent of the class of 2008 (undergraduate) carried some level of student loan debt, the average reaching $23,186 (Chaker, 2009). In spite of these increasing numbers, some still suggest that college is highly affordable for many at a majority of the available institutions (Gladieux et al., 2005).

Of students who borrow, many do so in order to allow them to better focus on their studies. If the story ended there, so too would this research. However, in addition to the borrowed monies from federal and private student lenders, most students have credit card debt (Kuzma et al., 2010). In 2008, nearly 84% of undergraduate students carried at least one credit card, half of whom maintained four or more (Kuzma et al., 2010). Upon graduating in that year, the students' average credit card debt was $4,100 (Kuzma et al., 2010). The alarming level of credit card debt is amplified in Bevill and Dale (2006); students who carry a large student loan amount are three times more likely to pay only the minimum monthly credit card payments, and carry twice as many credit cards as students with lower student debt.

These reported numbers on borrowing and students' debt lead to the conclusion that a large number of students either have poor knowledge of debt and personal finance, or are aware of their actions and believe that upon graduation a high paying career awaits them. With the current job market in the United States and abroad, the odds are severely stacked against this outcome. In 2009, only 46% of individuals in America between the ages of 16 to 24 had jobs (Kuzma et al., 2010). While this figure includes non-college graduates, consider that two years prior, over 84% of college graduates age 22–27 were employed compared to nearly 87%

of those aged 27–50. In the two years since 2007, that discrepancy has doubled (Kuzma et al., 2010). These figures add to the stress of obtaining meaningful employment for recent graduates who need to manage their student debt.

The Industry of Higher Education Is Mature

Levine (2001) attempted to explain why higher education has difficulty managing its budget and keeping costs down. As government support for higher education has decreased, two common rationales arise for an explanation. The first is that times are difficult and the government simply has less money to direct to higher education. The second explanation is that the government has different priorities. Where education used to be valued, today that value has shifted to prisons, transportation, healthcare, etc. (Levine, 2001). Levine (2001) offers a third rationale that is more permanent than the others: higher education has become a mature industry.

More than 60% of high school graduates go on to some form of college-level education (Levine, 2001). With that level of participation, higher education is reaching a point of market inelasticity; there is little desire on the part of the government to delegate funds to raise that number. This inelasticity is also why the federal student aid system has changed from grant-based to lending based (Levine, 2001).

In the early to mid-twentieth century, higher education was a growth industry. The government had as primary objectives to increase enrollment, increase college graduates, and expand the state and private institutions (Levine, 2001). Somewhere along the way, the focus shifted from the growth of the universities to the regulation of them. Government officials began asking hard questions about costs, efficiency, productivity, and effectiveness, seeking accountability on all issues. These are all clear indications of an industry that has transformed from growth to maturity (Levine, 2001).

The problem with higher education becoming a mature industry is that, for the most part, it is unaware of its situation. In order to cope, most institutions are shifting their focus from the process of education to the outcome (Levine, 2001). Institutions are discovering that in order to stand out from others, they must specialize. In the pursuit of specialization, budgetary constraints require an institution to terminate one program in order to create another (Levine, 2001). Higher education may be ripe for an overhaul.

How does this dilemma tie into the issue of rising student debt? Levine (2001) outlines the traditional cycle of budget shortfall dealings by higher education. Traditionally, the first step is to raise tuition and fees, requiring students to work, borrow, beg family for more money, or drop out (most opt for the first two options). The additional money allows the institution to hire development officers. The development officers raise funds to justify new hires. At the same time, the institution makes across-the-board cuts and initiates funding freezes. This causes departments to sacrifice the quality of teaching to avoid "rocking the boat" (Levine, 2001). The sad truth is that this cycle does not save or generate enough revenue to fully address the problem.

In addition to the common budgetary cycle, the world has moved from an industrial society (with power and wealth in labor and resources) to an informational one (with wealth in information and communication) (Levine, 2001). Today, most of the best careers require post-secondary education, creating the increased demand for higher education. Many traditional institutions are not equipped to handle the increase in enrollment and the demands for a more flexible schedule (Levine, 2001). As more students fit the working student model, they desire convenience, availability, and affordability (Levine, 2001). Add to this demand the fact that nearly one-third of all students require some form of remedial education, and the traditional institutions cannot keep up.

The demand of the students leads to a *consumer expectation* with which colleges must contend. Working students want "stripped-down" educations to avoid high costs. As a result of the necessary convenience and desire to avoid costs, distance education becomes paramount to an institution's success (Kinser, 2007; Levine, 2001). The inability of traditional institutions to meet the consumer demand is what gave rise to the proprietary colleges, born from the private sector view that higher education is poorly run, inefficient, and potentially lucrative (Levine, 2001). In order to compete with the for-profit sector, most traditional institutions are resorting to the standard action plan of raising tuition and fees in an attempt for the inefficient to be able to better compete with the efficient.

The Gainful Employment Act

The gainful employment concerns grew as a result of the rapid growth of the for-profit institutions in the 1980s (Johnson, 2011). During that era, the Department of Education began to monitor the cohort default rates of proprietary institutions' graduates (Johnson, 2011). In 1990, Title IV of the Higher Education Act was amended to include calculations for cohort default rates, designed to assess how many graduates with federally backed student loans were in default (Johnson, 2011). Congress hoped that the cohort default rate monitoring would identify which for-profit colleges were adequately preparing their graduates for employment that would allow them to fulfill their debt obligations, and which were not (Johnson, 2011; Lederman, 2009).

The version of the Higher Education Act, as renewed in 1990, led the Department of Education to create the cohort default rate threshold in 1991 as an instrument of governmental financial protection against schools with high default rates (Johnson, 2011). The threshold prevented any Title IV funding from being allocated to institutions with a cohort default rate in excess of 25% for three or more years in a row (Johnson, 2011). The cohort default rate considers all graduates who enter repayment status on their loans and then default within a specified period of time (Johnson, 2011, Student Assistance General Provisions, 2010). The current rule is any institution with a cohort default rate reaching 40%, or maintaining a level greater than 30% for three years, will lose Title IV funding (e.g., the ability to offer students federal financial aid) (Student Assistance General Provisions, 2010). The cohort default rate threshold has been successful in reducing the percentage of borrowers who default on student loans; however, the rate of proprietary college graduates who default is nearly double that of public college graduates (Johnson, 2011).

While the cohort default rates applies to all institutions of higher education offering federal student loans, the Higher Education Act requires proprietary institutions to prepare their students for gainful employment in ". . . a recognized occupation" (Higher Education Act, 1965). Congress's reason for the differential treatment of for-profit schools was because the students of proprietary or trade schools are learning skills for a specific vocation (Johnson, 2011). The law is intended to insure reasonable cost, for a reasonable education, for use in a valid career (Johnson, 2011).

After struggling for better than a decade to determine what gainful employment is, the Department of Education has a version that took effect on July 1, 2012. In addition to addressing incentive compensation for recruiters at proprietary colleges and graduation rates, the version for implementation contains two tests: the loan repayment rate test and the debt-to-income test (Johnson, 2011). At least one of these tests has already been scrutinized for being arbitrary (Fain, 2012).

Loan Repayment Test

The first test of the gainful employment act is the loan repayment test. This test determines whether a program offered by a proprietary institution is reasonable based on the ability of graduates to repay at a determined rate. The cost-to-repay rate deemed appropriate by Congress and the Department of Education is 45% (Johnson, 2011). This formula is applied by dividing the amount paid off on the note by the borrower over the last four years by the total amount borrowed to obtain the degree, training, or certification (Johnson, 2011). The Department of Education only considers money paid toward principal toward the equation, not those paying interest only or those in a forbearance period (Johnson, 2011). If a degree or certification program offered by a for-profit college meets this formula based on its graduates' payment history, then it is a viable program under Title IV of the Higher Education Act.

Debt-to-Income Test

This parameter of gainful employment requires the evaluator to look at the employment factors of the program's graduates—specifically, the average annual income for a degree earner employed in the field (Johnson, 2011). The Department of Education has determined the acceptable debt-to-income ratio is if the annual payments toward the principle of the note is 8% or less of the graduate's annual income (Johnson, 2011). By looking at the average income of program degree recipients over the previous three years and the loan payments made over the same time frame, the program can be deemed acceptable or cost prohibitive.

In some cases, a graduate will not meet the debt-to-income test in the first three years of employment and repayment because the specific professional field may start employees at a low wage, but increase income drastically later in the career. If a program offered fits the bill for this type of career preparation, the Department of Education can choose to extend the time for an additional three years, while possibly increasing the ratio above 8% (Johnson, 2011). This creates an incentive for a program's cost to remain reasonable, or for the proprietary college to remain in communication with the Department of Education to justify the costs of programs that prepare for higher paying careers over a longer Application of the Tests.

In applying the two tests to programs offered by subject campuses, the Department of Education considered the possibility of a program meeting one or the other test, or possibly satisfying both formulas. Any program offered by a for-profit institution that is able to pass both the loan repayment rate test and the debt-to-income test is able to offer loans under Title IV with no restriction. If a degree or certificate program only meets one of the two tests, then the institution must publish its current rates under both tests in order to be able to offer federal student loans (Johnson, 2011). In addition to the publication restrictions placed on institutions that meet one test, a duty arises for notification to prospective students that degree recipients from the subjected program may have difficulty meeting the repayment obligations of federal student loans offered for the program (Johnson, 2011).

The discussion about the passage of one or both of the tests opens the door for possible action by the Department of Education. If a program is unable to pass either the loan repayment test or the debt-to-income test, then the Department of Education intervenes. The intervention by the department can come in the form of a restricted status, or the institution can be found to be unable to offer federal student loans at all (Johnson, 2011). If the program is placed under restrictions, it can be required to notify prospective students that graduates will have difficulty paying loans off upon graduation. These notifications must be placed on recruitment literature, websites, etc., as well as presented to students upon enrollment (Johnson, 2011). In addition to the notification requirements, the total enrollment in a program can be capped by the Department of Education (Johnson, 2011). The restrictions and regulations on the proprietary colleges leave room for criticism that will come to light upon implementation of the policy.

A primary objection for critics of the gainful employment act is in its application solely to for-profit institutions. When Congress defined "gainful employment" the legislators were responding to the default rates from the students of proprietary colleges. The Department of Education is charged with an implementation that does not touch the nonprofit colleges (that have much greater rates of loan repayment) (Johnson, 2011).

Other critics wonder if the gainful employment act as written does enough to address the problem of federal student loan default (Adams, 2011). Under the two tests, an institution with a loan repayment rate less than 45% and a debt-to-income ratio of less than 8% is fully eligible for Title IV funding without restrictions. Graduates who make very little income may fall into default because they may not be able to afford the 8% payment (Johnson, 2011). Many low-paying jobs are unskilled labor positions, usually not requiring a degree or certificate for satisfactory job performance. In the face of criticism, there are those who oppose the act in its entirety.

The supporters of the proprietary institutions argue that any legislation against the common practices of the business colleges may severely limit access to higher education for millions and effectively impede economic progress (Association of Private Sector Colleges and Universities [ASPCU], 2011). Congress and the Department of Education would place more weight on this concern if the for-profit sector were more successful in decades past regulating their graduates' loan repayment progress. The concerns opposing the recent legislation of gainful employment are far outweighed by the policy grounds in favor of their implementation.

Conclusion

The degree-granting proprietary institution has evolved over time to become a major influence of modern higher education. As the for-profit has grown, the issues related to them have developed into more complex concerns. As the colleges learn to walk the line between regulation and corporate profitability, elected officials continue to attempt to implement policy in an attempt to respond to public sentiment.

From Congress's attempts to limit the cost of a for-profit education to its efforts to reduce financial aid fraud, it remains clear that proprietary institutions are hot beds for discussion. The Wall Street institutions wear several hats in the midst of the debate. As institutions of higher education there is a constant focus on student achievement and success. As publicly traded corporations, the duty of loyalty to shareholders is constantly in balance with educational principles and the Security Exchange Commission. As businesses relying on the students' ability to obtain federal financial aid, accreditation is paramount. By continuing to balance this equation and flexing to meet the challenges from Wall Street, Main Street, Capitol Hill, and the classroom, the for-profit college will continue to influence higher education.

References

Adams, C. (2011, June 15). "Gainful Employment" rules leave many disappointed. *Education Week,* 20–21.

Associated Press. (2008). Alabama chancellor cracking down on proprietary schools. *Community College Week, 20* (24), 10. Retrieved from http://www.ccweek.com/news/articlefiles/536–CCW081108–Allpgs.pdf

Association of Private Sector Colleges and Universities. (2011). *APSCU urges support for bipartisan amendment toblock federal funding of so-called "gainful employment" implementation.* Retrieved from http://www.highbeam.com

Berg, G. A. (2005). *Lessons from the edge: For-profit and non-traditional higher education in America.* Westport, CT: Praeger.

Bevill, S., & Dale, L. (2006). Students and the misuse of credit. *Proceedings of the Academy of Educational Leadership, 11* (2), 33–37.

Bollag, B. (2006, September 1). Controversial proposal fails to make panel's final report. *Chronicle of Higher Education, 53* (2), 35. Retrieved from http://web.ebscohost.com

Bollag, B., & Selingo, J. (2006, April 14). Federal panel floats plan to overhaul accreditation. *Chronicle of Higher Education, 52* (32), A1–A23. Retrieved from http://web.ebscohost.com

Burdman, P. (2005, October). *The student debt dilemma: Debt aversion as a barrier to college access* (Research and Occasional Paper Series CSHE. 13.05). Center for Studies in Higher Education, University of California, Berkeley.

Chaker, A. M. (2009, September 3). Students borrow more than ever for college. *The Wall Street Journal,* D1.

Cochrane, D., & Shireman, R. (2008). *Denied: Community college students lack access to affordable loans.* Berkeley, CA. The Project on Student Debt, Institute for College Access and Success.

Combe, P. (2009, May). What the federal government owes student borrowers. *Chronicle of Higher Education, 55* (36), 56. Retrieved from http://chronicle.com. proxy. lib. odu.edu/

Cunningham, A. F., & Santiago, D. A. (2008). *Student aversion to borrowing: Who borrows and who doesn't.* Washington, DC: Institute for Higher Education Policy.

Fain, P. (2012, July 3). Gainful employment's hazy next steps. *Inside Higher Education.* Retgrieved from www.insidehighed.com.

Floyd, C. E. (2005, April). *"State and federal policy of regulatory framework for for-profit degree granting institutions: How did we get where we are and where we are we going?"* Paper presented at the annual meeting of The Midwest Political Science Association, Chicago, IL. Retrieved fromhttp://www.allacademic.com

Gladieux, L. E., King, J. E., & Corrigan, M. E. (2005). *The federal government and higher education.* In P. G. Altbach, R. O. Berdahl, & P. Gumport (Eds.), *American higher education in the twenty-first century: Social, political, and economic challenges* (2nd ed.). Baltimore, MD: The Johns Hopkins University Press.

Greiner, K. (2007, October). *Student loan debt: Trends affecting the American dream.* Paper presented at the Iowa Higher Education Research Conference, Des Moines, IA. Higher Education Act, 20 U.S. C. § 1002 (1965).

Holtschneider, D. H. (2008, May). Colleges should teach students how to borrow wisely. *Chronicle of Higher Education, 54* (34). Retrieved from http://chronicle.com. proxy. lib. odu.edu/

Johnson, N. R. (2011). Phoenix rising: Default rates at proprietary institutions of higher education and what can be done to reduce them. *Journal of Law and Education, 40* (2), 225–271.

Kelly, K. F. (2001). Meeting needs and making profits: The rise of for-profit degree-granting institutions. Denver, CO: Education Commission of the States. Retrieved from www.ecs.org

King, J. E. (1999, September–October). Helping students balance work, borrowing, and college. *About Campus, 4* (4), 17–22.

Kinser, K. (2003, November). *A profile of regionally-accredited for-profit institutions of higher education.* Paper presented at the Annual Meeting of the Association for the Study of Higher Education, Portland, OR.

Kinser, K. (2005). A profile of regionally accredited for-profit institutions of higher education. In B. Pusser (Ed.), *Arenas of entrepreneurship: Where nonprofit and for-profitinstitutions compete* (pp. 69–84). San Francisco: Jossey-Bass.

Kinser, K. (Ed.) (2006a). From main street to Wall Street: The transformation of for profit education. *ASHE Higher Education Report, 31* (5), 1–155. Retrieved from Education Full Text Database.

Kinser, K. (2006b). Principles of student affairs in for-profit higher education. *NASPA Journal, 43* (2), 264–279.

Kinser, K. (2006c, July–August). What phoenix doesn't teach us about for-profit higher education. *Change: The Magazine of Higher Learning, 38* (4), 24–29.

Kinser, K. (2007, Spring). Dimensions of corporate ownership in for-profit higher education. *The Review of Higher Education, 30* (3), 217–245.

Kuzma, A. T., Kuzma, J. R., & Thiewes, H. F. (2010, April). An examination of business students' student loan debt and total debt. *American Journal of Business Education, 3* (4), 71–77.

Lederman, D. (2009, December 14). Defaults nearly double. *Inside Higher Ed*. Retrieved from www.insidehighered. com

Levine, A. (2001). Higher education as a mature industry. In P. G. Altbach, P. J. Gumport, & D. B. Johnstone (Eds.), *In defense of American higher education* (pp. 38–58). Baltimore, MD: The Johns Hopkins University Press.

Mangan, K. S. (1999, September 24). A struggling law school turns its management over to a chain of proprietary schools. *Chronicle of Higher Education, 46* (5), A52. Retrieved from http://web.ebscohost.com

Marriott, P. (2007, October). An analysis of first experience students' financial awareness and attitude to debt in a post-1992 UK university. *Higher Education Quarterly, 61* (4), 498–519.

Miller, M. H. (2005, March 28). Education committee may scrap "90–10" rule for proprietary schools. *Community College Week, 17* (17), 3–10.

Miller, H. N. (2007, August 3). Legislation can end bias against career colleges. *Chronicle of Higher Education, 53* (48), 44. Retrieved from http://web.ebscohost.com

Noone, L. P. (2004, Spring). A view from the for-profit edge. *Presidency, 7* (2), 18–22.

Saunders, D. (1997). *Student loan debt: Crisis or exaggeration?* Braintree, MA: Nellie Mae.

Sperling, J., & Tucker, R. W. (1997). *For-profit higher education: Developing a world-class workforce.* New Brunswick, NJ: Transaction.

Student Assistance General Provisions, 34 C. F. R. § 668 (2010)

United States Department of Education. (2012). Accreditation in the United States. Retrieved from http://www2. ed. gov/admins/finaid/accred/index.html

United States Department of Education, National Center for Educational Statistics. (1998). *National postsecondary student aid study: 1995–96.* Washington, DC: U.S. Government Printing Office.

Van Dyne, L. (1974). Accreditors drop ban on proprietaries. *Chronicle of Higher Education, 9* (13), 6.

CHAPTER TWENTY-NINE

Computing, Scholarship, and Learning

The Transformation of American Higher Education

EUGENE F. PROVENZO, JR.

If we persist in a conventional approach to these developments our traditional culture will be swept aside as scholasticism was in the sixteenth century. Had the Schoolmen with their complex oral culture understood the Gutenberg technology, they could have created a new synthesis of written and oral education, instead of bowing out of the picture and allowing the merely visual page to take over the educational enterprise. The oral Schoolmen did not meet the new visual challenge of print, and the resulting expansion or explosion of Gutenberg technology was in many respects an impoverishment of the culture.
—Marshall McLuhan, *Understanding Media: The Extensions of Man* (1964)

American higher education is at a unique moment in its history, one which is not necessarily sufficiently understood by either the administrative leadership of the Academy, the professorship, or the general public at large. It is the thesis of this chapter that university and college learning is at a very similar moment to the experience of the late medieval schoolmen, steeped in oral culture and memory-based learning, who in the sixteenth century were transformed by the Gutenberg technology of moveable type and the printed word. In several books and articles I have described the parallels between the Gutenberg print revolution of the late fifteenth century and the computer revolution that began in the period following the Second World War.[1] Most recently, I argue in a new book, *The Difference Engine: Computers, Knowledge and the Transformation of Literacy*, that since the early 1960s the assumptions underlying culture and education have dramatically changed.[2] The rapid evolution of new media such as television and film, and in particular the computer, have created a new cultural geography. I believe we are, in fact, well into a critical process in which our culture, and more specifically higher education, is moving from a modern into a postmodern culture—from a Gutenberg and typographic model of literacy, scholarship, and learning into a post-modern or post-typographic literacy.[3]

Concepts such as Hypertext, Hypermedia, Hyperreality, Augmented Intelligence, Cyberspace, the Internet, the World Wide Web, Networked Knowledge, Collective Intelligence, the Information Superhighway, Virtual Reality, Wikis and Mobile Computing—did not even exist a generation ago. At present, they are sweeping away traditional ways of knowing, learning and researching, just as the book and the printed word swept its way across the oral and memory-based traditions of the late Middle Ages. I use the term "Difference Engine" in my book to describe the phenomenon of what is going on in all aspects of learning as a result of the introduction of the models of computing that have come into existence in the past fifty years. The term "Difference Engine" is drawn from the work of the nineteenth century mathematician, philosopher and inventor Charles Babbage (1791–1871), who invented the first mechanical computer. Babbage's "engine" was a complex system of mechanical "mills" or computational units that, while theoretically sound, were limited by their mechanical construction.[4] I am drawn not only to the complex multivariate nature of the machine he created, but also to its possibilities as a metaphor to describe the current condition of computing and its role in shaping culture, knowledge, learning and scholarship.

I argue in *The Difference Engine* that there are seven elements of the post-modern model of computing that can be identified at this time. These include 1. Hypertext/Hypermedia—the eclectic combination of text, sound, graphics, animation, film and interactivity that is the foundation of the new electronic literacy; 2. Augmented Intelligence—the use of computers by humans as ways of enhancing cognition; 3. Networked Information and Communication Systems—online services such as the Internet and the World Wide Web, which are creating a highly interconnected worldwide information network; 4. Collective Intelligence—the linking of people electronically through connected systems of thought, organization, and action; 5. Hyperreality—the French theorist Jean Baudrillard's notion that we are creating an increasingly electronically mediated culture in which simulations are no longer referential beings or substances, but the main reality of our lives and experience; 6. the Panoptic Sort—the collection of electronic data that allows individuals to be observed, tracked, regulated, and controlled; and 7. Mobile Computing—the use of computing in transit. Each one of these seven elements is to varying degrees redefining the nature of higher education, in terms of the organization of knowledge, teaching, and scholarship. In the remainder of this chapter, I will analyze how each individual element is shaping our consciousness, learning, and approaches to research. Before doing so, I want to establish the idea that the condition we currently find ourselves in represents a cultural "singularity"—one that by definition is unique in its scope and nature.

Contemporary Computing as a Singularity

The idea of a "singularity" is that an event occurs that is so transformative it is not possible to talk about things in the same way after it has occurred.[5] The Gutenberg revolution of moveable type and its impact on the nature of scholarship, knowledge, and teaching was a singularity, as was the dropping of the atom bomb at Hiroshima in 1945. Singularities are rare, and their effects on traditional institutions and cultures are almost always, by definition, profound.

The computer technologies that have emerged in the past fifty or sixty years, and in particular during the last thirty years, such as the Internet and World Wide Web, Hypermedia, Virtual Reality, and Mobile Computing, represent, as a combined force, a singularity. What is so interesting is that because of computing this process is taking place simultaneously on multiple and interlocking levels (the phenomenon I describe as being the "Difference Engine").

Why has the process of computing, as a singularity, profoundly reshaping the fundamental nature of higher education not been looked at more carefully? Why has computing not been the primary focus of most aspects of teaching and research? Part of the problem may be Antonio Gramsci's observation that a fish is so immersed in water that it does not realize that it is wet. We may be so immersed in computing as part of our lives and knowledge systems that we are not even aware it is shaping us. Part of the problem may also be one of cultural lag—William Ogburn's notion that a culture needs a period of time to adjust socially and culturally to technological innovations and change.[6]

This is not to say that models of computing are not seen as being important, but in general they are understood in isolation and mostly as tools for increasing efficiency. The reality is more complex and nuanced than this. The technology of the computer creates tools that redefine the types and levels of inquiry that are now possible. This, in turn, reshapes how we teach, how students learn, and the politics of knowledge. An analogy with the early modern period is obvious. For example: How did the invention of the book change a field such as cartography? Beginning in the seventeenth century how did the telescope and microscope change fields such as astronomy and biology? Similarly in our own era, how does the new "knowledge space" created by the computer change the nature of teaching, learning, and research? In order to answer this question, I will look briefly at the seven elements that constitute what I describe as the "Difference Engine."

Hypertext/Hypermedia

Hypertext/Hypermedia is a concept that was first introduced in 1945 by the computer pioneer Vannevar Bush (1890–1974). Hypertext/Hypermedia does not lend itself to a simple definition. Ted Nelson defines hypertext by itself as *"non-sequential writing*—text that allows choice to the reader, best read as an interactive screen."[7] Popularly conceived, this represents "a series of text chunks connected by links which offer the reader different pathways."[8] George Landow, a literary scholar, art historian and pioneer in the use of hypertext systems, explains that "the defining characteristics of this new information medium derive from its combination of blocks of text joined by electronic links, for this combination emphasizes multiple connections rather than linear reading or organization."[9] Jeff Conklin describes hypertext as a system which makes possible "direct machine-supported references from one textual chunk to another; new interfaces provide the user with the ability to interact directly with these chunks and to establish new relationships between them."[10] According to Conklin: "The concept of hypertext is quite simple: Windows on the screen are associated with objects in a database and links are provided between these objects, both graphically (as labeled tokens) and in the database (as pointers)."[11]

The use of hypertext and hypermedia is ubiquitous, having become so widespread that they are now taken largely for granted in forms such as the hyperlinks in websites and in the use of streaming video. There is a profound transformation taking place however as a result of the introduction and use of hyperlinked materials. As an example, as I write this chapter I am finishing the editing of a college textbook about schooling and American culture that will be available not only as a printed document, but also as an Interactive PDF and E-pub product. In the print document, the book functions as a traditional textbook. It is read. The Interactive PDF and E-pub versions can be "read" using very different features. Besides accessing the print for the book, all of the text can be listened to in a digital audio file. The main concepts in the text can be "clicked on" to play brief video lectures and reviews provided by the author. Discussions of films portraying teachers and their work are linked to multimedia selections posted on YouTube and similar online sources. Government databases, which are referenced in the text, ranging from the Library of Congress to the U.S. Department of Education, are all hyperlinked and can be easily accessed. Primary source texts such as the 1692 *New England Primer* and John Dewey's 1896 article "My Pedagogic Creed" can be referenced directly from the text as well.

Such textbooks challenge traditional models of curriculum and instruction. Their availability raises fundamental questions. For example, is it important to have someone lecture in a college or university class when the author of the course's textbook is available to be listened to or viewed online at any time, in any place and as many times as is of interest to the student? Does the availability of this type of textbook, which only requires a computer or e-book reader and a web connection make the traditional classroom lecture obsolete? What now becomes the purpose of going to class? Should college instruction increasingly focus on discussion and analysis? How should it be integrated with this type of instructional material?

Augmented Intelligence

Augmented intelligence refers to the use of computers to enhance cognition. Although largely unrecognized, books have always done this. For example, books extend our "memory" making it possible to have huge amounts of information readily available to us that would be impossible to keep in our personal memory. Likewise, computers make it possible for us to add, subtract and multiply (calculate) or spell flawlessly. A key question increasingly comes to mind: What are the necessary knowledge and skills that now need to be learned as part of a college education? I know, for example, a very accomplished book designer and cover illustrator who readily confesses that she cannot draw. All of what she does involves manipulations through computer programs such as Adobe Photo Shop, Illustrator and InDesign. What does this mean for design education? How should university and college programs for graphic design be taught in the future? Should freehand drawing be required for artists, graphic design majors, or architects? Likewise, do English majors need to know how to spell or write grammatically, without the assistance of a computer, and if so, how much time should be devoted to such efforts?

Networked Information and Communication Systems

Networked Information and Communication Systems refer to online services such as the Internet and the World Wide Web. These systems redefine traditional research and scholarly exchange. When I began my work as an assistant professor in the mid-1970s, I spent a great deal of time going to archives and libraries around the country collecting visual sources as well as print documents related to my main specialty, the history of European and American Education. Most of those same sources are now available online through Google Books, Project Gutenberg and similar sources. A book on Florida and the Depression that I wrote with Michael Carlbach in the mid-1990s, *Farm Security Photographs of Florida*, required several extended visits to the Library of Congress Print and Photography Division in Washington,

D.C. Conducting the research was a laborious task. Individual photographs, from a collection of over 120,000 FSA images (of which approximately 2,000 were from Florida), had to be requested and brought to me and my co-researcher in the library's reading room by an attendant. The research was time consuming and expensive, taking approximately two years to complete. I am currently doing a similar book on Virginia and West Virginia during the Depression using the online collections of the Library of Congress. Compiling a selection of the core photographs for the book (choosing 150 images from a total of approximately 6,000 pictures taken in Virginia and West Virginia), together with their bibliographical citations, took me a long weekend of work.

I was trained in graduate school to work with actual documents in an archive or library. This skill is still essential for a good historian. New skills, however, are now also needed. How does one search for materials online? How does one cite them? What technical issues are involved in their collection and use? Are there ethical issues involved in their use, including issues of copyright, and so on? This suggests that training methods for researchers in college and university programs need to be carefully reworked.

Networked systems also provide means of scholarly communication and exchange. It is now possible to undertake collective editing projects much more easily. I was recently the editor of a three-volume encyclopedia on the Social and Cultural Foundations of Education.[12] The project, which involved hundreds of authors, took approximately three years to complete. If it had been done using non-electronic resources such as the phone and traditional mail, it would have probably taken three or four times as long to complete and interestingly would probably not have been as well done.

Collective Intelligence

Collective Intelligence—the linking of people electronically via the Internet through connected systems of thought, organization and action—changes the nature of research and potentially, teaching. Collaborative projects on a worldwide basis are now possible. Earlier this morning I spoke with a student from the University of Miami who is spending the summer in Egypt and who is creating a book dealing with children and environmental issues in the Arab world. The book, which will take the form of a traditional print project as well as an interactive PDF and E-pub format, is being created in Alexandria, Egypt. An Egyptian illustrator is being used for the project. Videos of street scenes in Alexandria will be imbedded in the book. Samples of videos and illustrations are being sent back to me at my home in Virginia. The final project will be assembled in Miami. Post-production may occur in Virginia and Miami. A wide range of collaborators, drawn from many different geographic sites, are involved in creating the final product.

Other examples—perhaps more specific to the concept of collective intelligence—can be cited. Perhaps the best example is wikis, which are collaborative writing and research projects done online. The most famous of these, of course, is *Wikipedia*, which is literally redefining the nature of encyclopedia writing. In essence, Wikipedia authors write anonymously on topics that are constantly in a process of review and revision. Hundreds of people can potentially contribute to the creation of a single online article. There is a constant refinement of the selected topic. No article is ever closed or complete, but subject to a constant process of revision.

In earlier encyclopedic projects—the eleventh edition of the *Encyclopedia Britannica* (1910–1911), for example—the world's leading authorities on virtually every known topic were consulted to provide comprehensive articles for what was to become one of the most respected reference works ever produced. The eleventh edition of the *Encyclopedia* was considered definitive and authoritative in nature, based on its distinguished contributors. Many of its articles are still considered authoritative.[13]

This authorial and authoritarian quality is lost with Wikipedia. Authors are anonymous. A much more democratic process is at work. The authorial or "authoritarian" role of the entries is lost. The articles are not necessarily written by "experts." Currently, there is considerable debate in academic circles as to the reliability and accuracy of Wikipedia articles. But this is a fluid and changing process—a new intellectual and publishing phenomenon. If the articles are inaccurate, the constant review process updates them until they reach an acceptable standard. A collective authority eventually underlies their content, one which may go beyond the potentially more limited views and perspectives provided by a single author. In addition, entries included in Wikipedia have the potential to be much more up-to-date. When the recent earthquakes struck Japan, for example, articles appeared within days describing the disaster. As the situation evolved, more data was added and continues to be added. In a more traditional print-based encyclopedia, such a document would have taken years to appear.

So, is scholarship done by a wiki type source considered a reasonable contribution for people working in the Academy? How is credit given for such work? In theory, there is no way of listing such activities on a vita, or of even identifying actual authorship, since authorship remains anonymous, following the Wikipedia model. The era of academics writing as authorities on topics for encyclopedias is rapidly coming to an end. What has been gained and what has been lost?

Hyperreality

Jean Baudrillard's notion of hyperreality is that we are creating an increasingly electronically mediated culture in which simulations are no longer referential beings or substances, but the main reality of our lives and experience. Simulations change the nature of instruction at all levels of the educational system. We can conduct complex experiments using simulated sources, such as the dissection of a frog or a human cadaver, or the modeling of a business or an economic plan.

Simulations require extensive programming. Once they are developed for an institution or classroom setting, they can be easily shared with other sites. They are very cost effective if they are produced on a large scale. Colleges, universities, foundations and the government increasingly need to consider how such materials can be supported in their development and distribution. Questions need to be carefully considered. For example, when does a simulated experience start to distort the reality that we are trying to demonstrate or teach? Having a gastro surgeon in training practice on doing endoscopic examinations with a simulator rather than on an actual human subject seems like a good idea. When is a simulation appropriate versus the reality? These are important questions for those concerned with instruction at the college and university level.

Panoptic Sort

The Panoptic Sort—the collection of electronic data that allows individuals to be observed, regulated and controlled—is an essential part of the mechanisms of the Difference Engine. Its use is highly problematic in college and university teaching and research—more so in authoritarian rather than democratic cultures. In a place such as China, for example, keeping the electronic interactions and exchanges of scholars and students for political purposes is potentially highly threatening. Are people reading politically correct books or engaging with subversive thinkers? One only needs to reference the work of George Orwell and his novel *1984* to understand the potential nightmare of this issue.

Standards for academic freedom will probably need to be greatly clarified in the future. Should colleges and universities as employers have the right to monitor academic correspondence in the age of e-mail? Under what circumstances and for what purpose? Does the university own rights to what an academic writes if it is stored in a university "cloud"? Do they have the right to review, censor or limit the expression of ideas in a classroom posting or as part of an e-mail exchange?

Mobile Computing

Mobile computing, the use of computers in transit, represents the most recently emerging (but certainly not the last) element of the Difference Engine. The use of mobile computers is almost completely unrecognized by colleges and universities, yet it is changing classroom practice and learning at a fundamental level. As a result of mobile computing, students now have access to computing at virtually any time and in any place. This seems obvious to anyone in a current classroom, but we have just begun to consider how such as access may play itself out in terms of instruction.

I find the availability of computers in the classroom while I teach changes the nature of discourse. Increasingly, as a university classroom teacher, I find myself wondering about the best ways to engage students in meaningful discussions and exchanges. I find digital dropboxes, where students comment on readings, to be tedious and mechanized. What are the possibilities for using instant messaging programs or twitter feeds in the classroom? Would these just be gimmicks, or could they revolutionize different aspects of classroom instruction?

A new phenomenon occurs when I ask a question in class: students now often respond by looking up something online with the computer they have brought with them to class. Thus, when I ask them to define what they understand a term such as "post-modernism" to mean and discuss its relevance to my course, I will increasingly have an answer read to me off a computer site that they have quickly, and often uncritically, accessed. I argue that students need to know certain basic things. But am I any different than the orally based scholar of the early modern period who argued that books were destroying the oral culture, memory and valid ways of knowing for their students?

Cyberscholars and the Implications of Cyberscholarship

All of this brings us to the question of what will be the nature of scholarship in the years to come? Computers clearly need to be thought of in ways that are different from in the past. As J. David Bolter argued in *Turing's Man*:

> The computer is a medium of communication as well as a scientific tool, and it can be used by humanists as well as scientists. It brings concepts of physics, mathematics and logic into the

humanist's world as no previous machine hasdone. Yet it can also serve to carry artistic and philosophical thinking into the scientific community.[14]

As should be clear from the first part of this chapter, the use of the computer in its manifestation as the Difference Engine has the potential to not only integrate fields of academic inquiry, but also to create new lines of research and new methods of teaching. The examples provided are limited, but many others could be included. A new type of scholarship and instruction is emerging that will represent a significant challenge to older models. The term I have invented to define this phenomenon is *cyberscholarship*, and the individuals engaged in its pursuit, *cyberscholars*.

My use of the term cyberscholarship is based on the word cybernetics, which was originally coined by Norbert Wiener, who derived the word from the Greek word *kubernnetes* or "steersman."[15] Cyberscholarship literally involves new ways of steering oneself through the collection of knowledge and the process of inquiry.

How is the process of scholarly inquiry and teaching being redefined by the various models and technologies that are part of the emerging phenomenon of cyberscholarship? I believe that the components of the Difference Engine, such as hypertext and hypermedia, as well the Internet and the World Wide Web, represent tools for the magnification and extension of ideas that are as important as the telescope was to the astronomer and the microscope to the biologist in the seventeenth century. Such technologies not only transformed their fields, but also created anew human environment. This point was made quite clearly nearly forty years ago by Marshall McLuhan, who argued that technological environments "are notmerely passive containers of people but are active processes that reshape peopleand other technologies alike."[16]

The introduction of printing in the fifteenth century, as pointed out by McLuhan, played an important role in instituting new patterns of culture and scholarship throughout Europe.[17] The Difference Engine is doing the same in our own era. It is already clear that these and related computer technologies will create not only new sources of information and new methods of analyzing data, but new ways of conceptualizing and symbolically constructing the world. New standards of scholarship will emerge. Likewise, new questions and debates will arise because the tools necessary to set the stage for such debates will be available. As J. David Bolter argues, the

> . . . humanist will not be able to ignore the medium with which he too will workdaily: it will shape his thought in subtle ways, suggest possibilities, and imposelimitations, as does any other medium of communication. . . . The scientist orphilosopher who works with such electronic tools will think in different waysfrom those who have worked at ordinary desks with paper and pencil, with stylus and parchment, or with papyrus. He will choose different problems and be satisfied with different solutions.[18]

In essence, the use of new computing technologies of the Difference Engine—particularly hypertext and hypermedia—transform traditionalscholarship and knowledge into a much more dynamic, analogic, metaphoric, comparative and encyclopedic process. The ways in which universities and colleges train students is being transformed as well. A new educational space is created by the various manifestations of the new computing environment.

In this context, the work of the literary scholar Richard Lanham is particularly interesting. For Lanham, who is focused as a professor and scholar on the process of writing and its resulting literature, the electronic text, and by association, the Difference Engine, "not only creates a new writing space, but a new educational space as well."[19] According to him, the computer frames inquiry differently than the printed book. As a rhetorical device, it allows thinking to occur in very specific ways—ones that potentially challenge older traditions. The traditional Western literary canon, for example, has been under considerable challenge in recent years as other literatures and cultures have been brought to light which question its dominance. What happens to Chaucer's *Canterbury Tales* when read on the computer screen? Using multimedia, the text can be read aloud and heard in Middle English properly pronounced as the author originally intended it. Lanham explains how an English teacher trying to diagram the Great Vowel Shift on the blackboard can now potentially "explain the vowel shift through a computer-graphics program that put sight, sound and phonological history together."[28]

The college or university professor's expertise, and in turn power, is potentially challenged in the new environment. What happens when this information becomes more easily available through sources such as the Internet? Likewise what happens when discourse occurs, at least in part, in an online context? Lanham, for example, argues that in a university classroom using networked computers the professor becomes one of many potential voices—not just simply the expert authority. New ways of being heard become possible. Voices that are normally too timid to speak out may be encouraged to reveal themselves in the computer mediated space of the online discussion.[20]

In all of this, the question arises as to what happens to colleges and universities, their traditions of scholarship and teaching? The emergence of new models of digital rhetoric, augmented and collective intelligence and cyberscholarship as part of the creation of the Difference Engine raises important questions for educators. How do we best educate and train students to meet the new models of scholarship? How will the rules of academic politics change? In what ways does it seem likely that the nature and character of college and university scholarship and teaching will change in years to come?

This is a complex process. The Difference Engine is, by definition, constantly evolving. It must be understood in the context of the cultural orientations that it reinforces. As such, it needs to be understood according to C. A. Bowers as

> . . . an integral part of a complex ecology that includes both the cultural and natural environment. This cultural pattern of thinking works, in a sense, like lenses that enable us to see certain entities while putting other aspects out of focus. When we think that expertise in the area of computers involves only a technical form of knowledge for usingand improving computers, we are, in fact, under the influence of the conceptual guidance system of our culture. In terms of the cultural bias built into our way of thinking, new ideas and technologies are understood as progressive by their very nature. But what is not as clearly recognized is that the new forms of knowledge and technologies often lead to unanticipated consequences whose disruption may outweigh any gains from the innovations.[21]

Like Prospero in Shakespeare's *The Tempest*, we must come to terms with a "brave new world" one that has been reinvented through the introduction of radical new technologies such as those that make up the "Difference Engine." Traditional studies in the computer field unfortunately do not provide adequate grounding to fully understand computer systems such as the ones I have outlined above and in my larger study.

The Difference Engine gives college and university educators "new freedoms" and "new dependencies."[22] Increasingly, we need to be aware that technologies such as the computer have the potential, if we do not employ their use carefully, to dehumanize us by separating us from nature and from our human selves. This is already happening in a number of different ways—some that do not include computers. As JosephWeizenbaum has argued in reference to the biofeedback movement: "man no longer even senses himself, his body, directly, but only through pointer readings, flashing lights, and buzzing sounds produced by instruments attached to him as speedometers, are attached to automobiles."[23]

We must not allow the Difference Engine to diminish or reduce our humanity. We must be aware of its limitations and its potential to distort and control us. Based on our previous adaptation of other technologies, I am not convinced that we will necessarily make the best and most effective use of this new technology. This is unfortunate in light of the new technology's potential to expand our awareness and better realize our human potential.

In this context, it is well worth reconsidering Marshall McLuhan's remarkable quote included at the beginning of this chapter:

> If we persist in a conventional approach to these developments our traditional culture will be swept aside as scholasticism was in the sixteenth century. Had the Schoolmen with their complex oral culture understood the Gutenberg technology, they could have created a new synthesis of written and oral education, instead of bowing out of the picture and allowing the merely visual page to take over the educational enterprise. The oral Schoolmen did not meet the new visual challenge of print, and the resulting expansion or explosion of Gutenberg technology was in many respects an impoverishment of the culture.

Are those of us in Higher Education truly meeting the challenge of the new technology? Do we really understand its implications and significance? What is undeniable is that we are involved in the invention of a new knowledge space—one based around the elements of the Difference Engine that represent a paradigm shift in our thinking about universities, information processing, scholarship, and teaching. We are clearly at a singular moment in the history of Higher Education.

Notes

This essay is based in large part on the author's work *The Difference Engine: Computers, Knowledge and the Transformation of Literacy* (Lanham, MD: Rowman & Littlefield, 2012).

1. See Eugene F. Provenzo, Jr., *Beyond the Gutenberg Galaxy: Microcomputers and the Emergence of Post-Typographic Culture* (New York: Teachers College Press, Columbia University, 1986); Eugene F. Provenzo, Jr., "Educational Technology and the Discourse of Education and Schooling," in*Power/Knowledge & The Politics of Educational Meaning: A Teacher's Guide*, ed. David Gabbard (Mahwah, NJ: Lawrence Erlbaum, 1999), pp. 297–302.
2. Eugene F. Provenzo, Jr., *The Difference Engine: Computers, Knowledge and the Transformation of Literacy* (Lanham, MD: Rowman & Littlefield, in press).
3. See Provenzo, *The Difference Engine*.
4. Babbage created a clockwork mechanism of gears in order to realize his computations. Driven by steam power, his device was too imprecise and slow to prove practical. What is remarkable is that Babbage managed, with the assistance of the poet Lord Byron's daughter Augusta Ada King, Countess of Lovelace (1815–1852), to outline a theoretically sound model of binary computing. It would take the invention of electronically based switching mechanisms—i.e., vacuum tubes and transistors—to make such a device actually work. For a fascinating alternative fictional history describing the potential of Babbage and Byron's invention, see the science fiction novel by William Gibson and Bruce Sterling *The Difference Engine* (London: Victor Gollancz, 1990).

5. The idea of a singularity is introduced by Vinge in his novella True *Names. . . and Other Dangers* (New York: Simon & Schuster, 1987), p. 1. Also see Vernor Vinge, "Hurtling Towards the Singularity" interview with Michael Synergy, *Mondo 2000* (1989). Vinge explains the situation as follows: "When a race succeeds in making creatures that are smarter than it is, then all the rules are changed. And from the standpoint of that race, you've gone through a Singularity. That's because it's not possible before that point to talk meaningfully about the issues that are important *after* that point" p. 116.

6. See William F. Ogburn, *Social Change: With Respect to Cultural and Original Nature* (Oxford: Delta Books, 1966). First published in 1922.

7. Theodor Holm Nelson, *Literary Machines, Edition 87. 1: The Report on, and of, Project Xanadu Concerning Word Processing, Electronic Publishing, Hypertext, Thinkertoys, Tomorrow's Intellectual Revolution, and Certain Other Topics Including Knowledge, Education and Freedom* (Bellevue, WA: MicrosoftPress, 1987), p. 2.

8. Ibid.

9. George P. Landow, "The Rhetoric of Hypermedia: Some Rules for Authors" *Journal of Computing in Higher Education*1, no. 1 (Spring 1989): 39.

10. Jeff Conklin, "Hypertext: An Introduction and Survey" *Computer* 20, no. 9: 17.

11. Ibid.

12. Eugene F. Provenzo, Jr., Editor-in-Chief, *The Sage Encyclopedia of the Social and Cultural Foundations of Education* (Thousand Oaks, CA: Sage, 2008). Three volumes.

13. For example, seeDavid Hannay, "American War of Independence"in *Encyclopædia Britannica*, vol. 1. 11th ed. (New York: Encyclopædia Britannica), p. 845.

14. J. David Bolter, *Turing's Man: Western Culture in the Computer Age* (Chapel Hill: The University of North Carolina Press, 1984), p. xi.

15. Norbert Wiener, *The Human Use of Human Beings: Cybernetics and Society* (New York: Avon Books, 1967), p. 24. Also see: Wiener, *Cybernetics, or Control and Communication in the Animal and theMachine*, 2nd ed. (Cambridge, MA: MIT Press, 1961).

16. Marshall McLuhan, *The Gutenberg Galaxy: The Making of Typographic Man* (Toronto: University of Toronto Press, 1962), page preceding Prologue, p. 1.

17. Ibid, p. 12.

18. Bolter, *Turing's Man*, pp. 6–8.

19. Richard A. Lanham, *The Electronic Word: Democracy, Technology, and the Arts* (Chicago: University of Chicago Press, 1993), p. xii.

20. Ibid., p. 79.

21. C. A. Bowers, *The Cultural Dimensions of Educational Computing* (New York: Teachers College Press, 1988), p. 2.

22. Stewart Brand, *The Media Lab: Inventing the Future at M. I. T.* (New York: Penguin Books, 1988), p. 256.

23. Joseph Weizenbaum, *Computer Power and Human Reason* (San Francisco: W. H. Freeman, 1976), p. 9.

CHAPTER THIRTY

The Transformative University Revisited

MAURICE R. BERUBE & CLAIR T. BERUBE

It seems that the question of university involvement in the social and political matrix of American society resurfaces every generation. Still, the evidence suggests that the paradigm of university involvement remains secure.

The Renewed Controversy

Stanley Fish, distinguished professor at Florida International University and academic scold, admonishes those bent on promoting the role of universities beyond teaching and research. In his challenging book *Save the World On Your Own Time* (2008), Fish argues that college and university teachers are only successful at "two things": namely, transmitting knowledge and developing analytical skills in students. Fish states that "anyone who asks for more has enlisted in the 'we-are-going-to-save-the world' army."[1]

Fish denounces the mission statement of practically every college and university that presumes "to think that it is the job of every institution of higher learning to cure every ill the world has ever known."[2] But he is realistic that his argument is "a minority view and that any number of objections to it have appeared in the literature."[3]

Indeed, Fish's view is a minority one and increasingly so as time progresses. Diametrically opposed to Fish's jeremiad is Evan S. Dobelle, president of Westfield State College, who not only presents an abstract rebuttal to Fish but, as an administrator, has been directly involved in rescuing an urban community through the power of the university. While President at Trinity College in Hartford, Connecticut, Dobelle engineered an imaginative restoration of the surrounding neighborhood community without displacing the poor.

Now, Dobelle and his staff monitor the social progress of colleges and universities and generate a ranked report. Begun in 2006 and followed up in 2009, the Dobelle ratings report on universities' activities in their respective cities. Criteria include "length of the involvement with the community" "catalyst effect on others" and "faculty and student involvement in community service."[4]

The activities are varied. For example, the 2009 report cites the University of Pittsburgh, whose "neighborhood collaborations have resulted in physically and economically revitalized neighborhoods."[5] The University of Southern California was cited in first place for having "transformed the neighborhood schools."[6]

And, in 1999, a group of academics created a program to bridge the town-gown divide at the University of Michigan. They named their effort *Imagining America: Artists andScholars in Public Life*. At this writing (2011), some 95 colleges and universities are affiliated with *Imagining America*. Each of these institutions has a variety of outreach programs for the community and nation. Their stated mission is to "animate and strengthen the public and civic purposes of humanities, artists and design, through mutually beneficial campus-community partnerships that advance democratic scholarship and practice."[7] This is to be accomplished by integrating "community and academic knowledge to help identify and solve significant community-identified real world problems."[8] *Imagining America* has a three-day annual conference for consortium members with a booklet of activities that consumes some 50 pages of events.

Moreover, the prestigious National Academy of Sciences is urging its members to engage in public discussions on their areas of expertise on science policy—and even to run for public office. Barbara A. Schaal, a biologist and Vice-President of the Academy, throws down the gauntlet to members: "We need to interact with the public for our good and the public good."[9] In 2011, only 31 of 435 members of the United States House of Representatives were scientists or engineers: one physicist, a chemist, a microbiologist, six engineers, and 22 with medical training.[10]

Seeking a Balance

University presidents who devote a share of their time and resources to their communities must do so without endangering their academic mission. The "bottom line" for Dobelle at the five institutions he guided was that "the absolute first priority must be the researchers, faculty and TA's. . . [because]. . . they inspire the students."[11] Dobelle considers the role of university presidents to be "an art and a science."[12]

There can be an occasional imbalance that might be detrimental to an institution. A recent case in point is what has happened at Syracuse University, a private university, under the leadership of Nancy Cantor. *The Chronicle of Higher Education* characterizes Chancellor Cantor's leadership as focusing "on the 'public good' [as]. . . Syracuse's reputation slides."[13]

After assuming the presidency of Syracuse seven years ago, Cantor embarked on an ambitious plan to revitalize a "sagging Rust Belt city."[14] Cantor devoted millions of dollars to revitalization by refurbishing parks and buying abandoned buildings to combat the local drugtrade, among other programs. She encouraged professors to "focus their research on the city, while giving free tuition to local high-school graduates."[15]

Meanwhile the academic mission suffered. According to rankings by *U.S. News & World Report*, Syracuse University went from a high of 40th best in the nation to 62 during Cantor's watch. The acceptance rate at Syracuse went from 50% of applicants to 60%. Moreover, SAT scores of Syracuse freshmen are now lower than several State University of New York campuses as well as such private urban universities as Boston University, the University of Pittsburgh, and George Washington University. Consequently, after 45 years of being a member of the prestigious Association of American Universities, Syracuse dropped out before it was to be thrown out.

Syracuse faculty are uneasy about the new urban focus. "Our primary mission is not managing cities" contends one political science professor.[16] Another professor, a biologist, charges that "my discipline is not the town of Syracuse [but]. . . scholarship all over the world."[17]

Dobelle would review the Syracuse experiment with alarm. Still, he feels that universities should continue to pursue social goals with their communities since "universities and their leaders are now the CEOs of their cities and that comes with assuming historic responsibilities formerly assumed by corporate entities."[18]

By contrast, the University of Notre Dame, a private Catholic school, blends student activity with social outreach to make it a model of a balanced university mission. Nearly 80% of undergraduate students are engaged in social service activities. In-house studies of student involvement indicate that this has long-term beneficial impact on students. Notre Dame is ranked 19th among national universities, according to the *U.S. News and World Report*. The University's endowment is $5. 3 billion, dwarfing Syracuse's nearly $700 million endowment. In short, one mission—that of social involvement—need not destroy the academic mission.[19]

The Evolution of an Idea

The idea of a university being involved in the public sphere was the legacy of the federal government establishing land grant universities in 1862 to shore up the national agricultural and industrial economy. The university, then, was directed to become involved in national economic policy.

By the end of the 19th century, the idea had evolved in some elite universities, such as Smith College, where the College enlarged its function by working in settlement houses in New York City with the city's poor Jews and Catholics. In the process of going beyond the ivory tower to confront real societal problems, the very definition of the university in America had changed. Added to the archetypes of the Cardinal Newman teaching university and the German research university was a new hybrid—unique to America—of the service university.

By the mid-20thcentury, the service university re-emerged in a historical context as the national demographics had increasingly shifted from a rural state to an urban one. Consequently, as Maurice Berube argued in *The Urban University in America* (1978), those changing demographics had resulted in a distinctly "urban university" with special responsibilities to its attendant urban communities. I concluded that "the urban college and university has great potential in playing an increasingly important role in the life of the city."[20]

The urban university idea was strongly rejected in some influential quarters in the United States. Harold L. Enarson , president of Ohio State University, in his review of Berube's book in *The Journal of Higher Education*, found the treatment to be a "simplistic either–or polemics."[21] Enarson went on to politely state it proposed a "plausible thesis" but was hopelessly misguided. His main objection to Berube's argument was that

The central difficulty in this provocative book is that the author loads upon a new imagined federal grant university all the reforms he wishes for American higher education. . . Today, the dream of a distinctly urban institution is more remote than ever before. And this is as it should be. . . It is essentially a bad idea whose time, fortunately, has passed.[22]

By contrast, the reception to the book abroad was more positive. Reviewing it in *Higher Education*, British scholar Sally Tomlinson, of the University of Lancaster, found it to be

a short lucid, readable book on the American urban university in its urban context. . . . it is a minor model of clarity in structure and presentation of argument. . . while readers may disagree with the prescriptions which Berube puts forward concerning urban universities, the book is thought-provoking. . . it is an informed and readable short volume on a crucial area of higher education in America.[23]

In time, the latter view of the book prevailed. For example, a generation later, Northeastern University would publish a brochure heralding their new Master's in Urban Studies program headed by former 1988 Democratic Presidential candidate Michael Dukakis. The brochure begins with a quote from *The Urban University in America*: "An urban university should be an institution developed specifically for the purpose of relating to the wide range of issues facing cities and their communities."[24] Under these words, Northeastern proudly noted that "For a hundred years, Northeastern University has been closely connected to the economic, social, and cultural life of Metropolitan Boston."[25]

The Social Spirit

There has been a tradition of viewing education as a transformative agent to reconstruct society—a grand tradition harkening back to John Dewey and George Counts and later reformulated by the Critical Theorists in more contemporary times.

Dewey was especially concerned with what he called "the social spirit" of schooling. He writes that "the measure of the worth of the administration, curriculum, and methods of instruction of the school is the extent to which they re animated by a social spirit."[26] He hoped that "enlightened" educational leaders would "conduct education so that humanity may improve."[27] Therefore, he concluded, that the task of philosopher and educatoris to embark on "the reconstruction of philosophy, of education, and of social ideals."[28]

Dewey's colleague and friend, George S. Counts, was also dedicated to social reconstruction through the power of educational institutions. In a famous address to members of the Progressive Education Association in 1932, he challenged fellow progressives to become the enlightened leaders that Dewey wanted to reform an inequitable society. His speech was provocatively titled *Dare the Schools Build a New Social Order?*

These social reconstructionists strongly influenced the generation of social minded critics of the 1970s and 1980s aptly named Critical Theorists. They included scholars such as Henry Giroux, Michael Apple, and Stanley Aronowitz, among others. This group focused on class, race, and gender inequities in public schooling by formulating a neo-Marxist analysis. One observer noted that this "radical critique has been increasingly well-known within the mainstream."[29] In short, they began a paradigm shift in social thinking within academe.

For example, Giroux follows Dewey's call for a core of "enlightened leaders" in his *Teachers as Transformative Intellectuals: Toward a Critical Pedagogy of Learning* (1988). Giroux writes that "the role that teachers and administrators must play is as transformative intellectuals" by inculcating social consciousness in their students.[30]

Although much of the work of Dewey and the social reconstructionists, as well as the Critical Theorists, concentrates on public schooling, the implication is that their agenda for social change also applies to colleges and universities. Indeed, some of the Critical Theorists have used their social critiques to dissect the world of higher education. Giroux criticizes the military-industrial-academic complex in his searing book *The University in Chains* (2007). Arguing for social involvement, Giroux urges the academic "public intellectual" to "take sides, speak out, and engage" in social actions.[31] Aronowitz would tackle corporate America's influence in higher education in his *The Knowledge Factory* (2000), in which he contends that universities mistakenly "tend to mirror the rest of society."[32]

The Future of the University and "the Real World"

The authors of this chapter sampled some leading academicians who have written about the need for social change, and who have been involved in social projects beyond their scholarship. We asked them different questions relating to the main theme of this essay in order to more fully understand this unique relationship. Each of the respondents had credentials that would make one consider them as part of the establishment. Yet, ironically, they are all endowed scholars at their universities.

The historian Maurice Isserman, a former member of Students for a Democratic Society and the author *of The Other American: The Life of Michael Harrington*, occupies an endowed chair at Hamilton College. Isserman argues that the next focus for universities regarding their cities is to "engage with pressing social issues, such as poverty."[33]

The sociologist Stanley Aronowitz, a distinguished professor at City University Graduate School in New York, has a three-point agenda for universities:

1. Put funds and other efforts into research on the past, present, and future of cities.

2. Encourage departments to offer curricula, majors and courses on the city.

3. Invite community organizations, especially activist in education, urban redevelopment, and immigration, to dialogue and otherwise participate in conferences, seminars and faculty development.[34]

Michael Berube, the Paterno Chair in Literature at Pennsylvania State University and President of the Modern Language Association, argues that

> Now, more than ever, you need a Morrill Act for urban universities even if that means bucking the tide of retrenchment and austerity politics nationwide at the moment. Today everybody understands the obligation of urban universities to be good citizens so a shot in the arm from the federal government would be all the more appropriate.[35]

Michael Apple, the John Bascomb Professor of Curriculum at the University of Wisconsin, Madison, "certainly agrees that the university should be involved in urban social issues."[36]

But he does not see faculty as the sole transforming agent. Rather he urges coalition building to achieve social change. He writes that

> As long as higher education remains gripped by the convulsions of neoliberal government and globalizing capitalism, individual and institutional self-determination will be increasingly curtailed. While the AAUP and other associations should continue to mount traditional defenses of academic freedom, these methods will not restore academic freedom, which is embedded in the nation's failing political and economic systems. Faculty members don't have the power to reform these systems, but we can attempt to make common cause with the many Americans who now realize that they don't share in the profits.[37]

The Limits of Social Engineering

Apple has placed in perspective the problem with university-led social change. Professors are not sufficiently organized either in trade unions like the American Federation of Teachers (AFT) or the Association of University Professors (AAUP)—their main organizations. Consequently, the impact of unplanned reform hinges on sporadic piecemeal change that is dependent on the whims of leaders of institutions of higher education.

Does that circumstance bode ill for Dewey's view of reconstructing society through education? Probably. The educational historian Diane Ravitch has often wondered why piecemeal change acquired such a bad reputation. We are thus saddled with what has been called a "happening"—a chimera of voices that are Babel-like.

Still one thing is assured: There is no turning back on America's college and universities in their pursuit of aiding society in some fashion. As this essay attests, the full contours and effects of that effort are yet to be decided.

Notes

1. Stanley Fish, *Save the World on Your Own Time* (New York: Oxford University Press, 2008), p. 13.
2. Ibid., p. 10.
3. Ibid., p. 15.
4. Evan S. Dobelle, "Saviors of Our Cities: Survey of Best Colleges and Universities" (unpublished report, Westfield State College, Westfield, MA, October2009).
5. Ibid.
6. Ibid.
7. *Imagining America*, Google, p. 201.
8. Ibid.
9. Cornelia Dean, "Groups Call for Scientists to Engage the Body Politic," *New York Times*, August 9, 2011, D1.
10. Maurice R. Berube, *The Urban University in America* (Westport, CT: Greenwood Press, 1978), p. 16.
11. Evan S. Dobelle email to Maurice R. Berube. October 4, 2011.
12. Ibid.
13. Robin Wilson, "Syracuse's Slide," *The Chronicle of Higher Education*, October 2, 2011, p. 1, http://chronicle.com/article/syracuses-slide/129238/.
14. Ibid.
15. Ibid.
16. Ibid., p. 5.
17. Ibid.
18. Dobelle, op. cit.
19. University of Notre Dame, "Best Colleges," *U.S. News and World Report*, http://colleges.usnews.rankingsandreviews.com/best-colleges/university-of-notre-dame-1840.
20. Maurice R. Berube, *The Urban University in America.* (Westport, CT: Greenwood Press, 1978), p. 16.

21. Harold L. Enarson, "Review" *Journal of Higher Education* 51, no. 1 (1980): 105.
22. Ibid., 104–5.
23. Sally Tomlinson, "Review," *Higher Education*8, no. 5 (1979): 594.
24. Brochure, Northeastern University, Boston, MA, 2000, p. 1.
25. Ibid.
26. John Dewey, *Democracy and Education* (New York: McMillan, 1916), p. 42.
27. Ibid.
28. Ibid.
29. Dennis Carlson, "Finding a Voice and Losing our Way," *Educational Theory* 48, no. 4 (1998): 506–541.
30. Henry A. Giroux, *Teachers as Transformational Intellectuals* (Westport, CT: Bergin &Garvey, 1988), p. 7.
31. Henry A. Giroux, *The University in Chains* (Boulder, CO: Paradigm, 2007), p. 206.
32. Stanley Aronowitz, *The Knowledge Factory* (Boston, MA: Beacon Press, 2000), p. 11.
33. Maurice Isserman to Maurice R. Berube, email, August 19, 2011.
34. Stanley Aronowitz to Maurice R. Berube, email, August 21, 2011.
35. Michael Berube to Maurice R. Berube, email, September 10, 2011.
36. Michael Apple to Maurice R. Berube, email, September 14, 2011.
37. Michael Apple, "Review," *Teachers College Record* June 24 (2010): 384.

Contributors

Baez, Benjamin. Benjamin Baez is an associate professor of higher education at Florida International University. His most recent book is *The Politics of Inquiry: Education Research and the "Culture of Science"* with Deron Boyles (SUNY Press, 2009). His academic interests include the politics of education, diversity, social justice, faculty employment issues (especially those relating to faculty of color), and legal issues in education (especially those relevant to race, class, and gender). He serves on the editorial board of *The Review of Higher Education*.

Bauer, Dan. Dan Bauer is an associate professor of middle grades education and English at Georgia College & State University in Milledgeville—a milieu that nurtured Flannery O'Connor, Jean Toomer, and Alice Walker, all of whom play pivotal roles in his studies. He works closely with pre-service middle school teachers in an intensive cohort model that has been cited for excellence by the National Association of Professors of Middle Level Education. He also co-directs the Central Georgia Writing Project. His academic interests focus on writing assessment; the crucial connection of composition and epistemology; and the legacy of public education on racial equity, opportunity, and curriculum. His articles appear in *College Composition and Communication* and *The Journal of Business and Technical Communication*, among other publications.

Berube, Clair T. Clair T. Berube is an assistant professor of education at Hampton University. Her academic interests include science education, gender issues, progressive education, critique of standardization in schools, and higher education. She is the co-author, with Maurice R. Berube, of *The Moral University* (Lanham, MD: Rowman & Littlefield, 2010) and the author of *The X Factor: Personality Traits of Exceptional Science Teachers* (Charlotte, NC: Information Age

Publishing, 2010) and *The Unfinished Quest: The Plight of Progressive Science Education in the Age of Standards* (Charlotte, NC: Information Age Publishing, 2008).

Berube, Maurice R. Maurice R. Berube is an eminent scholar emeritus of education at Old Dominion University. A wide-ranging interpreter and critic on important issues in P-12 schools and higher education, his most recent books are, with Clair T. Berube, *The Moral University* (Lanham, MD: Rowman& Littlefield, 2010) and *The End of School Reform* (Lanham, MD: Rowman & Littlefield, 2006). He is working on a book on President Barack Obama's educational policies.

Besosa, Mayra. Mayra Besosa is a full-time lecturer in Spanish at California State University, San Marcos, where she is Lecturer Representative and Faculty Rights Chair for the campus chapter of the California Faculty Association. At the national level, she co-chairs two committees of the American Association of University Professors (AAUP)—the Committees on Contingency and the Profession and Contingency and Governance—and is an elected member-at-large of the AAUP's Collective Bargaining Congress. She has presented at various regional and national AAUP meetings and organizing campaigns as well as at national and international conferences such as the AAUP Summer Institute, the Modern Language Association (MLA) annual convention, the City University of New York (CUNY) Collective Bargaining conference, and the Coalition of Contingent Academic Labor (COCAL).

Bieze, Michael Scott. Michael Scott Bieze is the chair of the Fine Arts Department at Marist School in Atlanta. His dissertation, "Booker T. Washington and the Art of Self-Representation" received the Dissertation of the Year Award from the History of Education Society in 2004. He is the co-editor, with Marybeth Gasman, of *Booker T. Washington Rediscovered* (Baltimore: The Johns Hopkins University Press, 2012) and the author of *Booker T. Washington and the Art of Self-Representation* (New York: Peter Lang Publishing, 2008).

Boeckenstedt, Jon. Jon Boeckenstedt is the Associate Vice President of Enrollment Management and Marketing at DePaul University in Chicago, where he focuses on enrollment policy and planning and oversees all undergraduate admissions functions and new student financial aid policies. He has worked in admissions at five different colleges and universities in his 30–year career in higher education and is the past-president of the National Catholic College Admissions Association. His undergraduate degree is in English literature and his master's degree is in marketing.

Brown, Scott C. Scott C. Brown is the Interim Vice President and Dean of the College at Colgate University. He was Director of the Career Development Center at Mount Holyoke College and held previous positions at the University of Maryland, the American Association for Higher Education, Dartmouth College, Indiana University, and the University of California, Irvine. He has developed, with Jeffrey A. Greene, the Wisdom Development Scale (WDS), served as an editorial board member of the *Journal of College Student Development*, and participated in a Fulbright Seminar Grant in Germany.

Burnett, Dana D. Dana D. Burnett is a professor of higher education at Old Dominion University. He has served as a department chair and previously held one of the best administrative jobs on any campus—Vice President for Student Affairs and Dean of Students—for a combined 34 years. His current areas of scholarly interest include privatization in higher education and themes emerging from a comprehensive review of the counseling literature.

Clopton, Aaron W. Aaron W. Clopton is an associate professor and program director for Sport Management at the University of Kansas. He is also the director of the University's Laboratory for the Study of Sport Management (LSSM). His research agenda focuses on the impact of sport on social networks and organizations. He has published in numerous outlets, including *Community Development, College Student Affairs Journal, Journal for the Study of Sports and Athletes in Education,* and *Journal of Intercollegiate Sport.* Prior to his current appointment, he held a similar position at Louisiana State University. He has also taught at Marshall University.

Cooley, Aaron. Aaron Cooley received his Ph.D. from the University of North Carolina at Chapel Hill. He has taught undergraduate and graduate courses in political science, education, and critical thinking. His governmental experience includes working in the North Carolina Governor's Office of Education Policy and for the North Carolina General Assembly. His research focuses on democracy, education, and public policy. His articles and reviews have appeared in *Educational Research Quarterly, Educational Studies, Southern California Interdisciplinary Law Journal, Journal of Educational Policy, International Journal of Philosophical Studies, Journal of Popular Culture,* and *Political Studies Review.* He serves on the editorial board of *The Journal of Educational Foundations* and the review board of *Educational Theory.*

DeVitis, Joseph L. Joseph L. DeVitis is a visiting professor of Educational Foundations and Higher Education at Old Dominion University. He is a past president of the American Educational Studies Association (AESA), the Council of Learned Societies in Education, and the Society of Professors of Education. He is the recipient of the Distinguished Alumni Award from the College of Education, University of Illinois at Urbana-Champaign. Author or editor of 13 books, he has written extensively on moral development, liberal education, and collegiate service-learning. He has edited a series of recent notable readers for Peter Lang Publishing: *Critical Civic Literacy* (2011); *Character and Moral Education* (2011), with Tianlong Yu; and, with Linda Irwin-DeVitis, *Adolescent Education* (2010). The latter two books won AESA Critics Choice Awards as outstanding books of the year.

Floyd, Deborah L. Deborah L. Floyd is a professor of higher education leadership at Florida Atlantic University. She has published over 70 works and is the editor-in-chief of *The Community College Journal of Research and Practice.* She has spent 20 years in community colleges as a president, vice president, dean, and director in Texas, Iowa, and Kentucky. For eight years she was a community college president in rural Appalachia, where she followed a long-term president and led the college through an era of change. She has also served as a Senior Fellow with the Association of American Colleges and Universities, past president of the Council for the Study of Community Colleges, secretary of the American College Personnel Association, and on the Board of Directors of the American Association of Community Colleges.

Gasman, Marybeth. Marybeth Gasman is a professor of higher education at the University of Pennsylvania. Her expertise pertains to African American higher education, leadership, and philanthropy. She is the author of *The Morehouse Mystique: Becoming a Doctor at the Nation's Newest African American Medical School* (Baltimore: The Johns Hopkins University Press,

2012); *A Guide to Fundraising at Historically Black Colleges and Universities: An All Campus Approach* (London: Routledge, 2011); *The History of U.S. Higher Education: Methods for Understanding the Past* (London: Routledge, 2010); *Understanding Minority-Serving* Institutions, with Benjamin Baez and Caroline Sotello Turner (Albany: SUNY Press, 2008); *Historically Black Colleges and Universities: Triumphs, Troubles, and Taboos*, with Christopher L. Tudico (New York; Palgrave Macmillan, 2008); and *Envisioning Black Colleges: A History of the United Negro College Fund* (Baltimore: The Johns Hopkins University Press, 2007). She is also the co-editor, with Michael Scott Bieze, of *Booker T. Washington Rediscovered* (Baltimore: The Johns Hopkins University Press, 2012).

Gregory, Dennis E. Dennis E. Gregory is an associate professor of higher education at Old Dominion University. He has served in numerous student affairs leadership roles, including as a senior student affairs officer. He has authored or co-authored over 50 publications, including a book on Greek life. He has also made nearly 100 presentations on topics related to enrollment management, study abroad, and comparative education. He is a charter member and past president of the Association for Student Conduct Administration (ASCA) and the International Association of Student Affairs and Services (IASAS). He is a member of the editorial board of the *Journal of Counselling and Development in Higher Education, Southern Africa*.

Hutcheson, Philo A. Philo A. Hutcheson is a professor and chair in the Department of Educational Leadership, Policy and Technology at the University of Alabama, Tuscaloosa. He is the past president of the History of Education Society. He is the author of *A Professional Professoriate: Unionization, Bureaucratization, and the AAUP* (Nashville, TN: Vanderbilt University Press, 2000) and numerous book chapters and articles. He has completed a manuscript on the 1947 President's Commission on Higher Education and has a book contract with Routledge to write a history of United States higher education.

Leavitt, Stephen C. Stephen C. Leavitt is the Vice President for Student Affairs at Union College in Schenectady, New York. He has also been a professor of anthropology at Union with a specialty in psychological anthropology. His central research interests include religious conviction and the narrative construction of personal experience, focusing on Papua New Guinea. He has written on adolescence, sexuality, mourning, and religious experience. He edited *Adolescence in Pacific Island Societies* (Pittsburgh: University of Pittsburgh Press, 1998).

Leland, Dorothy. Dorothy Leland is the Chancellor of the University of California, Merced, which opened its doors to students in 2005 as the 10th campus of the University of California system. She previously served as president of Georgia College & State University and in various administrative capacities at Florida Atlantic University and Purdue University. Her scholarly work focuses on 20th-century continental philosophy.

Liston, Delores D. Delores D. Liston is a professor of curriculum, foundations, and reading at Georgia Southern University. She teaches primarily doctoral courses in philosophy of education and ethics and curriculum studies. Her current research interests include studies bridging the scholarship of teaching and learning and educational foundations, especially as related to social justice, and sexual harassment in schools. Her most recent books are *Pervasive Vulnerabilities: Sexual Harassment in School* (New York: Peter Lang Publishing, 2011), with Regina

Rahimi, and *Learning to Teach: A Critical Approach to Field Experiences*, 2nd ed. (Mahwah, NJ: Lawrence Erlbaum, 2005), with Natalie G. Adams, Christine M. Shea, and Bryan Deever.

Lovett. Thomas M. Thomas M. Lovett is a professor of business at the University of North Alabama, where he teaches law, ethics, and negotiation/conflict resolution. He holds both a J. D. degree and a doctorate in counselor education. He is a National Certified Counselor (NCC), a registered mediator, and has been admitted to practice law in Alabama and Arkansas. He has extensive experience in higher education administration and law, serving as a dean of students, vice president for student affairs, and university legal counsel. He is a longtime member of the National Association of College and University Attorneys and is currently chair of the board for the Center for Credentialing and Education, Inc., a subsidiary corporation of the National Board for Certified Counselors, Inc.

Lucas, Christopher J. Christopher J. Lucas is a professor of educational foundations and policy analysis at the University of Arkansas, Fayetteville. He is a past president of the Society of Professors of Education (SPE) and the American Educational Studies Association (AESA) and founding executive secretary (subsequently president) of the Council for Learned Societies in Education (CSLE). He is the author or editor of over a dozen books, including, most recently, with John W. Murry, *New Faculty: A Primer for Academic Beginners*, 2nd ed. (New York: Palgrave Macmillan, 2007), and is editor of the *Journal of Educational Research Policy Studies*.

Ludeman, Roger B. Roger B. Ludeman is the Executive Director of the International Association of Student Affairs and Services (IASAS). Following eight years as a school music teacher and guidance director, he spent over 30 years as a student affairs officer, with two decades focusing on how international educators and student affairs practitioners can collaborate to enhance international education. His three Fulbright grants (in Germany, Japan, and South Africa) sparked his interest in global education. He has contributed a number of articles to professional journals and books and most recently served as editor-in-chief of *Student Affairs and Services in Higher Education around the World: Foundations, Trends, and Best Practices* (UNESCO, 2009).

Maisto, Maria. Maria Maisto is a founding member and current President of the Board of Directors of the New Faculty Majority: The National Coalition for Adjunct and Contingent Faculty in the United States. An adjunct instructor of composition at Cuyahoga Community College in Cleveland, she is Co-Chair of the Ohio Conference AAUP Committee on Part-Time Faculty and a former administrative director of the American Conference of Academic Deans. She has been a member of the White House Community College Summit.

Margolis, Eric. Eric Margolis is a sociologist and associate professor of human communication at Arizona State University. He is president of the International Visual Sociology Association. His scholarly interests include the politics and hidden curriculum of higher education, visual research methods in general and visual ethnography in particular. His most recent book, edited with Luc Pauwels, is *The Sage Handbook of Visual Research* (London: Sage Publications, 2011). He has also edited, with Mary Romero, *The Blackwell Companion to Social Inequalities* (Malden, MA: Wiley-Blackwell, 2005) and *The Hidden Curriculum in Higher Education* (London: Routledge, 2001).

Nuckols, William L. William L. Nuckols is a doctoral candidate and graduate assistant in the Higher Education Administration program at Old Dominion University. He earned his Juris Doctorate in 2000 from Southern Illinois University and his B. A. in 1996 from Old Dominion University.

Paredes-Collins, Kristin. Kristin Paredes-Collins is the associate editor of *Christian Higher Education: A Journal of Research, Theory, and Practice*. Prior to her work with the journal, she served as the Director of Admission at Pepperdine University. She regularly hosts college essay writing workshops for high school seniors. Her research interests include campus climate for diversity at religious institutions, student spirituality, and access and equity in the college admission process.

Park, Julie J. Julie J. Park is an assistant professor of higher education (student affairs concentration) at the University of Maryland, College Park. Her primary research agenda addresses how race, religion, and social class affect diversity and equity in higher education, including the diverse experiences of Asian-American college students. Her work has been published in venues such as the *Journal of Higher Education*, *Teachers College Record*, and the *Review of Higher Education*.

Pittman, Jeffrey. Jeffrey Pittman is an associate professor of education at Regent University, where he teaches higher education administration, leadership, and educational philosophy courses. He has extensive administrative experience at Regent as the vice president for student services, associate dean for administration and academics, assistant vice president for administration and auxiliary services, and president of the Association of College Auxiliary Services (NACAS). Currently, he serves as a member of the board of directors of the Council for the Advancement of Students in Higher Education (CAS) and the NACAS Education Foundation.

Provenzo, Eugene F., Jr. Eugene F. Provenzo, Jr., is a professor of social and cultural foundations at the University of Miami. The author of over 100 books on education, culture, and technology, his most recent books are *The Difference Engine: Computers, Knowledge and the Transformation of Learning* (Lanham, MD: Rowman& Littlefield, 2012) and *Critical Literacy: what Every American Needs to Know* (Lanham, MD: Rowman & Littlefield, 2006). He received the University of Miami's Provost's Award for Scholarly Activity in 2008.

Rahimi, Regina. Regina Rahimi is an assistant professor of adolescent and adult learning at Armstrong Atlantic State University in Savannah, Georgia. She taught middle school for 15 years before entering academe. Her research interests include gender and sexuality in education and adolescent literacy. She most recently authored, with Delores D. Liston, *Pervasive Vulnerabilities: Sexual Harassment in School* (New York: Peter Lang Publishing, 2011).

Samuels, Robert. Robert Samuels is a lecturer in the Writing Programs at the University of California at Los Angeles and President of the University of California's American Federation of Teachers (AFT). His most recent books are *New Media, Cultural Studies, and Critical Theory after Postmodernism: Automodernity from Zizek to Laclau* (New York: Palgrave Macmillan, 2009); *Teaching the Rhetoric of Resistance: The PopularHolocaust and Social Change in a Post 9/11*

World (New York: Palgrave Macmillan, 2007); and *Integrating Hypertextual Subjects: Computers, Composition, and Academic Labor* (New York: Hampton Press, 2006).

Sasso, Pietro A. Pietro A. Sasso is an assistant professor of student affairs and college counseling at Monmouth University in New Jersey. His research focuses on masculinity in undergraduate students, alcohol use among college students, and student identity development. He has been a vice president for a national fraternity, has consulted for a national sorority, and has served as a Greek advisor. He has worked in student affairs and academic advising for several higher education institutions. He earned his doctorate in higher education administration from Old Dominion University in 2012.

Schubert, William H. William H. Schubert is a professor emeritus of curriculum and instruction and University Scholar, University of Illinois at Chicago, where he founded and coordinated the Ph.D. Program in Curriculum Studies and received university-wide awards for teaching and mentoring. Author or editor of 16 books and over 200 articles and chapters, he is a past vice president of the American Educational Research Association (AERA) and a past president of The John Dewey Society, the Society for the Study of Curriculum History, and the Society of Professors of Education (SPE). In 2004, he received the AERA Lifetime Achievement Award in Curriculum Studies and, in 2011, the SPE Charles DeGarmo Lecture Award. His most recent book is *Love, Justice, and Education: John Dewey and the Utopians* (Charlotte, NC: Information Age Publishing, 2009).

Scribner, Jay Paredes. Jay Paredes Scribner is a professor and Chair of the Department of Educational Foundations and Leadership at Old Dominion University. His research has focused on the professional learning of teachers and principals in PK-12 schools. His most recent research centers on strategic thinking and behavior in school districts. He has published in journals such as *Educational Administration Quarterly*, *Educational Policy*, and the *Journal of School Leadership*.

Sheffield, Eric C. Eric C. Sheffield is an associate professor of foundations of education at Missouri State University. He is the assistant director of the Academy for Educational Studies and serves as the editor for the Academy's online journal, *Critical Questions in Education*. His most recent books include *Dystopia and Education: Insights for Theory, Praxis, and Policy*, with Jessica A. Heybach (Charlotte, NC: Information Age Publishing, 2012); *Strong Community Service Learning: Philosophical Perspectives* (New York: Peter Lang Publishing, 2011); and *The Role of Religion in 21st Century Public Schools*, edited with Steven P. Jones (New York: Peter Lang Publishing, 2009).

Smyth, John. John Smyth is Research Professor of Education in the School of Education and Arts at the University of Ballarat, Victoria, Australia. He formerly held the Mitte Endowed Chair in School Improvement at Texas State University, San Marcos. He is the recipient of several research awards from the American Educational Research Association and is a Fellow of the Academy for Social Science in Australia. His research interests are in policy sociology, policy ethnography, social justice, and sociology of education. Among his recent books are *Silent Witnesses to Active Agents: Student Voice in Re-engaging with Learning*, with Peter McInerney (New York: Peter Lang Publishing, 2012), *Critical Voices in Teacher Education:*

Teaching for Social Justice in Conservative Times, with Barry Down (Berlin: Springer, 2012), *Critical Pedagogy for Social Justice* (New York: Continuum, 2011), and *"Hanging in with Kids" in Tough Times: Engagement in Contexts of Educational Disadvantage in the Relational School,* with Barry Down and Peter McInerney (New York: Peter Lang Publishing, 2010).

Wathington, Heather D. Heather D. Wathington is an assistant professor of education at the University of Virginia. Her scholarship centers on the academic achievement of low-income students and students of color in higher education, with a specific focus on understanding the educational contexts, levers, and practices that promote greater academic success for those students. Her research examines college access, matriculation, and persistence in higher education, and postgraduate study and research preparation. She has authored numerous reports with the National Center for Postsecondary Research, and her published articles appear in such journals as *The Journal of College Student Retention* and *Journal of Developmental Education.*

Williams, Mitchell R. Mitchell R. Williams is an associate professor of community college leadership at Old Dominion University. He teaches courses on politics and policy development in postsecondary education. He has over 15 years of experience in higher education and has published over 20 articles and book chapters on community college issues and adult education. His research interests include the role of community colleges in rural economic development and collaboration between two and four-year institutions of higher education.

Adolescent Cultures, School & Society

Joseph L. DeVitis & Linda Irwin-DeVitis

GENERAL EDITORS

As schools struggle to redefine and restructure themselves, they need to be aware of the new realities of adolescents. Thus, this series of monographs and texts is committed to depicting the variety of adolescent cultures that exist in today's troubled world. It is primarily a qualitative research, practice, and policy series devoted to contextual interpretation and analysis that encompasses a broad range of interdisciplinary critique. In addition, this series seeks to address issues of curriculum theory and practice; multicultural education; aggression, bullying, and violence; the media and arts; school dropouts; homeless and runaway youth; gangs and other alienated youth; at-risk adolescent populations; family structures and parental involvement; and race, ethnicity, class, and gender/LGBTQ studies.

Send proposals and manuscripts to the general editors at:
Joseph L. DeVitis & Linda Irwin-DeVitis
Darden College of Education
Old Dominion University
Norfolk, VA 23503

To order other books in this series, please contact our Customer Service Department at:
(800) 770-LANG (within the U.S.)
(212) 647-7706 (outside the U.S.)
(212) 647-7707 FAX

or browse online by series at:
WWW.PETERLANG.COM